VOLUM

Steadfast Adherence to th

Twelve Sermons on:

Let us hold fast the profession of our faith without wavering (for he is faithful that promised). Hebrews 10:23

One Sermon on:

And let us consider one another to provoke unto love and to good works. Hebrews 10:24

Four Sermons on:

By a new and living way, which he hath consecrated for us, through the veil, that is to say, his flesh. Hebrews 10:20

Four Sermons on:

And having a high priest over the house of God. Hebrews 10:21

Eleven Sermons on Important Subjects

Peter, an apostle of Jesus Christ, to the strangers scattered throughout Pontus, Galatia, Cappadocia, Asia, and Bithynia, Elect according to the foreknowledge of God the Father, through sanctification of the Spirit, unto obedience and sprinkling of the blood of Jesus Christ: Grace unto you, and peace, be multiplied. Blessed be the God and Father of our Lord Jesus Christ, which according to his abundant mercy hath begotten us again unto a lively hope by the resurrection of Jesus Christ from the dead, To an inheritance incorruptible, and undefiled, and that fadeth not away, reserved in heaven for you. 1 Peter 1:1-4

Righteousness in Christ

Six Sermons on:

I do not frustrate the grace of God: for if righteousness come by the law, then Christ is dead in vain. Galatians 2:21

A Letter from the Author to his Wife

A Letter from the Author to his Children

Additional Sermons

The Works of Robert Traill

The Works of Robert Traill

In Two Volumes

Vol. II.

Cui veritas comperta, sine Deo?
Cui Deus cognitus, sine Christo?
Cui Christus exploratus, sine Spiritu sancto?

For by whom has truth ever been discovered without God?
By whom has God ever been found without Christ?
By whom has Christ ever been explored without the Holy Spirit?

TERTULLIAN, *Treatise on the Soul.*

THE BANNER OF TRUTH TRUST

THE BANNER OF TRUTH TRUST

Head Office
3 Murrayfield Road
Edinburgh
EH12 6EL
UK

North America Office
PO Box 621
Carlisle
PA 17013
USA

banneroftruth.org

First published in four volumes by J. Ogle, London, 1810
Reprinted in two volumes by the Banner of Truth Trust 1975
This retypeset edition (with additional sermons) 2020

*

ISBN (Volume II.)
Print: 978-1-84871-982-8
EPUB: 978-1-84871-983-5
Kindle: 978-1-84871-984-2

ISBN (2-volume set)
978-1-84871-985-9

*

Typeset in 10.5/13.5 Adobe Garamond Pro
at The Banner of Truth Trust, Edinburgh

Printed in the USA by
Versa Press Inc.,
East Peoria, IL.

CONTENTS

STEDFAST ADHERENCE

TO THE

PROFESSION OF OUR FAITH

RECOMMENDED IN TWENTY-ONE SERMONS

STEDFAST ADHERENCE

TO THE

PROFESSION OF OUR FAITH

RECOMMENDED IN TWENTY-ONE SERMONS

SERMON I.

HEB. 10:23.

Let us hold fast the profession of our faith without wavering, etc.

HAVING insisted at so great length upon the first exhortation of the apostle, concerning drawing near to God, which is built upon the foundations of the Christian's privileges, that the apostle named, and that we have spoke of, from the 19th, 20th, and 21st verses; those exhortations that remain are deduced from the same foundation: wherefore I thought fit not to let them pass. The former exhortation was unto a duty with respect to God, drawing near to him, which the apostle requires to be performed in such a manner, that all Christians, and the best of them, must be learning to answer every day in their life, that they may come up more and more thereunto.

The other two exhortations are with respect to ourselves and others. The first is in the 23rd verse, with respect to our own profession; the other, in the 24th verse, is with respect to our brethren and fellow Christians.

The first of these exhortations, which is contained in this 23rd verse, plainly divides itself into the duty exhorted to, and the argument to enforce it. The duty is, *Let us hold fast the profession of our faith without wavering*. The argument to this duty is a strong and a proper one, *He is faithful that hath promised*. Our faith should always be built on God's promise; it is not the right faith if it be not so; and our faith on the promise should answer the faithfulness of the promiser; the strength of our believing the promise, should bear some proportion to the great faithfulness of the maker of it. Now, it is evident, that the apostle's argument is both pertinent and strong: *Let us hold fast the profession of our faith without wavering*, for God the promiser does not waver in what he has said.

I shall begin with the first of these at this time, The duty he exhorts to. And you may see here, as I observed from the former exhortations, that the apostle, the penman of this blessed portion of scripture, puts in himself in this exhortation: *Let us*, says he, *draw near*, etc. *And let us hold fast the profession of our faith without wavering*.

In this duty exhorted to, there are three things to be considered.

1. What that is which is, as it were, the subject-matter of this duty; and that is, *the profession of our faith*; so we translate it. The words in the Greek, in the original, are certainly the *confession of our hope*. What reason there hath been in the learned translators for altering it, I do not know. However, it is no great matter; for profession and confession, faith and hope, are closely knit together; they are but several words expressing the same thing. *Confession* and *profession* are frequently named one for another, and *faith* and *hope* are frequently named one for another, in the word of God.

2. The *second* thing is the act, that the apostle craves about this profession, and we read it, *Let us hold it fast*. As if the apostle had said, The profession of your faith is very precious, keep it well; it will be attempted upon by your spiritual enemies, and they will be endeavouring to pluck it from you; hold it fast, keep it firm.

3. There is the manner of this duty the apostle craves about your profession: *Hold it fast*, says he, *without wavering*, without declining, without turning it to the one hand or to the other, but holding it steady and even. These are the heads that I would discourse upon from this text.

And to begin with the *first* of these, that are in the duty itself exhorted to, *the profession of our faith*, the apostle, you see here, plainly signifies, that it was made already, it was that they had; they had profession formerly. Now, says the apostle, *let us hold fast this profession of our faith*. This is the subject-matter of the exhortation, the profession of faith. And to make the way yet plainer, unto what I would observe and discourse from it, I would speak a little to the opening of these two.

I. *What is in this faith, that is the matter of this profession.*

II. *What is in the profession of our faith, or of this hope, which is as the form of it.*

I. What is in this faith or hope. There is none can understand what it is to hold fast faith and hope, till they know what faith and hope is.

First, For faith and hope, for I would still take them in both together, and shew, as we go along, the very small difference that is betwixt them; we find *faith*, in the word of God, taken for the doctrine of faith, for the truth of God, that is to be received, taken up, and embraced by faith: *Do we make void the law through faith?* says the apostle. *God forbid, yea, we establish the law*, Rom. 3:31, where the meaning plainly is, Do we make void the law by this doctrine of faith? No; by no means, God forbid. Divine truth is necessarily supposed to be the ground of all divine faith; if there were not such a thing going before, as *Thus saith the Lord*, no amen of faith could ever follow.

Secondly, In the considering of that faith that we make the profession of, we must consider that God that is to be believed on. Faith natively, faith ultimately, terminates on God: *That your faith and hope might be in God*, 1 Pet. 1:21, where he joins them both together. There can be no believing where God is unknown, there is no believing in an unknown God. God cannot be known as the object of faith, but only as in Christ Jesus. It is impossible that God can be grasped, may I so speak, by the faith of a poor sinner, but only as this God reveals himself to us in Christ Jesus. There is no approaching to God by believing immediately: *but by him we believe in God, who raised him from the dead, and gave him glory, that your faith and hope might be in God*. There is divine faithfulness for the ground of our faith; there is God himself in Christ Jesus for the object of our faith.

Thirdly, In faith there is always an outgoing of the soul in desire and expectation of some good from him. This is believing, this is hoping. Now, this is inseparable from the former. Wherever divine truth is divinely believed to be true, and God in Christ is embraced by the faith of a poor creature, this is unavoidable; immediately there springs some expectation and hope of getting good from him, and that is believing. All the difference betwixt faith and hope is this, that faith goes first unto God in Christ, on the ground of the promise, for good; and hope goes forth to the same God, upon the same ground, in the expectation of that good that is believed. This is not so distinctly owned by every believer; for there are some that have true faith in them, who, through the weakness of their faith, and manifold temptations, nip the expectations of faith from budding. But this is a violence done thereto. Wherever a poor sinner hath taken the warrant of God's promise, and has sealed it with the poor weak amen of his faith, that this is true, and he is faithful that hath spoken it; how can he forbear to add, And therefore there will be a fulfilment, when the good word that is spoken will be accomplished, when the good thing spoken of will be given? The apostle Paul speaking of his own faith, gives it two special words, Phil. 1:20, *According to my earnest expectation and my hope* (he made no doubt, but all things would do well with him), *that in nothing I shall be ashamed, but that with all boldness, as always, so now also Christ shall be magnified in my body, whether it be by life or by death.* The word there *earnest expectation,* is the same word in the original and our translation, with that which is used of the expectation of the whole creation towards the day of the glorious liberty of the sons of God. It is an expression borrowed from an intent looking out as it were, and stretching forth of the neck, in looking to see a friend coming, that will be very welcome when he comes. This is faith, divine truth known, God in Christ received, grasped, laid hold of by faith; expectations raised thereupon, that the good will come unto us. Though many poor believers do not own their expectations, yet such expectations are there, and do discover themselves sufficiently.

II. The second thing is, *What is this profession of faith?* Certainly, profession and confession is a declaring of this expectation I have been speaking of; it is a public declaring it one way or other. The apostle speaks of such kind of confession and profession, Heb. 11:13. They *confessed that they were strangers and pilgrims on the earth*; they made an open public profession of it. Profession of faith is made two ways; it is made either by word, or by deed.

First, Profession is made with words. This the apostle does expressly limit to the tongue, Rom. 10:9-10, *If thou shall confess with thy mouth* (the same word with profession here in my text) *the Lord Jesus, and shalt believe in thine heart, that God hath raised him from the dead, thou shalt be saved. For with the heart man believeth unto righteousness, and with the mouth confession is made unto salvation.* Confession or profession by word is made several ways.

1. It is made unto God in prayer. All our prayers, and all our callings on the name of the Lord, are a confession; all that we say to him is a profession of our faith. *O my soul, thou hast said unto the Lord, Thou art my God.* What great matter is that? Yes, it was a great word, that David's soul could say to the Lord, *Thou art my God.* There is a duty lying upon Christians to profess their faith unto the Lord, to avow it before him. Our Lord will have a poor man do so. *Dost thou believe on the Son of God?* Why, was Christ ignorant whether he believed or no? No; he that was the Son of God knew whether the blind man had faith or no; but our Lord will have it out of his own mouth; he will have him profess it, and avow it: as accordingly he did, *Lord, I believe. And he worshipped him.*

2. Profession is made by the tongue. In that special case of confession, when gospel-truth is opposed, when it is made the state of suffering, then it is that confession is specially called for. It is with respect to this that our Lord's severe word is, Matt. 10:32, 33, *Whosoever shall confess me before men, him will I confess also before my Father which is in heaven. But whosoever shall deny me before men, him will I also deny before my Father which is in heaven.*

Secondly, The profession of our faith is made by deed. A man that cannot speak may make a profession of his faith. He cannot make it by words, but he may make it otherwise; I acknowledge not so easy, for the tongue is man's glory.

1. The outward attending on the means of grace is a profession of faith. Whoever they be that give but their bodily presence unto prayer and preaching of the word of God, and other institutions of Christ's appointment, they profess their faith of the gospel. A great many are

liars in so saying; for they profess what they have not, and God will judge them accordingly. There is more need to be afraid, than people commonly are aware of. It is the most dangerous employment that an unbeliever can be taken up in, to make a secure attendance on the means of faith, when the man knows in his own heart, that he neither hath faith, nor would have it.

2. People may and should make a profession of their faith in their conversations in their families. This is one part of Christian profession, that every one that has a family, that he is master or she is mistress of, are obliged to make profession of their faith there. The Christian conduct of a family is a very honourable way of professing faith. *I will behave myself wisely*, says David, *in a perfect way: O when wilt thou come unto me? I will walk within my house with a perfect heart*, Psa. 101:2. Several good words he speaks there of his purpose of owning of God, and declaring his respect to him, by his conduct in his family.

3. People make a profession of their faith by joining to and embodying themselves with the church of Christ. If there were no more but twenty believers in a city, I am persuaded that within a little time these twenty believers would quickly scrape up acquaintance one with another, and would unite themselves in the profession of their faith. Shall we receive faith, this great gift, and the honour of so near a relation to God and Christ Jesus as faith brings us to, and shall we not own it? It is remarkable the apostle takes notice of this, 2 Cor. 9:13, *They glorify God*, says he, *for your professed subjection unto the gospel of Christ*. The word in the Greek is more emphatical; it is *for the subjection or stooping of your profession to the gospel of Christ*, and your acknowledgment of it. Pray what great subjection is there here? Is it so low a stooping for a man to make profession of his faith, that it must be called a stooping? Is it any wonder that the apostle called it stooping to be subject to the gospel, when he says, Romans 10:3, that the proud self-justiciary will not submit to the righteousness of God? And it is the same word with subjection in the other place.

4. People make a profession of their faith by an holy conversation. A walk as it becometh the gospel, is a profession of our faith, an outward confession of it. All manner of godly conversation, and the adorning of the gospel of God our Saviour in all things, is what is required even

of servants, Titus 2:10. But, say you, what will the gospel be adorned, is there an ornament added as it were to the gospel, by the faithfulness and obedience of a poor mean servant? Yes, says the Spirit of God, you are to adorn the doctrine of God our Saviour in all things. We find it instructed in several very like things. There is the giving of charity to the relief of the saints: That is, says the apostle, *by the experiment of this ministration, they glorify God for your professed subjection unto the gospel of Christ*: and you prove your subjection by your liberal distribution to your poor brethren. Nay, to bring the matter yet lower, and I cannot bring it much lower, and that is even in women's apparel: says the apostle, 1 Tim. 2:9, 10, *Likewise let women adorn themselves, not with broidered hair, or gold, or pearls, or costly array, but* (which becometh women professing godliness) *with good works*. Let the ornament of a Christian that seeks to adorn the gospel be good works, rather than the vanities of this world, that are utterly unbecoming the gospel; that the gospel never taught, and that it frequently rebukes; for these vanities always bring reproach upon it, and upon men's profession too.

5. The last profession of our faith is the last thing we can do; that is, dying in faith. After profession, and adorning our profession all manner of ways, as long as we live; in due time, when God calls us, we are to make profession of our faith in dying. There is a dying faith, as the apostle says of the Old Testament saints, Heb. 11:13, *These all died in faith*. They confessed themselves, all their life long, to be strangers and pilgrims on the earth; and in the same faith that they professed that they were strangers and pilgrims on the earth, in the same faith they died, and went to heaven. This is the noblest of all; and if it be not only dying in faith, but dying for the faith, it is so much the more amiable. 2 Tim. 4:6, 7, *The time of my departure is at hand*, says the apostle, *I have fought a good fight, I have finished my course, I have kept the faith*. Well, had he no more to do with faith? No, but one bit. *Henceforth is laid up for me a crown of righteousness*, etc. I will die in the expectation of the crown, I will have no more to do with faith. So Stephen, the first confessor, the first professor of faith by his blood, Acts 7:59, *And they stoned Stephen, calling upon the Lord, and saying, Lord Jesus, receive my spirit*. 'I have confessed thy name before these enemies, and they are driving this soul of mine out of my body; now, Lord, receive it; I have

believed on thee, I suffer for thy sake, I commit this expelled soul unto thy care and conduct; *Lord Jesus, receive my spirit.*'

So much now for the explaining the matter of faith and profession. The truth that I would speak a little to, is this:

DOCT. *That whoever they be that have Christian faith and hope in them, should make a Christian confession or profession of it.*

It is implied in my text, that a profession of their faith, or a confession of their hope, was made, and the apostle exhorts them about the keeping of it. It is not, Let us therefore make profession, we have done that already; but, Let us hold it fast. When we first gave our name to the Lord, when we first left the Jewish religion, or Paganish idolatry, and turned to the true and living God and his Son Christ Jesus, we then made profession; now let us hold it fast.

He lies to God and to the world, that makes profession of faith, when he hath it not; he dissembles with God and the world, that has it, and does not profess it. We find much spoken of this profession in the word: Heb. 4:14, *Let us hold fast our profession*; a word much to the same purpose with this. This I thought to have confirmed in a few things, and so have made some application. I shall only give a few at this time of the grounds upon which this truth stands, That all that have Christian faith should make a Christian profession of it.

First, The honour of Christ calls for it, Christ's glory and honour. The truth of grace does most immediately tend unto the salvation of a sinner; but the profession of grace tends most immediately to the praise of Christ Jesus. Now remember what severe words I named already: *Whosoever shall he ashamed of me, and of my words, says our Lord, in this adulterous and sinful generation, of him also shall the Son of man be ashamed when be cometh in the glory of his Father, with the holy angels*, Mark 8:38. The glory of our Lord Jesus Christ is promoted by our professing of him. Do you think that Jesus Christ, and his saving truth, and his gracious work upon the heart, are matters to be ashamed of? Is it not a great sin whenever this is committed?

Secondly, The good of others calls for this. The truth of faith is profitable to us; the profession of faith is profitable to others. Were it possible that all the godly could keep in all their grace, that none in the world could see it but God and themselves, none in all the world would be a whit the better for it. It is the displaying of grace and of the faith that God has given, that is the great means of promoting the reputation of the gospel, and convincing of the world: Therefore, says our Lord, *let your light so shine before men that they may see your good works, and glorify your Father which is in heaven*, Matt. 5:16. In the very next chapter our Lord severely inveighs against the Pharisees, that managed their religious worship with a design only to be seen of men: that was all they craved, and their hypocrisy was discovered thereby. But our Lord himself craves this of his people, that their light should not only so shine as to direct their own ways, but so shine that others might see it, and be provoked thereby to glorify their Father which is in heaven. The apostle Peter speaks of a case, I am afraid the mean is seldom tried, and therefore it is no wonder that the effect is seldom found. The mean is a Christian conversation, the effect is conversion. It is the conversation of the wife for the gaining of the husband. Now, the apostle craves this, and hints a promise for it. You would think it strange, that the Christian and sober deportment of a poor woman at home may accomplish that work, that by the ordinary means of grace had been in vain attempted: *That if*, says the apostle, *any obey not the word*, etc. that is, it is possible sometimes that the Spirit and power of God may attend a gospel-like conversation, and make it do that which the gospel and ministerial dispensations have not done; *they may without the word be won*; not that there is any conversion without the word, but that there may be such measures of light and conviction, given by other means that God may bring in otherwise.

Thirdly, We find by this, that our Lord Jesus Christ has a great concern about our profession, Christ Jesus himself was the great professor: He was so great a professor of faith, that his wicked enemies reproached him for it when he was upon the cross, Matt. 27:42. *He trusted on the Lord that he would deliver him*, Psa. 22:8. The apostle calls him *the high-priest of our profession*. He made a profession of his own, 1 Tim. 6:13, *I give thee charge in the sight of God, and before Jesus Christ, who before Pontius Pilate witnessed a good confession*. He told them he was a King, and that he came into the world to set up his kingdom; but they greatly mistook it. Christ might reign in this world, and all the kings of the world might sit where they are. Christ is troublesome to none, but them that trouble him, and he will be too hard for them. We find our Lord frequently upon this in exacting profession, and none needed it less than he. When people came to him for healing, *What would you*, says he, *that I should do unto you?* They tell him; and then he adds, *Believe ye that I am able?* Now, any man might say, If thou be able, thou mayst cure whether I believe or no; but our Lord will have it out of their own mouths. He comes to one man after he had wrought a cure; our Lord finds him out; but the man had confessed Christ honestly, he was a sound believer, and he was cast out of the wicked church of the Jews, John 9. Christ found him when they had cast him out, and says to him, *Dost thou believe on the Son of God? Who is he, Lord, that I might believe on him?* says he. *And Jesus said unto him, Thou hast both seen him, and it is he that talketh with thee. Lord, I believe*, says he, *And he worshipped him*. When Peter is to be restored, our Lord will have it by a confession: he had given one great confession to Christ, *Thou art the Christ, the Son of the living God*, which our Lord praises him greatly for, but he had fallen foully when called to confess Christ in the high-priest's hall. There was no excuse for a man to deny that ever he had seen Christ Jesus, or been in his company. Poor wretched creature! if Christ had left him, if Christ had said, I do not know Peter, as Peter said he is not my master; if Christ had said, he is none of my disciples, what had become of him? Now our Lord is restoring him again (John 21), our Lord asks him one question, *Simon, son of Jonas, lovest thou me*; and *Lovest thou me?* etc. What wonder is it, that the man is grieved that he should come thrice upon him? *Ay, but*, says our Lord, *I will have thee say, Lord, thou knowest all things, thou knowest that I love thee*. This is nothing but a profession of his faith and love.

Lastly, Faith itself will work a profession in a manner, whether men will or no. It is impossible to keep the fire of faith without the smoke of profession, and it is impossible to smother this lamp. If God hath kindled this heavenly fire of faith, and of the hope of the gospel, in any of your hearts, it will break forth one way or other. They with whom you live will know it; your faith will break out sometimes in your tongue; and it will appear, for as modest, and secret, and bashful as the person is, that there is something of heavenly fire working in him. This now is the constant practice of all nations and all people; and the Christian is not to be exempted from this common necessity; every sort of people in the world make a profession of what their faith and hope is: *All people*, says the prophet, *will walk every one in the name of his god*, though they be false gods, *and we will walk in the name of the Lord our God for ever and ever*, Mic. 4:5. Shall a worshipper of Baal be more bold and confident in professing of an idol god, than Jehovah's worshippers? *We will walk in the name of the Lord our God*; we will go up and down, professing and declaring, in all prudent and fit ways, our respects to him. We have an observable word of Jephthah; and truly he was such an odd sort of man, that unless it were for Hebrews 11 and one or two good words in Judges 11, we should hardly own him a believer. One of the words is in verse 11. He *uttered all his words before the Lord in Mizpeh*; that looks something like. He was called extraordinarily to be the head of Israel for their recovery out of a distressed state, and before he attempts the work, he acquaints God. The words that I speak of, and bring to this purpose, are these, verse 24, it is in his message to the Ammonites, *Wilt not thou possess that which Chemosh thy god giveth thee to possess? So whomsoever the Lord our God shall drive out from before us, them will we possess*. Now, here was a great profession of the man's faith: 'You poor blinded idolaters, that call upon your idols, and if you have success in your way, will praise your idols, and keep that which they give you to possess: *Shall not we, keep that which the Lord our God giveth us to possess?*' And, says he, 'Be it known to you we will.' Try all the world over, I say, wherever there is a form of religion, true or false, a profession of it is always required. As far sunk as the Antichristian state is, yet when they admit infidels, and, according to their wickedness, when they drive Protestants to their communion, they crave something of profession of faith. But all these professions are rather professions of opinion. A great many, ask them what religion they are of, they can tell you; ask them the principles of religion, they can tell you them; there is one question still that a great many of our professors are puzzled with; 'Pray, what is your faith?' These truths are the truths of God, but what truth is there in your faith of them? The apostle requires to *be ready always to give an answer to them that shall ask a reason of the hope that is in you, with meekness and fear*. How many of our professors (and we have a great multitude more than the gospel is honoured by), how many of them are not able to give an account of the hope that is in them? Unless this religion be well founded in thy heart, it is none of thy religion; it is the religion only of those that believe. But unless the divine truths revealed in the word, be ingrafted in thy heart by a true and lively faith in them and on them, they are not thy religion, they are only thy opinion. Take heed; this matter of profession, and profession of faith, is not so slight and easy a matter as people imagine. There is a very great danger in folks professing to have faith, when they have it not. We think there was great severity in dealing with those two poor people, Ananias and Sapphira, in Acts 5. There was a custom then, and special reason for it, that several rich folks, in the prospect of the expected difficulties that were coming upon the church, sold their land; two people, man and wife, agreed to sell their land, and keep part of the price in case of necessity for their own relief. Here was but bare lying in this case. It is true, the apostle aggravates it, as it was lying to the Holy Ghost; and it may be, there was something of a design to try the apostles. But this was an innocent thing to what it is for a poor creature to make a profession of faith, when he knows he has it not. To make a profession of that he has not, is to boast of a vain gift. The Lord is strict in observing men's profession; a little thing will go in God's sight for a profession: and accordingly he will deal with men that are not sincere therein; but there is no true profession but that which is sound. A profession that is of truth, is not only, that a man professes to believe truth, but that he does truly believe that which he professes: therefore in the creed, commonly called the apostles creed, the first word in it, and which is the greatest mystery in it, is, 'I believe in God,' I believe that there is a God; 'and I believe in,' etc. Ay, but the main thing in thy creed is the first word, 'I believe this.' What conviction hath the Spirit of God made upon thy conscience of divine truth to enforce this belief? For saving faith is nothing else but the mark which a divine impression of divine truth hath made upon a man's heart.

SERMON II.

HEB. 10:23.

Let us hold fast the profession of our faith without wavering, etc.

I SHALL now proceed to make some practical improvement of what has been delivered in the former discourse.

APPLICATION. *First*, then, we see what a Christian profession is; it is a profession of faith. This is the name given to it in my text. In Heb. 4:14 it is only called *our profession*; sometimes without profession, it is called *our faith, our confidence*, ver. 35. *Cast not away, therefore, your confidence*, etc. To a Christian profession of faith, there are two things required: 1. That it be true. 2. That it be visible. 1. That it be true; that is, that not only it be a profession of divine truth, but that it be a profession of a true faith that men have in the truth. If people profess error instead of truth, they take God's name in vain; if they profess they have faith when they have not, they lie against God and themselves too. Profession must be sound and true; a man must profess what he hath, and no more. 2. Christian profession must be visible. Profession is mainly for others, as faith in the reality of it is mainly for ourselves: the apostle therefore, when he is speaking of the great profession of the faith of the patriarchs, saith, Heb. 11:13, 14, *They confessed that they were strangers and pilgrims on the earth*. And *they that say such things, declare plainly that they seek a country*. All who had known Abraham, and Isaac, and Jacob, who saw their way of living, who beheld their way of not mixing with the rest of the nations, who beheld their faith and hope; these might have seen plainly, these were men for another world than this. There can be no profession unless it be visible. This is so general and well known a thing, that a visible credible profession of Christianity is that only that deserves this name.

Secondly, We see hence, what reason and ground ministers and churches have to call for and require a confession of men's faith and hope. The apostle speaks of it here, as a thing that had passed all these believing Hebrews. He reckons that all of them who had faith, had one way or other made a profession of it. Ministers themselves are or should be eminent professors. Indeed their profession is very public; every time they preach, they profess. The apostle takes notice of this, 1 Tim. 6:12. Thou *hast professed a good profession before many witnesses*; and every time Timothy preached faith, and called others to the hope of eternal life, he did thereby witness to his own faith in so doing. Churches are societies appointed by Jesus Christ, wherein his name is to be held forth in the world; and there is high reason, that all who desire to join with them in partaking of gospel-privileges, should make to them a profession of their faith. Notwithstanding all the corruption that is this day in the world (for I choose rather to call it the world than the church), yet there is something of this remaining in all that pretend to the name of a church; only, that they account their profession is most wofully mistaken. There are a great many who reckon it profession enough, if people be born in a land where Christianity is the common and established profession. Thus it is in the Antichristian kingdom generally. Some reckon, that their outward attendance on ordinances, and outward attendance upon the established religion, is enough to get men the name of professors; it may do so, but this is still short of a profession of faith. Sometimes there is assent required to be expressed unto points of truth or doctrine that a particular church espouses; and if men pass that test, this is thought to be a profession by a great many. In the mean time, the thing in my text is still omitted, and that is, the profession of a man's faith. It is not only the profession of the truth of the point of doctrine he assents to, but of his assent in it, that is necessary. 1. It is greatly for the honour of Jesus Christ, that men should knit themselves visibly under his standard and banner. Our Lord Jesus Christ is no such master, that people should be ashamed to wear his livery, and give themselves to him. Again, it is greatly for the advantage of people too. You know there are two great plagues the church of Christ has been distressed by, and it will never be quite free from them; a multitude of hypocrites in a fair day, and a multitude of apostates in a foul day. When summer-weather is, hypocrites increase to a multitude; when a storm comes, they are blown away as chaff by the wind. What is likely to be the only way that can prevent the abounding of these dreadful scandals? If there were strictness in calling for the truth of people's faith, for the making of them give a true profession of it, if they had it, truly they would be found to adhere to the Lord, far more closely in a day of trial. It is thought to be an outward glory to the gospel and Jesus Christ, to have a great multitude of professors of his name; but the scandal that their conversation gives, and the grievous offences that their apostacy makes, countervail it wofully. Pray, what sort of advantage is it to a poor sinner, to be admitted and entertained in the fellowship of saints, who himself hath no faith at all? People are apt to think that the minister or church are very strict, or severe, that will not admit them to the Lord's table. Sirs, there is a great deal of love in this. What have you to do there, if you have not faith? It is but as it were tendering you poison; for so the special ordinances of the gospel are unto them that have not faith. Therefore,

Thirdly, You see hence what your duty is; to make a profession of faith. Do not look upon it as a matter indifferent, whether you profess it or no. Say you, If I have faith, that will save me; what matter is it, whether the world know it or no? Commonly they that have most of it, make the least noise of it; but it is a duty lying upon believers, to make profession of their faith. I will give you a few things for this. 1. Let us see the Old Testament precepts, that were typical of New Testament practices. There is a notable one in Deut. 26:3, 5-7. I will read it to you, because it hath something worth special regard: ver. 3, *And thou shalt go unto the priest that shall be in those days, and say unto him, I profess this day unto the Lord thy God, that I am come unto the country which the Lord sware unto our fathers for to give us*. They would have all the country know that they are there, and that all the kingdoms round about them might know that they are there; nay, but says the Lord, I will enjoin this upon you, that when you bring the first-fruits of the earth, you make this profession before God. And there is more of their profession, in ver. 5, *And thou shalt speak and say before the Lord thy God, A Syrian ready to perish was my father, and he went down into Egypt, and sojourned with a few, and became there a nation, great mighty, and populous*. Poor Jacob went down to Egypt for want of bread to eat, where God made him a great kingdom. Now, how easy is the spiritual application of this? A Christian is to profess before the Lord his God, that a Syrian ready to perish was his father, nay, not only ready to perish, but that had perished already, and was condemned by the righteous law of God, and yet the Lord had mercy, and gave his grace to him. 2. We find the Old Testament promises of the New Testament practices. Several of them speak forth this profession very peremptorily: Isa. 44:3, 5, *I will pour* (says the Lord) *water upon him that is thirsty, and floods upon the dry ground: I will pour my Spirit upon thy seed, and my blessing upon thine offspring.* And what shall come on it? *One shall say, I am the Lord's: and another shall call himself by the name of Jacob: and another shall subscribe with his hand unto the Lord, and surname himself by the name of Israel.* How explicit are these words, *One shall say, I am the Lord's*! It is not, that they shall only be the Lord's, but they shall say so. There is subscribing with the hand, there is changing of the name: He *shall subscribe with the hand unto the Lord, and surname himself by the name of Israel.* What can this be? Why, he will account himself of, he will enter by his own act and deed into the family of Israel. It is not, that he will compare himself with so great a man as Jacob, so mighty a prince and wrestler with God; nevertheless, to all the privileges he desires to lay claim, and to have the same God to be his God. There is only one word now that is commonly repeated, and as commonly ill understood, as any words we know in the mouths of people; it is the word in the creed as we call it. 'I believe in the holy catholic church, the communion of saints.' 'I believe in the holy catholic church,' is, I believe that Jesus Christ hath a holy church scattered up and down the earth. This 'communion of saints' is of another consideration, as it were one of the privileges of this great church. If there were no saints upon earth to have communion one with another, there would be no church on earth; the church would expire. Blessed be God, that can never be till the Judge come, when the communion of saints ceaseth, and endeth only. Now, here is a grievous fault amongst many people that make some kind of profession. First, some enter into a profession; they slip into it they do not know how; a great many years they have borne the name of professors. What said you? what did you? Do you think the bare crowding to assemblies, where the word of God and prayer is used, will make any think with themselves, This is a man that makes profession of faith? He should do so, and the very outward appearance should never be but with this design: but it is not enough to convey the conviction: for it is certain, that is done many times by them that are quite void of faith. Some again make a profession of their faith once, and they think that is enough for as long as they live; whereas, all our life long, we should be declaring the faith that is lodged in our heart. The whole course of our conversation is but going on in profession; yet many make a profession, and contradict it daily by their conversation. Now, it is a principle that the world will never beat out of wise men's minds, that always deeds will be regarded before words; we will prove men's minds rather by what they do, than by what they say. If a man have a profession of faith in his mouth, and have his conversation quite contrary, no man regards what he says, *Why call ye me Lord, Lord, and do not the things which I say?* says our Lord, Luke 6:46. *They profess,* says the apostle, *that they know God; but in works they deny him, being abominable, and disobedient, and unto every good work reprobate,* Titus 1:16. But so much now shall serve for this, the subject-matter of the apostle's exhortation, the profession of our faith.

The *second* thing in the exhortation, is, the duty itself about this profession that he enjoins; that is, *Holding it fast without wavering*; I take them both together. The thing that I am to speak to is this,

That Christians should be stedfast in their profession. Whatever faith or hope they make by word or deed, they should be stedfast in it, they should hold it fast: *Let us hold fast our profession,* says the apostle, Heb. 4:14.

In speaking to this, I would shew, what is to be held fast; why it is; and how: what is the matter of the duty; what the enforcements to it; and what the manner of it.

I. What it is that is to be held fast, when we are commanded to hold fast the profession of our faith.

1. Hold fast the truths professed. Whatever truths of God we have known and made profession of, we must be careful to hold them fast. This the apostle Paul enjoins to Timothy, 2 Tim. 1:13, *Hold fast the form of sound words, which thou hast heard of me, in faith and love which is in Christ Jesus.* Departing from the faith professed is a grievous transgression; and the apostle here, in this chapter, in these dreadful words that have been so frightful unto many a poor weak conscience, has his

eye upon this crime that I am warning you against: *If we sin wilfully after we have received the knowledge of the truth, there remains no more sacrifice for sin.* A word, I say, that has been grievously mistaken by many a poor exercised creature; a scripture the devil has made use of to disquiet many an honest heart. It is not, if we sin wilfully, if we sin against light and knowledge, that there remains no more sacrifice for sin; that were one of the most dreadful things that can be thought of. The apostle's meaning certainly is this, If we sin wilfully by abandoning the faith of Jesus Christ, who is the only propitiation for our sins, we shall find that there is no other sacrifice for sin: if we resist the only true One, the blood of the covenant, and the Spirit of grace working therewith, as he explaineth in the 29th verse, there is then no more sacrifice for sin, for the sinner then throws away the only sacrifice, there is none else to be had. Apostasy from the Lord, and letting our profession slip, hath begun many a time at some points of truth, which a great many Christians, it may be, thought of no great importance. With what severity does the apostle thunder against the Galatians for their error in point of justification; and that was this, that they would mix the works of the law with the righteousness of Christ in the gospel, chap. 1:6, 7, *I marvel* (says he) *that ye are so soon removed from him that called you into the grace of Christ, unto another gospel: which is not another; but there be some that trouble you, and would pervert the gospel of Christ.*

2. In the holding fast our profession, we should hold fast the communion of saints. Whoever they be that leave the communion of saints for the conversation of the wicked, that person does certainly forego his profession. It is impossible, unless through a strong temptation, that a true Christian can savour that delight to his heart in the conversation of the wicked, as in communion with the godly. Thereupon we find, that the apostle, in the 25th verse, does in a manner explain what he means by holding fast our profession: *Not forsaking the assembling of ourselves together, as the manner of some is*, etc. As if the apostle had said, 'If you forsake your Christian assemblies, your meetings together, your edifying and helping one another, if you forsake these, so far you forsake your profession.'

3. In holding fast the profession of our faith, this is required, that we hold fast the exercise of the grace of faith and hope. If this be not

minded, you will quickly find that all things else in a profession do wither and waste away. When you are called to hold fast your profession, you are called to hold on in believing, in the exercise of it.

II. The *second* thing is, Wherefore is it that Christians should be so careful to be stedfast in the profession of their faith?

1. Because there are a great many devices of Satan and the world to drive people from it. Holding fast does imply that there are endeavours to take things from us. That which none will pluck away, none needs to hold. There is resistance that is made from without, and great are those that are made by Satan and the world. *1st,* From Satan. The devil is a cruel, malicious, and envious enemy. We all have some sort of notion of these woful wickednesses in the spiritual adversaries. But there is one thing concerning the devil we do not duly consider; the devil is the most desperate sinner of all God's creatures. I mean not only desperate in wickedness, but destitute of all relief under it; and therefore the profession of faith and hope in a sinner, is the most grievous thing that the devil can behold. He once had all believers his captives, and would fain bring them back again into his bondage. There is nothing grates the devil more, than a sinner professing his hope in that glory he is fallen from. The devil is a desperate sinner, and he would fain drive all sinners into the same state with himself, and if it were not his cunning, that he knows the danger of awaking men. If the devil had his will, he would rather be glad that all sinners were despairing than flattering themselves with vain hopes; but because their security renders their state more desperate in the issue, therefore the devil befriends them, and keeps all in peace. *2dly,* From the world. You know what enmity the world has testified against the people of God; and all this enmity arises from profession. Let a man have never so much faith, if this faith never discovers itself, neither by word nor deed, the world would never have any sort of disturbance thereby, and would not be angry at men. It is the testimony of the witnesses that torments men that are upon the earth. What, think you, is the reason of all the persecution that you read of in the word, and the bloody persecution that hath been in this land, and several other places? The true reason is the profession of faith of the people of God. If believers would part with their profession, the world would part with their quarrels.

2. Christians should be very careful of their profession, to hold it fast; for the honour of God and his Son Jesus Christ is greatly concerned in it. It is all we can do for his glory. The highest glory that is given to Christ in this world, is by the stedfast maintaining of the profession of our faith. The greatest affront that can be done, is by people's abandoning the profession of that faith they once made. It is a horrible thing; a thing the Lord calls the heavens to be astonished at: *My people have forsaken me*, and have forsaken me upon some alleged fault also: *What iniquity have your fathers found in me, that they are gone far from me?* etc. Jer. 2:5, 12.

3. *Lastly*, Christians should be careful to maintain their profession, to hold it fast; for their peace and their salvation stands mightily on it. It is remarkable how the apostle divides believing and confession: Rom. 10:9, 10, *With the heart man believeth unto righteousness, and with the mouth confession is made unto salvation*. Pray observe, if a man believe with the heart, he is not only possessed of righteousness, and stands clothed with it before God; but salvation is secured to him, by virtue of that righteousness too. Yet you see, that the apostle carefully shuns the dividing these two, faith and confession, righteousness in the one, salvation in the other: *Confession is made*, says he, *unto salvation*. After we are once possessed of the righteousness of Christ by faith, we only want complete salvation, and we must go on confessing his name till we be possessed of it. It is observable, that of all the hells upon earth that ever a true believer fell into, most of them have been upon this account, when the violence of temptation hath prevailed upon the people of God, in a day of trial, to abandon their profession. What sad instances have we of some of the most eminent saints and servants of God, that have been left of God in a day of trial, that have left their profession, and have been tortured in their souls till they have returned to it again, though with the peril of their lives? A stout and free adhering to the profession of their faith, was commonly attended with joy and peace in believing: and denying thereof, and complying with the course of this world, what sad smart did it raise in their consciences.

III. The *third* and last thing is, How this is to be done? I shall not now insist upon all things I thought of, with respect to this, how a Christian is to hold fast his profession. I shall only direct the exhortation these three ways:—

1. Hold fast the profession of your faith before God. If you ever have called God your God and Father, never eat in these words again. How sorry and pitiful, but common a matter is it, that a believer will call God his God confidently in the morning, and may be in the dark evening call him by another name? *Thou shalt call me, My God, and shall not depart from me*: it is a promise the Lord makes; the Lord fulfil it to us.

2. We must learn to hold fast the profession of our faith before the devil. Whenever Satan and we come together, he begins to assault; then be sure to keep the profession of your faith; hold it fast. *Above all*, says the apostle Paul, *take the shield of faith, wherewith ye shall be able to quench all the fiery darts of the wicked*, Eph. 6:16. So also says the apostle Peter, 1 Pet. 5:9, *Whom resist stedfast in the faith, knowing that the same afflictions are accomplished in your brethren that are in the world.*

3. We should be careful to hold fast the profession of our faith before the world. The world has a sharp sight into the infirmities of the saints, but is quite blind as to their virtues: They cannot see these: they cannot see the beauty of the inward man; but they can see the spots in the conversation of the people of God, and they will be careful to take notice of them, and to make more of them than they are. The more captious the world be, the more careful saints should be in their conversations: *Be blameless and harmless, says the apostle, the sons of God, without rebuke, in the midst of a crooked, and perverse nation, holding forth the word of life, etc.* Phil. 2:15, 16.

I would only, before leaving this head, name a few things that make this holding fast of our profession very hard, and should make us the more diligent in the exercise of faith, that we may get strength from the author of our faith to maintain the profession of it.

1*st*, It is very hard to keep the profession of our faith without wavering, when sin is in the conscience. The law of God enters there, and a man sees his own iniquity. Peter perhaps had made no profession of his faith before; but if he had, he renounced it when he spoke those ungodly words, *Depart from me*. What! a Christian pray Christ to leave him; is that spoke like a believer? But the sense of sin was raised in him, upon the appearance of divine power in that great work of Christ.

2*dly*, It is very hard to keep the profession of our faith without wavering, when we see a rod in an angry God's hand, and feel the smart of it upon our own backs. To think the same thing of God, to have the same kind thoughts of Christ, and lively hopes of heaven, in this case as formerly, is hard indeed. Job was a man that held fast the profession of his faith, without wavering, at a mighty rate, when he said, *Though he slay me, yet will I trust in him; but I will maintain mine own ways before him. He also shall be my salvation: for an hypocrite shall not come before him* (Job 13:15, 16). As if he had said, 'I defy all hypocrites in the world to say so.' Is there any but a believer, and a stedfast one, who is able to say, A God slaying me shall be my God.

3dly, It is hard to keep the profession of our faith without wavering, when there is a furnace of men's wrath for our profession, and when there are great hazards a man is exposed to for his profession. This has tried many a man's profession. There are signal instances of this in the 3rd and 6th chapters of Daniel. The furious king and the fiery furnace was just before the three children: 'Now,' says Nebuchadnezzar, 'will you fall down, and worship my golden image, or no? Will you profess still your faith in God?' 'Yes,' say they, 'whether he deliver us, or no, we will not serve thy gods, nor worship the golden image which thou hast set up.' Daniel would not forbear his praying in usual times and places, and usual circumstances, for all the danger of death thereby. This was the confession of his faith.

4thly, It is hard to hold fast the profession of our faith without wavering, in the sight and feeling of unbelief. When a poor creature finds unbelief in him, yet, notwithstanding, to adhere to, and hold fast the profession of his faith, is no easy matter. He was a young believer for time, but an old skilful believer for stedfastness, that gave that answer to our Lord, *Lord, I believe, help thou mine unbelief*; 'I own faith in the face of unbelief, in the feeling of it.' Thereupon it is that that word turns; I suppose a good part of the meaning of it is this that I drive at, 2 Tim. 2:12, 13, *If we suffer, we shall also reign with him; if we deny him, he will also deny us: If we believe not, yet he abideth faithful; he cannot deny himself.* Pray observe, *If we believe not*, if we have not the faith, that strength of faith that the case calls for; yet his faithfulness will take care of securing a gracious issue: for the meaning cannot be, if you have no faith at all; but if your faith be weak, and be not in that high measure the case calls for, the Lord will take care to support it; and he has done so many times to many of his people, and they have been only obliged to God's faithfulness in keeping his word.

Lastly, It is hard to hold fast the profession of our faith without wavering, in the sight of death and judgment. That is the great trial of a man's profession of his faith: this is the great wind, and storm, and rain, that beats upon the house, and tries how well it is built. It is an easy matter to make a profession in a fair day, and keep to it; but when this storm comes, it is a great matter to hold it fast. How many sad instances are there? Many, nay most Christians unconcernedly sit down, and think sometimes that they have faith enough for their daily work; but they do not know what provision they have for this great trial, the very foresight of death and judgment. Death looks near, when it enters, as it were, deeply into the meditation and thought of the heart of a poor sinner. Canst thou maintain the hope thou professedst the other day? canst thou look on death and judgment as near at hand, and say, 'I retain the same confidence and hope of eternal life, that I had when I thought these things were afar off?' The apostle therefore did express his faith extraordinarily, and professed it highly, when he sang, *O death, where is thy sting? O grave, where is thy victory? The sting of death is sin; and the strength of sin is the law: but thanks be to God, which giveth us the victory, through our Lord Jesus Christ,* 1 Cor. 15:55-57. He reckons himself, by faith, as sure of the victory, as if already possessed of it. The believer can, by a strong faith, sing the praise of victory, before the battle be half ended: for the apostle Paul had not yet known what death and the grave were; he knew them only by faith, and knew who had overcome death, and knew that he had an interest in him that had overcome both.

SERMON III.

HEB. 10:23.

Let us hold fast the profession of our faith without wavering, for he is faithful that hath promised.

I HAVE spoke unto the exhortation to the duty that is in the first part of the verse, *Let us hold fast the profession of our faith without wavering.* The apostle, ye see, joins himself in the exhortation; and, as it were, exhorts himself, whilst he exhorts them. That great apostle, who had so much faith, who had made so noble a profession of it, joins himself with the rest of believers, *Let us hold fast,* etc. Paul's faith was greater than that of the Hebrews; his profession and confidence higher; his stock richer; he joins himself equally with them: let us all mind this. Upon this I have spoken unto these two things:—

1. That which is the matter that this exhortation is conversant about, and that is the profession of faith, or the confession of our hope; and of that I spoke under this note, *That whoever they be that have Christian faith and hope, they should make a Christian profession or confession of it.*

2. The *second* thing in the words is the duty he calls to, with respect to this profession; and that is, holding it fast without wavering; and of that I spake last day, that Christians should be stedfast in their profession, 'not moved away from the hope of the gospel,' Col. 1:23. This first part of the verse I shall dismiss with two things, and proceed to his argument.

The *first* is this, That it is a mighty hard thing to make a true profession of faith. *Secondly,* It is a mighty hard thing to keep it when it is made.

First, It is a mighty hard thing to make a true profession of faith. I do not mean it is hard for folks to say they believe, that is as easily said as another word is; but to make a true profession of faith, is a matter of great difficulty. No man can make a true profession of faith, but he that hath true faith. This is certain and evident in itself; for if a man make profession of what he hath not really, it is but a lie, and a lie of a gross sort. No man can make a true profession of faith, but the man who hath not only true faith, but hath some sort of knowledge that he hath it; for the profession of faith is something besides the acting of faith. The acting of faith is, that it be wrought in the heart; the profession of faith is, a confident owning of that act before God, and men, and devils. They are witnesses of men's profession, but the Lord only is the witness of the truth and sincerity of faith; but when faith is come to profession, it is known to more than God. Now, that I may illustrate this in a few things, That it is a hard thing to make a true profession of faith, I would speak a little to both the words, that in our translation, and that in the original. We call it *profession of faith*; the original is, *the confession of our hope*.

1*st*, To take it for profession of faith: *I believe*, the first word in the apostle's creed, applied to divine things, is in some the greatest lie in the world. Most persons are guilty of lying in saying, *I believe*; for God and their own consciences may tell them, that though their tongues speak the words, their souls are strangers to the power and truth of this believing. I will name some few of the heads that people commonly profess faith on; and when they are seriously considered, it will be found that the faith of them is very rare.

1. To begin with that which the apostle calls the first thing that a man must believe, that God is, Heb. 11:6, *He that cometh unto God, must believe that he is*. How uncharitably would people think themselves to be dealt with, if they were charged with want of faith as to God's being? How confident are people that they are sincere, at least in this, 'I believe that there is a God?' Pray consider what there is in this believing. *He dwelleth in light that no man can approach to; whom no man hath seen, nor can see*. Whenever his glory shines in any manner before the eyes of a creature, it is enough to confound him. Do men believe that there is a God, that live plainly as if there were none? Do men believe that there is a God, in whose presence they are continually, and in the mean time have no awful thoughts of him? The true faith of the being of a God would make the world a most miserable world, unless Christ were known, and God in Christ. There is nothing more terrible to a man, as a man, and as a sinner, than any displays of the glory of God, unless there be some discovery of this glory, as shining in grace towards men. There

is more spiritual sense, I believe, than commonly is conceived, in that Old Testament word, *I shall die, for I have seen God.* Jacob wondered at the matter, and *called the name of the place Peniel: for*, says he, *I have seen God face to face, and my life is preserved*, Gen. 32:30.

2. A future state, and the soul's immortality. How commonly do men pretend to believe that they know God in Christ, that they believe the truth of Christ, and the mystery of God manifest in the flesh? He that can believe this well, may believe any thing. Let people be firm in the spiritual belief of it, they are fit to believe any thing; that God became man, Luke 1:35, Gal. 4:4; that this man is God over all, blessed for ever; that this man came in the fulness of time, and laid down his life a ransom for many. There is nothing about Christ Jesus, or about the whole mystery of the gospel, but is incredible to a natural man, and to natural reason. When Paul spake about one point, the resurrection of the dead, *O king Agrippa*, says he, *why should it be thought a thing incredible with you, that God should raise the dead?* Acts 26:8. Here are matters far more incredible: That God should become man; that this man should be still God over all, blessed for ever; that this man is made the great ark for the salvation of all the elect of God. Do not run away easily with an imagination, that it is a common and ordinary thing to believe the truth of gospel-doctrine. People will say, it is very easy to believe what is written in the Bible; it is a hard matter to believe, they may say, their own salvation; and that the one is a great deal easier than the other. If there be a firm assent begotten by the Spirit of God upon the heart, as to the foundation-truth of the gospel, the particular application of that to thy soul for thy salvation will be found an easy thing. Pray now, wherefore is it said so often in the word, that faith is the gift of God; that faith is of the operation of God; that Jesus Christ is the author and finisher of faith? It certainly points forth this to you, That believing is a mighty hard thing; that divine power is needful to beget it, and bring it forward, and act it, and maintain it.

Again, take the matter as to our *hope*, there is great difficulty to avow the hope of eternal life. It is a hope of the greatest blessing that can be conceived, it is a hope bottomed only upon the pure word of God. When you examine your hearts, you find some hopes of being saved; and that, in the day of the Lord, you shall stand with peace and confidence before your judge; why so? wherefore do you hope for this? Is it not because God hath said it? is it not because the God that cannot lie hath spoken it? If you expect to be saved upon any other ground, but because God hath said it, ye must change your minds ere ever you be saved; for ye are off the rock, ye are off the sure foundation that all God's Israel must rest upon. This hope is a hard thing to have and to maintain, because it is a hope that is assaulted; there is no natural probability for it, and a great many difficulties lying in its way. What is there now that can befriend the matter in the eye of sense and reason? There is a poor creature under all the frailties of body and mind, that are either natural to us as men, or that grow and creep upon us by age, and that are in us because of sin; our hope is, that we shall be perfect in soul and body in the enjoyment of God. Now we are encumbered with imperfections every day, and nothing so common and sensible as distance from him, and there is no probability of coming nearer. It is a probable thing that a young child may live and grow to be a man or woman, it is probable that a young plant may grow to be a tree; these are the common works of God in his providence, in guiding of this world; but what is there of probability, by philosophy, by reason, or sense, unto a poor Christian's attaining the possession of his hope? There is none for it, but a great many, on the contrary, against it. There is the law, conscience, sin, Satan, and the world, all combating our hope every day. So that from this you may see it is a mighty difficult matter to make a true profession of faith; a man must have that faith or hope, before he can truly profess them, these things are hard to come by, and hard to keep.

Secondly, It is as hard to hold fast the profession of faith, after we have made it. When a believer hath made a true profession of his faith, and a true confession of his hope, and made it often, it is very hard to hold it fast. The greatest believers have failed here. I do not say failed quite, but they have stumbled shamefully. Who was a greater believer and confessor of his hope than Abraham? yet he stumbled by unbelief grievously, again and again; Isaac did so, Jacob did so. David, that great believer and confessor of his faith, says, *All men are liars*; nay, it were well if his unbelief spake no worse; it was, in effect, God is a liar. Samuel, and Gad, and Nathan, and the other prophets, spake to him in the name of the Lord: And yet, says he, *I said in my haste, All then are liars; and said, I shall one day fall by the hands of Saul*; for all the promises God had made, and for all the faith David had avowed. But above all poor Peter, who is commended above all men for his confession, Matt. 16, how does he fall from it? *Thou art Christ*, says he to our Lord, *the Son of the living God*, ver. 16. *Blessed art thou, Simon Bar-jona; for flesh and blood hath not revealed it unto thee, but my Father which is in heaven.* This great confessor, what a strange confession does he make to the maid! *Art thou one of his disciples?* says she. *I know not the man*, says he. It is impossible, that a believer can keep the profession of his faith stedfast, unless he keep the exercise of his faith constant; if faith decay in its exercise within, the beauty and stedfastness of profession will be marred abroad.

I come now to the *second* thing in the words, and that is, the apostle's argument by which he enforceth this exhortation: *For he is faithful that hath promised*; so we read it. Three things I would take notice of, in the consideration of the reading of the words as they lie here, before I take them up in themselves; three things I note in general.

1. The apostle names no person promising, only speaks in general of one that promises.

2. He speaks of no sort of promise, but only, that there is a promise.

3. This I note also, that the word which we have rendered, *He hath promised*, in the original is in the present time, *He is faithful that is promising*. The promise here is not spoken of as an act past and gone, but of that which was present.

(1.) We find here the apostle does not speak of any person that promises, but only says, *He is faithful that hath promised*. Who then is the promiser? You may be persuaded that it is a divine person; and it is no great matter which of the three we confine it to; for I know it is generally applied to Christ's promising. But we find, 1*st*, That the promises that are the ground of the Christian's faith, are the promises of the Father, as the author, as the grand contriver and original fountain of the covenant. So the apostle calls him, Titus 1:1, *In hope of eternal life, which God that cannot lie, promised before the world began.* 2*dly*, We find the promises ascribed unto Jesus Christ, and he is the promiser. So when he left his people and went out of this world, he left them with the opening of his heart to them in abundance of promises. And in his last prayer, that is as good as any promise in the word; Christ's prayer is as good as any promise in the Bible. The promises are also given by the Holy Ghost: He is called *the Spirit of promise*; both because he is promised, and because he is a promiser and performer too; for promising and performing are ascribed still to the same person, Heb. 10:15.

(2.) The apostle doth not tell us what is promised, but only says, *He is faithful that hath promised.* What then must we understand to be the meaning of this dark expression, when a promise is spoken of, and no particular blessing specified? It is easily gathered from the scope: for the apostle is bidding Christians *hold fast the profession of their faith*; the confession of their hope; for, says he, *He is faithful that promises*; he plainly implies, that what he means by the promise is as large and broad, as all the foundation of the faith and hope that a Christian has. God's promises and our faith are to be commensurate; we are to make our faith as large and wide as the promise; it is to be shapen as the promise.

(3.) The third thing that I note in general is, That the apostle's word in the original is, *He is faithful that is promising*, that is, in the act of promising; so it is in the original; he is faithful that is now, and presently promising; the same word, as in Heb. 11:11. The promises of God are not, as people imagine, things that are over and past, as soon as the word is out of his mouth; but they are continued, constant current streams that will carry on his people that are in them still, till they be accomplished fully. A promise never ends till there be performance; a promise is in act and motion still, till it be accomplished. The like word the apostle hath, 1 Thess. 2:12 and 5:24, *Faithful is he that calleth you, who also will do it*, as we translate it: there had been as good reason to translate it, *Faithful is he that is now calling you*: he called you at first, by the effectual working of his grace with the gospel; and that calling continues still, and it will never leave you, till it bring you to heaven. Just so it is with the promise. There are five places to God's promise, and we must have our eye distinctly upon them. 1*st*, God's promise, is in God's heart; and there it is, but a purpose unknown and unsearchable to all creatures whatsoever. This is called a promise; for it is said, *He promised* *before the world began*, Titus 1:2. 2*dly*, A promise is next considered, as it is in the word. There it is recorded, it is entered, and will never be repealed. 3*dly*, The promise of God is in Christ; that is another place for the promise: *All the promises of God in him are yea, and in him amen*, 2 Cor. 1:20. *The covenant is confirmed of God in Christ*, Gal. 3:17. There is no change here; a promise in God's heart will surely have effect from the word; performance of a promise in Christ's hand can never miscarry. 4*thly*, A promise comes to be in the hand of a believer's faith; and this is a shaking, trembling hand. As it is in God's hands, Christ's hands, or in the word, heaven, and earth, and hell cannot shake it; but as it is in a believer's hand, the least blast from either will shake it. A poor believer grasps the promise of God frequently very weakly; yet he take it, it is well, if he lay hold on it any manner of way. There would none of us ever come to heaven, if the promise of God did not keep us better by its grace and power, than we can keep it by our faith; for this is the order of God, his promise is a mean that catches a believer, and a believer catches the promise by faith. Our hold of the promise many times fails, but the promise to us never fails. If the promise of Christ's grace come and take hold of your hearts, it will hook you, and pull you, and keep you, and draw you certainly to glory; but our faith is off and on. *Lastly*, Believers sometimes have the promise of God in their hand; not only in the hand of faith, but, if I may so speak, in the hand of performance; then they think it is well. If I may use the expression, there was never a good man that had a more blessed armful and heartful than old Simeon; he had all the promises of the Old Testament, and all the blessings of the New Testament, and all grace on earth, and all the glory in heaven, at one time in his arms. When he took the child Jesus in his arms, *Lord*, says he, *now lettest thou thy servant depart in peace, according to thy word; for mine eyes have seen thy salvation*, Luke 2:29, 30. He had the covenant in his hand, he had all the blessings in possession. He might have said as Hannah, *For this child I prayed: and the Lord hath given me my petition which I asked of him*, 1 Sam. 1:27. Something like this believers sometimes have; the promise of God brings forth, and they have the birth in their arms; but this is not that we must live by.

The apostle says here, that God is promising: *Faithful is he that is promising*. I would warn believers of this common fault and failing, they look upon the promise of God as that which is past and over; they are many times saying, I had once a promise of God, I do not know what is become of it now. What, is it out of God's heart? out of the Bible? out of thy faith's hand? The Lord is still promising the promise of eternal life that thou didst lay hold upon in thy first venturing thy soul upon Christ Jesus. God is making that promise every day to you, and you should be believing it every day. We live by faith, and God keeps us in life by promising. His promise runs down through all states and conditions, and so should our faith do. So much now for the general things from the words.

There are several doctrines from it, that I intend, if the Lord will, to speak from.

1. The *first* note that I raise from the words, is (understand it well and wisely, it may be you will think it an odd observation), *The Christian's God is a promising God.* The apostle describes him by this: 'What is the God that I Paul depend upon? He that promises; I will and can have nothing to do with any God, but he that is promising.'

2. *God is faithful in all his promises.*

3. *The faith of his people in a promising God, should some way answer the faithfulness of God in his promises.*

4. *A bold avowing of our faith, is not bragging of ourselves, but a magnifying the faithfulness of the speaker.* This is plainly the scope of, 'Hold fast the profession of your faith without wavering;' for he is a faithful God you lean upon.

Of the *first* of these a little at this time, *The Christian's God is a promising God*; a God made known to us by promises, who comes to us in the mask, and under the veil of promises. Let us see a little how this comes about, and how the world is changed to our great advantage, and his great praise. This promising God was from eternity blessed in himself, and in the mutual communication of love and delight, and converse betwixt the blessed Three. He is also called a purposing God, Eph. 3:11, 2 Tim. 1:9. In the fulness of time he makes a world. He makes himself known in this world three ways. 1. He makes known himself to some creatures by their creation. There are some creatures that God made on purpose that they might know him. He made the greatest part of creatures in a manner only that God might be known by others, not by themselves. The heavens and earth, and all the host of them; this world, and all the creatures that are therein, save one sort, are all incapable of knowing God; but God is made known by them. The only creatures we know that are made capable of knowing God, are angels and men. The one sort, the glorious spirits, were made the first day of the creation; the other is man, half spirit, and half flesh, that was made on the last day of the creation. Now, as soon as these rational creatures start out of nothing, by the commanding word of their Maker; as soon as ever they come into being, immediately the Lord's glory, as a Creator, is staring them in the face. Adam is no sooner a man, than he is a knower of God, as his God Creator. 2. We find God making himself known to man (for it is about man we will keep ourselves confined) as a Lord Commander; and as he has made this creature, he will dispose of him as he sees good. He determines the place of his living; he determines his employment; he lays him under law, and gives him a just and righteous command. He made himself known to man as a threatener too: *In the day that thou eatest thereof, thou shalt surely die*. Ay, but, say you, was there no promise in the first covenant? Truly the word does not say there was any: but if people will needs have it that there was a promise, it is not worthy the name of a promise, in regard of what we have in the New Testament. That promise laboured under woful disadvantages, that we are now relieved from. 1*st*, That promise was a promise of continuance in that happy state he was made in, but no promise of a better. There was no promise of eternal life to the first Adam, as far as we can find in the terms of it. There was no more spoken of, but a continuance in that state: and this is implied in the threatening, *In the day thou eatest thereof, thou shalt die*; which implies, Until the day thou eatest thereof thou shalt live. But we have a promise in the new covenant of a far better state than that we are in. 2*dly*, If there was any promise, it was a conditional one, a promise upon the condition of perfect obedience. There was no promise but upon this condition, *Do this, and live*. Life was promised upon the condition of doing, but no promise of grace to enable a man to *do* it. But now we are brought under a promise, blessed be he that promiseth. Whatever is required to be done by the man that would have the blessing promised, grace to do that is promised by the promiser. Hath he required faith? He hath promised faith, and he works faith. Hath he required repentance? He promises, and gives it. Our Lord is a Prince and a Saviour, to give repentance and remission of sins to the house of Israel. Are we required to be holy in all manner of conversation? Hath he not promises to sanctify and make us holy? Hath he not prayed for this, that we may be sanctified? I told you but just now, Christ's prayer is as good as a promise. The best promises we have in the Bible are the promised made by the Father to the Son; and next to them, are those promises that we draw out of the Son's prayer to the Father. So that, upon these accounts, whatever there was in the first covenant, it is not to be called a promise. *3dly*, There was no mediator in the first covenant; and therefore it cannot be called a covenant of promise, like that we are now brought under. The mediator of a covenant is to see the terms kept on both parts, and to see the ground secure and safe, that the bargain may not go back on either side. This is our Lord's undertaking, and his work. Now you see, that as soon as sin came in, grace comes in with a promise. God made himself known to Adam as his creator, commander, and threatener of just punishment to him for his disobedience. As soon as he disobeyed, so soon is he convicted of guilt in his own conscience. As soon as ever he is arraigned before God, the womb of the promise is open; then the sluice of the promise was drawn up, and it hath been flowing to this day. It began with a promise. Adam and Eve were to know God now under no other name, but the God that said, *The seed of the woman shall bruise the serpent's head.* So it went on through all the Old Testament; that still went along by promise. *The Christian's God*, I say, *is a promising God.*

1. God cannot be known but as a *promising God.* There is no saving knowledge of him, but as he reveals himself in the promise of life through Christ Jesus. 2. There is no worshipping of him but in this way. The apostle joins them altogether, Rom. 10:13-17. How can they call on him of whom they have not heard? How can they believe on him? They cannot pray, they cannot believe, they cannot know him, unless it comes by the word of God. *Faith*, says he, *cometh by hearing, and hearing by the word of God*; that is, the word of promise: Faith never comes by the word of command; but it comes by the word of promise. God commands faith; but God never works faith by the commanding

of faith as any duty, but by the promise of faith as it is heard. The giving of faith, is the performance of the grand promise of faith. 3. There is no believing on God, but as a promising God; there is no loving God, but as a promising God. If you suffer your hearts to take a view of God out of a promise, you wander in a maze and wilderness: he is a consuming fire, except in a promise. The Lord hath framed us in that manner, that it is impossible that God can be loved, but by a person that takes up this God as a promising God. All mankind have either to do with God as promising, or threatening. The threatening God threatens the most dreadfully: the promising God promises the greatest good. It is impossible that there can be true and strong love fixed on that person from whom we do dread the greatest evil: therefore the Lord hath framed the matter so in the dispensing of his grace, in the call of the gospel, that he still tenders himself to his people, and at all times hath done since sin came into the world, under some gracious discovery of himself. *I am the God of Abraham, and the God of Isaac, and the God of Jacob*, saith the Lord to Moses. Even when the man is afraid to look upon God, saith the Lord, *Do not be afraid, I am the God of Abraham*, etc. 'I am the God of thy fathers, I appeared to them, I spake my good mind to them, and they lived and died in the promise and thou, Moses, art one that art concerned therein,' Exod. 3:3, 4.

Two things I shall conclude with at this time.

1. It is a marvellous condescension in God, that he hath come to us as a promising God. He might have stood upon his state, and throne, and dignity; he might have kept upon the throne of his glories: but in wonderful grace he comes down, if I may so speak, as an equal; and he comes into covenant with us, and plights his troth. Is not this wonderful? Solomon wondered: *Will God indeed dwell with men.* No wonder if God will command men; no wonder if God will threaten sinners; these things become God, and are like him, and are suited to his nature; but will God promise to man: *Will he make a covenant with man.* Job 41:3, 4. So Ezek. 16:6-9.

2. As it is a great condescension in God to reveal himself to us as a promising God, so it is a great duty upon his people to keep that name of God continually in their eye. Pray, what do you do in the word? in prayer? What is the God you deal with? Do you betake yourselves to

the word, to hear the word of God as a commander? Ay, but where is the strength for obedience? That is uncomfortable work then. Ay, but, saith the believer, God's promising for all that he hath done for his people before, and all that they have done in their actings of faith towards him, encourages me. Would it not put another sort of edge upon our prayers, were we to eye God as a promising God? What do we do in prayer; think you, what is the business of prayer? The main thing in prayer is to put God in mind of the promise. The great work of Christians is to turn promises into prayer, and God will turn both into performance. Every believer, you know, is to ask according to God's will. The asking according to God's will, is to ask in faith, James 1:5, 6. And not only to ask what God bids us ask, but to ask what God has commanded us to hope; and we know what to hope for, by what God has promised. If we stretch our hope beyond the promise, we are out of the way: but his promises are so large, that a believer needs not to fear but he hath room enough for his faith to work in, nay to run in. The faith of a believer hath room enough to treat with God in. Labour for this. All the disquiets that are in the minds of believers, all the changes that are in their thoughts about the God they have to deal with, all proceed from this. In the day of his love, in the day of their peace, he hath been made known to them as a promising God. Ay, but now there is a cloud comes upon their faith, and may be a veil upon his face; and he comes to them and appears as if he were a threatening or commanding God. No dealing with him in this case. Learn to mind God's true name, *He is a promising God.* The Lord teach you this.

SERMON IV.

HEB. 10:23.

For he is faithful that promised.

YOU heard that these words contain the argument by which the apostle presseth the preceding exhortation to Christians, *Let us hold fast the profession of our faith without wavering*; and the argument is very proper, and very strong, *Let us hold fast the profession of our faith*, for God holds fast his promises sufficiently. Yea, our faith is built upon his promises. It is time enough for faith to stagger when God fails, but never till then. If God could fail, then a believer's faith should fail, and never till then. With regard to this argument of the apostle's, I did first take a general view of it, with respect to something contained in the manner of speaking. 1. He speaks of a promiser, and names no person, only he that promises. He knew well enough, that Christians knew whom he meant, that it was God's promise; faith looks to that only. 2. The apostle doth not tell what he promises; but only he hath promised. And here now it is needful that we gather the extent of the promise, and the nature of the faith and hope that the apostle is exhorting them to maintain the profession of. God's promises, and the believer's faith and hope are justly and equally commensurate; all that we need to desire and hope for, God's promises secure. 3. I noted, that the word here in the original is, *Faithful is he that promises*, or, that is the promiser; or, that is as it were in the act of promising. The promises of God are not past things; they may seem so to us; but they are always current, and present, and acting, and working perpetually, till performance comes.

From the words themselves, I did propose several truths to be handled. The first that I began upon, was this: *That the Christian's God is a promising God.* The name that the apostle here by the Spirit gives him, is, *He that promises.* Besides what was spoken last day, I shall now further speak upon this truth, in handling these two things:—

I. I will shew you what is a promising God, to be considered therein.

II. What need we have of a promising God; that there is no other God can save us but a promising God.

Lastly, I shall make application of the point.

I. *What is a promising God?* It is the true God manifesting his grace and mercy to us, and securing that by his faithful word, that is a promising God; he is the true God, and Father of our Lord Jesus Christ.

1. Consider, in this matter, the high and eternal rise of all promises; and that is the infinite, unaccountable love of God unto the chosen. The promise of God is but the birth of the purpose of God. The purpose of God springs from nothing, the promise of God springs from somewhat. There had never been a word of good-will to the children of men spoken by God, if there had not been thoughts of good-will framed in his heart from eternity. This we find sometimes called the promise: *God that cannot lie, promised before the world began*, Titus 1:2. The meaning is, he purposed it before the world began, and as soon as the world began he revealed it. This is carefully to be taken notice of, That all the promises of God spring from this purpose of God, and are designed by our Lord in their true application to answer the purpose; that as the purpose of his grace is a sure and limited one, determined, and distinct; so the promise is of the same design. *Who hath saved us*, saith the apostle, *and called us with an holy calling, not according to our works, but according to his own purpose and grace, which was given us in Christ Jesus before the world began, but is now made manifest by the appearing of our Saviour Jesus Christ*, 2 Tim. 1:9, 10.

2. About this promising God and his promises, we are to consider the channel wherein they run; and this is all in and through Jesus Christ. That man looks with a bad eye upon any of the promises of God, that does not see Christ in them; and they do not see Christ rightly, unless they see all the promises in him. We see the covenant in him, and him in the covenant; all the promises of God are in him; he was promised himself, and all the blessings that are promised, are purchased by him, and left to his people as a legacy in his last will, confirmed by his own death.

3. The promises in this promising God, come to be considered as they lie before us in the word. There they are indited by the Holy Ghost, and written by holy men of God, that were acted by the Spirit of God; and, if I may so speak, there we have them in black and white.

4. We would consider the promise as the father of believers, or the mother in a figurative phrase. Every believer is a child of promise: *Now we brethren, as Isaac was, are the children of promise*, Gal. 4:28. Not only are we heirs of the promise, for that relates to the estate, Gal. 3:29, Heb. 6:17 and 11:7, 9; but children of the promise, begotten again to a lively hope through the promise. When a poor creature is converted, it is the promise of God that does it. The efficacy of the promise of God, in its begun performance, does change and renew the heart, James 1:18, 1 Pet. 1:23. The apostle, concerning his own conversion, says, *It pleased God, who separated me from my mother's womb, and called me by his grace*, Gal. 1:15. It was a kind of strange separation. The poor young man was left of God as eminently as any youth in all Judea; at his best he was a superstitious blinded Jew, and at his worst a bitter enemy to the name of Jesus Christ. Who would think now this man was separated from his mother's womb for God? he seemed to be separated from God, and separated to the vengeance of God. For all this, grace seized his heart, and he is called in due time. These things we are to conceive when we speak and think of a promising God: the rise of them, in the purpose of God's heart; the channel of all the promises, in and through the heart's blood of our Lord Jesus; recorded to us in the word, and in God's good time applied to the heart, to call in the heirs of promise, and to bring them home to possess their estate.

II. The *second* thing is, *What need we have of a promising God?* This must be a name peculiarly applied unto the God we call upon and believe in. Since sin hath come into the world, there is an absolute necessity of our having to do with a promising God, and of God's dealing with us as a promising God, otherwise there can be nothing but ruin on our part.

1. Because God cannot be savingly known but as a promising God. The promise of God is both a veil, and a glass that we perceive God in. It is a veil upon his inconceivable, unapproachable glory: it is a glass wherein we may perceive, and may get near to him. We cannot

possibly take up any comfortable, saving, right apprehensions of God, but as he is clothed and veiled to us in a promise. His own glory is unapproachable; his justice, his majesty, these great attributes of his, are all amazing and confounding to poor creatures. But when God comes near to us, and promises great and good things to us, then we come to know him. It is remarkable how Moses dealt with God, and God dealt with Moses, Exod. 33 from ver. 13 to the end. The man is there praying for Israel under their great sin, and under God's great wrath for it: *Shew me now thy ways*, says he, *that I may know thee, that I may find grace in thy sight*. At last he arises, *Shew me thy glory*, ver. 18. Whether Moses was led or left unto any unbecoming desire, to his desiring more than his present state could permit, we cannot peremptorily say. He was in a high degree of communion with God, as any mere man in this world ever was. The Lord answered him most graciously, and fitly to our purpose. Moses prays that he may behold God's glory. What! had he not seen enough already? He saw, with all the people, the glory of God in the giving of the law; he saw a great deal more in his more near approaches to God; he saw it yet more in his staying with God forty days in the mount; he saw the pattern of the temple in the mount. Moses yet, for all this, cries, *I beseech thee shew me thy glory*, as if he had never before seen any thing of the glory of the Lord. Says the Lord, *I will make all my goodness to pass before thee* (my greatness would confound thee), *and I will proclaim the name of the Lord before thee; and will be gracious to whom I will be gracious, and will shew mercy on whom I will shew mercy*. Accordingly the Lord proclaimed it, chap. 34:6, 7. Will you take in now this that I drive at from this quotation, that a clear perceiving by faith of the sovereign grace and goodness of God in his promises of grace and compassion to poor sinners, is the most beneficial and highest discovery of divine glory that sinners can arrive at, and that believers should desire in this world. When we pray that God would shew us his glory, the Lord will understand it thus, and answer it thus: *I will cause all my goodness to pass before thee*. The more we see of his goodness, the more we see of his glory.

2. God cannot be worshipped acceptably, but as a promising God. Says the apostle, It is required that every man that comes to God to worship, must believe that *God is, and that he is a rewarder of them that diligently seek him*, Heb. 11:6; that he is a gracious God, not only great

in his being, but good, and bountiful, and kind, and gracious to them that seek him.

3. God cannot be trusted in, unless he be known as a promising God. Trust in God, faith in him, is a special point of worship; it is not a duty of worship so much as it is a grace that should accompany every duty. Now, whence can faith in God arise unless God speak some good to us? Faith arising from any other spring, is a dream and vain imagination of our own minds, not bottomed upon the single, sole word of God. *They that know thy name will put their trust in thee: for thou, Lord, hast not forsaken them that seek thee*, Psa. 9:10. In Jacob's pleading, Gen. 32:9, 13, see how exactly he stands upon God's word. He not only calls God, the God of his father Abraham, and the God of his father Isaac, that was a promising God; but the God that said unto me, *Return unto thy country, and to thy kindred, and I will deal well with thee*, ver. 9. *And thou saidst, I will surely do thee good*, ver. 12. See how Jacob's wrestling stood, how, if I may so speak, the man behaved himself in his mighty wrestling with God, all with the force of his word; upon that word of his; saith he to the Lord, 'Lord, thou bidst me, I am in the way thou bidst me go in; *and thou saidst, I will surely do thee good.*'

4. God cannot be loved but as a promising God. Love to God is promised, and love to God arises from the discoveries of God's goodness to us: and the clearer these discoveries be, love still increases.

5. All the enjoyment we have of God in this life, is enjoying of him as a promising God. Pray now which way is it that there is that intercourse, and that familiarity, that mutual dealing between God and us, that is called by those blessed names in the word; *fellowship with* him, *enjoyment of* him, *finding of* him? All stands in this; we approach to God by the warrant of his promise, he draws near to us according to his promise, and in the fulfilment of it. The promise is as it were Jacob's ladder, by which God comes down to us, and we rise up to him again. The communion which believers have on earth is with God as a promising God; and the communion the glorified have with him above, is with God as a performing God; and, if I may so speak, until God has performed all he has promised, he must never lose the name of a promising God to a believer.

Lastly, In the great wisdom of God, this name of God is appointed to be the great name wherein he will be glorified. The greatest glory that is given to God, is given under the name of a promising God. What is the reason that Abraham is especially said to give glory to God? *He was strong in faith, giving glory to God*, Rom. 4:20. Believing is but thinking, it is no more; but it is a rare thing, it is a great thought; and a great many things seem far bigger than believing. Doing seems to be a great deal greater than believing. Abraham's offering his son Isaac was a great act; ay, but the excellency of it lay in the faith he did it by. The reason why believing is specially said to give glory to God, is, because the Lord hath a special mind and design to have himself glorified in the soul, under the name of a promising God: and all good things shall come to his people, to make them happy by virtue of the promise. But the maker of the promise, and the keeper of the promise, and the performer of the promise, must have all the glory. All that is in the promise is ours, but all the praise of making it is his; it is made by grace, kept by grace, performed by grace; all this glory is to be given to him.

Application. The *first* use is this. That the Christian's God is a promising God. I therefore call you to enquire and determine, before God and your consciences, whether you do know God under this name. Do you know God as a promising God? A great many Christians there are that know no such thing; they are called, but are not really so. The acquaintance that most Christians have with God (poor it is), is with him as a commanding God. But if this does not settle and fix ordinarily in your thoughts, and in all your dealings with God, *I have now to do with a promising God*, all you do is worth nothing.

1. If you have not to do with a promising God, you do not know God's mind. There is a great difference, you know, betwixt knowing a man's face, and shape of his body, his estate, and garb, and house, &c. and knowing his heart and thoughts, and how he stands affected towards us. All other speculations about God are tolerable pieces of philosophy to them that have no better; but the grand inquiry that should possess our hearts is, What does this God think of me? What does he intend to do with me? This cannot be known but by the promise. Unless I have some good word from this God to show his good-will towards me, what do I know more than the devils do? for the devils know God

better than any men in this world, saving that they know God's wrath is against them to eternity. But this name, *a promising God*, they know nothing of. A great mercy it is that ever God should be known as a promising God to sinful men. God was never revealed as a promising God to fallen angels, but he was so to fallen man.

2. Unless you know God as a promising God, you cannot know God in Christ; and you do not know the true God, unless you do know God in Christ; unless your determinate knowledge of God, be of that God that shines in his glory to us in the face of Jesus Christ. We must look upon no God out of this face; for there is no eye that can perceive God, but as he shines this way, says the apostle, *We know, that the Son of God is come, and hath given us an understanding, that we may know him that is true: and we are in him that is true, even in his Son Jesus Christ. This is the true God and eternal life*, 1 John 5:20.

3. If you do not know God as a promising God, you know nothing of the marrow and substance of the Bible. Take away God's promises out of the Bible, and there is nothing left in it, but bones, and stones, and poison, and darts for poor man. If you do not see God as promising, you do not know the marrow of the scripture; for the heart and marrow of the will of God lies there.

Lastly, If you do not know God as a promising God, you cannot deal with God about salvation. Pray now, which way is it that men deal with God about their salvation? I do acknowledge, that there are some people that make a fashion of dealing with God about their salvation, who do not understand the way of God's dealing with them about salvation. Such kind of dealers spend their time to no purpose. All right dealing with God about our salvation, is in answering of God's dealing with us in that matter. Now, all the Lord's way of dealing with us about salvation is by his promises; he promises eternal life, he sends this promise to us in the gospel; we must lay hold on this, or we cannot deal with God, as he deals with us, Psa. 27:8, Eph. 4:32, Rom. 4:13, Hos. 2:23.

Secondly, I would add an exhortation or two unto Christians. Is the Christian's God a promising God? Keep always this name of God in your heart and eye. You will find no great ease in this work; it is a hard work to keep God as a promising God still in the eye, but it is very needful.

1st, Do not you find God began with you this way, and you began this way with God? You that are true Christians, that have been born again, that have been transplanted out of the old stock into the new, do not you know something of this, that as long as God was known to you only as a commanding God, and as a threatening God, there was nothing but death, and ruin, and damnation in your eye? but when he was revealed as a promising God, then light, and life, and hope, and liberty began to arise. Was there ever a distressed conscience in the world truly pacified without a promise? If it were without a promise from God, the devil was the doctor, and the disease is worse than ever it was. If ever thou hast been afraid of the wrath of God for thy sin, if thy mind has been quiet without a promise of God through Christ Jesus, you are but dreaming still; such a cure is worse than the disease. The apostle tells how it was with him: *When the commandment came*, says he, *sin revived, and I died*, Rom. 7:8, 9. There was woful work when the commandment came. When God is only known to you as a commanding God, sins grow greater, and appear exceeding sinful: but when grace comes, when the promise comes, the matter is altered, the prisoner is rescued. *Before faith came*, says he, *we were kept under the law*, Gal. 3:21-24. We were prisoners till Christ came, and the promise came, and faith came; for they are all three come together. Christ comes by the promises, and the promises are received by faith, and the prisoner is made whole by faith.

2dly, You must mind this constantly, for all believers must live by faith; and if so be we are called to live by faith, surely we must remember that God is a promising God; this is necessarily implied. To live by faith, implies these four things. (1.) That a poor believer in himself is a poor empty creature; he hath nothing at home to live by in his house, Isa. 3:7. And since there is no bread within, he must live abroad. (2.) It implies, that the stock that a believer is to live upon is elsewhere; it is without him, it is with God in Christ, Col. 3:3. (3.) It implies, that there are ways, issues, vents, by which he may go out for it, or it may come in to him; passages by which communication of this fulness in Christ comes in to the actual possession of the believer. There were no living by faith, unless the stock that is in Christ had ways of venting itself, of being brought down unto the hand, unto the use and benefit of the poor believer; and this is by the promise. And therefore it follows (4.) That the daily and constant work of a believer, is to be pleading these promises for his supply. *I live,* saith the apostle, *yet not I, but Christ liveth in me: and the life that I now live in the flesh, I live by the faith of the Son of God, who loved me, and gave himself for me,* Gal. 2:20. *Lastly,* He finds the good of it, Psa. 27:3, 28:7.

Lastly, Mind this frequently, that God is a promising God; for as you must live by faith on a promising God, so you must die and go before him under this name. The great appearance must be ventured upon under this name. There are few folks, Sirs, that are so happy, as to make their approaches to God by faith, with that dread, and reverence, and awe, that the last approach requires: we should then act firm faith frequently; we must die in this, with this God in our eye, as a promising God. We have a remarkable instance of this in those two good men, the father and the son, good Jacob 147 years old, and good Joseph 110 years old: *Behold,* saith Jacob to Joseph, *I die, but God shall be with you,* Gen. 48:21 and 49:25, Luke 2:30, and as if Joseph had learned it of his father, he tells his brethren that survived him, when he came to die, Gen. 50:24, *I die,* says he, *and God will surely visit you, and bring you out of this land, unto the land which he sware to Abraham,* etc. As if these two holy patriarchs had said, 'Now we die, but our promising God lives still, and the promise lives, and will have its accomplishment in due time.' It is upon this, that David amongst his last words spake that great word, 2 Sam. 23:5, *Although my house be not so with God; yet he hath made with me an everlasting covenant, ordered in all things and sure.* An ill-ordered house, but a well-ordered covenant; many things amiss in the one, but nothing amiss in the other, said the believer. So must you die, breathing out, 1. Your soul, Psalm 31:5. 2. Leaving your body in the dust, Psalm 16:9. 3. Your present enjoyments, 2 Sam. 33:5. 4. All your sinful infirmities.

The *second* exhortation is this, Make use of this name of God as a promising God, carefully and wisely. How you should use this name of God, I would instruct you in a few things.

1. In all your extremities mind this name only.

2. In all your walk, or ordinary cases, mind it mainly.

1. In all your extremities mind this name of God only; there is no

other name then to be minded. There are two sorts of extremities that Christians feel; and it is their great wisdom, when in them, to use this name. *1st,* There are extremities of conscience. *2dly,* Extremities of distress and dispensations. In extremities of conscience, people must be very careful to remember no name of God, but the name of the promising God; all is terrifying but only this. I hinted but just now, that the promise of the gospel is the only plaister for a wounded conscience, and when God lays it on and blesses it, it is marvellous what a sudden cure it will do. Health and peace quickly will follow this application. In extremities of distress, it is to be only minded, when people are borne down quite, and know not what to do. Saith Jehoshaphat, *If when evil cometh upon us, we cry unto thee in our affliction, then thou wilt hear and help,* 2 Chron. 20:9. Good Hezekiah was a follower of him in this practice. *O Lord,* says he, *I am oppressed, undertake for me,* Isa. 38:14. I may allude to the meaning of the word; undertaking there is undertaking as a surety; I may compare it with the same his great-grandfather David useth, Psa. 119:122, *Be surety for thy servant.* O what a prayer is that! The good man is in deep distress; as if he should say, 'My word signifies nothing before God, nor men, nor devils; it will not pacify God, nor quiet conscience, nor stop the devil's mouth; *Lord, be surety for thy servant,* speak a good word for me, thou art a promising God.' It is great boldness of faith for a believer to come to God to pass his word for him, to be surety for him.

2. In ordinary cases, we must mind this mainly. There are several other names of God by which he is known to us in the word; and in his dealings with us, we must give them their due room; but this must be the main still. As for instance, God is known to us as a commanding Lord and God, that reveals his will about our work and duty, hath proclaimed his mind, and calls for our obedience. Your duty with respect to this is, *1st,* Take the commands of God out of the hand of a promising God; This is not a bare commanding God, but it is a promising God that does command me. And unless you look thus on God's law, you may quickly over-stress yourselves in your endeavours after obedience, and yet do nothing to any purpose. See how observable this is in the giving of the law. God's glory was displayed, Israel and Moses trembling, Heb. 12:15, etc., yet I am your God. *I am the Lord*

thy God, which brought thee out of the land of Egypt, out of the house of bondage; thou shalt do so and so. Observe now the preface to the commandments (see Deut. 26:16-19). It is not, Thou shalt do so and so, and then I will be thy God; the Lord does not first reveal himself to them as a commanding God, and promise that, upon their obedience, he will become a promising God; but he reveals himself as a promising God, and upon that requires their obedience to him as a commanding God: *Because I was thy God, I brought thee out of the land of Egypt*; and after I have brought thee out of the land of Egypt, I tell thee my mind about thy duty. Oh that some Christians (if I may so speak) could find as much gospel in the preaching of the gospel, as is plainly here in the preface of the law; but some will make gospel-promises come in after obedience to gospel-precepts. There is no obedience that ever was performed by man rightly, nor graciously accepted by God, but that obedience that was performed to the commands of God, as a promising God. Again, we are not only to take a command out of his hand, as a promising God, but we are to turn the commands back again, for grace to perform them, Psa. 119:6-8. As soon as ever God reveals his mind to us about our duty by a command, we are immediately to turn the command upon him in prayer: *Lord, perform thy words; write them in my heart, that I may keep them*, for that is the promise. Psa. 143:10. What a great word is that, *Teach me to do thy will, for thou art my God!* It is not, to know or love thy will, though that is needed and begged, Psa. 119; it is not, Teach me to do thy will, that thou mayst be my God; but, *Teach me to do thy will, for thou art my God.* Faith in God animates his prayer for grace to yield obedience to it. God reveals himself sometimes to us as a threatening God. Threatenings and promises seem to be very cross to one another. It is the promising God that does threaten, and the Lord knows very well how to make his promises and his threatenings agree together, if we were wise to make them agree together in our faith. *If his children forsake my law*, etc. *I will visit their transgressions with the rod, and their iniquities with stripes. Nevertheless, my loving-kindness will I not utterly take from him*, Psa. 89:30-34. It were well for us, if we were as able to believe the standing of promises, and the love in his heart, notwithstanding the threatenings and the strokes of his hand; if we could in some measure do that, as well as he can make all his ways towards us to be mercy and truth. *All the paths of the Lord are mercy and truth unto such as keep his covenant, and his testimonies*, Psa. 25:10. We cannot easily see it, but God can easily do it. Sometimes God is manifesting himself to his people as a hiding God; that is a sad discovery, if it should be properly such; but it is a name of God oft known: *Verily*, saith the church, *thou art a God that hidest thyself, O God of Israel the Saviour*, Isa. 45:15. *I will wait upon the Lord that hideth his face from the house of Jacob, and I will look for him*, Isa. 8:17, Job 23:3-13. The sum of all this now is, that this name of God, *the promising God*, is the leading name that should mainly be minded by Christians in all his appearances. We take his commands, threatenings, rods, and corrections, we must use them all, as remembering that all these are from a *promising God*. If the commands were alone without a promise, who could perform them? If the threatenings were alone without a promise to sweeten them, and take away the poison of them, who could endure them? But all this is consistent with his love, and therefore should not shake the faith of a believer.

SERMON V.

Heb. 10:23.

He is faithful that promised.

YOU have heard again and again, that these words are the argument by which the apostle presseth the exhortation unto the duty of Christians *holding fast their profession of faith without wavering*. The argument is strong in itself, and pertinent to the apostle's scope, and is an argument that has a great deal of good truth in it, with respect to its contents. I have shewn what is in these words, *He is faithful that promises*. I first spake last day to this truth, *That a Christian's God is a promising God*. The name the apostle here gives him is, *He that promiseth*. He promiseth like himself, like a God. He is known by his promises.

The *second* thing that I am now to speak to is this, *That this promising God is faithful in his promises: He is faithful that promises.* This is a name of God frequently given to him in the word, both in the Old and New Testament. The prophet hath a great word about it, *Great is thy faithfulness. His mercies are renewed towards us every morning. His compassions fail not,* Lam. 3:3. In the New Testament it is frequently used also: 1 Cor. 1:9, *God is faithful, by whom ye were called unto the fellowship of his Son Jesus Christ our Lord.* 1 Thess. 5:24, *Faithful is he that calleth you, who also will do it.* 2 Thess. 3:3, *But the Lord is faithful, who shall establish you, and keep you from evil.* And I name these rather in the New Testament, because in all these three places that I have named, the word in the Greek is the same with that in my text. This is a name of God that all believers know, and all that would be believers must study. There is never a believer in the world but knows that God is faithful; and if they knew it better, they would be better believers: and no man can be a believer, till he know that his God is faithful. There is no trust given to him, till his trustiness be known.

I shall therefore, in handling this name of the Lord our God, *A faithful God that promises,* give you, *First,* The meaning of it; *Secondly,* The grounds of it: the meaning, that you may understand it; and the grounds of it, that you may believe it the better.

I. The meaning of this word, this name of God, *that he is faithful,* contains these things:

1. He promiseth who purposeth, neither rashly nor hastily. All his promises are from eternity.

2. God speaks as he thinks. It is one of the greatest and worst pieces of dishonesty in promising, when people promise what they think never to do; that is, lying. There is lying in promising, when people do not intend to perform: as well as in asserting that to be true, when they know it to be false. The wise man takes notice that there are such kind of folks in the world, Prov. 23:7. But when God promises, he speaks as he thinks.

3. God is faithful in this sense, that he remembers always what he says. There are some rash folks that promise a great deal more than they perform, because they forget a great deal of what they promised. Our Lord never forgets a word of his promise. Whenever he has made

a promise to a believer, it is fixed perpetually in his heart. Forgetfulness is not to be ascribed to God. I know believers sometimes, in fits of unbelief, have charged God this way: *Hath God forgotten to be gracious? Will the promise fail for evermore?* So in the Hebrew, Psa. 77:7. But that is the infirmity of the speaker. We find sometimes also, the people of God putting God in mind of his promises; yea the Lord calling them so to do: *Put me in remembrance*, Isa. 43:26. But this putting God in remembrance is required of us, and to be performed by us, not to help God's memory, but to exercise our faith: *Keep not silence, till he establish and make Jerusalem a praise in the earth*, Isa. 42:6. *Remember*, says the Psalmist, *the word unto thy servant, upon which thou hast caused me to hope*, Psa. 119:49. The Spirit of God tells us of the exactness of God's remembrance many times. His mercy towards his people is expressed this way. This is one of his names, *He remembers his mercy to them that fear him, he is mindful of his covenant*, Psa. 111:5. Nay, as to his people, it is spoken also, that there was *a book of remembrance written before the Lord, for them that feared the Lord, and thought on his name*, Mal. 3:16. I argue from that, that if so be the Lord keeps so exact an account of the poor slender thoughts that his poor people have of him, how much more will he keep a good remembrance of all his own precious thoughts concerning them, and of all the good words he passeth to them: Psa. 40:5 and 139:17.

4. God is faithful in this sense, that he never changeth his mind. Poor frail men may sometimes promise with an honest mind, and they may see good reason for the changing of it. Sometimes it is lawful to change in some cases, sometimes not. There may be sin in giving a rash promise, that may be greater than the breaking of it. The Lord never changes his mind. Balaam is called a false prophet by Peter; but the meaning is, he was not a false prophet in his prophesying, but a false prophet that prophesied. The Spirit of God spake by him, but never touched the graceless man's heart: *God is not a man, that he should lie, neither the son of man, that he should repent: hath he said, and shall he not do it? or hath he spoken, and shall he not make it good?* Num. 23:19, Job 23:13. God never changeth his mind, never comes to be in another mind, than that wherein he made his promise unto his poor children. Whatever changes there be in his dispensations, there is no change in

his mind, *If his children forsake my law*, etc. *I will visit their transgressions with the rod, and their iniquity with stripes.* Here is a great change in God's dispensations; instead of heaping loving-kindness upon them, he is visiting them with rods and stripes. *Nevertheless, my loving-kindness will I not utterly take from him, nor suffer my faithfulness to fail*, etc. *Once have I sworn by my holiness, that I will not lie unto David*, Psa. 89:30-35.

Lastly, God is faithful in promising, because he always performs what he promises; he always does as he says, speaks as he thinks, remembers what he says, never changes his mind, and always performs his word. What the testimony was, that Joshua exacted of the consciences of the Israelites, when he possessed the land of Canaan, our true Joshua, Jesus, will exact and get of all the true Israel, when they come to the true Canaan: Josh. 23:14, *And ye know*, says he, *in all your hearts, and in all your souls, that not one thing hath failed of all the good things which the Lord your God spake concerning you; all are come to pass unto you, and not one thing hath failed thereof.* This is briefly the meaning of this great name of the Lord our God, a faithful God, faithful in his promises.

II. The *second* thing is, to give you some grounds for our faith concerning this: for it is no small matter to have a firm faith of God's faithfulness. All faith is bottomed upon the promises, and all faith in the promises is founded upon the faithfulness of the maker of them. Though the promise be never so good, yet if the maker of the promise be not faithful, it is no security to the man that gets it.

I am to shew what grounds there are that we may use, and are given us in the word of God, for the clearing our understanding, and fixing our faith on this name of God: *That this promiser is faithful.*

1. The *first* I shall name is taken from the *nature of God.* Faithfulness is inseparable from his nature, as inseparable as any other name that can be given him. Omnipotency is of the nature of God; a weak God is no God, but an idol. Truth and faithfulness are in the nature of a God; a false god is an idol. Therefore, when the apostle would aggravate unbelief, gospel unbelief, he aggravates it by this; *He that believeth not God, hath made him a liar, because he believeth not the record that God gave of his Son*, 1 John 5:10. What is it to make God a liar? It is impossible for a creature to do so; but they account him so, that is the meaning of it. When we do not take God's promise, it is to make God a liar, it is to

make God a devil; for the devil *is a liar, and the father of it*, John 8:44. See what rank wickedness there is in unbelief, Jer. 15:18, Psa. 77:7-10.

2. We find this, the *unchangeableness of God* is another ground of his faithfulness: *With whom is no variableness, neither shadow of turning*, James 1:17. Changing is always a creature infirmity; it is impossible for a creature but to be changeable. Unchangeableness is a divine property, and cannot be communicated to any creature. Changing is twofold, 1*st*, From worse to better. 2*dly*, From better to worse. Neither of which can be in him. Whatever there is of fixedness in the state of believers, it is not unchangeableness; but it is a communicated security by the grace of God, the giver of it. All questioning of the promises of God always charges him with being changeable. He is the same that he was, whatever the unbeliever, or the unbelieving, doubtful believer may think. He is so as to established angels, and saints in glory now, and to eternity.

3. The great room that grace hath in the promises, is one good ground for our faith, as to the faithfulness of God in the making of them. And this is twofold. 1*st*, Grace is the spring of all the promises. 2*dly*, The glory of grace is the design of all the making of promises, and performance of all the promises: *Therefore it is of faith, that it might be by grace; to the end the promise might be sure to all the seed*, Rom. 4:16. It is by promise; this promise is by grace, that it may be sure to all the seed. If the promise were given upon any other account, and did flow from any other spring but the grace of God, it might grow dry. If God promised to us upon the account of any condition that might be wrought by us, the promise might not be sure; but this springing from the good-will and grace of God himself, as long as that remains they must stand. The design of all the performance of promises is the glory of grace. Our Lord speaks many good words to us in the scripture, he makes these warm sometimes upon the heart of his people in their faith, and at last, when all these good words shall come to good deeds, and shall shine forth in their glory, what a wonderful sight will that be, to see every poor believer have in his face, his heart, his soul, and body, all the promises of God fulfilled to him! Then the question will be, Why hath God done all this? why hath he rescued, and scraped, as it were, a company of vile sinners out of the bottom of hell, to fill them

with so much glory, and that to eternity; all to the praise of the glory of his grace, wherein we are accepted in the Beloved! Therefore are we adopted, therefore are we elected, therefore are we justified, therefore are we sanctified, and therefore are we glorified, that it might be *to the glory of his grace*, Eph. 1:4-14 and 2:7.

4. The great room Jesus Christ hath in the promises is one ground of our faith, that God is faithful in them, and that they shall fulfilled. Christ's room in the covenant is so great, that in effect he is it, and he is called the *covenant*, Isa. 42:6, 49:8. He is also called the *promise*, when the Father sent him into the world: *He hath raised up an horn of salvation for us*, says Zacharias, Luke 1:69. Christ's interest in the covenant and in the promise is great: they are said by the apostle to be all *in him yea, and in him amen, unto the glory of God by us*, 2 Cor. 1:20. God's glory wants sinners to work upon. If there were not lost sinners in this world, promises of grace could have none to work upon. If we were all perfectly holy, what hath the promise of forgiveness to do in this world. Says the apostle, They *are all in him yea, and in him amen, unto the glory of God by us.* We in our sins, infirmities, weaknesses, are the field wherein the glory of God's promises is displayed and advanced, and all this in Christ Jesus. Christ's interest in the promise is threefold. 1*st*, Christ hath bought all the blessings in the promise, and all the heirs of the promise; he hath bought us for the promise, and the blessings for us. His interest then must be very great. There is never a blessing that a poor believer partakes of, but Christ's blood went for it; it went for your daily bread, and for more grace and glory. He is blessed that believes, that his outward mercies and afflictions, etc. are all by promise. Whatever we have is by promise and purpose, Phil. 1:29. And never man received a promise, but he that Christ bought to be the heir of it. We are heirs of promise, because in Christ Jesus. We are all *the children of God by faith in Christ Jesus; and if children, then heirs*, Rom. 8:17, Gal. 3:29. 2*dly*, Our Lord Jesus Christ hath this interest in the promises, that his blood went for the confirming of the whole covenant. The whole book of the promises, Christ's blood sealed it all; therefore it is called *the blood of the everlasting covenant.* The testament of the covenant is made sure by the blood of the testator; no man must add any thing to it. There is a curse unto them that shall add or pare any thing from the

whole canon of scripture, Rev. 22:18, 19. How much more unsufferable to add or pare from our Lord's testament? *The covenant was confirmed before of God in Christ*, Gal. 3:17. By his mediation at last, as mediator of the covenant, he confirmed it by his blood. 3*dly*, A *third* interest that Christ hath in the covenant is, that he is *the surety of it*. He is to see the bargain kept on both sides, that God may not cast us off for our iniquities, and that we may not leave God by our unbelief. Christ is engaged on both; and, if I may so speak, he has a hard task of it, to keep devouring justice from consuming stubble fully dry. It is a task only fit for him, and he only fit for it; a task he cheerfully undertook and perfectly fulfilled, and is now fulfilling.

5. The high engagements of divine truth in the promises, are great confirmations for our faith in God's faithfulness. Promises are made by the Lord so deliberately; he goes so high in them, that we must believe he is faithful, and will perform them. See how the apostle discourses to the Hebrews, chap. 6, when he is exhorting believers to be followers of them *who through faith and patience have inherited the promises*: as if the apostle had said, 'Be not slothful, take pains, follow on; all those that have tried this course of faith and patience, have inherited the promises. And so will you:' why so? because when God made the promise to Abraham, because he could swear by no greater, he sware by himself; saying, *Surely, blessing, I will bless thee*, etc. There are several things of great consideration in that scripture, 1*st*, That there is double security, word, and oath. The least hint of good-will from so great a God, as our God is, should engage all the dependence of his children; nay, if it came but to only a may-be, God's may-be is enough for our reverend waiting on him. God not only speaks, but he swears. Now observe, how the apostle speaks, *Because he could swear by no greater, he sware by himself*; as if the apostle had said, 'If it had been possible for God to have gone higher, he would have gone higher.' How does God swear by himself? *As I live*; he swears by his *life*; he swears by his *being*; he swears by his *Godhead*. As true as I am God, *I will bless thee*, says he to Abraham. What is all this to us now? God testifies a singular respect unto an eminent man, upon a singular testimony of the man's respect to him; one of the most eminent acts of faith, and of obedience that ever was performed by a mere man, to offer up freely to God his only son now

grown a man. Here was a noble act of obedience; but the Lord testifies a special regard to this man, and gives him this oath. What is that to you and me? Now, says the apostle, this concerns you and me, that *have fled for refuge, to lay hold on the hope set before us*; he leads us to this, that every poor creature that has a mind for salvation through Jesus Christ, should say in himself, As sure as God said and swore to Abraham, so surely hath God said and sworn to me, that I shall be blessed with eternal salvation in flying for refuge to his own Son. So the apostle applies it, *That by two immutable things, in which it was impossible for God to lie, we might have a strong consolation, who hath fled for refuge to lay hold on the hope set before us.* Observe the vast difference. Abraham yields a grand act of obedience, and lifts up his knife to cut the throat of his own son at God's command: A poor sinner what does he? A sinner chased by the torments of his own conscience, and the threatenings of the law; he runs to Christ for salvation: he is a self-seeker, if I may so speak; he is seeking the salvation of his own soul: nay, says the apostle, he that does so, shall get that same security for his salvation that Abraham got. It is a great point, and only fit for Paul's divinity, to spell so great a matter out of that extraordinary testimony that God gave to Abraham. Though the service that God craved of Abraham be not craved of us, yet the privilege is allowed to every believer; so that if you fly to Christ Jesus, there is not a poor believer, that hath laid hold on the horns of God's altar, but that poor creature shall be as sure of God's eternal blessing as great Abraham was, when he heard God swearing to him. This is what the apostle teaches; the Lord help us to practise it.

6. There is *divine foresight* of all possible and future impediments of performance, which is a great argument of God's faithfulness. That proves to us, that God is faithful in his promises. An honest man may make a promise upon his best understanding, but the providence of God may render it quite impossible to perform it. Now, there is no such thing can befall the Lord our God. Here is a great argument for your faith in God's faithfulness: he foresaw all things that shall come, or can come to pass, that look like impediments. All your sinning, all your fainting, all your unbelief, all your murmurings, all your turnings and temptings of the Lord, poor believer, they were all foreseen by

God, yet he made the promise, and therefore he will keep it. I believe we are such poor believers, that if we had the foresight of all that comes in the way to hinder, we would never believe. A poor believer, if in the day that he gives the hand unto the Lord, in the day that he marries his soul unto Christ Jesus, in the day that he engages to expect life, and righteousness, and salvation in this Holy One of Israel; I say, if this man, could foresee all the sin, and all the miscarriages and weaknesses that will be found in him for but seven years to come, he would draw back his hand, and be ashamed to say, *I believe*. The reason why I say so is this, because when a few of these come in our way, they shake our faith. The children of God have one advantage in their weakness, that our future things are hid from us; things that shall come to pass we do not know, but the Lord sees them all, and in sight of them all he makes the promise, and therefore, notwithstanding them all, he keeps the promise, Isa. 48:18, 19, Psa. 69:5.

7. The *mighty power of God* is that which we should ground our faith of his faithfulness upon. *Omnipotency* must be engaged to fulfil the *promises*, and omnipotency must be acted upon in believing the promise: 2 Tim. 1:12, *I know whom I have believed, and I am persuaded that he is able to keep that which I have committed unto him against that day*. Abraham offered up his son Isaac, accounting that God was able to raise him from the dead. He had a promise, *That in Isaac his seed should be called*; God bid Abraham cut his throat, and burn (not bury) his body: says Abraham, 'That I will do,' accounting that he was able to raise him up from the dead. How frequently do we find faith fixed this way upon divine power? Rom. 11:23. As to the Jews, they shall be grafted in; why so? God is able to graft them in: as to a weak believer, it is far more easy, Rom. 14:4, *He shall be holden up*: for God is able to make him stand. Sirs, your faith will never behave well, till you have a view of omnipotency. That faith is never soundly tried, till it is brought into that distress that nothing but omnipotency can relieve out of; and that faith is not cleanly acted, that does not act purely upon omnipotency. Wherefore do I believe the promise? Because he is the Lord of hosts, for whom nothing is too hard, that promises; it is with this the Lord chides Sarah's unbelief, *Is any thing too hard for the Lord?* Gen. 18:4, Jer. 32:17, 27.

Lastly, There is something in the *very nature of the promises* that speaks forth the certainty of their fulfilment. Ye may know by the nature of the promises, that he is a faithful God that made them. One is the *absoluteness* of the main promise. That I call an absolute promise, wherein the whole of the care and charge is God's. When God says, I will, they shall; *I will be your God, and ye shall be my people*; and if I will be your God, no man shall say he shall not be my God; and if thou say, We shall be thy people, none shall say, We shall not be thy people. There is again the *wisdom of the order of the promises*, that there is some begun performance of the promises; the performance of the promise of grace is in a good way to the performance of the promise of glory.

Application. 1. Learn to magnify this name. God hath magnified it himself, and so should we; Psa. 138:2, *I will praise thy name, for thy loving-kindness, and for thy truth: for thou hast magnified thy word above all thy name*. Magnifying of God's faithfulness stands principally in praising for it. Praise him for all the promises he hath made, and praise him for all the performance he hath given, and praise him for all the performance that shall be given.

2. As you must praise him for it, so *you must count God faithful*. This is a great matter. May I speak it in more plain homely words: Every one of you must count *God honest*, an *honest, faithful, true God*; that never deceived any that trusted in him, that is never worse than his word; always a great deal better. It is remarked concerning Sarah, Heb. 11:11, that *she judged him faithful who had promised*. She is one of the women that are named there in that short catalogue of believers; and it is well for her she was named there, for indeed the account we have of her in Genesis is not so much to her honour; when the promise is made in Genesis, it is said, *Sarah laughed*, Gen. 17:17 and 18:12.

When do ye think Sarah believed? I really think she believed when she was reproved for her unbelief. What is her believing called? *Through faith also Sarah herself received strength to conceive seed, because she judged him faithful who had promised*. She accounted the promiser faithful, that is faith; to account the promises faithful, that is believing. Is it not a reasonable thing to crave this of you? You must account him faithful or unfaithful, there is no medium: if you do not give him the positive testimony of faithfulness, you reflect upon him the blasphemy of unfaithfulness. Now this would bring me to the third thing, *viz.* That the faith of believers should in some measure answer the faithfulness of God. See that your believing answer the promise, as your believing is bottomed upon the promise. See Acts 16:15, Lydia's charge to Paul.

This accounting him faithful craves two things; 1*st*, That you must learn, in the main matter of salvation, to take his word alone. We reckon always, that that person is jealous of another, that is not willing to take his word. It is true, that, on earth, men may pretend prudence for their distrust; but in dealing with God, it is an abomination, a prudence that comes from hell, James 3:15. If we account him faithful that promises, we should seek no more, and should crave no more. Believers that have their multiplied props from sense for their faith, labour under the disadvantage of a secret charge of unfaithfulness in God. Will you offer to bring any creature to confirm God's testimony? 2*dly*, Account him faithful that exacts this of us, that as soon as ever we get the promise, we should rejoice in hope of performance. *God hath spoken in his holiness, I will rejoice*, says David; 'I have got God's word, that is enough of joy to me,' Psa. 60:6.

SERMON VI.

HEB. 10:23.

For he is faithful that promised.

FROM the last words of this verse, which is the apostle's argument to press Christians *to hold fast the profession of their faith without wavering*, I have spoke already unto two notes that I observed therefrom; as, 1. It is a name here given to God, *he that promises*; and from this I shewed, that the Christian's God is a promising God, and he that knows not God by this name *of a promising God*, does not know the true God; no man can take up God aright, but in the veil of a promise; no man can draw near to God aright, but in and by the encouragement of a promise.

2. The second note was this, That this *promising God is faithful in his promises*, this promiser is faithful. To this I spoke last day, and shall add but a little to it, and proceed to the third thing.

I know that there are a great many professors that bear the name of Christians (God knows how little they deserve it, to him they stand or fall), who wonder, why there should be so much in the word spoken of faith; and that some ministers, in their doctrine should insist so much upon believing: Why not, say they, upon doing? Is not believing doing? The greatest doing that ever was done by a sinner is believing, and all the right doing of obedience flows from believing. Whoever they be that know what it is to be a Christian, know that their life is a life of faith; they live by faith, even as we live our natural life by breathing. It is as impossible, that a Christian can preserve his spiritual life, without repeated acts of believing, as it is for us to preserve our natural life, without putting forth and sucking in the air we breathe in. Therefore it is, that such as know what the life of faith is, that is, the Christian's life, never can think enough, they never can hear enough, because they can never do enough about believing. For this end, I have spoke unto this great name of the Lord our God, *That he is faithful in his promises*. I did, last day, 1. Shew you that the meaning of this is, what our thoughts of God's faithfulness do contain by the warrant of the word, and I gave you four particulars. Next, I shewed you the grounds, rather of your faith on God's faithfulness, than the grounds of his faithfulness. The Psalmist leads us to this, Psa. 138:2, *Thou hast magnified thy word above all thy name*. God makes all his name some way serviceable for the advancement of the glory of his word, and his faithfulness in his word is a main part of the glory of it. Several of the names of God that are useful for the strengthening of our faith, as to his faithfulness, I mentioned last day; and shall add two or three more, and go forward.

The first is his *holiness*. His holiness is a great ground of faith as to his faithfulness: *God hath spoken in his holiness, I will rejoice*, says the Psalmist, Psa. 60:6. *Once have I sworn by my holiness, that I will not lie unto David*, Psa. 89:35. Holiness is a name of God hateful to all sinners, and very awful to believers. When the purity, the spotlessness of his holiness is seen, what sad reflections usually does it occasion? *But thou art holy: But I am a worm*, says the Psalmist, *and no man*, Psa. 22:3, 6.

When God's holiness was proclaimed before Isaiah, *Wo is me*, says he, *for I am undone*, Isa. 6:5. Can there be any encouragement for faith from God's holiness? A great many Christians' main fear arises from his holiness. Now I am to show you, that the name of his holiness is a great consideration for strengthening faith. Faithfulness, if I may so call it, is a piece of holiness; faithfulness is a branch of holiness, so that as God cannot do any thing that is evil, so he cannot break his word. Then he swears by his holiness; as if he would say, 'Take me for no holy God, if ever I fall short of my word of promise.'

2. The second name of God is his *wisdom*. He makes promises in wisdom; he makes promises about blessings that he means to give, and knows, and hath appointed when and how to perform. We, that are poor creatures, that live in time, think a little time a long while, *viz.* from the beginning of the promise in Gen. 3:15 unto the end of time, and that is a great while after the end of the Revelation. You think it a long while betwixt God's first promise, and his last performance; but it is nothing with him, in the point of promise. Saith the apostle, *One day is with the Lord as a thousand years, and a thousand years as one day*, 2 Pet. 3:8, Isa. 54:8. There are a great many ten thousand days in a thousand years; there is a great inequality betwixt these, but both alike to God. We measure time, as it were, by our own duration; but he that inhabiteth eternity does not so. The wise God, I say, hath made all his promises in wisdom. In his eye, betwixt the making of them and the performance of them, there is no kind of distance at all.

3. *Lastly*, The name of his *love* is a great encouragement to faith in his faithfulness. Love made the promises, and love will see to the fulfilling of them; therefore the Psalmist says, *I will praise thy name, for thy loving-kindness, and for thy truth*, Psa. 138:2. The more love there be in making the promise, the more certainty there is of the fulfilment of it. Surely promises of love, free love, rich and eternal love, are made in love, Jer. 31:3, and will be fulfilled.

III. The *third* thing now that I would speak upon, and that I observed from these words, *He is faithful that promises*, is, That the believer's faith should answer God's faithfulness. The stedfastness of our believing should answer the faithfulness of God in promising; for this is the apostle's argument, *Let us hold fast the profession of our faith*, or the confession of our hope, *without wavering; for he is faithful that promised.* Your hope is fixed upon his promises: hold fast your faith therefore, for he will hold fast his word: *He is faithful that promises.* Be you stedfast in believing; the promise is a strong promise; it is the promise of a strong God; that faith that should be given to it, should be a strong faith. This is the glory of believing. Abraham gave glory to God. What way? He was strong in faith; and he was fully persuaded that the promise would hold good, for God was able to perform it, Rom. 4:20. From this truth I would speak a little to these two things. 1. Why our faith must answer God's faithfulness. 2. How it can do it.

First, Why the believer's faith must answer God's faithfulness.

1. The *first* reason is, because faith and God's faithfulness are relatives; they are necessarily related one to another. There were no use for divine faithfulness declared, no promise in time had been made, unless for some that should believe, John 17:20; there were no use in this world for faith, if there were not some appearance of divine faithfulness for faith to act upon. God's faithfulness is revealed on purpose that it may be believed. Faith is given on purpose, that divine faithfulness may be trusted in, and rested on, and applied. They relate one to another as necessarily as the eye and light do, and these are mighty like. If God had created creatures with eyes, and colours, or any other visible things, and no light to see by, it might be said, Wherefore gave he them eyes? The case is just so here: All the breakings forth of divine faithfulness are for faith's sake, that it may work upon it; and all the giving of faith is for faithfulness' sake, that it may act upon it.

2. Divine faithfulness is the ground of faith, and the only ground of faith, therefore faith must answer it. All the expectations of good from God, all the warm applications made to God are all bottomed upon, *Thus saith the Lord.* If God's faithfulness be the ground of faith, surely then faith should answer the ground. If so be a person could believe as firmly, and build as strongly as the ground will bear him, he might do great things.

3. God's faithfulness is the author of faith; it is not only the ground of faith, that lays us under an obligation to believe when he speaks, but the very author and worker of faith. I do not mean only that God grants and works faith in his faithfulness; but my meaning is more strict, that all faith is wrought in the soul by some discovery of divine faithfulness

at first, and in all the after-actings of it. We see that there are great multitudes that have the word of God alike, they have the same Bible, and the same ministers, and the same sermons; some believe, and some do not believe; some obtain grace to believe, and others not. Whence comes it? Wherefore is it, that ever at any time a poor self-condemned sinner trusts Christ Jesus with his salvation upon the warrant of the gospel-promise? When is it he does so? Always then, and never till then, that he gets a discovery of the faithfulness of God in the contrivance of the gospel. When God stamps his own faithfulness and truth upon the gospel, then the man believes it, and trusts it: *This is a faithful saying, and worthy of all acceptation, that Christ Jesus came into the world to save sinners; of whom I am chief*, 1 Tim. 1:15. What is the reason there is so great difference amongst believers at one time and another, that the same promise of God at one time is strong under them like a pillar of brass; at another time it is weak, or they think it weak as a broken reed? The true reason is this: At all times they have the word of the promise; but it is not at all times they see the glory and faithfulness of the speaker. When the promise appears in the glory of the truth of the speaker, it is impossible but it must be believed. When God takes his own word in his own hand, and stamps it down as the word of God upon the heart, then that mark is faith. Believing is another sort of business than a great many pretended professors of it know, or take it to be. The faithfulness of God is the cause of believing, 1 Thess. 2:13.

4. *Lastly*, Faith is God's appointed way for the performance of his promise. He will have glory by his people's believing, before he give them that satisfaction that they expect, and desire in his performance. That rebuke our Lord gave to Martha, John 11:40, is of lasting use in the church of Christ, *Said I not unto thee, that if thou wouldst believe, thou shouldst see the glory of God?* 'Did not I tell thee before, that if thou wouldst but trust in me, and wait quietly to see the issue, thou shouldst see the glory of God, for all the appearance to the contrary?'

The *second* thing is, *How ought our faith to answer God's faithfulness?* Here some things must be premised for caution, that we do not carry the matter farther than the balance of the sanctuary will admit.

1. You must not imagine, that any man's faith can answer God's faithfulness *fully*: that is impossible. God's faithfulness is an infinite perfection in itself; our faith is a finite grace, given to a poor shallow

creature. Our faith can answer his faithfulness no more, than our holiness can answer his holiness, though we are commanded to be holy, as he is holy. We are to take the pattern of our holiness from his holiness; and we are to study conformity to his holiness: but perfect conformity is impossible; and even sinlessness, which is impossible here, would not bring us to perfect conformity to God's holiness. We must not think to answer God's faithfulness with our faith in a perfect equality.

2. Neither doth a believer answer God's faithfulness with faith as he ought. We do not pay all the faith that we owe to the truth of God. It is as impossible for a believer to perform the obedience of faith required in the gospel perfectly, as it is for an unbeliever to perform obedience to the law perfectly. Indeed an unbeliever can obey nothing. Even the obedience of faith, the obeying of the gospel, by believing of it, needs gospel-grace for the forgiveness of the sin of believing, or the sin in believing. There is never a believer that believed at first, but there was sin in that believing: there are none that do rely upon the word of God so firmly, as that noble sure foundation deserveth.

3. There is no believer believes so firmly as he would: he does not answer God's faithfulness by his faith so well as he would. Whoever they be that think they believe as they desire to believe, I dare say they never believed, and never will learn to believe as long as they are of that mind. That poor man spoke as if he understood faith well, Mark 9:24, *Lord, I believe; help thou mine unbelief.* Believers are called to answer God's faithfulness by their faith, but they must not think that they shall ever attain to so much as they would: they must still go on growing in believing, as well as in any other grace. *The righteousness of God is revealed from faith to faith*, Rom. 1:17. We must go on believing daily.

4. Faith in all believers does not equally answer God's faithfulness. True faith is built upon it, but every one's faith does not alike equally answer it. There are some *strong in faith*, and some *weak in faith*. These are words in the scripture. Abraham is called *strong in faith*, young believers are called *weak in faith*, Rom. 14:1. Nay, the same man is not alike *strong in faith*, or *weak in faith*, at all times; sometimes the *strong* may grow *weak*, and the *weak* may grow *strong*, though they have both true faith, and that built upon God's faithfulness.

These things I premise, for the preventing any mistake in the resolving this question, what way our faith is to answer God's faithfulness? Our trust in believing, is to answer God's trustiness in promising.

1st, It is to answer it by a sudden taking of God's word of promise, and resting on it. There is no delay for this. There is no time, no moment of time wherein a man is allowed to toss this question, Is God to be trusted, or no? This is an abomination to conceive that the Lord will ever suffer a man to spend one moment in making this question, Shall I take God's word, or no? Does he deserve to be trusted? This is wickedness to think of, or to put it to the question. Sudden receiving of God's word is the glory we owe to the faithfulness of it. Our Lord found fault with the disciples, that they were fools, and slow in heart to believe: they would take time to consider, before they would believe. This is sin. The apostle commends the Colossians for their faith, for their hope laid up in heaven. When began it? *Since the day ye heard of it, and knew the grace of God in truth*, Col. 1:6. *That very day ye heard the word with power, the grace of God came along with it*. Our Lord takes notice of this, in John 1:50, 51. So runs the promise, Psa. 18:44.

2dly, By taking the least hint of God's word for our encouragement. This is to give glory by our faith to his faithfulness. The least appearance of his faithful word should be enough to engage our hearts. The great faith our Lord commends so highly, *I have not found so great faith, no not in Israel*, is exemplified by this, Matt. 8:8, *Lord*, says the centurion, *I am not worthy that thou shouldst come under my roof: but speak the word only, and my servant shall be healed*. As if the good man would say, 'Lord, I know that thou dost use to go to some men's houses, and visit the sick, and heal them; but I am a poor man, unworthy of this favour.' But is he unwilling to receive Christ's grace: No; he was far from thinking so; the poor man had a mind to Christ's grace; *Lord, speak the word only, and my servant shall be healed*. This faith is commended in the nobleman, John 4:50, *Go thy way*, saith our Lord, *thy son liveth. And the man believed the word that Jesus had spoken unto him, and he went his way*. You may be sure he went believing all the way, till he came near home, till his servants came and told him, *Thy son liveth*; then he believed over again, and believed better. There is a great failing in the faith of the people of God in this point, That they offer sometimes, in the vanity and pride of their hearts and unbelief, to tell God which way he should engage his faithfulness. The least hint of Christ's faithfulness should serve, if you have a mind to glorify the faithfulness of God.

3dly, Faith is to answer God's faithfulness in the full extent of it; that is, in believing in length and breadth, according to the largeness and wideness of the promise. Now, here is a great duty that we are very dark and ignorant about. When a believer believes rightly, he is to believe every thing God says. A great many things we believe, we do not know what they are; we are to believe them notwithstanding. When thou dost believe eternal salvation through Christ Jesus, dost thou know what weight there is in the crown of glory? what entertainment is with them that behold the face of God, and of the Lamb? what is done? what is fed on? and what is enjoyed? what is said within the veil? We know none of these things; but we must believe them notwithstanding. We are to believe the full extent of the promise; that there shall be a performance, though we do not know yet what it shall be. *Now we are the sons of God, but it does not yet appear what we shall be*. But does that shake their faith? No, says the apostle; *we know that when he shall appear, we shall be like him; for we shall see him as he is*, 1 John 3:2. And with the apostle's leave, for as great a divine as he was, what seeing him as he is, and what being like him as he is in heaven, the good divine John did not know on earth, and tells us that he did not know; only in these general words he tells us, in Christ's words, *That he should be with him, and behold him*; and his faith goes forth accordingly.

4thly, Answering God's faithfulness by our faith, is to lay all our weight upon the promise of God, and upon it only; every thing that concerns us for our souls and eternal salvation, for our outward concerns, for Zion, for the church and people of God; it is to glorify divine faithfulness, to lay all these burdens upon the back of the promises, not doubting but it shall bear them; laying it upon the promise alone. It is a great matter for a believer to think God's faithfulness security alone, that there needs nothing to prop it and hold it up. We many times sinfully crave props of sense to support our faith; but the matter indeed is to support the promise; therefore we would fain that God should give something to support us; all this, like Naaman, 2 Kings 5, is unbelief. We must lay all our weights and burdens upon the faithfulness of God: so says dying David, 2 Sam. 23:5, *Although my house be not so with*

God; yet he hath made with me an everlasting covenant, ordered in all things and sure; for this is all my salvation, and all my desire. As if David, in his last words, had left this his legacy to all believers in after ages, that now when a dying man, 'I have,' says he, 'seen a great deal of sin and wickedness in my family, in my heart and life, and in the land of Israel: in the cases of Uriah, Absalom, Amnon, Tamar, Adonijah; but I now die satisfied with this only, *He hath made with me an everlasting covenant*, etc. Here is *all my salvation, and all my desire.*'

5thly, The answering God's faithfulness by our faith, is in the avowing our faith to God and men. God avows his promise publicly, Isa. 45:19. It is not enough that we believe, but we must not be ashamed to own it. How frequently do we find the saints owning it to God? Psa. 57:1-3, *Be merciful unto me, O God, be merciful unto me, for my soul trusteth in thee. I will cry unto God most high; unto God that performeth all things for me. He shall send from heaven, and save me from the reproach of him that would swallow me up; Selah. God shall send forth his mercy and his truth.* Oh, what a blessed song is this! He prays for mercy, because he trusts in it: and he adds this, *God shall send forth his mercy and his truth.* If I may so speak, these two messengers, mercy and truth, are enough to pluck a man out of the jaws of death and hell itself; if God send them, they come; and if they come, they save one, that is certain. The psalmist complains most grievously of their reflecting upon his God; it was as a sword in his bones, while they reproached him for trusting in his God. Psalm 11, he is so confident he will reproach them for it, ver. 1, *In the Lord put I my trust: how say ye to my soul, Flee as a bird to your mountain?* 'Are ye not ashamed,' would David say, 'to look upon me as a forlorn person, and tell me to flee to the mountains for help, when I have a refuge in my God?'

Lastly, God's faithfulness should be answered by our faith, in our constant keeping upon this foundation. Faith and patience is required in order to the inheriting of the promise. Performance comes not immediately as the promise is made, nor as soon as it is believed, Acts 7:17, Psa. 31:15. Believing must be drawn forth God's full time, till performance ripen the ground. Why we should believe God's faithfulness, is, because God's faithfulness is a constant thing itself. If the Lord's faithfulness did change, a believer's faith might change lawfully; if there were any shaking in the word of God, it were no sin for a believer to doubt in that word. The aggravation of unbelief is, because we change in our faith, when God is unchangeable in his faithfulness.

APPLICATION. If believers' faith should answer God's faithfulness,

1. Then, what can the unbeliever do that has no faith? God's faithfulness is before him, the faithfulness of God is seen in his threatenings and promises: the faithfulness of God is seen in the law, and in the gospel; the unbeliever hath faith for neither. When God threatens the unbeliever with everlasting destruction for his sin in the law, every secure sinner says, God is a liar. Fearlessness of wrath, when a man is under the lash of God's threatening, is a certain proof that he believes not what he speaks. There is no word of threatening shall come short of its fulfilment, no more than a word of promise. The unbeliever hath no entertainment to give to the promise of the gospel, because he hath not faith; what then must the issue of it be? A man that hath no faith, is under these two things; one at present, and the other a coming, if God prevent it not. First, Every man that is an unbeliever must blaspheme God now, whatever he does when he goes to hell. There is no greater blasphemy against God, than to say he lies. A poor lying man, through the custom and fashion of this world, looks upon it as one of the greatest provocations that can be given in words, to say in his face, he lies. Every poor sinner that hears the law and the gospel, and neither trembles at threatenings, nor rejoices at promises, says every day to God, he lies. *He that receives not his testimony, has made God a liar*, 1 John 5:10. *And he that receives his testimony, hath set to his seal, that God is true*, John 3:33. People that have not faith, have great need to cry for faith, to beg that God would give it. I have nothing to entertain God's faithfulness with, I have no hand to take a word from God, if I have not faith.

2. How justly chargeable are believers themselves, if their faith should not answer God's faithfulness? How guilty are most believers in this matter? An unbelieving believer is a monster, not for the rarity of it, but for the ugliness of it; for there is nothing more common amongst believers, than to be acting unbelief. There are few believers, but do act more unbelief than faith; they unbelieve, if I may so speak, ten times for their believing once. Now, the great aggravation of this their sin is, that not only God's faithfulness is engaged for their faith to act on, but God hath wrought faith in them: therefore the guilt of believers is very

great upon this account. Shall a man that is in this case be still acting unbelief? Too frequently they do so, but I will name a few things, and conclude at this time.

1st, How many believers act their unbelief, and are convicted from this point, in their fearing to believe, when they are called to lay hold on the hope set before them, and to lay the stress of their eternal salvation upon the faithful promise of God? They are afraid they shall sin to believe. I pray now is this a mannerly question, Shall I sin in trusting God? Is not this a fearful thing? Is there any danger of sinning in my taking God's word? I am sure, the greatest sin is in refusing it, and there can be none in taking of it. It is nothing but the power and strength of unbelief that makes so much fear in believers. In putting forth the hand of faith, they seem to put forth their hand to God, as he is a consuming fire, Heb. 12:29, and not as he is in his Son reconciling us to himself.

2dly, Not only are they very fearful to believe, but very weak in believing. A great many believers (if I may use such a homely similitude) walk upon the promise at God's call in the way to heaven, even as a child upon weak ice, which they are afraid will crack under them, and leave them in the depth. What can there be but unbelief in the weak trust we have in the promise of God? Art thou sure, that thou hast trusted thy soul upon the word of God? Do not reply, there is no more betwixt thee and eternal ruin, but a bare word of God; for can that word fail? is it possible, that it can miscarry? Why then should we not believe more firmly? There is a silly practice amongst us, I shall not speak my mind about it, I only speak of it now with respect to my present purpose: A great many believers do even venture in their believing upon the word of God, as too many idle people do upon their lotteries, they will try; but they do not know whether they shall get a blank or a benefit. Is this believing and giving glory to the faithfulness of God?

3dly, There is doubting after believing. When a poor believer hath once cast his burden upon the word of God, a cloud comes on, and he begins to question, whether he did well in trusting God or no; this is the English of it, Did I well to trust God? *We trusted that it had been he which should have redeemed Israel*, Luke 24:21, but was it well done, thus to repent of their trust?

4thly, Believers are many times in danger, by using sinful shifts to obtain the thing promised, as in Gen. 16:2. David would not do so, as you may see, 2 Sam. 1.

Lastly, Believers are guilty of great unbelief, in pleading the cause of their unbelief; they not only doubt, but they will argue for their doubting. Now, all objections of unbelief are arguments against faith; they are all great reflections on God's faithfulness, and are only to be answered by God's faithfulness: and we must take this as an universal answer to them all. All the pleas that the carnal unbelieving heart of a Christian can frame for the fencing himself in unbelief, are all to be broken upon the rock of God's unchangeable faithfulness. I will name some of their objections.

1. I do not know, if the promise be to me; if I were sure that the promise were to me, I would believe it better than I do. I answer, is the law to thee? is the command to thee? Does the law of God threaten thee in the first Adam? and is not the gospel to thee also in the second Adam? Is not the promise thine, if it be believed? What is the meaning of the preaching of the gospel? but only this, Preach the gospel to every creature, and tell them, He that believes, shall be saved. Whoever they be that will venture their salvation upon the man slain at Jerusalem, and expect God's favour, and eternal life for his sake tendered to them, believe it that will, if they take it, it is theirs.

2. A second objection is, I am a vile, filthy, guilty creature, how dare I believe? Satan and unbelief will multiply things here, and make a hideous appearance to a poor creature; as indeed, if the devil get leave to draw a person's own picture, and to set it before his eyes, or to write the history of his life, this will be a very dreadful thing; some have seen it, and felt the terror of it. But what is this to the faithfulness of God? Is God unfaithful in his promise, because I am a great sinner? No such thing; nay, *Let God be true, and every man a liar.* Is this an argument, Because I am very sick, therefore Jesus Christ the Physician will take no care of me: I dare not employ him, because I am very sick? Assure yourselves of this, Wherever sin is a man's disease, there Jesus Christ has been already the Physician, and will certainly cure it. I do not say, where sin is a man's delight, wherever

sin is a man's truce; but wherever sin is a poor creature's sickness, and when they are groaning towards Christ, the Physician, our Lord Jesus hath begun to cure them, and will perfect it infallibly.

3. Another objection that unbelieving believers make, is, I am a backsliding creature, I have been mighty unfaithful to God. What then? It may be God will deal with you, as he did with the backsliders of old. See how he calls them, *Return, ye backsliding children, I will heal your backslidings: Behold, we come unto thee, for thou art the Lord our God*, Jer. 3:22. The name the Lord gives them is, *backsliding children*; the promise he makes them is, he *will heal their backslidings*. Both these are entertained by an assent of faith, *Behold, we come unto thee; for thou art the Lord our God*, that only canst heal us. Sometimes they will plead, God is very angry, and hides himself. What then? He is not unfaithful for all that, the promise stands sure. *Verily thou art a God that hidest thyself, O God of Israel the Saviour*, Isa. 45:15; see also Psa. 119:75. I can assure you, Christians, that that faith is very weak, and that believer will lead but a poor sorry life, that hath not learned to believe in the dark, as well as in the light of his countenance. We must not believe by day-light only, we must learn to believe in the dark. The greatest part of the way to heaven lies in the dark; if we have not this light of faith, we are but in a bad case. Some may say, they see no appearance of performance; they have tried the promise of God, and it is as unlikely as it was at first; the complete salvation of their soul is far off; the growth of their corruptions appears daily; their consciences sometimes making as dreadful an alarm as in the days of their former darkness. This is a very common and ordinary exercise, and the cure of it is very easy; the remedy is near at hand. We are not to judge of the certainty of the fulfilment of the word of promise, by the appearances that are in providence towards us, but we are to build all upon the faithfulness of the speaker. Though *clouds and darkness be round about him, righteousness and judgment are the habitation of his throne*, Psa. 97:2. The word stands firmly, whatever darkness there be in his works; wait a while, and but a little while (Heb. 10:37), give him time, and give him trust, and none that believe in him shall ever be ashamed.

SERMON VII.

HEB. 10:23.

He is faithful that promised.

THE apostle tells us in Romans 10:17, that *faith cometh by hearing, and hearing by the word of God.* Faith both comes by hearing, and grows by hearing. There is no part of divine truth that is more profitable for the growing in faith, than the doctrine of faith; it is therefore a great pity, and a great miscarriage, that when people hear much of faith, they do not practise much. Every thing that is spoken of faith, is spoken of it, that ye should be always doing; that as the ear takes in the report of the doctrine of faith, the heart may be exercised in the acting of it. With respect unto this, I have several times spoke already, upon this latter part of this verse, which is the apostle's argument, by which he enforceth the exhortation he gave in the preceding part; and from this argument I have observed three things.

1. That the Christian's God is a promising God. He is called here by the apostle, *He that promises*; and the apostle knew well God's names, and which it is that is fittest to be used on every occasion.

2. That this promising God is faithful in all his promises, which he hath promised from the beginning of the world to this day. There have been some in all ages, and a great many in some ages, that have trusted God upon his promises; but there hath not been one that could ever justly charge God with failing.

3. The *third* thing that I spoke to was, That the Christian's faith should answer God's faithfulness; that as our faith is fixed on God's promises, faith should some way be as firm as the promises. A Christian is called faithful, because he is a *believer*; God is called faithful, because he is a *fulfiller*; he keeps his word by *doing* it, believers are faithful in *trusting* it. Upon this note I shewed (1.) Why the Christian's faith should answer God's faithfulness. (2.) How it may and ought so to do. Some ways it cannot, some ways it must.

1. I concluded with a double reflection; one upon the sinful miserable state of unbelievers. They have nothing to answer God's faithfulness; they must perish, because they have not faith; they dishonour God highly, because of their unbelief. The true state of the matter is this: Our first father and mother, Adam and Eve, if I may so speak, by their sin leapt over-board, they cast themselves under the wrath and curse of God. In this state all we their posterity are born; the Lord, in great mercy through Christ Jesus, casts forth the rope of his promise; now, what is an unbeliever, but like a poor drowning man? there is a rope cast out that may save him, the poor man has no hands to catch at it, therefore must perish; and to perish in the view of a promise, is a sad case; but to the believer, the Lord will stretch out his hand to help him.

2. I made a little reflection upon the unbelief of believers. Believers themselves are wofully guilty sometimes in this matter, and their faith is far from answering the faithfulness of God. Compare his faithfulness with their faith, and you would think they do not relate to one another at all. Strong ground, strong foundation, but sorry building upon it! I named four of their common failings, which I shall have occasion to insist more upon on the other head. Sometimes they fear to believe, as if there were any sin in trusting God; when distrust is the greatest sin; they believe fearfully and weakly, as if the ground would not bear them: they believe and doubt, and recall their believing: they plead sometimes the cause of their unbelief in many of their ungodly objections against faith.

That which I would now do in the prosecuting this point, and with respect to all the three, shall be to give you, first, Some doctrinal inferences from this point; then, if the Lord will, we may come to make some practical exhortations unto duty therefrom.

As to these inferences I shall speak to a few of them at this time.

First, Hence we see, what the strict and true nature of faith is. The doctrine is, *That believers' faith should answer God's faithfulness.* We hence infer the strict and true nature of saving faith; which is certainly this: It is a trusting of God's word for his own faithfulness in speaking it, a trusting God's promise for the faithfulness of the speaker; that is strictly the nature of faith. It is a pity, but a pity that you will have occasion to exercise as long as you live in the world, that faith is so mightily mistaken by so many people. People can talk of faith, can dispute of faith, and in the mean time they are in a cloud, in a maze about the thing itself, and know not what believing is.

1st, Believing is not doing, but trusting. It is opposed to doing and working, *But to him that worketh not, but believeth on him that justifieth the ungodly, his faith is counted for righteousness*, Rom. 4:5, John 6:26, 29. *The just lives by faith*, but the law is not of faith: the law requires doing, Gal. 3:10-12. Faith is God's commandment, that is certain. The first precept in the decalogue is for faith, *Thou shalt have no other gods but me*; the positive part of it is, Thou shalt take me by faith to be the Lord thy God. Faith is never put forth as obedience; the strict nature of faith is trusting the speaker. The apostle speaks in Heb. 6:18 of faith under a blessed similitude, as *flying for refuge to lay hold upon the hope set before us*. Now pray consider what the state of the man that fled for refuge was. There was no other appointment of God left for him, but only the next city of refuge. The man that had shed innocent blood casually, for that was the case under the law, there was nothing else required in order to his safety, but running with speed to the next city of refuge. The man must not go to the temple, or altar, and pray, or offer sacrifice there for his life, he must not go home to his house, and mind his business and affairs; there was only one thing required of him, if he would be safe from the avenger of blood; to the city of refuge he must fly. A man must not go to save his life by doing some great act of valour for his country, against the enemies of it. Flying was the only shift, if I may so speak, that God fixed, and he must make use of. Believing is commanded, but it is always acted in trust.

2dly, Faith is not a notional assent to a divine truth, but it is an assent with the heart to the good-will of God. Pray take heed to this; true faith gives an assent unto all that God says, unto all that God reveals; but if you come to the strict nature of saving faith, it is only a trusting of a promising God, it is only a hearty affiance in God, in, and under, and by virtue of his promises. To believe, is not only to say, God has said this, and therefore it is true; but it is to believe that what God says, he says to me. What good-will hath God declared in the word concerning me? A believing of that is this faith that we are speaking of. Thus, I say, you are to take up the strict nature of faith; the proper nature of it is trusting God's promises, for God's faithfulness that speaks it. And thus we have these advantages by this strict notion of faith, and these confirmations of its being right.

(1.) Thus it is distinguished from all false faith. There is a great deal of faith in this world that is little worth; there is a great deal more in the next world that is less worth. In this world a great many of the ungodly have a kind of faith, such as it is; they know divine truth, they give an assent to it; this assent may be so strong sometimes, that it may work some alteration in their conversations, they may escape the corruptions of the world through the knowledge of our Lord and Saviour Jesus Christ, when, in the mean time, they have no faith for all that; they are dogs and swine still, as the apostle calls them, 2 Pet. 2:20-22. The great difference that is betwixt all the unsound faith of hypocrites, and the true faith of a believer, is to be determined from the proper nature of believing. There is no unbeliever that ever takes God's word for his security, barely as it is God's word; there is never an unbeliever that trusts God's promise, because God makes it; the promise is never seen by such a one as it is in the hand of the faithful promiser; and therefore the man never believes with the heart, and therefore never believes truly. Again, there is a great deal of faith in the other world. The devil hath faith, all the damned in hell have faith, but a woful faith it is; God save us from ever knowing what it means. The devil knows the mind of God in the word better than any minister this day in the world; he knows God, and he knows Christ wofully: *What have I to do with thee, Jesus, thou Son of the most high God?* Mark 5:7. The devil knows the gospel; Acts 16:17, *These men are the servants of the most high God, which shew unto us the way of salvation.* What better can be said of the gospel than this, to call it *the way of salvation*; and to call the servants that preach it, *the servants of the most high God*, that have it for their employment, *to shew men the way of salvation*? All the damned in hell are great believers, but woful ones. They know certainly that there is a God, for they feel his displeasure; they know certainly he is a just God, for they lie under the lashes of his justice for ever; they believe firmly the day of judgment, for they tremble in the fears and approaches of it: but there is no sound faith there; why? Because there is no promise there. If there was a promise let down to them that are in hell, faith might be there; if the same God would give the promise and work faith, it might be acted there; but there is no promise there, and therefore there is no faith there, there is no deliverance from that prison, Luke 12:59.

(2.) This is a fit description of the strict nature of faith, because it answers the first expression of faith, that is in all the word of God. I do not say, that Abraham was the first believer; but this you may find, that he is the first man that is spoken of as a believer. It is true, in the next chapter of this epistle, there are some believers named before him; Abel was a believer, Enoch and Noah were believers; but the first faith spoken of in the word expressly is Abraham's; and you know how much use is made of Abraham's faith, and practice, and example, in the New Testament, Gen. 15:4-6. The word of the Lord came to Abraham, and said to him, *Look now toward heaven, and tell the stars, if thou be able to number them. And he said unto him, so shall thy seed be. And he believed in the Lord; and he counted it to him for righteousness.* What was this believing in the Lord, but the believing with the heart, the truth of what God spoke? And ye know, by Paul's help, what a great deal of gospel there was in this word, *So shall thy seed be.*

(3.) It answers the frequent name that is given to the revelation of God's will, that is, *the way of our salvation*. It is called the gospel, that is, *good tidings*; and what are *good tidings*, unless they be believed? It is called a *promise*; and what signifies a promise unless trusted? It is called a *covenant*; and what signifies a covenant, unless subscribed unto, unless a man enter into it? The entering into it is by believing him that promises.

(4.) This is a right notion of faith, because it answers all faith, all sorts of faith whatsoever. It answers the faith of the strongest, and the faith of the weakest; it answers Abraham's faith, and it answers them of little faith. What is the reason of this distinction, that there are some strong in the faith, but because they put a strong trust in God's strong faithfulness? What is the reason some are called weak in the faith, but because they give a weak, wavering, staggering trust to the faithfulness of God? It answers all sorts of faith; faith for justification; faith for sanctification; faith for our comfortable support in our pilgrimage; faith for our safe landing at heaven. All these consist in our trusting

God's promise for his sake who gave the promise: as I shall shew more at large, when I come to lay before you your duty of believing. Only this shall serve for the first inference, that we may hence see, what the strict nature of believing is; it is trusting God upon his promise, it is taking God upon his word.

Secondly, We see hence what the reasonableness of believing is; of strong believing; why? Because it is trusting God's faithfulness. What can be more reasonable than this? I know that sense and carnal reason are the greatest enemies of true believing; but there is nothing unreasonable in believing; nay, pure spiritual reason is highly for it. Can there be any thing more reasonable than this, to trust one that cannot lie? to take an immutable foundation to build our confidence upon? So the apostle Paul expresses it, when pleading his cause before Agrippa, and Festus, and Bernice (a great many great folks were there): Acts 26:8. He has this expression to king Agrippa, *Why should it be thought a thing incredible with you, that God should raise the dead?* The apostle's scope there, is not to discourse that head of divinity about the resurrection of the dead, that was not his principal design; but here lay the grand matter, that Paul laboured to pinch their consciences by, that our Lord and Master Jesus Christ, that died for our sins, was risen again for our justification; the unbelieving world that saw him before he died, and saw him die, did not see him after he was risen again; now, says Paul, *why should it seem a thing incredible*, etc.? The words before, and those following, shew they had a promise for it, and that all the people of Israel had hope in the promise that God had made; thereupon, in ver. 27, he drives the matter most closely upon the conscience of that great man, *King Agrippa, believest thou the prophets? I know that thou believest*; as if Paul would say, 'Thou assentest to this, that the prophets spake the mind of God by inspiration: dost thou believe that I preach nothing else but what the prophets foretold, and what I know is fulfilled; that God hath raised his Son Christ Jesus?' *Almost*, saith Agrippa, *thou persuadest me to be a Christian*. The highest reason for the believing any thing is, *Thus saith the Lord*; the most certain reason that a future thing shall be, is, that the Lord hath said it shall be. Therefore now we should tread down carnal reason, and yield to this main grand reason, Thus saith the Lord; God hath spoken, and it must be true, because he saith it; and I will trust it, because it is true. Consider an instance of Abraham's faith with respect of issue from Sarah, Rom. 4:18, 19, *Who against hope believed in hope, that he might become the father of many nations.—He considered not his own body now dead, when he was about an hundred years old, neither yet the deadness of Sarah's womb. He staggered not at the promise of God through unbelief; but was strong in faith, giving glory to God.* Pray observe, Abraham in this case must believe against sense, against reason, and against all experience; though it is likely that, before the flood, women were fruitful, when they were a great deal older than Sarah was; but a little while after the flood, men and women's lives and vigour were contracted to much the same bounds as at this day. Abraham considered not that Sarah was ninety years old: 'Nay,' would the man say, 'if she were ninescore, or nine hundred years old, God hath said it, and I believe it.' Now, the grand matter was not barely and simply, that Abraham should be a father of a son, that he should be a father of many nations: but in this great promise of issue from God Christ was comprehended, who was to be the eternal salvation of the whole church of God. He was to spring from Sarah's womb, and Abraham had the promise of it, and against all sense, reason, and experience, he will believe it. Now observe what use the apostle makes of it: *It was not written for his sake alone, that it was imputed to him; but for us also, to whom it shall be imputed, if we believe on him that raised up Jesus our Lord from the dead, who was delivered for our offences, and was raised again for our justification*, ver. 23-25. Pray, observe what I drive at is this, That the apostle brings in every believer on Jesus Christ for salvation, in the same list of enjoying the blessing with great Abraham, that believed so strange a thing about Sarah. And the truth is, that the salvation of a sinner, dead in sins and trespasses, by Christ Jesus, is a greater wonder and miracle, than Sarah's dead womb bringing forth a living child: that, in a manner, was a work of wonder, wrought by the God of nature according to his word; and this is a work of wonderful grace against the course of sinful nature, for the overthrowing of it.

Thirdly, Hence we see why faith is said to *give glory to God*: the reason is, because faith answers God's faithfulness. Great faith is said to give glory to God; one of the special commendations of Abraham's faith is, *He was strong in faith, giving glory to God*, Rom. 4:20. God magnifies his name of faithfulness above all his names; the believer magnifies his faithfulness by his believing, therefore he gives glory to God. There are three honourable services that some men get put into their hands, and which are denied to angels. There is preaching of Christ, suffering for Christ, and believing in him: these are three honourable pieces of service, that only poor mortal men are intrusted with. The apostle reckons he had got a great grace, when he had got that of preaching Christ, and that too the unsearchable riches of Christ. When an angel was sent to Cornelius, he was not sent to preach the gospel to him, but to tell him where a gospel-preacher was, Acts 10. Suffering for Christ is a great honour; angels are not capable of it, it does not stand with their blessed state. The apostle seems to call this a higher matter, than the honour of believing, Phil. 1:29, *For unto you it is given in the behalf of Christ, not only to believe on him, but also to suffer for his sake.* Let us pass these, and consider wherein there is an honouring of God by believing; for it is a point very rarely believed. Who is there of believers that think, that by bare believing they give God more glory, than any other way they can do?

1st, Faith gives glory to God, because it brings nothing to him, but poverty, want, and emptiness. All graces bring something to God, but faith brings nothing. Love brings a flaming, burning heart to God; repentance brings a bleeding, broken heart to God; obedience brings a working hand to God; patience brings, as it were, a broad back to God, let him lay on what he will; poor faith brings just nothing, but the poor man's bare hand and empty dish. The poorer man comes to God, the more glory to God. It is remarkable, that in those cases, wherein we bring something to God, we are very apt to carry away something of the glory that belongs to him: faith brings nothing at all to God; it brings no more than broken bones, and sores to the great Physician. As a condemned prisoner, it brings his chains and fetters to the great Redeemer, but nothing to commend him to God, nor carries away any thing from God.

2dly, Faith glorifies God; for it seeks all in him, and from him; as it brings nothing to him, so it expects every thing from him, whatever its wants be. The language of faith is, 'All my wants be upon thee, O Lord;'

there is no other way of bearing them; it expects all from him, and from the single warrant of his word.

3dly, Faith always glorifies God, for it ventures its all upon his word. The believer is still in this frame, in the exercise of faith: 'Now here I have God's faithful promise; and if it should fail me, I should certainly sink for ever. My soul, body, reputation, privileges of the gospel, all my concerns whatsoever, are all laid upon the faithfulness of God; they are all put in that bottom of the ship: if I miscarry, I am gone for ever.' Who is there of believers that believes this, that a bare adventuring of thy eternal salvation upon the Son of God, by virtue of the promise of God, brings more glory to God, than all things else can do?

Lastly, Faith glorifies God, because all other acts of glorifying God are only so as faith is in them, and as they spring from faith. When the apostle is commending the great exploits of believers, Heb. 11, he saith, they *all obtained a good report through faith*. If their works had been done without faith, there is never a good word to be said of them, whatever they did. All our duties, obedience, sufferings, the great things that are done for God, only tend to the glory of God, as they are spirited and enlivened by faith. Take away faith from your prayers and God gets no glory, and you no comfort, by your praying, James 1:5-7. Let faith be separated from the word, and God gets no glory by your hearing. Whatever you do, there is no glorifying God, unless in the doing of the thing you do believe: *Whatsoever is not of faith, is sin*, Rom. 14:23, Heb. 11:6.

Fourthly, Hence we see how faith is said to have the soul, because it answers God's faithfulness. Such is approaching to the saving God, and its nearest abode with him. It is running to, and abiding with him. It is going in the nearest way to heaven: Heb. 10:39, *We are not of them*, says the apostle, *who draw back unto perdition, but of them that believe, to the saving of the soul*. The poor jailor asks a question, *What shall I do to be saved? Believe on the Lord Jesus Christ, and thou shalt be saved*, says Paul. Pray now, what is the meaning of this? 'There is a man, Jesus Christ, whose servant I am,' would Paul say; 'and thou hast persecuted me for his sake, and for preaching of him; now believe on him, venture thy soul on him, take his word for thy salvation, his righteousness for thy clothing, his Spirit for thy sanctification, and thou shalt certainly be saved as well as I, or any others.' I need not insist upon the frequent connections that are in the gospel, betwixt believing and salvation; this only is that which I drive at, to shew you, how faith comes to be saving to the soul; it is an echoing to God's faithfulness. Take the matter in these four plain principles, to begin at the top. *1st*, My eternal salvation stands in the enjoyment of God. *2dly*, This God comes down to me in Christ Jesus, for otherwise he is not to be known, not to be enjoyed. *3dly*, This Christ Jesus comes to me in the promise of the gospel, otherwise he is not to be known, he is not to be received. *4thly*, This promise, in the day of God's power, is joined with my faith, and my faith with it. It came to me, and I received it. See for this Gal. 3:23, 25. Hence the believer rises up again, and says, God has wrought faith in me: Therefore (1.) The promise is mine. (2.) Christ inseparable from the promise is mine, and then God inseparable from Christ is mine, and I must be saved for ever. So that wherever the believer begins, at the top, at God; or at the bottom, at the dependence of his soul on God, the reason backward or forward holds perpetually: now, there is no parting of any of these; God never revealed himself a faithful God to any, but in Christ; Christ never revealed himself as a Saviour to any, but in the promise; the promise does no good to any, but a believer. It is true, God in his great wisdom makes use of the promise, as the means of faith, as well as the ground of faith. The reason why faith saves the soul, is not because of any mighty thing in faith, for faith is a poor weak thing; but it is fixed to the faithfulness of God, and the faithfulness of God through Christ is in it, and God is in it. You may take faithfulness from God the Father, as soon as take salvation from a believer in Christ Jesus. Hence comes it, I say, that faith is saving. The rope of salvation is in the promise; the poor believer hath but a trembling hand in catching hold of it; but, if I may so speak, the higher end of the rope is in heaven, at the right hand of God, and it catches hold of the believer; unless it break, saved he must be; break it cannot, and therefore saved he must be. See Phil. 3:12.

Fifthly, I might add, Hence we may see something of the *easiness of believing*. I do not say, it is an easy thing for a man to believe; this a deceiving flattery of wicked, ungodly men. I intend, if the Lord will, to prove the contrary, that there is great *difficulty* in the working of faith. All my meaning is, that it is an easy thing to act faith, where God hath wrought it already. In this case, it is but the soul's echo to the faithfulness of God, it is only the soul's saying amen when God promises. I hear the word of him that cannot lie, amen, so be it; that if I may compare this ordinary instance with an extraordinary one, Luke 1:38. The angel of the Lord that brought the virgin Mary the tidings of the conception of our blessed Saviour, he sent her the news; she staggers at it at first, through unbelief, at last, by the power of God, faith is begotten in her: *Behold the handmaid of the Lord, be it unto me according to thy word*; that, if I may so speak, was the very consent of faith, that the miraculous conception of the Son of God began with. So may it be with us, if the Lord will put that life, and power, and stamp on the promise of the gospel, that here is life, and salvation, and righteousness, and all good, both of grace and glory, tendered to faith through Christ Jesus. Trust him, trust God's word, and it shall be done. *Behold the handmaid of the Lord, be it unto me according to thy word.* Though there be nothing more incredible, though there is nothing that is more impossible, than that such a vile creature as I am should be saved; yet God hath said it, God hath bid me believe it, and believe it I must, or call the speaker a liar. Believing is hard only to the unbeliever: but let the Spirit of faith (as the apostle calls it) be stirring, and a believer cannot forbear to believe. Let the word of God be heard as the word of God, and this is by the preaching it as his word, 1 Thess. 1:5, and the assent of true faith will be given to it, 1 Thess. 2:13. And thus will its fruit be both unknown to the unbeliever, and to the non-feeling believer.

Lastly, Hence we see why so much is spoken of faith in our Saviour, John 3:36, *He that believeth on the Son, hath everlasting life: and he that believeth not the Son, shall not see life; but the wrath of God abideth on him.*

SERMON VIII.

HEB. 10:23.

For he is faithful that promised.

THE faithfulness of God is one of his great and glorious names. Whenever he makes it appear before the eyes of a poor sinner, when he proclaims this name, then they believe, but never till then. It is a sad thing to consider, that when there is so much of faith spoken of in the word, there should be so little of it in the exercise of Christians. The New Testament name that is given to the godly, is that of believers. A man is not called a believer, because he hath faith, or because he once acted faith; as long as he lives, he should be still believing.

1. We find the gospel is called *the word of faith*. The apostle speaks of it expressly in distinction from the law, Rom. 10:8, *The word of faith which we preach*, Gal. 3:2, it is called *the hearing of faith*; that is, the doctrine of faith. The gospel is called the word of faith, as it is the only ground of faith. All the hope that is raised in the heart of man, as to good in time, or as to eternity, is all founded upon the bare word of God. We can believe nothing but his word; and we believe it, because it is his word. Again, it is called the word of faith, because it is the means of faith, and begets faith. What think you is faith? but only the impression, the stamp, that the word of the gospel, when brought home with power, leaves upon the soul. It is the heart's echo to the voice of salvation by Christ in the gospel; and when the Lord proclaims it, as he can, and always does to the chosen, this echo will still follow. Again, it is the word of faith, because it is the food of faith, that which we are to desire, *that we may grow thereby*, 1 Pet. 2:2. The whole gospel is the word of faith; people get no good by the gospel unless they get faith; they cannot profit by the gospel but by faith, and by the increase of that faith.

2. We find Christ gets a name from faith. Heb. 12:2. He is *the author and finisher of our faith*. When we think of the many names and offices of our Lord, some of which have a great deal of visible glory in them,

how shall we conceive of this, that our Lord Jesus should be denominated the author and finisher of our faith! that Christ should get a name, as it were, in the word, from the begetting and cherishing, and preserving, and perfecting of faith in a poor creature!

3. We find the Holy Ghost called the *Spirit of faith. We having the same Spirit of faith, according as it is written, I believed, and therefore have I spoken; we also believe, and therefore speak*, 2 Cor. 4:13. We find farther in the word a *work of faith* spoken of, a work of God's working, 2 Thess. 1:11, *The work of faith with power*. We find also *a good fight of faith* spoken of.

Now, from all these things you may plainly see, that people do not know what pertains to the gospel; they know not Jesus Christ, they know not the promise; they know not the Holy Spirit; they know nothing of a work of God upon their hearts, unless they know something of a work of faith. Alas! many poor creatures are wofully deceived about their souls. Some have had experience of this, and they think it a great experience, that whereas they were ungodly, and carnal, and secure, and walked loosely; strong convictions of sin came upon them, and some reformation from sin followed after; they immediately think they are good Christians (many such good Christians are in hell), but in the mean time have no sense of this Spirit of faith. What have you found of the Spirit of God as a Spirit of faith, carrying on a work of faith in your souls, and drawing forth your hearts, that are naturally unbelieving, unto a trusting in God through our Lord Jesus Christ?

We find farther *a door of faith* spoken of, Acts 14:27—*And how he had opened the door of faith unto the Gentiles.* See Heb. 4:1-3, 11. A poor unbeliever is a prisoner under the law, a prisoner under the chain of God's curse, and he can do nothing but stay there; for remove he cannot, until the devil come to drag him out to hell. In this miserable state, the Lord opens a door of faith, that the poor prisoner may get out, and get into the open air, and come to partake of the glorious liberty of the sons of God: Gal. 3:23, *But before faith came, we were kept under the law, and shut up unto the faith which should afterwards be revealed*; that is, we were prisoners till that faith came, then we had our liberty.

We find likewise the *footsteps of faith* spoken of. There are no true Christians, but must know something of this:—*And the father of circumcision to them who are not of the circumcision only, but also walk in the steps of that faith of our father Abraham, which he had being yet uncircumcised*, Rom. 4:12. He had the blessing of the covenant before he had the seal of it. Now, Abraham's footsteps were strong ones, steady ones, and, if I may so speak, they were wide steps that he took in the way of faith. It is a hard matter for you and me to follow him; ay, but though we cannot walk so fast, nor so strongly as he did, yet we must walk in the footsteps of the same faith. When our faith and his are compared, our steps and his compared, it is a shame to think what a great difference there is betwixt them; but this way we must walk in; a child may follow the footsteps of a strong man.

Lastly, There is an *end of faith* spoken of: *Receiving the end of your faith, even the salvation of your souls*, 1 Pet. 1:9. The end of faith is that which faith aims at, that which faith attains, and that with which faith hath no more to do, when it hath got it; for there is no proper believing in heaven; and there is no true believer, but he believes till then. There is also (1.) The mystery of faith, 1 Tim. 3:9. (2.) The law of faith, Rom. 3:27. (3.) The work of faith, 1 Tim. 1:11. (4.) Household of faith, Gal. 6:10. (5.) Fight of faith, 1 Tim. 6:12.

So much now is said concerning faith in the word, and of its great influence on all things that pertain to this life, and that to come, that sure no true Christian can possibly be unconcerned about this affair.

In speaking to this word, as I have done several times, *Faithful is he that promises*, I have spoken, 1. To the promising God, as the name of our God. 2. Unto the faithfulness of this promising God. 3. That the faith of believers should answer the faithfulness of God, that as all our faith is built upon his promises, so our faith should be built firm, because the promise is firm. I did propose, in the application of these truths, some doctrinal inferences to be drawn therefrom, then an exhortation unto believing inferred from all.

Of the doctrinal inferences, I named four last day, and entered a little upon the fifth, which I would now speak farther to.

1. Hence we may see the true nature of faith, that it is an answering God's faithfulness. I shewed then, 2. The reasonableness of believing,

that though corrupt reason be a great enemy to faith, yet there is nothing more reasonable, that a reasonable creature can do, than trust the infallible God. 3. I shewed you, that hence you may see how faith glorifies God. 4. How it is that it conduces so much to the saving of the soul; it is called therefore frequently by Christians *saving faith*; we are saved by faith, kept by the power of God through faith unto salvation; and believe to the saving of the soul.

5. The *fifth* thing was, to speak a little of the easiness of faith. If so be, that true faith be an answering of God's faithfulness, and trusting of God's word, it seems then to be a very easy act. I told you, that it is not easy to come by it, neither is it easy to act it, but it is easy in the acting. To prevent mistakes about this on either hand, I would give you but these few things:—

1*st*, Believing is hard and utterly impossible to every unrenewed, ungodly man: *No man can come to me, except the Father, which hath sent me, draw him*, says our Lord, John 6:44. This word did break the necks of a great many of Christ's hearers: and in ver. 65 it is repeated, *Therefore said I unto you*, says he, when they began to murmur, *that no man can come unto me, except it were given unto him of my Father*. A little now of this. Believing, as hath been said, is but a trusting God's faithfulness in a promise of salvation by Christ; it seems to be marvellous, that this should be impossible to a natural man; naturally men think it is very easy, all the ungodly think they can believe when they will. But how grossly are they mistaken about it! I would therefore shew a little whence it comes that it is impossible for a natural man to believe. That he cannot believe, is frequently spoken of in the scripture, John 5:44, *How can ye believe?* John 12:39, *Therefore they could not believe*; the same truth is held forth in both places, they could not believe.

(1.) All natural men are unconcerned about those great things, which trusting in God is concerned about. Trusting in God, that is, true faith, is trusting in him through Christ Jesus, for the great concernment of our eternal salvation, which is the pardoning of our guilty souls, and washing of them from all their defilements, with the subduing of all their corruptions. Now, do you not see plainly, that it is impossible, that a man should trust God for those things, when he has no heart-concern about them? The matters that faith is employed about, and which trusting in God hath in its eye, are altogether remote from the thought and mind of a natural man; therefore they do but lie against God and themselves, that say they trust God with their eternal salvation upon his word, when their consciences tell them that their eternal salvation was never so weighty with them, as the concerns of this poor frail life; and that they never were in so much earnest in saying, *What shall I do to be saved?* as they are daily in saying, *What shall I eat? and what shall I drink? and wherewithal shall I be clothed?*

(2.) The natural man is ignorant of God, and trusting in God is impossible to all that do not know him. There is no trusting of an unknown God. Poor Pagans may worship an unknown God, but it is unacceptable worship, Acts 17:23. Formal hypocrites perform several duties of worship to God, though unknown; they may obey a commanding God, though unknown; all these are but sinful practices: but trusting in an unknown God is impossible: *They that know thy name, wilt put their trust in thee*, says the Psalmist, Psa. 9:10. The reverse of it is very plain: They that know not thy name, will not put their trust in thee. When Paul gives an account of his faith, *I know*, says he, *whom I have believed*, 2 Tim. 1:12.

(3.) All natural men are possessed with that which is inconsistent with believing in God, with believing his word, or the truths contained in it. Hence is that great word of our Lord, John 5:44, *How can ye believe*, says he, *which receive honour one of another, and seek not the honour that cometh from God only?* Pray observe, that there is a greater depth of spirituality in these words of our Lord, than ordinary readers do perceive. It hath but a very bare and harsh sound, for to make it to be this, How can you believe that seek honour and applause from men? The meaning principally of it is this, How can you believe as long as this is in your frame, that the honour that comes from God to you, and the honour given to God by faith, is not more dear to you than any thing else? A natural man can never give God the honour due to the name of his truth, and he cannot set all his rest and confidence upon that honour and reputation that the free grace of God in the gospel brings to him. *How can ye believe*, then, says Christ, etc.? Nay, a natural man hath not only unbelief in him, but the nature of the natural man is unbelief. The apostle cautions all of this, Heb. 3:12, *Take heed, brethren, lest there be in any of you an evil heart of unbelief.* The apostle speaks of unbelief now, not only as a heart-sin, but as if the heart of the unbeliever were made up of unbelief, as if there were nothing in it but unbelief. In such there is no disposition to trust God upon his word; all the trust of the heart is lodged on creatures, it is lodged upon things of nought. This is the first thing, though I say believing is easy, you must not think that it is easy to a natural man, for to him it is impossible.

2*dly*, Neither is believing easy to a believer; otherwise what need is there of *the fight of faith*, as I named but just now? The fight of faith, and the warfare of faith, do not only stand in faith's fighting against all the impediments that are in its way, but in faith's fighting against the unbelief that is lodged in the same heart with it. The believer is not perfectly renewed; there are remnants of the heart of unbelief in him; and from these remnants it comes, that he neither can believe when he would, nor can he at any time believe as he would. *I believe*, says the good man, *Lord, help my unbelief.* He speaks like a man that knew this point well: 'I believe, and I have unbelief for all that; I will not deny my faith, because of my unbelief; I will not conceal my unbelief, because of my faith; I will acknowledge the one to thy praise, and the other to my own shame; Lord, help my unbelief,' Mark 9:24. The thing then that I mean, when I say faith is easy, is, that it is easy in the acting; there is no great difficulty in the acting of it, when once received. This I would shew you in two particulars.

1. Faith is sweetly drawn forth. 2. It sweetly acts when it is drawn forth.

(1.) Faith is sweetly drawn forth. The hand that works faith, deals gently with the soul. It is a drawing with *lovingkindness*, Jer. 31:3; it is a causing of a man to *approach* to God, Psalm 65:4; it is a drawing with such an arm of love and power, as there is no pain in it, but a great deal of pleasure; there is a heavenly pleasure in feeling, as it were, the hand of God drawing the soul sweetly and kindly to himself; it is a gentle motion. Now, here is the mystery of the wisdom of the grace of God: A natural heart is averse from faith; but when the Lord comes to work faith, he offers no violence unto the nature of the man; the way whereby he overcomes unbelief, is by an overpowering, gracious influence of his Spirit, whereby people are made willing. This day of power makes a man willing, as the promise is, which, blessed be God, hath been often fulfilled, *Thy people shall be willing in the day of thy power*, Psa. 110:3.

(2.) It is kindly acted too: as the Lord works it kindly, so does the believer act it kindly. What is there in believing, that should not be very kindly and sweetly done? There is no other relief found for the distressed soul, but only in God through Christ Jesus. This relief is found to be a very amiable and taking one. Is there any pain, think you; is there any trouble; is there any regret seizing upon the spirit of a poor creature, when he gives his consent to a blessed bargain? When the condemned prisoner takes his pardon, what pain is there? is it not an easy thing to accept of pardon? the captive is willing to have his chains loosed, and loosed by him that can take them off sweetly. Sirs, the thing that I drive at is only this, and in it I do appeal unto all the consciences of them that hear me, that ever knew what believing is, That when God proclaims his name, and shines in his glory in the promise, and draws the heart sweetly towards himself, was there ever any thing you did in all your life more sweetly done than to trust God? It is one of the most cheerful acts that ever the soul put forth.

6. The *sixth* inference is about the sensibleness of faith. If so be that faith answers God's faithfulness, why, then, surely it seems faith may be a sensible thing; my meaning is, that a man may know it when he does it. I know there are a great many believers who are very doubtful of their faith, and I believe they will be doubtful as long as they live, if they go that way to work that commonly they do. They want a clearer discovery of the causes and grounds of their faith, they want a clearer discovery of the fruits of their faith, and truly both the one and the other are pretty hard to be obtained. May I now offer an advice, that may be shorter than this, and that is, *Look to faith itself.* The Spirit of God calls faith *an evidence*, Heb. 11:1; and is it so mystical, so involved, so intricate a thing, that people must go so far about, as it were, to find it out? Pray go to faith itself: It is *the evidence of things not seen*, says the apostle. Faith brings light to dark things, but dark things will not bring light to it. I know the Spirit of God can shine upon faith, and the grounds of faith, and can make the fruits of faith appear to the comfort of his people; but in the ordinary practice of believers, if they would mind the acting of their faith more, they would come better to

understand, whether they have it or not. It is a great word the apostle hath, 1 John 5:10, *He that believeth on the Son of God*, says he, *hath the witness in himself.* The words in the original had been better translated, if it had been, *He that believes, hath the testimony in himself*; for witness sometimes signifies the person, and so people commonly mistake it; but the words are, *He that believes, hath the testimony in himself*; his faith receives the testimony of God about the truth of the gospel, so that the man relies upon his faith, apprehends and has it. Now, to bring this matter unto conviction, that faith is a sensible thing, I would only ask you these two things, Do you know what you think? and do you know what you do? Surely, if people can know neither of these, they can pretend to know nothing. But if you do know what you think, and what you do, I must infer this, that you must know when you believe, if you do believe. 1*st*, What do you think? What think you of God, and of his faithful promise? Do you in your heart account him faithful? and do you account the promises sure in your heart and thought? So faith is described in the words, *Sarah judged him faithful who had promised*, Heb. 11:11. So that, in a manner, if Sarah had been to examine herself, Whether have I faith in God? the matter was to be determined thus, What dost thou think of God? He hath passed his word to thee, dost thou judge him faithful? *David thought him so*, 2 Sam. 23:5, Psa. 50:10. Paul thought him so, 2 Tim. 1:12. Cannot a man tell whether he judges God faithful in his great promises of salvation through Christ Jesus? 2*dly*, Cannot you tell what you do? In all other things people know what they do. A poor child can tell you plainly, as soon as it is able to speak, whom it trusts for its daily bread and raiment. It is careless and thoughtless about the things of this life; and the ground the child can give, is this; My parents take care of me. Shall a child, as soon as come to the use of reason, argue so plainly as this? and shall not a child of God be able to do so too? Cannot you tell where you have lodged your great salvation? where you have lodged your darling? It is marvellous if people cannot do this; but I know and shall speak farther of it. There are a great many Christians dare not deny, that there is in them the direct act of faith, who yet, for the want of other things they would fain have, complain that they have not the comfort of the truth of their faith.

7. Hence we may see the greatness of the sin of unbelief, so much spoken of in the word. Faith answers God's faithfulness; unbelief will not stir, but reflects on God's faithfulness: *He that believeth not God*, says the apostle, 1 John 5:10, *hath made him a liar*; made God a liar! A hard word. If it had been, He that believes not, is afraid that God is a liar, that is bad enough; and, He that believes not, calls God a liar, that is yet worse; but this is a dreadful word. He that believes not, hath made God a liar. It is impossible he can make him so, it is impossible, for God to lie; but the poor man does all he can to make him so, and shall be reckoned as if he had done the greatest wrong and hurt to God imaginable. Unbelief is aggravated by two things up and down the world. 1*st*, That it is the boldest and most provoking affront that a sinful creature can give to God, not to believe his word. To call God weak, is blasphemy; to call him foolish, is blasphemy; to deny him his eternal power and Godhead, all these are blasphemy: but to deny his truth, is something above these. See how it is among poor silly men. There is many a man will think it no great affront to be called poor; another will think it no great affront to be called weak and foolish, a man of small parts to be called shallow; but to call a man that hath any thing of a principle of honesty in him, a liar, this is not well to be endured. A man that hath a great many other infirmities, yet may be one that makes conscience of what he says, Rom. 3:4. Now, shall the pride of man rise so readily against reflections of lying cast upon him by his fellow-creatures, and yet shall he cast this unsufferable affront upon the God of truth? The grand transgression is to disbelieve God; and all that do not believe, do so. 2*dly*, Unbelief hath this in it, that it is the most certain, the most sure, and dreadful way of ruin to men; it brings destruction upon men with a special vengeance. *If ye believe not that I am he*, says our Lord, *ye shall die in your sins*, John 8:24. *If I had not come, and spoken unto them, they had not had sin: but now they have no cloak for their sin*, John 15:22. See also verse 24.

Now, of this inference, that is so native, concerning the greatness of the sin of unbelief, there are two things mightily to be regarded. (1.) As great as this sin is, and as surely damning as it is, yet it never disturbs the conscience of a natural ungodly man. He may be disturbed in his mind for sin, he may be disturbed in his conscience for his own lying, but is never disturbed in his conscience for calling God a liar; he may be disturbed in his conscience for his disobeying God's law, but never thinks it a sin to disbelieve God's promise; shaking off of God's authority and yoke of obedience, he may have some challenges for, but in despising God's grace and the offers of it in the gospel, he is never disquieted; therefore sometimes you may marvel, whence this comes. A great many people, may be, have a hell-storm raised in their consciences, but wait a little while, and you will find, in many cases, it comes to nothing; they are only sea-sick, it is the effect only of some sharp affliction or some temptation, or some alarm upon conscience: when they come to shore, and the weather grows fair, and the wind down, they are as quiet, and secure, and harder than ever they were. The reason is, because they never were convinced of the sin of unbelief; they never felt any thing in their exercise about this, that they have been great sinners before God; because this grace offered to them in Christ Jesus was not made precious to them. More hopeful a great deal is the state of that person who is bewailing the heart of unbelief, than of those that are bewailing a covetous, worldly, proud, and filthy heart; though these deserve their own bemoanings in their own places. (2.) As great as this sin is, and as much as there is of it in the godly, yet it is a sin that very rarely disquiets even godly men's consciences. This is sad, that Christians are seldom troubled about their unbelief. Our Lord speaks concerning it, John 16:9, that he will send the Comforter to convince the world of sin, *because*, says he, *they believe not on me*. Moses may convince men of sin, of murder, of adultery, of swearing falsely, of profaning the holy day of God; Moses may convince them of a great many transgressions against the law; but the Spirit of God only can convince a believer of the sin of unbelief. Judge you now how rare this is, in all the professions, in all the humblings of believers, when they are alone. I pose your consciences about it; what Christian is there to be found? Not one among a thousand have their hearts broken, their consciences disquieting them, as broken bones within them, because of their unbelief, their jealousies of Christ's love, their doubting of the faithfulness of the promises: nay, of the same promises that they have believed formerly, and have given glory to God by believing, they take back again the glory by unbelieving. The most spiritual attainment of a Christian in the world, the most spiritual, evangelical mourning and repentance that can be acted by a Christian, is a mourning over his unbelief; that the word of the Lord is not more precious to him; that he cannot trust God's word barely without props; that he doubts of it so often, when darkness comes on; that he lets go his hold of this great rock, the faithfulness of God.

7. And *lastly*, The last inference is, That here we may see the wonderful wisdom of God, in twisting his glory with the eternal concerns of the children of men, and that both in the saving of the elect, and in the perdition of the unhappy remnant; for the elect are sometimes called *the remnant*, and the reprobates are sometimes also called by the same name. *The remnant are blinded*, says Paul, Rom. 11:7. In the same place, within two or three verses, the elect are called *the remnant according to the election of grace*, and the reprobates are called the *rest that were blinded*. The Lord, I say, hath herein linked his glory marvellously with the eternal concernments of men. Thus, as to the salvation of the elect, God gives Christ for them, according to the eternal promise of his heart: he gives the purpose to them; he gives them faith, to lay hold on the promise; and he glorifies himself, and saves them in the performance of the promise: all these things are framed so together, that the glory of God shall be greatly advanced in saving of poor man. There is glory in electing love, there is glory in redeeming grace, there is glory in God's faithfulness in his word, this is glorified by the believing of the perishing sinner; and in and upon this believing, the performance of the promise, the applying of the redemption, the accomplishment of the purpose of his grace, is at last reached. On the other hand, a great many under the gospel perish. Christ was never given for them, but he is offered unto them. The promises were never meant for them, but they are offered to them. No man perishes, because Christ died not for him; no man misses of the performance of the promise, because the promise was not made to him; but he perishes because of his unbelief, because the testimony of God was not looked upon as sufficient ground to venture his soul upon, therefore he perishes. And thus the Lord gets the glory of his justice and faithfulness upon those wretches, that have denied to trust him. The apostle joins both in 2 Thess. 1:8-10. Our Lord is to take *vengeance on them that know not God, and that obey not the gospel of our Lord Jesus Christ*; and this, *when he shall come*, says he, *to be glorified in his saints, and to be admired in all them that believe*

(because our testimony among you was believed), in that day. 'You that have believed the testimony of God in the gospel,' says the apostle, 'our Lord will be admired in you, and glorified in that day.' So much shall serve for the doctrinal inferences from this truth.

There is only one practical exhortation, but it is a large one, that I would deduce from it, and name it now; that is, Since believers should answer the faithfulness of God, I exhort you in the Lord's name, to come with your faith and answer this faithfulness; believe as he hath promised.

I shall not enter upon the particulars of it now, only conclude in general with these three:—

1. If you would answer the faithfulness of God by your faith, you must believe much, for God hath promised a great deal; our faith, I say, must be a great one, it must be a large one, we must believe a great many things, for God hath promised greatly; the covenant, if I may so speak, is a large charter, and our faith must seal every word in it; we must put the amen of our faith unto every true and faithful saying of God, Rev. 19:9, 21:5 and 22:6.

2. If you would answer the faithfulness of God by your faith, you must believe greatly; not only much, but strongly. The promises are strong in themselves, so should your faith be.

3. You must believe long. If your faith answers God's faithfulness as it ought, you must believe always, as long as promises are promises; and promises are promises still, till they be performed; and therefore faith should be faith still, and acted still, till the performance come. *Ye have need of patience*, says the apostle, *that after ye have done the will of God, ye might receive the promise*, Heb. 10:36. God's promises are for a great while to come, as David's word is concerning the Lord's kindness to him, *Thou hast spoken also of thy servant's house, for a great while to come*, 2 Sam. 7:9. So that the answering of God's faithfulness by our faith, should bear proportion unto the greatness, largeness, freeness, and length of the promise. We should look to the promise, and say, Here is a great blessing, when is it to be? Here is a promise leads into eternity, I will believe till then, says the believer; till I launch into eternity; for there the grand expectation of the main fulfilments is to be.

SERMON IX.

HEB. 10:23.

For he is faithful that promised.

YOU have all great need to study your Bibles well. According to their diligence in using of the word of God, is the thriving of men's souls. There are these four things, that should still be minded in our using the Bible:—

1. To look on it all as the word of God. When this is impressed on the soul by faith upon opening the book. All this is the word of God, this is scripture inspired by the Holy Ghost, what a great savour does it leave upon the heart!

2. In using your Bibles, be sure to pick out the promises thereof. This is the main thing in the word, the testimonies of God's good-will to the children of men. People's spirits are discerned by this, what it is in that word they chiefly mind. Some folks read the Bible as they read another history, and the historical part they like very well; some like the wise precepts of the word for the conduct of their lives, of which the scripture is full. But if so be you be Christians indeed, the main thing you will spy out in the word, is, Where does God's good-will appear? What has God said for me? What good word has God passed that I may trust to, and be saved by?

3. When we have picked out the promises, we must then lay them to the heart; they never do good till they meet with the heart. What gracious changes hath God wrought, when he hath laid a warm promise to a cold heart! The fire of heaven kindles immediately. We cannot put life into the promise, that is God's gift; we cannot put life into our own hearts, that is God's gift too; but we should strive to bring the heart and God's promise as near as may be. *Thy word have I hid in mine heart*, says David, Psa. 119:11. God's people do as it were eat the word, Jer. 15:16.

4. *Lastly*, In using your Bibles, be sure to pray over the promises. I assure you, wherever faith hath got but a bit of the bread of life in the promise, it will immediately lift itself upwards in desires, and in

breathings towards the Lord for performance. *For thou, O Lord of hosts, God of Israel, hast revealed to thy servant, saying, I will build thee an house, therefore hath thy servant found in his heart to pray this prayer unto thee.* David was a great believer, and he argues like one, 2 Sam. 7:27. David needed those blessings that God promised, and in the sense of his need of them, he should, and did pray for them: but when God gives him a promise, he prays then better for performance; and it is more of the nature of faith to pray upon a promise, than to pray for the supply of a want. The desires of supplies of wants are somewhat of the voice of nature, but breathings for the performance of promises are the very breathings of faith itself.

Now, this text that I have spoken from to you so often, is indeed but a short one, but it is in a manner the key of the Bible, *Faithful is he that promised.* I have spoke at large unto the observations from these words, besides what was taken notice of in the words with respect to their scope; as,

1. That the Christian's God is a promising God; he is made known by promising; and he is never rightly known, but when known as a promising God.

2. That this promising God is faithful in all his promises.

3. That the faith of believers should answer the faithfulness of God; their faith should come up in some measure of correspondency with the faithfulness of the promiser. Of this last I have spoke several times in opening up the doctrine, and began to apply it first in doctrinal inferences.

My work now is to enter upon the exhortation unto this answering of divine faithfulness by your faith, and I would extend it to these three:—

1. Answer divine faithfulness in the promise of salvation by Christ in the gospel. This is the beginning of faith, Heb. 3:14.

2. Answer divine faithfulness in all the promises of grace and glory made to believers. This is the course and race of faith, Heb. 12:1, 1 Cor. 9:24, 26.

3. Answer the faithfulness of God in the grand promise of eternal life, to be possessed upon our departure out of this body. This is the beginning, this is the life, and this is the end of believing, 1 Pet. 1:9.

For the first of these, the exhortation is this (and it is an exhortation to every one of you, whether you be believers or unbelievers): Answer the faithfulness of God in the promise of salvation by Christ in the gospel, answer it by faith. This is that which is the scope of all the gospel, this is the design of God in writing to us the gospel. *But these are written*, saith the apostle, *that ye might believe that Jesus is the Christ, the Son of God, and that believing ye might have life through his name*, John 20:30. This is what our Lord charges his apostles with: *Go*, saith he, *and preach the gospel to every creature*; and as the apostle saith, *which was preached to every creature which is under heaven*, Col. 1:23: that is, Every man and woman that lives in this world, preach the gospel to them; what gospel? Tell them that there is life and salvation for them in Jesus Christ; if they will believe it, well and good; if not, they *shall be damned*, Mark 16:15, 16. Upon this now, because it is a matter of great concernment unto people to be well informed about it, to be well roused up unto the practice of it, I would shew,

1. The nature of this promise that is to be believed.

2. The nature of that faith which is to answer the faithfulness of God in the promise.

First, For the nature of the promise of salvation by Christ in the gospel, which is the sum and substance of all the right preaching of the gospel, there are three mistakes very usual amongst people about it.

1. This promise is no declaring the eternal purpose of election. Though I know that the promise flows from the purpose, and is a proof that there is an election, yet the promise is no declaring of the particular purpose of election to any particular person. You are not commanded to believe the gospel because you are elected, but you are commanded to believe the gospel that you may know your election, and that of God. No man is cast into hell because not elected (though all that are not so, shall be sent thither); but men under the gospel are damned, because they are unbelievers, and receive not the testimony of God.

2. Neither is this promise a declaration of the design of the redemption of Christ. A promise of the gospel does not declare nor determine whom Christ died for; it is not the nature of this promise, nor the design of it to do that. Christ hath laid down his life for his

sheep; the promise is made to all, though none but his sheep will receive it: *Ye believe not*, says our Lord, *because ye are not of my sheep*, John 10:26.

3. Neither is the promise of the gospel, the declaring of the effectual working of the Spirit upon the heart. It is the means that God works by, but it is not that which does declare the work. It is a bad argument for one to say, I know I am elected, and redeemed by Christ, and sanctified and changed by the Holy Ghost, because I have the promise of salvation by Christ in the gospel. Indeed, if you can say, I have received the promise by faith, you speak according to the word; then all the former are evident, the saving operation of the Spirit appears, thy interest in Christ's redemption appears; thy name is written in the book of life, and thou mayst read it.

What then is the promise, if it be not a declaring of any of these? The promise of the gospel is a declaration of God's good-will to save men by Christ Jesus, and to this declaration he requires their faith. This good-will of God is tendered to men by promise, for wise ends.

1. By this means God brings in all the elect; by the means of the declaring his good-will in a promise. *1st*, The promise is the means of their faith, and therefore is a ground of their faith. When the Lord, in the day of his power, makes use of the word, and sends it home upon the heart, it begets faith; and as soon as faith is begotten, it acts upon the same word of promise from whence it sprang. Now, here is the great wisdom of God. His purposes are all kept hid with himself; he hath determined from eternity, in his own thoughts and decrees, the eternal state of all men, and his counsel will stand; he hath his people whom he hath a mind to save, lying scattered up and down the world. There is no mark upon them that is visible to any creature; they are in the same mass, of the same lump, in the same state, children of wrath even as others, as ripe for hell as any man. The Lord, to accomplish the purpose of his grace, sends the gospel to them. The promise is no more to them in the dispensation of it, than it is to any body else. I know the promise in God's purpose is otherwise designed for them than others; but this promise is cast abroad as an equal ground of security for all that will lay hold of it; and the poor elect man, when he ventures upon the promise of God, hath nothing before his eye but only the promise: 'It is

a true and faithful saying, worthy of all acceptation, and therefore worthy of mine; I will give it due attention, and lay hold of it.'

2. By this means God stops the mouths of the condemned remnant of gospel-despisers. Pray observe the word that is in the parable, Matt. 22:10, 11. Though parables, you know, are not to be so strictly urged, yet there are some things that are to be applied, and that is what serves the scope of them: When the King came to view his guests, he spied one without a *wedding-garment; and he saith unto him, Friend, how camest thou in hither, not having a wedding-garment? And he was speechless.* Pray observe; we find in the same feast the invitation is given to all sorts, the invitation is to good and bad; so the word is; and it is made effectual upon the lame, and blind, and halt, and most miserable that could be found by the hedges and highway-side, as Luke hath it, Luke 14:16, where the same parable is. Now, what can be the meaning of this, *Friend, how camest thou in hither, not having a wedding-garment?* Why, if the poor man had not a wedding-garment, whence should he get it? Should he not have sought it? All that makes us amiable and acceptable before God, is of the gift of his grace on us. That which is the perdition of the ungodly unbelievers of the gospel, is, because they do not receive the testimony of God; they dare not, they are not able, they are not willing to trust their eternal salvation upon God's bare word. So much now for the nature of this promise. The promise is Christ's, and that which he casts forth in the dispensation of the gospel, and gathers in men thereby. Where the power of the promise reaches the heart, it draws in the chosen; where only a common power reaches carnal men, they are only drawn into a profession, and are *cast away* as lost, as our Lord speaks of the kingdom of heaven under the similitude of a net to catch fish, Matt. 13:47, 48.

The *second* thing to be spoke to is, What is that faith that is to answer the faithfulness of God in the promise, the general promise of salvation in the gospel?

1. It is to believe the gospel-report firmly concerning Jesus Christ, and God's great salvation in him and by him; that there is life enough in Christ for men, 1 John 5:11. It is to believe the report concerning Christ, according to the prophet Isaiah, chap. 53:1. Which words our Lord applies unto the gospel, more plainly to himself, John 12:40, where he

applies the words of the same Isaiah unto the unbelievers that were in his own days. Some folks may possibly think there is no great difficulty in this matter; but it is because they are ignorant, and have never been tried. How hard a matter is it to believe the mystery of the gospel, that the Father hath sent the Son to be the Saviour of the world; that he came in the appointed time, that he did all his work, and obtained eternal redemption for us; that he bought all his sheep by the price of his blood, and by that blood entered into heaven to make intercession for us? and that because he is there, *he is able save them to the uttermost, that come unto God by him?* as in Heb. 7:25. Pray observe this, when a great many Christians' doubtings are thoroughly sifted and convassed,[1] it will be found that the shaking of their faith, as to their interest in Christ, proceeds much from the weakness of their faith as to the gospel-report concerning him. If people did firmly believe all that is said in the Old and New Testament, concerning that righteousness and salvation wrought out by the Son of God, they would find it an easier matter to apply it to themselves, and say, Surely (1.) I have no righteousness of my own. (2.) Nor can any creature procure it for me. (3.) Enough is in Christ. (4.) All is offered to me in the gospel. (5.) My soul likes the offer. (6.) I willingly accept him for my only Saviour. *Surely, shall one say, in the Lord have I righteousness and strength,* Isa. 45:24.

2. It is to believe firmly the truth and the sincerity of God in the offer of this Saviour, and of all his salvation as offered to men. Pray observe, here we shall come to that which does pinch the consciences of many Christians. Ye are required by the Lord, and in his name, by them that preach the gospel, to believe the truth and the sincerity of the offer of Christ and all his salvation to thee in particular. You are to think thus within yourselves, Verily this Saviour, and all his great salvation is offered to me. Pray what conceptions have you of the gospel, if you do not admit this? For you to run away with an imagination, that Christ is offered unto the church, that he is offered unto his people, is wrong. I tell you, in the gospel he is offered to you in particular; and there are none that believe in him, until they take it up so. Says the poor jailor, *What shall I do to be saved? Believe thou on the Lord Jesus,* says Paul to him, *and thou shall be saved.* I am preaching Christ, and I have got

[1] [That is, examined.]

bonds for my reward; but if thou wouldst be saved, remember that I in prison offer this Saviour to thee: *Believe thou on the Lord Jesus, and thou shalt be saved.* Unless people do come this length of faith, firmly to believe, that God fairly and honestly, and with an upright meaning, makes free offer and tender of Christ and of all his salvation to them; they never will be believers, they never will believe the scriptures aright.

3. You are to believe that there is no impediment nor hindrance, neither on God's part nor thine, to hinder thee from partaking of Christ, if thou be willing. This is a part of that faith that answers the faithfulness of God in the promise of the gospel, and which a poor creature should believe firmly; that there is no impediment on God's part, nor on my part to hinder my partaking of Christ, according to God's offer, if I accept of him. The impediment on our part is sin, the impediments on God's part are the law and justice. The Lord hath declared these shall not stand. The law and justice stands in no man's way to hinder him from partaking of Christ, if he will accept thereof. Neither shall sin hinder him, for the offer is made to all men as sinners, whatsoever they have been, and whatsoever they are; but none will accept it but enlightened sinners.

4. You are required to venture your salvation on Jesus Christ, according to the warrant of this offer, and according to the truth of this promise. As you believe the doctrine of Christ, and believe the offer of God, and the sincerity, and freedom, and largeness of the offer, you are to accept thereof, and to venture your all upon it. This is believing. God has given his promise of life in Christ Jesus, as the foundation of all our hope of salvation; we should answer his faithfulness by building all our hopes upon that bottom. Lay hold therefore on this cord of salvation, and ye cannot miscarry. No man can receive Christ out of a promise, no man can receive a promise of salvation out of Christ; no man can do both, no man can do any one of them without faith; for believing is receiving; and none who believe on him can perish, but shall *have eternal life*, John 3:14-20.

5. *Lastly*, You are to believe firmly, that if you be willing, the Lord is willing, and you shall be welcome; nay, you are now welcome at this present on believing. I say you are to believe firmly, that when your hearts are drawn forth to accept of him, the Lord will accept of

you, and to be confident of it too. Now, I shall offer for the clearing of this, as far as some ordinary transactions amongst men may help, some instances which the Spirit of God makes use of in the word to illustrate this affair, this first believing the promise of Jesus Christ, or a poor sinner's first believing. I know all similitudes that are used in the word, or can be contrived by us, are but like parables, they do not quadrate fully; but I shall use them no farther, than as shall serve the scope and drift of this doctrine.

The *first* is a common transaction of mankind, that of *marriage*. You all know how this matter is carried on. The transaction with God in Christ Jesus for our eternal salvation, is frequently expressed by this similitude: *I will betroth thee unto me for ever; yea, I will betroth thee unto me in righteousness, and in judgment, and in loving-kindness, and in mercies,—and thou shalt know the Lord*, Hosea 2:19, 20. *I have espoused you*, says the apostle, *to one husband, that I may present you as a chaste virgin to Christ*, 2 Cor. 11:2. The expressions are manifold up and down the word, both in the Old and New Testament, about this similitude. Now, to bring it to my purpose, you know when a marriage is made up, especially of them that are vastly unequal, as it is here, the man declares his love, courts the party, affirms, that if she will give her consent to be his, he is heartily willing to be hers. The promise upon the man's side makes no marriage; but the promise duly declared by the man, and duly accepted by the woman, makes one. The promise of the gospel comes this way to you, sinners; it is the faithful promise of God in Christ Jesus; that if you will accept of him through Christ for your God and portion, he will be yours; give but your consent and the match is made. But if the party that is courted say or think (1.) That either the bargain is not good; or (2.) That the man that promises is not true; or (3.) If her affections are set on another; or (4.) If she be married to another, Rom. 7:6; or (5.) If she hate him, Prov. 8:36: in these cases she will withhold her consent. In like manner assure yourselves, that all gospel-hearers who do not give their hearty consent to be the Lord's, will be chargeable with some of these; for either they think, that the bargain is not good, or that he that promises is not true, or their affections are set on other objects, or they hate the ways of the Lord.

2dly, There is a transaction spoken of in the word under the notion of *adoption*. It is now out of use in the world, but it was customary of old, when a man did adopt another's child, and brought in that child to possess the inheritance, to bear his name, and to be his heir. There were usual formalities, as good reason there should be, where such matters are; the consent of the child was required; Are you willing to be such a man's? to be under his conduct? to be his heir? to be possessed of his estate? The very declaring of the consent is that which makes up the relation.

The *third* instance shall be that of the *King's pardon* given to a company of rebels. So the gospel is God's act of grace unto a company of sinners: it is proclaimed as publicly as may be; and the more sinners that hear it, the better, if they would believe. Now, suppose there be such a thing as proclamation of free pardon to a company of rebels, it is unavoidable, that their not accepting of it must be, either, 1. Because they think their cause is just, and themselves not to be rebels; or, 2. That they have strength enough to fight it out; and if they come in, they shall be hanged; if so, they will rather die in their arms, they will *stand upon their sword*, as the word of the prophet is, rather than accept of it. But if they have any hopes of pardon upon their submission, and believe the person who promises pardon on such terms, will stand to his word; they will accept of it, and embrace it. The case is just so here: Proclamation of God's free grace and pardon through Christ Jesus, is tendered to the children of men; it is necessarily required to the accepting it, that you have a trust in the good-will of the proclaimer, as well as confidence, that the mercy is great that is tendered.

We shall consider this contract, *4thly*, as in the case of *surety* and *debtor*, for it is so represented to us in the word. Our Lord Jesus Christ is the great Surety; we are great debtors, not able to pay; Christ offers to pay our debts; there is no more required, when the law and justice condemn us to hell prison, but, *Lord, take bail of thy own Son for me*. But if men will pay part of the debt, and work out the rest, they despise the gospel; as too many do.

There is a *fifth* similitude common amongst us, and that is of *buyer* and *seller*, all managed by faith. In buying and selling, you know how frequently this is used amongst men. (1.) We will suppose we know this, that the man that sells, is willing to part with his goods at the price named, otherwise he is a deceitful man that offers things to sell, and will not part with them. (2.) We all know this, that if I come up to the price demanded, and pay it down, the goods are mine. Bring this matter to our purpose: The great goods are Christ and salvation, the price is nothing, the poor sinner is the buyer; now, this little price; this no price, this no money, is so great a matter, that proud poor man is very unwilling to lay it down. *Ho, every one that thirsteth, come ye to the waters, and he that hath no money, come ye, buy and eat, buy wine and milk without money, and without price*, Isa. 55:1. *I counsel thee to buy of me*, Rev. 3:18. Then if they be buyers, they had something to buy with; no, they had nothing; for our Lord tells them in the verse just before, that they were *wretched, and miserable, and poor, and blind, and naked.* Now, what can such folks have to buy with? Gospel-buying is nothing else but honest begging. But notwithstanding the gospel be so freely offered, many say to God, as Abraham said to the king of Sodom, *I will not take any thing that is thine, lest thou shouldst say, I have made Abraham rich*, Gen. 14:23.

Begging is a *sixth* similitude by which this matter is expressed; *begging* and *receiving*. God offers, we beg; God gives, we take; and all begging of God is in faith. We have some kind of faith, that God hath these good things to give, and is willing to give, else wherefore do we ask them? When he gives them, we receive them. Have you received Christ Jesus the Lord? *As ye have received him, so walk ye in him*, says the apostle, Col. 2:6. From all these now you see, that the transactions amongst men, in all sorts of affairs almost, do discover the relation that is entered into, and that covenants are made amongst men by mutual trust; that we trust him that promises, and accept the bargain because we do so: So must there be here. Only there are two great differences in this great bargain of the gospel, which are beyond all that we can gather out of any similitude. (1.) That the consenting trust of the receiver, is the work of the offerer; this trust, this faith, this receiving that we have spoken of, is God's work. He that proposes a good bargain to another, hath no power over him to persuade him, infallibly to give his consent; but the Lord hath this power. (2.) The nature of God's proffer, and his promise, are the means by which he works the principle of acceptance.

When the sinner is rebellious (as all men by nature are, till grace tame them), the Lord can deliver the promise of salvation by Christ Jesus in that beauty and glory, and with that power and strength, that no man can resist it: *Thy people shall be willing in the day of thy power*, Psa. 110:3. If the Lord put forth this power, this willingness, this trust, that I am calling for, will infallibly be produced.

So much now for the explaining of these things, what the promise of salvation by Christ in the gospel is, that we should glorify God's faithfulness in, and what that faith is that we should meet this promise with.

Application. 1. Hence you may see the marvellous way of saving us by Christ Jesus. What wonderful grace and wisdom shines here! All this salvation was prepared in God's counsel before the foundation of the world was laid, we had nothing to do with it; all this salvation was wrought out in God's time, by the life, and death, and sufferings of our Lord Jesus; that which we had no hand in, and in which all our salvation stands; for all that, all this grace and mercy, and salvation comes streaming unto us in a bare promise of God; the Lord proclaims it; this is the call of the gospel, He that dares trust Christ with his soul, upon the warrant of the gospel, shall be saved for ever. The Lord tries people this way. We have no more to do but take pen in hand, and say, Amen, O Lord; it is a good bargain, and a true word, and I will trust my soul on it. This is believing.

2. See, Sirs, what you have been doing under the gospel all your days. I know that this assembly, as most weekly assemblies are, is made up of a sort of people that spend a great part of their time in hearing. For God's sake tell me, what you have been doing all this while. Have you put the main matter of your salvation out of the devil's reach? Have you made conscience of this, of giving glory to God's faithfulness in the grand promise of salvation by Christ? Have you learned to know Christ? Have you learned to talk of him? Have you learned to understand the gospel? to talk, to reason, to discourse of it? But is this all? Have you never been exercised about this, about putting your own seal to the gospel? *He that hath received his testimony, hath set to his seal, that God is true.* God will be true, whether we set our seal to it or no; but God's truth will not be to our interest and advantage, unless we

set to our seal. Take heed, there are few folks, whose conscience falls under conviction of duty in this matter; that they are bound before God to believe on Christ Jesus for eternal life. People will not believe, that they should believe; and can there be any hope that ever they will believe, who are of this mind? How hard is it to persuade people that they should believe; that upon the preaching of the word, and the proclamation of God's salvation by Christ Jesus, they must venture upon it! Say some, 'I know not whether the promise be to me.' Is it not to you as much as ever it was to any? Is it not to you as much as ever it hath been to any sinner, the hour before he was converted? The promise will never be more to you, till it be believed, than it is now. *Repent*, says the apostle to the murderers of Christ, *for the promise is unto you*, Acts 2:38, 39. Ye killed the promiser just now, yet for all that you shall be saved, if you repent; one of the strangest repentance that ever was required in this world! The very exacting repentance from them was expressly exacting of faith; for it was impossible for any man to repent of killing Christ, but he that believed he was the Son of God; therefore, says the apostle, *the promise is unto you, and to your children.* Say you, 'Natural men are without the promise, and strangers from the covenants of promise,' Eph. 2:12. And what then? If they be, what will you infer from that? I am a poor natural creature, a stranger from that covenant of promise. But I pray, how shall this strangeness be removed? Just as if a poor man, standing without like to starve with hunger and cold, should say, Alas! I shall die in this place, without the house. Why, the door is open, in God's name enter. We enter by faith; the promise is God's door cast open, that poor men may enter in. Pray now consider that place, which I will speak a little to, as well as from the preceding and following words: Heb. 4:1, *Let us therefore fear, lest a promise being left us of entering into his rest, any of you should seem to come short of it.* The thing that the apostle deduceth his exhortation from, is a most awful instance; the instance of the people of Israel in the wilderness. Take notice of the passage, and of the Spirit of God's using it. God had said to Moses, that, at the appointed time, he would bring the children of Israel out of Egypt. He appeared with them, and for them, in ten great wonders and miracles, that they might know his calling to be of God, and his message from God. The people believe at last; they believe that God had a good mind towards them, and would bring them into the land of Canaan, according to his promise; but when they are a little way got through the Red-sea, difficulties meet them, unbelief arises, and they hardened their hearts, and tempted God; from whence we may observe, *How long*, says the Lord, *refuse ye to keep my commandments, and my laws?* That which they were bound to believe, was this, That God meant well and honestly with them in the promise of bringing them to the land of Canaan; and because they did not believe it, God sware, that not one of them from twenty years old should enter into it. Upon this instance the apostle makes his exhortation: *Let us therefore fear, lest a promise being left us of entering into his rest, any of you should come short of it.* Alas! the rest we are called to, is a far greater rest than the rest of Canaan, the promise is a promise more sure. Ay, but says the apostle, *Let us fear, lest a promise being left us of entering into his rest, any of you should seem to come short of it*, lest we should *fall after the same example of unbelief*, as he has it in verse 11. The case then, as to us, is this, The Lord hath proclaimed to us in the gospel, his good-will in high and great promises, to save us by Jesus Christ. He proclaims it thus, that whosoever will trust him, and take his promise, shall certainly come to heaven. There are some of the children of men, whom God hath a mind to bring to heaven, and a great many others have the promise in their hand, as well as they, but have not faith in their hearts; they let the promise slip, and the promise lets them slip; and, if I may so speak, to hell they fall; but there is no fault in the promise, it is because they do not build upon it.

Some may say, 'I am not qualified for the promise, I am not so good as I should be.' *Answer*, Are you qualified for hell or no? No man shall be in heaven but he that sees himself fully qualified for hell, as a faggot that is bound up for eternal burnings, unless mercy pluck the brand out of the fire. Instead of these objections, I will tell you better, 1. What think you? Is Christ a fit Saviour for you? Christ is exactly shapen, as fit for a sinner as possibly he can be. God, in making and framing his Son for a Saviour, consulted to make him as fit to be a Saviour for sinners, as divine wisdom could make him. 2. Ask this question, whether there be no promise in the new covenant that looks towards you? Are there no streams in this great well of salvation? Yes, surely, the covenant streams out towards thee. Pray now can you find nothing in the promise of the new covenant that suits you exactly? *I will pour clean water upon you*: who needs this more than the filthy? *From all their iniquities will I cleanse them. I will take away the heart of stone*, etc. If you have a heart of stone, your cure is in the covenant. My meaning is, that you, feeling the heart of stone, may plead this promise. I know no body that hath a hard heart can plead this promise; they that have a truly hard heart, think nothing ails them. 3. The third question you should ask yourselves is this, Whether there is any trust in your heart working towards God? Shall all the promises of the gospel be proclaimed to men every day, and no thoughts of trusting in him arise? That he is a faithful speaker, is plain; therefore his message should be received. The mystery of saving particular persons by the application of divine grace, is greater than any can fathom, with respect to themselves, but more or less they can search it with respect to others. All the faith that ever was wrought in the hearts of believers, to make unbelievers believers, and make believers better believers, was evermore wrought by the appearance of divine faithfulness in the promise. The better you know the promise, the better believers you will be; therefore make conscience of this. Think that your eternal state depends upon this, how the gospel hath been received by faith. Secure sinners find no difficulty in believing, but poor awakened sinners find it the greatest difficulty in the world. A natural man finds no difficulty in believing, because he is not concerned about salvation; a poor awakened sinner finds it a hard matter to believe, because he is deeply concerned about salvation. Nothing can save us but only the bare promise. This promise can save no man till it hath laid hold on him, and till it hath put forth its power upon him. It usually appears but a weak and slender thing for a man to trust his all upon. How slightly do unbelievers think of the promise of God? There is not an ungodly man in the world, but he reckons a rich man's promise to provide for him in this world, is a great deal better than all the promises in the Bible. But this is a sign the poor creature hath no true faith in a faithful God, whatever false trust he may have in man, who is not only a *liar*, Rom. 3:4. but a *lie*, Psa. 62:9.

SERMON X.

HEB. 10:23.

For he is faithful that promised.

LITTLE do many people know that daily hear the gospel, what the gospel is, and what hearing of it should be. The gospel is a divine proclamation of God's good-will towards perishing sinners, delivered to us in many words in the scriptures. The sum of it is in this offer, That whosoever they be, and whatever they have been, that are content to take Christ for their guide, and his fulness and grace for their stock, and God's faithful promise for their security, as sure as God lives they shall be saved for ever. This is the gospel which is preached in many forms of words, but the substance is the same. How many are they that do not know what they are doing when they hear? It is a proclamation that is either received to God's highest praise by faith, or is rejected to his greatest dishonour, and to men's most certain ruin. It is the Lord's great wisdom that the gospel should be preached, and that it should be preached by men, by sinful men that are believers themselves; and they should recommend the same way of salvation to the faith of others, that they have taken to themselves.

Upon these words you know that I have spoken several times concerning the promising God, his faithfulness in his promises, and the duty of his people to answer his faithfulness by their faith. The last day I proposed the application of this whole matter in three exhortations, and spake unto the first last day; I shall now add a little more, and proceed.

1. The first exhortation was to this duty, That you should all answer the faithfulness of God in the great promise of salvation by Jesus Christ in the gospel; for in a manner this is the promise that faith first meets with, and first fixes on; faith is begotten by it, and faith receives the new life in it, and by it.

2. The second exhortation is, That believers must answer the faithfulness of this promising God, in the expecting of all good by the way.

3. That believers should answer the faithfulness of God, in a firm expectation of the inheritance at last.

Of the first of these I spoke some time last day, and shewed you (1.) What the nature of this promise of salvation is, that our faith first should take hold of. (2.) Wherein the answering of faith to the faithfulness of God does consist. *1st*, In believing the truth of the gospel-record and report, that there is life in Christ for men. *2dly*, It is a believing of the truth and sincerity of God in the offer of it. *3dly*, A believing that there is now no impediment on God's part, or on ours, that shall hinder the partaking of the blessing promised, if we will be willing to trust. The last is, by venturing our eternal salvation upon it; that is believing, taking up, taking in the truth of the gospel-promise of salvation by Christ, that the heart is resolved here to settle, and here to adventure its all. *Lord, to whom shall we go?* says Peter; *thou hast the words of eternal life*: we will lodge our eternal life on thee, and upon thy word; no where else can we find them, and they are sufficiently with thee for our trust; for *we believe, and are sure, that thou art that Christ the Son of the living God*, John 6:69. The only thing I would do, before I leave this first exhortation, shall be a little more fully to bring this matter near to your conscience, searching and trying of you, whether you have given this faithfulness of God a meeting; the question is a question of the greatest importance. All things else, that you may be concerned about, and there are a great many other things that people may lawfully be concerned about under the gospel; all things else, I say, are either trifles in themselves in regard to this, or very unreasonably started, till this grand question be determined, Have I entertained God's offer and promise of eternal life by Christ Jesus with true faith or no? The importance is obvious, for our eternal salvation stands upon it. The question is not only important, but it seems easily resolved, it seems to be a great deal harder one way to conceive how a believer should be ignorant of his believing, than how it should be that he should know it: though I do acknowledge that many believers are ignorant that they are believers. The apostle's word puts it out of question, 1 John 5:13, *These things have I written unto you that believe on the name of the Son of God; that ye may know that ye have eternal life, and that ye may believe on the name of the Son of God*; that is, that ye may believe better, that ye may know ye believed, and that ye may know what ye have in and by believing. The apostle seems to speak of it as a matter of wonder that people should not know it. *Examine yourselves, whether ye be in the faith; prove your own selves; know ye not your own selves, how that Jesus Christ is in you, except ye be reprobates?* Only now a few things concerning this matter, that will make it on a little inquiry appear at least to be easily resolved.

1. The greatness of the matter intrusted in this believing. The more considerable the matter of trust is, the better people usually know where they trust it, and when they trust it. If a man trust his wife and children, his estate, his house, and all his business, he knows very well when he trusts that which is so dear to him; but, alas! a great many never knew they had souls, the preciousness of their immortal souls was never felt by them; these folks can never trust, or know whom they trust.

2. The party trusted is one, one only. When our trust is scattered, as it were, people may forget where one part of it is lodged, and where another part; but where it is all unitedly centered in one hand, why should people not know where it is? *I know*, says the apostle, *whom I have believed*, 2 Tim. 1:12. O how blessedly these two words answer one another, *Faithful is he that promised*, and *I know*, etc. There is God's name, and there is the faith of the Christian concerning this God: It is he whom I have trusted, he that promises, is he whom I have believed; whereas *a double-minded man is unstable in all his ways*, James 1:8.

3. The warrant of this trust is single; it is upheld by the word of promise, and that alone, that separate from all things else. All our hopes are founded barely upon the word of God; and the more we strive (as you have heard already) to add supports to the word, for the imaginary strengthening of our faith, the more we weaken our faith, and the more we dishonour the word. If God's word of promise cannot bear thee up, though all the shoulders of all the angels in heaven should prop thee up, thou wouldst sink under them.

4. The influence and power that is needful for the drawing forth this trust, makes it remarkable also. When God *causes* us to *hope*, as David speaks, Psa. 119:49, this makes the matter yet more remarkable. If faith and trust in God were a plant that could grow up in our hearts daily, it might spring up unobserved, as a great many other things do.

There are a great many seeds of knowledge and understanding, that do naturally grow up in children, as they grow in years, from the stock of natural parts that God gave them in their first frame; but faith is none of these things. This trusting is never without a causing, a causing to approach to him; it is never without a drawing. Therefore believers are more sensible of the power that works faith, than of that faith working in themselves, they are more sensible of the pains God hath been at to draw forth faith, than of the living acts of faith in themselves.

5. The fight of faith is to be taken notice of; as in Genesis 25:22, 23.

6. *Lastly*, The grand expectation of faith is of that nature, that we cannot tell how it can be acted, though it may be known after it hath been acted. What do we take Christ's word for, and set our seal to it, but for everlasting salvation, for a glory to be revealed at the appearing of Jesus Christ, beyond what our ear hath heard, or tongue can tell, or heart can conceive? *And now, Lord, what wait I for? My hope is in thee*, Psa. 39:7. *We are not of them who draw back into perdition, but of them that believe, to the saving of the soul*, Heb. 10:39. *We are looking for the mercy of our Lord Jesus Christ, unto eternal life*, Jude, ver. 21. Now, may not one know these things, think ye? Nay, there is a special weakness in faith, a special cunning of our adversary the devil, that makes this believing not more frequently known by believers, that we do not know that we trust, when we trust. The matter is so considerable, the acts so formally and deliberately put forth, that a man may believe, and yet not be sensible of it, but by the fruits and effects of believing, which are the ordinary ways by which we come to know it. Therefore, now, unto such of you as can with some confidence avow it before God, that the gospel-promise of salvation by Christ Jesus hath been so warm upon your hearts, that you have built your everlasting hopes upon it, only three words, and I proceed.

1*st*, Bless the Lord, the great promiser, for the work of faith, and that on his promises. Praise is due upon both accounts. His grace made the promises, and his grace works upon the heart, which is always needful to embrace the promise; and the heart that partakes of the blessing, should entertain a due sense of its great debt to God, and pay it in praise: that is all the payment we can give, though praising is rather owning a debt than paying it.

2dly, You that have built your salvation and eternal hopes upon the promise of the gospel, rest yourselves on him. Whatever your state and condition in the world be, you are blessed by God, and should own it: *Blessed is she that believed, for there shall be a performance*, Luke 1:45. How many blessednesses are ascribed unto believing and trusting in God? *Blessed are all they that put their trust in him*, Psalm 2:12. Here now is a fault that is very frequent with the godly; they are ready to be sensible of mercy, and to bless God for mercy; they are sensible of promises, they bless God for making of them; and when God makes a performance of a promise, they bless him for that too. This is the thing I find fault with, that few Christians are heartily thankful to God for trusting, for believing. A poor child of God can look upon the promise, and say, Here is a full promise, but no performance, no appearance in the world for performance; yet God be thanked, I can trust it, and believe his faithful word, and wait till his time comes.

Lastly, You that have built your salvation and eternal hopes upon the promise of the gospel, never recall that trust, but re-act it every day. The righteousness of God is revealed from faith to faith, and believers should go on believing the promise of salvation that we believed at first believing. We are to believe still more and more, growing in faith; for faith is a grace to be grown in as well as knowledge, and repentance, and holiness. How many believers are there that are sensible of the one, and insensible of the other? They are easily convinced that they can never be holy enough, but they are not easily convinced, that they cannot believe strongly enough, that there is something still lacking in their faith, that they should labour to build up and to advance in more and more. If I may so speak, faith is something like a believer, believing is like a believer, a believer is never perfect till he is dead, and faith is never perfect till it is done. I mean, there is always some failing in our believing till believing is ended, and seeing comes in its room: *As ye have therefore received Christ Jesus the Lord, so walk ye in him: Rooted and built up in him, and stablished in the faith, as ye have been taught, abounding therein with thanksgivings*, Col. 2:6, 7. Wherein observe the variety of expressions concerning faith. 1. There is *Receiving*. 2. *Walking*. 3. *Rooting*. 4. *Building*. 5. *Stablishing*. 6. *Abounding*. To which is added, 7. *Thanksgiving*.

This leads me to the second exhortation, and that is, *that we should answer the faithfulness of God by believing, that all promised good things shall be given unto you by the way*. This is a needful answering the faithfulness of God, to believe all good by the way, and to believe nothing but good. This is believing, to expect all good by the way from God, and nothing but good. So his promise runs; and Oh! That our faith could fasten upon it, and kindle with that gracious promise a flame of love. If fire from heaven would fill the altar and kindle the sacrifice, to wit, our faith, what a blessed meeting would it be? *And I will make an everlasting covenant with them, that I will not turn away from them, to do them good; but I will put my fear in their hearts, that they shall not depart from me*, Jer. 32:40. Pray observe, we are not only to expect all good from God, but are to expect from God that all good shall be with us; we are not only to believe he will do us always good, but we are to believe, we shall believe, we are to believe our faith shall never fail, for that is a part of the promise: *I will put my fear in their hearts, that they shall not depart from me*. God's faithfulness is equally engaged in keeping his people from departing from him, as it is engaged in his not departing from them. He that says, *I will not turn away from them to do them good*, has also said, *they shall not depart from me*. Now, what follows, ver. 41, *Yea, I will rejoice over them to do them good, and I will plant them in this land* (that is a part of the Old Testament type from the body of the new covenant), *assuredly, with my whole heart, and with my whole soul*. Were ever such words spoken by God, *with my whole heart, and with my whole soul?* Now, who can understand what is in this? God's whole heart, God's whole soul is in this promising; and should not the believer's whole heart and whole soul be in the believing of it? Why, this is but reasonable, that we should give God a meeting. 'This way has he promised to do me good, with his whole heart and his whole soul, and shall not I trust him with my whole heart and with my whole soul?' Psa. 119:58, Prov. 3:6, this is soon said, but is not so soon done.

I shall therefore upon this exhortation speak a little to these two particulars:—

1. The grounds of this faith that I am calling for.
2. The cases wherein this is especially to be acted.

First, As to the grounds of this faith that I am calling for, the answering God's faithfulness in the promise, in expecting good from him; they are two.

1*st,* From the state of the believer. 2*dly,* From the nature, and order, and condition of the covenant.

1*st,* From the state of the believer, what sort of a man is a believer? He is one that is brought within the chariot *paved with love, for the daughters of Jerusalem,* Song of Sol. 3:10. Every one that is brought to heaven, is carried in that chariot, love all over, bottom and top, and all the sides of it; every believer is a prisoner of love, he is guarded by love, till he come to heaven. Every believer is an heir of promise; the promises are his, he may count them in his estate; all the charter we have, is the promise. God is our father, Christ is our redeemer, the Holy Ghost is our sanctifier, heaven is our inheritance, promises are our charter: Such a man as this, that is an heir of promise, surely he should expect the fulfilling of the promises, the estate his father has given him, and may expect to be dealt with accordingly.

2*dly,* The nature of the covenant calls for the answering of our faith unto God's faithfulness, as to all good by the way.

1. All good, and nothing but good is in the covenant; all blessings are in it; and every thing that is in it, is a blessing, because it is in it. If the rod be in the covenant, as it is, it is good, because it is there; and it will be found to be good when we meet it. *I know, O Lord, that thy judgments are right, and that thou in faithfulness hast afflicted me,* thou hast kept thy promise to me, Psalm 119:75, and ver. 65, *Thou hast dealt well with thy servant, O Lord, according unto thy word.*

2. There is this in the covenant, that trust is God's appointed way for the getting the performance. The Lord hath given many great promises to us in the covenant, and he expects to be trusted when he promises, if we would have the accomplishment of what we want. Besides all the great promises of the new covenant, observe those mentioned in Ezekiel 36:25-37, *Then will I sprinkle clean water upon you, and ye shall be clean: from all your filthiness, and from all your idols will I cleanse you,* etc. After all which is added, *Thus saith the Lord God, I will yet for this be inquired of by the house of Israel, to do it for them.* It was for Israel's sake that the promise was made, yet he will have Israel's faith and prayers called upon and brought forth, in order to the accomplishment of

them. As the brazen serpent healed those that beheld it, Num. 21:9, and as Jordan healed Naaman, after he had *dipped himself seven times*, 2 Kings 5:14, or as Elisha's staff would not raise up the dead son, 2 Kings 4:31. So, unless we address ourselves to God by prayer for the performance of his promises, which cannot be done without trusting in him, we cannot expect to receive any real advantages by the promises: But if we do make our supplications unto him, we shall undoubtedly partake of the promised rewards.

3. There is this in the covenant, that the promiser and fulfiller is the same. God does not intrust the fulfilling of his promises to any body else; we are not to take God's promise as a bill, and call upon another man to pay it: no, we are to bring them all to himself, he is the fulfiller. What a blessed saying is that of good Hezekiah, Isa. 38:15, *What shall I say? He hath both spoken unto me, and himself hath done it?* I got the word from him, and I got the deed from him; the words were the words of his mouth, and the deeds were the work of his hands: *He hath both spoken unto me, and himself hath done it.* Here is a remarkable emphasis, a spiritual eyeing that this godly man had of the eminent hand of God in fulfilling his gracious word to him.

Lastly, The great Mediator of this covenant obliges us to faith mightily. I defy a believer to take a look on Christ Jesus by faith, but in and by that look he will find ground for better believing. Look on him which way you will, so it will be found. I will name a few things concerning this, how our faith should be strengthened in the expecting of all good things, according to God's covenant, because of Christ's interests in it.

(1.) The promises are in the hand of Jesus Christ: this covenant is established in the hand of a Mediator, he gets the promises. You think this strange; the promise of the forgiveness of your sins, of the sanctifying of your nature, of the bringing you safe to the kingdom of glory, are first Christ's promises; they are made to him for us, and he is first intrusted with them; but the covenant is confirmed before of God in Christ. The promise is made unto the same Christ personal and Christ mystical, the head of the body, as the apostle saith of it, Gal. 3:17-19.

(2.) Our Lord is not only the receiver of the promises, but he hath already fulfilled the grand condition of the covenant, the proper strict condition of the covenant, whereupon, without any more, an immediate access to all the blessings is given to every believer upon his pleading. *When thou shalt make his soul an offering for sin*, that is the condition, *he shall see his seed, he shall prolong his days, and the pleasure of the Lord shall prosper in his hands. He shall see of the travail of his soul, and shall be satisfied*, Isa. 53:10, 11. So that now when you are to believe the promises, you are to exercise your faith thus: 'This promise hath a great blessing, that I stand greatly in need of; our Lord Jesus Christ hath fulfilled the grand condition of the promise, and all the blessings that are in the promise, are now made over to me in the last will and testament of our Lord Jesus Christ, confirmed by his blood; that as sure as Christ was dead and is alive, so surely is the New Testament and all the blessings of it confirmed and sealed already.' Our charters for heaven are sealed by our Lord's blood, we have no seal to put to them, but the seal of our poor faith.

(3.) Our Lord is ministering in the sanctuary above. If Christ were not interceding in heaven, a poor Christian would have a comfortless work in believing on earth: but our poor believing and his grand intercession, when they chime, if I may so speak, make wonderful music above. He sends his Spirit to work in us those desires after covenant-blessings, that he is pleading for in the virtue of his blood, in the highest sanctuary. Let your faith then argue thus: 'Jesus Christ is at the Father's right hand: I am a poor pleader at the footstool, but there is a strong pleader at the King's elbow, if I may so speak, in the highest court, and it is his business to mind my affairs.' How strongly would believers plead, how believingly would they send up their broken desires to heaven, if they did duly know, that all their petitions must be sent up to God through Christ, and be perfumed with another kind of incense than they can give! So much for this, on what ground believers should expect all good from God by the way.

Secondly, What are the cases wherein this believing and glorifying God's faithfulness is to be acted? The answer is, in every thing. I shall only name a few particulars, which as they are the great trying of faith, wherein believing is most difficult, so they are triumphs of faith, and believing is most noble, when in these cases.

1st, In case of great affliction from the hand of God. That is a case wherein believers are called to expect good from God, when things to sense and reason, and to common observation, seem to go against us; we say such an one is in affliction. They are called evil things sometimes by saints themselves: *Shall we receive good at the hand of God, and shall we not receive evil?* says patient Job, chap. 2:10. But believers should learn to name things as God names them, and as the covenant names them; we are to learn to name God's works by his word, and not to name his word by his works. Afflictions are very common, and they are very many; the heads of them are many, the various sorts of them are innumerable: I will only name a few things concerning them, that are commonly most trying to faith, and name them to press believing the more earnestly.

(1.) There is the surprising unexpectedness of affliction, when it comes from a quarter that people did not expect it to come from. The apostle warns Christians as to this: *Beloved, think it not strange concerning the fiery trial, which is to try you, as though some strange thing happened unto you*, 1 Pet. 4:12. It is very observable, that there is hardly a person that is soundly afflicted, that is smartly afflicted, but he apprehends there is something special in his case, which never was in any before. A man that hath a true sight of his sins, thinks they are the greatest that ever were; a man that rightly sees his own mercies, thinks those the most special mercies that ever were; a man that narrowly looks upon his own afflictions, sometimes thinks them so too. Surprising, unexpected, unaccountable afflictions, are commonly very trying; and usually this is in them, that the man thinks them greater than have befallen others. The infinite wisdom of God can shape and frame afflictions; those which seem to be common, yet by some form, by some reason, by some circumstances of them, he shall make them as singular, as if they had never been felt by any; this is a part of the wisdom of God. Our Lord speaks of a man taking up his *cross*. What, does not God give a common cross to a great many? No; every one hath his own, and the Lord makes it, and shapes it, and fits that cross, which is fittest to be laid upon the back of his poor child.

(2.) There is an oppressing affliction, that is a great trial, that seems to threaten all things, and to cut down the very root of all. A poor creature expects that the tree will be cut down from the very root of it, and that it will be quite plucked up. Lopping off the branches is not so formidable: *I am oppressed*, says Hezekiah, *Lord, undertake for me*. Sometimes a dark and dumb affliction is a very great trial of faith, and a great many of the children of God meet with such. Says the poor creature, I have had such an affliction a long while upon me, and I have many times laid my ear to it, to hear what it says, and there is no voice, if I may so speak. If you cannot hear the rod's voice, pray hear God's voice in the word. Sometimes the rod cries aloud, and speaks God's mind in the word; sometimes we must bring the word to the rod, and see if we can put the rod upon the rack, and make it speak what God means thereby. Now, in all these cases, in any sort of affliction, let it be surprising and strange, let it be oppressive, let it be dark, let it be dumb and speak nothing, believers must believe still.

(1.) Believe that whatever changes there are in God's way to you, there is none in his heart. The Lord hath changed his countenance, the Lord hath changed his hand, only his heart remains unchangeable, still that is to be firmly believed: *As many as I love, I rebuke and chasten*. People commonly think, as soon as Christ begins to rebuke and chasten, he begins to cease to love; but our Lord says just the contrary, Rev. 3:19. See also Prov. 27:6, Psa. 119:75.

(2.) Believe this firmly, that God's wisdom is never puzzled or nonplussed, though you be. The Lord knows his matters, and he will not give you an account of them; but we are to believe he knows what he does, and he has a wise end before him. Christians do commonly imagine they are so wise, that if there were any possible good, that could be the fruit of such a dispensation, they could perceive it, but, after all their studying, they cannot find what good this can turn to. *If it be marvellous in the eyes of the remnant of this people in those days, saith the Lord, should it also be marvellous in mine eyes?* Zech. 8:6. A severe rebuke given to an unbelieving people. *Quest*. Do you think God's eyes are no better than yours?

(3.) In all the trials of your faith by affliction, believe this, that God's eye is on you, when you cannot see him: *Behold*, says Job, *I go forward, but he is not there; and backward, but I cannot perceive him: On the left hand where he doth work, but I cannot behold him: He hideth himself on the right hand, that I cannot see him*, Job 23:8, 9. I take it, says he, when I am tried, I shall come forth as gold.

Lastly, In all your afflictions believe a safe issue, that you shall get well out of all: *Many are the afflictions of the righteous; but the Lord delivereth him out of them all*, Psa. 34:19. *These are they which come out of great tribulation*, says the angel to John, Rev. 7:14. There is no affliction can enter heaven, but I believe the best talking of affliction that ever was, is in heaven. All the glorified in heaven understand better all God's way with them. They were, many of them, plagued every morning, and chastened every moment; their souls were filled with bitterness and sorrow all their life long; yet there is never a one there, but sees that every thing was well done, there was nothing that they could have been without; their guide guided them well, and there is nothing amiss, nothing crooked in all God's way. It is with respect to this, that the apostle calls to believers, to *rejoice*, though in the midst of *manifold temptations*; why so? knowing that the *trial of your faith* shall turn to *praise*, 1 Pet. 1:6, 7. *Ye are in heaviness, through manifold temptations*, that is, as to the things of sense; but, says the apostle, *ye rejoice with joy unspeakable*, as Christians; and wherefore rejoice in the midst of heaviness? Because your faith, though much exercised now, will make a glorious appearance at the last day. One of the greatest praises that can be given to the Lord by his people, is, that their faith glorified his faithfulness, whilst on earth, in the midst of their greatest distress.

2*dly*, People should act their faith on God's faithfulness in case of desertion, when our Lord hides himself. Our Lord Jesus went before us as a pattern in this, *My God, my God, why hast thou forsaken me?* To put a *my* to a forsaking God, is brave believing. Our Lord's case, I know, is altogether singular, but many believers have had some measure of his Spirit in using that word in their own case. When a man *walks in darkness, and has no light*, what shall he do then? *Let him trust in the name of the Lord, and stay upon his God*, Isa. 50:10. If a man forbear trusting in the Lord, till darkness be scattered, and light come, and if he says it is time enough for me to believe, when God lights the candle; no, says the Spirit of God, *When he walks in darkness, and hath no light, let him then trust in the name of the Lord.*

3*dly*, In the case of temptation (I name these things which are so common, that, in truth believers' lives are spent about them), temptations from Satan. Sirs, if Christians were wise, they would learn, if I may so speak, of the devil; the more the Lord loves us, the more the devil hates us; and the more the devil hates us, the more we should love the Lord. As soon as a Christian gets faith, the devil falls upon him; and when the devil falls upon him, he should believe the more. The time was, saith a believer, when he let me alone; what makes this great change, that he is turned to a roaring lion? It is because I left his camp, and turned to another master. Faith is especially to be acted in temptation, and victory over temptation is by faith. When our Lord said to Peter, *Simon, Simon, behold Satan hath desired to have you, that he may sift you as wheat*; our Lord adds, *But I have prayed for thee, that thy faith fail not*; and if thy faith do not fail, the devil will get the worst of the bargain, Luke 22:32. The apostle puts a special mark upon this piece of the Christian armour: *Above all*, says he, *taking the shield of faith, wherewith ye shall be able to quench all the fiery darts of the wicked*, Eph. 6:16. That *above all* does not only point forth the eminent use of faith, in the warfare of faith, but it seems to set forth the excellency of a Christian's armour in this matter. When Satan and a poor Christian engage together, the devil would first have the shield of faith laid down, and then he would be too hard for any of the children of God, for commonly one temptation comes not alone. Now thou art put upon examining and trying whether thou hast any faith. Question all, doubt all, says the devil, and let us argue upon the point. But if you enter with the devil upon these terms, he will certainly be too hard for you; lay down the conclusion of faith firmly, and tell the devil, I have entrusted my soul with Christ Jesus, what hast thou to say to that? will he fail me or no? If thou speakest any evil of my Lord, thou speakest like the devil, and I do not regard thee; but if thou speak evil of me, I will believe thee, and can speak of it myself, and tell it to my Lord, Psa. 42:5, 6. The question that we are to propose in the warfare of faith with the devil, is, Is God true or no? If he be true in his promises, I will believe them, and believe none that contradict them, and in all my adversities will I take *the shield of faith*. See Eph. 6:18 and Psalm 91:4.

4thly, In the case of manifold delays and disappointments, as to the performance of pleaded promises; in this case, I say, you are still to believe. If though you have taken the promise, though you have believed it, though you have prayed upon it, though you have been looking out and waiting for the fulfilment of it, still delays come in the way, believe still. The Lord in his wisdom has reserved times and seasons for our mercies, and for his fulfilling his word, all to himself. He hath told his people what he will do for them, but he hath not told them when. Though he made a great promise to Abraham, yet he did not tell him when he would perform it; that great believer must wait twenty-five years from the promise, till the performance came, yet no doubt he believed the promise every day.

5thly, In cases of challenges of conscience for sin. Believers must learn to exercise their faith upon this faithfulness of God, in the view and in the face of challenges of conscience for sin. *Iniquities prevail against me*, says the psalmist, Psa. 65:3. What could a man say after this? What could you expect should be the next word? Must it not be, And therefore wrath shall come upon me? No such thing: *As for our transgressions, thou shalt purge them away. If thou, Lord, shouldst mark iniquities, O Lord, who shall stand? But there is forgiveness with thee, that thou mayest be feared*, Psa. 130:3, 4. Our consciences are sometimes disturbed with challenges for old sins long since committed, which, according to a similitude that a holy saint of God gives us in his letters, *like the ghost of a dead friend, continually haunt us*. An old subdued, pardoned sin, may fright one terribly; we have great need, if I may so speak, of strong faith, to converse without fear with this ghost, the ghost of an old transgression. A sin that is twenty years old may appear as formidable as the devil himself; but if we do not learn to believe and maintain confidence of faith, notwithstanding challenges for sin, who can believe at all?

Lastly, In case of God's calling us unto any special piece of service, some special piece of hard, singular work, that we were never called to before; in this case faith is to be exercised, for help in time of need shall be given us; if the service be required of you, the assistance for it shall be given to you; really the faith of Christians is tried greatly with the change of work that God puts in their hands. They think they have some tolerable measure of faith for their daily and usual work; but if God call them to that they never acted before, to some new singular piece of work, then believing is specially called for, to help out in this time of need; as we are to crave help in all times of need, so we are to crave special help in times of special need; I named these six, as being those in which the life of Christians is mainly spent. Take away the Christian's afflictions and desertions, his temptations, challenges of conscience, delays in promises, and special turns of God's hand towards him, and pray what is left in a Christian's life, that is so difficult? And since our life is spent about these things, we must live by faith, we are to exercise faith in and about all those things, that our life is mainly spent in; how blessed a thing is it for a believer to go on towards heaven, and in every step of the way to be able to say, Though God hath changed his way towards me many times, though he hath brought me into many by-paths, yet, blessed be his name, there was never a path I was in, but I believed in him, and if it were an evil one, I hoped to be delivered out of it; but if a good one, I believed it would advance me towards heaven, I believed and praised; and in every one I believed it would turn to my salvation. I knew they would bring me nearer to God; that they would at last bring me to heaven, where I hope eternally to bless him for them!

SERMON XI.

HEB. 10:23.

For he is faithful that promised.

FROM these words I have spoke unto three doctrines, and they having been again and again repeated unto you, you may easily remember them; 1. *That the Christian's God is a promising God.* 2. *That this promising God is faithful in all his promises.* And, 3. *That the faith of believers should answer the faithfulness of God in the promises.* I referred the main application of the whole doctrine unto this, last head, in laying the duty before you that this truth does exact and crave of you. I named three things, wherein our faith should answer the faithfulness of God, and have already spoke unto two of them.

The *first* was, That our faith should answer the faithfulness of God, in the grand general promise of salvation by Christ Jesus. This is that faith that the word calls so much for; it calls for it from unbelievers;

and this call is God's appointed means for working the faith that it calls for; *faith cometh by hearing, and hearing by the word of God*; the word of God tells us what we should believe, and the word of God, in the name of God, commands us to believe what God says. This I did insist sometime upon. I know there are some who think it needless to press people to believe, and to put forth faith; at first a great many poor creatures think it an easy thing to believe, whereas it is a hard matter to awaken the conscience; but when the conscience is awakened, they think it an easy matter to believe, but they only think so that never knew what an awakened conscience was; let a poor sinner see nothing before him but hell, and nothing within him but what deserves hell, it is only the wonderful power of God that can make this sinner trust Christ upon a bare word for his eternal salvation. Believing and trusting the soul on Christ Jesus is found a mighty difficulty by all them that are concerned about their salvation. Some think this answering of God's promise in the gospel, improper to be laid before sinners at first; these people imagine, that there is something that sinners should be called to before believing. But as long as these two principles of truth remain, and remain they will, as long as the world lasts, this is always a vain objection: *First*, That no man can do any good, nor get any good, but in and from Christ Jesus. *Secondly*, That no man can do any good with Christ, nor get any good from him, but in the way of believing: and if so, will our Lord give his help to them that will not give trust to him?

The *second* thing I was last day exhorting you to, was this, To answer the faithfulness of God in believing for all covenant-blessings by the way. This is properly the life of faith, and a great work this is to believe, as large as the whole covenant: to believe as firmly, as the promises are firm; to believe as long as until the promises turn to performances, how much of divine power is needful for this work! Justly does the apostle call the work of faith *a work of faith with power*, 2 Thess. 1:11; in which not only power is put forth by the creature that acts it, but there is power put forth by God to draw it forth, and to keep it up. Of this I spake last day.

The *third* exhortation that remains to be handled, and that I shall insist on, if the Lord will, a little more, is, That believers should answer the faithfulness of God in the promise of eternal life, by believing the *prize* and *hope of our calling*, as the apostle calls it. The Spirit of God calls this eternal life, *the promise*, as if all were contained in it; 1 John 2:25, *And this is the promise that he hath promised us, even eternal life.* Faith in this case that I am to speak of, is faith which *entereth into that within the veil*, as the apostle saith of *hope*, Heb. 6:19. I am now to direct this exhortation unto them that have some confidence and good conscience towards God; that have, in some measure, regarded the former and performed it, and that desire more and more to be in it; such as have intrusted their souls by faith in Christ's hand, upon the warrant of the promise of the gospel; such as are exercised in living by faith upon the promises of the new covenant; it is upon them that I lay this burden, and a sweet one it is; that you should believe eternal life. The apostle John, chap. 5:13,[2] speaks something to the same purpose: *These things have I written unto you* (says he) *that believe on the name of the Son of God; that ye may know that ye have eternal life, and that ye may believe on the name of the Son of God.* The apostle's meaning certainly was not, to persuade them to believe that they were in heaven, for he and they both knew the contrary sufficiently; but he calls them to believe that they had eternal life, that they had already a hold of it by faith; that they had it in the root by Christ's dwelling in their hearts by faith; that they had it in the foundation of it, by their believing the record that God gave of his Son; as is plain from the context.

In prosecuting of this exhortation, there are three things that I shall have some respect unto, and handle.

1. What is to be believed, or how it is that a Christian in the way of duty must answer the faithfulness of God, in the promise of eternal life.

2. What are the difficulties that lie in a Christian's way which makes this believing so rare and so hard.

3. What the grounds of this faith are, that believers should improve, and in the improving of them triumph over all the difficulties that are in the way.

First, What it is believers are to believe, when they are called to believe eternal life. I take it, as you may perceive, strictly, as contradistinguished from all the covenant-blessings that believers have a right to in this life, and have a begun possession of, that they should live by

[2] [That is, 1 John 5:13.]

that faith, of which I spake in the former part. But I shall now respect only *the prize of our high calling, the mark* that God has set before us to run towards, to cheer ourselves with the faith of it before we come at it. And surely the speaking and hearing of heaven should be a pleasing subject unto all them that have any hope to be in it; the speaking of it is sometimes blessed by the Lord to make them mind it, that never thought of it before. The sum of it is in these four principles:

1. In the way of duty, in answering the faithfulness of God, believers should believe this, that as soon as the soul departs from the body, it is immediately received by Christ. A believer is to honour God's faithfulness in believing this, that as soon as the soul and body are parted by death, the soul is immediately with the Lord. This the Spirit of God, by Paul's pen, teaches us, in two places, very fully, 2 Cor. 5:1-8 and Phil. 1:23. In the former the apostle expressly asserts this doctrine: *For we know*, says he, *that if our earthly house of this tabernacle were dissolved, we have a building of God, an house not made with hands, eternal in the heavens; knowing that whilst we are at home in the body, we are absent from the Lord.—We are confident, I say, and willing rather to be absent from the body, and to be present with the Lord.* By how many words does the apostle expressly teach us that the state of absence from the body to a believer, is immediately attended with a state of presence with the Lord! And in Phil. 1:23 he says, *For I am in a strait betwixt two, having a desire to depart, and to be with Christ. Departing* and *being with Christ*, are joined together, as inseparable. As soon as Paul is gone out of this world, he is with Christ. Our Lord gave a very great promise to the believing thief, for he was then a great believer, though once as great a thief, Luke 23:42, *Today*, says he, *shalt thou be with me in paradise.* 'Thou art dying, thou art drawing near to thy end, as I am, but this day thou and I shall be together in a better state.'

2. Believers must believe, and glorify God's faithfulness in believing, that the bodies they leave shall be raised up again glorious bodies, at the appearing of Christ. This is as plain as any thing can be expressed to be in the word, that the body the believer leaves, as it were, in the dust, which death hath dominion over, which rottenness and corruption triumph over, the same body shall live again, and be raised by his mighty power: *Knowing that he which raised up the Lord Jesus, shall*

raise us up also by Jesus, and shall present us with you, 2 Cor. 4:14. *For if we believe that Jesus died, and rose again, even so them also which sleep in Jesus, will God bring with him*, 1 Thess. 4:14. See also 1 Cor. 15:58. This faith Job also acted, and it is one of the singular expressions of a New Testament faith in the Old Testament times: *For I know* (says he, chap. 19:25, 26) *that my Redeemer liveth, and that he shall stand at the latter day upon the earth. And though after my skin, worms destroy this body, yet in my flesh shall I see God.* A great part of the meaning of which is: Job had, by this loathsome disease that was sent upon him, in a manner death beginning to prey upon him; now, says the good man, though worms should go on, and after they have destroyed my skin, they should destroy my flesh also, yet in *my flesh shall I see God; whom I shall see for myself and mine eyes shall behold, and not another, though my reins be consumed within me*, ver. 27. The faith of the resurrection of the dead, though plainly revealed in the word, is not a matter so easily attained, there needs a great deal of faith to believe it firmly. How quietly, how patiently, how cheerfully would believers look upon death seizing them, and coming in upon them, either gradually by age and the infirmities of it, or more violently and speedily by sickness and diseases; how quietly would they look upon the tumbling down of this earthly tabernacle, if they believed this firmly? *For our conversation is in heaven, from whence also we look for the Saviour, the Lord Jesus Christ:* what will he do when he comes? Here is one thing, says the apostle, he will do, he will *change our vile body, that it may be fashioned like unto his glorious body, according to the working whereby he is able even to subdue all things unto himself*, Phil. 3:20, 21. The faith of the resurrection of the dead can never stand, but upon the prop of Divine omnipotency. It is founded upon this, That he has said it that can do every thing. Thereupon when our Lord checks the Sadducees for their infidelity, he saith, *Ye do err, not knowing the scriptures, nor the power of God*, Matt. 22:29. If you understood the scriptures spiritually, you would not have asked such a question in derision of the resurrection; if you knew the power of God, you would firmly believe that God can perform it. Our Lord tries Martha with this, John 11:25, 26, *I am the resurrection, and the life: he that believeth in me, though he were dead, yet shall he live; and whosoever liveth and believeth in me, shall never die. Believest thou this?*

Our Lord, in the questioning of it, hints the difficulty that was in it, and some backwardness unto this believing that he perceived in the good woman. See also Luke 20:33, 36.

3. That the departed soul and the raised body shall be eternally united together. This is a part of that faith that we owe to the faithfulness of God in the promise of eternal life, that not only the body shall be raised, but that our spirit shall again, by the mighty power of God, take possession of these same bodies. It is the same body the apostle still speaks of, when he saith, *It is sown in dishonour, it is raised in glory; it is sown in weakness, it is raised in power; it is sown a natural body, it is raised a spiritual body*, 1 Cor. 15:43, 44, etc.

4. That this united soul and body shall be unspeakably blessed in the highest heavens with that that is called the reward of eternal life. This, I say, is the sum of what we are called to believe, and is the duty of every believer to believe, in answering the faithfulness of God in the promise that he hath promised; that when he sees good we shall live here no longer, he will immediately receive our departing souls; *Lord Jesus, receive my spirit*; that when his appointed time comes, when the morning comes, he will also in power and mercy visit our rottenness and dust in the grave, and raise up a glorious tabernacle, and unite the soul therewith, and bless both body and soul, the whole man, in the enjoyment of himself. These are the common plain truths that are in this promise of eternal life; but this I would not leave thus; therefore we will take a little farther notice of this great blessing, according to what we gather of it from the word; for whoever they be that are called to the exercise of faith, they had need distinctly to know what it is they are to believe for, as well as what is the ground to believe upon. We find this great prize of our calling spoken of to us in the word, three ways, and I would handle it a little in all these three respects.

1*st*, It is spoken of *negatively*, by removing all the known evils from that state, that we know to be evils in this state; this is a way, I say, whereby the Lord helps our weak shallow apprehensions about the prize of eternal life, that it is a state separate from, and altogether above all the miseries, calamities, and evils that are afflicting and disturbing in this present state. So we find in Rev. 21:4, *And God shall wipe away all tears from their eyes, and there shall be no more death, neither sorrow, nor* *crying, neither shall there be any more pain: for the former things are passed away.* Sorrow and cause of sorrow are so inseparable from the state we live in, that in a manner we do not know how to live without them, nor to think of our life, as separate from them; we all know how natural it is for people to frame apprehensions of a happy state, by removing of miseries from their thoughts and desires: Now, take all the heaps of miseries you know, and concerning these you may say, None of these things are there, there is no sin, there is no sorrow, there is no sickness, there is no disturbance without nor within, there is nothing at all of those things, that we are now daily exercised with, and bewail before God and men; now, this negative notion of it leads no further than we can distinctly know. We know what an evil these things are, but we do not know what a great happiness it is to be quite rid of them all, we know what a trouble pain is, and what a blessing ease is, what a trouble there is in sickness, what a comfort in health, what trouble there is in crosses, losses, disturbances, in this world, we know a little of the misery of them, and the happiness of being rid of them; but we cannot conceive a right notion of that state, wherein all things that are evil shall be quite removed; therefore you may find all along the believer's faith goes beyond his knowledge in the believing of eternal life. We believe what we cannot fully know, 1 Cor. 2:9. But as it is written, *Eye hath not seen, nor ear heard, neither have entered into the heart of man, the things which God hath prepared for them that love him.* It is but a small portion thereof that we come to attain the knowledge of.

2dly, This prize of our calling is known *comparatively*, by comparing it with other things. We know it a little negatively, by removing all the evil from it we know. We know it comparatively, when we prefer it to all the good we know: now, there are three things which bear the name of good, and some of them undeservedly, that it is to be compared with, and greatly preferred above.

(1.) The first is the portion of the men of this world. This eternal life that we believe and hope for, is a great deal bigger higher, and better than that. *Lord, deliver me*, says the Psalmist, *from the men of the world, which have their portion in this life.* As for me, says he, I expect better things than this world can afford, Psa. 17:14, 15. The portion of the men of this world is such a prize, that the greatest part of the world run after it all their life long. What pain, what care, what thoughts are spent about these things? And when they have got them, what have they got? How poor and empty are they? The believer's portion even in this life is a great deal better than that of the wicked. Better is that little the righteous man hath, than many revenues of the wicked; how much more must the prize of the high calling be? We would not, as it were, disgrace our prize so much as to compare it with the portion of the men of the world, and yet what a believer hath in time, is beyond what they have.

(2.) We compare this with the spiritual allowance of believers in this life. There is a gracious allowance of spiritual blessings given to believers in this life. We are to compare this with what remains, and to prefer our expectations to our possessions; there is something of the earnest of the inheritance given now, Eph. 1:14, 15. There is something of communion with Christ now that fills the heart *with joy unspeakable, and full of glory*, 1 Pet. 1:8. And what is that now to what remains? There have been believers that have had heaven upon earth in this world, but when they came to enjoy heaven in heaven, they doubtless found a vast difference. *At that day*, says our Lord, *ye shall know, that I am in my Father, and you in me, and I in you*, John 14:20. You shall know it in a better manner, than now you can imagine; all the enjoyments that God affords unto his people here, are all helps whereby believers may come to know and guess better what heaven is: they should not say, It is good to be here, because of these, but he is good that gives that good here, and there are better things prepared that we should desire the more fervently; all spiritual enjoyments that are given in time are for the sharpening the believers' appetite, and raising their spirits in desire of heaven the more fervently.

(3.) We are to compare the prize of our calling, with the desire and longing of believers: our desires are larger than our possessions. There is never a believer but knows this in experience, that he can desire a great deal more than he can hold. The reward of eternal life goes beyond our desires. The Lord works in us, and *does for us exceeding abundantly above all that we ask or think*, Eph. 3:20. What use should a man make of this name of God? Think as much as you can, and ask as much as you can, and in the faith of that asking, and in the faith joined to that thinking, expect some blessing that is beyond both, beyond both our asking, and our thinking. This is a second consideration, whereby we come to know what the prize of the high calling of God is, that we are called to believe, by comparing it either with the poor portion of the men of this world, or the spiritual allowance of believers, or the extended desire of Christians.

3dly, The word of God speaks *positively* of it, and we are to learn something of it this way. But as positive as the Spirit of God is in speaking of it, we are still very short of being able to apprehend it, there is a great deal more spoken of heaven in the word, than any saint out of heaven can ever understand; may I so speak, we shall understand the Bible a great deal better when we come to heaven, especially that part of it that speaks of heaven; the blessing of eternal life, the greatness, the sweetness, the vastness of it, is best known by enjoying of it. Of the positive account that we have in the word, concerning the state of believers in eternal life, I would give you some hints from the word of God, in these six or seven things:—

(1.) There is a glorious appearing and manifestation of Jesus Christ spoken of; from him grace begins, by him grace is carried on, with him glory begins, and continues for ever; it is called the *blessed hope, and the glorious appearing of the great God, and our Saviour Jesus Christ*, Titus 2:13. The appearance, I say, of Jesus Christ in his highest glory. All the appearances that Christ hath made, have been some way under a veil, and under some eclipse, therefore is it that he is so despised. In the first appearance that Christ made in the flesh, what a thick veil of infirmity was upon it? *The word was made flesh*, says the Holy Ghost, *and dwelt among us (and we beheld his glory, the glory as of the only begotten of the Father) full of grace and truth*, John 1:14. Every one could not do so. He was made flesh, this is called an appearance of Christ. He hath *brought life and immortality to light* by this appearance of his, 2 Tim. 1:1. Christ makes an appearance unto his chosen, first in calling them, afterwards in visiting of them. When he first comes to call a poor creature, this appearance of Jesus Christ is under a veil; still it is Christ in the word, Christ under the veil of ordinances, Christ in the means; many times he is not known, when he does appear. Many poor sinners Christ hath appeared to in his working upon them, and he hath carried on his work a good while before they knew who it was that worked upon them; his appearing afterwards to his people in love-visits, is more sensible, but far short of this; *I will manifest myself to him*, John 14:21, 23. There are some appearances and manifestations of Christ unto the souls of his people, not wherein they see any thing with their bodily eyes, or hear any voice with their bodily ears; but in and under the form of prayer, the means of his appointment, there is a gracious display of all the glory that passes like a beam upon their souls, that they can say, This is the Lord, this is Christ, this is he I have waited for. The state of eternal life is incomparably beyond all this; there is a glorious appearance of Christ; the word speaks of it so, as if Christ had never appeared before; Col. 3:4, *When Christ who is our life shall appear, then shall ye also appear with him in glory*. 1 John 3:2, *We know, that when he shall appear, we shall be like him, for we shall see him as he is*.

(2.) The word speaks of this blessed state, that is the hope of our calling, under the notion of a full vision of him, or of seeing him; he not only appears in his glory, but that glory is seen by his people; thence springs their happiness. Our Lord Christ knew best what heaven was; it is best learning what it is by his speaking of it. See how he prays, John 17:24, *Father, I will that they also whom thou hast given me, be with me where I am; that they may behold my glory which thou hast given me*. Observe, Christ there plainly shews us, what is his great design in desiring to have all his people with him, and what way it is he intends to make them blessed, by beholding the glory the Father hath given him. Now when we are living in this body, and are compassed about with frailty without, and sin within, any singular appearance of his glory is disturbing and dreadful to us; may I speak such a word, and you understand it rightly, there is never a believer so comfortable, but Jesus Christ could render that person a very miserable creature, by a display of his glory; saints may desire more now than they are able to take in. *I beseech thee shew me thy glory*, saith Moses; but the Lord answers him, *Thou canst not see my face, for there shall no man see me, and live*, Exod. 33:18, 20. Observe, the vision that the Prophet Isaiah had, was a sight of Christ, and was a sight of his glory too, Isa. 6:1, 5, commented upon by the Holy Ghost, John 12:41, *These things*, said Esaias, *when he saw his glory, and spake of him*. Now, surely you would think, that when there is a discovery made of the glory of Christ unto such a man as Isaiah, so long before, that there should be a very great contentment therewith.

Why, Abraham saw Christ's day afar off, and was glad; Abraham's heart was cheered by believing Christ's day, and seeing his glory afar off. But when this glory shone, if I may so speak, in those beams that mortal eyes were not able to receive, Isaiah saith, *Wo is me, for I am undone,—for mine eyes have seen the King, the Lord of hosts.* Here is a sight not fit for a sinner to bear, the frailty, I say, of our flesh, with the remaining corruption that is in our natures, makes the full visions of the glory of Christ very unfit for us, and we for them; but this is the state promised to us in the gospel, *When he shall appear, we shall be like him, for we shall see him as he is,* 1 John 3:2. What, have we never seen Christ, as he is, before? No, ye only see him in the glass of the gospel; ye only see him under the veil, and in that shadow that is fitted for our present state. Hence it comes to pass, that it is said concerning believers in this day, *That Christ shall be glorified in his saints, and admired in all them that believe,* 2 Thess. 1:10.

(3.) In this state there is full conformity to a seen Christ. Christ in his glory is fully seen by the glorified eye, and perfect conformity to him resulteth therefrom. For according to the measures of clearness with which we see Christ by faith, are the measures of our conformity to him now: 2 Cor. 3:18, *But we all with open face, beholding as in a glass the glory of the Lord, are changed into the same image, from glory to glory, even as by the Spirit of the Lord.* Pray, observe the gradual progress of sanctification in a renewed man; it is carried on by the visions of Christ by faith now; the more clearly the eye of faith takes up Christ, the more strong and abiding impressions of likeness are upon the soul. But what perfect conformity to him is, we cannot yet conceive. If I may offer such a similitude, we are such dunghills, so dark, that when the Sun of righteousness shines upon us, there is but a little beam left, just enough to testify that the sun hath shone upon us; but the state of glory will render a believer, both in soul and body, like a crystal wall, that will reflect the image of the Sun of righteousness most purely and resplendently. The state of happiness and eternal life consists in being like Christ: *We shall be like him, for we shall see him as he is;* the conformity is carried on by that seeing: *I shall be satisfied, when I awake, with thy likeness,* Psa. 17:15.

(4.) There is a state of constant serving him spoken of, a state of unwearied delightful serving of Jesus Christ. Heaven would not be heaven to a heavenly mind, if there were no service to Christ in it. It is strange to see how the apostle values service to Christ on earth so highly, that he lays it in the balance with the enjoyment of Christ in heaven, and he cannot tell well which to choose: *I am in a strait betwixt two*, says he, *having a desire to depart, and to be with Christ; which is far better: Nevertheless, to abide in the flesh, is more needful for you.* It is natural, I say, to a saint to love service. It is promised, that *they shall see his face, and his name shall be in their foreheads.—His servants shall serve him*, Rev. 21:3, 4. See also chap. 4:10. Little we can do for Christ and his glory while we are here, and we should be deeply humbled that we can do so little. Christians, lay firm hold upon eternal life by strong faith. You shall bring more glory to Christ the first half-hour in heaven, than ever you did, if you lived fourscore years, in believing, and praying, and wrestling here on earth. There is pure sinless serving that is tendered with delight, and received accordingly.

(5.) There is inexpressible satisfaction and contentment in this blessed state. It is properly called happiness. Whatever there be of goodness, the relish of that goodness stands in the soul's contentment: *And ye now therefore have sorrow*, says our Lord, when about to depart, to his disciples: *but I*, says he, *will see you again, and your heart shall rejoice, and your joy no man taketh from you. Your heart shall rejoice*, John 16:22. A heart full of joy is not to be expected by believers till this great day come; but then the heart shall be so full of joy, that there shall be no room for any thing else. I know there are some sudden floods of joy that the Lord gives even here, and such as there seems to be no room left for any thing else; but though this joy fill the whole heart, yet stay a little while, and the flood will dry, the flood will grow smaller and smaller, and the old darkness will enter again. This joy will be taken away, one way or other; but in the state above, our joy shall have no end.

Lastly, To complete all, there is eternity in this blessedness. *Ever* and *ever* are the main things in heaven and hell. Take eternity out of heaven, it would turn heaven into an hell: take eternity out of hell, and it would turn hell into a heaven. Eternity is the joy of heaven, and the torment of hell. Poor Peter was little time in heaven, as he thought: *Lord*, says he, *it is good to be here*. But all that are got up yonder may say rightly, *It is good to be here, and good to be eternally here*, to be ever with the Lord. The greater any blessedness be, it is greatly enhanced by its lasting; the greater any misery be, it is greatly aggravated by its continuance. Where the greatest good comes to be enjoyed with the longest duration, even eternity, what inexpressible joy is there! But where the greatest misery is to be inflicted unto eternity, what vast heightening is it of the misery! So much now shall serve for the first thing, what it is that we are to believe, when we are called to glorify God's faithfulness in believing the prize of our calling, that after we have given glory to God, by believing for all the good things by the way, we may glorify him, by believing the good home he hath prepared for us.

Application. I ask you, in the first place, Do you believe that there is such a hope of this calling? Christianity is a despised thing. Christians are a despised people, because the prize is unknown to the despisers. Do you believe firmly, I say, that there is such a state, and that all that are departed in the Lord are blessed, because they are entered upon the enjoyment of it; and that all that believe on him, shall certainly enjoy it in his good time? I would reckon that that man were fairly setting out for heaven, who firmly believes that there is one, and hath his heart filled with a sense of it, as a great invaluable blessing above all that time can talk of.

2. Must not an interest in this prize of our calling be well worthy the having, and the knowledge of it well worthy the seeking? Are heaven and hell so small things, and these different states so like one another, that people should be unconcerned which of them be their lot? Indeed, the greatest part of people live as if they had laid down this conclusion, I care not whether I come to heaven or hell.

3. Should not Jesus Christ our Lord be very precious to us? Whenever we think of the prize of our calling, we must always remember Christ, and our debt to him; he bought this prize by his blood; heaven is a fruit of the price of Christ's blood, heaven is a palace built upon the foundation of the blood of the Son of God; he hath bought it by his blood, and he offers it freely to us by his grace: Whoever accepts his offer, he takes them and leads them kindly by the hand; he *brings many sons unto glory*, Heb. 2:10, and at last, when he hath brought them through all, he himself puts the crown on with his own hands: *Looking*,

says the apostle, *for the mercy of our Lord Jesus Christ, unto eternal life*. Ye have got a deal of mercy from him before, but the grand gift of mercy will be, when the believer shall kneel at Christ's feet, and receive the crown of glory at his hands. It is impossible that a man can have right thoughts of heaven that has not right thoughts of Jesus Christ; and it is impossible that a man can have right thoughts of Jesus Christ, but his heart will be filled with heaven.

SERMON XII.

HEB. 10:23.

For he is faithful that promised.

THOUGH you had heard these words but once, if you be true Christians, you would never forget them; how much more should they be well remembered when they have been so often repeated, and so long spoken to. That which remains now is a part of the application of the truths proposed from these words. I did propose three exhortations in the conclusion of the application of this doctrine.

1. That you should answer the faithfulness of God, by believing the promise of salvation by Christ Jesus. This is the first act of faith that God craves of all them to whom the gospel is preached. Wherever the apostles came with the glad tidings of salvation by Christ Jesus, their application was to all, *Believe*; believe this doctrine with the heart, and ye shall be saved.

2. I was calling believers unto the answering of God's faithfulness, by trusting him for all covenant-blessings by the way. And,

3. By answering God's faithfulness by faith, as to the end, eternal life, the great hope of our calling; *the hope of eternal life*, as the apostle Paul calls it, *which God that cannot lie, promised before the world began*, Titus 1:1, 2. In the handling this exhortation, there were three heads I proposed to speak to.

First, What is to be believed, when a believer is called to believe eternal life promised to him in the gospel; and this I spent the last time in discoursing to. Believers are called to believe, that as soon as the soul is dislodged from the body, it is present with the Lord. They are to believe, that the same body that is laid in the grave, and rots there, shall be raised again in glory, at the appearance of Jesus Christ. They are to believe, that this departed soul, and this body raised again, shall be eternally united, never to part more. *Lastly*, That, in this state of perfection, we shall be eternally blessed in the enjoyment of God in Christ Jesus above. Of the particulars of which I discoursed the last day.

The *second*, that now remains to be spoke to, is about the difficulty of believing this. Shall I prove that it is difficult? Is there not proof enough, that this faith is so very rare? It may be, you may think it an unreasonable surmise and jealousy, but let every one's conscience answer for themselves. It may be (I do not know that it is), that, in all this assembly, there is not one person that can tell when they spent a calm sweet hour in the hope of the glory of God, when they had a satisfying rejoicing in the hope of this great prize of our calling. If this be rare, surely the faith of it is rare; for it is impossible that the faith of the glory to come can be strong in the heart, but joy will spring up therefrom: *By whom also we have access by faith into this grace wherein we stand, and rejoice in hope of the glory of God*, Rom. 5:2. Christians know this well enough, that when they have tried their faith upon a great many promises of the word, sometimes upon the promise of God's hearing prayer, that their faith does pretty well there; sometimes upon the promises of pardon of sin through the blood of Jesus Christ, and their faith answers: but bring them close to believing the prize and crown of glory, there frequently their faith fails them, they cannot draw it forth so confidently as they would. That it is difficult and rare, I take for granted, and shall not spend time to prove that which almost every exercised conscience in the company has a witness within to the truth of. My work then shall be to shew you, whence it comes that believing of eternal life is so very hard to be got, and is so rarely found with Christians.

1. Because this great thing, *eternal life*, is greatly unknown to us. *It doth not yet appear what we shall be*, says the apostle, 1 John 3:2.—*Neither have entered into the heart of man, the things which God hath*

prepared for them that love him, 1 Cor. 2:9. Now, it is true the apostle says, that it is *made manifest by the appearing of our Saviour Jesus Christ, who hath abolished death, and hath brought life and immortality to light, through the gospel*, 2 Tim. 1:10. Yet though it be made manifest, we are rather told that it is, than what it is. This glory to come is yet *within the veil*, as the apostle saith of it, Heb. 6:19, where Christ is, *whither the forerunner is for us entered*. There is an express allusion to the typical high-priest, who, when he had offered the blood of atonement upon the altar, carried that blood within the veil to the mercy-seat; then he was quite out of the sight of the people, for he must go in alone, and none else could look after him. Now, how easy is it to conceive this, that the darker the thing believed be to us, the harder believing is? Mercies that we cannot well tell how to conceive of, is it any wonder, we cannot tell how to believe them firmly? For believing has an expectation of a blessing, as well as it has in it a trusting in the truth of the promiser. Heaven to every believer is more strange, than Canaan was to Abraham, who by faith, when he was called of God, went into that place, *and he went out, not knowing whither he went*; he was called to go to a land which he never saw before; only the difference is great in this, that though it was a better spot of the earth, than that where he was born or dwelt, yet it was a spot of the same earth, but heaven is a quite different country, Heb. 11:8.

2. The vast greatness and goodness of this prize, makes some difficulty to the faith of the people of God. It is so great, so good, that they find it hard to believe the expressions thereof in the word, which are great and many. The hearts of believers are many times so taken with them, and that deservedly, when they have expatiated in their thoughts about the greatness of the hope of their calling, that they are ready sometimes to say, And will God give such a blessing to me? You know what is said of the disciples, and it is one of the oddest accounts that can be given of unbelief, that while they beheld him, *they believed not for joy*, Luke 24:41. They loved Christ so well, they sorrowed for his death so deeply, and were so overjoyed at the sight of him risen again, that they could not tell how to believe their own eyes, as we usually say; the news was, as they thought, too good to be true. People are sometimes slacker to believe that which they would very fain have come

to pass. Thus Jacob's *heart fainted*, when he was told that his son Joseph was yet alive, and more than that, was *governor over all the land of Egypt*, Gen. 45:26.

3. The awfulness of the passage to eternal life, makes the faith of it yet harder. If all believers were dealt with as Elijah was, that after they have accomplished their course of service and suffering upon the earth, they should be sent for, as it were in a chariot of fire, to be carried up to heaven; it would be an exit, if I may so speak, suitable to their expectations. But now for a poor believer, that hath been fed all his life long with the promises of eternal life in the gospel, and has been cheering his heart thereby, that this man should lie down in the dust, should walk through the vale and shadow of death, should leave his body a prey to worms and rottenness in the grave, this seemeth very hard. Will not every one say, Is this the way to eternal life? This is a strange way to heaven, that lies through death and the grave, and through the lowest and most abject state that a man can be in. Yet thus our Lord went into his glory, only bating the corruption of the grave, which he could not suffer; but through death, and sufferings, and groanings, and pain, he yielded up the ghost, was buried, and lay under the power of death, until the time appointed of the Father for his resurrection out of it. There is no Christian, but finds this to be true which I speak, that the dark black passage of death makes the difficulty great in believing eternal life. How far remote is it from all our reason, and from all our desires, that the last step in our journey to heaven, should be through so thick and deep a mire as death itself is?

4. The mystery of the title and right that a believer hath in eternal life, makes the believing of it the harder still. His title and right to it lies in another, and not in himself; it lies in the righteousness, and worth, and purchase, and merit of the Son of God; so that the faith of eternal life cannot be kept clear in the heart of a believer, unless Christ, who is the hope of glory, be kept clear in our eye by faith.

5. There are many misgivings of heart that believers cannot well avoid; and if they cannot avoid them, they must meet them; and when they meet them, they must wrestle with them, and overcome them. The poor Israelites are not to be excused, but are much to be pitied; they were brought out of the land of Egypt with a high hand, God granted them

a great deliverance through the Red-sea, they sung joyfully upon the other side in the view of the great discomfiture of all their enemies, and like enough they expected nothing, but very quickly they should come to the borders of the good land. But when God led them about and tried them, they sinned; when they sinned, he punished them; under their punishment they repine and rebel, they vex him, and a great deal of sorrow came thereupon. Believers are in great danger of something like this; many faintings and misgivings of heart seize upon believers as to the hope of their calling. (1.) Conscience of utter unworthiness. (2.) Sense of great unmeetness for it. 1. Conscience of utter unworthiness of this great prize, and every Christian hath this. No man will ever get to heaven that thinks he deserves it; for it is certain, whoever thinks he deserves heaven, may conclude from the word of God, there is a bar and bolt drawn upon heaven's gates against that proud sinner; for it is the gift of God through Jesus Christ our Lord. But this is not usually so hard; this temptation does not so frequently distress believers, as the other; they know the reward of eternal life is a reward of grace; they know that it was dearly bought, freely promised, and is graciously given unto the seed of Christ: but here comes in the *second.* A sense of great unmeetness for it, says the poor Christian; I know I am unworthy of it. And so was Paul; the last hour of Paul's life, he was unworthy of heaven. But, say you, here is the great discouragement, I am unmeet for it. But consider, that God works meetness in his people for heaven: *Giving thanks unto the Father, which hath made us meet to be partakers of the inheritance of the saints in light*, Col. 1:12. Though I know that the word there in the original might be very well otherwise rendered, who hath *graced* us and privileged us with his favour, as it may also be rendered in 2 Cor. 3:6. But now this only I would have to be considered about meetness; it is certain that none are possessed of heaven, but they that are meet for it; it is as certain that all believers, when they come to lay their claim to eternal life, are all alike unmeet in their own apprehensions. There is a great difference between some and others, as to their meetness for heaven: an ordinary Christian must not pretend to be as meet for heaven as Paul was; but there is not a Christian but stands upon the same level with Paul, as to his pretensions and claim to eternal life. What would Paul be at? He would be *found in him, not having his own righteousness*; and so would every believer be. God works meetness for heaven in them, that he makes possessors of it in a deep mysterious way. The sense of this meetness is, that that is never to obstruct pure and mere faith. Suppose, and it is a case that I wish it were not a bare supposition, but were more frequent and with a good foundation; suppose, I say, that the grace of God seize a poor young creature, call him early, prevent him from wallowing in the puddle and mire of the world's wickedness; suppose still the same grace sanctify him, and this sanctified creature should grow up more and more unto the stature of a grown Christian for many years in the house of God: now, you will say, this man is meet for heaven; he is so, God hath made him so. Pray now let this man be examined about his meetness, and let his last plea, as it were, be heard, when he is knocking at heaven's gate for entry at last. It is only upon the account of the common foundation that every believer's faith is fixed upon; God will save none but those he sanctifies; but eternal life follows more immediately upon justification; our title to eternal life comes from the same righteousness that the forgiveness of our sins flows from.

6. There is a special activity of Satan in tempting believers, that makes this work yet the harder. The devil's great work in this world is to increase bad works, and to hinder good works; to keep them that are bad, bad still, and make them worse; and to hinder them that are bad from being good, and the good from growing better, and the best from being perfect. Believers are the special mark of the devil's malice; and there are two times wherein, be sure, if the devil may have his will, and he hath a great deal lent him by our Lord; there are two times wherein a poor child of God may be sure to meet with the devil, if the devil be not bound by more than ordinary restraint. The first time is, when the poor elect child of God is stepping out of nature into grace; the other is, when he is stepping out of grace up to glory. If the devil can possibly have his will, and it is rarely denied him, he will shoot his fiery darts in these cases. When a poor sinner is leaving Satan's camp, and going over into Christ's kingdom, when he is just upon delivery from the power of darkness, and of being translated into the kingdom of his dear Son, then the devil bends his bow, and lets fly thick and apace. A great many poor creatures that never knew there was a devil in hell, or out of hell, till this time, as long as they were in nature and quiet, the devil was quiet too; but when Christ came to pull them, and

draw them, and bring them home to himself, they then found they had been under the keeping of an enemy, that was loth to part with them. The last case is much the same: When a poor creature is going over to Christ, the devil is losing his right; when going to heaven, the devil is losing all opportunity against him. There are few of the people of God that, in walking through the vale of the shadow of death, do not feel this serpent bruising their heel; but if they once be well landed, the smart will quickly be gone.

Lastly, There is some wise deep contrivance of God in this matter. The Lord hath ordered the matter of our salvation so, that believing shall be hard, and the last believing still hardest; so he hath ordered our right to eternal life: all is lying in another, nothing in us; we have a right in and by Christ, our charter of eternal life lies in God's word. In the conducting of the people of God, the Lord guides them so, that pure believing is never put out of its office: whatever he give, whatever path he leads them in, this remains continually useful and needful to them, that they must still go out of themselves, and exercise dependence upon another, upon the Lord alone. The whole contrivance of the way of our salvation, I mean the way of God's working with us about salvation, is framed for this end, that believing shall be perpetually used; the contrivance of the way of salvation for us, is made on purpose for the glory of God's grace through Christ Jesus; it is contrived for this purpose, that all the way we should believe; whatever we receive, we must trust still, for the great hope of our calling. So much for this second thing, What the difficulties are of believing eternal life.

The *third* thing is, How these are to be overcome; where is the victory that believers must have over all these difficulties? *And this is the victory that overcometh the world, even our faith*, 1 John 5:4. The victory lies in this word, 'Faithful is he that promised.' Let the difficulties that lie in the way of believing be never so great, we must hold up this as a shield against them all, *Faithful is he that promised*; and in order to guide you in the right way of using it, I would offer you four or five things.

1. Muse, think often, both on the promise, and on the promiser. They whose minds and thoughts are not much taken up about the faithful God, and the faithful promise of God, how can it be expected

that they should believe well? Entertain, I say, a frequent savoury remembrance both of the promise and promiser. Our Lord charges his disciples with this, *And now I have told you before it come to pass, that when it is come to pass, ye might believe*, John 14:29 and 16:4. Remember it then, that you may believe more. Can you imagine it possible, that faith should flourish in the heart, when the promise and promiser is out of the eye, and out of the mind? That is utterly impossible.

2. Pray to the promiser upon the promise. He that prays much, believes well; and no man that neglects prayer, can act faith. We pray upon the promise to the promiser: *Remember the word unto thy servant*, says David, *upon which thou hast caused me to hope*, Psa. 119:49. The promises are given for our faith, and our faith is to be acted in praying upon them; and when we pray upon the promises, we pray to him that made them, and he that made them can certainly perform them.

3. Build upon the promises, lay your weight on them. The apostle Jude requires us to *build up ourselves in our most holy faith*. Faith is on the promises; and our building ourselves upon our most holy faith, is building on the promises by faith. The promise of God can bear every thing, any thing, and we must lay all upon it; we must lay every thing whatsoever upon the promise of God, all our desires, all our cares, all our weights, all our burdens, but especially of eternal life, which, as you know, we cannot bear ourselves; let the promise of God bear them; and in this matter of our eternal salvation, we know we cannot bear it of ourselves. This burden we must lay upon the promise, since it must be borne, or we are undone utterly. If this great affair of our eternal salvation be not laid upon a solid and good foundation, we are gone for ever; there is no foundation, but the foundation of God, that standeth sure, that of his faithful word.

4. You must learn to reason and argue upon the promises. A blessed way of exercising faith is to be reasoning by faith. There are faith's reasonings that have a great deal of excellency in them, a great deal of use. If I may so speak, it is a sort of pity that such good words should ever come out of so wicked a mouth as Balaam's; the man spoke words of faith, that he knew nothing of; Num. 23:19, *God is not a man that he should lie, neither the son of man that he should repent: hath he said, and shall he not do it? or he hath spoken, and shall he not make it good?* With

a better heart use these blessed words. The Spirit of God over-awed the man's tongue to speak them, and the Spirit of God guided Moses's pen to write them; therefore, though they are spoken by a false prophet, it is a part of precious scripture, it is of the arguings of faith: *Hath God said, and shall he not do it?* There is never a man nor all the devils in hell shall be able to say, Here is a word of God which he did not make good. See also 1 Sam. 15:29. I would only help you to a few of these reasonings of faith, that you may think of and use at any time, as God inclines your hearts.

1st, God knew what he promised, when he promised. Though God promised me eternal life, I do not know what is in this eternal life, but God knows full well. We are puzzled, we are darkened in the studying the doctrine of grace, and the great prize of our calling; but God knows it well; he promises no blessing unknown to himself, though it be unknown to us.

2dly, He knew to whom he gave the promise, he knew what they were, he knew what they would be, he knew what they would prove. When God delivered to me, saith a poor believer, the promise of eternal life in the gospel, he knew what I was, in the day I laid hold of it, John 13:36, 38; 14:18; 16:31.

3dly, This is arguing of faith, when the promise and promiser hath engaged our trust and confidence in any case, we may argue upon that; he hath not only promised, but he hath begotten expectations in our hearts concerning the thing he hath spoken of, and will he fail in the word upon which he has caused us to hope? Hast thou added the power with the word, so as to make me hope in it, and wilt thou not perform it? Psa. 119:49, 2 Sam. 7:20, 27.

4thly, Has not God begun to perform his promises to us; and should we not argue by faith, that we should trust in them more and more? The promise of eternal life is begun to all believers: He hath *quickened us together with Christ, and hath raised us up together* in regeneration, *and made us sit together in heavenly places* in him as our head; and will not the rest come on then? *Being confident*, says the apostle, *of this very thing, that he which hath begun a good work in you, will perform it until the day of Jesus Christ*, Phil. 1:6; 1 Thess. 5:23, 24.

Lastly, This is an arguing of faith, God's design in making, keeping, and performing his promise, is the same with the believer's design in receiving and resting on the promise; the same thing that God designed in the making, and keeping, and fulfilling his word; the same thing the believer designs in his taking, and trusting, and waiting for the performance of the word. What is God's great design? God's great design is to glorify *the exceeding riches of his kindness towards us in Jesus Christ*, as the apostle tells us, Eph. 2:7. What does the believer design? He designs the same thing. God promises us eternal life to the praise of the glory of his grace in Christ Jesus; what more would the believer have? In the day that he lays hold on the promise by faith, he means nothing else but this; he seeks nothing else, but that he may have eternal life, to the praise of God's grace in Christ Jesus. Hath God designed, in making the promise, to glorify his faithfulness? I, in believing the promise, design the same thing. Now, whenever God and a poor believer jump in the same design, it is impossible that it should miscarry. Indeed, if God designed one thing, and we another, God would reach his end, and we should lament our folly; but if we intend the same thing in all our faith in the promises, that God intends in making them, a disappointment is impossible. See Phil. 3:12, 1 Peter 5:10.

The *last* thing is, That you must take this truth of God, *Faithful is he that promises*, and keep it in the hand of your faith, in life and in death; hold it fast continually, keep it still as your anchor. When the body is decayed, when Satan is tempting, when the heart is misgiving, when pale death settles upon your eye-lids, when an awful judgment is staring you in the face, nothing but this, *Faithful is he that promises*, will support us. Weak is the believer, but faithful is the Promiser. So much for these three exhortations that I promised, and have now spoke to from these words.

There is one more, and that I would conclude with. I have been exhorting you to glorify God's faithfulness, by venturing on the promise of salvation by Christ in the gospel; to glorify God's faithfulness, by believing all covenant-blessings by the way; and to glorify God's faithfulness, by believing eternal life in the end. Only one word more, and that is the greatest of all. Glorify God's faithfulness by believing the promises about Sion and Christ's kingdom, though its state be ever so low. It was a good saying of a believer, in dark and dismal times, 'Now it is time to believe.' The great believer had a kind of joy in dark hours, because there was such a fair field for faith to act on God's faithfulness.

I believe many of you do not know much of the state of the work of Christ abroad in the world, and a great many are little careful to know it that should; but, by all the little hints that we have any manner of way, it is exceeding low at this day: let us believe, notwithstanding, it shall be well; this great faithful promiser hath promised great things about Christ's kingdom, and we must believe greatly about them; the strongest faith should be put forth here.

1. The promises that we are to believe on for Christ's kingdom, are Christ's promises. My meaning is, not only that they are by Christ, for all are so: but they are made to him; so, in some sense, all are too; but they are made to him primarily, they are made to him for his body's sake, the church. Shall we not believe firmly the promises of the Father to the Son? *Of the increase of his government and peace there shall be no end, upon the throne of David, and upon his kingdom, to order it, and to establish it with judgment and with justice, from henceforth even for ever: the zeal of the Lord of hosts will perform this*, Isa. 9:7. Let the faith of believers believe it then.

2. These great promises we are to believe about Christ's kingdom, are most free to the church, but they are most dear to Christ Jesus, and he hath already paid the price for them; he hath bought the kingdom already, and all that glory that is given him; *that name which is above every name, that at the name of Jesus every knee should bow, of things in heaven, and things in earth, and things under the earth; and that every tongue shall confess, that Jesus Christ is Lord, to the glory of God the Father*, Phil. 2:10, 11.

3. These promises are greatly fulfilled already, and we should believe them the more firmly upon that account. Our Lord himself, the great heir of the promises, is, as well as we can wish him, and better than we can think, exalted at the Father's right hand above all his enemies. If there were a host of all Christ's enemies together, it may be, they would be as bold as ever; but if all the devils in hell, and all wicked men on earth, were conjoined against him, yet a sight of his glory would chase them into hell, Eph. 3:20.

4. Believe these promises, for they are the largest and most comprehensive of all. The promises of Christ's kingdom, are the stock of all the faith of God's children in all ages. Pray, whence comes thy conversion,

justification, calling, or being brought home to God? It came out of the womb of the promises of the Father made to his Son: *He shall see his seed, he shall prolong his days, and the pleasure of the Lord shall prosper in his hand. By his knowledge shall my righteous servant justify many, for he shall bear their iniquities.* All the saving grace that we receive, comes from these promises that are made to Christ; and what we desire now, is but the fulfilling of them. What is there that we desire in all this world but this, that a great many ungodly people may be converted, and that all the godly may be eminent in grace, and at last ripe for glory? All these are contained in Christ's promises, these promises wherein the faithfulness of God is engaged: he hath promised this to David, that he will *establish his seed for ever, and build up his throne to all generations,* Psa. 89:4. You have ground sure enough for your faith, and you cannot be more happy than to have faith enough for your work. The Lord furnish you with it.

SERMON XIII.

HEB. 10:24.

And let us consider one another to provoke unto love, and to good works.

HAVING spoken so long upon the preceding verses, I thought fit, before I left this scripture, not to pass this that follows. The apostle, from these grounds that you have heard at great length, from the 19th, 20th, and 21st verses, draws three exhortations. The first is with respect to our duty, in the 22nd verse, That we should draw near to him. The second exhortation is to a duty that respects ourselves, and our profession of faith, in the 23rd verse, which I have stood long upon. The third exhortation is in the words read, and that is to a duty that respecteth others. This is indeed the right method, that conscience be made of what we owe to God, and care be taken of what concerneth ourselves, before we be in a case to discharge any Christian duty towards others.

This scripture I mean to speak but a little to, and was something doubtful in speaking to it at all, not from any doubt of its pertinency, but from a mighty doubt of its fruit; for the duty called to in this verse is so neglected, that it is not readily to be hoped people will much mind it, when they hear of it, till at least they begin to know faith, the spring of it: but when I considered that these two things, love and good works, are so very scarce, and that Christian fellowship is so worn out of use amongst them that are called Christians, I thought something should be said of them, though I were never so afraid that little good would be done by it; and therefore for once I will speak a little to it.

In this verse therefore lying before us, there is an exhortation to a duty that is very remarkably expressed by the apostle. There is, 1. The matter of the duty in general, to *consider one another*. 'Let us,' would the apostle say, 'that are brethren, and that know the way to the holiest of all, who have some faith, a sprinkled conscience, and clean conversation, and have made profession of our faith, let us consider one another.' The original imports a narrow locking one to another.

2. There is the end that this duty is enjoined for; and that is, *to provoke us unto love, and to good works*, so we read it; but the word in the original is far more significant than our translation carrieth it: Consider one another in order to a paroxysm, or high hot fit of love and good works, to stir up mightily thereto.

I would at this time speak a little to both these.

1. To the matter of the duty, *Considering one another*; then, 2. The end of it, *provoking unto love, and to good works.*

First, The duty, *Considering one another*. This implieth,

1. That there is a plurality of Christians. If so be there were but one Christian in one place, he would have nothing to do with such a place of scripture; he is only to walk wisely to them that are without, where the providence of God calls him; but this considering one another is no work for him.

2. It implies, that they are known one to another. When the apostle bids us consider one another, it necessarily implies, that we may know one another; and truly Christians are easily known one to another. I do not mean them that go with the herd, that call themselves Christians out of compliment, or fashion, or are Christians by reason the place

where they were born professeth Christianity; if this be all, it is no easy matter to know them: but such as have the power of the grace of God at work on their heart; and even here it is not so hard a matter for one Christian to know another.

3. Here is implied, and follows in the text, their meeting together; this is a part of their profession, *Not forsaking the assembling of yourselves together, as the manner of some is.* This considering, that implies these things, is spoken with respect to our Lord the head, with respect to ourselves, and with respect to our brethren. The same apostle bids us *consider the Apostle and High Priest of our profession Christ Jesus*, Heb. 3:1. That is a blessed consideration, with respect to patience in suffering: *Consider him that endured such contradiction of sinners against himself, lest ye be wearied and faint in your minds*, Heb. 12:3. As if the apostle would say, 'If you would use to ponder how Christ was used in the world, and how many foul tongues were employed against him, ye would think little of all the contradictions you meet with.' For one sinner to contradict another sinner, is no great matter; for a sinner to contradict a saint, no great matter neither: but for wicked sinners to contradict the Saviour, is the wonder. We are bid to consider ourselves, that *if any see another overtaken in a fault, we might restore such an one in the spirit of meekness, considering ourselves, lest we be also tempted.*

Now particularly what this considering of others is, will you hear of it, and mind it a little more, what that Christian duty of considering Christians aright is. You know, that considering is a serious employment of the mind; this employment is about other folks, and this employment must be about every thing in them and about them that we can discern. These I would reduce to three heads, their good, their bad, and what is indifferent, neither good nor bad in itself, but as it is guided.

1st, In considering of other Christians, ye should consider their good. I will not say, that always it is the wisest work for a man, in considering himself, to begin with considering his good; but I dare say, it is the wisest work in considering others, to do so. Our Lord, in the seven letters he wrote to the seven churches in Asia, begins always with their good, if there were any good in them, and commends them, before he takes notice of, and reproves for their faults. A Christian is very ill considered, if all his good and the best things in him is forgot. Amongst those good things that are to be considered, in order to *provoke unto love, and to good works,*

(1.) We should consider the grace of God that is in them, when it becomes visible, and visible it will be, if of the right kind. Barnabas saw the grace of God among them at Antioch, Acts 11:25. The apostles saw the grace of God that was given to Paul, Gal. 2:8, 9. Sirs, communion of saints is one of the articles of our creed, as we call it; and there is so much spoken of it in the word, and it is so great a blessing, that it is a thing impossible, that grace in saints should not be knowable by saints. If no man could know the grace of God in any other but himself, that man indeed might have communion with God, but he could have no communion with the saints. The main thing that we are to regard and to consider in Christians, is the truth of the grace of God in them, their shining in the image of their heavenly Father, and their partaking of the Spirit of Jesus. Wherever these characters and signatures are, a spiritual eye can discern them.

(2.) We should consider the station they have in the body of Jesus Christ, and that also is discernible; I mean, what state, what place, what room, the Lord hath called them to, or placed them in; not with respect to their office in the church, that is a thing of another consideration; but with respect to honourable service. The Lord gives his grace in various measures to his people, and in some it is a matter very remarkable, that quickly after the Lord hath begun to communicate of his grace to them, he intends to prove them in a higher sphere than ordinary; we must consider, what marks the Lord hath put on them that we know to be Christians of a more than ordinary stature, and usefulness, and service in the body of Christ, of which the apostle speaks so much, 1 Corinthians 12, almost throughout.

2dly, We are to consider Christians in their bad things. Can there be any provoking unto love and good works, in seeing of their bad things? Yes, a great deal. Amongst the bad things in Christians, I reckon,

(1.) Their sins and their infirmities; these are to be tenderly regarded, and looked upon, their weakness, their stumbling; the apostle calls much for a spirit of meekness towards such; a great deal of tenderness must be used. Happy are they that can represent and express the tender heart of Jesus Christ towards sinners in a Christian-like tenderness, towards sinning and stumbling believers. See what tenderness the apostle requires as to this, 1 Cor. 8. There is a poor weak Christian, it may be, stumbled, when he saw people making use of what was ordinarily bought in the market; it may be a great deal of the meat that was sold there, had first been shown before their idols, and presented in their temples, and the poor weak Christian scrupled this, and thought it a sad thing for a Christian to make use of his liberty this way: says the apostle, *Through thy knowledge shall the weak brother perish, for whom Christ died?* ver. 11. *For my part*, says he, *I will eat no flesh while the world standeth, lest I make my brother to offend,* ver. 13.

(2.) We should consider folks' temptations and afflictions, we should look on them so as *to provoke unto love, and to good works*. The more tempted and afflicted they are, the more need have they of pity from the Lord their head, and of compassion from all their brethren. The apostle Paul expressed this tenderness of spirit, and oh for some measure of it among us! 2 Cor. 11:29. Besides all his own sufferings, of which he names a great many, as perils by sea and land, and from his own countrymen, as well as heathens, nay, all sorts of distresses, besides all these things, he had the care of all the churches devolved upon him. What sort of care was this think you? Was this like the Pope's care that he pretends to have over the face of the earth, wherever the name of a Christian is? This was not thought of by the apostle; the care of all the churches was only a care of tenderness and sympathy, like the care of a mother to her children, when any of them are sick: *Who is weak*, says he, *and I am not weak? Who is offended, and I burn not?* What a brave spirit is here! Did not a distress come upon any Christian, the apostle knew of, but his heart felt the smart of it?

3dly, There are some things that we are to consider in Christians, that are in themselves neither good nor bad, but are of an indifferent nature, yet are to be considered, and are of great use to *provoke to love, and to good works*.

(1.) There is a consideration to be had of a Christian's education, of the place of his conversation, and of the means and helps that he hath or wants. There is a great matter in this. I do not say, that always such Christians are of the best complexion, as to their inner man, that are born again under the greatest advantages of the gospel means; only this is that I drive at, that the truth of the grace of God may be planted in the heart of a poor creature, where the means of grace have been but small, and his helps and advantages but few. Now, a great deal of tenderness is to be exercised towards such a one. The apostle takes frequent notice of it, as to himself, though indeed the grace of God to him was extraordinary, Acts 22. I do not mean, that the apostle does think to extenuate his sin before God by the mentioning it, but rather he mentions it to enhance the grace of God that took hold of him; that it was a sufficient ground for abating the severity of censure from other Christians, when they reflected upon his former conversation.

(2.) We should in things indifferent consider their natural temper. Tempers of mind vary as much as features of the face. We commonly observe it with great wonder, that there are not to be seen in a whole kingdom two faces so exactly alike, but that we discern some difference, and there is as great a difference in the natural tempers of folks' minds. Where the grace of God is grafted upon a good natural temper, it does set it off, I acknowledge, very beautifully; abundance of grace sown in them that have an equal temper of mind, makes a Christian appear very amiable: but the grace of God does not ordinarily fall there; the Lord commonly sows his grace in the worst soil. The heart of every man by nature is bad enough, but there are some worse than ordinary, and God plants his grace frequently there. Now, when the grace of God comes, it is appointed to change our natural state, as we are sinners, and to make us believers, of sinners to make us saints; but it was never appointed to change our natural temper. He that is born, as it were, with a hasty, hot, warm temper, the grace of God may guide that, and put it into a right channel; but rarely, if ever, does remove it. Now, it is to be observed, that a great many of the offences that Christians take one at another, are upon the account of the breakings out of their natural tempers; but we should give an allowance to these things. It is very likely, that our Lord, in calling his disciples, had regard unto this, and names them accordingly. Peter seems to be a forward, zealous, bold man; James and John seem to have been warm hot men; they are called sons of thunder; would our Lord say, 'I will graft my grace upon these men, and I will make use of their natural temper for the setting forth some piece of work, that such and such are fittest for.' We see then the wonderful wisdom of God, in guiding the corruptions of his people; and should we wonder at this, that the same wisdom should guide the natural infirmities of his people, and make them serviceable so much the more in their time? We must consider, I say, one another's natural temper, and give some grains of allowance thereto.

(3.) Among the things indifferent, I reckon people's outward estate in the world: *Not many wise after the flesh, not many noble, not many rich, and not many mighty are called*; but now and then some be. And it is very observable, that through want of a due consideration of this, a Christian that is very high, and rich, and wise in this world, and a poor low weak Christian as to his condition and natural parts, are usually very bad company; they are very apt not duly to consider one another, with respect to this; the poor are apt to envy them that are above them, and they that are high, to despise them that are below them. The word of God warns against both.

(4.) People's age and standing in Christ's house, is to be considered by us. When we consider one another, we are not, we must not expect those experiences and attainments in a novice, and one that is newly come to the faith, that we may look for, and expect in them that are of long standing in the house of the Lord. The apostle takes notice of this, and he checks them that had this standing. *For when for the time*, says he, *ye ought to be teachers, ye have need that one teach you again, which be the first principles of the oracles of God; and are become such as have need of milk, and not of strong meat.* See how the Spirit of God by Paul directs Timothy to his carriage, *Rebuke not an elder*, says he, *but entreat him as a father, and the younger men as brethren; the elder women as mothers, the younger as sisters, with all purity*, 1 Tim. 5:1. How distinctly does the apostle direct his discourse unto fathers, and young men, and children!

Lastly, Christians' different light about smaller matters should be considered, in order to provoking 'unto love, and to good works.' If people lay aside the duty of love, till they be all of one mind in all things, they may leave love till they come to heaven, and truly they look unlike them, that ever will be in heaven, that are strangers to love when they be on earth. How tenderly does the apostle apply himself unto this! Rom. 14:1-5; 15:1-4. *Him that is weak in the faith*, says he, *receive you, but not to doubtful disputations*. What were those doubtful disputations? These were not whether we are justified by Christ, or by good works, or by both together; they were about small little things; they were about food, some would eat nothing but herbs, and had no liberty to eat flesh; there were others that were strong, and they could eat freely any thing. But, says the apostle, *Let not him that eateth, despise him that eateth not*; that is his weakness; and let not him which eateth not, judge him that eateth, for the man walks according to his light, and indeed according to truth. One observes a day, and another not; his non-observing is an act of worship to the Lord. How excellently does the apostle comment upon these things! The meaning was this, In the beginning of Christianity, there was some of the Christians, that had been Jews, and were not yet altogether so far reformed from what they had professed before, but that they still retained, and were fond of their old ceremonies and customs; wherefore the apostle exhorts them to bear, with love and tenderness, with all such persons. The apostle therefore in some places did tolerate their weakness; yet, notwithstanding, when these small things are brought in upon an high account, how does he thunder against them! He speaks so tenderly to the Romans, to doubtful believers, yet to some that would observe days, and abstain from meats, he is as severe, *Ye observe days, and months, and times, and years*, etc. Ye are men that are parting from Christ, says he; why so? Because they did place a piece of their worship therein, and thought they would render them acceptable to God, and therefore brought in these Jewish rites and ceremonies into the matter of justification before God. The Lord hath not given all his people the same light; we are to be fully persuaded in our own minds about our own light: *Let every man be fully persuaded in his own mind*, Rom. 14:5. But that is but an ill sort of being persuaded in our own mind, that brings this persuasion also, that they who are not of our mind, are not right before God. So much for the *first* thing, the matter of the duty, *considering one another*.

The *second* thing to be spoken to, is what the end of this is, *To provoke unto love, and to good works*.

1. The first thing I note in this end is, You find love and good works joined together. Good works, or holiness, will never thrive amongst

Christians, where love is under a decay. *Where envying and strife*, says the apostle James, *there is confusion, and every evil work*, chap. 3:16, not only *there is an evil work*, but there is *every evil work*. The edifying and building up of the church by their mutual communion, as well as by communications from the head, Eph. 4:16, is expressly determined to be in this, *edifying of itself in love. From whom the whole body, fitly joined together, and compacted by that which every joint supplieth, according to the effectual working, in the measure of every part, maketh increase of the body, unto the edifying of itself in love*: as if the apostle had expressly pointed forth, that the general spirit of love is as it were the cement, and nutriment of the whole body of Jesus Christ; grace from the head, and spiritual love of the members one to another, is as the spring to their growth.

2. We find that the increase of love and holiness, is the proper and right end of Christian communion. For this end churches are appointed by Jesus Christ, that they may be societies for building up a company that he calls out of the world in love to God and to one another in holiness, till he transplant them to the church above.

3. The making this the end, speaks forth this, that the best of Christians stand in need of being mightily stirred up unto love, and to good works, or why stood the Hebrews in need of being so stirred up? We have the same word in the original, in 2 Cor. 9:2, *Your zeal hath provoked very many*. The grace of God, and the Spirit of holiness is ingrafted in the hearts of every Christian; but notwithstanding, every one should make conscience to water this, to stir it up, to blow upon this little fire, and to increase it.

Application. The first word shall be a word of reproof or lamentation. How sadly is it to be bewailed, that love and good works are so rare, and the means for them so neglected? that there is so little considering one another, *to provoke unto love, and to good works?* If it were not for the name of churches that is amongst us, one would hardly understand, that there is such a company of Christians amongst us; that considering one another *to provoke unto love, and to good works*, the Lord knows how few mind. How many are there of our Christians, that are not a bit the better for their fellow Christians, since the day God gave grace to them? Is there no Christian of your acquaintance, that you can labour to do good to? I never expect that person is fit to get good from others, that is not ready to do good to others. The spirit of humility, that makes us ready to receive good from others, will work a spirit of love in readiness to do good to others. Now, that this matter is neglected, is not all we have to complain of; but the contrary thereto is that which I would bewail and reprove, and the Lord make reproof light where it is most justly deserved.

1. There are a great many people, that consider one another's infirmities to blaze them abroad; instead of considering one another *to provoke unto love, and to good works,* they consider their infirmities to take notice of them, and to blow a trumpet upon their failings. I have often seen, and you may observe it, and may have found, that very often such professors as have been given much to the observing of the infirmities of saints, and then publishing of them, have been left of God to be apostates from the truth of the gospel themselves. It is a greater transgression than you are aware of, to observe the infirmities of saints, on purpose as it were to crow over the profession, because of the faults of them that make it. Let us always be tender of the name of Jesus Christ. If men that are not Christians are yet called so, and fall, let them get their just shame; the way of the Lord is not a whit the worse because a transgressor falls therein; the fault is not in the way, but in the walker. *Who is wise, and he shall understand these things? prudent, and he shall know them? for the ways of the Lord are right, and the just shall walk in them: but the transgressors shall fall therein,* Hosea 14:9.

2. Some consider one another's infirmities to imitate them, and to excuse themselves in the like practice. This is just contrary to what is in my text. Instead of considering one another to *provoke unto love, and to good works,* they consider others in their failings and infirmities, they take notice of a great many infirmities in the people of God; they think with themselves, Why may not I do so too? Such a minister or Christian has done so and so; why may not I? This is a most dangerous practice, for people to take notice of the infirmities and failings of saints, to imitate them, and never take notice of their virtues to imitate them: therefore the apostle warns them in this manner, *Whose faith follow,* says he, *considering the end of their conversation*; regard their doctrine, regard their practice, imitate their faith. The wisest observing

of one another, is to spy out one another's good, and labour to imitate it immediately. Wherever you see faith, and repentance, and believing, and holy walking with God, set about the imitating that. May I speak of the lowest, of the meanest, and of the most foolish practice amongst us, a practice that, I am afraid, is a great deal too common in this place? Instead of considering one another *to provoke unto love, and to good works*, many consider one another to provoke to vanity and to superfluity. Instead of taking notice of the virtue of believers, it may be people take notice of their way of living, of their garb; it is well if a great many be not hardened thereby: If one wear such a garb, why may not I? The righteous judgment of God will ever follow, where one Christian makes not conscience to observe and imitate the virtues of another, they shall be left of God, to observe and imitate the corruptions of one another. Let me therefore press it with these few, that you would mind well the plain words of the text, *to consider one another*, etc., all the Christians ye know, consider in such a manner, as that you may stir them up to love and holiness.

1st, Is not this commanded by God? There is none that can read the New Testament, and not find this commanded frequently, as Col. 3:16, 17; 1 Cor. 1:5-7, and a great many other places.

2dly, Hath not this been practised by the saints of God in all ages? There was never a generation of believers that lived in any time of the world, but if they could converse together, they would. There were a company of them long since in the Old Testament, that *feared the Lord, and thought on his name, that talked often one to another*. There were a company when Christ was born, and yet it was as dark a day as ever came upon the church, there was a company for all that, Luke 2:30, that were *waiting for the consolation of Israel*; and Anna, the old prophetess, knew them, and went to speak to all of them; like enough, she knew where to find them that waited for redemption in Jerusalem. This is a duty now to be practised, and there was never more need of it. What our Lord said as a prophecy, hath been plentifully fulfilled in our day: *Because iniquity shall abound, the love of many shall wax cold*, Matt. 24:12, 13. It is a duty the Lord hath always put a special remark upon, and hath taken great notice of, and for which *a book of remembrance was written*, Malachi 3:16. For those that had sighed and cried, because of all the abominations done in Jerusalem, these are men marked, set apart for special mercy. I shall leave this matter with three or four notes.

(1.) Never did the grace of God reach a poor creature's heart, but with it there came an instinct after converse with them of its own nature. Whenever one is made a new creature, they begin to look upon them that are new creatures in another manner, and a warmer way, than they did before.

(2.) Wherever the power of godliness is spreading, Christian communion always is. Never did the power of godliness flourish, where this was neglected. Therefore I look upon it as one of the sad signs that the power of Christianity and the efficacy of the gospel is greatly withdrawn from us, because Christian fellowship is so greatly neglected. I shall not tell you whence it comes particularly, and how it may be mended; much may be done to the mending of it. The Lord incline their hearts in whose hand it lies.

(3.) Where love and holiness is not, the single end of Christian fellowship, the fellowship of Christians, is a most dangerous snare. The communion of Christians one with another is the most dangerous company one can be in, if so be that this be not the grand design, to promote love and holiness. There have been such meetings amongst us, among them that are called Christians, and it may be are truly so; many people of different persuasions have met together for disputation; a most vain sinful practice, that always flows from corruption, and always issues in destruction; so far from good works, that it was never found to fail to provoke to hatred and ill works. It were far better that Christians should soberly retain their particular sentiments.

Lastly, Where Christians are a plague to one another, it is a sad sign that God hath a mind to plague them all together. Where people neglect to do good to one another, where Christians are hindrances one to another in the righteous ways of God, it portends that God will plague them all together. That is a sad threatening, Ezek. 22:18, *Son of man, the house of Israel is to me become dross*; what shall I do to them? says the Lord, *as they gather silver, and brass, and lead, and tin into the midst of the furnace, to blow the fire upon it, to melt it; so will I gather you in mine anger, and in my fury, and I will leave you there, and melt you*, good and bad in the same furnace, the silver and brass, and tin and iron. It is a fatal signification, when the institutions of Christ's appointment are not only forgot, but when they are perverted to contrary ends, than he hath appointed them for; it is a sad signification what the issue may be.

SERMON XIV.

Heb. 10:20.

By a new and living way, which he hath consecrated for us, through the vail, that is to say, his flesh.

THE sum of Christianity is to know Christ, and to use him; to know him for use, is to use him as known; his name sounds daily in the ears of multitudes, whose hearts never did once make use of him in the thing, if I may so speak, that our Lord only is useful for them in, and that is, his great calling to salvation. The apostle in the context is upon both these; he is both upon the doctrine of Christ, and the improvement of it; in the doctrine of Christ, he does discover and reveal this great usefulness for us in the matters of salvation, that the entry to the holiest of all is through his blood, that the way to the holiest of all is through his flesh, that he himself is the great High Priest set over the house of God; these are in the 19th, 20th, and 21st verses. From this 20th verse, I take notice of three things to be spoken to.

First, Where lies the way to heaven? How may a man find it? When is it one may be sure he is in it? Says the apostle, it is *through the vail* of the flesh of Christ. They that know not Christ, whatever they may pretend to, as to the knowledge of God or heaven, know nothing of either; and this I was speaking to last day, That the way to heaven lies through the vail of the flesh of Christ. Our Lord, in his helpfulness to us in our getting to heaven, is many ways spoken of in the word. Sometimes this great usefulness is expressed of his *person*, he is the *peace*; sometimes it is expressed concerning his *office*, he is the *Saviour*; sometimes it is spoken of his *life*, and sometimes of his *death*;

sometimes of his *flesh*, and sometimes of his *blood*. But whatever the words be that are used in the scripture, concerning our Lord in his calling as a Saviour, we are to take none of them apart, but to take all together; for Christ is not divided. His flesh that is here spoken of, is his human nature offered in sacrifice unto God, for the sins and souls of his elect; and through this we must pass, if we have a mind to heaven. It was an old custom, it is likely its original was from an institution, but it is very visible that it was several times practised of old before the Levitical law, and that it was a ceremony in making of covenants, that some living creature should be divided into two, and that the covenanting persons passed through the parts thereof; which had a great secret imprecation in the oath, that so God might do to them as was done to the beast, if they did falsify their engagements; and this the Lord by the prophet charges severely upon the people of Israel, for breaking his covenant: Jer. 34:18, *When they divided the calf in twain, and passed between the parts thereof.* Our divided and our slain Lord Jesus is the great covenant-mean betwixt the Lord and us; and all that seek their peace with God and entrance to the heavenly kingdom, must pass, if I may so speak, through the parts of this divided and slain Son of God. Christ's flesh is called the *veil*, because it hides his glory; it is a veil, because the passage to heaven lies through it; though the veil of the temple covered the holiest of all from the eyes of all the people, yet through it a passage was for the High Priest at the appointed time. There are three things simply needful, not only needful to our salvation, but grand pieces of salvation. *The saving knowledge of God*; *acceptable worshipping of God*; and all enjoyment of him. In the saving knowledge of God, all graces are exercised, in acceptable worship all duties are performed, in the enjoyment of God all blessings and mercies are received. These three have all a mutual influence one upon another; the more there is of saving knowledge, the more there is of acceptable worship; and the more there is of both these, the more of communion with God. And thus it is both on earth and in heaven; only there is a wonderful difference in degree, for all these are low here, but are perfect above; our knowledge is dark, our worship is faulty, our enjoyment scanty, small, and quickly passes away; our vessel is narrow, and cannot receive much; and leaking, and cannot hold much; what it is they know above, and what worship they perform, and what enjoyment of good they receive; is above our knowledge. Of their knowledge too the apostle speaks singularly, *For now we see through a glass darkly; but then face to face: now I know in part; but then shall I know even as also I am known*, 1 Cor. 13:12. The words that the apostle hath there, are very hard to be understood; but we might know something of them by the former part of them; we know what it is *to know in part*, we know a little what it is to *see through a glass darkly*: but what face to face knowledge of God is, and what to 'know' even 'as also we are known,' we do not know. What is more common in the sense and thoughts of believers than this, even in their nearest approaches to God, even in their clearest views of him. It is but a little that I know of him, but he knows me perfectly? Will ever that day be, that Paul shall know Christ as well as Christ knew Paul? I shall know even as also I am known, as clearly, as satisfyingly, as far beyond what our present knowledge is, as any thing can be. *We shall be like him*, says the apostle John; *for we shall see him as he is*, 1 John 3:2. *Beloved*, says he, *now are we the sons of God, and it doth not yet appear what we shall be*. Ay, but it will ever appear? Yes, says he, it will appear; when he shall appear, then we shall be like him, *for we shall see him as he is*. The knowledge we have of God and of Christ Jesus now, is through the glass of the gospel, 2 Cor. 3:18. And the more that God shines upon that glass, and the more that he enlightens the eyes of our minds in beholding it, the more we perceive it; but now what a wonderful knowledge of Christ must that be, that is gathered and learned out of his blessed face, when we shall see him as he is! Christ is a great deal better than the Bible; the Bible is a creature, the Bible is a created manifestation of the will of God; all our knowledge now of God and Christ must be bounded with that, must be determined by that, must be ought from it; but the apostle tells us, there is another sort of knowledge of Christ, to be hereafter, when we shall see him as he is. How they worship, we do not know, we know what worshipping in a temple is, but we do not know what worshipping is without it, where *the Lord God almighty, and the Lamb, are the temple thereof*, Rev. 21:22. I only take notice of these things, because I was saying that these were the main parts of salvation, and that we come only to them through Christ Jesus. We cannot worship God acceptably but in Christ; we cannot enjoy God, but in Christ; never was there a gracious communication of God's love given unto men, but through Jesus. The application of this truth, that the way to heaven lies through the veil of Christ's flesh, I shall forbear until I have gone through the words of the text, upon the second thing, which is *the properties of this way*. The way is through his flesh, but what sort of a way is it? The apostle gives us here three properties of it, and I will take one of them to speak to at this time.

It is called *a new way*, it is called *a living way*, and it is called *a consecrated way* for us. We would have no need of Christ's flesh, or of its being made a vail, unless it had been the purpose of his grace to save a multitude of poor lost sinners in a way 'consecrated for us.'

Of the *first* of these, it is *a new way*. The meaning of this, is what I would discourse a little to.

First, To avoid mistakes; I shall remove those things that this word may lead people to, and tell you what is not the meaning of the newness of this way, then positively what it is.

1. This is not a new way, as if it were of a new invention, a late contrivance and device of God; but is as old as eternity; and there can be nothing before nor after in eternity. Our Lord is the way to heaven; he is the *Lamb slain from the foundation of the world*, and that in a usual scripture-sense, as much as to say, *from eternity*, Rev. 13:8. *I was set up from everlasting, from the beginning, or ever the earth was*, Prov. 8:24. *His ways are from everlasting*, Micah 5:2. The way of saving men by Christ Jesus is not a way of late invention: *It is according to the eternal purpose, which he purposed in Christ Jesus our Lord*, Eph. 3:11, 2 Tim. 1:9.

2. Neither is it a new way, as if it were newly revealed, as if it were of late revelation; for this way of saving men by the Son of God, is as old as sin is, and was revealed immediately upon sinning, in that way that we shall further hear of. Adam knew this way, Abel knew this way, and Enoch; and Abraham saw Christ's day, and Christ was before him: *Before Abraham was, I am*, says our Lord, John 8:58.

3. Neither is it of late as to the use of it, for the benefit has been received by multitudes; all along by Abraham, and Isaac, and Jacob, and all the prophets that are in the kingdom of God. There is but one way to heaven, though this seems strange to us. Adam died some

thousands of years before Christ came in to the world, before this vail was actually made; so did Abraham, so did the Old Testament church, according to the order of their generations, some a longer, and some a shorter while before: But they had the way for substance revealed to them; there was a revelation of God's good will towards them in such ways as he thought good, whereby his pardoning grace and acceptance, through a mediator, was pointed out to them; they had the same hope that we have, and the same faith that we have; only with this difference, their faith was to look forward, and our faith is to look backward; their faith was in the Messiah to come, and our faith is in the Messiah which is come. Their faith was in the veil of that flesh that was to be reared up, and our faith is in the veil of his flesh that has been reared up, and is now gone up to heaven: the same faith we have, saith the apostle, *the same spirit of faith*, 2 Cor. 4:13. We find there is a great difference between David and Paul, as to their expressions of godliness, and as to the clearness of their knowledge: ay, but, says the apostle, we have the same spirit of faith with David; David said, I believed, and therefore have I spoken; says the apostle Paul, The same spirit of faith is in us. These are the things that are to be removed, when Christ as to heaven is come to be a new way; not that it is newly devised, or newly revealed, nor newly used. It is called positively *a new way*.

1*st*, Because it comes after another, as the apostle teaches us to argue, Heb. 8:13, *In that he saith, A new covenant, he hath made the first old*. So may we say, when Christ is said to be a new way, there hath been then some way before, that is now made void, and made void by it, as this was. There was a way by the first covenant, wherein sinless man might have been saved and happy. This was a way God never intended to bring one man to heaven by. Do not imagine, that God did ever design that which he never effected. When the Lord made the first covenant with Adam, he foresaw the event. If I may so speak, the first covenant was but a scaffold reared up a little while, that the glory of the new might be displayed. The first covenant was (1.) A covenant without a mediator, God and man treated immediately together; sinless creatures made in so great perfection, as God made them, were in case, if I may so speak, of treating with God. (2.) This covenant was made upon condition, that is to say, the blessings of that covenant were suspended until the duty of that covenant was fulfilled. (3.) There were peremptory threatenings that did make all void, whenever it was incurred, *In the day thou eatest thereof, thou shalt die.* Sin broke this quite to pieces, this covenant of works, this covenant without a mediator, this covenant upon conditions, this covenant that might be broken by sin, is altogether removed, and no man can ever get good by it. The bridge is quite broke down; but such is the folly of this blind world, that multitudes will labour to build up this bridge again; whereas the day of the Lord, or a storm, will quickly discover how rotten it is.

2dly, It is called *new*, because of its great light in the revelation of it under the gospel, because it is newly revealed in greater light than it was before. There is a pregnant place to this purpose, Heb. 9:8. The apostle is speaking upon the same thing that I am, *The Holy Ghost this signifying, that the way into the holiest of all was not yet made manifest, while as the first tabernacle was yet standing.* Pray observe it, it is a great scripture; the Holy Ghost by these things taught the church of the Jews; the holiest of all was a type of heaven, there was an entrance into this typical heaven for the high-priest, in the name of all Israel; the Holy Ghost signified to them, that there was greater light to come in the way to heaven, but that the first tabernacle must be removed before that light come. How much does the apostle speak, 2 Cor. 3:6, to the end, of the difference betwixt the Old Testament and New Testament dispensation? He depresseth the one, and raiseth and exalteth the other greatly, both in the power and glory of the one beyond the other. Let us now consider this matter a little more narrowly, because it is of considerable use for directing our path, in order to make us thankful for the blessing of our lot in the New Testament day. You heard there was a revelation of Christ, and the way to heaven; there were promises, there was worship, there was faith, and there was salvation under the Old Testament, but how vastly preferable is our state beyond theirs? (1.) As to the doctrine of Christ, see how the matter was discovered to Adam and Eve. He was to be the seed of the woman, that is all we find they knew, that was to break the head of the serpent; there was to be a child born into the world, that should defeat all that the devil had done in destroying mankind in the first brood. Our Lord Jesus was to Abraham the seed of the woman, in whom all the nations of the earth should be blessed; to Jacob he was Shiloh, Gen. 49:10, 11,

Binding his fole into the vine, and in Acts 7:37 he is a Prophet raised up like unto Moses, as Moses foretold in Deuteronomy 18. If we go further, he was to David the son of David; if we go on to the Prophets, Isaiah speaks greatly of him, chap. 9:6. He was *to be a child given to us, a Son born to us; his name was to be called Wonderful*, etc. chap. 53. He was to be *a man afflicted of God, he was to be slain*, etc. And, Micah 5:2, *But thou, Bethlehem Ephratah, though thou be little among the thousands of Judah, yet out of thee shall he come forth unto me, that is to be ruler in Israel.* These are several of the brightest dawnings of the light, and the knowledge of Christ in the Old Testament: but pray what are all these to one word that John Baptist speaks, *Behold the Lamb of God, which taketh away the sin of the world*, John 1:29? And therefore he is greater than all the Prophets, that is, all the Old Testament Prophets, until the testimony of the apostles: *That which was from the beginning, which we have heard, which we have seen with our eyes, which we have looked upon, and our hands have handled of the word of life*, 1 John 1:1. Thereupon it was that our Lord said, *Blessed are your eyes, for they see; and your ears, for they hear. For verily I say unto you, that many prophets and righteous men have desired to see those things which ye see, and have not seen them; and to hear those things which ye hear, and have not heard them*, Matt. 13:16, 17. Certainly there was, if I may so speak, a greater temptation unto the Old Testament saints, to desire to see Christ in the flesh, than there is to New Testament saints, to long impatiently for his second coming. Surely the strong faith of Abraham, that saw Christ's day near two thousand years before he came, had great desires to have seen him in person, and the Lord was pleased to gratify him in some measure; for even the Son of God in all appearance did take on him the form of a man, in appearance, not really, not the nature of a man, but the form of a man, and did converse with the prophets of old. The happiest man that we find in the Old Testament, as to this point, was old Simeon; he was both an Old Testament saint and a New, he had it revealed unto him, that he should not see death before he had seen the Lord's Christ. I only touch on these things, to shew that the doctrine of Christ is a great deal more clearly revealed to us than to them; therefore the way may be called new. Next, as to their worship, they had in the wilderness a curious tabernacle, in Canaan a stately temple, and there was a multitude of glorious ornaments in the outside and in the inside;

there were courts, there were washings, there was incense, there was blood, sprinkling with blood; and what signified these things? Since we have got *the true tabernacle which the Lord pitched, and not man*, Heb. 8:2. We worship towards the true tabernacle, that their tabernacle was but a type of. How weak a type and resemblance was that of a great house of threescore cubits long, twenty cubits broad, and thirty cubits high, 1 Kings 6:2, etc. what sort of resemblance was this to a man like to this? But it was so, and all that they had. Our Lord is the minister of the true tabernacle, which the Lord pitched, and not man; all their washings and sacrifices were but shadows of that, of which we have got the substance; these were all the *shadows of things to come, but the body is of Christ*, Col. 2:17. So I may say as to their promises; they had promises, but there was something of a veil even upon the promises of the Old Testament; a great many spiritual promises were veiled under temporal blessings. The apostle saith concerning them, *These all died in faith, not having received the promises, but having seen them afar off*, Heb. 11:13. That is the second, the way is called new, because it is of a new, lightsome, glorious revelation, under the gospel. The apostle Paul saith, *Be it known unto you, men and brethren, that through this man is preached unto you the forgiveness of sins*, Acts 13:38, 39.

What great difference is there between Paul's preaching, and the bringing of a beast upon the altar? and the sinner laying his hand upon his head, and the priest cutting his throat? What a poor thing was this, in regard of the plain gospel-revelation of Jesus Christ's sacrifice?

3dly, It is said to be a *new way*, because it is newly and lately made: and the word in the original has something in it, that favours this sense. Some read it a *new slain way*. It is a way that comes by blood, that blood is newly shed; there is no abatement of the virtue of Christ's death, his blood is as warm, cries as loud this day, as the day it was shed: yet, notwithstanding, it had something in it to work upon people the more readily, because it was newly done at this time. Now, when we come to a matter of sixteen hundred years, we are apt to think that the virtue is in a great measure impaired; but this is our sin and folly.

4thly, It is a *new way*, because it is always new, and never gives place to another. It is never called old, for that which is old is ready to decay, and to vanish away; it is called new, because there is never to be another way to heaven. People had need take heed how they improve this. *If we sin wilfully after that we have received the knowledge of the truth, there remaineth no more sacrifices for sins*, Heb. 10:26. A scripture that, by the cunning of Satan, and by the darkness of the minds of many good people, has raised a storm in many good people's consciences without ground. The meaning is this, God will never provide another way to the end of the world, but only this one way.

Lastly, It is a *new way*, because it is well prepared, as new ways use to be. In the order that God gives about the city of refuge, Deut. 19:3, 4, *Thou shalt prepare thee a way*, says the Lord; thou shalt make a new way on purpose, a way that a man may easily find, a way that may be distinguished from all other ways, that may direct itself to the passenger; whenever a man should stand in need of the city of refuge, that he may find the way ready before him. Christ as slain as the new way to heaven, that is, well prepared, all impediments being removed out of the way, and all furtherances being in it; every thing that may hinder is removed, justice, the law, conscience condemning, and sin working; of all these we find plenty spoken of in the word of God. The Lord puts away sin by the sacrifice of himself, he sprinkles conscience, and gives full assurances of faith; but some of these I have spoken to already. Only now a little of the positive furtherances that are in this way, or the properties of it, as it is a new prepared way.

1. Christ Jesus is a safe and sure way, so that a man needs fear nothing, if he be in Christ: *Who shall separate us from the love of Christ?* says the apostle, Rom. 8:35. I know that they that are in Christ will fear often, but that is their weakness. It is a reflection on our Lord Jesus, as to this sure way to heaven, to have trembling travellers walking in it; people should walk confidently, the way is sure and safe. There are many enemies in it, that is certain; but they are not properly in the way, but are in our way as we travel in it; so that believers cannot walk quietly to heaven for them, but they walk safely for all that. The devil has been busy for above these five thousand years upon the road to heaven, yet he never slew one believer to this day. If a man be in Christ, the ark, he is certainly safe: he may be frightened, he may be disturbed, he may apprehend danger, but he shall feel none.

2. This way is a well-provided way. If a man have a great way to go, if there be danger of his being starved by the way, he is in a poor case; but there is no danger of being starved, if we walk in Christ. Here, if I

may so speak, we may live upon the way; here is a cordial to the soul, food to the soul. Remember our Lord's body was given for us, his blood was shed for us; the eating his flesh and drinking his blood, is food to the traveller in this way.

3. It is a very pleasant way. All they that know it find it to be pleasing both to God, and to his people. May we conceive, Sirs, how pleasing it is to the God and Father of our Lord Jesus Christ, to see multitudes of poor sinners coming home to heaven in the arms and heart of his own Son? to see the strayed sheep come home upon the good Shepherd's shoulders? to hear him say, *Behold, Here am I, and the children thou hast given me?* It is pleasant also to all believers; there is no believer that usually hath great trouble, but either when his interest in Christ is hid, or when his enjoyment of Christ is small. When we know we are in him, and when we do feel the blessedness of being in him, it is not ordinary affliction that will work much upon the soul of a believer. With what contempt does the apostle speak of all afflictions? *I know*, says he, *and am persuaded, that they are not able to separate me from the love of God which is in Christ Jesus.* He was walking in the way, and encompassed with the love of God in Christ Jesus; therefore he gives a defiance to things present, and things to come, as not being able to hinder him from reaching to his journey's end.

4. Christ is the way to heaven, and he is prepared as a near way. It is not far betwixt Christ and heaven; for as soon as ever a believer sets foot in Christ as the way, he is immediately possessed of begun eternal life. We are to lay hold of eternal life; that eternal *life is in his Son, and he that hath the Son, hath life*, saith the apostle, 1 John 5:11, 12. Alas, poor people commonly misreckon most wofully, that we are so far from heaven as from death and the grave; for though heaven's full enjoyment lies beyond both, and such as be young may possibly be a good many years from heaven; yet if so be that you be truly in Christ, Christ is now in heaven, and heaven is in him: we receive eternal life by receiving him; we do not receive the full enjoyment of it, but we receive a right to it, and earnest of it. It is a near way, for a man may see heaven when he is in the way. There is a promise in the prophet Isaiah that has its vail on it: *Thine eyes shall see the king in his beauty, and they shall behold the land that is very far off*, Isa. 33:17. All that I allude to is, that as soon as a believer by faith takes up Christ Jesus as his Lord and Saviour,

immediately he sees the land that is far off; for there is no man can have a believing look of Christ Jesus, but he must see heaven and salvation in his face. *We have access*, says the apostle, *by faith into this grace, wherein we stand, and rejoice in hope of the glory of God*, Rom. 5:2.

SERMON XV.

Heb. 10:20.

By a new and living way, which he hath consecrated for us, through the vail, that is to say, his flesh.

THERE are two things, that if they were more upon our hearts and minds, would make both the speaking and hearing of this subject sweet and savoury. If our hearts were set on heaven, it would be delightful to hear of the way to it; and if our hearts were filled with love to Christ Jesus, his most lovely appearing would be very desirable; and the most useful and sweetest sight that believers can have of Jesus Christ, till they come before his throne, is to see him, as by his death and blood, making his way to heaven for them. Christ crucified and Christ glorified is all that we are to study; the one we are to study as long as we are on earth, and the other we shall be admitted to study when we get well to heaven. It is upon this theme I have been speaking again and again, and, if the Lord will, shall do it yet farther, That Jesus Christ as slain is the way to heaven; or, That the flesh of the slain Son of God is the vail through which we must pass to heaven. This point I have opened in several things; and before I come to the large application of it that I design, I thought fit first to speak of the commendations of this way, that are in the text, and last day spake to the first of them, That it is called a *new way, new* not for its being newly contrived, for the contrivance of this way is as old as eternity; it was an eternal purpose, that God purposed in himself, about bringing the elect number of Adam's fallen seed to glory by his Son Christ Jesus. It is not new in the revelation of it; for it was revealed as soon as sin came into the world, and sin is as old as the world, within a week or little more. I mean sin is as old as any creature is; it may be that sin was on the sixth day, or at least the seventh, it was very quickly. As soon as sin came in, the revelation of this way comes in also. It is not new for the use and benefit of it; it is not this day, nor yesterday, nor from the death of Christ, that believers get entrance to heaven, but from the beginning, from Abel the righteous, unto Zechariah that was slain betwixt the altar and the temple; and in all the Old Testament times, the access to heaven was the same as it is now. Why then is it called a *new way?* It is neither newly contrived, nor lately revealed, nor lately felt in the profit of it. It is new, because there was another before it; there was a way to heaven before it; but never man got to heaven that way, and never man shall. God never meant that ever man should perfect obedience unto himself by the terms of the first covenant; though life was promised by it, yet the least disobedience was threatened with death. It is *new*, because it is so clearly and newly revealed in the gospel; therefore the gospel, in the declaration that we have of it, is called the *New Testament*. It is new, because it was but lately that this way was actually declared, and made known by the death of the Son of God. It is new, because it is constantly fresh, and is never to give place to a successor; as long as the world lasts, God will never contrive another way to bring men unto eternal life, but this through his Son shall remain for ever. If men sin wilfully in the contempt of this, says the apostle, there is no more sacrifice for sin; God will never provide another sacrifice for them that contemn this. It is new, because it is well prepared, and made fit with all the encouragements that may be to the traveller. Of these things I have spoken already.

It remains, that I speak of the second property of this way, it is a *living way*. Christ slain as the way to heaven is a living way. Now, this is a more marvellous property than the former. Here is, in the preceding verse, a man whose blood was shed and all of it, and by blood shedding he was slain; in this verse here is a man whose life was taken away, and his flesh rent, so the word implies in the original, his body and soul were plucked asunder by violence. That our Lord Jesus as slain is the way to heaven, and a living way, is what we would inquire into the sense of, and see what we are taught thereby.

First, Christ as slain is a living way to heaven, because there was great life in his death, mighty power, mighty effects, it did great things.

The apostle Paul was a great divine, you know; O what a blessing were it to the world, if there were but one man in it that knew Jesus Christ but half as well as Paul did! Now, what was this great man's study all his life, but to know him? *That I may know him, and the power of his resurrection, and the fellowship of his sufferings, being made conformable unto his death*, Phil. 3:10. Observe, every body knew as well as Paul, that Christ had died and was buried, that Christ had suffered and had risen again; but, says the apostle, I do not study that, that I know sufficiently; there is something else about it, there is power and virtue in that death, and suffering, and resurrection, that every day I am studying more and more. See now how the apostle does most excellently and elegantly vary the word. The general word is, *That I may know him*, that is, Christ: the particulars are various; *that I may know his resurrection, and the power of it,* that is one phrase; *that I may know his sufferings in their power*, is another; and the third is, *That I may know his death in being conformable to it.* The fellowship of his sufferings, conformity to his death, and the power of his resurrection, are but various words expressing the same great fruit, that the apostle aimed at in his knowledge of Jesus Christ. When I am dead to sin as he was; when I am like him in suffering and weanedness from this world; when I know his resurrection, in being raised up to newness of life, as he was raised up, by the glory of the Father, to a new resurrection. There was never a death in this world, that had life and power in it, but Christ's; God be thanked, death is the way to life, and we pass through death unto life; but there is no life in the death of martyrs, when slain for Christ's sake, as Abel the righteous was; when they are dead, their blood cries for vengeance; but in the very death of our Lord there were great and mighty effects, there were great acts of life. I will name them for our study and use in our spiritual knowledge, for in this exercise of our faith should be our daily employment.

1*st*, There was life in Christ's death, for by it he reconciled us to God. There is a great word to this purpose: *And having made peace*, says the apostle, *through the blood of his cross, by him to reconcile all things unto himself*, Col. 1:20. The greatest quarrel that ever was in the world, or ever will be, is that betwixt God and sinners, taking up of which is the greatest difficulty; the quarrel is just on God's side, for he is offended; the quarrel is unjust on man's side, for the fault is his; the parties are mightily unequally matched, the Almighty God and a frail worm. But our Lord by death made up this quarrel, and there was no way of making it up but only this. Now, we commonly know this, and say it, that we are reconciled to God by the death of his Son; but this matter should be distinctly known, and narrowly thought upon; we should have our faith exercised so about it, as that we may be able to improve it a little. I would therefore shew you now, how Christ, by his death, reconciled us to God. He did this,

(1.) In that he satisfied divine justice by his death. There can be no peace betwixt God and men, as long as God's justice is demanding vengeance; as long as the justice of God has any thing to crave, there is no man can stand before him. Now, there are only two ways of satisfying divine justice, and there will never be a third. If all the devils in hell or men on earth should study to devise one, it will be impossible to find it. Divine justice is either satisfied by falling upon the sinner himself, or the surety for him: when justice falls upon the sinner, and exacts payment of him, the poor wretch must be perpetually paying, because he can never pay to purpose: a great reason why hell's torments are eternal, is, because justice can never get enough of them. But the satisfaction that justice got of our Lord Jesus, was full measure heaped up and running over; he offered himself a sacrifice to God for a sweet smelling savour; justice was pacified and satisfied, and love got a vent towards men.

(2.) The law must be fulfilled before there can be any reconciliation with God. The law of God is not to be shifted off or put by; God's holy law is a perpetual bar in the way of all men to heaven, unless Christ remove it and take it out of the way. God's law demands a perfect obedience or death. Our Lord Jesus comes in and gives both, on the behalf of those that he redeemed; he was made under the law, and came under the curse, that we might receive the blessing, and that the curse might be diverted from us.

(3.) Sin must be taken out of the way. Justice was not only to be satisfied, and the law honourably fulfilled, but sin must be taken away, in order to our salvation and to our reconciliation with God. About this great work of our Lord, and that he did it by his death, the word speaks great things: *But now once in the end of the world, hath he appeared to put away sin by the sacrifice of himself*, Heb. 9:26. He hath done it for ever; sin is sufficiently put away. But how is sin put away? Sin by Christ's death is not put out of the world, but remains still in the world, and is greatly aggravated by Christ's death: *If I had not come and done amongst them the works that never man did, they had not had sin.* Small sins get great advantage this way, upon gospel-despisers. Christ did not come then to put sin out of the world, neither did his death put sin altogether out of his people. Where his death and the virtue of it is applied, sin is subdued, but is not expelled. The Canaanites were worsted, but were not quite put out of their coasts. Much less is sin by Christ's death put away as to its vile nature, but remains still wherever it is, a vile loathsome thing to God. Neither did Christ put away the deservings of sin. What then did he? Christ put away the condemning power of sin, that it shall no more be an impediment to the peace and reconciliation of believers. Therefore, says the apostle, *There is therefore now no condemnation to them, which are in Christ Jesus*, Rom. 8:1. The second word of Christ's death about sin is, that he *condemned sin, he condemned sin in his flesh*. Sin is a word that is too well understood even by those that are unacquainted with both the Hebrew and Greek. All sin requires a sacrifice for its expiation: *He condemned sin in the flesh*. There is nothing more reasonable in all the world, than for a poor creature to fear that sin should condemn him, that he should be condemned for sin, there is nothing more known in the scriptures than that Christ died for our sins. Then it would seem that sin condemned Christ; how then did he condemn it? Let us consider now for this where the strength of sin lies. The apostle tells us, *The strength of sin is the law*, 1 Cor. 15:56. That which makes sin able to bind a man over to eternal vengeance, is the strength and power of God's law; and God's law is as strong as God himself, for almighty power is engaged to see the law fulfilled. Now, when Christ engages with sin's strength, and hath overcome that, may it not well be understood, that he did condemn sin? All sin's power to condemn, is from the law. Our Lord hath taken that out of the way, he hath satisfied it fully. The law demands blood for transgression; it is granted, it is given, and blood of a high sort, even the blood of the Son of God. So much for this first thing, *Christ as slain is a living way, for there was life in his death*, as appears in his reconciling us to God by his death. But never shall a man, to the end of the world, if it should last as long as it hath already (and blessed be God, it shall never last long) get God's peace and favour, but that man whose peace with God was bought by this blood.

2dly, There was great power and life in Christ's death, in his overcoming the power of hell; he did it by his death. A great many words there are in the scripture about this. Hell never did act more like hell, than in slaying the Son of God; hell was never so rampant as it was at that time, Luke 22:53, says our Lord, *This is your hour, and the power of darkness*, your sad hour of temptation; the devil's great power is exercised now Christ is taken, and to be condemned. It is strange, if the devil were ignorant of the consequences of this thing; he that entered into Peter, and got hold of his tongue for to persuade Christ not to go to Jerusalem, where he was to die; our Lord perceives the devil's hand in it, and calls Peter *Satan* for his pains. Is it not marvellous now, that this wicked one should have entered into the heart of Judas to betray him, and should have stirred up the chief priests and people to cry, *Crucify him?* Like enough the devil thought he had done a greater exploit than in throwing down the first Adam; and what says our Lord concerning it? *Now is the judgment of this world: Now shall the prince of this world be cast out*, John 12:31. Our Lord prophesied of his own death in these words, *And I, if I be lifted up from the earth, will draw all men unto me*, John 12:32. And in another place he tells us, *The prince of this world is judged*, John 16:11. This now we would consider, what way this power of our Lord's death appeared in the conquering of Satan: and in order to this, we would shew where Satan's armour lies, if I may allude to that word, for that word is spoken of the same wicked person, the devil, Luke 11:22. *When a stronger than he shall come upon him, and overcome him, he taketh from him all his armour wherein he trusted, and divideth his spoils*. Pray what is the devil's armour, think you? Where lies his strength. His strength lies in sin, which is his seed and offspring; his strength lies in the law, whereof he is the hangman and executioner; his strength lies in the justice of God, wherein sometimes he is the instrument: therefore, because of this, the apostle says expressly, Heb. 2:14, that our Lord took part of flesh and blood, *that through death he might destroy him that hath the power of death, that is, the devil.* How came the devil to have the power of death? According to his interest in sin, according to his interest in the executing of God's vengeance, he has the power of death; but our Lord through death overcame him: Col. 2:15, *And having spoiled principalities and powers, he made a shew of them openly, triumphing over them in it.* Though death and hell united their powers against him, he proved too strong for them, and by dying overcame them. Hereby also he rent the vail betwixt Jew and Gentile; and because the Spirit of God does expressly and particularly mention it, therefore we may. It was a greater matter at first than now, through time, it is with Christians; we do not sufficiently ponder this great blessing: *For he is our peace, who hath made both one, and hath broken down the middle wall of partition between us; having abolished in his flesh the enmity, even the law of commandments, contained in ordinances, for to make in himself of twain, one new man, so making peace; and that he might reconcile both unto God in one body by the cross, having slain the enmity thereby*, Eph. 2:14-16. When Christ died, the veil of the temple was rent from top to bottom, Matt. 27:51. Here now our Lord Jesus' flesh was the vail that we must go to heaven by. When Christ the true veil was rent and died, immediately the typical veil was rent also; as if God had said, Now let all men know, upon the death of my Son, that all the partitions betwixt Jew and Gentile are removed. But this was a great mystery for a good while in the church, and Paul reckons upon his knowledge in this mystery of Christ, Eph. 3:4, 5, *Whereby when ye read ye may understand my knowledge in the mystery of Christ, which in other ages was not made known unto the sons of men, as it is now revealed unto his holy apostles and prophets by the Spirit; that the Gentiles should be fellow-heirs, and of the same body, and partakers of his promise in Christ, by the gospel.* So much for this first thing, Christ as slain, is called a living way, for there were great works of life even in his death.

Secondly, He is the living way, because all the life of man is lodged in him. Whatsoever extent life is drawn to, whatever sense we put upon this word *life*, as to all blessings for this and the other world, they are all contained together in Christ Jesus; so contained in him, as to be found no where else. He is *that living bread that came down from heaven, that gave his flesh for the life of the world*, John 6:51. The brazen serpent was a type of this. As the life of the stung Israelites stood in that ordinance of God, so the life of poor sinners stands in this grand ordinance of God, his slain son. *The first man Adam*, says the apostle, *was made a living soul, the last Adam was made a quickening spirit*, 1 Cor. 15:45. Surely all the natural life that is in the world, of sense, and reason, and understanding, is derived from the first Adam: he hath made of one blood all nations upon the face of the earth. Adam appears to have been a very fruitful root; the world now for almost six thousand years, has been filled with his offspring, for of two there sprung all mankind that are upon the face of the earth; but there is no quickening here, for all this. *The second Adam*, says the apostle, *was a quickening spirit*; he alone gives the quickening spirit to this mighty offspring of the first Adam.

Thirdly, Christ is a living way, because all that are in him, as soon as they are in him live. That is one of the meanings of this word. There is no dead man can be in this way. Do not ask the question, for it is a very idle one, Whether is a man quickened before he is in Christ, or whether he is in Christ before he is quickened? Neither the one or other, but both together; his life comes by being in Christ. How can men conceive of quickening now? Quickening is a work of God. Can it be said, that he quickens before we have life, or that we have life before he quickens? We can easily perceive, that we act life by his quickening, but the Lord quickens not a moment before we are alive. How did the Lord raise Lazarus? There went life-giving power along with the word, by which life was received, and the voice was heard, as our Lord calls it; *the dead shall hear the voice of the Son of God, and live*; they must live before they hear; for hearing is an act of life, and they receive life by the powerful word of Christ.

Fourthly, He is a living way, because he lives for ever to be the way. There is continual virtue in Christ's death, which perpetually issues forth, in order to the salvation of all his people. You would think it strange, if one should ask, What is heaven? What is eternal life? Why, it is Jesus Christ, that is eternal life; it is one of Christ's names: *And we know that the Son of God is come, and hath given us an understanding, that we may know him that is true; and we are in him that is true, even in his Son Jesus Christ. This is the true God, and eternal life*, 1 John 5:20. This way lives for ever, to preserve all his people; he lives *for ever to make intercession for them*, Heb. 7:25. Nay, if I may so speak, even in heaven, this way is not forgotten, I mean in the songs of the glorified; the song of the Lamb is perpetual: they sang the song of Moses and of the Lamb. What is in the song of the Lamb, think ye? *Worthy is the Lamb that was slain, to receive power, and riches, and wisdom, and strength, and honour, and glory, and blessing*, Rev. 5:12. Christ's blood in heaven, in the virtue and life of it, raises the notes of perpetual praises most highly. I know the book of the Revelation is a mysterious one, and every word of it is to be narrowly canvassed:—*And in the midst of the elders, stood a Lamb as it had been slain*, Rev. 5:6, so that though there be no appearance, nor will be, of any infirmity that attended the low estate of the Son of God, when he dwelt in mortal flesh, yet there will be a perpetual remembrance of the dearest acts of his love, and richest acts of his grace towards us, in loving us, and giving himself for us.

Fifthly, It is a living way, for no man can die in this way. That way may be called a living way indeed, if there were such a one that led to a good place that no traveller in it could die, and would be a great temptation for people to undertake it. There are some places in the world where riches and honours are, that people run towards, and run through a great many dangers for; but they may die in that way, but never a man dies in this way, they sleep in Jesus, but they die not. *I am the resurrection, and the life*, says he: *he that believeth in me, though he were dead, yet shall he live; and whosoever liveth, and believeth in me, shall never die. Believest thou this?* John 11:25, 26. O how sweet a question is that, *Believest thou this*, that a believer in Christ can never die? Wherefore now, since our Lord died, death hath got a more sweet name. It is called sleeping, and sleeping in the Lord. Thus it is said of Stephen, that he was stoned, calling upon God, and saying, *Lord Jesus, receive my spirit.—And when he has said this, he fell asleep*, Acts 7:59, 60. It is called *sleeping in Jesus*, 1 Thess. 4:14, 15. Do not you see, say you, that believers die like other men? Yes; but then they die in Christ Jesus; they only fall asleep in the way. And the Lord, the way, will awake in a little while, and raise them up again, and bring them their new apparel, their house from heaven, 2 Cor. 5:1-3.

Lastly, It is a living way, because the traveller must live upon this way. Here is a marvellous living way; the traveller must live upon this way; he lives as soon as he is in it, and he lives as long as he is in it, for he cannot die in it, and he lives upon it while he is in it. My meaning is, that all the fare that believers must cherish their new life with, is Christ himself. Therefore our Lord speaks of it so frequently: *Verily, verily, I say unto you, except ye eat the flesh of the Son of man, and drink his blood, ye have no life in you. For my flesh is meat indeed, and my blood is drink indeed,* John 6:53, 55. Blessed are they that can eat and drink plentifully of it. When the faint and weary traveller walks in Christ as the way to heaven, and has any thing that overtakes him, any faintness, any distemper that seizes upon him, nothing is he to do, but only to fall upon Christ by faith, and to live upon him, and to eat and drink this blessed way. This was Paul's life: *The life which I now live in the flesh, I live by the faith of the Son of God, who loved me, and gave himself for me,* Gal. 2:20, as if the apostle had said, The stay of my life, the comfort my life, the security and continuance of my life, depends upon this; whenever I can get but a look, whenever I can get but hold of this love of Christ, that *loved me, and gave himself for me,* life, and strength, and vigour return upon me. So much for this second property of the way, that it is a living way. There was life in his death; all our life is lodged in it, as soon as we are in him, we live. Whenever a poor sinner is drawn to Christ as the way to heaven, he comes and lives, and lives and comes, and comes by life, and lives by coming. Turn it which way you will, the truth lies equally sure on all hands. This way is living, because Christ as the way lives for ever; because no man that walks in it, can die; and because a believer can live upon this way, as long as he is in this world. Never bid better fare to a child of God, than more of Christ, more of the sap and virtue of a crucified Saviour. If there were more of that among us, our souls would be more fat and flourishing.

A word or two only, at this time, of APPLICATION, before I proceed to the third property.

1. Is Christ a living way to heaven? Is a slain Christ for us, the living way in which we must walk to heaven? Then surely it should be very pleasant to the people of God to go to heaven. What is there to make it irksome to a believer? What is going to heaven? It is nothing but walking in Christ towards Christ, to be ever with Christ; that is going to heaven; our way is walking in him, our way is walking towards him, our hope is to be ever with him. I know that there are a great many

impediments and hindrances in the way, and yet these Christ has disarmed and removed by his death; they may make an appearance that may be frightful to such weak people as we be; weak believers take the shadow for an armed man, and are afraid many times unreasonably; but how pleasant will it be, I say, for a believer to find himself guarded from all attempts against him in his way to heaven? *As ye have received Christ Jesus the Lord, so walk ye in him; rooted and built up in him*, Col. 2:6, 7. Fix your root in him, and draw your fruit from him.

2. Is Christ a living way to heaven? Then what a sorry pitiful case are they in, that walk in the ways of death, that despise this way of life? It is very common, and it does not cease to be the more sad, because it is common, but is so much the more grievous, that persons love death rather than life. The matter now is balanced thus: every sinner is by nature dead in sin; if he continues in that state, he dies in his sin, and dying in his sin, he dies for ever, for his sin: this miserable case now is to be balanced with what our Lord proffers, that he will give the light of life, that he offers to lead men to heaven; that if they will but set foot in him, set their hearts on him, lodge their faith on him, and put all their trust in him, he will guide them safe thither. You should reckon it a mercy, that you have sinners to preach to you; if it were not, that we have the experience of that rebellion of the natural heart in ourselves, ministers would be mighty impatient in dealing with ungodly persons. What ails men, that they refuse Christ Jesus? What madness possesses the hearts of men, that they will rather go to hell, with the devil, than to heaven with Christ Jesus? Do not they well deserve to be in hell for ever, that make such an abominable choice? Yet every natural man does so, every natural man prefers the way of death to the way of life, and prefers Satan's driving to hell, unto Christ's gracious and blessed leading to heaven.

SERMON XVI.

HEB. 10:20.

By a new and living way, which he hath consecrated for us, through the vail, that is to say, his flesh.

I HAVE spoke, upon the 20th verse, of the way that is made to heaven, as the apostle does delightfully and wisely by the Spirit of God teach it; the various aspects, as it were, that Christ hath on our salvation, which we must have in our faith on him for salvation. I told you from this verse, that the way to heaven lies through the vail of the flesh of a slain Saviour, and this is the only way. I proposed to handle the properties of this way, before I came to the large application that so great a theme calls for. I have spoke of the first of them, That it is a new way, a new slain way. Last day I spake of this property of the way, That it is a living way. Jesus Christ as the way to heaven is a very great mystery; take but the words now as they are in our text. This sense of them is inseparable from them; and can there be any thing more mysterious than they do express, that a slain Christ is a living way for dead sinners to walk in unto eternal life? Who understands this? who believes this? I spake of the signification of this property at some length last day, how that Christ as slain is a living way to heaven. 1. In that there was life in his death. He was crucified through weakness, as to outward appearance of his low state; yet the great things that were done by that powerful death, are unspeakably mighty and many. He hath reconciled us to God, he overcame Satan, he overcame death in dying; death was never conquered until it got one man in its hands, that was our Lord Jesus; and from that day to this, it is able to master none that believes on him, but must make an entrance for them to the heavenly kingdom. Death cannot stop a believer in Christ from going on to heaven, but rather it is made now one of the last dark gates that we must pass through. 2. He is a living way, in that all the life of poor man, all saving spiritual and eternal life, is lodged in the Son of God: *This is the record that God hath given of his Son, that he hath given us eternal life, and this life is in his Son*, 1 John 5:11.

There is nobody makes a question of that, that call themselves by that common name of Christians, that all life is from Christ; and there are but few, but know that all life is in him, and that men get life by being in him; that they have it when they have him. 3. He is a living way, in that, as soon as a man is in Christ, he is made alive. When that power of divine grace draws a poor wandering sinner, and puts him in the way of Christ, he is made alive immediately to God. 4. He is a living way, because he lives for ever. The virtue and savour of his sacrifice is as fresh in heaven, as in the day wherein it was offered. 5. He is a living way, because all that are in him shall live for ever; never can a man die in Christ. I know that we sometimes use the word *dying* so frequently that this phrase is common amongst Christians, *living in the Lord, and dying in the Lord*; but the New Testament phrase is fitter; believers in Christ only *sleep* in the Lord: *They that sleep in Jesus, will God bring with him. Lastly*, He is a living way, because the walker in Christ lives upon the way, the way is food to him. The same sacrifice of atonement before God is made a feast for the believer. As under the law and before the law, in peace-offerings, by which covenants of peace were confirmed, there was some part thereof that was to be made a feast of; so this flesh and blood of our Lord that is rent for us for a propitiation, is made a feast unto our faith: *Except ye eat the flesh of the Son of man, and drink his blood, ye have no life in you*, John 6:53.

The *third* property of this way remains now to be spoke to; that it is a *consecrated way*: *By a new and living way, which he hath consecrated for us*. The words as they run in the original have *consecrated* before the other two properties, and may be equally fairly rendered, *which he hath consecrated for us, to be a new and living way*; and that consecrating relates not only to the substance of Christ's being the way, but to his being a new and living way.

There are three things that I would discourse to you from these words.

1. Of Christ's consecration.

2. His own interest in it, his hand in it; so it is told us in the text, *By a new and living way which he hath consecrated for us*.

3. For whom it is that this way, this consecrated way is; it is consecrated for some body; it is consecrated for us, for our sakes, for our benefit, for our advantage.

First, Of Christ's consecration. This word *consecrate* as it is in the English, is not in all the New Testament, that I know of, but in this epistle; and it is twice in this epistle, though not the same Greek word in both places. See Heb. 7:28. Consecrate in the Old Testament is very frequent; and you know that the apostle, as hath been frequently observed to you, in this epistle, and particularly in this part of the epistle, has wisely accommodated himself to those he wrote to, who understood these words a great deal better than we do, for they knew well whence they were borrowed; they were borrowed from the temple, and tabernacle, and Old Testament worship, where consecrating was used about every thing. Consecrating is dedicating and devoting a person or thing to a special or holy service; so we find consecrating or dedicating of things and places. There was the book of the covenant, and there was the tabernacle, and all the utensils thereof, all of them dedicated with blood; and this ceremony in their consecration was used, that, by being sprinkled with blood, they were dedicated to the holy use and service God appointed them for. So was it also as to persons: we find it especially concerning Aaron, the high-priest, who was the first type, and concerning his sons that were under him; they were separated and set apart by divine appointment for a special use, none else were appointed for it. The sense then of this word is, That Christ's consecration is, that he is devoted, and appointed, and dedicated to, for a special use, and that is, to be the way to heaven, that by him men may come to God. John Baptist understood this when he preached Christ: *Behold the Lamb of God*, says he, *which taketh away the sin of the world*, John 1:29. Here comes the true sacrifice, who bears the iniquity of his people. The apostle, in Heb. 9:22, makes a deep and excellent use of this consecration: *Almost all things are by the law purged with blood*; purging there is partly in the same sense with our consecrating. *It was therefore necessary that the patterns of things in the heavens should be purified with these; but the heavenly things themselves with better sacrifices than these.* What were the patterns of the things in the heavens? The holiest of all was the grand one; the high-priest was a pattern of our Lord Jesus Christ; the temple was a pattern of the heavenly things; yet these were but shadows of them; the things themselves must be purified with better sacrifices than these, even with the blood of the Son of God. We find therefore the truth of consecrating, and devoting, and dedicating our Lord Jesus to be the way to heaven; it is frequently in the word, and used upon many accounts. We will therefore take notice, that it is the Father hath dedicated him to be the way; for this is of great use in the exercise of our faith, to know our Lord Jesus under this name, That he is the consecrated way to heaven.

1. He is consecrated by the oath of God; as in Psa. 110:4, *The Lord hath sworn, and will not repent, Thou art a priest for ever after the order of Melchisedec.* And this the apostle discourses of at great length in chap. 7 of this epistle, and makes one of the grand differences betwixt his priesthood and all that went before, to consist in this, That they were made without an oath; hinting there was a time when they should cease; but when he made our Lord Jesus a Priest, it was by an oath; which was a demonstration, that he was to continue for ever in that employment. Therefore in the conclusion of that chapter, he says, *For the law maketh men high priests, which have infirmity; but the word of the oath, which was since the law, maketh the Son who is consecrated for evermore.* Take in this matter now by a true faith, and it may be that some time or other you will find food for your faith from it, That, by the oath and appointment of Jehovah, the God and Father of our Lord Jesus Christ, Christ the Son is sworn and appointed to be the only way to bring sinners to glory.

2. Our Lord Jesus is dedicated and consecrated to be the way to heaven, by the preparing him a body to suffer in. The covenant betwixt the Father and Son had all the blessings therein secured, by the mutual faithfulness betwixt Father and Son; but the way by which these were to be brought about, was the sacrifice of the Son in man's nature; therefore his consecration is carried on by his getting a human body: verse 5 of this chapter, *Sacrifice and offering thou wouldst not, but a body hast thou prepared me.* Did not God will and command sacrifices? Yes, but never out of his Son Christ Jesus; these were all but shadows and types of the great one, and there was no such thing required of our Lord Jesus, neither did he offer any such thing; but, *A body,* says he, *hast thou prepared me.*

3. By the commission and charge that our Lord had for the setting about this great work of redemption. He not only had a body to suffer

in, but was commanded by the Father to lay down his life for his people. This our Lord frequently takes notice of: *This commandment have I received of my Father*, John 10:17, 18.

4. He is dedicated by the holy anointing. One of the grand ceremonies of consecrating a person under the Old Testament, was by anointing. Aaron was to be anointed, and his sons; when they came in to be priests of God's appointment, they were God's anointed. And all this is typical of the true anointing of our Lord Jesus. The anointing of Christ is the fulness of the Holy Ghost, and his pouring upon him: 'Therefore God, thy God hath anointed thee with the oil of gladness above thy fellows,' Psa. 45:7.

Lastly, By giving him all power over all persons and things, in order to the accomplishment of his work. All judgment is committed to him: *As thou hast given him power over all flesh, that he should give eternal life to as many as thou hast given him*, John 5:21; Matt. 28:18; John 17:2.

Secondly, How is it that Christ hath a hand in his own consecration? The word is, He hath *consecrated himself to be the new and living way.*

1. Christ devotes and consecrates himself to be the way to heaven, in a cheerful and willing compliance with all the will of his Father about him. In order to his being the way, the Lord God his Father opened his ears, and he was not rebellious; it was his delight to do his will; and in compliance with the divine will a great matter of his consecration stood; by the which will we are sanctified; the Father's will willing him to come, the Son's will willing him to come willingly.

2. By his dying. Our Lord Jesus died willingly, in another manner than any of us either can or should. He laid down that life that he could keep, if he would; he laid it down as an act of great obedience unto the will of his Father; he died cheerfully, and died willingly. See what he says of it before-hand: *And for their sakes I sanctify myself, that they also might be sanctified through the truth*, John 17:19. What is that sanctifying of himself? A sacrificing of himself, devoting of himself to be a sacrifice for the saving of his sheep. They could never come to that sanctification, by gospel-devotedness to God, unless our Lord Jesus had devoted himself to death.

Lastly, He consecrates and devotes himself by the consequent practice and exercise of his office. Every poor sinner upon whom our Lord Jesus puts forth his skill in saving him, is a display of his authority to save, is a further declaration of the power and might that he was clothed with in bringing men to glory. Therefore, says the apostle, *it became him, for whom are all things, and by whom are all things, in bringing many sons unto glory, to make the captain of their salvation perfect through sufferings*, Heb. 2:10. He was made perfect through sufferings, to the end that he might bring many sons to glory; and the more he brings, this perfection is the more evident in him.

The *third* thing in the words to be explained is, For whom is this consecrating of Christ? The apostle says, he has consecrated this way for us, for a particular sort of people, for some of the children of men. Christ did not consecrate and make himself a way to heaven, and send the gospel into the world, that men, according as they incline, and according to the direction of their free-will, might come in and get life and salvation by him. Our Lord Jesus went about his work more knowingly, more fixedly than that; he knew what would come of it. It is done, I say, for particular persons. Consider, with respect to this,

1. That all the springs of salvation are towards particular persons.

2. That the covenant, the charter of salvation, is with, and for, and to particular persons.

3. The possession of it is by, and for particular persons.

1st. The great springs of salvation are all for particular persons; the three grand springs of salvation, are the election of the Father, the redemption of the Son, and the sanctification of the Holy Ghost. Now, all these are determined towards distinct and particular persons. *1st,* The election of grace is upon persons; there is no election of qualifications, the election is of persons. Wherever it is spoken in the word, it is spoken of persons: *He has chosen us in him before the foundation of the world. Give diligence to make your calling and election sure. God hath not appointed us to wrath, but to obtain salvation by our Lord Jesus Christ.* The election is all of persons.

2dly, The grace of redemption by our Lord, with his redeeming love, is of persons: *He laid down his life for his sheep*, and, *I know you are not of my sheep*, says our Lord. That was a not Christ could speak; but none of his servants must ever offer to speak after him; never was there an apostle could say so in an assembly of people concerning one particular person, *I know they are none of Christ's sheep*, that is only for the great shepherd to say. The chief shepherd can only tell his sheep exactly.

3*dly*, The sanctification of the Spirit, which is the great spring of salvation, as it is begun in us, is of persons. There is a devoting of the whole church, the body of Christ. But as it is a work on particular persons, this work must pass upon particular men; the springs must work in every man that is called to this salvation. *For we ourselves were sometimes foolish, disobedient, deceived, serving divers lusts and pleasures, living in malice and envy, hateful and hating one another*. So that we find, I say, that the springs of salvation are all about particular persons. The springs run in one distinct channel towards particular persons, and always answer the same. Every one that is elected by the grace of the Father, is redeemed by the blood of his Son; every one that is elected and redeemed, is sanctified by the inhabitation of the Holy Ghost; they are not equally visible, but equally certain.

2. The charter of salvation is to particular persons. Every one must have God's covenant made with himself. None are saved by a general covenant of God with a body of people. A church covenant under the gospel signifies nothing at all in matters of salvation; it may be of good use in church-order. But every one in particular must have salvation come to him, through the channel of a particular covenant betwixt God and him: *He has made with me*, says David, *an everlasting covenant*. If it had been only with Israel in general, it had been a cold business for a dying man's comfort; but *he has made with me*, as particularly with me, as if there were not another man in all the world that God covenanted with.

3. The possession of salvation is by particular persons. People are not saved in crowds and corporations. There are bodies of Christian churches, as they are called, that are to attend to the means of grace and mutual edification, according to the Lord's appointment; but when we come to partake of begun, or of complete salvation, every one must have it for himself; no other body's salvation can serve him. This is the substance of the meaning of this word, that our Lord as slain is consecrated, and hath consecrated himself to be the way to heaven for his people.

I would make some little use of this at this time, and reserve the more general application of this slain Christ, as the way to heaven, unto another opportunity. Two things I shall infer from hence, and speak to at this time.

1. Is Christ a consecrated way to heaven, and hath he consecrated himself for his people? Then *behold how he loved them!* If the Jews said so of Christ's weeping at Lazarus's grave, what must we say of our Lord's consecrating himself to the death for us, that he might make a way to heaven for us? *Jesus wept*, John 11:35. The Jews said, *Behold how he loved him!* We find most frequently in the word, when either this great devoting of Christ to death is spoken of in general as to churches, or applied in particular to particular persons, it is still ascribed to love as its spring. *Husbands*, says the apostle, *love your wives, as Christ also loved the church, and gave himself for it*, Eph. 5:25. *He loved me, and gave himself for me*, says the apostle, Gal. 2:20. Great must that love be, when the love-gift is so great. It must be a strong love that must give so great a gift, *Who loved us, and washed us from our sins in his own blood*, Rev. 1:5, 6. The love of Christ constrained us, because we thus judge, *that if one died for all, then were all dead*, etc. 2 Cor. 5:14. This I would speak a little to in a few particulars, this consecrating himself to be the new and living way to heaven.

1st, Our Lord Jesus did consult the necessity of his people out of mere pure love. He was upon the Father's counsel from eternity about the way of saving man; he is the wisdom of God, and hath an interest in the contriving of it; the eternal purpose was purposed in Christ Jesus our Lord: The contrivance was, What way may poor fallen sinners be brought well and safe to glory? They are fallen by sin, conquered by Satan, proclaimed rebels by God, attainted and condemned by God's holy law, are beggared and impoverished, and cannot pay a farthing to divine justice. The law must not be broken, justice must not be affronted, God's power cannot be resisted: How then can man be saved? It is impossible but only this way; here is the mystery of our Christianity. It is impossible that a man can be brought up to God, until God come down to man, and become man for him; and that God-man is made the great mean to bring all his people up again to God; the sacrifice of the man, and the power of God, and the merit of that sacrifice of that God-man, is made an everlasting chariot, that will carry all that believe on him certainly safe to glory. He consulted, I say, our necessity in great love. He consulted not his own conveniency at all: *Even Christ pleased not himself,* etc. O what an argument is here! The apostle brings the sweetest arguments sometimes to press the easiest ordinary duties. *Let us not please ourselves, but every one another, for edification*; that is wholesome advice, but the argument is beyond it, *even Christ pleased not himself.*

2*dly*, Our Lord's love in being thus a consecrated way appears in this, that he draws all his redeemed to himself. Christ being the way to heaven is no man's way till he be in it; no man is brought to heaven by Christ, till he be in him. Therefore our Lord, knowing this, draws them to himself: *And I, if I be lifted up, will draw all men to me*; that is, all that I have laid down my life for.

3*dly*, This love appears not only in drawing them, but in preserving them to the heavenly kingdom. We do not fall out with ourselves so much as we ought; but we were in a bad case if Christ should fall out with us, as often as we do with ourselves; if the Lord Jesus had had the same thoughts of us, that we ought to have of ourselves, where had we been? But he pities and spares in his great love, and by his great might keeps his poor people in the way, and gives them the crown in the end, Rev. 2:7, *To him that over cometh will I give to eat of the tree of life, which is in the midst of the paradise of God.*

Sirs, Christ's love is a blessed thing. If a poor believer can but see it through a glass darkly, and perceive something of the stream of it, he is joyful. But Christ's love as a Saviour will never appear in its glory, till the crown of glory comes out of his own hand; when a believer, if I may so speak, kneels before the throne of God and of the Lamb, and receives the crown of eternal life; our Lord may well say then, *Hereby thou mayest know how I have loved thee*. Christ consecrated himself to be the way to heaven, and a great demonstration of his love we should gather out of it. See Rev. 3:9.

2. Did Christ consecrate himself to be the way to heaven? Then surely men may boldly use him as the way; he is devoted for this end. There are two grand abuses of consecrated things, When they either are not used for that end they were consecrated for, or when they are abused to another end.

Is our Lord consecrated to be the way to heaven? Men must boldly by faith make use of him. See our Lord's own argument, John 6:27, *Labour not for the meat which perisheth, but for that meat which endureth unto everlasting life, which the Son of man shall give unto you: For him hath God the Father sealed.* He hath consecrated him, set him apart to be the bread of life, and giver thereof. This now I would only branch out in two particulars.

1st, Christ as the way to heaven maketh us bold in entering by him; he is consecrated for this end. There is a boldness of faith, that in the day of God's power is practicable. At first believing some have found it. I will not say very many. The very first adventure of a sinner, that has been despairing of all relief before, may trust with a great confidence upon Jesus Christ, as the consecrated way to heaven. But, say you, I do not know that he has been consecrated for me. I know that he is consecrated to be the only way to heaven; but is he consecrated for me? I answer (1.) No man ever did, and no man can, and you never will be able to know that Christ is consecrated for you, till you be in him. This is the great wisdom of God. God's great book of life, I say, is not to be read by any eyes, but the eyes of a believer; and when he reads the book, he can only read his own name in it. But indeed Paul, by an apostolic spirit and discerning charity, might speak as he did, *Whose names are written in the book of life.* The book of election, and the book of Christ's sheep, can be read by no eyes but the eyes of a believer; and this is enough, we need no more. It would be enough to confound all things in the church of Christ, if so be that the secret books of God's purposes were visible unto and legible by believers. If I may so speak, there would be no living in the world, if men knew who were elected, and who not. The very doctrine thereof, you see how many tumults it raises; how much more would it be, if they saw the thing? Take heed, remember that Christ is consecrated to be the way to heaven; he is consecrated to be so for a particular number of men; no man can know himself to be of that number, but a believer, and every believer may. Whenever a poor creature can assure his heart before God, that he, in the sense and plain conviction of his deserving hell, and of his being utterly unable to do any thing to bring him to heaven, takes Christ as God's appointed way, and ventures his all upon the slain Son of God, this man is a believer, and the way was consecrated for him; as soon as he is in it, he may know it. Make but your calling sure, and you make your election sure thereby. (2.) Whatever darkness there be about this, whether the way was consecrated for you, you have encouragement to venture upon the way by all the scripture. It is not the doctrine of the purpose of God on the death of Christ, that is the ground of our faith; it is the doctrine about the sufficiency of Christ's death; it is the doctrine of the gospel, wherein the tender of the Saviour and great salvation is brought to every man's door so closely, that the issue must be either an acceptance unto salvation, or a refusal with the great aggravation of condemnation; and so will the judgment at the last day proceed.

2dly, In using Christ as the way to heaven, we must not only, because he is consecrated for this end, venture on him boldly, but we must walk in him confidently.

(1.) Without fear of enemies; I do not say without apprehension; there is an apprehension of enemies, that is an act of wisdom and faith, in order to prepare for the encounter. Take ye the whole armour of God, we have need of it, for there are great enemies; not flesh and blood only, but greater enemies we have to fight with. Remember this, that you cannot get to heaven in that road that the devil does not haunt; there is no path lies to heaven that the devil cannot meet a walker in it. We must not expect to get to heaven without meeting him by the way; but let us remember this, I am upon consecrated ground; if I be in Christ, Satan cannot prevail against me: And the more confidence we have of our security in Jesus Christ, the more courage and strength we have against Satan.

(2.) Fear nor miscarrying at last, if ye be in Christ. It is a pitiful case that a great many believers are in; there are believers, God help them, that are so weak, they believe all their days, and they unbelieve all their days; they walk on in Christ, and fear they shall never come to the end. What, art thou in Christ, and yet fearest thy missing heaven? Whither can Christ the way lead a believer, but home to himself? *Father, I will that they also whom thou hast given me, be with me where I am; that they may behold my glory which thou hast given me: For thou lovedet me before the foundation of the world*, John 17:24. I will not lose a bit of them, I will not lose the man, notwithstanding his temptations, corruptions, and weakness in grace. I will make the poor creature get good of all. It will be seen when our Lord has perfected his work, that he has lost nothing of all that was given him.

Lastly, Walk confidently in Christ, and do not fear wandering. Believers have the promise of the Spirit to lead them into all truth. If they be in Christ, Christ will keep them. I do not say, but many believers may be left to great mistakes and errors about several things of smaller moment. But every believer that is in Christ, as to greater matters, is kept in the truth as it is in Jesus. O that this were duly minded! How wisely does the apostle speak of this point, Eph. 4:14-16. compared with ver. 19, 20. and onward of Col. 2? The thing that I observe from both these places is, the instruction the Holy Ghost gives us of the spring of error in the church. The apostle cautions us, that we be not overtaken with the cunning craftiness of them that lie in wait to deceive. How shall we know them? would the poor man say. Know them? Always by this, they do not hold the head, says he: *Not holding the head, from which all the body by joints and bands having nourishment ministered, and knit together, increaseth with the increase of God*, Col. 2:19. As long as a believer is in Christ as the way, he can never miscarry, never wander totally; he may mistake in something in his way, but he is in the right way in the great matters of salvation, and shall be safely landed at last.

SERMON XVII.

Heb. 10:20.

By a new and living way, which he hath consecrated for us, through the vail, that is to say, his flesh.

THIS is the second encouragement, that the apostle, by the direction of the Spirit of God, gives in encouraging Christians to approach to God. They are all drawn from Christ Jesus; and all our encouragements for faith are in Christ alone; nothing that is in him, but is encouraging to faith; and nothing that can encourage faith is out of him, or any where else to be had. The first is, That there is an entrance allowed to us by the blood of Jesus Christ, ver. 19. The second is, That there is a way prepared, and consecrated for us through the vail; that is Christ too. And the third encouragement is, That we have an High Priest himself, set over the house of God.

Upon this second encouragement from the 20th verse, I have been several days speaking upon this truth, That the way to heaven is through the vail of the slain Son of God, it is through the vail of his flesh; and upon it, at several times, I have shewn, what is meant by Christ's flesh; it is his human nature offered in sacrifice to God for the salvation of his people, with all its spirit, and power, and virtue. Next, I shewed, why this flesh is called the vail. It hid and covered the glory of his Godhead, and yet makes a passage unto us by faith to approach to God; for an immediate approach to God, now that sin hath entered in to the world, is impossible; therefore all our approaches must be by a mediator, and this Mediator did mediate mainly by his blood and sacrifice. What sort of a way this is, has been spoke to, both in general, and according to the three properties of it in the text: That it is a new way, a living way, and a way of Christ's own consecrating for us; and upon each of these some little application has been made suitable to the doctrine that has been discoursed to. I design now, as I promised, to make some more large application of this great truth, That our Lord Jesus as slain is the way to heaven: though I know the apostle makes the grand application in the 22nd verse, for he points forth the use we should make thereof, *to draw near to God.*

I will, notwithstanding, as the Lord shall help, speak something of application previous unto that; and it shall be only in two particulars.

First, If Christ be the way to heaven, we may plainly see how fatally and wofully the greatest part of the world are mistaken about the way; and if mistaken about the way, they must miss of the end. If one do not take the right way to heaven, he can never come at it. This is an inference that is very plain, and very sad. There are two false sorts of religions in the world, I mean that almost all the rest are reducible to two. There is natural religion; and there is the Antichristian one, which is but a grand corruption of Christianity, and a changing of it some way into the old Pagans' natural religion, and many gross things therein. I would speak but briefly unto both of them, and reduce what I mean mainly to warn you of, as inferences from thence.

1. There is natural religion. I call it by that name, because something of it is every where, and it is only what remains in that fallen state that man is come into. We will see now what this is made up of, what are those principles that are so deeply engraven in the hearts of men, that they do fill all the inhabitants of the earth with some form of religion. Wherever travellers have come, and observations have been made, among the most savage people, there is something left of some notions of religion; forms of it, though very sorry ones they be, it is acknowledged. You had need consider this, for this kind of religion is in every one of your hearts; but unless the grace of God, and the light of the gospel expel it, and plant something better in its room, you are lost for ever. Natural religion has in it these particulars.

1*st*, Some notion of the being of a God, that there is a God, and that this God is to be worshipped, and served, and obeyed. All the world own something of this. *The invisible things of him from the creation of the world are clearly seen, being understood by the things that are made, even his eternal power and God-head; so that they are without excuse*, Rom. 1:20. There is nothing more invisible than the God-head; eternal power is also invisible: but, says the apostle, the very Heathens have these things made visible by the mighty works of God; and their natural reason can instruct them so far, that the rearing up of this glorious canopy of the heavens, the frame of the earth, the making of these great seas, and the making of so many beautiful creatures upon the earth, must be the work of some great, powerful, wise agent. Atheism is against nature, and is no where found, but where the principles of natural religion are extinguished by the power of the devil, and the justice of God by men's abuse of revealed religion. When men come to struggle with the right way of the knowledge of God revealed in the word, and shut their eyes against that, God suffers them to be blinded, as to those things that the very Heathens have more light in. I believe that there are more Atheists in England, than among all the Pagan nations through the whole earth. A place where the gospel-light doth shine, and men rebel against it, is the only place where such monsters are bred.

2dly, In natural religion, there is always some distinction made about good and evil, some light about good and evil, and some conscience there is exercised about these. Conscience is as natural to us, as understanding, and will, and memory are. It is as natural to us to have a conscience, as it is to be men and women, or to have reason; for conscience is nothing else but the exercise of reason about the greatest concernments; it is only a man's judging himself, according as he stands before a greater and supreme judge. Therefore the apostle speaks thus of the Heathen: *These having not the law, are a law unto themselves: which shew*, says he, *the work of the law written in their hearts*, Rom. 2:14, 15. Pray observe, one of the grand promises of the new covenant, is God's writing his laws in our hearts. Here the apostle speaks of the law of nature, as written in the heart of a Heathen, *their conscience in the mean while*, says he, *accusing, or else excusing one another*, according to the light that they receive.

3dly, There is amongst all natural men, and a natural religion, some notion of forgiveness, and pardoning mercy and goodness in God. Amidst all their darkness about God, yet they do know, that it is a great excellency, and all excellencies they will ascribe to God, to be good and gracious, and ready to forgive. As there is a conscience of sin amongst all men, so they do give this praise to God, that he is a God that can forgive; thereupon they address to him, in their several ways, for it. All the Heathen have some sense of judgment to come; and from these principles all the fabrics of natural religion are reared up in the world. Now, where this natural religion comes to be polished by the light of the word, it will look a great deal better, and a great many are deceived by it.

What then are the grand wants and defects that are in a natural religion, which must certainly leave a man that has no more, in a condemned state?

(1.) With all their light, and all the knowledge they have of God, they do not know the true God; they do not know the God and Father of our Lord Jesus Christ, they do not know God in Christ. All gods not seen in Christ are the idols of the nations. It is a deep word that the apostle has, *For after that, in the wisdom of God, the world by wisdom knew not God, it pleased God by the foolishness of preaching to save them that believe*, 1 Cor. 1:21. All their wisdom could not bring them to know God, because they did not know God in Christ.

(2.) All natural men, whatever thoughts they may have of God's goodness in saving and forgiving, yet know nothing of God's way of doing it; and if they do not know of God's doing of it, how can they come by it? They do not know God's forgiving through a satisfaction, they do not know of God's saving men by a mediator; and a great many that hear of these things every day, seem to know it as little as they; I mean, though they subscribe to the notion, the power of the truth is as little upon their hearts as upon the Heathens. Therefore all this natural religion, that fills the nations of the earth, is nothing but a dark and dim light, a false fire that leads men into the pit, and never did lead a man to heaven; for no man can be made wise to salvation, but by the revelation of the word of God; and no man can savingly know the word of God, but by the revelation of the Spirit of God.

2. The second great religion that fills the world is Popery, as we commonly call it, Antichrist's religion. They call it the way to heaven; but the word of God calls it *the mystery of iniquity*, and the head of it, *the son of perdition*, 2 Thess. 2:3, and *man of sin*. The spirit of Popery lies in this, in inventing, devising, and imposing of false ways to heaven. All their several religions, as they call them, are but so many ways to lead people from Jesus Christ. There is a way to heaven that they propose by the merit of good works, sometimes by our own, and sometimes by those of others; there is a way to heaven by the intercession of saints or angels, thereupon they pray to them, and expect relief from them; there is a way to heaven in that pardon that they stand much upon, and that is by the absolution of a sinful priest like themselves. Really it is amazing to behold the judgment of God, that so many of the wise, and prudent, and great, of the kings, and princes, and learned of the earth, have been so long bewitched with these sorceries. They have another way to salvation which is yet worse, and more dangerous, because it comes nearer the true one; and that is, their carnal representing the true way to heaven, that is, Christ crucified. Here lies a great part of the mystery of Antichristianism. If so be that this were laid quite aside,

that Christ is the way to heaven, Christianity were firmly and in plain terms laid aside; therefore they are left to be so gross in their life to serve their design. In the mean time, Antichrist does so paint forth and represent Jesus Christ to poor people, that quite enervates and spoils all the virtue of this great contrivance of God. There is representing him by an image and picture; they worship the picture of a man extended upon the cross, and this is called by them their saviour; but the Spirit of God calls it a devil; for every image or every creature that becomes the worship of man in the stead and room of God, is called worshipping of devils, worshipping stocks, and stones, and devils. Another gross abuse of Christianity is this, that is reckoned one of their great ways to heaven; and that is, they turn the memorial of the death of our Lord, that is to be perpetually kept up in the church, into a propitiatory sacrifice for the sins of the quick and dead; besides the other abominable things that are therein, is that of transubstantiation. But that which serves my purpose is mainly the sacrifice of it. The design of our Lord Jesus in appointing his last supper was, that bread might be eaten, and wine drunk amongst believers in the churches of Christ, in the remembrance of Christ's death, till he come again; a plain naked teaching thing, and has its own signification in the institution of it. Instead of this, they have the bread turned, as they fancy, into the flesh and body of a man, and this body eaten; and this they reckon the way to eternal life, when the abuse of it is a sin, enough to damn men. But now, say you, what does all this serve for? We are neither Pagans nor Papists. But notwithstanding there is not one of you, but are in some danger this way; for, from a mixture of natural and Antichristian religion, there spring up a great many sorts of people among us.

1. There is the superstitious formalist. These are in all sorts of religion. They imagine, that because they are in the true church, therefore they shall be saved. The true church is not the way to heaven, but Christ is the way to heaven; and all that are in Christ will betake themselves to that church that is true. They commonly lay a great stress upon their outward performances and duties, and many times on the smallest.

2. There is the moralist. Would any believe it, unless they read it in books and in some men's preaching, that in such a land as England is and has been, there should be in it either man or woman, or child of

seven years of age, that should drink in this dreadful notion, that if I do justly, and do as I would be done by, I shall surely be saved? But thou shalt surely be damned, if thou dost no more. Is not this a wonder, that after all the light that has shone from the word of God about the way of salvation by the slain Son of God, that civility that is to be found amongst Heathens is all a great many have for their title to eternal life!

3. There is the self-righteous legalist; a man that goes beyond the former: he will not stint himself in the matter of his salvation, and lodge it in the form of his profession, but will bring it farther to the exercise of his conscience, and the employment of his heart about good works, about striving to please God; he is about the establishing his own righteousness, and he will find out a way to heaven for himself. Much is said against this in the word of God, and much should be daily said against it by the ministers of the word. There are some men so impatient in hearing any speak against self-righteousness, as though it were not a sin, and nobody were in danger to be ruined by it; when it is the sin that is the last strong hold of Satan, and that keeps many men in, that the word of God hath ferreted out of others. What can be the grand reason of this, that men should fall into so many fatal mistakes about the way to heaven? I do not speak of them that want the light of the word, nor of Popery; but that there should be so many of these remaining mistakes where the light of the word is, is strange. The reason is only this, the great darkness that men naturally labour under as to the way to heaven; this darkness leads men to mistake it, and to take up other ways, because they do not know the true way. Every body thinks that it is very hard to get to heaven, and it will cost a great deal of time and pains, and struggling before they get thither; but here is the mischief of it; people do not know it is hard to know the way to heaven, they are not convinced of this, that unless a beam of light shine in upon thy heart, thou mayest hear of the way to heaven all thy life long, and not know it. There is the Spirit of wisdom and revelation in the knowledge of Christ, that every one had need to pray for. I might instance a great many of the ordinary simple mistakes of people. Some do imagine, that any way that is contrary to the way to hell, is the way to heaven; a great mistake. Every sin is the way to hell, will you say, every duty is the way to heaven. Any sin may ruin a man, but nothing can save him but

Christ Jesus. Intemperance, drunkenness, etc. is the way to hell; but is there any so unreasonable as therefore to think, that soberness is the way to heaven? It is a duty, it is that which God commands of them that are in the way; and some imagine, that what every one that is in the way to heaven does, is the way. But the way to heaven still is through Christ himself; for though all this walking is to be in the way, yet walking is not the way; we are to walk in holiness, but this is but our walking in the way of Christ; none can walk in him, but they are sanctified; and the more they are sanctified, the more they partake of him. That which is reckoned a very abominable heresy amongst the Socinians, is indeed that which is very natural amongst many that would be reckoned good Christians, that our Lord Jesus Christ came to shew the way to heaven; but they do not believe, he came to be the way to heaven; they think he came to tell us the way to heaven, and to make a way for us; but they cannot understand, that he came to be the way to heaven, that we cannot get to heaven, unless we be in him. So much for the first, That the way to heaven is through the vail of the flesh of the slain Son of God. There are many in the world that are most wofully and fatally mistaken, and we may make use of our Lord's words and arguments in this point, there are few that find this way: *Broad is the way that leadeth to destruction, and many there be which go in thereat*: why so? *Because strait is the gate, and narrow is the way which leadeth unto life, and few there be that find it*, Matt. 7:13, 14.

The *second* word that I would give in application of this truth, That Christ as slain is the way to heaven, shall be in exhorting of you to take this way. Labour to be acquainted with a crucified Saviour. The apostle Paul was a better preacher than any one in England: He determined to know nothing but Christ, and him crucified, and he knew his work, he knew wherein profitable preaching lay. You must labour, I say, to be in him; see that you be in the way. This I would exhort unto, and enforce upon you in a few things, if the Lord give them force, for it is in his hand only.

1. Consider, and be serious in this matter, whether you have a mind to be in heaven or no. Sirs, ministers are deceived wofully here; we expect when we come to preach to people, and study for them, and pray for them, we expect the company has a mind to go to heaven;

but the matter is otherwise. A great part of our work is to persuade people to have a mind to be in heaven; but if you have a mind to be in heaven, have you ever been at that question, *What shall I do to be saved?* Would you pretend to be Christians, or, for God's sake, would you have any to think you Christians, that have not come this length, Oh what shall we do to be saved? Do you think, that any man will ever come to heaven, that never thought of it before he came thither? How God deals with infants, we do not know; but for persons that live under the means of grace, the salvation of folks that are mindless of salvation is impossible. God never designed it, and will never perform it. This is the first consideration. Enter into your own hearts, and think with yourselves, what an answer ye can give to so plain a question as this is, Is hell the most unholy and unhappy place of all? Is heaven the holiest and happiest place of all? Is it lovely above all other lovely things to you? Then here is the way to it: Labour to get into Christ Jesus.

2. Consider, that if you have a mind to be in heaven, you must be in that way wherein you may be safe against all that can assault you. Have you a mind in earnest to be at heaven, to be surely there? You must be in that way wherein you may be safe against all assaults from enemies; you must be found there where you shall be surely safe. This made the apostle Paul so desirous to be *found in him.* I fear nothing, if I be found in him, Phil. 3:9; found in him, there lies the business. I shall but run through, and name a few of those difficulties that you will have to encounter withal, and that you can be no way secured against, but by being in Christ as the way.

1*st*, You have the world to oppose you; and the world is too hard for any man that is out of Christ. The world has been too hard for a great many that thought themselves strong enough for it; its cunning, its wiles, its violence, its temptations, have overcome a great many. There is no overcoming the world but through him that has overcome it for us, John 16:33. We have the devil to oppose us, and we must be in that way, wherein we can be safe against him. If you be in Christ, the gates of hell shall not prevail against you: *Greater is he that is in you, than he that is in the world,* 1 John 4:4. You had need to be in that way, wherein you can give an answer to your consciences. How needful is it to have something that can stop the mouth of the most craving clamourous conscience, that can answer it satisfyingly. So that it shall speak no more? What can that can be? *The answer of a good conscience towards God, by the resurrection of Jesus Christ*, 1 Pet. 3:21. People will imagine now that the grand security is the answer of a good conscience towards God, as to our conversation, heart, and way: that indeed has its own use, and an inferior use; but when men come to reckon with conscience, truly there is nothing but the sprinkling of the blood of Jesus upon it, that can make it good. But here is more, I will not say worse, but more dreadful than all this; God's holy nature, God's holy law, God's spotless justice, they will appear against you in the way to heaven; unless you be in Christ the way, there is no standing before these. When a man is in Christ, he has a ready answer, I do not fear God's holy nature, for he hath provided a Saviour; I do not fear the law, Christ, in whom I am, has fulfilled it; I do not fear the justice of God, for Christ has satisfied that to the full. When death, judgment, and awful eternity stares a man in the face, he had need to be sure that he is in Christ. Death, that is the greatest terror to all natural men, to a believer is looked upon as overcome by Christ. This is the great comfort of a believer, I know I must die; but Christ has died, and has overcome him that had the power of death. And why should a believer be afraid of judgment, who is in the way, walking towards him who is the Judge? *We must all appear before the judgment seat of Christ*, 2 Cor. 5:10. *If any man be in Christ, he is a new creature*. Do you think a man that is in Christ, has reason to be afraid to stand before the judgment-seat of Christ? No; a believer reckons thus with himself, He that spared not his own Son, the Son that spared not his own blood, will he not give a favourable sentence in that day? And for eternity, that awful endless thing, that we can never fathom in our thoughts, the believer looks upon as a very amiable thing: This eternity that confounds other folks, to the believer is the great joy of his heart; for there, and through all the ages of it, will he be with the Lord, praising him, enjoying his company, and partaking of his fellowship. This is the second consideration. You should be sure, I say, to be in Christ the only way to heaven, where you may be safe against all you can encounter with. Whenever people come to have an awful prospect of these things, of God's holy nature, law, and justice; of death, judgment, and eternity;

when their consciences are truly awakened, all the fig-leaf coverings that men used to cover their nakedness with, are all blown off. It is only men's trifling thoughts of heaven, and of these awful things, that make Christ so much despised.

3. Consider this, what a great sin it is, how extraordinarily damnable and damning, to neglect Christ as the way to heaven; a sin, as our Lord seems to call it the only sin: *If I had not come*, says he, *and spoken unto them, they had not had sin; but now they have no cloak for their sin*. They had been an innocent kind of people, if Christ had never come amongst them: John 15:22, 24, *This is the condemnation, that light is come into the world, and men love darkness rather than light, because their deeds were evil*. Christ came into the world, lightening them in the way to heaven, and they will not make use of him. There are three most sacred things; and whosoever stumbles at any one of them, is broken in pieces, if they stumble finally at one or at all. The first is, The rich grace of God the Father, in providing the way to heaven by his Son. The second is, The blood of the Son of God, that made the way to heaven. The third is, The gracious strivings of the Spirit of grace in the gospel to bring men to walk in this way. Whoever they be that live and die under the gospel, and do not make use of Christ as the only way to heaven, they are chargeable with all these; they frustrate the grace of God; they trample upon the blood of Christ; and do violence and despite to the Spirit of grace; which are the highest expressions of wickedness that are in all the Bible, though I know the highest degree of them is applied to the grand unpardonable sin.

Lastly, Consider, that all excuses are taken off. Nothing can justify a man in refusing to betake himself to Christ as the way. The Lord has provided and framed the gospel, by which he deals with men so, that they must be rendered inexcusable, that do not embrace it, and venture on Christ offered therein. For consider, the light of nature makes men inexcusable, the light of God's law stops men's mouths, and all the world are guilty before him. The light of the gospel is also framed so, that it much more stops all men's mouths, and provides an answer for every thing. And indeed men are very fruitful in these objections: 'I am a singular sinner, therefore I dare not venture to come into Christ as the way to heaven.' What sort of an objection is this? Art thou a singular sinner? Why, Jesus Christ is a singular Saviour; let that stand against that; and his business was with sinners; he came into the world to save sinners; and all sinners that are in the world, and hear of him, should come to him for salvation, then there is a happy meeting. 'I am a vile sinful creature.' What then? We are called to come to a fountain that is opened for sin, and for uncleanness, if I may so speak. Come in filthy, and go out clean: *Come now and let us reason together, saith the Lord, though your sins be as scarlet, they shall be as white as snow; though they be red like crimson, they shall be as wool*, Isa. 1:18. What reason has God to argue thus with poor sinners? That he should reason thus with unreasonable sinners? That he should freely offer his pardoning mercy to those that are altogether undeserving of it? As if God should say, I know all that you can speak must only be from your sins; I know them better than you do; come hearken to me, take my counsel, your sins shall be no hindrance, they shall be removed quickly. But, say you now, what shall a poor creature do that would be in Christ as the way to heaven? He is sensible that he must be in him, how shall he do to get into him?

First, Be willing to be taken by him. All that are saved are begun to be saved when Christ begins to lay hold of them. The first act that is upon a sinner, is of Christ's putting forth: *That I may apprehend that*, says the apostle, *for which also I am apprehended of Christ Jesus*. I was a poor wandering creature, as if the apostle had said, one time and for a long time; but, at last, Christ laid hold of me. He remembered time, and place, and day, as long as he lived. *Believing* is sometimes denoted by the name of coming, so it be by him. Would you be acquainted with Christ Jesus, and be in him as the way? Resolve to say thus much, Though I cannot climb to Christ Jesus, and though I cannot find him; yet, by God's grace, I will not run away further from him, I will stay and long for his laying hold on me. The misery of people is this, they are constantly striving against Christ's saving of them. Whenever a poor sinner is broke as to this resolved resisting of the grace of God, grace does overpower him immediately. Be therefore willing to be taken by him.

2dly, Is it a hard matter to look on Christ Jesus and be saved? A man may look on one that he cannot come to. Look upon him as the way. If people do but get a view of Jesus Christ as the way to heaven, their hearts will follow their eyes immediately; but this eye to see him is of his own giving; and he has an eye-salve to give to make us see, as he promises, Rev. 3:18.

3dly, Love Christ as the way to heaven, and you shall be in him; nay, you are in him, when you love him. It is impossible, that a man that loves Christ Jesus, should ever go to hell; it is impossible, that ever a man can love Christ Jesus, but one that is beloved of him. But now the love of Jesus Christ, though it be the most sensible of all graces, it is very hard to own it, because believers would fain love him more and better; they cannot tell how to own they love him at all. I would ask you but one question, Can you read, and seal, and subscribe your name, and put your amen to two verses in the Bible? I dare warrant you your eternal salvation, if you can do so. The first is a dreadful word. *If any man love not the Lord Jesus Christ, let him be an Anathema Maranatha.* Amen, says the poor believer: if God curse him, it is no wonder. What! not love the Lord Jesus? The other is, Rev. 5:12, *Worthy is the Lamb that was slain, to receive power, and riches, and wisdom, and strength, and honour, and glory, and blessing.* Amen, says the believer. That heart, I say, that is taken up with the love of Christ Jesus as the way to heaven, that is bent to his praise, is one that is in him.

4thly, If you can trust Christ Jesus as the way to heaven, you are in him. Do you know what trusting is? You know what it is in matters of money and trade; it is just the same thing in matters of your salvation. Do you know in whom you have laid your great stress, of bringing you to heaven? Say to yourselves, I do not know a better hand in heaven or earth, to lodge my immortal soul in, than in Christ Jesus the Son of God. We come to him by faith, and we go on in him by trusting: *I know whom I have believed, and I am persuaded, that he is able to keep that which I have committed unto him against that day.* I know my friend, would the apostle say, and I am sure he will give a good account of all I have trusted him with, 2 Tim. 1:12.

SERMON XVIII.

HEB. 10:21, 22.

And having an high priest over the house of God: let us draw near with a true heart, in full assurance of faith, having our hearts sprinkled from an evil conscience, and our bodies washed with pure water.

APPROACHING to God is a very awful and dangerous thing. Many are undone thereby, as truly, as readily, as the poor curious priers into the ark were. There is nothing more common in people's practice, especially amongst us, than forms of approaching to God; little fear upon men's hearts in the work, and little profit by it. There is need of great encouragement unto a serious and sensible person to support his heart in drawing near to God. The prophet brings in men in distress, saying, *Wherewith shall I come before the Lord, and bow myself before the high God?* Mic. 6:6. Where the majesty of God is seen, and our own vileness seen also, it must be a great thing that can encourage such a creature as a sinner is, to approach to such a God as our God is. All the encouragements for approaching to God are in Christ Jesus, and from him; every thing that is in him is encouraging, and every thing that is revealed of him is encouraging, and there is no encouragement elsewhere to be had. Our apostle is here taking several views of Jesus Christ, with an eye to this scope, to encourage us to draw nigh to God. We have spoke to two of them already.

1. As his blood makes the entrance to the holiest. 2. As his slain body is the vail we must pass through.

We now come to the third encouragement, which is taken from Jesus Christ, with respect to his grand office of being a Priest: *Having an high-priest*, says the apostle, *over the house of God*. He doth not name who this high-priest is, neither needed he, for he had spoken so much of him before, that none that read this could doubt that this high-priest, though unnamed, is Jesus Christ our Lord.

In these words are three things I would take notice of, and speak to in order.

1. The name of the office of our Lord; he is an *High Priest*, and expressed in a singular manner. An high-priest we read it; but the word in the original is not *an high-priest* but a *great priest*. It is not the usual Greek word, that the apostle uses in this epistle frequently, when he speaks of Christ the High Priest after the order of Melchisedec, chap. 6:20, and several times in chap. 7, 8, and 9. It is a special phrase here: he is a great Priest; there is something very singular in it, something above all that we can conceive.

2. Where his charge lies. Says the apostle, He is *an High Priest over the house of God*. The house of God, in the New Testament phrase, has two proper significations. (1.) The things that pertain to God, as the apostle expresses it, Heb. 2:17, *That he might be a merciful and faithful high-priest, in things pertaining to God. Every high-priest, taken from among men*, says he, *is ordained for men, in things pertaining to God*, chap. 5:1. (2.) God's house in the New Testament, and in this epistle, is God's church and people, that is, believers. So the apostle explains it, chap. 3:6—*Whose house are we, if we hold fast the confidence, and rejoicing of the hope firm unto the end.* He is a Son and Lord over his own house; *whose house are we*, says he. So the church is called *the house of God*, 1 Tim. 3:15. Hereabout then lies the charge of our Lord as Priest; it is in things pertaining to God, for his people: this is a matter that is to be frequently and seriously minded, for it is of great use for the directing the exercise of our faith. Ye all know that our Lord Jesus, in his great work of Mediator and Redeemer, is clothed with three offices, Prophet, Priest, and King; and in two of them he deals with us from God, and in one of them he deals with God for us. As a Prophet he reveals God's mind from God to us; as a King he puts forth God's divine authority upon us, and over us, and all things else; but as a Priest our Lord's business is only with God for us. In all the exercise of our faith, the faith of a poor creature that flies to Christ for righteousness and eternal salvation, minds him mainly, in that office wherein Christ deals with God for us.

3. The *third* thing that we have in the words, is the interest that the church hath in this High Priest: *Having an High Priest*, says the apostle: the word having is not in the original, but it is necessarily supplied, to make our language run intelligible; and it relates to the former *having*,

ver. 19, *Having therefore boldness*; and here again, *Having therefore an High Priest*. He is not an high-priest to be provided, nor to be got, nor to be sought, but he is already: every one has him not; but, says the apostle, we have him already; he says he is in his office, he has done the greatest part of it, and is ready to complete it quite. So much for the heads of what I would discourse upon from this verse.

The *first* shall be to discourse to you something of the priesthood of Christ; then afterwards of the singularity of it, and charge of it, and of the interest the church hath in it.

The truth that I am to speak to is this, That our Lord Jesus Christ, as the Saviour of the body, is a true and proper Priest. So the apostle calls him, and so the apostle proves him to be at more length, and with more words in this epistle, than is any where else in all the Bible. Though this office of his be touched upon both by the prophets and by our Lord himself, and by the other apostles in other epistles, yet this epistle is principally written to shew forth the priesthood of our Lord Jesus. Concerning this I would give you a few things to be considered.

1. We must consider Christ's instalment, when and how it was that he was installed the great Priest over the house of God. He did not take this honour to himself, but was called of God as was Aaron; *He glorified not himself to be made an High Priest, but he that said to him, Thou art my Son, this day have I begotten thee*, Heb. 5:4, 5. Christ's instalment into the office is by oath: and this oath was a declaration, not only of the authority that was derived upon him, but of his continuance in it, and that he should have none to succeed him therein: *Those priests*, says the apostle, chap. 7:21, *were made without an oath, but this with an oath*: therefore is he surety of a better testament. The words of the oath consecrated and made the Son Priest, who is so for evermore. The great charge as Priest over the house of God was derived upon the Son of God in the eternal counsels of the Trinity, that in time, as soon as sin entered into the world, he should enter upon his office.

2. We are to consider the types of it; and when the truth is come, the shadows maybe the better known; we may understand better by the antitype, what the types did signify. The greatest part of God's worship of old, until Christ came, did consist in a great many shadows of Christ's coming; they are called *shadows of good things to come, but*

the body is of Christ, Heb. 10:1; they are the shadows, but not the very image of the things. Of priesthoods we find three in the word; they do all shadow forth the priesthood of our Lord Jesus.

The *first* was the patriarchal priesthood, the priesthood of the fathers; for the first word you read in all the Bible of worship to God is expressed by *sacrifice*; the first word of God's good-will towards men, is in the promise of Christ, Gen. 3:15. The first expression of worship to God is in offering sacrifice, by Cain and Abel; and it is not unlike but Adam was the priest. Adam, and Noah, and Abraham, these fathers that were acquainted with God, were all priests by office, neither of the one order, nor of the other; yet notwithstanding they were priests, and did perform sacrifice: and all these sacrifices were shadows of the grand one that was to be offered by our Lord Jesus.

The *second* is the priesthood of Aaron. There is a great deal written of it in the word; the book of Leviticus is in a manner all of this priesthood: they were distinguished into many sorts; there was a high-priest over all, that had some of the holy things to manage, which none else should meddle with; there was the common priest, that ordinary sacrifices were to be slain by, and offered up according to the law. This was a shadow of Christ's coming, of his being a sacrifice, as the apostle at length in this epistle proves.

The *third* sort of priest is that of Melchisedec, that this apostle in chap. 7, is very exact in the examining of. There are but two places in the Old Testament that speak of him, yet what great matter does the apostle draw from these two scriptures! He leaves nothing that concerns the man without a mystery. He is *Melchisedec*, he gathers a mystery out of his name; he is *king of righteousness*, he gathers a mystery out of the kingdom, that he was king of; he was *king of Salem*, that is, *king of peace*, says he; so Christ was: he gathers a grand mystery out of the scripture-silence concerning him; the scripture neither tells when he was born, nor who were his parents, nor when he died; in this, saith he, he was made like unto the Son of God, without father, without mother, having neither beginning of days nor end of life: he gathers a grand mystery out of his blessing Abraham, and out of his receiving the tithes of the spoils of Abraham; and from thence proves, that he was a great priest indeed, when he was greater than Abraham himself, when he received the tithes of Levi, that was then in Abraham's loins; and here he shews that Melchisedec was high beyond that of Aaron. Yet all this was but a type of Jesus Christ; and there is no doubt to be made but this Melchisedec was a man, and was born, and did die, and was buried like other men; but because the scripture speaks of him no otherwise, than by way of silence in these things, therefore the apostle gathers wisely from the scripture-silence, those things that were typical of our Lord Jesus.

3. We are to consider the parts of the priestly office, wherein it did consist. These we shall bring to our purpose, and to our Lord's priesthood. The parts of the priestly office were especially two; oblation and intercession, offering a sacrifice, and the making intercession in and by the virtue of that sacrifice. *Every high-priest taken from among men, says the apostle, that he may offer gifts and sacrifices, is ordained for men in things pertaining to God, that he may offer both gifts and sacrifices for sins*, chap. 5:1. *Every high-priest is ordained to offer gifts and sacrifices; wherefore it is of necessity, that this man have somewhat also to offer*. See how the apostle argues. Is Christ called a High Priest? Then he must have something to offer; the offering that the priests of Aaron offered, he could not offer, for he was sprung of the tribe of Judah, of which the Holy Ghost speaks nothing of priesthood; nay, if he were on earth, he must not be a priest, not a priest of the order of Aaron.

1*st*, Then of Christ's oblation, the sacrifice he offered was himself; the sacrifice of his own body, of his own soul: *He made his soul an offering for sin; he poured out his soul unto death*, are the Old Testament expressions of that sacrifice, Isa. 53:11, 12. Here now is the most common word in all Christianity; Christ died for us, and the very soul of Christianity lies in the believing improvement of it. The meaning of the word is, Christ died for us, Christ Jesus was offered in sacrifice to God for us; he did not die only in love for us, and he did not die only to give an example for us, and he did not die only for our good; but he *died in our stead*, he died as a sacrifice dies. The way in which the beast that was to be sacrificed died, was this; there was a transferring of the guilt of the master of him upon his head; that guilt deserved death by the law, and this death was inflicted upon the poor innocent creature; this was a shadow of that great sacrifice that the Son of God was to offer. *Neither* *by the blood of goats and calves, but by his own blood, he entered in once into the holy place, having obtained eternal redemption for us*, chap. 9:11, 12. Here we would consider, in order to the fixing and feeding our faith on this,

(1.) The vast dignity and preciousness of this sacrifice, the person who did assume this nature, that it was which raised its value and dignity infinitely; the comparison is very mean betwixt a man and a beast. The poor idolaters that fell into that dreadful blindness and wickedness, as to offer unto God the fruit of their bodies, for the sin of their souls; they did fall into that abominable wickedness upon this same principle; they thought always the more excellent the sacrifice was, the more pleasing it would be to God; if the Lord required the blood of a beast for man's sin, would he not much more be pleased with the blood of a child? *Shall I give my first-born for my transgressions?* Will not he accept of the fruit of my body for the sin of my soul? It is marvellous to think, how strong the spirit of idolatry has been in the world. What a strong desire hath there been of peace with God! What a strong sense of sin hath been in these blinded idolaters, that run into these ways of atonement! The Lord condemns them utterly, because they were all invented, he never commanded them. Now, the sacrifice is always, if commanded, the more excellent because of its native dignity. If God commanded the life of man for a sacrifice, it had been much more than that of a beast; but here the life of one that is more than a man is commanded, it is given, therefore it is of infinite dignity. You do not imagine, it may be, some of you, what you may feel before you die, even of the great difficulty of having faith firmly fixed, that the death of our Lord upon the cross, without the gates of Jerusalem, should be a sufficient atonement to God, for all the provocations that he hath received: yet in truth ye believe nothing, unless you believe that, ye believe nothing that will stand you in stead in a great storm. The man that was sacrificed was in human nature; but the divine person that assumed it, made it of infinite dignity; therefore it is called, the blood of God; *the precious blood of Christ, as of a lamb without blemish and without spot.*

2dly, This sacrifice that Christ made an oblation of, was commanded, and required; and covenanted, upon the terms of our salvation; the conditions of it were adjusted from eternity; the decree of election adjusted it, the covenant of redemption adjusted it, that when Christ should *make his soul an offering for sin, he should see his seed, he should prolong his days, and the pleasure of the Lord should prosper in his hand.* Thereupon we find, that the apostle brings Christ, as coming into the world with this, *Sacrifice and offering thou wouldst not, a body hast thou prepared me*: as if the apostle would direct us to this, that Christ's thoughts were according to that appointment: 'Father, I know, I am not coming into the world to be a priest after the order of Aaron, to offer bullocks and goats on the altar at Jerusalem; but I am to offer that body which thou hast prepared me upon the altar of my Godhead, for the satisfying thy justice, and saving thy elect.' These thoughts were in his heart.

3dly, The power that our Lord had to do it. Never had any man, no mere man, power over his own life. We have neither physical nor moral power; we can neither lay it down lawfully, when we will, nor can we keep it as long as we will; but in the keeping, and having, and losing it, we are under the law, under his appointment, and under the conduct of his word. Our Lord Jesus was the only man that had power over his own life; *I have power to lay it down, and I have power to take it again*, John 10:18.

Lastly, The last virtue and grand effect of this sacrifice is, that that should be in our eyes when we think of our Lord's priesthood, he offered a sacrifice, he gave himself a sacrifice to God of a sweet-smelling savour; the greatest things that ever were done in this world, were done by our Lord upon the cross: The law fulfilled, justice satisfied, heaven appeased, God reconciled, the world of the elect redeemed, eternal redemption brought in, salvation in God's covenant for us ratified and made unalterable by this blood. This was a great sacrifice, and great effects it had.

The *second* part of the priestly office is intercession. Intercession is nothing else but the application of the virtue of that sacrifice, according to the appointment of God. The intercession of the high-priest under the law was explained and expressed to us, by his entering with the blood of the sin-offering into the holiest of all, and anointing the corners of the mercy-seat therewith, for an atonement for all the children of Israel, that they might be cleansed from all their transgressions. Now, this was a shadow, I say, of the intercession of our great High-priest, Christ Jesus. I shall speak a little of this intercession, and consider it in three seasons.

1. Before he came into the world. 2. While in the world. 3. After he went out of it; for, in all these seasons, our Lord was a priest, and managed intercession.

1. Before he came into the world. Pray observe, we touched a little upon Christ's being installed in the office of high-priest. There could be no exercise of this office, till there were sinners; what use could a priest be of, till there were sinners, and some elect sinners in the world? We hope in God, the first pair that lived in it were of that number, I mean our first parents. Pray observe this, all the salvation, and pardon of sin, and entrance to heaven, that was given to the fathers before Christ came, was all given in the view, and in the virtue of the death of our Lord, who was to die once for sin. Abel, Enoch, Noah, and all the saints of old, had their peace with God, those large measures of the love and favour of God and salvation in the end dispensed to them, through the virtue of the sacrifice of Christ not yet offered. The Father trusted his Son firmly, that in the fulness of time he would pay the debt. The discharge is given before the payment, the discharge is given to the criminal before the payment is made by the surety. The believers before Christ came, looked to him as come; and according to that small light that they had in that time, so was their faith. Now, if salvation and all spiritual blessing were given to believers before Christ's coming, before he was in the flesh, we may well conceive, that the intercession, which was a part of his office, and which he was to discharge in heaven, was not unminded by him.

2. When he was in the world, when he was in the flesh, we find he was greatly given to prayer. We find him spending several nights alone in prayer to God. Were it lawful to wish, and may be it is not; but surely, if it had been lawful to wish it, and if it had been attained, and if grace had been given to guide it, the most happy opportunity that ever was in the world, had been to have heard our Lord Jesus praying a whole night to the Father. The scripture does not tell us what he prayed for; but we are sure of this, that he prayed for his sheep: *I pray not for*

the world, but for them which thou hast given me; for they are thine, John 17:9. Somewhat our Lord used to utter, and to pour forth his heart to his Father about. Many prayers he put up for himself; Christ made no sacrifice for himself, but he put up many prayers for himself: *Who in the days of his flesh, when he had offered up prayers and supplications, with strong crying and tears, unto him that was able to save him from death, and he was heard, in that he feared*, Heb. 5:7.

3. The *third* season is, Christ's intercession in heaven, when he went out of the world into his exalted state; and that is the word most commonly used in the scriptures about his intercession. His intercession is frequently both in the Old and New Testament subjoined to his sacrifice; *He hath poured out his soul unto death: And he was numbered with the transgressors, and he bare the sins of many, and made intercession for the transgressors*, Isa. 53:12. *It is Christ that died, yea rather, that is risen again, who is even at the right hand of God, who also maketh intercession for us*, Rom. 8:34. *He ever liveth to make intercession*, Heb. 7:25. Of this intercession of our Lord, as managed in his exalted state, we find several expressions in the scripture, and I choose rather, and will advise you accordingly to confine your thoughts to scripture phrase, about these things, wherein we may overdo, and overthink, and think amiss.

1*st*, His intercession stands in his entering into heaven in our name, and in our room. See how the apostle expresses it, Heb. 9:12, 24. The most glorious, the most powerful entrance, the stateliest thing that we can imagine next to his return again, was when a slain, quickened, ascended Lord Jesus in man's nature entered into the heavenly places; not the *places made with hands, but into heaven itself*, says the apostle. As long as he is there we are there, for all his people's cases will be minded effectually.

2*dly*, It is called appearing before God for us; not only entering in our name, but staying there on our behalf, for our good. To this purpose seems the word of our Lord to point: *The spirit shall convince the world of righteousness*; why so? *Because I go to my Father, and ye see me no more*, John 16:10. This is a dark expression, *I go to my Father, and ye see me no more*. The meaning of it is plainly this, that the certainty of our justification by the virtue of the righteousness of Jesus Christ stands in this, that the person whose blood wrought out this righteousness is gone into heaven, and is not returned again. Pray observe, the high-priest under the law was to go in, and to accomplish righteousness for the atoning of God's anger against Israel, in the seventh month once; and he was to come out again, the poor man was not to stay there: but our grand High-priest is to stay for ever in heaven, until all the virtue of his death is fully applied to them that it was appointed for: when all that is done, then he comes out of his throne, in the clouds to gather all his people.

3dly, His intercession is expressed to us by his knowledge and sympathy with the ails, wants, and infirmities of his people. So the apostle argues, *Seeing then that we have a great High-priest, that is passed into the heavens, Jesus the Son of God, let us hold fast our profession*, Heb. 4:14. But, might the poor believer say, Our dear Lord is passed into heaven, and we are here in this miserable world; how shall there be converse betwixt him and us? *We have not*, says he, *an high-priest which cannot be touched with the feeling of our infirmities; but was in all points tempted like as we are, yet without sin*, ver. 15. Pray observe, that of the apostle's argument, the main thing is implied, the other things are but the outside of it. The thing that is the outside, is, Christ was once tempted as we are; the apostle's argument from thence is, Therefore we have an high-priest that can be touched with the feeling of our infirmities; but the force and scope of it is, for our consolation, that he is *touched* with them. What his glorified state does admit of, is what we cannot conceive of, but what our necessities crave, our faith is allowed to expect. Our Lord will not cry and weep at Lazarus's grave now; he will not grieve in himself, because of the hardness and unbelief of their hearts, as he did when on earth; he does not bear our infirmities, nor feel them with that afflicting sense and sorrow that he had in the days of his flesh; but every thing that ails a poor believer, is as well felt and as really known by our Lord Jesus, as if Christ and the man were in one place and room together.

Lastly, His intercession stands in blessing, and wishing well. These wishes and this blessing rise upward to the Father, and come downwards to us; he wishes as it were, he wishes and wills that all the blessings purchased by his death may be bestowed on all them for whom his blood was shed. See how he expresses it in his intercession on earth, how he prays, *Father, I will, that they also whom thou hast given me, be with me where I am*, John 17:24. Is that a word for a man in prayer to say, *Lord, I will?* You see how in some cases our Lord with the deepest humility addresses to the Father, *I thank thee, O Father, Lord of heaven and earth*, Matt. 11:25. But here now, when he is giving us a copy of his intercession, and is fore-acting his intercession in heaven, he puts on the authority that in his glorified state he is fully clothed with: *I will, that they also whom thou hast given me, be with me where I am; that they may behold my glory which thou hast given me.* Christ's blessing of his people is the virtue of his intercession; when his wishes as it were, and his will is delivered to his Father, then the blessing wished for comes down upon us. The last thing our Lord did on earth should be dear to us, to think how Christ and his people parted; he lifted up his hands and blessed them, that they might remember him as long as they lived. Christ came into the world to bless his people, and died to obtain a blessing; and when he went to heaven, he left his blessing upon them; and it was the last thing he did upon earth.

Application. Is Christ a proper priest, a true priest? 1. Be very thankful to God for this provision, that we have an high-priest. 2. Be careful to make use of him.

1. Be highly thankful to God for Christ, as a High-priest. The provision made is absolutely needful, no dealing with God but by him. It is provision that is made in mere grace and mercy; nothing is in us to move God to it but mere mercy. It is provision that is made very costly. To be a high-priest cost our Lord a great deal: *he made himself of no reputation, and took on him the form of a servant, and became obedient unto death, even the death of the cross*, Phil. 2:7, 8. It is however such a provision as brought a great deal of honour to Christ: *he glorified not himself, to be made an high-priest*, but his Father glorified him; this is a very strange word, Heb. 5:5. This high-priest was to be made a sacrifice; was there any great glory in being made a sacrifice? To be made sin, to be made a curse, to be made shame, to be made, as it were, the channel of the wrath and displeasure of God, for all the sins of the people of God; where is the honour of all this? But look through this; there is grand honour, he is to be the reconciler of all things to God, the great umpire of heaven and earth, the great purchaser of eternal salvation for all the elect. The condescension and lowness that our Lord stooped to in undertaking

this office, had great dignity in it; and so it appears in the issue, and will appear more when all is done.

2. Be careful to use Christ as an High-priest. Wo to them that do not know Christ; but a great deal more wo to them that know any thing of him, and do not make use of him. Every believer hath need of every thing that Christ has to give. Christ's fulness was never so laid open before the eyes of a believer, but the more he sees Christ hath, the more the man is convinced of his need of every thing he sees. In this using of Christ as an High-priest, only take notice of these two particulars:—

1st, Never deal with God without him in any thing. It is only the pride, and ignorance, and folly of the children of men, that they dare venture into God's presence without Christ Jesus. An understanding believer cannot do so. He dares not come into God's presence, but in the hand of this great high-priest, and with him upon his heart. Do not offer, I say, in any concern, to deal with God without this high-priest. Judge ye what would have been done in the state of the church of the Jews, if any man had brought his sacrifice to the altar, and laid his own hands upon it, and said, This sacrifice is mine, and I will be priest myself. That soul had been cut off from amongst his people. This was but typical of the severe charge we lie under. In all things that pertain to God, we must still bring Christ along with us. I will name some of those things that we must not deal with God in without him, and that we must deal with God by him, and with him.

(1.) When we draw nigh to God for the acceptance of our persons, and obtaining peace with God; this must be by our great High-priest, for it is in the beloved only that we are accepted, Eph. 1:6. It is in his Son only that he is well pleased. If ever you think to bring that to God that may make him love you, or that will render you lovely in his sight without Christ Jesus, you will find yourselves dreadfully mistaken, when it comes to the issue.

(2.) In all the offerings of service to him, let them be all by the hand of this High-priest. If you pray, pray in his name, and not in your own; if you offer the sacrifice of praise, do it by him: *By him let us offer the sacrifice of thanksgiving.* Whatever you do, do all in the name of the Lord Jesus. This great high-priest must receive all our services and sacrifices, and he only must present them, if ever they be accepted, Heb. 13:15.

(3.) In all your expectations of good from God; let all those expectations be through Christ, if there be any looking and working of heart, as there will be if you be believers, in begging something, and looking for somewhat. There is no Christian that is exercised in begging much, but that poor creature will find some expectation and hope rising, that there shall be an answer of peace, there will come some good, some blessing will be returned. Now, take heed of this in all these expectations, let the answer of them all be through Christ.

In sum, The eyes of a believer are to be fixed on Christ, in all his dealings with God (if I may divide them so, and this dividing is but uniting the eyes of faith that are fixed on Christ). The one eye is to be set on his oblation, and the other on his intercession; and when your eyes are fixed, serve God as painfully, and expect as highly as you please; ask as largely, and expect as confidently according to his word. Then your eyes are singly upon this high-priest set over the house of God when your hearts bear you witness; and you are persuaded in yourselves, that there is nothing in you, nothing done by you, that can ever turn to a good account in God's sight, unless this great High-priest put incense thereto, and obtain acceptance from God for you.

SERMON XIX.

HEB. 10:21.

Having an high priest over the house of God.

THE apostle pressing the great duty of drawing near to God, presses it from mighty arguments. The strength and multitude of the arguments are so many implied proofs of the backwardness of our hearts unto this great work, and of their great indisposition for it. His arguments, as you have heard, are all taken from Jesus Christ, concerning whom the apostle speaks and holds forth the mysteries of the gospel, under the vail of the expressions of the law; that, by the blood of our Lord, access with boldness is made unto the holiest; that through the vail of his flesh, that is, him as slain, we have a new and living way consecrated for us.

The third encouragement is, That this Jesus is a great Priest over the house of God. There was no approaching to God's worship under the law but by the priests; the altar was not to be approached to, nor sacrifice to be offered by any hand but that of the priests; the holiest of all was not to be approached but only by the high-priest. This the apostle here alludes to: We have, saith he, an High Priest over the house of God. All the Jewish priests, all of the order of Aaron are removed, and the use of the temple is removed also, and all the service and ceremonies that belonged to it, are removed also: but the substance that they all signified we have; we have Christ as an High Priest over the house of God. From this argument for our encouragement, that the apostle here gives us, I did take up three things to be spoke to in order.

1. The office of our Lord Jesus, that though he be not named, yet he is named immediately before and quickly after, and all the apostle's discourse was of him: therefore there was no hazard of any man's mistaking; when the apostle named the High Priest, every Christian would understand whom he meant.

2. We have the extent of his charge in his office; *it is over the house of God.*

3. We have the church's interest in him: *Having an High Priest.* It is true, that word in the original is wanting, which is to be drawn from the preceding verse; but it is necessarily implied; this is certain in the sense of it, we have an High Priest.

Of the first of these, Christ's office, I spake last day, That our Lord Jesus Christ, in the great work of saving of men, was and is a true and proper Priest. I spake both of his instalment in his office, of the types and shadows of his office, and the parts of his office in the oblation that he made, and in the intercession that he doth daily make, for our Lord is about part of his priestly office now. These things I did speak to, and entered a little upon the application thereof.

Now it remains to take a little further notice of a word I observed to you before, because it is singular, I would not pass it, but speak something to it apart. The note is this, That our Lord Jesus Christ is a great Priest. I told you that this word that we read here in our translation *an High Priest*, is not the ordinary Greek word by which the high-priest is expressed; but it is a singular word, very different what we find in other places of scripture, *a great Priest*. There is something singular to be observed in every iota, in the smallest particle of the word of God. This then is that that I would speak to, what is pointed forth to us about Christ's priesthood, when he is called *a great Priest*.

1. He is a great Priest, because he is a great person. He is God's own Son, God's own equal. Though he be man, and conversed among men, the person is more than man, he is God. If we therefore consider this, that this Priest, Christ Jesus, is God, he must be a great one. The greatest priests that ever were in the world were men. Melchisedec was certainly a man, though we know nothing of his pedigree; the Holy Ghost conceal it, and makes good use of that concealment, he being the grand type of the priesthood of Jesus Christ.

2. Our Lord Jesus is a great Priest, for, by the virtue of his priesthood, he makes all whom he undertakes for priests: *For he hath made us kings and priests unto God and his Father*, Rev. 1:6. *He hath made us kings and priests unto God*, Rev. 5:10. *Ye are an holy priesthood*, 1 Pet. 2:5, 9. These things I pass, as not conceiving them to be of so much importance at present.

3. Then and mainly Christ is a great Priest, because of his greatness in his office, or the greatness of the office he was clothed with. A proper priest as under the law, was a sort of mediator betwixt God and men; and this mediation was most eminently and solemnly acted and performed in the great day of atonement, when the high-priest entered into the holiest of all in the name of all Israel, and with their names upon his breast; never a one of them upon pain of death must follow him; he brought back the answer of peace from God to them. Our Lord is a greater High Priest; Israel's fate depended on his welcome in the holiest of all, upon the account of a far greater office than this. Let us consider, for the shewing of the greatness of the office of Christ as High Priest,

1st, The greatness of the parties he deals betwixt: he deals betwixt God and creatures; that is great, but there is a great deal more; he deals betwixt an angry God and provoking sinners. That is Christ's work, I say, that he is a mediator bewixt God and men, the man Christ Jesus;

a work that never any was fit for, and never any called to, but he alone. They were but little inferior shadows that were acted by some of the saints of old. We find indeed in the Old Testament (and there is no reason to question, but some may be again in the New, in our days), that some have stood, by faith and prayer, betwixt the dead and the living, and stayed the plague; that when God hath been angry, and his anger hath begun to burn, some of his servants have stood in the breach before him to turn his anger away, Psa. 106:23. That is recorded to the praise of Moses, *Therefore he said that he would destroy them, had not Moses his chosen stood before him in the breach, to turn away his wrath, lest he should destroy them.* If I may so speak, there was but temporal anger, and a temporal judgment threatened, and a temporal mediator, and a temporal mercy obtained; but the mercy is far otherwise here, Christ undertakes as Priest betwixt these two great parties, an offended God and a sinful people.

2*dly*, His greatness in his office appears in the great work he doth in it; and that is, to reconcile both, to make up the peace: *We are reconciled to God by the death of his Son*, Rom. 5:10. *Therefore being justified by his blood, we are reconciled to God by the blood of his cross*, Col 1:20. What a marvellous way was this, the taking up this controversy, that this great High Priest's undertaking in this manner should bring about, which otherwise was utterly impossible!

3*dly*, His greatness in his office appears in the greatness of the sacrifice that he offered; he offered himself; but who knows the value and worth of that *self? He gave himself a ransom for all*, 1 Tim. 2:6. Immediately after that he had said, that *there is one God, and one mediator betwixt God and men, the man Christ Jesus.* Sirs, the people that lived when Christ was in the world, and saw him, and heard him preach, that saw him eat and drink, the greatest part of them thought with themselves they saw no more but a man; they could not see through the vail of his flesh, to see who dwelt in that temple; yet there were a few that did see: *The Word was made flesh, and we beheld his glory; the glory as of the only begotten of the Father, full of grace and truth*, John 1:14. The sacrifice that Christ offered was himself; thereupon the apostle prefers him greatly unto all the priests of old; for it was but the blood of bulls, or calves, or goats, of creatures meaner and lower than themselves, that they offered in sacrifice to God; but our Lord Jesus Christ becomes a greater Priest by a greater offering. Nothing but the human nature of Christ could be the sacrifice; there was more than the man Christ that was the priest: *He offered himself up to God through the eternal Spirit without spot*, Heb. 9:14. I would be loath to draw people's imaginations unto the knowing of Christ after the flesh: but whosoever he be that believeth not that Jesus is come in the flesh, is a man not born of God. We must know Christ's flesh, we must know the sacrifice, and what made it to be so great. If Christ had been only a man, his blood had been no more than the blood of another man, only because it was a sinless man, that made it better: as we may say of the sacrifices that were offered to the praise and service of God, by the blood and sufferings of many witnesses of Jesus, they are called sacrifices in the word; but there is nothing of priesthood here, they are not sacrifices of atonement nor propitiation, they are but sacrifices of praise and testimony. The great view that we have, and that our faith should feed on about the sacrifice of our Lord, is this, That there was a piece of man's nature, by the extraordinary operation of the Holy Ghost, framed in the womb of the virgin, and which was assumed by the Son of God, and made the temple wherein God dwelt; there dwelled the fulness of the Godhead bodily; it is this temple of his body that was the great sacrifice, to which all the worship, and trust, and adoration of his people was rightly directed. For it is certain, that if our Lord Jesus Christ were in his human nature on earth, he in that nature is to be immediately, and formally, and directly adored and worshipped; they are never reproved that did so. When he was in his low estate, the poor woman fell down and worshipped him, crying, *Lord, help me*, Matt. 15:25. Christ never found fault with that; but when any poor believers, in the height of their zeal or respect, either to apostles or angels, did so, they were checked immediately: *Stand up*, said Peter to the centurion, *I myself also am a man*, Acts 10:26. *See thou do it not*, says the angel, *I am thy fellow-servant, and of thy brethren*, Rev. 19:10 and 22:9.

Lastly, Christ's greatness in his office appears in the great glory that accrues to him in it, and by it.

(1.) He in and by this office is made the head of the new creation; Christ is made the head of the new world. As God equal with the Father, and as the eternal Word of God, he made all things, and without him was nothing made that was made; by him were created all things, both angels, and principalities, and powers, all things were created by him and for him, Col. 1:15, 16. But now, if I may so speak, there hath entered one thing into the world, that hath marred all the creation; that is sin: Our Lord came to repair this with advantage. For be persuaded of it, that unless the Lord had contrived to have brought more glory to his name by sin's entrance into the world, than its entrance could bring dishonour to him, it had never entered: for he does all things for himself; and the very permitting of sin was an act of infinite wisdom in God, willing his own glory; and by Jesus Christ, as the great High Priest, is this end reached; he is made the head of the whole creation; all things are reconciled, all things are set to rights in him, all things are to be gathered together unto an head in him as the head.

(2.) There is this glory to our Lord as Priest, that makes him a great one, that the everlasting salvation of all the elect and redeemed is purchased by him. What an unspeakable honour is this? He is the proper cause of the salvation of all that are saved; he becomes the captain, head, and author of our salvation: He is *the author of eternal salvation*, Heb. 5:9. *He hath obtained eternal redemption for us*, Heb. 9:12. This I would consider a little more particularly, namely, the glory that comes to our great High Priest, by his being the author of eternal salvation.

[1.] We find that all faith in approaches to God is to be made through him; all acts of trust Godward are to be made through him: *No man cometh to the Father but by him. He saves them that come unto God by him*, Heb. 7:25. *By him we believe in God, that raised him from the dead, and gave him glory*, 1 Peter 1:21. This is proper divine honour to be a mean of peace with God; and that person that is the mean of approaching to God, and that is the object of our faith, is always divine. We can approach to God by no creature, it is an honour too big for them: but we may approach to God by Christ Jesus, for the Father hath consecrated him in this station: *He suffered the just for the unjust, that he might bring us to God*, 1 Peter 3:18.

[2.] All the gracious communications that are betwixt God and men, is all through this great High Priest. This is his glory, this makes him a great one. All the gracious communications and fellowship, either of God's giving to us, or our returning again to him, are all through this great High Priest; the communications, and blessings, and privileges to us, and the return of praise to God again, are all through Christ.

(i.) The communications that are from God to us, do all come from Christ. If you receive them, you know which way they come, for they taste of the channel.

(*a.*) Our justification. This is by the redemption that is in Christ Jesus, Rom. 3:24. Whenever a sinner stands accepted before God, that state of acceptance is owing to this great High Priest; if God look graciously upon him, if we may stand with confidence in his presence, it is all through Jesus Christ.

(*b.*) Our sanctification is by the Spirit of Jesus. Whenever sanctification is begun, Christ is formed within; whenever sanctification goes on, conformity to Christ is advanced, and we are going on towards perfection. What is perfect holiness, but only conformity to the image of his Son? And to this the Lord hath predestinated all his chosen, Rom. 8:29.

(*c.*) Our adoption is through this great Priest also: *He hath redeemed them that were under the law, that they might receive the adoption of sons*, Gal. 4:5.

(*d.*) Our perseverance is only owing to Christ's grace and power. He is able to make us stand, and he will make us stand. See what the apostle says concerning the poor weak tottering Christian, that is weak in the faith, Rom. 14:4. Our supports and encouragements under all our temptations and difficulties are owing to Christ; and eternal glory at last is owing to him also; he purchased it for us, he hath possessed it in our room, and receives us to himself at last; *that where he is, there we may be also*, as his own words are. So,

(ii.) Is it as to all returns of service unto God again. These are all to the honour of our great High Priest; that as God dispenses all his good-will and favour through Christ, we are to return all service and worship to God in him. This I would explain to you in these things:—

(*a.*) That all the adoration, and worship, and obedience, and service, call them by what name you will, that is now given by Christians, is given at the command of our Lord Jesus. We must take this great High Priest's will as the rule of our worship. *So the Lord hath commanded*, is enough for a Christian's conscience; and where the Lord hath not commanded, no tender conscience will act. Let men talk what they will, let the authority of men, either of churchmen or statesmen, work as they will, if they be in matters of the worship of God, our great High Priest must command it, or we dare not do it. It had been a great deal better for the interest of Christ's church in the earth, if the great High Priest had been better consulted. *Consider*, says the apostle, *the High Priest and Apostle of our profession*. How many names hath the Lord Jesus Christ in the word? He is called the Apostle and the High Priest of our profession; he is the Lord our righteousness. We must profess nothing but what he enjoins, believe nothing but what he reveals, do nothing but what he commands.

(*b*.) Not only must all worship, and service, and obedience, be done as obedience to him, but it must be all done in his name; that is more, not only at his command, but in his name. If we pray, it is in the name of our Lord Jesus Christ, John 14:13. If we offer up spiritual sacrifices unto God, it is by Christ our great High Priest, that we are to offer them, Heb. 13:15. To offer worship to God in the name of Christ, is another sort of business than people commonly imagine; it is to set about the performance with an eye to the great undertaking of this great High Priest.

(*c*.) It tends to his glory not a little, that the eternal praises of the saints in heaven will all depend, and border, and rest upon this great Priest our Lord Jesus; that when the heirs of glory are come to the possession of the inheritance that is purchased for them, the praise of this grace will be eternally sung by them. That song in Rev. 5:9, 11, is a song of praise to this great Priest, *Worthy is the Lamb that was slain, to receive power, and riches, and wisdom, and strength, and honour, and glory, and blessing. Thou hast redeemed us to God by thy blood*, says he. Must not then Christ be a great Priest, when all the salvation that is dispensed on earth is all owing to him, and all the praise that will be given in heaven will be all paid to him? Thereupon the apostle hath that word, 2 Thess. 1:17. *When he shall come* (speaking of our Lord's second coming), *to be glorified in his saints*. The greatness of Christ's priesthood will never appear so fully, as when the whole virtue of his sacrifice shall be seen, when all the heirs that his blood has bought shall appear together, and all the glory and the possessors thereof.

Application. Our Lord Jesus is a great Priest. 1. Then let him be great in your eye. He is great in himself, great in his office, great in his Father's eye; let him be also great in yours. Low and common, and mean thoughts of Christ are very ordinary, and very sinful. If people would take the apostle's exhortation, Heb. 3:1, *Consider the High Priest of our profession*; if people would take a more near and close view of Jesus Christ in his office of a priest, what a beautiful sight would they see? Christ always rises in men's esteem, according as he is bright or dark in their eyes. Every man esteems Christ highly, that knows him clearly. It is impossible, but the beams of the saving discovery of Christ must imprint upon the soul unspeakable apprehensions of his greatness and value. See how the apostle speaks of him; that very word is enough to make one have high thoughts of Christ, if they were heard by faith: Heb. 1:2, 3, *God—hath in these last days spoken unto us by his Son, whom he hath appointed heir of all things, by whom also he made the worlds. Who being the brightness of his glory, and the express image of his person, and upholding all things by the word of his power.* Must not this be a great person now, that is the very brightness of the Father's glory? that is, another person, but the same God? and exactly like him? What does this great one now? He upholds all things by the word of his power; he made all things of nothing in the beginning, and, by the same word of power, keeps all things from dropping again into nothing. What more stately can be said in the word of the divine dignity of his person? Now, in the next word, he comes to speak of his office, *when he had by himself purged our sins.* How marvellous was it so great a person should come down for so mean and sordid an employment as to purge our sins? A prince removing dung from his own stable is a mean thing in regard of this: he did not commit this great work to another, but he did it himself; he purged our sins by himself, that is, himself offered in sacrifice for sins.

2. Have a care that you make use of Jesus Christ as a great Priest.

1*st*, Bind this matter upon your consciences, that the greatest sin, or the greatest duty, that is committed or performed by men, lies here. The greatest sin is not improving Christ, the greatest duty is using him in that station the Father hath set him in. *See*, says the apostle, *that ye refuse not him that speaketh*, Heb. 12:25. Pray, observe what the connection is. *Ye are come*, saith he, *unto Jesus the Mediator of the new covenant, and to the blood of sprinkling, that speaketh better things than that of Abel. See then that ye refuse not him that speaketh*, Heb. 12:24. If Christ come to speak to you as a Priest, if Christ come to you by his blood; take heed, that you refuse not him that speaketh: there is no escaping, if you turn away from him that speaketh from heaven.

2dly, As you would be careful to make use of Christ as a Priest to you, so you should learn to do it confidently. We shall have further occasion to speak of the confidence of faith which is allowed, in the next verse; yet I would not pass it now, when it is so needful to speak of this great duty, this great grace of making use of and improving of this great Priest. It should be done with confidence.

1. With confidence as to the greatness of his office, and the sufficiency of his sacrifice. Lay that down and settle upon it, whenever you come to act faith on Christ for the pardon of your sins, and bringing you into the favour of God. Remember, you come before God in the name of a High Priest, whose sacrifice is great. There are many great objections that hinder confidence: I will name a few of them, and I will tell you where their answer only lies. You may try and search for other answers, and the answers may please sometimes for a little while.

The first objection is this, 'Shall I draw near to God? I have to do with a great God.' So you have; in all your dealings with God about salvation, you have to do with a great God; his majesty when it is discovered, unless Christ be discovered also, is one of the grandest shakings of faith: *Wo is me*, saith Isaiah, *I have seen the holy one of Israel.*

The second objection is, 'I am a great sinner.'

The third is, 'That the law is a great and awful law, that I am to answer to.'

All this is true. What shall a man do with this? Will God grow less, will the law be unbinded, or thy sin removed? No; they stand all as they are, an infinitely great God, a vile guilty sinner, a righteous holy law, that cannot be defeated.

The only answer is here, if I have a great God to deal with, and if I am a great sinner, and if a great law to reckon with; I have a great

High priest, and I can set this alone against all these; he is a High Priest whose sacrifice is of a sweet-smelling savour before the great God; the virtue of it cleanseth sin, and the virtue of it fulfils the law. The apostle therefore, when he is giving the grand foundations of a Christian's faith, lodges it all upon this great High Priest: *Who shall lay any thing to the charge of God's elect? It is God that justifieth.* But how can God justify? *It is Christ that died,* says he, *yea rather, that is risen again, who is even at the right hand of God, who also maketh intercession for us.* His dying is the oblation of this great High Priest, his rising again is the application thereof, Rom 8:33, 34.

2. In your making use of Christ as High Priest betwixt God and you, you must do it not only with confidence of the worth and virtue of the sacrifice, but with confidence as to your right to make use of it. Here is a common deceit that Satan hinders the peace of many a poor Christian by; the greater our shame; his cunning is not so great as our folly is great. The common thought of men is this, there is no doubt, but that Christ is a great Priest, and that his sacrifice is a great sacrifice, happy are they that have the virtue of it; but what right have I to make use of it. The meaning of this question, What right have I? is commonly this, May I adventure upon it without sin? This is undeniable that thou mayest; for there are these three things I would lay before you:—

(1.) God commands thee, whoever thou art, to deal with him about salvation. Pray lay down this for a conclusion; it is the certain revealed mind and will of God, that every man and woman, how great sinners soever they be, should deal with him about their salvation. God never allows men to run to hell, neither in security, nor in despair; but he proclaims his displeasure against those that do either way. If men run to hell sleeping or roaring, and depart from God with a tormenting conscience, they are both condemned justly. This then is a principle, that is some way befriended by the light of nature, the only true God commands me in his word to deal with him about salvation; and since his patience has kept me out of hell, he allows me to lay hold of his grace, for the preventing of that dreadful ruin.

(2.) God forbids thee to deal with him about salvation in any other name, but in Christ's name. That is as plain as the other. As God would have men mind their salvation, and glorify him in seeking for it from him; so he forbids them expressly, to come about salvation in any name but Christ's: *There is no salvation in any other: for there is none other name under heaven given among men whereby we must be saved,* Acts 4:12. There are two things that are pretty plain: God commands us to deal with him about salvation, and not to go to hell quietly and tamely; and he forbids us to deal with him about salvation in any name but Christ's.

(3.) He has revealed and set forth Christ Jesus unto men in the gospel to be thus made use of: Rom. 3:25, *Whom God hath set forth to be a propitiation, through faith in his blood.* As really as the brazen serpent was erected upon the pole, that the stung Israelites might look and live; so truly is Christ Jesus held forth in the gospel, that every man that has a mind to salvation may look to him and get it. All men that live where the gospel is preached have alike right to believe on Christ Jesus; no man has a right in Christ, till he is a believer. There are secret purposes and thoughts in God's heart where to apply his grace; but in the public dispensations of it, all men are alike afar off, and all have alike equal right to believe. There is not a poor creature upon the face of the earth, that lives where the gospel is preached, but he has as much right to believe on Christ for the salvation of his soul, as Saul had when he went to Damascus. Indeed an actual right follows faith. Does God command you to treat about salvation with him? doth he forbid thee to treat in any other, but in Christ's name? hath he revealed Christ Jesus in the gospel, for this end to be made use of? How can the devil prevail with any creature ever to fall into this dreadful imagination, I am afraid God will be angry, if I should venture the burden of my lost soul upon Christ Jesus? Be ye persuaded of it, that murder and adultery, and the greatest abominations, are not more displeasing, by virtue of that command of the law, than a bare not improving of the Son of God for salvation, is by virtue of the gospel. This is the condemnation, this is that which sends multitudes of poor sinners to hell, if I may so speak; it sends more to hell in London, than all the profaneness in the midst of us; and until the power of the gospel be sent more into the hearts of the people; these open sorts of profaneness will never be destroyed. This confidence is so far from pride, that it is a great act of humility; and it is only the pride of men's hearts that hinders this confidence; they are unwilling to cast themselves upon this plea alone, to intrust the whole burden of their salvation upon this great Priest alone; that is the way to make all miscarry.

3dly, Make use of this great High Priest entirely in all things, in all things wherein you need him, in all things wherein he may be useful to you. We must use our High Priest about our good things, as well as about our bad. A great many poor creatures are so ignorant, I hope some may be Christians that are so ignorant, but this may be, and it is certain with many of them, that whenever they come to treat with God about their sin, then they know they must treat with him by Christ Jesus; but when they treat with God about their services, and when they present their grace, and faith, and repentance, and love, and worship, they do not see so much need of the High Priest. If you make right use of Christ as the High Priest over the house of God, remember this, that you must use him as really, as humbly, as entirely, in presenting your good works to God for acceptance, as in pleading for pardon for your bad ones.

4thly, Make use of Christ as a High Priest constantly. There may be such a weakness amongst some believers, that they think, that when they began first upon godliness, they stood in need daily of the High Priest, they are weak and feeble: but after they have got a great deal of experience, they hope that that experience and the means of grace may do pretty well with them. And that is the reason, why so many do so very ill. No Christian can ever outlive the necessity of employing Christ as High Priest in all the steps of his life; and in the last step through death we must still lean upon this High Priest; we go by our High Priest within the vail, leaning and going through the vail of his flesh. And truly I am afraid, the Lord prevent it in you mercifully and graciously, there are many worse things to be afraid of; I am afraid of some Christians, that their best acts of faith on Christ Jesus are at their last, that their believing through the course of their pilgrimage is a little mingled and mixed with something of themselves; and when they come to the awful and dreadful step, and look death and judgment in the face, then they throw all away to the moles and bats; then their renouncing their own righteousness is no great business to a believer.

Lastly, Use him delightfully, use him with pleasure. Sirs, the constraint of conscience is good where there can be no better: but I would lead you to a better constraint, and that is the constraint of love: *The love of Christ constrains me*, says the apostle, *to live to him*. There is no man ever will be in heaven, but he that loves heaven, and no man walks in the way to heaven, but he that loves that way. There is a perverse love of heaven, and a mistaken love of the way to it; and if people would examine their hearts, and find the matter thus with them, I may say, in a word, there is a determination about your state. A Christian loves heaven because Christ is there, and there he is seen and enjoyed; and a Christian loves the way to heaven, because it all lies through Christ: *I live by the faith of the Son of God, who loved me, and gave himself for me*. The virtue of the sacrifice, giving himself for me, is the very strength of my life; whenever I would be recovered, and refreshed, and strengthened, I take a meal by faith of this love, and of his giving himself for me, and do it delightfully. I know that there is something of the new nature, that does prompt every believer to some spiritual pleasure in all actings of faith; but sometimes this is not so very remarkable. Says the apostle, *Ye fled for refuge to lay hold on the hope set before you*. Great dangers constrain people in a manner to take the first way of escape; but the believer comes to see what a glorious refuge Christ is, that not only is he a sure defence, but a glorious habitation; he blesses the danger that drove him, as well as the grace that welcomes him; he in a manner blesses the disease, that hath sent him to so sweet a physician. A great many make use of Christ as a Priest, when they cannot help themselves otherwise. Let it be your thought, If there were a possibility of doing my matters with God about salvation, otherwise than by Jesus Christ, I would renounce them all, and take Jesus Christ. But this is the only way; it should be as our meat and drink. Believing on the Son of God, will never be strongly done till delightfully done. When the weary traveller casts himself with delight, as well as with confidence, upon the stone laid in Zion, he then feels the benefit of rest.

SERMON XX.

HEB. 10:21.

And having an high priest over the house of God.

THIS verse contains the third encouragement which the apostle draws from Jesus Christ, to stir up believers to approach to God in the right manner. I did propose three things to be spoke to; I have spoke to the first of them. The first thing is this encouragement is taken from Christ's office; he is a Priest, and a great one. Accordingly I spoke to these two: 1. That our Lord Jesus Christ as a Saviour is a true and proper Priest betwixt God and men. 2. That he is a great one; as it is his office to be a Priest, he is a great one in that office. From these I have spoke.

The second thing in the verse, is that which follows now to be discoursed of; and that is our Lord's charge in this office. We are told by the Spirit of God in the word, that he is a *Priest over the house of God*, in it, towards it, and over it. On this truth, That Christ is a great Priest over the house of God, I would spend this time in speaking, and would do it in this order.

I. Shew you, what is the house of God that Christ's charge is in and over.

II. What sort of charge and authority he hath in it and over it.

Then apply it.

First, What is the house of God that Christ's charge lies about and over? We all know, that there was of old a typical house, and it had a typical priest, which was the chief officer over it. Of this there was a change in the wilderness, and a good many years after they came to Canaan; the tabernacle was removed in all their journeyings in the wilderness, and was removed according to God's ordinance and appointment several times; in the land of promise it was sometimes in Kirjath-jearim; the ark was a while in captivity; it was at last brought; to the city of David, then settled by Solomon in the temple, which the

Lord calls his house, 2 Sam. 7:6, 7. This house of God, the temple, was a type of Christ's body. So our Lord uses it of his natural body, if I may so call it: *Destroy this temple*, says our Lord, *and I will raise it again in three days; but he spake of the temple of his body*, John 2:19-21. All the glory that was in the temple, was but so many shadows of the great glory of that tabernacle wherein God was to dwell, where the fulness of the Godhead was to dwell in the man Christ. This temple was typical also of Christ's mystical body, the church: therefore we find the church often called by this name, *the temple of the living God: Ye are the temple of the living God*. Our bodies are so, the whole man is so: 1 Tim. 3:15, *That thou mayest know, how thou oughtest to behave thyself in the house of God, which is the church of the living God*. That we have now no more to do with this typical temple, it pleased the Lord, in the depth of his providence, a little while after our Lord Jesus came in the flesh, and after he had gone to heaven, and had fulfilled all righteousness, and had dispatched all his work; it pleased God, I say, to lay this temple desolate by the hands of strangers, and it remains a ruin to this day; and so perhaps it will to the last day. There is now no house can be called the house of God, as the temple at Jerusalem was. Typical temples and typical priests are all expired with the ceasing of the Levitical service; and it is but an aping of this, that Antichrist, and they that would work after the same spirit, labour to rear up in the church of Christ. What then is the true house of God? The apostle certainly had no thoughts to draw the minds of these Hebrews unto the doting upon the outward worldly temple, that he knew was shortly to be removed and destroyed. By the house of God, that Christ's charge is about and over, we are to understand two things, 1. All the matters; and, 2. All the people of God.

1. All the matters of God. All those things wherein God deals with us, and we with him, our Lord is concerned about them all: *He is a merciful and faithful High Priest in things pertaining to God*, Heb. 2:17. Every high priest is chosen from amongst men for things pertaining to God, Heb. 5:1. Let us look a little to this.

1*st*, In all God's dealing with us, he deals with us altogether by this High Priest. The Lord hath resolved, and he keeps his purpose, that he never will treat graciously with men, but only in, and through, and by Christ Jesus. (1.) In all the revealings of his mind to us, they are in and by Christ Jesus. If ever God manifest his will, if he speak forth all his mind unto the children of men, it is by his Son, as the apostle tells us, Heb. 1:2. (2.) In all his ruling, and managing, and guiding of his church and people, it is all done by Christ Jesus. (3.) In all the communications of his love, and grace, and mercy to the children of men, they are all given through Christ Jesus. Never did any man obtain a saving blessing immediately out of God's hand, it is all given by Christ Jesus.

2dly, In all our dealings with God, we must do so too. If God deal with us only by Christ Jesus, we must deal with him, and thereby acknowledge this power that our Lord hath over the house of God. As for instance (1.) If ever we set about the knowing of God, or thinking on him, or studying of him, we must do it all by Christ Jesus. There is nothing so hard to bring your hearts to; I know it well by my own; and every one that knows his own heart, will find it so; there is nothing so hard as for a person to confine all his meditations and thoughts of God unto those discoveries that are made of God in the face of Christ Jesus. There are some natural notions we have of God, and by the light of the word; these are polished in a great many people; thereupon you will find, that the religion of a great many folks (a great part of it) who bear their heads high in Christianity before men, lies wholly and altogether, if I may so call them, in a company of philosophical thoughts, of the majesty, and power, and attributes of God, and never a thought of God in Christ. Whenever a man thinks of God out of Christ, he enters immediately into a maze and labyrinth, and he will be confounded and wander unavoidably: *The light of the knowledge of the glory of God shines to us in the face of Christ Jesus*, 2 Cor. 4:6. *If thou hast seen me*, saith our Lord, *thou hast seen the Father also: believest thou this?* John 14:9. (2.) In all our treatings with God for reconciliation, they must all be managed in Christ Jesus. This is one of the matters, that God is specially concerned in in this office. It is a great reflection on Christ as a High Priest over the house of God, when a sinner offers to make his peace, or seek his peace from God, without Christ. No man can come to the Father but by him; he is the only introducer of poor men into God's favour and friendship. (3.) In all the exercise of grace and performance of worship and duty, these are matters of God, these are things wherein we have to do with God, and in all these we must deal with God through Christ Jesus. Whatever our sacrifices be, they must all be offered up in and by the hand of this great High Priest. Never was there a man in this world, that had so good a gift to give to God, as that he durst give it out of his own hand. No, we must put it in Christ's hand; and till it come out of his own hand, it can never be accepted of God: We are *built up a spiritual house, to offer up spiritual sacrifices, acceptable to God by Jesus Christ*, 1 Peter 2:4, 5. So also as to all our expectations from God, all the hopes that we have of good things from God, are all to be in Christ Jesus; the apostle therefore does well call him *Jesus Christ, who is our hope*, 1 Tim. 1:1. That is the first thing that is to be understood by the house of God; all the matters of God, all things that pertain to God, every thing wherein God deals with men, and wherein men deal with God, he deals with us by this Mediator and High Priest, and we must deal with him so too. He knows we cannot bear his immediate dealings with us, and we should know that we are not able to deal with him; therefore the Mediator is betwixt God and men, that all the affairs of God and men may be well and fitly managed.

2. By the house of God, is understood, in the word, the people, the church of God, a company of people that our Lord hath chosen and gathered unto himself in every age. Sometimes they have been fewer, and sometimes they have been more; but it is a plantation that hath been of so long standing, and there have been so many in every age, that doubtless when they come all together, there will be a great and goodly company; they are the house of God: *In whom you also are budded together*, says he, *for an habitation of God through the Spirit*, Eph. 2:22. So much for this thing, What this house of God is, that Christ's charge is over; all matters of God, and all the people of God.

II. The *second* thing to be spoke to is, what is this authority that Christ has over this house of God? I will name a few of the general properties of it, and give you a few of the instances thereof, that may give some understanding of the nature of it.

1. This authority that our Lord hath is divine, though delegated, though commissioned. All commission from God is not divine, is not so divine as Christ's authority is. The apostles had their authority from Jesus Christ, yet their authority was but that of men; whatever power they were clothed with, it was still in the name of another, in the name

of God. But our Lord Jesus comes in his own name, and in the name of his Father; his power, though delegated, is divine, because the person is so; so that all the respect that we owe to divine authority in its most glorious exertings and exercises, is due to the Son of God. He hath committed all power to him, *that all men should honour the Son, as they honour the Father. He that honoureth not the Son, honoureth not the Father which hath sent him*, John 5:23.

2. This authority of our Lord's is universal and absolute; it is over all things, it is over all things with reference to his church and people. The immediate exercise of his charge as Priest is about the house of God, but every thing besides, as it may serve that. So says the apostle,—*And hath put all things under his feet, and gave him to be the head over all things to the church*, Eph. 1:21, 22. He hath put all things under his feet; therefore it is evident, that there is nothing that is not put under him, as the apostle exactly reasons upon Psa. 8 in Heb. 2:8, *In that he saith all things are put under him, it is evident, that there is nothing left that is not put under him*; where we have the Spirit of God, in the New Testament, giving a full meaning of the Spirit in the Old. This authority that Christ hath over the house of God, is altogether incommunicable; there is none but he that is God's fellow and equal, that is worthy of this honour, nor able to manage this great trust; there is none capable of this trust but Christ Jesus; no men, no angels have a share in it. None of the apostles ever had a share in an authority over the house of God; they had but the power of servants and ministers in the house; they were not lords in it: as the same apostle in Hebrews 3 does most elegantly compare Moses and Christ: *Moses was faithful in all his house*; but how? *as a servant*, saith he; *but Christ as a Son over his own house*; *whose house are we*, ver. 6. This now is the general nature of this great authority that our Lord Jesus, as High Priest, hath over the house of God; it is divine, it is absolute in all things, it is communicable to none, it passes not from him to any body. The first typical priesthood was put into Aaron's hands; when he died, it was left to his son, and so from one to another's son; says the apostle, *They could not continue in their office by reason of death: but this man, because he continueth ever, hath an unchangeable priesthood*, Heb. 7:24. It were well then, if so be, that the name of a priest had been buried in the

ruins of the temple at Jerusalem: for that name and the office did alone belong to that constitution, and is quite foreign to the ministry of the gospel: but Antichrist hath brought it in, as he makes himself the grand high-priest, and ordinary ministers as underlings unto him; and he hath framed a sacrifice for them, which is the very abomination of abominable Popery, he has a priest, and altar, and sacrifice, for they will be perpetually together; where there is no altar, nor sacrifice, wherefore should there be a priest? If our Lord hath offered the grand sacrifice, and be the everlasting Priest, and about his work in heaven, and has ended all his work on earth, there is no work for any man under that name, and in that office upon earth.

Now, the other thing that I promised to speak to about the power of our Lord, is to shew you some particular instances of it, that we may not rest only in generals about Christ's power over the house of God.

1. Christ's power over the house of God is seen in this, that he calleth and bringeth into the house of God whom he will; he calls strangers, he hath the key of the house of David, and he opens when he will, and shuts when he will, Rev. 3:7. Do any of you partake of the grace of God? are you brought in truly to this spiritual house of God? All the thanks is owing to this great High Priest. Our Lord puts forth his power and saves whom he will; he brings men to God; he follows after strangers; he knows them well. There is not an elect person in the purpose of God, and there is not a redeemed person in the design of Christ's dying, but our Lord knows them, and will pursue them, and follow them, and overtake them and bring them in: *Other sheep*, says he, *I have, which are not of this fold; them also I must bring, and they shall hear my voice*, John 10:16.

2. Christ's power over the house of God is seen in this, that he dispenses and disposes the treasure of the house as he sees good. All the riches of this great house of God are given forth by our Lord Jesus, as he thinks good: *Unto every one of us*, saith the apostle, *is given grace, according to the measure of the gift of Christ*, Eph. 4:7. No wonder that our Lord has great power in dispensing his grace, for it is all his own; all that is given out of his house is the purchase of his blood, and what he hath dearly bought, that he might be the Lord thereof: *Of his fulness have all we received, and grace for grace.*

3. Christ's power over the house of God is seen in this, that he welcomes all his people to the mansions in his Father's house, which he has prepared for them. After he hath brought them into the lower house here, and hath enriched them as he sees good, he at last brings them into his presence above, and they enter by him as the gate. John 14:2, 3, our Lord speaks of his going to prepare a place for them, and of his receiving them to himself. The crown of eternal life is given particularly by Christ Jesus to every saved one, as certainly as every bit of saving grace is Christ's free gift. Now, the crown of eternal glory is his free gift: *Looking for the mercy of our Lord Jesus Christ unto eternal life*, saith the apostle, Jude 21. They are vain lookers for the mercy of our Lord Jesus Christ unto eternal life, that are rejecters of the mercy of our Lord Jesus in fitting us for eternal life now. But a poor believer that hath partaked of eternal life in its seed, and hath received a great deal of Christ's mercy, this man may easily expect, and confidently look for the greatest at last; he that hath lived upon Christ's grace and mercy all his days, may expect the last gift when he stands in need of it, and when our Lord's time is to give it.

Lastly, The last instance of Christ's great power over the house of God is in his coming again, and fetching the whole family together. Now heaven is filled with the spirits of just men made perfect, as Christ calls them. We do not know how heaven is filled now; sometimes we see believers expiring, and they breathe out their breath, and leave a carcase lying upon the bed; we can see no further; how the immortal soul maketh its passage into the heavens, and is received there, passeth our understandings. But there is one filling of heaven that is a coming, which every one of you will be witnesses of, God grant you may be joyful witnesses thereof; that is, when our Lord shall come again, and gather the dust of his people, and raise up glorious temples out of their vile bodies, and shall carry up soul and body to heaven. This is a proof, I say, of the last great instance of Christ's power over the house of God, that as he did ascend himself, and entered heaven with his own blood, having obtained eternal redemption; so the day is coming, and may be nearer than you apprehend, when he shall come again and gather all his people, and judge them, and save them, and carry them up to heaven, and present them to the Father. The one is as sure as the other. *And as it is appointed unto men once to die, but after this the judgment: so Christ was once offered to bear the sins of many; and unto them that look for him shall he appear the second time, without sin unto salvation.* As if the apostle had said, As sure as Christ died without the gates of Jerusalem, and there were thousands then alive that knew it, and saw it, as sure as that was, he will make another appearance without sin to salvation, to all them that look for him. This is the last act of our Lord's conduct in his great guidance of the house of God, that he then puts down all power, and authority, and rule, and lays aside his own mediatory dispensation of the kingdom, that God may be all in all, as the apostle speaks of it, 1 Cor. 15:26.

Application. Is Christ a great Priest over the house of God? Then I would, 1. Exhort you to have great and high thoughts of Christ Jesus. Pay a great deal of honour to him. Never think so highly of Christ as to be afraid to employ him; but, in all your employings of him, have a great sense of his grandeur and power. With what reverence, and adoration, and submission, should we employ him, when we exercise faith on him! Believing on Jesus Christ, and exercising faith on him, trusting him with the concerns of our eternal salvation, is one of the most bold and familiar, and also one of the most reverent and awful things that a poor creature can do.

2. Learn to pay your due respect unto the true house of God, because of its Master's sake. Every thing that concerns the house of God should be regarded reverently by us, because it is Christ's charge.

1*st*, All the orders, and all the ordinances of the house of God are to be reverently regarded, because they are under Christ's charge; he is the Lord and Master of them all. All gospel-ordinances are Christ's appointments, and they are to be used as such; and we are to submit to them, and use them reverently as such. What our Lord said of his supper, may be said of every appointment, *Do this*, saith our Lord, *in remembrance of me*; hear the word in remembrance of Christ that appointed it; pray in remembrance of him that commands men every where to follow his example, and to lift up holy hands without wrath and doubting. All the ordinances and order of his house are to be reverently regarded, because of the Master thereof. The word is the word of Christ: *Let the word of Christ dwell in you richly*, Col. 3:16. This would make your Bibles dearer to you, and make you use them spiritually, if every time you open your books, you thought, This is Christ's will, and this is a letter to me sent by Jesus Christ from heaven; and he by his Spirit can speak them to me, and I by faith may vent that back in prayer, that may make as true comfort and converse with him, as if he were upon the earth.

2nd, There is in Christ's house the dwellers, the inhabitants; his people are of the house, they dwell there. That charge our Lord gave, and the Lord grant its power may reach our hearts: *Take heed*, says he, *that ye despise not one of these little ones that believe on me*, Matt. 18:6, 10. They are little, they are weak as to a great many things; wherefore they may be despised. There is a deep providence of God in this, that there is not a perfect sinless Christian on the earth. I do not believe the world would like them the better, if they were so; I do believe, if there were a perfectly holy person upon earth, that perfectly holy person would be more perfectly hated by all the ungodly than any. But whatever the infirmities and weaknesses of the children of God are, which things commonly make them to be despised, our Lord warns against it. Now, if I may so speak, our Lord's argument is not so great, though it be a good one, as that which this text does afford. Our Lord's argument is only drawn from a smaller thing: *Take heed, that ye despise not one of these little ones that believe on me*; for as mean as they be, their angels behold the face of my father which is in heaven. You would think it a great thing to have the company of an angel, you would be loath to despise an angel; but you can despise a weak silly believer, says our Lord; that weak one that believes in me is under the guard of these angels, yea of him who is the Master of angels, of our Lord Jesus, who is the head of all principalities and powers; take heed therefore you despise not such a believer.

3dly, There are the concerns of the house of God, that you should be concerned about greatly. It is a shame to think, how we are outstripped by Old Testament saints in this point. What great things are spoken of the zeal of the people of God of old! *The zeal of thine house hath eaten me up*, saith David, typically of Christ. And, Psa. 122:7, 8, *For my brethren and companions' sakes, I will now say, Peace be within thee; peace be within thy walls, and prosperity within thy palaces*. How much more may we say, for our Lord's sake, who is the Master of his house, we wish well to the church of Christ. There is a great want of public-spiritedness, and it is a great sign that God hath no great mind to do any great public work for his glory, and for his people, in that he hath restrained the spirit of due concernment about the house and interest of Christ. All men seek their own things, but no man the things of Jesus Christ. If a particular church, and a particular city or land have the gospel in any tolerable quietness amongst them, and all is well with them, very unconcerned are they about the great dishonour that Christ sustains in the world. For Christ's sake we should be concerned about all the affairs of his house, about the prosperity and adversity of it; rejoice when it is well with Zion, and mourn when it is otherwise.

3. You that have a mind to be in the house of God, to be brought into his favour now, and into his presence hereafter; you must mind Christ Jesus, make use of him, for he is set over the house of God; you must enter by him, or you can never come into this house. If you enter not by him that is the door, ye are but thieves and robbers, and will be punished for your trespass, rather than commendably entertained. Now, how shameful is the practice of a great many in this particular? There are many that do think they are in God's house already, as far as God's house is to be entered into by men on earth, and they hope they shall be in God's house above for ever; whereas in the mean time they have no acquaintance with Jesus Christ, and no employment for him. See now how men mistake. There are some that think they are born in God's house, and therefore they shall be well, because they are born of godly parents. There is no man born in God's house, no man born in God's inward house; a great many are born in the outer courts. There is no man born to good purpose, unless he be born again. There is no man born in God's house; though I acknowledge, that there is an external federal right which the children of believers may have.

Some think they are in God's house by education; they have light and knowledge, and have been instructed in the ways and things of God from their youth and childhood: and by the fruits of these, they begin to imagine that surely they are in God's house. There are some that go yet further, and they think they are entered into the house of God by their profession, by their professed subjection to the gospel of Christ; and I acknowledge, that where this is sincerely done, it goes a great way: but that is not a man's entering into this spiritual house, but a man's declaring that he is in it already, and that he desires to be trained up in it. Unless you have a particular exercise in the employing Christ to introduce you into God's presence; unless you have particular experience, that Christ hath taken you by the hand, and hath brought you in, you have little to say for your being Christ's. Our Lord Jesus Christ is the only man that can introduce a man into God's presence; and O how sweetly can he do it! When we speak, we must consider that we frame our words with reverence. Our Lord Jesus, in presenting a sinner to his Father, says in a manner, 'Father, here is a poor one that thou hast given me, and that I have redeemed; he has been wandering from me, and I have pursued, and overtaken, and found, and brought him home, and now I present him unto thee; Father, welcome this lost sheep.' O, when our Lord as it were takes a sinner in his own hand, and presents him to his Father as a returning sheep, as the apostle saith, *You were sometimes gone astray, but are now returned to the Shepherd and Bishop of your souls*, 1 Peter 2:25, how sweet, how great, and how sure is the welcome!

SERMON XXI.

HEB. 10:21.

And having an high priest over the house of God.

YOU have heard again and again, that the scope of the apostle, and of the Spirit of God that guided him in this context, is to encourage believers in approaching to God, by several great discoveries of Jesus Christ, and of the great provision made in him for them.

1. That the entrance to the holiest is made by his blood.

2. That the way that leads unto the holiest of all, is through the vail of his flesh.

3. That he is a High Priest to introduce us, and to bring us unto God. From this third argument of encouragement that is contained in this verse, I proposed three things to be spoke to.

1. What that office is that the apostle here holds forth Christ to be in; he is a High Priest, a great one; the word here is only in the original *a great priest*, our translators have rendered it an *high priest*; the same apostle in Hebrews 4:14 calls him *a great High Priest.*

2. I have spoke something of Christ's charge, whereabout it lies. It is, saith the apostle, over, or upon, or in the house of God. What this house of God, and what Christ's power and authority in it, and over it is, I spake to you last day. The house of God, is all the matters of God, and all the people of God, and all things wherein God deals with us. He deals with us by Christ; and in all matters wherein we deal with God, we must deal with him by Christ. The high-priest under the law, was a kind of mediator betwixt God and men. The immediate approaches unto Israel's God, were not to be made by the people immediately, but by the high-priest; and the answers of peace were to be returned by him, when he came forth from the holiest of all.

This I shall dismiss with a word or two more of application; and that is, Since believers are the house of God, they that are such should mind their duty. A great duty lies on them by this name, that they are of the house of God.

I will name a few things that are plainly contained in it, and may be strongly urged from it. I speak now to them that are true believers, that are Christ's special charge.

1. You that are the house of God by faith in Christ Jesus, know humbly and remember frequently your great debt unto our Lord Jesus. I do not believe that ever there was a believer on earth, that had that sense that the greatness of the matter calls for, that sense of thankfulness for the marvellous change that grace makes when it plucks us out of nature, and brings us into Christ, that the case requires. To *be translated from the power of darkness into the kingdom of God's dear Son*, as the apostle's phrase is, Col. 1:12, 13, is a just ground of great thanksgiving. Every one by nature is not only in the house of the devil, that is bad enough; but every one by nature is the devil's house; that is a great deal worse: it is a great deal worse to have him duelling in us, than to have us dwelling with him: *Ye walked according to the course of this world, according to the prince of the power of the air, the spirit that now worketh in the children of disobedience*, Eph. 2:2. Is it not wonderful grace, that

our Lord Jesus Christ will make that heart to be the temple of the Holy Ghost, that was, till he entered, the habitation of the devil, and under the power of sin, and dominion of Satan! For sin, and Satan the father of sin, are perpetually inseparable. If a man be sin's captive, he is the devil's, and taken captive by him at his will, as the apostle's phrase is. Therefore you that have this change wrought in you, that are made the house of God, and are brought under the charge of our Lord Jesus, should humbly and heartily own his great goodness in this dispensation.

2. You should know where your standing is, what foundation you stand upon. All grace comes from Christ Jesus; and the end of his giving of grace is, that he may be more improved and used by his people; for all the saving graces of the Spirit of God, are but like so many various tools and instruments, by which the new creature acts towards its original. Now, here is a woful course of a great many; when Christ bestows his grace, grace many a time is put in his own room; when he makes his grace to dwell in us, we are apt to forget that our standing is in himself alone, that created, and infused, and dispensed the grace that is lodged in us. As we are made vessels of grace, we are as feeble as ever; no dispensation of grace was ever given in this world for that end; and if it be used for that end, it is grossly abused. That a believer should live the less dependent upon Jesus Christ, is a snare that you have great need all of you to take good heed of, and beware of. Remember that you do not live, and that you do not stand by the grace that is in you, but only by the grace that is in him. Our strength stands in the fountain: *Be strong in the grace that is in Christ Jesus.* A believer thinks himself exceeding weak, when he can see nothing of Christ's grace in himself; but that is a great mistake; that man is exceeding weak indeed, that can see no grace in Christ Jesus; that man is fallen wofully. How excellently does the apostle speak of it: 2 Cor. 12:9, 10, *Most gladly therefore will I glory in my infirmities, that the power of Christ may rest upon me. For when I am weak, then am I strong*. It is best with me when I am nothing. What a mighty word is that, *Though I be nothing*, ver. 11!

3. You that are made the house of God, the charge of this great High Priest, mind the perfection of your state, press towards that. Though believers are the house of God now, and he dwells in them, yet there

is another house and another sort of dwelling, that they do expect and should long for. All dispensations of grace unto the children of God, are not only given in order to prepare them for glory, but in order to enable them to press further to the obtaining of the glory of God. *Wherefore receive ye one another, as Christ also received us, to the glory of God*, Rom. 15:7. As soon as Christ's call has reached the heart of a poor sinner, immediately he should be thinking within himself, What is that I am called to? I am called to heaven, I am called to march towards heaven, and I have Christ, and the Spirit, and promise, and all dispensations of grace as seals and earnests of that great profession. There are some things, Sirs, that are needful to make a lovely Christian, and I am afraid, that we may go far, and search long before we can find any of them; but we hope some such there are. A lovely Christian is a man whose root is deep in Christ, *rooted and built up in him*, Col. 2:7. People will not perceive it, until many sad experiences make them to feel it; there are many things amiss with many Christians, and they are full of complaints; they do not fully ponder this, that the root is not deep enough, they have not taken deep root in Christ Jesus. Again, a lovely Christian is one whose fruit abounds: *That your fruit may abound through him. Abide in me, and I in you,* says our Lord, *so shall you bear much fruit. Herein is my Father glorified, that you bear much fruit, so shall ye be my disciples*, John 15:8; and several places in the same chapter. The third property of a lovely Christian is, that his leaf is green, his profession fair, and clean, and not withered. It is said of the happy man in the first psalm, *His leaf fadeth not*; he is well planted, and he brings forth much fruit in season. Alas! fruit is in a great measure gone, and the beauty of the leaves of our profession is in a great measure withdrawn also. How few can speak David's words, Psa. 52:8, *But I am like a green olive-tree in the house of God.* The loveliness of our profession tends to our Lord's praise, and our fruitfulness therein not only to his praise, but to our advantage. The last thing in a beautiful Christian is, that I may allude to the word of the prophet Daniel to Nebuchadnezzar, that his *branches reach to heaven*. My meaning is this, that there should be breathings and pantings after perfection, and there should be springings up towards eternal life. Examine yourselves now about this point. I dare say, that the greatest part of Christians, sound honest Christians, have more mind to beg grace of God, that they may glorify him here, than they feel of any great desires of enjoying a perfect state hereafter. It is a shame, Sirs, to think, how many Christians are plucked to heaven against their will; my meaning is, before they would be there. They would be there at last; but the shame is, that we should be so unwilling to be there, whenever he calls. A believer, an heir of heaven, to be sorry to leave this earth, is a most shameful thing; but the churches of Christ are full of such shameful things. It was wont to be otherwise, and God can make it otherwise again. *We groan within ourselves, being burdened,* says the apostle. Why, what burdened the man? Did his afflictions burden him? No; he gloried in them. Was it his temptations burdened him? No; he rejoiced in them too. His burden was, that he was out of heaven, 2 Cor. 5:2, 4.

Lastly, You that are the house of God and believers, concern yourselves in the prosperity of the great house of God. Every believer is a temple of God, and the whole church is the great one. Is Christ set over the house of God as great Priest; is his charge lying there? and should not the care of our hearts go where Christ's charge is?

1st, Walk honourably, you that are the house of God; do not disgrace and disparage the temple of God: *Know ye not, that ye are the temple of God, and that the Spirit of God dwelleth in you? If any man defile the temple of God, him shall God destroy.* The true spring of true tenderness and holiness in all manner of conversation, is the faith of those privileges that by the grace of God we are possessed of.

2dly, You that are the house of God and believers, labour to bring in many to the same house with you. The leavening power of godliness is greatly gone: time hath been when it was otherwise, when the enemies took notice of it, that Christianity was in a manner catching wherever it came; that some Christians, by their conversations and by their example, by their exhortations, and speakings, and teachings of others, have been of great use to bring in many strangers to the house. O that that were more minded!

Lastly, Let us all pray more for the prosperity and increasing of the house of God. There is room enough in this house for Jew and Gentile. The great High Priest is able to take care of them all, and he will take care of all that are given him; they shall be spoke for, and brought in, in his time. So much now for this second thing.

The *third* thing in the verse, and which I would dispatch also at this time, is the interest that the church hath in the High Priest: *Having an High Priest over the house of God.* Christ is the High Priest, the house of God is his charge, all his people have him; that is what the apostle speaks. It is not, seeing there is an high-priest, though that is something; but it is an argument of far greater force, having him. But though the word having be not in the original here, it is necessarily understood from the 19th verse, and is expressed chap. 4:14. That which I am to speak to then is this, That the church of believers has a true and certain interest in and possession of Jesus Christ, as their High Priest. I shall only speak unto this, and then make application, What that interest is that believers have in Jesus Christ as a High Priest, how far we may carry this word having.

1. We have this High Priest taken from amongst men. He is a man as we are; he is one of our nature, though not of our condition. *Every high-priest,* says the apostle, is taken from amongst men in things pertaining to God, Heb. 5:1. So Jesus Christ must be taken from among men.

2. We have this High Priest, as the Spirit of God calls it, with us: *He shall be called Emmanuel, God with us,* Matt. 1:23, taken from Isa. 7:14; with us not only in the union of nature, but with us in another union, as he is our Lord, and head, as he is the head, and surety, and undertaker for his people.

3. We have him made, and framed, and shapen for us. What did Jesus Christ do in the world, and what had he to do to be a High Priest, but only for his people? *In all things it behoved him to be like unto his brethren; that he might be a merciful and faithful High Priest, in things pertaining to God, to make reconciliation for the sins of the people,* Heb. 2:17. There is a greater word in Heb. 7:26, *For such an High Priest became us.* Pray what doth become us? Nothing doth become a sinner, as a sinner, but hell; that he deserves, and that he is ripe for: but, says the apostle, *such an High Priest became us, who is holy, harmless, undefiled, separate from sinners, and made higher than the heavens*; such a High Priest became us. In the framing of our Lord Jesus as a High Priest, and as a Mediator, the infinite wisdom of God consulted what was fit, and meet, and needful for poor men. Thereupon, says the apostle, *He is made unto us of God, wisdom, and righteousness, and sanctification,*

and redemption, 1 Cor. 1:30. So that if we must conceive, as indeed we must some way, of the works of God, according to the weak thought that we are capable of bestowing upon them, the Father, in framing his Son Christ, considered what man needed; and whatever was needful, and wanting in them, as all good was, that Christ was made to be. If they are fools, he is made wisdom; if they are guilty sinners, he is made righteousness; if they are defiled creatures, he is made sanctification; if they be captives and slaves, he is made redemption.

4. We have him not only made thus, but sent, sent with the highest authority, coming in his Father's name; as he says himself, *I am come unto you in my Father's name*: he is consecrated by the word of the oath for evermore, Heb. 7:21, 28. This man is made a Priest by an oath, *by him that said unto him, The Lord sware, and will not repent, Thou art a Priest for ever after the order of Melchisedec.*

5. We have this Priest with the greatest part of his work done already, and the rest he is daily doing. The comfortable doctrine of Christ's priestly office was not so clearly known, until he had done the greatest part of it. It is marvellous to think what dreadful darkness was in the minds of believers before he died. Peter very readily saith, *Thou art Christ, the Son of the living God*, Matt. 16:16. And the Lord owns him a blessed man for so saying, and tells him, that the Father had revealed this to him; that it was true faith he had, and that it was of a divine original; so that it was an infallible evidence, that the man was a believer: but as soon as Christ comes immediately after to preach to them the doctrine of his sufferings, that he was to be a sacrifice, and was to go up to Jerusalem, and there was to be delivered into the hands of sinful men, and to be slain, *Be it far from thee*, says Peter. Accordingly you know how sharply he was reproved by our Lord. But we need not aggravate the wickedness of that word of the good man; for their darkness was such that they commonly stumbled in these things grievously. What! speak against Christ's offering the grand sacrifice, by the virtue whereof Peter himself was to get eternal life! But so it was with him. But now we have this advantage, that the main, the hardest part of it is past: *We have a great High Priest*, saith the apostle, *the Son of God, that is passed into the heavens*. There were some that saw him upon the cross, that beheld our Lord in his agony, that saw him paying that

price to divine justice, by the sacrifice of himself. *We see Jesus*, saith the apostle, *who was a little lower than the angels, for the suffering of death, crowned with glory and honour, that he by the grace of God should taste death for every man*, Heb. 2:9. As for his intercession, he is daily about it.

Lastly, Every true believer hath Jesus Christ given to him, and he is possessed of him, with all the virtues and benefits of his great office, the virtues of his sacrifice, and the benefits of his daily intercession; the virtue of that one offering, and the benefit of his interceding before God, this is the proper and complete meaning of this word, *We have an High Priest*; we have an interest in him, we have all the benefit of this great office the Father hath set him in.

Thus I have gone through these arguments of the apostles. What follows in the following verses, is the proper use the apostle makes of this doctrine; yet as I have, upon every one of the particular arguments and branches of them, made some little use thereof; so would I of this.

The only thing I would speak to you about from this truth is, That since believers have Christ the High Priest, I would exhort you to try and see carefully whether you have him or no. That is a plain question, Have you Christ or no? Christ saves none but them that have him: Christ saves no man at a distance; he enters into us, and we into him; and, if I may so speak, we go to heaven together. The question is this now, and it is a very plain one, and an important one; and it is a pity that the question is not more frequently put, and seriously considered, and that there are so few can truly answer it, Whether you have Christ or no? I believe if there were one to stand at the door as you go out, and ask every one this question, whether you have Christ or no, there would be confounded answers. You can tell what you have, and what you want of worldly things; cannot you tell, whether you have Christ or no? The importance of this inquiry should prompt you highly to the resolution of it.

1. It is certain, that Jesus Christ is come into the world, and did all his work he came for, and that he is gone to heaven, and is about that work he has there, and will quickly finish it, and return again: *Behold, I come quickly*.

The inference I draw from it, as to this question, is, If Christ be certainly an High Priest of good things to come, it is mighty important for people to know, whether they have a special interest in him; for Christ's coming does not make it absolutely necessary, that all that are in the world after his coming should be in heaven; but multitudes perish, notwithstanding the light is come into the world, and many perish thereby, through the corruption of their hearts, refusing this tender of the grace of God.

2. It is certain, that you have heard of Jesus Christ as a great High Priest, and this is a great blessing that many want, and perish for the want of it. Now, to hear daily of Jesus Christ, and not to have him, is a grievous thing. The Lord has ways unknown to us to justify himself, when he shall judge the Heathen world: but the greatest judgment will be upon them that daily have heard of Christ, and never labour to get him.

3. There is more than that, it is sure that you have had the offer of him. The gospel is properly made up of two things, a declaring of what Christ is by the Father's appointment, and the tendering of him. As the Father hath made him unto sinners according to their need; so in preaching of the gospel, is the offering of Christ to all men. In all the preaching of the word that you hear, you never hear a word with one exception; you never hear our Lord commanding his servants to preach the gospel with any exception; but preach the gospel, and whoever believes and is baptized, shall be saved. The tender of Christ as a High Priest is a great matter. Now, to have Christ offered, and not to have him, is worse than not to hear of him, and not to have him. This gospel-offer of Jesus Christ is of that nature, that every thing in it, look on it which way you will, makes the sin of refusing him very dreadful; especially if we consider, who it is that makes the offer, God the Father, Son, and Holy Ghost; all three are witnesses to it; and if we consider what that offer is, how great, how taking. Christ Jesus deals wonderfully with them he has a mind to save; Christ courts his bride, if I may so speak, always in his blood; and to a believer, Christ is never more beautiful, than when his garments are stained or adorned with his own blood for our redemption. Christ is made a feast to us in his death: *Therefore let us keep that feast*, says the apostle; why, what

feast? *Christ our passover is sacrificed for us*, 1 Cor. 5:7, 8. That person is in a very poor case, stark dead in sin, and may be dead, and in hell within a little while, unless God prevent it by his grace, to whom Jesus Christ was never beautiful in his bloody garments, in his working out eternal salvation for us. The offer is an offer also that is most fit and suitable for us. What can be more fit for them that cannot deal with God, and cannot bear God's dealing with them, than to have an High Priest that can undertake for both, that can speak from God to us, so that we shall not be confounded, and carry our mind to God, so as we shall not be rejected? If God should deal with us out of a mediator, we should be confounded with his glory; and should we deal with God out of a mediator, he would abhor us, and all our attempts, and all our services.

Lastly, It is certain, you all make profession to have Christ. Pray take heed to this, that when you have the offer of the gospel, and the offer of Christ in it, that you get the thing offered, that you have the thing you profess to have. Pray, what is the profession of a Christian? What is it to be a professor of Christianity? Is it to make parties in the church of Christ? We know a great many things a man may profess, but take the matter of Christianity simply, What is it that man professes? He professeth he hath Christ. A Christian without Christ is a monster of hypocrisy, a piece of contradiction. Men must either make sure, that they have Christ, or, I assure you, it were good manners for them to renounce the name of Christianity. Why should I be called a Christian, and have not Jesus Christ? The advantage of this reasonable name is from the possessing the person. A Christian is a man that hath, and is possessed of, and by Christ. How may one know that he hath Christ as an High Priest? I will name a few things concerning this, and they shall not be very hard, nor very high.

1*st*, Do you love to have him? Do you look upon the possession of Jesus Christ, as that part which would make you completely happy? Paul proved his sincerity this way: *That I may win Christ*, says he. Why, had he not won him long since, and got him long since? Yes; but the man is for winning him still, Phil. 3:8, 9. Abraham's word has more gospel in it, than a great many carnal professors understand, Gen. 15:2. When the Lord comforts him after the slaughter of the kings, *Fear* *not, Abraham, I am thy shield, and thy exceeding great reward. Lord,* says Abraham, *what wilt thou give me, seeing I go childless?* Pray observe, our Lord could give him safety from his enemies without children. Here lay the stress of the matter, the gospel had been preached to Abraham before; as the apostle Paul tells us, and the gospel that was preached to Abraham was this, *In thy seed shall all the nations of the earth be blessed,* Gal. 3:8. Christ was preached to Abraham, as one that was to spring out of his loins. Now, *Lord, what wilt thou give me, seeing I go childless?* It is like Abraham did not well know, how many generations the Messiah was to come after him; it may be he expected his coming sooner than it was; like enough he knew it would be a good while: but here lay the grand trial of the man's faith; God hath promised, that in my seed all the families of the earth shall be blessed; the universal blessing upon poor man after sin came into the world, is to come into the world by a certain one, that is to be born of my posterity: this is that which Abraham had in his eye: Now, *Lord,* says he, *what wilt thou give me, seeing I go childless?* In a manner the force lay here; Lord, what wilt thou give me, seeing I go Christless; where is the blessing of all the families of the earth? Sirs, if you can turn this now into the spiritual sense of it, and your hearts can deal so with God, if the Lord should give you riches, and long life, and posterity, and all the comforts of this life, Lord, what wilt thou give me, nay, what canst thou give me, that can be a blessing to me, if I do not receive Jesus Christ?

2dly, You may know, whether you have Christ or no by this; what is it that you are aiming at and catching at in the gospel? I would fain know, what people come to hear for, what is the inward thought of your heart to this, and the other places? Is it, O that I may get hold of Jesus Christ? If I may but lay hold of the skirt of this Jew, this great High Priest over the house of God, it is enough? Our work in hearing the gospel, is to see if we can get hold of Christ Jesus; he comes near to us in the word, and sometimes comes so near, that a poor creature is enabled to get hold of him. Many ways do poor believers lay hold on Christ; he is only laid hold on by faith, but faith acts and works many ways; faith works many times strong desires; pantings and breathings after him, so frequently expressed by our Lord, *by hungering and thirsting after him*; but the proper meaning of this, is accepting

Christ in the gospel. Try yourselves by it. Can you trust Christ Jesus this great High Priest with all your affairs? If you can trust him, you have him, for he is possessed by trusting. When the matter of your eternal salvation is great in your eye, when you know the preciousness of your immortal souls, when you see the multitude of those sins you have to answer for, and fear the strength of corruption that is raging in you, and see the power of temptation that surrounds you; now, in all this, can you, with the heart, trust this great High Priest that is set over the house of God, to cast yourself alone upon him, and to seek no relief elsewhere, knowing that you need no more than what he is willing to give? Trusting in Christ Jesus is a very deliberate act, and a very determinate act. That man that trusts in Christ Jesus, can trust in nothing else in that act wherewith he trusts him. People that are trifling, whose hearts are secure and carnal, can easily join these two together as they imagine; they can trust in Christ, and in themselves too. But it is impossible; trust must be always determined upon one single foot of account; it must be undivided. Certainly every man may know this easily, upon what account it is that he lodges that safety of his soul. *I know in whom I have believed, and I am persuaded he is able to keep that which I have committed to him.*

3dly, You may know if you have Christ by this, Hath he done any thing in you? We have not only a great High Priest for us, but this great High Priest does many things in us, and by that we know we have him. Whenever Christ comes to take possession of the heart, he does something in the heart that will easily make a difference betwixt Christ the new possessor, and the devil that was the old one. You will find that the savour of his sacrifice hath been powerful upon your hearts; you will find the benefit of his intercession has been many times perceived by you. Every child of God finds frequently experience of the thing. They many times pray and pray poorly, and are heard graciously; they wonder, they are surprised with mercies they did not look for; they admire whence they flow. Alas, the poor creature does not know, that there is a great friend in heaven that remembers them, and these are the fruits of his remembrance.

Lastly, You may know if you have Christ thus; if you have daily work for him, you have him; for if you understand it rightly, it is a certain truth, that the employing of Christ is the possessing of him, the employing of him is the enjoying of him. It is impossible, that any can employ Christ in any part of his office, that has not Christ in that office really bestowed upon them. If therefore you have Christ, this will unavoidably be; you have an evidence, that you have him by this, that you have daily work for this great High Priest, you need the sprinkling of his blood for your daily transgressions, and need the efficacy of his grace for your daily wants. Never bid a worse sign for a man that has not Christ, than that he has no sense of the want of him. He that has no work for Christ, is yet without God and Christ in the world; and a poor believer that groans in a sense of his need of Christ, is, oftentimes discouraged, when it should be an argument of encouragement. Believers, if they be lively and growing, will find the universal sense of all of them is: In truth I find I have far more need of Christ than I had twenty, thirty years ago. As his fulness is discovered, and our emptiness discovered to us, our employing him does increase, as well as our enjoyment of him.

ELEVEN

SERMONS

ON

IMPORTANT SUBJECTS

FROM

1 PETER 1:1-4

SERMON I.[1]

1 PET. 1:1, 2.

Peter an apostle of Jesus Christ, to the strangers scattered throughout Pontus, Galatia, Cappadocia, Asia, and Bithynia, Elect according to the foreknowledge of God the Father, through sanctification of the Spirit, unto obedience, and sprinkling ling of the blood of Jesus Christ: Grace unto you, and peace be multiplied.

I DESIGN (if the Lord will) to speak on some verses of this chapter. I thought it fit not to pass by even the preface of the apostle to this epistle, which is contained in the verses that I have now read unto you. And there are three things in these verses that I would labour to speak something unto. *1st*, The penman, or the writer of this blessed letter, *Peter an apostle of Jesus Christ*. *2dly*, The parties to whom this epistle is directed; and they are described in these two verses, as *strangers scattered throughout several countries*, but yet *elect according to the foreknowledge of God the Father*, etc. *3dly*, There is the apostolic wish and prayer for them, *Grace unto you, and peace be multiplied.*

I. I would speak a little concerning the first of these, the penman of this epistle, *Peter an apostle of Jesus Christ*. He describes himself from his *name* and also from his *office*. His *name* was Peter: this was a name that Christ gave him, and therefore you may well think that the man would remember it; his own name (if I may so say), his Christian name. His circumcision name was Simon, and Jonas was his father; and of this our Lord puts him in mind, John 21:15-17, Mark 3:16, *Simon son of Jonas, lovest thou me?* Peter was the name that Christ gave him, *Simon whom he surnamed Peter*, recorded by all the Evangelists.

[1] These eleven sermons are fairly transcribed from Mr Traill's own hand-writing, by the late Rev. Mr Davidson of Braintree; and the savoury Spirit of godliness that runs through them cannot fail to render them acceptable to every attentive reader.

Again. We have a description of the man from his *office: An apostle of Jesus Christ.* I shall not now speak of his apostolic office; it died with him, and I believe will never rise again: for it was an office only adapted to a particular state of the church of Christ: which state will never return, and therefore the like officers will never be renewed again; Acts 1:21, 22: for the apostolic office was (as you have often heard) to be a witness unto, and the apostle, one of personal acquaintance with the man Christ, both before and after his death and resurrection.

But, however, there are several things concerning this man, the author of this epistle, that I would take notice of for your edification. As,

1*st.* The strange way of the man's calling; how he was called to be an apostle: an extraordinary miracle was wrought, and extraordinary terror seized on him when he was thus wrought upon; it is said, Luke 5:8, 9, that he *was astonished, and fell down at Jesus' knees, and said, Depart from me, for I am a sinful man, O Lord.* Is there any hope that Christ and this man will ever be acquainted together, when at his first meeting, the first prayer that the man makes is, Lord, be gone, and leave me?

2. Another great fault that we find in this man, was the bad counsel that he gave to his master, for which the meek Jesus called him by the name of the Devil. Matt. 16:22, 23, *Get thee behind me, Satan; for thou savourest not the things that be of God, but the things that be of men.* I confess the sin was great, the folly and the forwardness of the man was great. It is said in the text, *then Peter took Christ*; the meaning is, that he took him aside from the company; the bold man would deliver a rebuke to Christ: *he took him, and began to rebuke him, saying, Be it far from thee, Lord; this shall not be unto thee.*

3. Another thing concerning this man, was his woful denial of his Master; now who would think that ever this man should be an apostle of Jesus Christ, that had denied his master so dreadfully? Three of the Evangelists make mention of the history of it, Matthew, Mark, and Luke: Matt. 26, Mark 14, Luke 22; and John makes mention of the threatenings of it, John 13:38. Peter's denying of Christ was a dreadful sin, and there were prodigious aggravations of it. 1*st*, Christ warned him of it, and he did not believe his master. It is a sad matter, sirs, when Christians (for Peter was so, and a good one too, notwithstanding all

these sins), when Christians, I say, will hold up their good thoughts of themselves against all the awful warnings of the word of God. *Though all men deny thee, yet will not I*; 'it may be the rest will do so, but, Lord, do not suspect the like of me:' Peter refused to take in the warnings Christ gave him. 2*dly*, He fell on a slight and slender temptation, only the voice of a damsel in charging him to be one of them. Peter would have fared never the worse, if he had said, 'Yes, I am one of them, and I count it my glory to belong to such a master;' he would have had never the worse fare: for he had his master's pass, *If ye seek me, let these go their way*, John 18:8: that was a security sufficient for them all. 3*dly*, His sin was greatly aggravated, in that it was a repeated transgression; thrice did he do this: had he only denied his blessed Lord and Master through a sudden pang of fear, he might have recovered himself again on better thoughts; but a good while after he doth it again, and a little while after that, he doth it a third time, with cursing and swearing. 4*thly*, The worst of all was, that all this was done when his master was at his lowest, and done in his hearing too: for his master was but at a very little distance from him; it may be there stood only a small guard between our blessed Lord and Peter, and behind that woful company the man was denying his master. It is said, Luke 22:61, *The Lord turned and looked on him*; to be sure he was within his eye, if not within his hearing: from whence take this observation, It is certainly a great aggravation of sin, when it is committed in the special presence of God; then it is in a special way provoking.

4. We have another thing remarkable in Peter, namely, his being restored again: notwithstanding all this, the man became an apostle of Jesus Christ! Peter, the denier of Jesus Christ, is Peter an apostle of Jesus Christ! How came this man to be raised again? What assurance have we from the word, that the man after his awful fall was well raised up again? 1st, He was raised up again to his apostolical office, in the beginning of it, by Christ's looking on him, and looking repentance into him. Luke 22:61, 62, *The Lord turned and looked on Peter, and Peter remembered the word of the Lord, how he had said unto him, Before the cock crow, thou shalt deny me thrice; and Peter went out and wept bitterly*. 2*dly*, We find that he was restored again by that gentle message that the angel sent by the women, Mark 16:7, *Tell his disciples and Peter*: it shewed the Lord's

special remembrance of Peter; it spoke forth certainly Christ's special minding of him: for the angel delivered nothing but what was the mind of Christ. 3*dly*, Our Lord restored him thrice very solemnly, suitable to his threefold denial of him. Christ asked him three questions, and Peter returneth him an answer to each; and Christ sends him back to his apostolical office upon his reply. *Simon, son of Jonas, lovest thou me more than these? Lord*, saith the man, *thou knowest all things; thou knowest that I love thee*. Well, would our Lord say, art thou risen so far as to be a sound-hearted lover of me? Go, take care of my people, feed my sheep, feed my lambs, John 21:15-17. 4*thly*, The apostle Peter was specially installed, and owned in his apostolic office, by a signal testimony of the Holy Ghost, in the second of the Acts: and it may be from that day to this (and there have been a great many years since), never was there any preaching that had so much of the divine power going along with it; with one sermon three thousand were converted! Well might the man be called an apostle of Jesus; he was indeed a messenger of Christ, and had his master's presence with him. 5*thly*, We have another evidence of this, and that concerns us; the first fruit of the Gentiles was committed to him, Acts 10. He had the honour of converting and bringing into Christ the first fruits of the Gentiles. The first church could hardly bear the thoughts of this; and this he remembered many years after. *Brethren*, saith he, *Ye know, how that a good while ago, God made choice among us, that the Gentiles by my mouth should hear the word of the gospel and believe*, Acts 15:7.

There are only two words that I would say, as the USE you should learn to make of such an explained history.

1. Learn to know how far the corruption that is in the hearts of believers may go in a day of God's leaving them, and in a day of great temptation; the corruption, I say, that remains in a true believer, who is sanctified in part, but who is justified wholly; the corruption that is lodged in a true believer may work very strongly. God save any of you from making a bad use of this! It is a certain truth, No creature knows how bad even a good man may be if God leaves him; what dreadful sins a believer himself may commit if God leaves him to himself. Therefore it was a grave rebuke that a foul malefactor, condemned for his wickedness, gave to one who checked him, and asked him, how

he could do such wickedness? the poor wretch replied, *What will not that man do whom God leaves?* A most savoury and true answer. Let no persons therefore settle themselves upon this, that their state is good, and that a saving change is wrought in them by the Spirit of God; all this may be true, and yet you may be left of God to do very wicked things. Peter abhorred the thoughts of denying Christ, and resolved rather to die than do it, and yet did it, because he was then left of God.

2. You are from hence called to admire the grace of God, and the sovereign grace of our Lord Jesus Christ, in passing by one, and in taking up another, by preventing utter ruin when some of his people were very near to it: none in all the world can tell how many times they have been just on the brink of hell, and our Lord Jesus Christ hath put forth his hand and supported them, that they fell not quite in. Peter was in this case: and truly, if we weigh the matter in a just balance, there was but one thing wanting that Judas had; Judas did not betray his Master for any hatred he bore him, nor did he betray him with a design of having him killed: for we find that the man was surprised when he saw that Christ was condemned, and brought back the money again to the high-priest. The poor wretch only betrayed him for the lucre of a little money; he thought to cheat the chief priests of so much money, he would put Christ into their hands, and supposed that he would get out again, and there would be an end of it. Judas' design in betraying Christ was not so naughty as people commonly imagine; and really, sirs, abstracting from the circumstances of men, how little difference was there between Judas's going to the chief priests, and speaking a few words, and making a bargain about the taking of Christ; and Peter's denying and foreswearing that ever he knew Christ, and yet Judas stumbled and fell, and was never recovered: but when Peter fell, grace rescued him, and plucked him back, and made him again an apostle of Jesus Christ. The word is to be observed that this apostle himself used concerning Judas, Acts 1:25, *From which ministry and apostleship Judas by transgression fell.* Peter might have remembered, and no doubt but he did remember, that in the justice of God, he also fell from his office by transgression, and it was only his Master's grace that prevented the same dreadful issue. So much for the first thing in these words, the author of this epistle; Peter an apostle of Jesus Christ.

II. The next thing to be considered in these words is, *the parties* to whom this epistle is written; and they are described to us two ways: from their condition before men, and from their condition before God; in their condition before men they were strangers scattered through several kingdoms: but their condition before God was the best that could be, with respect to *All the blessed Three*. They were elect, according to the foreknowledge of God, sharers of God's everlasting love: sanctified by the Holy Ghost, and justified by the sprinkling of the blood of Jesus.

1*st*, Their outward condition before the world was that of strangers and pilgrims. You know, without any great need of being told, that a great deal of holy scripture was written to particular persons and people, about some particular cases, yet it was designed for the public good of all; and so, though this epistle be directed to the scattered Jews, yet in the wisdom of God, it was designed for the use of us Gentiles. And it may be that this is the meaning of that dark place, 2 Pet. 1:21, *No prophecy of the scripture is of any private interpretation*; that is, no man applies the scripture well, that applies it to one person, or to one time: for it was designed for common public good to all who read it, to the ends of the world. *These things*, saith the apostle, *were written for our admonition, upon whom the ends of the world are come*, 1 Cor. 10:11. I would not stand long upon this: these strangers here spoken of, as to their outward condition before men may be taken either literally as to their outward state, or spiritually as relating to their inward state as Christians.

You may take it *literally*, and then it is, that those believing Jews that Peter here writes to, were scattered in their habitation through several parts of the world. This apostle had the ministry of circumcision committed especially to him, and therefore he not only laboured among them in Judea, but he sometimes made visits to them in other places; it is said, Peter was come to Antioch, Gal. 2:11, which was a good way distant from Jerusalem. What I would mainly observe from hence is, that wheresoever the elect of God are, gospel-grace will find them out. Here are many countries mentioned by the apostle, throughout which they were scattered, Pontus, Galatia, Cappadocia, Asia, and Bithynia: how this scattering came, is not for us to determine; but one of these things certainly attended it; either it was the judgment of God upon them, in driving them from their own land; and so it was with many of them: or else it was their sin, in choosing to live out of the holy land: for it was a great sin for a Jew, before Christ came, to live contentedly for his accommodation any where but in the holy land. You may read how the Lord threatened such of the Jews that would go down to Egypt, Jer. 42; for the holy land, before Christ came, was a type of their hope of a better life; and in it God's ordinances were to be enjoyed, and therefore a willing estrangement from that land was their great sin. Also it was their great unhappiness to be out of the land of Judea in those times that Christ lived in it: for they wanted that blessing which Christ pronounced, Luke 10:23, *Blessed are the eyes that see the things that ye see.* And the apostle seems to have a reflection on their unhappiness on this account, in the following words, ver. 8, *Whom having not seen ye love*: 'If you had been in the land of Judea you might have seen him; for he lived there and died there in your time.' But yet notwithstanding all this, gospel-grace reaches them. Wheresoever any of the elect of God are, gospel-grace will reach them; either they shall be brought where the light shines, or the light shall be sent after them to find them out. This is expressed by our Lord in two parables, Luke 15, the man seeking his lost sheep, and the woman looking for her lost piece of silver. Sometimes the elect are brought where the gospel is; and it is remarkable that the pouring out of the Spirit was adapted to the time of Pentecost: when there was the greatest assembly of the Jews from all parts of the world to worship there; then and there Christ and his gospel met them, Acts 2:1. This is a matter of great consolation; gospel-grace will find out all the elect of God, wheresoever they are scattered; either the gospel shall be sent after them and find them out, or they shall be brought where it is.

Let us now consider the *spiritual* meaning of these words, with respect to their Christian state; for I judge there is something more than their bare outward state meant here by the apostle, because he names it so frequently in his epistle; they are called *strangers scattered*, ver. 1. They are also called *sojourners*, ver. 17, *Pass the time of your sojourning in fear.* He calls them *strangers and pilgrims*, chap. 2:11, and warns them to *abstain from fleshly lusts which war against the soul*; which fairly relates to their spiritual state.

That which I would speak a little to from these words is this, *That Christ's people are strangers in this world.* Let them live where they will, whether at home in their own land, or in any other place, they are strangers still; they are never at home till they are in heaven. A great deal of the faith of the Patriarchs appeared in this; *They declared plainly*, saith the Holy Ghost, *that they sought a country, a better, that is a heavenly country,* Heb. 11:14, 16. Abraham, Isaac, and Jacob, proclaimed themselves to be strangers on earth, Gen. 23:4, it was their boast before all men. So said Abraham to the children of Heth, *I am a stranger and a sojourner with you.* So it is said, that Isaac *sojourned in the land of Gerah with Abimelech*, Gen. 26:3. So saith Jacob also, concerning himself, to Pharaoh, Gen. 46:9, *The days of the years of my pilgrimage are an hundred and thirty years: few and evil have the days of the years of my life been, and I have not attained unto the days of the years of the life of my fathers, in the days of their pilgrimage.* Strange! what running is there upon this pilgrimage, that in this short answer to the king he hath it up two or three times over! But now, lest any man should think that they were indeed strangers, whilst they only sojourned in the land of promise, because that was not God's time for them to possess it; but that surely they thought themselves well at home when they were settled in the land of promise, and that God had given it them to possess it; see what David saith, 1 Chron. 29:15, *For we are strangers before thee, and sojourners, as were all our fathers.* Quoted also in the Psalms, Psa. 39:12. A little to this now, that true Christians are strangers in this world.

1st, They are not born here, that is one thing that makes them strangers, they are not born in this world: they have indeed their natural being here as other men have, but their spiritual being is from above; they are not children of this world, but of another; they have the spring of their being from above. Whensoever any poor sinner is made a partaker of the heavenly nature, that will make him a stranger in this world as long as he lives, and it cannot be otherwise.

2dly, Christians must be strangers, for they have received another spirit than the men of the world have: *We have not received*, saith the apostle, *the spirit of the world, but the spirit that is of God*, 1 Cor. 2:12. The world and we should agree well enough, if their spirit and ours were of the same sort; but, saith the apostle, *We have received the spirit of God*; and the spirit of this world and the spirit of God, are constant, perpetual opposites.

3dly, That they are strangers appears in this, that they have another language, which the men of this world do not understand. Never an unbeliever can understand the language of a believer, though they are both Englishmen, and both of them speak English; they may indeed understand the words, but yet let a believer speak of the things of God, and of another world, the unbeliever (though the English be ever so plain) cannot understand a word of it; the thing is still strange to him; there is something lying under the shadow of those words, that no natural man can conceive. Every unbeliever in the world is convinced in himself, that there is something in the ordinary spiritual language of a Christian that they do not understand, therefore they call it cant: a profane word flowing from a profane heart. For a man to speak of the things of God, and the work of God, and of matters of experience according to those words that the Holy Ghost directs, and uses in the holy scriptures, for them to reproach this as cant, is as much as if they should say, 'This is a strange language that we do not understand.' So let them say, and thereby be convinced that they belong to another world than believers do.

4thly, Believers are strangers here, for they have strange apparel, such as this world can neither perceive nor like. A believer hath two sorts of clothing, the one the world cannot see, and the other they cannot love though they do see it. The one is their clothing before God, and that is the righteousness of Jesus Christ by faith; this the world cannot see, they do not understand it; they never saw how a soul is beautified in the sight of God, by the righteousness of another, even of Jesus Christ. The other garment of a believer, is that wherewith he is clothed before the world, and that is holiness; this indeed the world sees, but they cannot abide it. Sirs, if it were possible that true faith in Christ could be smothered, and not break forth in good works, believers would then meet with nothing of the hatred of this world; for they cannot hate an unseen thing. The state of a believer, as standing justified in the righteousness of Christ, an unbeliever cannot see it, nor can he hate it, although he hates the expressions of it; but when holiness shines forth in all manner of conversation, this is what the ungodly world cannot abide. *Because I have chosen you out of the world, therefore doth the world hate you*, saith our Lord, John 15:18. I might speak of several other things concerning this matter, but I pass them. I shall only add a word or two of use upon this head, and then proceed.

Use first, If believers are strangers in this world, we need not wonder at the bad entertainment that they meet with in it. It is a wonder of divine power and wisdom, that a poor believer gets leave to live in this wicked world; it is a wonder that they are not all knocked on the head and murdered. The devil has many times cut off thousands of them, and indeed we may well wonder that any of them are suffered to live in this wicked world, that know the godly better than many of them know themselves, and they hate them when they know them. *Think it not strange*, saith the apostle, *of the fiery trial that is to try you, as though some strange thing had happened to you*: it is the common and ordinary lot of all the people of God.

2*dly*, If believers are strangers on earth, then no wonder that they be so often solitary and heavy. This is one offence that men now take at the godly, they are solitary folks, and very sorrowful; and is there not good reason for it? they are strangers, and not at home: if you could but see them at home, never was there a merrier company seen in this world, than they will be when they are got on Mount Sion with the Lamb; then there will be a joyful company indeed; but now they are strangers, and therefore their cheer is here but small.

3*dly*, Let every believer take care to answer his name; it is given to you, and you should remember it that you are but *strangers*, and therefore prove yourselves to be so, by an estrangement of affection from this world; and by a warm heart towards heaven. This is the way to prove yourselves strangers, by being mortified to things below, and having your affections set on things above. (1.) If you are strangers in this world, then let your affections be weaned from the things that are here below. When a man is posting from one kingdom to another, he will not care much about what he meets with by the way; if he gets a bad lodging tonight, he thinks he will get a better tomorrow, and a few days more be out of that strange land. So it is with the believer, he meets with bad entertainment here; well, a little time will put an end to all. *Our light afflictions, which are but for a moment, shall* *work for us a far more exceeding and eternal weight of glory*, 2 Cor. 4:17. (2.) Prove yourselves to be strangers by your warm thoughts of heaven; strangers should love their home. If heaven be our inheritance, how delighted should we be with the thoughts of it? how frequently should we converse with it? how often should we send to it? Do ye belong to heaven, and are you strangers on earth? then, whilst we are denied entrance to our home, let us entertain correspondence with it, like a child that is sent by his father to travel in a strange land; whilst he is denied his father's sight, he will yet entertain correspondence with him by letters.

I would now speak a word or two to the next word, that they are strangers scattered. The original word is *strangers of the dispersion*; and this was a common word among the Jews, by which they did express that number of their countrymen who were scattered among the nations round about, *Will he go to the dispersed among the Gentiles?* say they of Christ, John 7:35.

The only thing I would note from hence is, *That Christ's people hitherto are scattered abroad*; they were never yet gathered all together, nor ever will till the last day. They have been scattering (if I may so say) for these six thousand years; one generation goes and another comes: and they are also scattered through many countries; many of them never yet saw one another's faces, and if they should see one another, they would not understand one another's speech; and the Lord has ordered this in great wisdom, that his elect shall be scattered, and not confined to one place, it may be you would think it a brave thing, if all the elect of God were confined to this land, or to the neighbouring nation, and that they were all brought forth in one age; you would think that to be a lovely land indeed, if all the inhabitants in it were truly godly; but the wisdom of God sees it far fitter as it is, that the elect should spring up in every age as he sees good. They are scattered now, some spring up in one part of the world and some in another, but they shall be brought all together, to the praise of his grace. *They shall come from the east and from the west, and from the north and from the south, and shall sit down in the kingdom of God*, Luke 13:29. *He shall send his angels with a great sound of a trumpet, and they shall gather together his elect from the four winds, from one end of heaven to another*, Matt.

24:31. But I shall not stand on this: for it is a plain noted truth, that the elect of God are a scattered company through all ages, and through all parts of the world, as God sees good. Their gathering together begins in churches; that is something like a gathering them together: *The Lord added to the church daily such as should be saved*, Acts 2:47, that is, the scattered elect were gathered together to that first church. *For as many as were ordained to eternal life believed*, Acts 13:48. But the great day of gathering them together, is at the coming of our Lord Jesus Christ; it is the apostle's expression, 2 Thess. 2:1, *I beseech you, brethren, by the coming of our Lord Jesus Christ, and by our gathering together unto him.* The apostle calls this great and last day by this name; it is not only the day of the appearance of our Lord Jesus Christ, but it is the day also for gathering all his people to him. This gathering together is also spoken of by our Lord himself, John 10:16, *I have other sheep, them also I must bring in, and there shall be one fold and one shepherd.*

All the USE I shall make from this head is this, Are the elect of God a *scattered company* through the world? See what your estate is like to be then by what it is now; though believers are scattered through the nations, yet they are all centred in one head; though they do not know one another, yet they all know or shall know Jesus Christ, and he knows them exactly; though they have not communion with all the members of the body, yet they have all communion with the head; what then should be people's great concern, but to labour to know this about themselves, that they are of the scattered remnant that shall be gathered together into one at that day? It will be a sad charge, if Christ shall have to give it in against any of you, Matt. 23:31, *How often would I have gathered you, and ye would not?* Christians should cheer their hearts, and rejoice their spirits, in the lively hope of this blessed gathering together, when all the elect of God shall be gathered together into one place, never to be scattered any more. So much for this first thing; the first description of these strangers scattered abroad, as relating to their outward condition in the world.

The second description of them is from what they were before God; they were a company of distressed and dispersed strangers, but yet they were God's elect ones. *They were elect according to the foreknowledge of God the Father, and elect to the sanctification of the Spirit, and elect to the sprinkling of the blood of Jesus*; a strange description of election! Election is properly of eternal life, and to the utmost period of it, saith the apostle, 2 Thess. 2:13, *God hath from the beginning chosen you to salvation*. But the apostle here speaks of election to justification and to sanctification: here he comprehends the steps and methods and means by which the purpose of election is made effectual. The last design of election is to possess the elected of eternal life; but not by skipping immediately from the grace of election to the state of glory; no, there are several steps between them, Rom. 8:30, *Whom he did predestinate, them he also called: and whom he called, them he also justified: and whom he justified, them he also glorified*. But I cannot enter on these things now, and shall only add a word or two in general.

The Lord needed not us, nor any of those creatures that are better than we; his setting his love upon a company of the children of men, and giving them to the Son to be redeemed by him, is an act to be wondered at in time and to eternity; it is wondered at on earth, and will be more and better wondered at in heaven. The Lord now and then takes a few, and picks them up through the nations where they are scattered; they were all of the same mass, of the same lump, lying in the same pit; Peter was no better than Judas, nor Judas any worse than Peter; Cain was no worse than Abel, and Abel was no better than Cain, till grace made the difference. Jacob and Esau were alike, till grace made the difference; when they were in the same womb, at the same time, yet, saith the Lord, *Jacob have I loved, and Esau have I hated*. Unaccountable love! and unaccountable hatred too! Deep! *O how deep are the ways of God, and his judgments past finding out? Who hath known the mind of the Lord? or who being his counsellor hath instructed him? he is in one mind, and who can turn him? and what his soul desireth that he doth*. For bold ignorant creatures to open their mouth against God, is but like the clay grumbling against the potter; wo be unto them that strive with the Lord: we should not strive with our Maker, but lie down and look with wonder at the inconceivable depth of his wisdom; and we should learn to say over our Lord's thanksgiving, Luke 10:21, *We thank thee, O Father, Lord of heaven and earth, that thou hast hidden these things from the wise and prudent, and hast revealed them to babes*. There are but few of the great and the wise, the mighty men after the flesh that are called; *But God hath chosen the weak and the foolish, and the things that are not, to confound the things that are mighty, that no flesh might glory in his presence, but that he who glorieth might glory in the Lord*, 1 Cor. 1:27, 28.—The Lord hath revealed to us in his word, and he makes it good to us in his daily dealings, that his people are a scattered company throughout this world; but it will be a lovely sight to see them all together, to see them complete, to see them gathered together into Christ the head; such a head! and such a body! will be a marvellous sight indeed! never was any thing like it seen since the creation. It was doubtless a lovely sight, if there had been any with the *Divine Being*, to have looked and seen all things starting from nothing: to see the heavens extended, and the earth established; to see the sun, the moon, and the stars starting up and shining at the commanding word of their maker. It was a great change, from the chaos and the confusion of the first mass, to that beautiful world God made; but there will be a far greater and a more notable change between the state of the church militant, that are fighting and suffering and strangers here below, and that glory which is to be revealed at the appearing of Christ, when he comes in his own and in his Father's glory. A poor believer now seems to be a distressed creature, despised of men; but he is precious in God's sight: where there is but the least drop of the sprinkling of the blood of Jesus, there God's heart is; that covers all, that ennobles all: if we are but sprinkled with the blood of Jesus Christ we need fear nothing; we may keep the passover and the sprinkling of blood, and the destroying angel shall not touch us.

The next thing that the apostle speaks of is the *sanctification of the Spirit*, which is given to all the people of God, as though yet in small measures; it is but like a little leaven in a great deal of meal, and we are to wait for the blessing of God till it leavens the whole, and we be sanctified throughout.

SERMON II.

1 Pet. 1:1, 2.

Peter an apostle of Jesus Christ, to the strangers scattered throughout Pontus, Galatia, Cappadocia, Asia, and Bithynia, Elect according to the foreknowledge of God the Father, through sanctification of the Spirit, unto obedience, and sprinkling of the blood of Jesus Christ: Grace unto you, and peace be multiplied.

THESE words, which are the apostle's preface to this epistle, contain three things. 1*st*, The penman, how he is described, an apostle of Jesus Christ: what sins this man was guilty of, and what grace he met with to raise him again to this dignity, I spoke to in the former discourse. 2*dly*, I also made some entrance upon the second thing, the description of the parties to whom the epistle is directed; and they are described two ways: 1*st*, As to their condition before the world: they were strangers, and strangers scattered abroad; and here are no less than five different countries named, that they were scattered in, Pontus, Galatia, Cappadocia, Asia, and Bithynia. Never a word of England here, no, there was nothing but darkness in this land at that time: we should reckon it a great comfort and honour, if the name of the land that we were born and live in, was found in the holy scriptures. There is not the name of any country, that hath the gospel in any measure flourishing in it at this day, that is named in all the New Testament. There is Italy named there, and Rome, that is now the seat of the beast; there is Spain named there, that is now the darkest kingdom in all the world that bears the name of Christian: Greece and Illyricum are named in the New Testament, and many other places that are now under the dominion of the Turks. Those strangers that the apostle writes to were scattered through the countries here. I showed you how they were strangers, and how they were scattered strangers; all believers are strangers whilst they are here, and generally they are scattered through several parts of the world; but there is a day coming, when they shall all be gathered together into one. Thus far I have gone. 2*dly*, The persons that he writes to, though they are described as strangers in the world, yet they were not so with relation to God: They were strangers scattered; but were they strangers to God too? no, far from it. For they are said here to be 'elect according to the foreknowledge of God the Father, through sanctification of the Spirit, unto obedience, and sprinkling of the blood of Jesus Christ.' There are several things that I would first take notice of in general from the view of these words, before I enter on any of the three particulars in them. We find in this description, a plain hint of that divine truth, the Trinity of persons in one God: the blessed three are all here named, God the Father, God the Son Jesus Christ, and God the Holy Ghost, the Spirit, with a distinct regard to poor sinners; the Father electing, the Son redeeming, and the Spirit sanctifying. This is a mystery of faith plainly revealed in the word, but is plainly knowable by no man: for always the nearer that a divine mystery lies to the being of God, the greater depth it is. The will of God about our duty is not without a mystery; his will about the lot of men, according to his own sovereign counsel (of which we shall have occasion to speak), is yet a deeper mystery; but revelations about himself, are yet a great deal deeper than any of them. The word reveals them, *There are three that bear record in heaven, the Father, the Word, and the Holy Ghost, and these three are one*, 1 John 5:7. A place of scripture, that the devil's diligence hath not been small to weaken, and to beat out of the Bible, though in vain. When our Lord was going to heaven, he charged his disciples *to baptize men in the name of the Father, and of the Son, and of the Holy Ghost*; these are three names; but these three names have but one name; the great name of God is ascribed to them all. There has been a great deal of disturbance given to the church of Christ in several ages, on account of the faith of this truth; the wisdom of corrupt men is a very fertile soil in objections and quarrellings, with divine unsearchable truths; the plain course of a Christian is to believe and adore what is plainly revealed, though it cannot be perfectly known.

II. I would note from these words in general, that these three have a distinct part about man's salvation; I say these three, they have each of them a distinct part about man's salvation, and thence they come to be known best to us, as their power is felt and experienced by us: I make no doubt but there were undeniable proofs in the Old

Testament of a trinity of persons. Divine power and godhead is ascribed to one, and to another, and to a third; frequently it is so in the Old Testament, but this is plain, that the light about this great doctrine of the Trinity, broke forth more especially when Christ came into the world. The Son of God came from the Father, and the Son as from the Father sends the Spirit. This is Christ's own testimony of himself; *I come forth from the Father*, John 16:26. 'You call him your God; he sent me; and I as his Son, send the Spirit.' The church of God, in the Old Testament times, had but small light about the doctrine of the Trinity, in comparison of what came into the world with Jesus Christ; and therefore we find this broke forth in his conception, and yet more at his baptism, when *the Father from heaven owned him to be his Son, and the Holy Ghost descended like a dove and lighted upon him*, Matt. 3:16, 17. This doctrine of the Trinity appears in the threefold share that they have in man's salvation; election is ascribed to the Father, redemption to the Son, and sanctification to the Holy Ghost. Not only did this doctrine appear more brightly when Christ came into the world, but it appears most of all to people when salvation comes to them. A great many persons think that this doctrine of the Trinity is a vast deep, and so it is, and they think it is not a subject to be preached on, and that there is danger of unsavoury, unwarrantable, and presumptuous thoughts about it; I do acknowledge something of all this to be true, that there is danger in it, and that it should be warily handled; but when is it that poor souls begin to find the doctrine of the Trinity true, and believe it, and know their concern in it, but only when the salvation of Christ is begun to be applied to them? Whensoever this salvation is applied to the poor soul, then immediately the believer begins to be concerned about all the Three; then he begins to be concerned about the Father's electing love, and to be concerned about the redeeming grace of the Son, for an interest therein; then he begins to be concerned about the sanctification of the Spirit, and the influences of his grace; there is never a believer in all the world, but his daily exercise lies about all these three. As the blessed Three in the Godhead have a distinct part in the work of our salvation, so every believer has a distinct exercise about each of these distinct persons.

III. These distinct parts that the blessed Three have about man's salvation, are always towards the same persons: the same that are elected according to the foreknowledge of the Father, the same are sanctified by the Spirit, and sprinkled with the blood of Jesus Christ. There is no difference in these things; there is not one man sprinkled by the blood of Jesus Christ, and another man sanctified by the Spirit, and a third man elected according to the foreknowledge of God the Father, but all that have either have all; all the elect are justified and sanctified.

IV. These distinct parts that the blessed Three have in our salvation, each of them is a divine act, and proves the person that acts it, to be a divine person. This I gather from the running of the words; these three things, election, justification, and sanctification, are distinct acts of distinct Persons in the Godhead, and the very acts prove that they are acts of God. Election is an act of a God of infinite divine sovereignty (of which I shall speak more by and by). The sprinkling of blood is an act of God (of the God) Jesus Christ the Son: for there is no other person in the Godhead that hath the blood of a man: *For he took part of flesh and blood, that in all things he might be made like unto his brethren*, Heb. 2:14, 17. And his blood was the blood of God, because it was the blood of that man, that was personally united to the Son of God. *Feed the church of God*, saith the apostle, *which he hath purchased with his own blood*, Acts 20:28. So sanctification is a divine act, and it is only a divine person that can effect it; for wheresoever omnipotent power is put forth in an act, the agent must be God: for omnipotency belongs to God only. Now the sanctifying a creature that is all over so filthy, so foul, and so defiled, is a work that craves no less than creating power, and creating power belongs to God only. Eph. 2:5, 10, and 24; Col. 3:10.

V. The distinct parts that these Three in the Godhead have in our salvation, have their order and their dependence; they have their order and their dependence one upon another; this is plainly asserted here by the apostle. Election is the spring; sanctification of the Spirit, and the sprinkling of the blood of Jesus, are the streams. The first spring of our salvation lies in the good-will of the Father in election, and this flows down to us through the redemption of the Son, and this redemption is applied by the sanctification of the Spirit.

VI. *And last,* These acts of God thus passing upon men, are their great distinguishing glory and dignity, and therefore doth the apostle name them here: You are indeed strangers, scattered throughout many places of the world; but here is your honour, you are elected according to the foreknowledge of God the Father, sprinkled by the blood of Jesus, and sanctified by the Spirit; and whosoever are partakers of these three blessed acts of the blessed Three, and yet but One, about their salvation, they are honourably distinguished thereby, let their circumstances be what they will; and therefore, saith the Psalmist, *Blessed is the man whom thou choosest, and causest to approach unto thee,* Psa. 65:4. So much in general from the words.

It now follows, to enter a little on the first particular in them: *Elect according to the foreknowledge of God the Father.* I am well aware, that this business of election is a great deep of God, and a great many poor creatures have been drowned in this deep, for want of light and knowledge about it, and about the right guiding it. I would therefore speak a few things concerning it, as they lie before us in the word of God.

1st, Election always passes upon persons; it is never spoken of, either in the New Testament or the Old, but as an act of grace falling upon persons: Election, I say, is of persons, and not of qualifications and conditions. There is an Arminian notion drank in by a great many ignorant people, that God hath chosen them to salvation, who he foresees shall believe and persevere in faith and holiness; they will own that all such are chosen, but this is to choose nobody: Election falls on persons, that they may believe, and that they may persevere. Faith and holiness are not the causes but the fruits of election.

2dly, Election not only falls on persons, but it always falls on them with a distinction, with a discrimination and difference; election, I say, always makes a difference: If any are elected, then surely all are not elected; if some are elected, then some are surely passed by; the apostle calls them *the rest. The election hath obtained it, and the rest were blinded,* Rom. 11:7. Oh, how hard is it for proud self-conceited man to receive and submit to this awful truth of God, that election passes upon some and passes by others, and no account at all to be given of it!

3dly, Election here in my text, is plainly ascribed to God the Father, as his special part in the business of our salvation. Election, I say, is frequently ascribed to the Father, both in the Old and New Testament. Our Lord takes frequent notice of this; *I have manifested thy name unto the men that thou hast given me out of the world*, John 17:6; that is election. I would speak very soberly and warily about this; but you will find one thing, if you take notice of it, in the economy (as they call it), the dispensation of God towards men in the matters of salvation, it doth answer mightily the interest and the influence, that the three blessed Persons have one upon another. The Father is independent, and therefore the sovereignty of election is ascribed to him; the Son is of the Father, as he is the Son, and therefore redemption is accordingly committed to him; and the Spirit, as he is the third Person, proceeds from the Father and the Son, and therefore in the work of sanctification, he is sent from the Father and the Son. I say, the dispensation of God in the matters of salvation, doth resemble, represent, and answer, the mutual influence that there is between the blessed three Persons in the Godhead.

4thly, Election is in my text ascribed to the foreknowledge of this God the Father; this is the same word that the apostle Paul useth, Rom. 8:29, *Whom he did foreknow he also did predestinate*; and in Acts 2:23, *Him being delivered by the determinate counsel and foreknowledge of God, ye have taken*, speaking of our Lord's death. Of this foreknowledge of God, I shall speak but a very little: I know blind ignorant mortals can make but poor guesses at the knowledge of God, far less are they able to guess at his foreknowledge; only this is plain, *All God's works are known to him from the beginning of the world*, as James saith in the assembly of apostles and elders and brethren, Acts 15:18, *Known unto God are all his works from the beginning of the world*; and according to his foreknowledge he hath determined all the issues of all the works of his hands. He knew all the creatures that he was to make before he made them, and he foresaw all their issues, and determined them: for divine prescience and divine ordination, are but different words for one and the same thing, and therefore his decrees are said to be according to the counsel of his own will. There is will as a sovereign act, and COUNSEL as a wise knowing one; so that the reasons are not knowable by us, yet there is infinite wisdom in all the determinations of divine purpose.

5thly, This great purpose of God about men in electing them is knowable, and it is of great use when it is known; therefore it is that the word of God speaks of it so often; and therefore it is that the apostle here speaks of it as to be known; but it is only knowable by the first fruits of it; we cannot know it any other way: for election is the eternal purpose of God in his own heart, and unless he had revealed it no man could know it. *Who hath known the mind of the Lord? or who hath been his counsellor?* saith the apostle, speaking of the depth of the riches both of the knowledge and wisdom of God, Rom. 11:33, 34. We find (1.) that election is knowable by a man for himself, blessed be God for it; that a man may know that he is elected, though it be only by the fruits of it, and these are mentioned in the text. Is a man sprinkled with the blood of Jesus Christ, and sanctified by the Spirit? then he may know that he is chosen: for, saith the apostle, *He hath chosen you to salvation through sanctification of the Spirit, and belief of the truth*, 2 Thess. 2:13. (2.) This election may be known as to other persons also; so we find it in the text, the apostle calls them Elect: *remembering without ceasing your work of faith, and labour of love, and patience of hope in our Lord Jesus Christ, in the sight of God and our Father: knowing, brethren beloved, your election of God; for our gospel came not unto you in word only, but also in power, and in the Holy Ghost, and in much assurance*; and thereby we know our election, 1 Thess. 1:3-5.

6th, and *lastly*. This great purpose of God in election, is not only to the end, but also to the means in order to the end; and if this were but duly considered, it would remove many cavils in the hearts of men against this truth. I say, election is not only to the end, but also to the means; in my text the end is concealed, and the means only expressed; but in some other places of scripture, the end only is expressed, and the means are concealed, but they should still be joined together. Election, properly, is the appointing of some to eternal life, for that is the end of election: so saith the apostle, 1 Thess. 5:9, *God hath not appointed us to wrath, but to obtain salvation by our Lord Jesus Christ*. There the end is only mentioned, and not the means. Sometimes the means are only expressed, as here in my text, *Elect to the sanctification of the Spirit, and the sprinkling of the blood of Jesus*, where he only names the means, but not the end; though he names it a little after ver. 4, *Unto an inheritance incorruptible and undefiled, that fadeth not away, reserved in the heavens for you.* Remember this always, that the purpose of God, according to his foreknowledge, is an appointment with respect to the end and the means also: It is a purpose of God falling on persons in great wisdom, and in great sovereignty, and it is always unto the end with the means; we are elected to the end, and to the means, in order to the reaching that end. There are three things that I would say by way of use, from this general glance that I have given you of these words, *Elect according to the foreknowledge of God the Father*; and so shall conclude at this time.

Use first. Learn to adore and worship an electing God. Here is the name of God shining forth; he doth whatsoever seemeth good in his sight: Our Lord Jesus Christ himself adores his Father on this account, Luke 10:21, *I thank thee, O Father, Lord of heaven and earth, that thou hast hid these things from the wise and prudent, and hast revealed them to babes; even so, Father, for so it seemed good in thy sight.* That *Even so, Father,* is, *Amen, Father*; 'I pay my praise to thy name for doing so, and I put my amen to thy determinations.' Adore, I say, an electing God. *Who art thou, O man, that repliest against God? Shall the thing formed, say unto him that formed it, Why hast thou made me thus? Hath not the potter power over the clay?* Rom. 9:21. Shall God, in the infiniteness of his wisdom and good-will, make a world of creatures, and shall he not have the disposing of them, and all that belong to them? Sirs, there is the height of corruption working in that heart which cannot stoop to an electing God, to a God, determining the final and the eternal issue of all the works of his hands.

Use second. Admire electing love: as you are to adore an electing love, so you are to admire electing love. Electing love hath no cause at all for it; redeeming love hath no cause in us, but it hath a cause; sanctifying grace hath no cause in us, but it hath a cause. Let us consider a little how this matter rises; a poor believer is brought to the possession of eternal life because he is a man in Christ; when Christ redeemed this poor creature, there was no cause at all in the man, but there was a good cause for the thing. *For this cause,* saith our Lord, *came I unto this hour,* John 12:37, viz. his Father's will. Why a believer in Christ Jesus should be admitted to glory, there is a good cause for it; it is promised that a man in Christ Jesus shall not perish: Why did Christ die? there was no cause at all in us, for we were a company of poor lost creatures, but Christ had good cause for it; *This commandment*, saith he, *have I received of my Father*, John 10:18, 'and I must obey it.' But if we rise higher to electing love, there is no cause at all for that; when we come to the top, there indeed we are swallowed up, only this, *Even so, for so it seemed good in thy sight.* Electing love is a marvellous thing, and therefore though it be a sovereign thing, it is always managed in the depth of love, saith the apostle, Eph. 2:4, 5, *God who is rich in mercy, for his great love wherewith he loved us.* When did he love us with that great love? From everlasting; and that love broke forth in quickening them together with Christ.

Use third. Wisely search into your own concern in this matter; learn I say, to search wisely into your own concern in this great deep of election; do the other two things, and you will find this to be the easier. Learn to adore the great God, in his choosing and doing with his own creatures as he will; and admire that marvellous love, which acts in choosing some to everlasting life, and then come in and search for your own concern in this matter wisely. Election is a great height; it is, if I may so say, the uppermost round of the ladder of salvation: all comes down from that to us, but we must not strive to set our foot first upon that, no, we must rise up to it by sanctification of the Spirit, and by the sprinkling of the blood of Jesus Christ; it is by the fruits of electing love that we must come to know it: so saith the apostle, 2 Thess. 2:13, *God hath chosen you from the beginning to salvation, through sanctification of the Spirit and belief of the truth.* When faith on the truth of the gospel, and the sanctification of the Holy Spirit is wrought in the heart, then the poor creature may say, 'Now I see that I have an interest in the electing love of God:' and as salvation comes this first way, and hath its first spring in electing love, so at last it issues in it. The glory of salvation shines in this: so saith our Lord, Matt. 25, *Come, ye blessed of my Father, inherit the kingdom prepared for you from the foundation of the world*: as if our Lord should say, 'You were many times in the dark, and oftentimes doubted what my Father's love and purpose were about you; but now I bring you to the kingdom of glory, and tell you it was prepared for you by my Father from the foundation of the world.' But as yet we can only see into the borders of this depth. Oh! what an ocean is the wisdom and knowledge and counsel of a sovereign God! how unsearchable are his ways, and his judgments past finding out? It is long since that he said to Moses, *I will have mercy upon whom I will have mercy, and I will have compassion upon whom I will have compassion; so that it is not of him that willeth, nor of him that runneth, but of God that sheweth mercy*, Rom. 9:15, 16. *We should bless God for this doctrine of election*; so doth the apostle, Eph. 1:3-5. *Blessed be the God and Father of our Lord Jesus Christ, that hath chosen us in him before the foundation of the world, that we might be holy and without blame before him in love; having predestinated us to the adoption of children by Jesus Christ to himself that we might be to the praise of the glory of his grace. To him be glory for ever. Amen.*

SERMON III.

1 Pet. 1:2.

Elect according to the foreknowledge of God the Father, through sanctification of the Spirit, unto obedience, and sprinkling of the blood of Jesus Christ: Grace unto you, and peace be multiplied.

YOU have heard of the penman of this epistle, Peter an apostle of Jesus Christ: you have heard also the description of the parties to whom it was written, namely, to the scattered Jews in several parts of the world; and he describes them, as ye have heard, two ways: 1*st*, From their outward condition before the world, they were scattered strangers. 2*dly*, He describes them from their state in God's sight, and in this view they are described as *elect*, as *sanctified*, and as *redeemed*. The first part of this description, I have spoken to, *Elect according to the foreknowledge of God the Father*: a deep truth that should be firmly believed, and not curiously pried into. This electing love and grace is the part of God the Father in our salvation.

I would now, in the next place, speak unto the part of the Son of God in our salvation, from that clause, *the sprinkling of the blood of Jesus*. I know that this is the third thing in the order of the words, but it is the second thing in the order of nature: for the sprinkling of the blood of Jesus Christ doth necessarily precede, and go before the sanctification of the Spirit; and therefore (not only because the natural order is so, but also because of the work we have this day to do in remembering this blood of our Lord) I shall first speak to this latter part of the text, *The sprinkling of the blood of Jesus.*

And I would in the first place lay this before you, that the apostle Peter was a Jew, and is here writing to the Jews, who well understood the Old Testament, and knew by the apostle's words, what this sprinkling did respect and allude to: therefore I would take a little notice of those sprinklings of blood that we find in the Old Testament; those sprinklings that were typical of our Lord Jesus Christ: and those the apostle doth certainly refer unto in this expression, *the sprinkling of blood.*

1*st*, The first sprinkling of blood that we find in scripture, was the sprinkling the blood of the *Paschal Lamb* at the first passover; for it is not certain whether ever the same practice was used afterwards. Though the Paschal Lamb was eaten for many ages after, yet the sprinkling of the blood thereof upon the threshold, I do not find by the word of God, that ever it was practised but the first time, and there was a special reason for it: the reason of that appointment was this; the first passover that ever was kept, was kept by the children of Israel in Egypt; and it was on the same night in which the hand of God went forth in destroying all the first-born in Egypt; the eldest in every family was slain by the angel of the Lord, and immediately on that they were delivered.

They eat the passover for their supper, and at midnight the angel slew the first-born; and immediately on that there was a cry of death throughout all the land of Egypt; and the Israelites were thrust out, and Pharaoh sent them away free. You may find the institution of this ordinance, Exod. 12:6, 7, 12, 13, *And ye shall kill it in the evening, and they shall take of the blood, and strike it on the two side-posts, and on the upper door-posts of the houses; for I will pass through the land of Egypt this night, and will smite all the first-born in the land of Egypt; and the blood shall be to you for a token upon the houses where you are; and when I see the blood, I will pass over you, and the plague shall not be upon you to destroy you when I smite the land of Egypt.* And it is again repeated, ver.

22, 23, *And you shall take a bunch of hyssop, and dip it in the blood that is in the bason, and strike the lintel, and the two side-posts, with the blood that is in the bason; and none of you shall go out at the door of his house until the morning; for the Lord will pass through to smite the Egyptians: and when he seeth the blood upon the lintel and on the two side-posts, the Lord will pass over the door, and will not suffer the destroyer to come into your houses to smite you.* What a clear type was this of Jesus Christ! the sprinkling of the blood of the true passover, was declared hereby to be the only preservative from the destroying angel; so that let it be an Israelite, of what family soever he was, yet if the blood was not upon his house, the destroying angel would certainly have come in. It is with respect to this that the apostle speaks of Moses, *Through faith he kept the passover, and the sprinkling of blood, lest he that destroyed the firstborn should touch them*, Heb. 11:28. 'Through faith he kept the passover:' What an unlikely mean was this (but by God's appointment) that the sprinkling of a little blood upon the doors, should be a preservative against the destroying angel! but it was a mean of God's appointment, and by faith they used it, and the blessing followed.

2*dly*, The next sprinkling of blood that we find in the Old Testament, was at Mount Sinai, which was one of the most solemn appearances of God that ever was in the world: there was some abatement of the rigour and severity of the Mount Sinai dispensation, in that second visit which God made to them, and allowed them to make to him. *And Moses took half of the blood, and put it in basons, and half of the blood he sprinkled on the altar; and he took the book of the covenant, and read in the audience of the people: and they said, All that the Lord hath said we will do, and be obedient. And Moses took the blood and sprinkled it on the people, and said, Behold the blood of the covenant, which the Lord hath made with you concerning all these words*, Exod. 24:6-8. This solemn action of sprinkling the blood of the covenant, the apostle to the Hebrews describes expressly and fully, nay, more fully than it is recorded in Exodus. Heb. 9:18-20, *Neither was the first Testament dedicated without blood: for when Moses had spoken every precept to all the people according to the law, he took the blood of calves and of goats, with water, and scarlet wool, and hyssop, and sprinkled both the book, and all the people, saying, This is the blood of the Testament, which God hath enjoined unto you*: so that even in the giving of the law in that most solemn appearance of God, there was a hinting of this, that the acceptance of the people must be in the virtue of this sprinkled blood.

3dly, The next sprinkling of blood we find was in their daily sacrifices, and that was a sprinkling of the blood of the sacrifice on the altar, Lev. 1:5, *And he shall kill the bullock before the Lord: and the priests, Aaron's sons, shall bring the blood, and sprinkle the blood round about upon the altar, that is by the door of the tabernacle of the congregation*. And again, you find it enjoined in another offering, ver. 11, *And he shall kill it on the side of the altar northward before the Lord: and the priests, Aaron's sons, shall sprinkle his blood round about upon the altar*: and this was in order to an atonement. Now this the Jews knew very well, for it was their daily practice; for there were two sacrifices to be offered up daily, every morning and evening, besides occasional sacrifices to be offered by the people upon conviction of any sin against the law.

4thly, The most solemn typical sprinkling of blood, was that on the great day of atonement; they had one grand yearly sacrifice in the seventh month, which the apostle to the Hebrews marks, chap. 9:7, *The high-priest went alone once every year not without blood*. You have a large account of this in the sixteenth chapter of Leviticus; a chapter that has a great deal more of the gospel in it than many New Testament Christians understand. There are three sprinklings of blood there spoken of: (1.) The sprinkling of the blood of the bullock for the sins of Aaron and his house; Lev. 16:14, *And he shall take of the blood of the bullock, and sprinkle it with his finger on the mercy-seat eastward, and before the mercy-seat shall he sprinkle of the blood with his finger seven times*. (2.) The next sprinkled blood was that of the goat, to whose lot it fell to be slain; for on that day of atonement, there were two goats set before the Lord alive, and the lot was cast between them, and that goat upon which the lot fell was to be slain, and the other was to escape; ver. 15, *Then shall he kill the goat of the sin-offering that is for the people, and bring his blood within the vail, and sprinkle it on the mercy-seat and before it*. It was only on this solemn day of atonement that the mercy-seat was to be sprinkled with blood; for never in all the year did the high-priest enter into the holy of holies but on that day. (3.) We find the sprinkling of blood spoken of again; ver. 18, 19, *And he shall go out unto the altar that is before the Lord, and make an atonement for it; and he shall take of the blood of the bullock and of the goat, and put it upon the horns of the altar round about, and shall sprinkle of the blood upon it with his finger seven times, and cleanse it, and hallow it from the uncleanness of the children of Israel.* The other goat that was left alive, was sent away with the sins of Israel confessed over it: this deep type of one of the goats being made a sin-offering, and the other live goat being sent away with the sins of all Israel, seemed to have a clear meaning this way; the goat, that was slain, pointed forth the death of our Lord Jesus Christ; and the live goat, that carried away the transgressions of Israel, pointed to the resurrection of our Lord Jesus Christ: *For we are justified by his blood, and saved much more by his life,* as the apostle's expression is, Rom. 5:9, 10. These sprinklings of blood were a great deal better known to the Jews than they can be to us: one of them was done every year, and some of them very frequently, though it is likely that the sprinkling of the blood of the paschal lamb was done but once.

Concerning all these sprinklings of blood, there are three things that you must remember and know full well; and when they are rightly known, you will the more easily understand the meaning of the apostle in these words of my text, *the sprinkling of the blood of Jesus.* (1.) This blood that was sprinkled, was always the life-blood of the sacrifice; the blood that was shed when its life was taken away: for the life is in the blood, and that blood must be shed. (2.) This sprinkling of blood under the Old Testament, was always the priest's act; the man brought his sacrifice to the altar, he laid his hand upon it, and acknowledged his sin over it, and offered the atonement before the Lord; but the priest slew it, and he only sprinkled the blood of it. (3.) All the sprinkling of blood under the Old Testament, was for atonement and expiation; and therefore, concerning that solemn day of atonement, it is said, Lev. 16:30, *On that day shall the priest make an atonement for you, to cleanse you, that ye may be clean from all your sins before the Lord.* This is expressed by the apostle to the Hebrews, chap. 9:22, *And almost all things are by the law purged with blood, and without shedding of blood is no remission.* And therefore it was needful that the blood of Christ should be shed; for all the sheddings of blood under the Old Testament were but typical of this. So much for the account that is given us in the

Old Testament of the sprinkling of blood. I would now come to speak to this sprinkling in my text; the sprinkling of the blood of Jesus: and there are two things that I would discourse on; 1*st*, Of the sprinkling of the blood of Jesus in itself, and then, 2*dly*, I would speak to the relation and respect that electing grace hath to it; for it is said in the text, *that we are elected to the sprinkling of the blood of Jesus.*

1*st*, Concerning the sprinkling of the blood of Jesus in itself: and here there are three things. 1*st*, I would speak of the blood of Jesus Christ, and what it is. 2*dly*, Of the shedding of that blood; for there could be no sprinkling of blood till it was shed. 3*dly*, I would speak to the sprinkling of it.

1*st*, The blood of Jesus Christ is the life-blood of that man Jesus Christ the Son of God (which he assumed into personal union with himself): they are but ridiculous and Popish notions that many people have of the blood of Christ. This blood was shed many ways; it was shed in circumcision; it was shed in the garden when he was in an agony; it was shed by scourging, and shed by the crown of thorns on his head. But the blood that we mean here was the life-blood of the man Christ Jesus; that blood which is called by our apostle, 1 Pet. 1:19, *The precious blood of Christ, as of a lamb without blemish, and without spot.* The same blood is called the blood of God. Acts 20:28, *Feed the church of God, which he hath purchased with his own blood.* And therefore whosoever they are that do deny or doubt that Jesus Christ is a true man, or deny that Jesus Christ is true God, they are not to be called Christians; call them what you will, Christians they are not; call them Pagans, Heathens, Mahometans, give them what name you will, they are no Christians that do not believe Jesus Christ is come in the flesh, and that he was God before he came into flesh, that he was truly God in the flesh, and that the Godhead remained united with the flesh as our great Emmanuel.

2*dly*, How came Christ's blood to be shed? for it could not be sprinkled unless it was shed. If I may so say, as long as Christ's blood ran in his veins, it could sprinkle none. How Christ's blood came to be shed, every one, even carnal Protestants and Papists know, and can give a ready answer to it. As that Christ's blood was shed by the cruelty of barbarous people, who murdered him by nailing him to the cross, where he bled to death in great torment, according to the nature of that violent death. But how far is this from the gospel account of it? from what Christ and his servants say of it? *The Son of man*, saith our Lord, Matt. 20:28, *came to give his life a ransom for many. Christ died*, saith the apostle, 1 Cor. 15:3, *for our sins, according to the Scriptures.* Of this blood-shedding take these four or five things, and lay them together. 1*st*, That Jesus Christ the Son of God was sent into the world in the room and in the stead of his elect. He did not come as a single person into the world, but he came as a public person, representing a great many, even all that were given to him by his father; *for their sakes*, saith our Lord, *do I sanctify myself*, John 17:19. 2*dly*, By virtue of this substitution of Jesus Christ, all that the elect were indebted for, was justly charged on him: I say, by virtue of his coming in their place, in their name and stead, all that was owing by them to the law and justice of God, was justly exacted of him; and therefore it is said, *That he died for our sins*, 1 Cor. 15:3, because our sins were charged on him: if he had no relation to our sins, there could be no justice in punishing him for them. He had indeed no guilty relation to them, but he had a near and gracious relation to them: for they were debts that he undertook to pay. 3*dly*, This debt that was exacted of Christ, and which he paid, was for our disobedience to the law of God, and for the punishment due to us for that disobedience. The law saith, *Do and live; Sin and die*; and therefore our Lord's undertaking was made up of two parts, a perfect obedience to the precept of the law, and a severe punishment according to the threatening of the law, commonly called the active and passive obedience of Jesus Christ, by both which he brought in that righteousness that we are saved by. 4*thly*, The debt of sin being death, Christ therefore died: he owed death to the law of God; he had never transgressed it, but he bore the sins of many transgressors: *He was numbered with transgressors*, Isa. 53:12, and dealt with as a transgressor, and died as a transgressor. The justice of God can slay no man, nor smite any man but for sin; it would cease to be the sword of justice if it should fall upon any that were perfectly innocent. Indeed the Son of God was perfectly innocent in himself, but as he stood in our room and place, he was the greatest of all transgressors. Saith the apostle, 2 Cor. 5:21, *He hath made him to be sin for us that knew no sin, that we might* *be made the righteousness of God in him. 5thly*, This debt that Christ owed to the law, as our surety, was brought upon him by the surest way, of blood-shedding; the surest way of dying in the world, is when all the blood in the body is shed; and our Lord died by this violent sort of death, blood-shedding: our Lord's blood was shed. If people regard only the Jews, and Pilate, and the soldiers that stood round about him, and look upon them as the only persons concerned in the shedding of Christ's blood, if they look no higher they can see no good at all in this blood-shedding.

Whensoever you think and read of our Lord's blood being shed, there are two things that should always be in your eye. *1st*, Who was the highest author of it. *2dly*, What were the blessed ends of it. The highest author of it was the justice of God; this cup, bitter as it was, was the cup that his Father gave him to drink. His Father's hand was in it; *The cup which my Father hath given me, shall I not drink it?* saith our Lord, John 18:11. Christians, in looking on Christ's death, should learn to see these two things; to see the Father slaying his Son Christ Jesus, and to see our salvation springing up from his death: *Who his ownself*, saith the apostle, 1 Pet. 2:24, *bare our sins in his own body on the tree, that we being dead to sin, should live to righteousness: by whose stripes ye were healed.* Where is our faith that should see this? I cannot tell whether there was any faith so active at our Lord's death, as to believe and rejoice on this account. Here is the justice of God taking a true sacrifice, and we shall be saved by the virtue of it; the believing thief bid fairest for it of any; the very disciples knew it not at that time, though they knew it well afterwards.

3dly, What is the sprinkling of this blood of Christ thus shed? You understand what the sprinkling the typical blood of the sacrifices was; it was the natural blood of a poor beast that was sacrificed, sprinkled by the hands of the priest on the altar and on the mercy-seat: But what is the sprinkling of this blood of Jesus? The sprinkling of the blood of Jesus Christ is nothing else but this, the spiritual application of its power and virtue. It is an old doting dream of the Antichristian party, to make a great deal of noise about the material blood of Christ; it is probable that the natural blood of Christ sprinkled the garments of many of his murderers, who were never a whit the better for it; and that the earth drank it in, like the blood of another man; but the spiritual heavenly virtue of it is quite another thing. This is what we are to speak to, what the sprinkling of the blood of Jesus Christ is? that is, wherein was this virtuous blood applied. *1st*, This blood of Jesus Christ sprinkled the altar of justice, at which it was shed for atonement and propitiation. I say, the blood of Jesus Christ sprinkled the altar of justice; that is, the power and virtue of it made satisfaction to the justice of God for sin: it was a satisfaction to justice and the law, for an atonement for all his people. The law and justice of God shed this blood, and the virtue of it satisfied both. Eph. 5:2, *It was a sacrifice of a sweet-swelling savour to God*; so that justice had no more to crave, and sin had no more to oppose: *for he put away sin by the sacrifice of himself*, Heb. 9:26. *He was offered to bear the sins of many*, Heb. 9:28, and by bearing of sin he took it away, so that from the day our Lord died, sin shall never be a powerful impediment in the way to heaven to a believer in Christ; and the reason is, because Christ has condemned sin, as the apostle discourses at large; Rom. 8:1-3, *There is therefore now no condemnation to them which are in Christ Jesus, who walk not after the flesh, but after the spirit: for the law of the spirit of life, in Christ Jesus, hath made me free from the law of sin and death: for what the law could not do, in that it was weak through the flesh, God sending his own Son, in the likeness of sinful flesh, and for sin condemned sin in the flesh. 2dly*, The sprinkling of the blood of Jesus Christ, that is, the power and virtue of it, reaches heaven. Heb. 9:12, *Neither by the blood of goats and calves, but by his own blood, he entered in once into the holy place, having obtained eternal redemption for us*; ver. 24, *For Christ is not entered into the holy places made with hands, which are the figures of the true: but into heaven itself, now to appear in the presence of God for us*. Sirs, when we say that Christ entered into heaven with his own blood, it would be a foolish thing for any body to imagine that our Lord ascended into heaven in a state of infirmity, and in that weakness of flesh in which he died; no, our Lord Jesus was glorified, and he went in glory to glory. But Christ's entering into heaven with his own blood, was an allusion to the high priest's entering into the holiest of all with the blood of the sacrifice, and points forth to us the virtue of the blood of Jesus Christ, making heaven patent to us, like a victorious head opening the door to all that were to follow through faith in him. *3dly*, The sprinkling of the blood of Jesus is upon the new covenant. This the apostle to the Hebrews speaks of, chap. 9:15, *For this cause he is the mediator of the New Testament, that by means of death, for the transgressions that were under the first Testament, they which are called might receive the promise of an eternal inheritance.* Christ's blood, I say, sprinkled the new covenant, it was the seal of it; it was sprinkled on it, if I may so say, to seal it (as the blood of the sacrifice was called the blood of the old covenant, so the blood of Christ is called the blood of the new and everlasting covenant). Oh that believers would learn to know what the promises are, and learn to read the promises well, and look well on them. We look upon the promises thus: This is God's word, and this word of God holds forth great blessings to me, and these blessings I very much need, and therefore I pray upon the promise; and all this is well done: Aye, but when do ye see the promises sprinkled with the blood of Jesus Christ? That is a work for your faith; every promise in the Bible, the blood of Christ is upon it, to seal it, to purchase the blessings contained in it, and to secure the performance of it to every one that believes. *4th*, and lastly, The virtue of the blood of Christ is sprinkled upon believers, upon their persons and upon their consciences. Of this the apostle to the Hebrews speaks, chap. 9:14, *How much more shall the blood of Christ purge your consciences from dead works to serve the living God?* And this is what we should seek to feel. What Christ did to justice is a matter of faith; the satisfaction that his blood gave to justice: what Christ doth in heaven by the virtue of his blood, that is matter of faith; he makes intercession there in virtue of his blood: what Christ doth with respect to the new covenant, this is also a matter of faith: but the power and virtue of the blood of Christ on the conscience, is not only a matter of faith, but it is also a matter of feeling; that which we must feel ourselves, the virtue of the blood of Christ purging our consciences: therefore the apostle, in that place I last quoted, speaks of it with a *How much more*; how much more shall the blood of Christ do it? Surely the blood of bulls and of goats was far inferior to the blood of Christ, and the purifying the flesh was a far inferior effect to the purging of the conscience; but yet the apostle lays a stress upon this word, How much more shall Christ's blood do so? If the Lord was pleased to appoint such an ordinance, that the sprinkling of the blood of certain beasts should convey along with it a sort of Levitical cleanness, much more shall the blood of Christ have its spiritual saving gospel effect in purging and sprinkling the conscience; and this is that which gives a man confidence towards God. The law of God is backed by the justice of God, and the law of God is levelled at the conscience of a sinner; the law saith, The sinner shall die; conscience saith, I am a sinner, and I must die; it is only having the conscience purged by the blood of the sinless Son of God, that can give us confidence towards God, though we are guilty in ourselves.

A few words by way of Application.

Use 1. Learn to come to this blood of sprinkling. It is a duty, and the great privilege of true believers, expressed by the apostle, Heb. 12:24. *But ye are come to Jesus, the mediator of the new covenant,* he is good company; well, what great thing do ye mind when you come to Christ? *Ye are come to the blood of sprinkling, that speaketh better things than that of Abel.* It is the blood of sprinkling, and it is blood that hath a voice (blessed are the ears that can hear it!), it is only the ear of faith that can hear what mighty shouts arise from this blood of sprinkling; what great and good things it speaks for poor sinners; it speaks to God for them. A few things concerning this coming to the blood of sprinkling.

1*st,* You that would set about coming to the blood of sprinkling, that it may be upon you, learn to know and lay to heart your own filth and defilement. There was no sprinkling of blood but in the case of sin; the sprinkling of blood was for atonement, and the user of it was to acknowledge his sins: they who are too high and too proud to own themselves to be sinners, will not be found too good to go to hell: all such shall perish. Christ came into the world to save sinners, and no man can come to him to be saved but a sinner.

2*dly,* You must be persuaded of this, that nothing cleanses you from sin but the sprinkling of this blood, and that this can do it effectually. When the stain of sin is seen upon people's consciences, there are a great many wells of water that the devil and the world dig up; they think to cleanse themselves in their duties, and in their performances, their vows, their purposes, their resolutions, their praying, reading, hearing, and meditating; these are used by a great many, just as water, to wash away the stain of sin on their consciences. Vain, dangerous, wicked ways! things not wicked in themselves, but most wicked as so used. Prayer is a duty, but to put prayer in Christ's place is an abomination. All the ordinances of the gospel are things commanded us, but to use them so as to keep at a distance from this blood of sprinkling, is to pervert them to our destruction. It is a great matter to believe firmly, that nothing but this blood of sprinkling can justify and cleanse us; and it is also a great matter to believe that this can do it effectually. The poor creature thinks it is now about seventeen hundred years since Christ's blood was shed at Jerusalem, and so it is; but what then? the virtue of it is everlasting to cleanse us from all sin. *The blood of Jesus Christ his Son cleanseth us from all sin*, 1 John 1:7.

3dly, If you would come to this blood of sprinkling, that it may be upon you, you must adventure upon it, and place all your confidence in it, and make it your only plea for your acceptance and justification before God. *We are justified by his blood*, saith the apostle, Rom. 5:9. The believer is to see his justification streaming from the life-blood of the Son of God. When a poor creature sees the holiness of God's law, and the severity of his justice, and feels a disturbance in his own conscience, it is no easy matter to believe that the blood that was shed without the gates of Jerusalem, in the day when this great sacrifice was offered up, is able to wash away all our sins; and that we have nothing else to betake ourselves to; God would have nothing else. Christ tells his Father, Heb. 10:5, *Sacrifice and offering thou wouldest not, but a body hast thou prepared me*: burnt-offerings and sacrifices of the law, the Father would take none of these of Christ, but he took his own sweet life, he took his own heart blood for the expiation of the sins of his people.

4thly, In coming to this blood of sprinkling, I would give you this advice: Attend upon all the means of Christ's appointment, in order to the getting the sensible sprinkling of this blood upon your consciences. When you believe its great power and virtue, you must put in for a share therein; and the Lord's appointed means for this end they should all be well used. When you come to pray, it should be in virtue of this blood, that you may feel more of it, and be brought nearer to God by it; for if ever you have any communion with God, it must all be through the virtue of this blood; if we are brought near to him, it is by the blood of Jesus. Eph. 2:13, *But now in Christ Jesus, ye who sometimes were far off are made nigh by the blood of Christ.* Ye were without Christ, and without hope, and without God in the world, but now the matter is far changed, ye are brought near by the blood of Christ. This should be especially minded when we come to the Lord's table; the great thing we come there for is to remember our Lord's death, to his praise and to our profit: all the saving blessings that we stand in need of for time and for eternity, are all the fruits of his death. This is the first exhortation, *Come to the blood of sprinkling.*

Use 2. Abide by this blood of sprinkling, stay and dwell by it; this fountain is opened for sin and uncleanness, and as long as sin and uncleanness remain in us, we have work and employment still for this blood of Jesus. Take heed to yourselves, that ye fall not in the crying sin of this day: Sirs, there is a plague growing in the land and city we live in, and a dreadful one it is; I will take the liberty to speak of it, for it has been many times the very thoughts of my heart, That never were there so many guilty of sin against the Holy Ghost at any time, or in any place, as are now in London. Read what the apostle saith of them, Heb. 10:29, *Of how much sorer punishment, suppose ye, shall he be thought worthy, who hath trodden under foot the Son of God, and hath counted the blood of the covenant wherewith he was sanctified, an unholy thing, and hath despite unto the spirit of grace?* These three go together, treading under foot the Son of God, counting the blood of the covenant an unholy thing, and doing despite to the spirit of grace. These blasphemies that are daily sounding in our ears, that Jesus Christ is but a mere man, are here charged by the apostle to be a treading under foot the Son of God; but he will have them under his foot ere long; *His foes shall be made his footstool,* Psa. 110:1. The Son of God and all his enemies, were they ever so many, are a very unequal match. Let believers cry to him to assert his own name, his interest and glory, and to trample upon his enemies in his fury. It is here charged on them, that they count the blood of the covenant an unholy thing, that is, they count it to be a common thing. Those are grievous apostates indeed, that count no more of the blood of Christ, than of the blood of a good honest man, shed by the hands of wicked men for the truth's sake. They reckon that the blood of Jesus Christ hath no more power for the saving of men than the blood of one of the martyrs; and it is said of these, that they do despite to the spirit of grace. Take heed to yourselves, there is a great snare and a great danger here; remember it, Your salvation, if ever you come by it, must come by the sprinkling of the blood of Jesus; and the sprinkling of the blood of Jesus could never have saved any man, except it had been the sprinkling of the blood of God. Acts 20:28.

Use 3d and last. As to this blood of sprinkling, you must not only come to it and abide by it, but you must learn to die in it, and pass to heaven in it. Jesus Christ entered into heaven with his own blood, and we must imitate him, and follow him with his own blood; that is, if I may so say, we must take and keep the mark of the sprinkled blood of Jesus upon our consciences, as our grand pass for heaven and eternal life. The poor dying believer thinks with himself, 'I have nothing to trust to but the blood of Jesus Christ; I have ventured on it, and the virtue of it hath reached my conscience many times, and now I would go down to the grave, and rise again in judgment, with this sprinkling of the blood of Jesus upon me, as my only ornament, my only plea, and my only praise, to eternity.' We want to have the virtue of this blood more and more sprinkled upon our consciences, that we may lift up our faces with confidence towards God through our Lord Jesus Christ, through whom we have received the atonement.

SERMON IV.

1 Pet. 1:2.

Elect according to the foreknowledge of God the Father, through sanctification of the Spirit, unto obedience, and sprinkling of the blood of Jesus Christ: Grace unto you, and peace be multiplied.

I TOOK up the preface to this epistle, contained in the two first verses of it, in three things; 1*st*, the name of the penman or writer of it, *Peter an apostle of Jesus Christ*; what he was by nature, and what he was raised to by grace. How he fell, and how he was raised again, I have spoken to.—The second thing in the words is the description of the parties that he writes this epistle to; and they are described by their state before the world, *strangers scattered through several countries*; that I have also considered. They are also described further by their state before God; *Elect according to the foreknowledge of God the Father, through sanctification of the Spirit, and sprinkling of the blood of Jesus.*—Of the first of these, the first spring of eternal salvation, the election of grace, I formerly discoursed. There is a great reverence to be paid to this unsearchable counsel of God; it is to be firmly believed, it is plainly to be declared, but it is not curiously to be inquired into. The next thing in the description of the parties here written unto, and to which election has a respect, is the blood of Jesus Christ, and the sprinkling of it; for though it is the third thing in the order of the words, yet because it is the next in the order of nature, I thought fit to consider it in the second place. The last occasion, I discoursed something concerning this, though but briefly, in regard of the greatness and weight of the theme. I told you what the blood of Jesus was, and how he came by it; God's own Son did partake of flesh and blood, in God's wisdom and wise counsel about our salvation. How it was shed, and what the sprinkling of it was I spoke to; the sprinkling of the blood of Jesus is nothing else but the displaying and exerting of its merit, power, and virtue: for the blood of Christ, when it was shed on the cross, fared just as did the blood of another man, when drawn forth by violence out of his veins; it poured down on the earth, and by that blood-shedding he did die; just as another man would have died: but the sprinkling power and virtue of it, was of greater extent than any created blood could ever have. Abel's blood had a voice in it; *The voice of thy brother's blood crieth unto me from the ground*, said the Lord to his bloody murderer Cain, Gen. 4:10. The meaning was, that his crime in shedding it did cry to the righteous Judge of the earth, for vengeance on the shedder of it. And it is this blood only, so far as I remember, that is spoken of in the word as having a voice in it; and it is twice spoken of, Gen. 4:10 and Heb. 12:24. And some think there was something of this meant in those words, *He being dead yet speaketh*, spoken also of Abel, Heb. 11:4.

Application. I would speak a few more things in the application of this truth, That the sprinkled blood of Jesus is one great mean of our salvation, that is, the Son's part; there is the part of the Father in our salvation, in his gracious choosing us; and there is the Son's part, in his gracious redeeming us by his blood; and there is the Holy Ghost's part, in sanctifying by his grace; and all these three are in our text. The first is an eternal act of God the Father; the second is an act of God the Son, done at once in the fulness of time; the third is a constant act of God the Holy Ghost towards all the heirs of eternal life. All that were chosen, were chosen from eternity, and all that were redeemed were bought in one moment by the blood-shedding and death of the Son of God; but sanctification is a work on our persons and on our nature, and is a constant work throughout all ages and generations. The Father's election was at once from eternity, the Son's redemption was at once, in one act in time: *By one offering*, saith the apostle, Heb. 10:14, *he hath perfected for ever them that are sanctified*; but the sanctification of the Spirit, that comes upon the heirs of glory from one age to another. The Holy Ghost is still sanctifying, but Christ is not still redeeming, far less is the Father still electing; there is no time-election, though there is time-sanctification.

Use 1. The first use that I would now make of this truth, That the sprinkled blood of Jesus Christ hath so great a hand in our salvation, and is so great a part of it, shall be to call upon you to a holy wondering and admiring at this strange way of our salvation; at this saving us by the sprinkling of the blood of Jesus! A great many people are minding heaven, and praying to be in heaven, and hoping for heaven, that yet to this day never knew the way to heaven; but think the way to heaven is to be good, to pray, to be holy as they call it: these things indeed are the exercise of a man that is in the way to heaven, but these are not the way to heaven; the way to heaven is Jesus Christ; *I am the way, the truth, and the life*, saith our Lord to Thomas, John 14:6, and Christ is the way to heaven, as a slain Saviour; but how few are there that know him? Therefore our first exhortation is, To take a view of this sprinkling of the blood of Jesus, and wonder at it, that this should have so great a hand in our salvation. I shall offer a few things about it.

1*st*, There appears in this way most wonderful love towards persons. Pray observe what I say, in making this sprinkling of the blood of Jesus to be the grand means of our salvation, there appears to be wonderful love towards persons. Jesus Christ did not die at a peradventure, the great price of his blood was not laid down and he ignorant of what should come of it: he knew exactly (if I may so say) every penny that he laid down, and every redeemed soul that he was to take up. *He gave his life a ransom for many*, Matt. 20:28, and every one of those many were known unto him. *I know my sheep*, saith our Lord, *and I lay down my life for them*, John 10:14, 15. Oh what rotten doctrine is that which possesses the minds of a great many people, who think that the Son of God laid down his life to be a sufficient price for the saving of men, and then left it to men to improve this price, according as their own free-will should incline them; so that at this rate Christ might have died and no man been saved by him. If I may so say, this was to make Christ die as a fool dieth; but he is infinitely wise, and knew well wherefore he laid down his life. There was love in it to persons, therefore you still find it running this way, *he loved* ME, *and gave himself for* ME, Gal. 2:20. 'If he had not loved me he had never died for me.' Rev. 1:5, *To him that loved us, and washed us from our sins in his own blood*; if I may so say, all the life-blood of the Son of God was drawn out of his veins, by the force of the love of his heart. *Husbands, love your wives*, saith the apostle, Eph. 5:25, *as Christ loved the church, and gave himself for it*. Whenever you read this word, the sprinkling of the blood of Jesus, and hear of its great interest in our salvation, you should say, *Behold how he loved us!*

2*dly*, There is herein to be observed the most wonderful abasement and condescension of Jesus Christ, that he should stoop so low as to shed his blood that it might be sprinkled upon ungodly sinners. There is none that the Father loves so as he did his Son, and there is nothing that he hates as he doth sin; now, that the only beloved of the Father's soul should be given for the expiation of the only thing that his soul abhorreth, what marvellous condescension is here! That Christ himself should stoop so low, *who was in the form of God, and thought it not robbery to be equal with God, or as God*, Phil. 2:6, 7; that he should stoop so low as *to be made of no reputation, and to take upon him the form of a servant*; that this great one should count it no shame to be made sin, and to be made a curse for us, 2 Cor. 5:21, Gal. 3:13. What wonderful condescension is this! *Who being the brightness of his Father's glory, and the express image of his person, and upholding all things by the word of his power, he by himself*, saith the apostle, Heb. 1:3, *purged our sins*. You would think that the purging such an abominable kennel as our sins, was a work base enough, and low enough for a devil; aye, but the Son of God himself stooped to this, and his condescension was his glory.

3dly, In this interest that the sprinkling of Christ's blood hath in the way of our salvation, there is the infinite wisdom of God to be seen. It is called *the manifold wisdom of God*, Eph. 3:10. *Christ crucified* is called *the wisdom of God*, 1 Cor. 1:24. Wisdom among men is seen in bringing about effectually impossible-like matters: he is a wise man who can do that; who can reconcile things plainly discordant; things plainly cross one to another; it is great wisdom to reconcile such things: and all this is done by the sprinkling of the blood of Jesus Christ. There is justice and mercy in God, that do here kiss one another. Justice in God is natively directed to the destroying of a sinner; and the mercy of God is directed to the saving of a sinner; now, how mercy can save without reflecting upon justice, and how justice can be satisfied without consuming the sinner, here lay the difficulty that Christ's blood only could reconcile. *Being justified freely by his grace, through the redemption that is in Jesus Christ; whom God hath set forth to be a propitiation, through faith in his blood, to declare his righteousness for the remission of sins that are past, through the forbearance of God; to declare, I say, at this time, his righteousness; that he might be just, and the justifier of him which believeth in Jesus*, Rom. 3:24-26.

4thly, In this interest that Christ's blood hath in our salvation we may perceive, for the raising our faith and wonder, a new way to heaven that is now reared up, a way to heaven that every one who is good is pleased with it. The apostle speaks of this way, Heb. 10:19, *Having therefore, brethren, boldness to enter into the holiest by the blood of Jesus, by a new and living way, which he hath consecrated for us, through the veil, that is to say, his flesh*; his rent flesh, that is the meaning of it. I shall speak a little further concerning this new way to heaven; for it will be my main work, in prosecuting this exhortation, to press you to take it. All who are good are pleased with it. 1. The justice of God is pleased with it: that the justice of God should be pleased with a way to heaven for sinners is a marvellous thing; but justice is pleased with this; for hereby it gets a full satisfaction. The justice of God never got such a satisfaction as by the blood of Christ. Blinded sinners think to appease the justice of God, and to atone it by their own little doings; but justice never got a satisfaction but by the shedding of this blood. 2. The law is satisfied and pleased with this way to heaven. I do not say the law of God tells us the way to heaven, it is the gospel only that reveals this; but when the law sees the way to heaven revealed in the gospel, it hath nothing to say against it. *The righteousness of God without the law is manifested, being witnessed by the law and the prophets*, Rom. 3:21. We do not destroy the law by this way. *Do we then make void the law through faith? God forbid, yea, we establish the law*, Rom. 3:31. God's law never got so much honour in this world, and never will get so much honour in the next world, as it did by shedding the blood of Jesus Christ. When the law sheds the blood of a sinner, it gets some glory; but how small is that honour which arises to the law from the destruction of a criminal? Aye, but when God's own Son comes to offer to the law the blood of God, what a dignity is this to the law? That the law hath this, as it were, to record, 'I have not only sent multitudes of sinners to hell, but I punished God's own Son in man's nature; he fulfilled all the righteousness that I demanded, and performed all the obedience that I craved.' All the punishment that the law inflicted he bore; he was made under the law, and fulfilled the whole law. 3. This new way to heaven, by the sprinkling of the blood of Jesus, is pleasing to all the BLESSED THREE, to FATHER, SON, and SPIRIT. The Father is pleased with this way of salvation by the sprinkling of the blood of Jesus; for it was his own contrivance, it was his own act, his own pleasure: it is called the pleasure of JEHOVAH, Isa. 53:10. *It pleased the Lord to bruise him, and the pleasure of the Lord shall prosper in his hand.* How did the Lord's pleasure prosper in Christ's hand? If I may so say, the pleasure of the Lord could not have prospered in Christ's hands till the pleasure of the Lord had been in shedding his blood; and thus the pleasure of the Lord prospered in his hands. Our Lord himself was pleased with it, it was his delight; he died cheerfully and willingly; this lay at his heart: *Sacrifice and offering thou didst not desire, burnt offering and sin-offering hast thou not required; then said I, lo! I come: in the volume of thy book it is written of me, I delight to do thy will, O my God: yea, thy law is within my heart*, Psa. 40:6, 7, Heb. 10:8, 9. The Holy Ghost is also well pleased with it; for he sanctified him, and witnessed to him at his death, but more especially at his resurrection. 4. We may go further about this; all the angels in heaven are satisfied with this new way of salvation: they are mightily pleased with it; though it is not the way of their salvation, it is a way they are highly pleased with: they pry into it, and they give praise for it, 1 Pet. 1:12. The suffering of Christ, and the glory that shall follow, are things that the angels desire to look into. *To the intent*, saith the apostle, *that now unto principalities and powers in heavenly places, might be known by the church the manifold wisdom of God*, Eph. 3:10. And they praise in heaven on this account; Rev. 5:11, 12. *And I beheld, and heard the voice of many angels about the throne, and the living creatures, and the elders; and the number of them was ten thousand times ten thousand, and thousands of thousands; saying with a loud voice, Worthy is the Lamb that was slain, to receive power, and riches, and wisdom, and strength, and honour, and glory, and blessing.* We do not know that the angels get any good by Christ's death; they did not stand in need of the sprinkling of the blood of Jesus Christ, but they stood in need of confirming grace from their great head; for our Lord Jesus Christ is the head of principalities and powers, Col. 2:10. The angels are part of the triumphant church above, and are under the headship of Jesus Christ, as the word frequently speaks. The angels in heaven are pleased with this new way; for there is joy in heaven, in the presence of the angels of God, over one sinner that repenteth and is brought home to God by Jesus Christ. 5. All the glorified saints in heaven are pleased with this way to heaven, by the sprinkling of the blood of Christ: and of this there is no doubt; for their everlasting praise proceeds on this account. Rev. 5:9, *They sung a new song, saying, Thou art worthy to take the book, and to open the seals thereof: for thou wast slain, and hast redeemed us to God by thy blood, out of every kindred, and tongue, and people, and nation*: from thence rises their song of praise. 6. This way of salvation is pleasing to all believers that are on the face of the earth. To be saved, to come to heaven, by the sprinkling of the blood of Jesus, is pleasing to every believer; nay more, if I may so say, it is their being heartily pleased with this that makes them believers; for believing stands in a heart-satisfaction with the sprinkled blood of Jesus. Aye, but are there none who are displeased with this way of salvation? Yes, there are; and their being displeased with it is the praise of it. All the devils are bitterly displeased with this sprinkling of the blood of Christ upon sinners; for they know they have no share in it: the greatest enmity that the devil hath is against Jesus Christ as a Saviour. All the damned in hell are displeased at this; for they are past all hopes of benefit thereby. And all unbelievers upon earth are displeased with it; because they do not know it. So that this way of salvation by the sprinkling of the blood of Jesus, is pleasing to all heaven, and only displeasing to hell, and to poor blind unbelievers here upon earth. So much for this first Use.—Learn to admire at this strange way of salvation, to save us by the sprinkling of the blood of Jesus Christ!

Use 2. I would now, in the next place, lead you to the examining and trying yourselves, whether this sprinkling hath come upon you or not; a very important matter this to be managed by every one! 'Hath this sprinkling of the blood of Jesus come upon me? Am I sprinkled by it?' It is not enough that Christ's blood was shed, and that you know wherefore, to sprinkle the altar above for satisfaction; to sprinkle heaven to make an entrance therein for poor sinners; to sprinkle the covenant, and to seal it for a charter and testament of Jesus Christ; but you must labour to know whether this sprinkling hath come upon you. It is not enough that you sit under the gospel and the preaching of it: truly the preaching of the gospel rightly, is like the bunch of hyssop that Moses put into the bason of the blood of the covenant, and sprinkled it round among the people; and the preaching of the gospel is as it were the scattering of the virtue of the blood of Jesus upon all them that will receive it by faith; but a great many hear, that are not partakers of it, for all that. It is not enough that you come under the sacraments, and use them, though they are the means of the sprinkling of the blood of Jesus. Baptism is a representation of the washing virtue of this blood; the Lord's supper, especially the cup in it, is a representation of the nourishing virtue of this blood shed for the sins of men; yet people may be under both these, they may be baptised, and receive the Lord's supper frequently, and yet not be sprinkled with the blood of Christ. The apostle speaks of an Old Testament instance, and applies it with respect to New Testament professors, 1 Cor. 10:1-5, *Moreover, brethren, I would not that ye should be ignorant, how that all our fathers were under the cloud, and all passed through the sea; and went all baptised unto Moses in the cloud, and in the sea; and did all eat the spiritual meat, and did all drink the same spiritual drink.* Why doth the apostle call it spiritual meat, and spiritual drink? Was it not true, real, nourishing bread that fell from heaven? and was it not true, wholesome water that flowed from the rock? Surely they were not fed by dreams and imaginations, but they were real creatures of God; and it may be bread better than ever man eat, and water better than ever man drank: for the more eminently the hand of God appeared in forming those creatures, the better it is likely they were. Why then doth the apostle call them spiritual meat, and spiritual drink? Because they were of a spiritual signification: *For they drank of that spiritual rock that followed them, and that rock was Christ.* Never a time that an Israelite was hungry but he did eat Christ; never a time that he was thirsty but he drank Christ; that is, spiritually and typically. But notwithstanding this, the apostle adds, *With many of them God was not well pleased: for they were overthrown in the wilderness.* They liked the waters well enough, and were nourished and refreshed by them, but the spiritual signification of them they did not understand; and God was not well pleased with them, and they were overthrown for their rebellion. And just so is it with professors now. We have a great many words and much talking about the seals of the covenant, baptism and the Lord's supper; about the way, time, means, and methods of them; but here is the main business, Where is the sprinkling of the blood of Jesus? hath the virtue of this blood come on you or not? that is the main question: a question I would say these two things about. It is of the greatest importance, and of great difficulty. 1*st*, It is of the greatest importance to be determined; for our eternal state stands and depends upon it. You will not say any man can be saved that is not elected; so no man can be saved who is not sprinkled with the blood of Jesus; and who is not sanctified by the Spirit: for all these three are of equal necessity about our salvation. 2*dly*, This is a matter of *great difficulty* to be resolved, because it is about a great mystery. People commonly mistake about mysteries, and are in the dark concerning them. Jesus Christ himself is a great mystery, and the communication of his virtue to men is a great mystery; and the application of it to the soul is a great mystery. Indeed, Sirs, it is but in the dark that we know how we are saved; we know that Jesus Christ is the only Saviour, and that his saving power is put forth upon us, or we cannot be saved; but how this is done, who can tell? The poor creature that touched the hem of Christ's garment, found virtue coming forth from him, Mark 5:28, 29, for the cure of her body; and Christ found virtue going from him on her faith; but the poor woman could not give a rational account how this came to pass, that her touching by faith the hem of Christ's garment should bring in this saving, healing power to her body. Many touched Christ as well as she, but none touched him so as she did: she had a special errand to him, and special business with him, and made a special application to him: that touch she gave with her finger to the border of his garment reached secretly and powerfully to the heart and love of our Lord Jesus Christ, and drew forth relief immediately. Of these three things that are in my text, the greatest difficulty lies in knowing the two first; for election is never rightly known immediately by itself, but by its effects; and the sprinkling of blood cannot be immediately known by us, but by our application to it, and the fruits of it upon us. But the sanctification of the Spirit is quite another thing; it is something that falls upon ourselves, and upon our nature, regenerating us, and framing us to a newness of life. I shall offer a few things at this time concerning the sprinkling of the blood of Jesus; whereby you may know whether you have gotten it or not.

1st, All high-prizers of, and praisers for it, have this sprinkling of the blood of Christ upon them. This I will prove; for wheresoever the virtue of Christ's blood is put forth, there it is known, and wheresoever it is known, it is highly esteemed. I do not say, that the man knows he hath got it; but he that hath it feels something that makes him prize it greatly. *We preach Christ crucified*, saith the apostle, *to the Jews a stumbling-block, and to the Greeks foolishness*, 1 Cor. 1:23. They saw nothing at all in Christ crucified, in a man that was slain and hanged on a tree without the gates of Jerusalem, that the apostles should go up and down the world and preach salvation through him; they saw nothing of glory in this; *But*, saith the apostle, *to them that are called, Christ the wisdom of God and the power of God*. 'In that day that I was in the dark,' would the apostle say, 'I was an enemy to Jesus Christ, and I thought as little of him as any of you now do; but after I was called by his grace, the matter was quite otherwise; Christ was then to me the power of God, and the wisdom of God.' God never did a wiser thing in this world than in saving men by Christ Jesus; and God never put forth his power more effectually than in making Jesus Christ the great mean of saving a lost world.

2dly, Would you know whether you ever had any thing of the sprinkling of the blood of Christ upon you, enquire, whether ever you had any thing that this blood is sprinkled upon; What is that? It is upon a guilty conscience. The blood of Christ is only applied, and only applicable to a guilty conscience; to a man condemned by the law, seeing and judging himself as ripe and ready for hell: this is the only man that can be sprinkled by the blood of Jesus. *How much more*, saith the apostle, Heb. 9:14, *shall the blood of Christ purge your conscience from dead works?* 'You were wearied with dead works, and burdened thereby, and then this sprinkling came upon you.' Oh what a trifling creature is a man with a secure conscience! he plays, as it were, with Jesus Christ. He may talk of Jesus Christ, and commend him as Lord and King; but for the blood of Jesus Christ, he sees no need of it, nor has he any use for it. No man can apply to this blood but a man who finds he has a guilty conscience; that hath his conscience as a serpent or vulture gnawing within; this is the man that values the blood of sprinkling: *For without the shedding of blood, there could be no remission of sins*, Heb. 9:22.

3dly, Would you know whether this blood of sprinkling hath come upon you, and that its virtue has reached you, you may know it this way; Are you come to it, and are you users of it? Christ has many sweet names, engaging names, to poor sinners to make an errand to him. Every name that Christ hath, a poor sinner should make an errand to him under that name. But the chief errand that every poor sinner should have to Christ is in respect to his own sins; now it is this name of the sprinkling of the blood of Jesus that makes him amiable to a poor sinner, and therefore he would fain come near to him that he may get it. To give you a similitude: When Moses sprinkled the blood of the covenant upon the people, Exod. 24:6-8, you must not think that this blood of the goat or bullock could go any great way in sprinkling the people; there was no necessity that every one of the Israelites should have the mark of the blood on their raiment; but it was their duty to get as near as they could to that external sprinkling, that sanctified to the purifying of the flesh. So in this gospel Christ's blood is held forth; and people should come as near to it as they can, praying and looking that the virtue of it may reach them. *Ye are come*, saith the apostle, Heb. 12:24, *to the blood of sprinkling,* That is your part and duty; and if this blood of sprinkling comes on you, ye are saved, and that is your mercy. We should labour to get nearer to Jesus, and we should reckon it a great happiness if we might but once touch the hem of his garment; but to touch his heart, to touch his heart's blood that was shed for the remission of the sins of many! blessed be the shedder; blessed be the sender; blessed be the comer! The Lord hath bought his flock with his own blood, and a great many of them are got safe to heaven, and the rest are following and will be quickly there; and we should long for the day when the Redeemer and the redeemed shall be seen together.

SERMON V.

1 Pet. 1:2

Elect according the foreknowledge of God the Father, through sanctification of the Spirit, unto obedience, and sprinkling of the blood of Jesus Christ: Grace unto you, and peace be multiplied.

YOU have heard in the opening of these words what respect they have to the preceding. The sprinkling of the blood of Christ is to be understood as relating to the first words of the verse, *Elect according to the foreknowledge of God the Father; and not unto the sanctification of the Spirit.* The sprinkling of the blood of Jesus doth necessarily precede the sanctification of the Spirit: upon that account it was, that I entered on the handling of it before the other. You have heard of the blood of Jesus Christ, and of the sprinkling of it, and of the great interest that it hath in our salvation. I began to apply this, and insisted on two uses. 1*st*, I called you to a spiritual right, the admiring this great work of God, that our salvation comes by the sprinkled blood of Jesus. When sin came into the world, no sinful person could be saved, unless a sinless man had died for him; and a sinless man's dying could never have saved them; but this man must be God, or rather God's own Son must be man, and so shed the blood of God. I know we live in a corrupt day, wherein the grand fundamentals of the gospel are warmly debated, and most wickedly opposed, and this virtuous blood of Christ most wickedly blasphemed; an abomination that God will visit for, in his own time: happy they who are innocent of the guilt! *2dly*, I called you to try, whether or not this blood of Christ be sprinkled on you: Be persuaded, that it was of absolute necessity to the salvation of the elect, that the blood of the Son of God should be shed for them; so it is of as great necessity to the salvation of every particular believer, that the virtue of this blood should be upon them.

There are two heads of exhortation that I would now farther speak to.

First, To believers that are sprinkled by this blood of Jesus; who not only were elected to it, but on whom purpose of election hath taken place. Every believer in Jesus Christ hath it, though every believer does not know he is a believer; and therefore he cannot know all the privileges that belong to believers. But every poor sinner that ventures his eternal salvation on this blood shed, the sprinkled virtue of it is upon him, according to the manifold promises given by our Lord, that whosoever believeth on him hath everlasting life, John 6:47. There are two or three things that I would say to such. To them, *1st*, that though they dare not say boldly that they are believers, yet they can call God to witness, that all their hopes towards God for time and eternity, for the remission of their sins now, and the admission of their persons to eternal life hereafter, they are all bottomed and placed on the blood of Jesus Christ: such are believers, whether they think so or not.

1st, It is required of them who are believers, and sprinkled with the blood of Jesus Christ, that they should give praise and thanks for it. Spiritual mercies are great mercies, and they should be greatly praised for. This is the greatest of all mercies, to be sprinkled with the blood of Jesus Christ. Christians should bewail their ignorance of their spiritual state on this account; not only because they want that peace which the knowledge of their state would bring them, but also because the Lord calls for that praise, which the knowledge of our state would incline us to give him. Peter, in this epistle, and the apostle Paul, in almost every one of his epistles, begins with thanksgiving on the account of the grace of God bestowed on him, and on the rest of believers to whom he writes. I shall never reckon that Christian in a very spiritual frame, who hath not a deep sense of the debt of mercy, and a strong inclination to pay that debt in praise. I know that generally Christians are of another temper, though that is not a very good sign: if they can but tenderly and feelingly complain; if they can but pray heartily, and beg blessings greedily from the hand of God, then they think they are in a good frame; and indeed I do not deny but there is something of goodness in that frame.—But how few are there who have this sense upon their spirits? 'How many mercies have I received from the Lord, and how seldom have I praised him for them?' Shall so great a blessing as the virtue of the blood of Christ pass upon the soul, and shall not a man praise the Lord heartily for it? We find the apostle, in the next verse to my text, blessing *the God and Father of our Lord Jesus Christ, for begetting us again to a lively hope, through the resurrection of Christ from the dead*, ver. 3. And whosoever are thankful for the virtue of Christ's resurrection, it is impossible but they must also be thankful for the virtue of his death: for Christ's death, and the virtue of it, are implied in his resurrection. What needed Christ's resurrection, unless he had been dead? and therefore the purchase of our blessings come by the death of Christ, and the application of them by his resurrection. So saith the apostle, Rom. 4:25, *He was delivered for our offences, and raised again for our justification.* This is the first exhortation; Give hearty praise for this blood of sprinkling; bind it as a duty upon our consciences, and set about it; and I can assure you that you will find great advantage by it. Many Christians have tried it, and I can appeal to the experience of several here, who know what this means, when they have been in a vein of complaining, that hardness of heart, and dulness and deadness, have prevailed strangely; but when the poor creatures have been by the hand of God inclined and turned to think of the great bounty of God towards them, and have begun to be exercised in the work of praise, they have presently found their bonds to be loosed, and that the Spirit of life hath entered, and they have found sweet communion with God therein.

2dly, You that have had the blood of sprinkling passing upon you through faith in Christ Jesus, *stand in it before God.* Whensoever this thought enters into your mind, 'The eye of the all-seeing God is now upon me, and this great God judges all things, and determines concerning my present state; what case then should I desire to stand in before him?' Only in this blood of sprinkling; as if the poor believer should say, 'Let God never cast his eye upon me, but that he may always see the sprinkled blood of Christ upon me!' There are two things I would say concerning it. This sprinkling of the blood of Jesus is our only guard against justice and ruin; and it is our only ornament to commend us to the acceptance of God. 1. It is our only guard against the justice and law of God. You have heard of the typical blood of the paschal lamb, that was sprinkled upon the posts of the Israelites' doors; what a vain thing had it been for an Israelite to stand in his arms at his door, to guard his house against the avenging angel? alas! the destroying angel went to Pharaoh's house, and despised his guards, and executed the judgments of God according to his commission. The only guard that the poor Israelites had, was to sprinkle the blood of the paschal lamb on the posts of their doors; and if the destroying angel was not kept back by that, they had nothing else to trust to. So, whenever you think of standing before a holy and just God, it is this sprinkling of the blood of Jesus that must be your only guard: for most assuredly the sword of justice will pierce and draw the blood of that soul which hath not this blood sprinkled upon it. 2. This is our only ornament in the sight of God. There are two things that we should still desire in all our thoughts of God: the one is, to be safe from his displeasure; and the other is, to be amiable and pleasing in his sight. A natural man cares for no more from God than what will save him from being ruined by him; but a spiritual man desires not only to be saved from destruction by the Almighty, but he also desires to be in terms of peace with God; that God may look graciously on him, and that he may stand with acceptance in his sight: now nothing else can procure this, nor obtain it, but this sprinkling of the blood of Christ. *We are accepted*, saith the apostle, *in that beloved*, Eph. 1:6, 7. But how came ye to be accepted in the beloved? what did it cost that beloved to make you accepted? *In whom we have redemption through his blood, the forgiveness of sins, according to the riches of his grace.* Rich grace, and dear blood, there stands our safety; it was rich grace that sent the person to die, and it was rich grace that accepted the blood for our sake, and for our advantage; and the virtue of this blood is reckoned to us for the forgiveness of our sins.

3dly, Not only stand before God in this sprinkled blood of Christ, but plead with God in every case upon the account of this blood. I say, you must learn to plead with God in every case upon the account of this blood. You think, and you think rightly, that Jesus Christ is a great intercessor in heaven; that he is a powerful pleader, and so he is; but what is the great argument that he pleads upon? What is it that makes all his pleadings successful, and that secures answers of peace to all whom he pleads for? It is from the virtue of this blood of his; he pleads upon his own blood, and we that are poor sinners must do so too. *By his own blood*, saith the apostle, Heb. 9:12, *he entered in once into the holy place, having obtained eternal redemption for us*; and in the power and virtue of that blood he still appears before God for us. Whatsoever you ask, you must ask it in the name of our Lord Jesus Christ: But, if I may so say, what is the main letter in the name of Jesus, that the eye of our faith is to be mainly to be upon in all our pleadings with God? It is the name of this blood, he that shed his blood for all the blessings that we beg of God. There are three things chiefly that discourage believers in their pleadings with God, and they are all three answered from this blood of sprinkling. (1.) When we plead with God, we are apt to think with ourselves that God is great: *With God is terrible majesty*, Job 37:22. He is so far above us, that we are confounded when we speak to him. Good Abraham our father, that great believer, had a deep sense of this, Gen. 18:27, *Behold now I have taken upon me to speak unto the Lord, who am but dust and ashes*. Now, what ground of boldness can a poor creature, and a great sinner, have in approaching to God? Only this, We bring the blood of God with us; if I may say so, we bring the blood of one as great as he is, to whom we come. (2.) Believers are discouraged in praying sometimes, from the greatness of the things that they ask; we ask blessings that are vastly great, pardon of sin, peace with God; we ask no less than the Spirit of God, nothing less than an eternal crown of glory. What is it that makes us so bold, to beg so great blessings as these are? Only because we come in the name of that blood which is a just price for the biggest of them. Though we have not one farthing of our own to give towards the least of them, yet by the virtue of this blood of Jesus we produce, as it were, and lay before the Lord, a price big enough for the greatest of them. This blood of Christ is a sufficient price for all the pardons that are obtained upon earth, and for all the supplies of grace that believers receive now, and for all the crowns of glory that they will be partakers of hereafter; Christ's blood is worth them all. (3.) Believers are often discouraged in their pleadings with God, from their own sinfulness, and the sinfulness of their way of pleading; both the supplicants, and their supplications, afford us great matter of fear. When a man knows what himself is, and knows what his performances are, so poor, so sorry, so pitiful, this thought presently arises in our hearts, Will the great God ever accept such persons as we are? No, never, if we come in our own name; but if we come sprinkled with the blood of Jesus Christ, that is the only thing regarded in us; all things in us, and all things in our supplications are covered and clothed thereby.

Lastly, You that are sprinkled with the blood of Jesus Christ, take good heed that you do not defile and stain it. Take heed that you do not defile the blood of Christ by loose, careless, and unholy walking. The apostle charges a kind of Christians that were in his day, with this, *Do they not blaspheme that worthy name by which ye are called?* If it were only a reproach to yourselves, it would be but a small matter, but they blaspheme the name of your Lord and Master on your account. There are two things that I would fain have Christians take notice of about this. (1.) The smart that is given to a tender conscience from the dishonour that is done to the name of Christ. I could wish that people had a greater sense of this than of their own damnation; it should wound the heart of a tender Christian more, to be the occasion of reproach to the name of Christ, than to be the occasion of endangering his own eternal salvation; even as his glory should be dearer to us than all things else which concern ourselves. (2.) I would fain have Christians know also, the force there is in faith on the blood of sprinkling constraining the soul to the study of holiness: for my part, I shall never expect to see the holiness that is worth a farthing amongst Christians (not only that it will not be accepted with God, but it will have no beauty before men), till it derive its original from this spring, the believing of the virtue of the sprinkled blood of Christ. Oh what a mighty constraining thing is that to a man to be holy! *The love of Christ constraineth us*, saith the apostle, *because we thus judge, that if one died for all, then were all dead*, 2 Cor. 5:14. I know the common topics for holiness that are mainly managed by preachers, and that are mightily relished by many hearers: Such and such things are plainly commanded by God, therefore do them; such things are plainly threatened by God, therefore forbear them; such a practice is encouraged by a promise, therefore engage in it. These are the common topics of holiness, and a natural man may have some gust and relish of such things; but the grand gospel motive to holiness, none but a believer can have any sense of: 'I am sprinkled by the blood of Jesus Christ, therefore I must be holy; I am delivered by Christ from all sin, therefore I must be holy.' *How shall we that are dead to sin, live any longer therein?* saith the apostle, Rom. 6:2. 'And how came we to be dead to sin, but by Christ's dying for us in our sins, and thereby delivering us from our sins; and therefore we will cast them off by the help of his grace.' It is the promise, *Sin shall not have dominion over you; for ye are not under the law, but under grace*, Rom. 6:14, this is an argument of special force, but its force is only known and felt by a lively believer. But I shall pass this at present, because we shall have farther occasion to speak more to it, when we come to treat of the sanctification of the Spirit. So much for this *first* branch of the exhortation to believers.

2*dly*, I am now to speak a word of exhortation to *unbelievers*, to people who never had any business all their life-time about this blood of sprinkling; who read of it in their Bibles, but never felt any thing of it in their exercise, never felt any thing of the power of it.

I would first reason a few things with such sort of persons. 1. Do not you know that you are sinners? There are none of you that will deny that you are sinners; but there are many that say they are sinners, who never knew what it was to be a sinner. They know what it is to sin, but they do not know what it is to be a sinner. Whosoever knows himself to be a sinner, knows himself to be the vilest creature in the world, save the devil, and indeed some way worse than he: for none of us but are guilty of those sins the devil is free of. The devil was never guilty of the sin of unbelief in this world; for a Saviour was never in his offer, and was never despised by him. I know he hates the Saviour, but the Saviour was never in his offer; gospel-unbelief is none of the devil's sins; although there is corruption enough in the devil to act any villainy, but yet this is quite out of his reach. 2. Do ye not know what sin deserves? do ye not consider that you have many thousand times over deserved eternal ruin? *For the wages of sin is death*, Rom. 6:23. 3. Do ye not know that Jesus Christ is the only Saviour of sinners? These three things every one will say they know: That they are sinners; that sin deserves wrath; and that it is Jesus Christ only can save from this wrath. Then proceed to inquire, in the 4th place, How it is that Jesus Christ saves sinners from wrath? There are many that will say, Christ saves us by dying for us. This is a good answer; but do ye understand what there is in this dying for us! He came in his people's room, he came in their stead, he took upon him their persons, their guilty condemned persons, and was dealt with by law and justice accordingly: Our Lord Jesus Christ in saving us from wrath had a very hard task of it. 5. Do ye know what Christ doth in and for them that he saves? What our Lord did when he was here upon earth, was to offer an universal atonement for all his people, a great part of whom were not to live in the world till a long time after he died. Now our Lord Jesus Christ, that he might be a complete Saviour, besides what he did then in redemption, hath a great deal of work to do about every particular believer; and therefore it is not enough to know that Christ saves sinners by dying for them, but you must also know what he doth actually in them whom he saves; to whom he applies what he wrought out; he comes near to the soul, and puts forth his virtue upon it, and unites it to himself: *And he that is joined to the Lord is one Spirit*, 1 Cor. 6:17. 6. Do ye know what Christ requires of them who partake of this saving power of his? They must believe on him, and come to him, and trust in him, and adventure their souls upon him. So that granting your assent to all these six things: That you are sinners; that sin deserves wrath; that Christ is the only Saviour from this wrath; that he saves the whole body, his church, by his death; that he applies this death to particular persons by the power of his Spirit; and that every one who would have this blessing must make application to him for it by faith; from all these things there remains one question, and let your consciences answer it as in the sight of God, Have you done so? There is the blood of sprinkling here spoken of, Have you betaken yourselves to it? You have prayed many times, it may be, and come to the ordinances of the gospel many times; but have you ever made a particular errand to Jesus Christ about this? 'Here is a guilty conscience of mine, that shall never be quiet till this blood of Jesus Christ purgeth it by an effectual application.'

I would, in the next place, commend this question to your consideration, that you may be careful how to get an answer to it, Whether you have ever made an application to this blood of sprinkling? This question hath three things to commend it to your consideration. 1*st*, Our standing before God for peace and acceptance to all eternity, depends upon this alone; make but this sure, that the blood of sprinkling hath been upon you, never make any question of your possessing eternal life. 2*dly*, Your place in Christ's church depends upon this: What is the reasonable condition that is required of any man that offers himself to a well ordered church? It is this, that the person declares truly and plainly that he is a lost sinner, and that all his hope of salvation is from the virtue of the blood of Jesus Christ. Let a man declare this in what words he pleases, that one may reasonably and charitably believe him, and there is no more required of him. But if a person should be so far left of God, as to declare, either by words or deeds, that he hath no kind of trust in the sprinkling of the blood of Christ, there is no right ordered church but would cast him out immediately. What hath the church of Christ to do with any, but with them who fairly profess, that all their hope of eternal life flows from the sprinkling of the blood of Christ? You first give yourselves up to the Lord, and then to each other, to be for the Lord and not for another. 3*dly*, The solid peace of your conscience depends on your answering this question. I know not what sort of consciences some persons have, that are sometimes quickly disturbed with that which is of no great concernment, and sometimes they are as quickly pacified with that which is also of no great concernment. Imaginary sins sometimes disturb weak consciences; and that which is more common and worse, imaginary relief sometimes pacifies deluded consciences. But this is what I declare unto you, in the name of Christ, that whensoever you come to know what true soul-trouble, what true sickness of conscience, is, you will find that all the ministers in the world cannot send you true consolation, but what arises from the virtue of this blood of sprinkling: and therefore you may see of what great concernment it is for men to know whether they have come to this blood of sprinkling or not. If you are come to it by faith, it is upon you; and if it be upon you, your state is secure to all eternity.

I would now, in order to stir you up to a right application to this blood of sprinkling, just lay before you these five or six considerations, and then proceed.

1st, Consider, Jesus Christ in and with his blood is proposed and set forth to you in the gospel; remember this, Jesus Christ with his blood is set forth to you in the gospel. *God hath set him forth to be a propitiation, through faith in his blood, to declare his righteousness, for the remission of sins that are past, through the forbearance of God*, Rom. 5:25. Pray observe; the law comes and declares righteousness in charging men's sins upon them, and the gospel comes and declares God's righteousness, in a blessed way of absolving men from that charge; and this way is declared to us in the gospel, to be through Christ Jesus. This propitiation is wrought by his blood, and this blood is that which faith must take hold of and rest upon. The apostle Paul tells the Galatians, *That Christ Jesus was evidently set forth crucified before their eyes*, Gal. 3:1. What a blessed crucifier of Christ was the apostle Paul! he was daily, as it were, preaching over again the death of our Lord Jesus Christ, and diffusing, as far as he could, the power and virtue of it upon poor sinners. You would think it a strange thing now, if in the camp of the Israelites, when the brazen serpent was set up by God's appointment, with this proclamation going along with it, 'That whosoever in the camp were stung by the fiery serpents, let him but come to his tent-door, and look up to the brazen serpent, and he shall be a whole man immediately;' you would think it a strange thing that a poor Israelite, groaning to death within his tent, should refuse to come forth, and make use of this great appointment for his cure. The case is just the same: our Lord Jesus Christ is as this brazen serpent, and he is lifted up in the gospel; but for all that, a great many people have no business with him; though he be held forth to men in the gospel, they have no heart-dealing with him.

2dly, Jesus Christ deals with us in the gospel, and shall not we deal with him? Christ speaks to us two ways, he speaks to us in his own blood, and he speaks to us in our blood; in our blood of filth and defilement, Ezek. 16:6, and in his own blood of atonement. *When I passed by thee, and saw thee polluted in thy own blood, I said unto thee when thou wast in thy blood, Live; yea, I said unto thee when thou wast in thy blood, Live.* Christ also pleads with us in his own blood, this is the great argument that he deals with men by; he loved us, and shed his blood for us, and therefore prays us to be reconciled to him.

3dly, We should consider Christ's patience in dealing with us; this is a great reproach to them that have no heart to deal with him. Christ's patience towards sinners is a wonderful blessing; he waits a long while upon men; none can set bounds to his patience; none can tell how long it will last; none can promise himself a day more of Christ's patience: but yet his patience is a wonderful blessing. *Behold I stand at the door and knock*, Rev. 3:20, 'and I have staid a long while:' And truly I am afraid there are a great many grey-headed, and dim-eyed sinners too, in London, that have had Christ knocking at the door of their hearts all their days, and they have never thought of opening to him; they have never thought of dealing with him for eternal life: And should not these perish? One would almost say, it is pity such persons should not go to hell, who have had Christ beseeching and praying them, all their life long, to take salvation from him, and they have no heart to receive it. *I have spread out my hands all the day to a rebellious people; I said, Behold me, behold me, to a nation that was not called by my name*, Isa. 65:1, 2. 'I craved no great matter of them, no more but this, to open their eyes and see the Saviour, and to live by the sight of him.'

4thly, Christ deals with us about salvation and this consideration should make them ashamed that have no dealing with him. Be you persuaded of this, that whosoever lives under the rightly-preached gospel, at one time or another of their lives; they are brought under some conviction of this: 'Surely Jesus Christ is dealing with me about salvation; Why else doth he call, and wait, and knock, and entreat, and command, and threaten, and promise, and use all the means that can be used, but that he is dealing with me about salvation?' And if Christ be thus dealing with us, should not we deal with him? When Christ is trying so many cords of love, should not our hearts once yield a good return, and say, Behold I come, Lord, draw me nearer?

5thly, Consider this, that when Christ in this gospel is pleading in the virtue of his blood, he takes a most exact and careful notice of people's behaviour. When people attend public worship, sometimes they hear, and sometimes they do not; sometimes they wake, and sometimes they sleep, as the mood takes them; and indeed were it only creatures like yourselves that spoke to you, the matter would not be very great; but here is the weighty business, 'It is Jesus Christ that in this gospel is dealing with me about eternal salvation; and he takes exact notice how the frame of my heart stands towards him; if I slight and despise him, and neglect him and his great salvation, Heb. 2:3; if his precious blood be undervalued by me, these things, Christ remarks, and I shall hear of it another time.' Sirs, I am persuaded of this, there are many poor creatures who sit quietly under the preaching of the word, by a man like themselves, that yet in the carelessness of their hearts, and in the estrangedness of their thoughts from Jesus Christ, do commit a greater sin, and that they will make a more dreadful charge in their indictment, than any sin that ever they committed all their days. *I send the Spirit*, saith our Lord, John 16:9, *to convince the world of sin, because they believe not on me*. And that is only a sin of not doing something good; it is not, 'I will send the Spirit to convince them of sin, because they have broken the law of Moses,' but, *I will send the Spirit to convince them of sin, because they believe not on me*; because they have not their hearts kindly affected with desires after Jesus Christ. It is a sin of omission, and a most dreadful one.

Lastly, As Christ regards what entertainment he meets with from men now, so at the last day he will declare the same in judgment. *I came not to judge the world, the word that I have spoken, the same shall judge him in the last day*, John 12:48. This same word whereby you have been offered eternal life, will be a dreadful aggravation of your condemnation at last. Sirs, Christ and his despised blood will make a more dreadful cry of vengeance against the damned, than all the roarings of the devil and their fellow-damned in hell. Hear the voice of Christ's despised blood crying against men, when at the last day the judge shall say, 'This man was a despiser of my blood, which was tendered and offered to him all the days of his life, and yet never made an errand to it, and never desired to be sprinkled with it, and therefore shall be made a sacrifice to justice.' Therefore prevent all this, by making an application to the blood of sprinkling; which is nothing less, and nothing more, than for a poor sinner to come as a sinner, to a Saviour dying for sin, and saving him by his dying. Christ saves us by his dying, and the lost sinner must come to him for salvation. Therefore, Sirs, let there be a heart-dealing between Christ and you: you have often been told, that a profession is not worth taking up, and it is not worth the keeping, if the all of it stands in the view of the world; that the family knows, the congregation knows all that belongs to the man's godliness: that godliness is not worth the having. The beginning, the substance, the root of all true Christianity lies in these two things: What Christ by his Spirit deals with thy heart, and what thy heart by the same Spirit deals with Jesus Christ; and all the world can never know either the one or the other of these. The operation of the Spirit of Jesus Christ on the heart of a sinner, and the operation of the sinner's heart towards Jesus Christ; these two are the source and the spring of all true Christianity and godliness: and whatsoever a man hath without these, is worth nothing at all; but whosoever hath these things, truly there will be much besides them, flowing from them, that is worth something. Therefore now I would exhort you to make use of this sprinkling of the blood of Jesus, that is, that you may have a communication of the virtue and all the saving benefits of it, which secures our eternal state, and commends us to God. I shall offer three or four ways wherein you should do this.

1st, Deal with this blood of sprinkling by obedience to his commands, this is one thing. That person is in a hopeful way to salvation who is brought to this resolution, 'I now see by the gospel that I must intrust Jesus Christ with my soul, or I must provoke him; one of these two must be; and because his command is peremptory, every lost sinner, that sees himself to be so, should intrust his eternal salvation with him by faith.'

2dly, Employ Jesus Christ as Saviour, with the virtue of his blood, from mere necessity. I know there are better springs than this, but it is well if any thing will make a man come to Jesus Christ. Fell necessity, desperate necessity, should enforce us. When a poor sinner sees his case so bad that there is no hope for him; but only one heavenly remedy, the blood of Jesus Christ, that alone can put a stop to the quarrel between heaven and him: and therefore, saith the poor soul, I will try it from mere necessity.

3dly, Try to do this out of love; Oh! that all the world would believe on Jesus Christ merely from love to him. Jesus Christ, if I may so say, is a great vessel which will carry all that are in it safe to heaven: therefore let us embark in him, not only because we would not be drowned by the way, but because we love to be in him. There is a love to Jesus Christ that flows from faith, or that makes the following acts of faith more sensible to believers. Therefore,

Lastly, This employing of Christ must be by an adventuring trust: an adventure is that which a man hath some uncertainty about; I do not say, it should be so, but many times it is so. This is our trusting, it is a committing our greatest concern to this only safe hand to keep it. See now, how narrowly this matter is brought: Whensoever any of you have, at any time, any heart-concern about your salvation, remember now, hereafter, and at death, the matter can be only secured by a bold adventuring on the sprinkling of the blood of Jesus. 'I am such a sinner, saith the man, so undone, so distressed, so destroyed, so endangered by the law of God because of sin, that if the sprinkling of the blood of Jesus Christ be not able, to bear me out, I must sink to eternity under the burden of it.' Every one that adventures upon this should do it confidently, though but few can till they have tried the trade of believing for a time. It is a great work to save a sinner; and it is well that it is put into so great a hand; never had a sinner been saved unless Christ had been the Saviour. We have been speaking of employing Christ by faith, and this very faith Christ must be the author of. Oh that Christ might grow in our hearts, that holy one of God! Oh what reason have we to be ashamed of the bad entertainment that we have given to the Son of God! The Lord forgive and help us, and grant that the life that we live in the flesh may be by the faith of the Son of God!

SERMON VI.

1 PET. 1:2.

Elect according to the foreknowledge of God the Father, through sanctification of the Spirit, unto obedience, and sprinkling of the blood of Jesus Christ: Grace unto you, and peace be multiplied.

YOU have heard that this description of the parties which the apostle here writes to, is not only a discrimination of the persons, but it hath in it an account of all the great work of God about the salvation of his people. The election of the Father; the sanctification of the Spirit; and the sprinkling of the blood of Jesus. This sprinkling of the blood of Jesus is by the apostle put in the last place; yet because in the order of nature it hath indeed the second place in the dispensation of grace about our salvation, therefore I spoke unto it in the second place: and two things I proposed to handle upon it; 1*st*, The sprinkling of the blood of Jesus itself; 2*dly*, The respect that electing love and grace hath to it. To the former of these I have spoken at some length; I shall pass by the other at present, until I have spoken to the third thing, viz. the sanctification of the Spirit, and then I shall jointly handle the respect that electing grace hath to both. I come now to this third thing in the order of nature, though it be the second thing in the order of words; *the sanctification of the Spirit unto obedience*: so it is expressed. And here we have three things to discourse of. 1*st*, The sanctification itself. 2*dly*, The sanctification of the Spirit; what is to be understood when sanctification is thus expressed to us, *The sanctification of the Spirit*. 3*dly*, The end of this sanctification of the Spirit, it is sanctification of the Spirit *unto obedience*. It is not sanctification of the Spirit that is got by obedience, but it is sanctification of the Spirit that works obedience. Of these in order.

I. Of *sanctification itself*. There is a sanctification that is the same with justification, mentioned expressly by the apostle to the Hebrews, 10:10, *By the which will we are sanctified, through the offering of the body of Jesus once for all.* Sanctification is also an Old Testament phrase, whereby special devotedness to the Lord is expressed. Concerning sanctification, there are three things that I would speak to. 1*st*, What sanctification is. 2*dly*, Wherein it agrees with justification. 3*dly*, Wherein it differs from justification. And then I shall make some application of it for your edification.

1*st*, What sanctification is. It is a great deal better to feel it than to express it. Sanctification is the same with regeneration; the same with the renovation of the whole man; sanctification is the forming and the framing of the new creature; it is the implanting and engraving the image of Christ upon the poor soul. It is what the apostle breathed after, *That Christ might be formed in them*, Gal. 4:19. *That they might bear the image of the heavenly*, 1 Cor. 15:49. Sirs, there are but two men only that all the world is like; and so will it fare with them, as they are like the one, or like the other: the first Adam, and the second Adam. Every man by nature is like the first Adam, and like the devil: for the devil and the first fallen Adam were just like one another. *Ye are of your father the devil*, saith our Lord, John 8:44, *and he was a murderer from the beginning*. All the children of the first Adam are the devil's children, there is no difference here. And all the children of the other sort, are like to Jesus Christ, the second Adam; and when his image shall be perfected in them, then they shall be perfectly happy. *As we have also borne the image of the earthly, so shall we also bear the image of the heavenly*, 1 Cor. 15:49. Pray observe; We bear the image of the earthly by being born in sin and misery; we bear the image of the earthly by living in sin and misery; we bear the image of the earthly by dying in sin and misery; and we bear the image of the earthly in the rottenness of the grave: and we bear the image of the heavenly Adam when we are sanctified by his Spirit. This image increases in us according to our growth in sanctification: and we perfectly bear the image of the heavenly Adam when we are just like the man Christ, both in soul and body, perfectly happy, and perfectly holy; when we have overcome death by his grace, as he overcame it by his own strength. It will never be known how like believers are to Jesus Christ, till they are risen again: when they shall arise from their graves, like so many little suns shining in glory and brightness; Oh! how like will they then be to Jesus Christ! though his personal transcendent glory will be his property and prerogative to all eternity.

2*dly*, Wherein are justification and sanctification alike? We find them both in the text; the sprinkling of the blood of Jesus is justification; justification is an effect of the sprinkled blood of Jesus. Sanctification is also spoken of here, Wherein are these alike one to the other? I answer, in many things. 1*st*, They are like one another as they are the same in their author; it is God that justifieth, and it is God that sanctifies. Rom. 8:33, *Who shall lay any thing to the charge of God's elect? it is God that justifieth. I am the Lord that doth sanctify you*, is a common word in the Old Testament. Exod. 31:13, Lev. 20:8. 2*dly*, They are alike and the same in their rise, being both of free grace; justification is an act of free grace, and sanctification is the same. *Not by works of righteousness which we have done, but according to his mercy, he saved us by the washing of regeneration, and the renewing of the Holy Ghost*, Titus 3:5. They are both of grace. 3*dly*, They are alike in that they are both towards the same persons. Never a man is justified but he is also sanctified; and never a man is sanctified but he is also justified; all the elect of God, all the redeemed, have both these blessings passing upon them. 4*thly*, They are alike as to the time, they are the same in time. It is a hard matter for us to talk or think of time, when we are speaking of the works of God: these saving works of his are always done at the same time; a man is not justified before he is sanctified, though it may be conceived so in order of nature, yet at the same time, the same grace works both. *Such were some of you*, saith the apostle, 1 Cor. 6:11, *but ye are washed, but ye are sanctified, but ye are justified, in the name of the Lord Jesus, and by the Spirit of our God*. 5*thly*, They are the same as to the operation of them by the same means, that is, by the word of God: we are justified by the word, sentencing us to eternal life by the promise; and we are also sanctified by the power of the same word. *Now ye are clean*, saith our Lord, *through the word that I have spoken unto you*, John 15:3. *That he might sanctify and cleanse his church*, saith the apostle, *with the washing of water by the word*, Eph. 5:26. *Lastly*, They are the same as to their equal *necessity* to eternal life; I do not say, as to their equal *order*, but as to their equal *necessity*; that is, as it is determined that no man who is not justified shall be saved, so it is determined that no man who is not sanctified shall be saved: no unjustified man can be saved, and no unsanctified man can be saved. They are of equal necessity in order to the possessing of eternal life.

3dly, Wherein do justification and sanctification differ? This is a matter of great concernment for people's practice and daily exercise; wherein they differ. They agree in many things, as has just now been declared, but they likewise differ vastly. *1st*, Justification is an act of God about the *state* of a man's *person*; but sanctification is the work of God about the *nature* of a man: and these two are very different, as I shall illustrate by a similitude. Justification is an act of God as a judge about a delinquent, absolving him from a sentence of death; but sanctification is an act of God about us, as a physician, in curing us of a mortal disease. There is a criminal that comes to the bar, and is arraigned for high-treason; the same criminal has a mortal disease, that he may die of, though there was no judge on the bench to pass the sentence of death upon him for his crime. It is an act of grace which absolves the man from the sentence of the law, that he shall not suffer death for his treason; that saves the man's life: but notwithstanding this, unless his disease be cured, he may die quickly after, for all the judged pardon. Therefore, I say, justification is an act of God as a gracious judge, sanctification is a work of God as a merciful physician; David joins them both together, Psa. 103:3, *Who forgiveth all thine iniquities, who healeth all thy diseases*. It is promised, *That iniquity shall not be your ruin*, Ezek. 18:30, in the guilt of it; that is justification: and it shall not be your ruin, in the *power* of it; there lies sanctification. *2dly*, Justification is an act of God's grace upon the account of the righteousness of another, but sanctification is a work of God, infusing a righteousness into us; now there is a great difference between these two: for the one is by imputation, the other by infusion. In justification the sentence of God proceeds this way: the righteousness that Christ wrought out by his life and death, and the obedience that he paid to the law of God, is reckoned to the guilty sinner for his absolution; so that when a sinner comes to stand at God's bar, when the question is asked, Hath not this man broken the law of God? Yes, saith God; yes, saith the conscience of the poor sinner, I have broken it innumerable ways: And doth not the law condemn thee to die for thy transgressions? Yes, saith the man;

yes, saith the law of God, the law knows nothing more but this; *The soul that sinneth must die.* Well then, but is there no hope in this case? Yes, and gospel grace reveals this hope; there is one that took sin on him, and died for our sins, and his righteousness is reckoned for the poor sinner's justification; and thus we are absolved. We are absolved in justification by God's reckoning on our account; on our behalf, and for our advantage, what Christ hath done and suffered for us; but in sanctification the Spirit of God infuses a holiness into the soul. I do not say, he infuses a righteousness; for I would fain have these words, *righteousness* and *holiness*, better distinguished than generally they are. Righteousness and holiness are, in this case, to be kept vastly asunder. All righteousness is without us; our holiness is within us, it is our own; the apostle plainly makes that distinction, Phil. 3:9, *Not having mine own righteousness*: it is our own, not originally, but our own inherently; not our own so as to be of our own working, but our own because it is indwelling in us. But our righteousness is neither our own originally nor inherently; it is neither wrought out by us, nor doth it dwell in us; but it is wrought out by Jesus Christ, and it eternally dwells in him, and is only to be pleaded by faith, by a poor creature. But our holiness, though it be not our own originally, yet it is our own inherently, it dwells in us: this is the distinction that the apostle makes, Phil. 3:9, *That I may be found in him, not having my own righteousness, which is of the law, but that which is through the faith of Christ, the righteousness which is of God by faith. 3dly*, Justification is perfect, but sanctification is imperfect; and here lies a great difference between them. Justification, I say, is perfect, and admits of no degrees; admits of no decays, admits of no intermission, nor of any intercession: but sanctification admits of all these. When I say justification is perfect, I mean, that every justified man is equally and perfectly justified. The poorest believer that is this day in the world, is justified as much as ever the apostle Paul was; and every true believer is as much justified now, as he will be a thousand years hence. Justification is perfect in all them that are partakers of it, and to all eternity; it admits of no degrees; and the plain reason of it is this—the ground of it is the perfect righteousness of Jesus Christ, and the entitling us to it is by an act of God the gracious Judge, and that act stands for ever; *And if God justifies, who is he that shall condemn?* Rom.

8:33. But sanctification is an imperfect, incomplete, changeable thing. One believer is more sanctified than another. I am apt to believe that the apostle Paul was more sanctified the first hour of his conversion, than any man this day in the world. Sanctification differs greatly as to the persons that are partakers of it; and it differs greatly too as to the same man; for a true believer, a truly sanctified man, may be more holy and sanctified at one time than at another. There is a work required of us, *To be perfecting holiness in the fear of God*, 2 Cor. 7:1, but we are no where required to be perfecting righteousness in the sight of God; for God hath brought in a perfect righteousness, in which we stand; but we are to take care, and to give diligence to perfect holiness in the fear of God. A saint in glory is more sanctified than ever he was; for he is perfectly so: but he is not more justified than he was; nay, a saint in heaven is not more justified than a believer on earth is: only they know it better, and the glory of that light in which they see it, discovers it more brightly and more clearly to them.

I shall add but two words of advice on this head, of the difference between justification and sanctification. Do not divide them. Do not confound them.

1*st*, Do not divide and separate them: no man can do so, but in dream and notion. Justification and sanctification God hath joined together, and no man can put them asunder. They are everlastingly united together, and every one that is a partaker of either is a partaker of both. 2*dly*, Do not confound them. I am persuaded that one of the main causes of the disorder that is in the spirits and the conversation of the most part of Christians, lies in their confounding these two great blessings. They do not give them their proper place; they are not rightly exercised about them in their due sphere; therefore I shall offer a word or two of advice for preventing this confounding of them. When you are seeking justification, let there be no mind of sanctification, I mean as to any merit; but when you are seeking sanctification, have a good mind to justification. To make this matter plain to you; when you are seeking justification, you should have no thought of sanctification; the reason is, because justification is an act of pure grace, that we must betake ourselves to God for, as poor condemned sinners. If men will perplex us with qualifications, pray let it run this way, What is it that qualifies a sinner for justification? it is this only, that he must be a condemned sinner; God's law must condemn him, and the man must come into God's court with this sentence in his hand, 'Lord, justify a poor sinner for Christ's sake; the law hath condemned me, and sentenced me to hell, and thither I must go except gospel grace relieves me in Christ Jesus.' When I say that in seeking justification you should have no mind of sanctification, my meaning is only this, that when you come to plead at God's bar for justification, do not dream of bringing your sanctification with you: for it is altogether improper and impertinent at this court. Let men varnish their doctrines which way they will, and cover them what pretences they please, they do but murder souls, who pretend to advise them to bring something with them to God for the grace of justification. Bring thy sins with thee, and bring the curse of the law upon thy conscience, and lay these before the Lord, saying, 'Lord, here is an undone sinner, have mercy upon me, for Christ's sake:' there should be nothing else heard there but that. But when you come for sanctification, you have good reason to mind justification, for it flows from it. When you would try your justification, in God's name try it by your sanctification, that is allowed you; the reason is, it is but a trying the tree by its fruit. If the question be, Am I a pardoned, forgiven, accepted sinner in the sight of God, through the righteousness of Christ? if that be the question, try it by your sanctification; for all who are justified by the grace of God in Christ Jesus, are also sanctified by the Spirit of God. Now sanctification being the work of God in us, is far more easily discernible than justification, which is an act of God about us. Justification is the sentence of a judge, but sanctification as you have heard, is a gracious work of God on the heart and soul of a poor sinner, and that may be more easily known: therefore try your justification by your sanctification. In short, they who bring sanctification as a title to their justification, they err the breadth of God's whole heavens: and they who pretend to the blessing of justification, and cannot justify it by the practice of sanctification, do but deceive themselves. *If any man*, saith the apostle, *abideth in him, he ought himself also so to walk, even as he walked*, 1 John 2:6. I would only add, it is the Spirit of God alone that can make the word of God, and the truths of it, powerful upon us; it is he alone that can let us into them, and make us know spiritually and savingly the great blessings of justification and sanctification; our acceptance with God through the righteousness of another, and our being adorned by the Spirit of God with a holiness of his own implanting in us. We must not make our holiness our righteousness, nor our righteousness our holiness; our righteousness belongs to another, and only the benefit of it accrues to us; our holiness is the work of the Spirit in us, and Christ is the root of both. He is the person we are justified by or through, and his Spirit is the root of all holiness in us; and both give us the possession of eternal life: justification, by the sentence of the judge, is the ground, and sanctification is that which makes us meet for it in his time and way.

So much for this first general, of sanctification itself, its agreement with, and its difference from justification.

II. The next thing in the words that I am now to speak to, is, *the sanctification of the Spirit*; what is to be understood when sanctification is thus expressed: *The sanctification of the Spirit.* There are three things contained in it that I would speak to. 1*st*, Sanctification of the Spirit respects the author of it, that is the fairest, fullest, and plainest meaning of the word; sanctifying a sinner is the work of the Spirit of God. 2*dly*, Sanctification of the Spirit relates to the *means* of it; it is wrought by the Holy Ghost, by means of the gospel, which is often called the Spirit in the word. 3*dly*, It may be taken as relating to the seat of it; it is called sanctification of the Spirit, in that is seated and lodged in the inmost part of the man, called *the spirit of the mind*, Eph. 4:23. *Be ye renewed in the spirit of your mind.*

1*st*, Sanctification is here called sanctification of the Spirit, to denote the author of it, the Holy Spirit of God. I told you before, that there were three blessed persons in the Godhead, and one God; and each of them has a distinct part in the work of man's salvation, here expressed in the text. Election is ascribed to the Father, redemption to the Son, and sanctification to the Holy Ghost. The same is also expressed by the apostle Paul, *God hath from the beginning chosen you unto salvation, through sanctification of the Spirit, and the belief of the truth*, 2 Thess. 2:13. A little concerning this, the operation of the Holy Ghost in the work of sanctification.

1*st*, Since a divine person hath the work in hand, it must be managed by sovereign grace; God works nothing from hire, or motive from the creature, more than he did the work of creation; no more doth he any thing since. When he raised all things from nothing, nothing moved God to make all things, but only his own will and pleasure: all divine operations must necessarily have their rise from sovereign will and grace: and this is ascribed to the Holy Ghost. *All these things worketh that one and the selfsame Spirit, dividing to every man severally as he will*, 1 Cor. 12:11. There is the sovereignty of the will and the grace of the Holy Ghost in this great work of sanctification.

2*dly*, As all divine acts are acts of sovereignty, flowing from his own will and pleasure, so they are always acts of an Almighty power. When we say, that it is the sanctification of the Spirit, and that the Holy Ghost works it, it is plain he works it with an Almighty and irresistible power; nothing but an Almighty power can sanctify a dead sinner; the same power that wrought in raising a dead Saviour, is needful for the raising a dead sinner, Eph. 1:19, 20, and hence it is that the power of the Holy Ghost is so much spoken of in the word.

3*dly*, This work of sanctification, ascribed to the Holy Ghost, shews that it is always done in infinite wisdom. All divine acts are wrought in wisdom; there is a depth in them all. There is wisdom as to the *persons*, and wisdom as to the way. There is wisdom as to the *persons*; all the elect of God, all the redeemed, and none but they, are sanctified. As the Redeemer knew who were given to him, and therefore he laid down his life for them; so the Holy Ghost knows who the Son redeems, and he sanctifies them to his praise. It is always done in great and unsearchable wisdom. No man knows this way of the Spirit; *Every one that is born of the Spirit is born that way*, John 3:8; he cannot tell how the work is wrought, and yet it is wrought, because an Almighty arm is at the working of it.

4*thly*, This work having so great a worker, doubtless hath a great effect. If I may so say, election has not so great an immediate effect; for there are a great many elected, who are a long while before they are called; the sprinkling of the blood of Jesus, and the virtue of his redemption, doth not reach its effect so quickly, because there are a great many whom Christ died for that are a long while before they come to him, and receive the power of his grace. But the operation of the Holy Ghost in sanctifying us, hath a sensible and an immediate effect. There is always something in it that may be presently, sensibly, and undeniably known. I do not say it is always so; but there is nothing spoken of in the word, as a more sensible thing than is the work of the Holy Ghost. It is expressed to us by all those words by which the greatest changes that ever were wrought are expressed. It is expressed by creation, 2 Cor. 4:6, *God, who commanded the light to shine out of darkness, hath shined in our hearts.* Was there ever so great a change in this world as creation? When nothing became all things, that was the greatest change imaginable; a change from nothing into being; this is the greatest change that can possibly enter into the mind of a man. It is expressed by the change from death to life, at the resurrection. And is not that a great change; when the body that hath lain in the rottenness of the grave for so many ages, shall be raised up a glorious temple to the Holy Ghost? It is also expressed by opening the eyes of the blind. You read in the gospel, John 11, of one who was born blind, whose eyes Christ opened: now let any of you enter into a serious consideration of the marvellous change that this man found; doubtless he had heard of the sun, and the moon, and the stars; and some dark notion he might have of them; but he could have no imagination at all of light and colours, he could form no proper idea of them: but now, when our Lord had opened his eyes, and he looked up to heaven and saw the glory of that creature the sun, which he never saw before; when he looked about him, and saw a world filled with fine things that he never saw before, doubtless he found a wonderful change; and it is a great wonder, if he came to himself in a long time after. So this change that is wrought by the Spirit in regeneration, is just like the opening of the eyes of a man born blind: he had heard tell of Jesus Christ, and the new world of grace, but he never saw it before, till the Spirit of wisdom and revelation in the knowledge of Christ came, and then the eyes of his understanding were opened. May the Lord so enlighten and enliven us by his Spirit! Amen.

SERMON VII.

1 Pet. 1:2.

Elect according to the foreknowledge of God the Father, through sanctification of the Spirit, unto obedience, and sprinkling of the blood of Jesus Christ: Grace unto you, and peace be multiplied.

THROUGH sanctification of the Spirit, unto obedience, is the clause I am now upon. I was speaking in my last discourse of this third work of the third person in the Godhead, in the salvation of a sinner. Election is ascribed to the Father, redemption by blood to the Son, and sanctification unto the Holy Ghost. Of this sanctification of the Spirit, that is the work of the third person in the Godhead about our salvation, I proposed to speak three things. 1*st*, Of sanctification itself. 2*dly*, That it is called sanctification of the Spirit. 3*dly*, That this sanctification is said in the text to be unto obedience. Of the first of these I have spoken all that I intended; both of the nature of sanctification itself, together with its agreement with the blessings of justification, and its difference therefrom. I began also to speak unto the second particular—that sanctification is here said to be of the Spirit. I mentioned three things, as contained in this, though indeed it is the first of them that is principally meant;—that this sanctification of the Spirit is chiefly to be understood with respect to its author, the Holy Ghost: and what that implied I then spoke to.

2*dly*, I am now to take notice of this word, *The sanctification of the Spirit,* as it denotes the means whereby this work is wrought; and the rather is this to be taken notice of, because the word Spirit is frequently ascribed to the gospel; more especially this expression is frequently used by the apostle: in 2 Cor. 3:6, *The letter killeth, but the Spirit giveth life*; and again, ver. 8, *How shall not the ministration of the Spirit be rather glorious?* and again, ver. 17, *Where the Spirit of the Lord is, there is liberty*; and again, in the last verse, *We are changed from glory to glory, even as by the Spirit of the Lord.* This great work of sanctification is managed by the word of God; now, What word is it that God makes use of to sanctify a man? It is by the word of the gospel; for that is specially called the Spirit: and here is a point that lies remote from the knowledge and observation of the greatest part. They think, and it is a very natural thought, that the law is the mean of sanctification; that the law commanding is the mean of it. I would therefore shew, that it is not, but that the gospel is so. Now this thought, that the law is the mean of sanctification, is greatly fortified by these two considerations: 1*st*, The law is the measure and rule of holiness; that is past question. When the enquiry is, What is holiness? What is pleasing to God? There is no answer can be given but this, 'That which is according to his will; the law is the certain sure rule of all holiness.' 2*dly*, The law commands holiness, and that in the most forcible manner, by the greatest promises, and by the greatest threatenings. *Fear* and *hope* are the great engines that set all mankind at work; there would be no stirring in this world if it were not for fear and hope. All men's natural, civil, and moral actions are moved this way; they flee from that which they apprehend to be hurtful, out of fear; and they pursue what they apprehend to be good, out of hope. Now the law is the sure rule of duty, and the law is the forcible commander of it; and therefore it is that men are so apt to think that the law is the mean of sanctification; every natural man thinks he may be made holy by the law.

I would therefore prove this matter both negatively and positively. 1*st*, That the law is not the mean of sanctification. 2*dly*, That the gospel is so. That the law is not the mean of sanctification, I would prove by two things. It was never designed so to be; and it never effected it. It was never designed to be so by the Law-giver, and it was never found to be so by the law-receiver: and when these two are plainly seen and proved, the negative part will be sufficiently confirmed—that the law is not the mean of sanctification. 1*st*, It was never made to be so; that is, the great and wise Law-giver never gave his law to be the mean of sanctification: you may think strange of this, but I will give you three instances of it, which will abundantly confirm it. 1*st*, When the law was first made, and given to innocent Adam, it was not given as a mean of sanctification at all. When God gave the law to the first Adam, it was never given to make the man holy; for he was made holy before the law was given him; he came holy, pure, and perfect from the hand of

God; the law was only given to be the rule of his conversation in that holy state, and the way of his continuance therein. Adam could not make himself holy by the law; sinless Adam could not; he was made holy before the law was given, and was to continue himself holy and happy by his obedience to the law. Oh that this were duly considered! that when God gave the law to the first man, it was not given, to make him holy; for he was made holy before. *2dly*, The law was given in a great copy of it, at Mount Sinai, to sinful Israel, to a sinful people that had been carried away with the abominations of the Egyptians; and, except their retaining circumcision, the sign of God's covenant with their fathers, we find but little that there was left amongst them: they were greatly corrupted before God gave them the law. What a great work was there about purifying them? Now when God gave the law at Mount Sinai, it was not given to make the people holy; pray take heed to this: it was never given to make an unholy man to be holy. *Wherefore then*, saith the apostle, *serveth the law? it was added because of transgressions, till the Seed should come, and was ordained by angels in the hand of a Mediator*, Gal. 3:19. The law was given at Mount Sinai, to convince the people of their sinfulness, that they might have recourse to their gospel, and their gospel was their sacrifices, which were typical of our Lord Jesus Christ. *3dly*, The law is written in the word of God, and is daily to be preached by his servants whom he sends, but never that it may make people holy; rather to make them see their vileness, to make them see their uncleanness, and the desperate wickedness that was in them till gospel-grace cures them. This is the first thing—the law was never designed by God to make men holy.

2dly, It never did so, and it never can do so. I know I am now teaching a doctrine that a great many do not understand, and will not like because they do not understand. I will tell you what the law of God can do separately from the gospel; I am sure much hurt it will do to them that betake themselves to it as a mean of sanctification. We find several things concerning the law, separate from the gospel, in the word. *1st*, It discovers sin; I say the law discovers sin; Now, saith the apostle, Rom. 3:20, it is evident, that *by the deeds of the law shall no flesh be justified in his sight*. Why, how comes this to be so evident to you, Paul? it is not evident to a great many people: *For by the law*, saith he, *is the knowledge of sin*. Now can ever any man be justified by that which in its native light tends to discover his vileness? *These things saith the law, to them that are under the law, that every mouth may be stopped, and that all the world may become guilty before God: therefore, by the deeds of the law shall no flesh be justified in his sight; for by the law is the knowledge of sin*. The apostle was a man like a great many in our days, for the righteousness of the law, as long as he was a Pharisee, and confident of speeding that way; but when the law came to deal with him in the spirituality of it, he tells us what he felt; *I had not known sin*, saith he, *but by the law, for I had not known lust, unless the law had said, Thou shalt not covet*, Rom. 7:7. There can be none of you so ignorant to think, but that the apostle Paul, when he was a Jew and a Pharisee, understood very well the tenth commandment, *Thou shalt not covet*; he read it, remembered it, and understood it perfectly, as a Pharisee; but when the spirituality of the law of God was discovered to him, shewing him, that the least inordinate rising of his heart towards that which was evil was forbidden therein, then the man was slain, his confidence was broken: he did not know sin till this came. Alas! Sirs, many do nothing but sin, and yet they do not know what sin is; if I may so say, they know nothing but sinning, yet they do not know what sin is. The discovery of sin is made by the brightness and the power of the law of God, when the spirituality of the law is discovered. 2*dly*, The law aggravates sin, it multiplies it, it increases it; *The law entered, that the offence might abound*, Rom. 5:20. Pray observe; the apostle is telling us, in the preceding verse, that one man's offence abounded to the condemning the whole world. Had not the offence abounded sufficiently then? Nay, saith the apostle, *the law entered that sin might abound*: that men might know and understand, how great their provocations were, what a holy God they had offended, what a righteous law they had broken, and thereby come to see the evil of sin to be a great deal bigger than ever they apprehended it to be before. And assure yourselves, Sirs, that unless the law of God be known unto you as the cause of the abounding of sin, as the cause of its growing bigger and greater in your eyes, you never yet knew the law of God rightly. 3*dly*, God's law doth irritate and provoke sin; not only doth it make the sin that a man committed to be greater than he apprehended it to be before, but really it makes the man sin the more.

The bare law of God—pray take heed to what I say—the bare law of God, without gospel grace applied to the heart of a sinner, to one that is a stranger to gospel grace, it will make his provocations more bitter and more grievous than ever they were before. So the apostle speaks, Rom. 7:11, *Sin, taking occasion by the commandment, deceived me, and by it slew me.* What occasion could sin take by the commandment? Pray mind; How could sin take occasion by the commandment? the commandment forbad sin, and the commandment threatened sin; what occasion then could sin take by the commandment? Just such an occasion as the building of a wall against a running river would be to its overflowing its banks; if any man does foolishly imagine to stop the course of a river by fencing against it with a wall, it will quickly rise higher and higher, and bound higher, and overtop that wall, and run more furiously than ever. Just so it is with a great many poor sinners; their consciences convince them of sin, and they are disquieted with the thoughts of it, and this and that and the other they will do, and this and that and the other sin they will forbear; they will set God's commands, and God's threatenings, in the way of their sins, and then they think surely they shall be sanctified: a vain dream! sin is stronger than the law, be you persuaded of it; I mean, sin is stronger this way, than to be bounded and stopped by the law of God: sanctification belongs only to the Spirit. 4*thly*, Law obedience doth increase the pride and stubbornness of the heart against God, which is the root of all sin. Pray take heed to what I say; I am not now speaking of a man's obeying the law in point of justification; that casts a reflection on the blood of Jesus Christ; but I am speaking of that obedience which a man strives to pay unto the law, in order to his sanctification; and whosoever labours to obey the law, without a due regard to the sanctifying influences of the grace of God, this man's pride will grow greater hereby, and his rebellion against God be acted the more. A poor sinner is never truly humbled till he knows that he deserves nothing which is good, and till he knows that he can do nothing that is good, and then he is broken indeed: he can deserve nothing that is good, and therefore must be beholden only to the good that is wrought out for him by another: he can do nothing that is good, and therefore must be beholden to grace to work that in him which he was never able to get. So much for this first thing—that the law is not the mean of sanctification: it is the rule of holy walking, but not the *mean* of it: for unless the Spirit of Christ works upon the heart, no man can be holy.

2dly, I am to prove that sanctification is by the Spirit, that it is wrought in the heart only by the grace of the gospel. *1st*, This only changeth the tree, this only changeth the man. The law deals with a man as it finds him, and leaves him as it finds him; it finds him a sinner, and leaves him a sinner; it finds him condemned, and it leaves him condemned; it finds him corrupted, and it leaves him corrupted; it finds him in his grave, and it leaves him there. The law finds a man in the grave, bound hand and foot, and commands him to do what it knows he cannot do; but gospel grace changes the man, and changes the tree. This is old doctrine, that a great many of our new preachers, and new Christians, know nothing of. *O generation of vipers! how can ye, being evil speak good things?* Matt. 12:34. This world will still run upon this, that a bad man may grow good by doing good things: our Lord tells us just the contrary, a man must first be good, before he can do any good thing. *Either make the tree good and his fruit good, or else make the tree corrupt and his fruit corrupt; for the tree is known by his fruit*, Matt. 12:33, Luke 6:43, as our Lord at large and plainly teaches. Gospel grace is the only mean of sanctification; for it alone changes a man, renews and quickens him. This is the commendation of it, in that place I now named, 2 Cor. 3:6, *The letter killeth, but the spirit giveth life.* The Spirit, that is, the gospel, giveth life; namely, when the Holy Ghost concurreth with it: for here it is spoken with respect to his concurring influence. *2dly*, Gospel grace takes away the sting from the law, and so makes it lovely to the soul. The sting of the law is the curse of it, there is nothing else in the law that is displeasing to a man that hath any thing of the grace of God in him; now the curse of the law is a dreadful thing; but gospel grace takes away the sting and the curse, and then becomes lovely and amiable to the believer. The law is a holy rule of practice, that is true; but the law that commandeth holy practice on the penalty of eternal death, that is removed to the believer, and thereupon holy practice begins to be amiable. *3dly*, The law by gospel grace is written upon the heart, and so the practice of it becomes lovely and amiable, according to God's covenant; Heb. 8:10. *I will put my law into their minds, and write it upon their hearts*; as if the Lord should have said, 'I formerly wrote my law on tables of stone, I proclaimed it in fire and thunder upon earth, but that did not do the business; now in these latter days I will write my law in their hearts:' and for God to write the law in the heart, is nothing but for God to make the law lovely to the heart, that the heart may be framed to a holy liking and loving of the law of God. 4*thly*, Gospel grace only, renders God lovely to the soul; now to have God to be lovely to us, is the spring of all holiness. You know how our Lord sums up the whole law, in this, *Thou shalt love the Lord thy God with all thy heart, and with all thy soul, and with all thy mind, and with all thy strength: this is the first commandment*, Mark 12:31. *Love*, saith the apostle, *is the fulfilling of the law*, Rom. 13:10. Pray take heed to this point; I am speaking of gospel grace as sanctifying a man, because it is that only which represents God as lovely to the soul. And truly, till the love of God be planted in the heart, it is impossible that a man can be holy: for whatsoever obedience is paid to God and his will, if not from love, is but provocation. Now the love of God cannot be planted in the heart, but by a discovery of the loveliness of God; and it is impossible that a man can love God, until he knows God to be love. *In this was manifested the love of God towards us*, saith the apostle, *because God sent his only-begotten Son into the world, that we might live through him. Herein is love, not that we loved God, but that he loved us, and sent his Son to be the propitiation for our sins*, 1 John 4:9, 10. Here is the way to make an end of sin; Christ being the propitiation for our sins, is the ground of justification; and a discovery of God's sending Christ to be a propitiation for our sins, is the motive of our sanctification. No man obeys God out of love, but that man who knows and believes the love that God hath towards him. *We have known and believed the love that God hath to us: God is love; and he that dwelleth in love, dwelleth in God, and God in him*, 1 John 4:16. What I have said is to point out these two things: 1*st*, All that are savingly won to Christ Jesus, they are won by arguments of love. Sirs, whatsoever use the Lord makes of the law (and a great deal of good use he makes of it), the Lord never convened a man by the law, nor ever will. Many are awakened by the law, and terrified by the law, but the law of God can do nothing else; it can never make a man a believer; it may awaken a secure sinner, and make the smoke of hell to arise in his throat, but it can never make a man a believer on Christ Jesus; it is impossible to make him such, till the amiableness of the Saviour be discovered to him in the glass of the gospel. 2*dly*, As Christians are first made Christians by the arguments of love, so all their obedience and holiness flows from the same spring. All that obedience and holiness which is right and acceptable in the sight of God, is from the same arguments of love. Christ craves it on this account, and they pay it on this account; and if their obedience and holiness be not thus paid, it is never accepted. What the apostle saith in another case, about giving alms, *God loveth a cheerful giver*, I may say, the Lord loveth a cheerful doer: all holy obedience is to be performed by the arguments drawn from love. Therefore now, whilst I am on this head, let me lead you a little to the searching of your own spirits, that you may see what spirit you are under, and what spirit you are led by. There are a great many arguments to duty in the gospel, and a great many in the law; and according as they have force and power upon you, so are you to judge of your spiritual frame.

I would speak a little more distinctly about the law's arguments to holiness, what they are, and what they do: the arguments that the law gives for obedience to God, they principally arise from these three heads. 1*st*, The greatness and majesty of a commanding God: the glory of God shined forth at the giving of the law, and whensoever the Lord sets home the same law upon the conscience of a man, there is also a discovery of the glory of the Law-giver. 2*dly*, The equity and righteousness of his will is another argument: if this be the will of God, it must be just, righteous, and equal; and this is a strong argument for obedience. 3*dly*, The danger of sinning, and the wrath that is due to every transgressor; this is another of the law's arguments: but what can all these do, let them be exerted to their utmost force? The glory of God as the speaker, the equity of what he speaks, and the danger of disobeying him; all that these arguments can do upon a sinner stands in these three things, that a great many people's religion all their days lies in them; a hating sin as hurtful to us; a loving holiness as profitable to us, and some weak, pitiful essays to shun the one and to do the other: and thus a great many are hammered by the law all their days, and they do just nothing at all. They sometimes see the glory of God, and their consciences subscribe to the equity of his will, and they are afraid of wrath to come; but knowing nothing but law-light, and law-relief (and truly that is nothing at all), they do just nothing at all to any purpose. But the arguments of the gospel to holiness, are quite of another nature. 1*st*, They are arguments to holiness from privileges: pray consider this; the grand arguments of the New Testament still run this way; arguing with men to the practice of holiness from their privileges; from the great things God hath done for them, and from the great things that he hath promised to them. The apostle gives us a large account of this in the 12th chapter of the Hebrews, verses 14, 18-24, *Follow peace with all men, and holiness, without which no man shall see the Lord.* Well, and what arguments hath he for this? 'For ye are not come to Mount Sinai,' to that terrible word of the law, of which he speaks there at great length, *but ye are come*, saith he, *to Mount Sion, to the blood of sprinkling, and to Jesus, the mediator of the* new covenant. 2*dly*, Gospel arguments have this in them, they are ordained for this end, and they reach it; both the master and the work is love, and therefore the work is done, and the master obeyed. Every natural man, that is under the law, thinks with himself that the way to please God is to do his will; but the believer under the gospel doth God's will, because he knows that God is pleased with him; he doth those things that are pleasing in the sight of God, from the faith of his person's being accepted with God. *Sin shall not have dominion over you*, saith the apostle, Rom. 6:14. Why so? *for ye are not under the law, but under grace*. There are two things that I would have you think on with respect to this, in trying your spirits about this; how you relish Christ's arguments, and whether you are led by law arguments, or by gospel ones. 1*st*, What is it you would be at, in order to your progress in sanctification, and all holy obedience towards God? There is one thing I would take notice of, and I do it the rather because I believe it is some people's snare; some persons imagine with themselves, and their imaginations sometimes come the length of their prayers, and they are foolish and wicked ones; 'Oh that God would discover the greatness of his glory, and the greatness of his wrath to me!' that he would open hell to them, and let them see it and fear; and then they think they should be a great deal more holy than they are. There is an evil spirit working in the design of this: we may not only give Christ's answer to his disciples to it, *Ye ask ye know not what*, Mark 10:38; but we may say, the very asking it is from an evil spirit. Is it not far more desirable, and should you not know that it would be far more profitable to you, if the Lord would reveal more of his love and kindness to you? that would quickly carry on the work of sanctification with greater ease and speed than all those other things that you would so fain be at. *2dly*, What things are there in the ministry of the word that relish best with your spirits? Clear discoveries of the anger of God against sin, and the desert of sin at the hand of God, these are useful things, and there is a measure of knowledge and sense of them that no man should be against: But are these all that you relish in the word of God? Have you never found any desires after greater manifestations of the love of God, that you may know Jesus Christ better? Sirs, though there be a wonderful variety in the Lord's way of dealing with his people, so that no one man's experience is to be made a measure or a rule for every one, yet I dare be bold to say, that in this matter the greatest part of Christians that are now alive in the world, will put their seal to this; they who have had experience of both; who have had their hearts pressed with the terror of God, and with the arguments of the law, and also have had their hearts melted with the love of Christ and with the arguments of the gospel, I am very confident that all of them will be able to witness to this, that these latter did promote sanctification and conformity to the image of Christ a deal more than the former. How many poor believers have there been, that have for a long time struggled with their stubborn corruption, that have hedged it in by the law, and the curses of it, with all manner of watchfulness, and yet but little efficacy hath been found in all; but when in a time of love the Lord hath drawn near to their souls, and hath sent in a warm beam of love, how greatly have they triumphed over that which they found to be a great deal too strong for them before!—So much for this second head, about sanctification of the Spirit, as it denotes the means of sanctification. Never wonder, Sirs, that there is so little holiness in the world, and so little holiness among professors; the reason is, they do not know whence it comes: the gospel, as the great mean of sanctification, they do not know, and because they do not use this mean, they go away without the blessing.

3dly, This phrase of the sanctification of the Spirit may be taken as it points forth the *seat* of this sanctification—as it points forth where true sanctification is lodged; in the spirit, in the heart, in the inward man; *Be ye renewed*, saith the apostle, *in the spirit of your mind*, Eph. 4:23. The mind is the common expression of the understanding part of the soul, which is a more refined faculty than that which we call the heart; whereby we fear, love, desire, or hate. Here the apostle calls it the spirit of the mind; had he only called it the spirit of the body, we know that the soul is the spirit of the body; 'but,' the apostle would say, 'it lies deeper than this, it is in the spirit of your minds, in the very soul of your souls; it is the renovation of the Holy Ghost, and lies very deep in the soul; not only in the heart and mind, but in the spirit of the mind.' But I pass this; and finish the second general head, Why it is called the sanctification of the Spirit:—to denote the author of it, and the means by which it is wrought, and the seat of it in the soul. I am now come to

The 3*d* and *last* thing about this sanctification, and that is the *end* of it, *to obedience*; it is the sanctification of the Spirit *unto obedience*. Obedience is here plainly said to be the end of this sanctification of Spirit, or the fruit of it; pray take heed to this; for here is another way that men pervert the ordinances of God: my text tells you, that all holy obedience paid by men to God, is the fruit, of the sanctification of the Spirit; but the ungodly, unbelieving world take the matter quite otherwise, and understand it thus, that obedience is the way to come by this sanctification of the Spirit; whereas the word tells us plainly, that this sanctification of the Spirit is the way whereby we come to obedience: it is the sanctification of the Spirit unto obedience. Never was there any piece of acceptable obedience paid to God, unless it flowed from the sanctification of the Spirit. A little unto this, and I shall apply the whole. 1*st*, Of this obedience more generally: And then, 2*dly*, I shall speak more particularly about it.

1*st*, For obedience more generally, take this brief and plain account of it. When God had made man upright, and created him perfectly holy in that happy state, he demanded obedience of him, and had that obedience paid cheerfully till sin came in; and upon man's sinning, the world broke out altogether in rebellion against God. The first Adam, upon his sinning, turned a rebel against God, and tainted all his children with his guilt and an inclination to this wickedness; and therefore it is said, *We are children of disobedience*, Eph. 2:2. And children of disobedience are a strange sort of children; children that have disobedience to be their father, that are born of disobedience, that have their original from disobedience. When it is said, *we are children of disobedience*, the meaning is, that we are the offspring of disobedient parents, and that they conveyed to us a disobedient nature. The first Adam sinned, *and by one man's disobedience, many* (nay all) *were made sinners*, Rom. 5:19. And this is the state that the world lives in, and that most of them die in. God and they are at variance; what he is for, they are against, and what he is against, they are for; and a little time is spent, the short time of man's life in this world is spent in this quarrel; men sin against God, and God witnesseth against them for their sinning: and God hath a great many ways of witnessing against them. He witnesseth against this disobedience in them that have no more but the light of nature: see what the apostle saith to the barbarous Lycaonians, that counted Paul a God, and Barnabas another God; *Nevertheless he left not himself without witness, in that he did good, and gave us rain from heaven, and fruitful seasons, filling our hearts with food and gladness.* You will think now that this was but a poor witness; the apostle reckons God's common providence in ordering the seasons of the year, and in making the earth fruitful and able to yield bread to mankind, as a witness for God, that people should know their duty to their great maker. God gives a farther witness by his word, to them that have it, against these rebels. He adds a farther witness by his Spirit striving with them. And farther yet he adds another witness, by his providences, in striving with them. How many poor sinners are there who live this way? God and they are at enmity, they hate God, and God hates them, and strives against them by his word, and sometimes by checks in their consciences, and many times by checks in his providences; and all to bring them over to obedience to his will; but they continue rebels still till death destroys them. They strive with God till God gets the mastery, as he always will, over them who strive with him; for wo be to them who strive with their Maker: and this is the issue of the controversy one way. But there are a few that saving grace comes in upon, and hold of, and changes their hearts, and brings them over to be loyal and obedient subjects and servants to

God, and to Jesus Christ: and thus it is that there is any difference made between the herd of the perishing world and those few that are saved.

Secondly, and more particularly, The obedience that the sanctification of the Spirit is directed to, may be comprehended under these three heads: 1*st*, There is the obedience that is given to a promising God, and this respects privileges; for all promises are of privileges. Now the obedience that is to be paid to a promising God is plainly the obedience of faith, which the apostle speaks of, Rom. 16:26, *God hath made known the gospel to all nations, for the obedience of faith*. Whensoever God promises, there is a debt laid upon men by his promising, to believe that he is true who speaks; and by virtue of the greatness of the truth of the speaker, there should be a great expectation of the good things that are promised. And herein lies the life of faith that Christians are called to. What think you is the life of faith? it is nothing at all but this, a life of looking for all those good things that God hath spoken. It is a life of expecting the great blessings which God hath promised; this is the obedience that is due to a promising God, the obedience of faith. 2*dly*, This obedience relates to the commands of God, to a God craving duty, worship, and service from us. These are called for, and every Christian is inclined to yield them. *Be not conformed to the world*, saith the apostle, Rom. 12:2, *but be ye transformed by the renewing of your mind, that ye may prove what is that good, and acceptable, and perfect will of God*. And they are strangers to the sanctification of the Spirit, who do not find this obedience working in them: for wheresoever this sanctification is, this obedience will be in greater or lesser measures; according to the measure of the one, such will be the measure of the other. 3*dly*, There is also obedience due to an afflicting, trying God: and these are the three grand appearances of God to us; a God promising good to us; a God commanding service from us; and a God inflicting trials on us, as he sees good: and this is the obedience which all believers owe to God, that when he smites them, and tries them, when he delays blessings, and threatens bad things to them, it is their duty to bear his hand quietly, and to glorify him by a quiet submission to his will. And whosoever they are that have in some measure reached to these three, they have that obedience which God calls for, and they have that sanctification of the Spirit, which is the cause and spring thereof.

Application. I would now make some application of this truth; and that I would speak to you about, shall be a word of trial. You have heard of the sanctification of the Spirit to obedience; pray try yourselves whether this be in you or not. You have heard it spoken of as a great part of our salvation. There are only two arguments by which I would enforce this searching upon you: *1st,* This sanctification of the Spirit is equally needful to salvation with any of the former. It is absurd to think, that a man shall be saved who is not elected according to the foreknowledge of God the Father; that would be as much as to think that a man might come to heaven without God's knowledge, and that would be a strange thing indeed. It is an absurd thing to think, that a man shall be saved who is not sprinkled with the blood of Jesus Christ. What! shall a man be saved that gets no good at all of the Saviour? that would be a strange thing: even so it is equally true in this case; no man can be saved who is not sanctified by the Holy Ghost. The apostle names salvation as if it was from this thing only, Titus 3:5, *He hath saved us by the washing of regeneration, and the renewing of the Holy Ghost.* So that an enquiry after sanctification is of as great concern as your eternal salvation. *2dly,* As it is needful as the former, so it is more evident than any of the former. Election is a purpose in the heart of God, that is utterly unknowable but by its fruit: the redemption of Jesus Christ is an act passing between the Father and the Son, and is not to be known by us, but by the effects of it: but sanctification is a work passing on us, and therefore may be far more easily known than the former; nay, it may be so far the more easily known, that it is the great mark to know the former by. When you would enquire after your interest in the redemption of Jesus, it is sanctification that is the fruit of it. When you would inquire about your interest in justification, it is sanctification that is a fruit and a plain mark of it. I would name a mark or two of this.

1st, Would you know whether you have partaken of the sanctification of the Spirit, try it this way: Hath the word of Christ in the gospel had any dealings with your hearts to change and renew you? This is the question; hath the Spirit, by the gospel, been dealing with your hearts to change and renew you? The sanctification of the Spirit is a work in and on a man; redemption is a work of Christ about a man; election is a purpose of God concerning a man; but sanctification is a work of the Spirit of God in a man. Now, hath the Spirit been at work upon you this way? There are many who have a feeling of some workings of the Spirit in a way of conviction, in some fears of hell, and in some desires after heaven; but hath the Spirit of Christ, by the power of the gospel, been at work to change your hearts, to make them new, to turn you quite about, so that you savour all things far otherwise than you did before? Do you think it, my brethren, to be possible that a man can live in a profession of godliness, and be really under the sanctification of the Spirit, and know nothing about it? I do not believe it, say it who will. I know many are under the sanctification of the Spirit, that yet have not confidence to own it, and to say that it is a true and thorough work; but that there is something felt wherever the Spirit of God works on the heart, is undeniable.

2dly, The great mark is that which you have in the text, *unto obedience*: Are you all obedience? A sanctified man is all obedience. I do not mean that he obeys in all things as he would, but he would obey in all things. He was a sanctified man, and sanctified by the Spirit to obedience, who said, *With my mind I serve the law of God, but with my flesh the law of sin*, Rom. 7:25. He had rebelling corruption remaining within him, and he had grace within him striving against it. There are many people who find it to be so with them; they have light and darkness, corruption and grace within them, 'How shall I know if mine be of the right sort?' There is one thing I would tell you, if, when you come far short of what you would be at, you are ashamed of it, and afraid of it, and are best pleased at heart when your obedience is greatest, and are most sorry when your disobedience is greatest, and when sin prevails, this is a mark that never fails: for an honest-hearted Christian, when sin is lowest, his heart is highest in joy. When grace is lowest, the man is lowest in his frame; he is rejoiced when he can get his enemies under his feet, and is ashamed when he is under theirs. When sin prevails, the man is abased, when grace prevails over sin, the man rejoices therein. The very name of this text may serve as a mark to help you in trying yourselves; it is sanctification of the Spirit unto obedience. There are three miserable sorts of persons, the Lord grant there may be none of them found amongst you! and then you will be a happy company indeed; and every one of these are worse than another.

1st, A great many hearers of the gospel live all their days contented strangers to the sanctification of the Spirit; they do not know what it is, and they do not care to know. These are miserable persons indeed, who can hear, learn, talk, think, and get increase of light; and knowledge, and gifts, but the sanctification of the Spirit is that which they can be without in their religion. The Lord save you from their religion who are contented strangers to the sanctification of the Spirit to obedience! they are a miserable people indeed, especially if they live under the preaching of the gospel. But there is a worse sort than these.

2dly, Who not only are strangers to it themselves, but are also mockers of it in others. They have no acquaintance with, no experience of the sanctification of the Spirit, and if any body do but pretend to it, he only makes himself a laughing-stock to them. So saith the apostle, Gal. 4:29, *As then he that was born after the flesh, persecuted him that was born after the Spirit, even so it is now.* Pray now, what great persecution was this? The apostle is there speaking of Ishmael and Isaac; Ishmael mocked Isaac; Ishmael was thirteen years old when Isaac was born, and he mocked Isaac, the heir of the promise; saith the apostle, *Even so is it now*; every man that is born after the flesh, and hath not the Spirit of Jesus dwelling in him, will always mock them that are born after the Spirit; them who place their righteousness in Christ only, and their sanctification in the efficacy of his Spirit upon them. *Even so is it now*, saith the apostle, in his time; and that was above sixteen hundred years ago; and we may say, 'Even so it is now;' and if the world should last sixteen hundred years longer, it would be still the same. They who are born after the flesh, will mock them who are born after the Spirit; and so it will be to the end of the world. This is a strange thing; I have many times thought it to be a strange thing, that there should be such wickedness in the world, as to mock at godliness; but I would fain have people forbear to mock at godliness till they feel it, and when they feel it, let them mock at it, I will not say in God's name, but in the devil's name. It is utterly impossible, that true godliness can season the heart of a man, but there will be an awful regard to it, in the man's respect to all the appearances of it in others; but they who do not know what it is, will mock at them who have it.

3dly, Can there be any worse than these, who have not the sanctification of the Spirit in them, and that mock at it in others? Yes, there is a worse sort than these (though indeed they commonly belong all to one person), and these are such as resist the sanctification of the Spirit in themselves. When the Holy Ghost comes near to them by his word, and by his motions upon the heart, they rise up in rebellion against the same. Stephen knew his hearers very well, and spake sharply and dreadfully to them, Acts 7:51, *Ye stiff-necked and uncircumcised in heart and ears, ye do always resist the Holy Ghost; as your fathers did, so do ye.* The blessed man was then full of the Holy Ghost, and he was pleading Christ's cause before that wicked company, and they themselves saw some singular appearance of God in him; it is said, *they that sat in the council, looking stedfastly on him, saw his face as it had been the face of an angel*, Acts 6:15. Stephen knew that the Holy Ghost was in him, animating him, and working in him, and drawing forth these words from him; and he knew by their behaviour that they resisted the Holy Ghost, and he charges them with it. Take heed to yourselves, Sirs, the greatest sins are quietly and quickly done; that knot which may tie you to everlasting destruction, may be knit by an evil thought under this gospel. If the Spirit of God comes near to you at any time, and persuades you that there must be a work of sanctification passing upon you, and you rebel against the same, you do resist the Holy Ghost, and will be found amongst the worst of sinners. Be you persuaded of this,—whether you will believe it or not,—the gospel brings all the hearers of it, whether they will or not, to the brink of eternal salvation, or to the brink of eternal damnation: and so it will fare with you to eternity, according to your present entertainment of Christ's calls. People do not know how near they may be to heaven, or how near they may be to hell. When Christ is at the door, give him but a hearty welcome, and salvation is secured; give him but a silent, trifling refusal, and God knows but it may be the utter undoing of thy soul. The greatest mercies are secured, on our part, by a very small, silent act of the mind; and the greatest judgment is also inflicted and incurred by a very small act of the mind. It seems to be no very great matter, when a poor sinner is reading, thinking, and hearing of Jesus Christ in the gospel; it seems to be no great matter, when their hearts begin to grow warm within them, and this Saviour and his salvation appears to be lovely to him, and the poor creature resolves to venture his all on the Son of God; there seems to be no great matter in this; it is quietly and silently done: and yet this may be the subscribing of the everlasting marriage-covenant between Christ and the soul. So, on the other side, a poor sinner under the gospel, is calm in making slight of all that he hears, he only stands remote and aloof from all; you would think there is no great matter here: only they do not mind, only they do not think; Is there any great fault here? Alas! the poor creature is hereby ripening his condemnation more than you can imagine. Sirs, take heed to yourselves; a poor creature may run faster to hell in an hour spent in hearing a gospel-sermon, than in a whole week's profane walking. A person may make a greater leap to the pit by a silent rejecting of the offer of the gospel, than by all his law-transgressions.—So much for the *third thing* in the text, the *sanctification of the Spirit to obedience.*

It would follow now, to speak of the respect that electing grace hath, in this text, to the sanctification of the Spirit, and the sprinkling of the blood of Jesus: for though they are all absolutely necessary in order to salvation, yet there is a becoming order. Election leads the van, the sprinkling of the blood of Jesus follows next; and, in the third place, the sanctification of the Spirit; and then, in God's good time, everlasting glory. But I cannot enter on any of these things at present, only a word or two in general. It is, it should be, and it will be the everlasting wonder of our hearts, that God should take so much pains to save sinners; that he thought of them from eternity; that he sent his Son to redeem them by his blood, and that he sends his Spirit to sanctify them by his grace; and that he keeps his hand about them with so much tenderness and care, till he has brought them into his kingdom and glory. If we had faith, we would wonder at it now, but we shall wonder better at it when we come to heaven. When at any time we are awakened and enlightened to see what vile creatures we are, how incredible is it that God should take any pains about us! Why should not God frown such wretches as we are into eternal ruin? It is an easy thing with God to send a sinner to hell; for we all deserve it; but God waits upon us, and strives and labours with us, as if we were worth the having: but, alas! we are worth nothing, only as grace makes us the field from whence the praise and glory of grace shall spring up to eternity. When we come to heaven, if the inhabitants there knew what we had been upon earth, would they not wonder that ever we should come there? But they are all saved by the same grace, all the redeemed offspring of fallen Adam are saved the same way. Will not the angels wonder, that sinners of mankind are saved, and their brethren passed by? that so many of Adam's lost seed should be brought to that upper house above, and the fallen angels are left to eternal ruin? We have nothing to say to this, but *Even so, Father, for so it seemed good in thy sight*. The Lord will give no man a reason of his doings; but they are all done in wisdom, and the wisdom of them will appear in his due time.

SERMON VIII.

1 Pet. 1:2.

Elect according to the foreknowledge of God the Father, through sanctification of the Spirit, unto obedience, and sprinkling of the blood of Jesus Christ; Grace unto you, and peace be multiplied.

WHEN I first entered on the preface to this epistle, contained in these verses, I took it up in three things; 1*st*, A description of the writer of it, *Peter an apostle of Jesus Christ*; 2*dly*, A description of the parties that he writes to, and they are described two ways; as to their outward condition before the world, *strangers*, and scattered abroad through several countries. Again, they are described as to their state before God, *Elect according to his foreknowledge, through sanctification of the Spirit, and sprinkling of the blood of Jesus*. To this I have spoken all that I intend, saving one thing I promised to speak to, and would now remember, and then proceed to the last clause of the verse, *Grace unto you, and peace be multiplied*. I have spoken a little respecting election according to the foreknowledge of God the Father; and also to the sprinkling of the blood of Jesus, and to the sanctification of the Spirit unto obedience. That which now remains for me to speak to, is the respect, interest, and influence, that the first blessing hath on all the rest. This is plainly hinted in the text, that election is unto sanctification of the Spirit, and the sprinkling of the blood of Jesus; all the grand blessings of justification by the virtue of Christ's blood, and sanctification by the power of his Spirit, these all flow from election. This now I would say something to; that election is the grand leading benefit to all the rest which flow from it: *For whom he did foreknow, he also did predestinate, and them he also called; and whom he called, them he also justified; and whom he justified, them he also glorified*, Rom. 8:29, 30. Effectual calling, justification, and eternal glory, all flow from predestination. I would, therefore, in discoursing on this point, take a sober and wary view of the fountain itself, and then come down to the streams that flow from this fountain; to electing grace, and to what it produces and brings forth.

1st, Then, as to this fountain-grace of election, we find concerning it in the word, that is *eternal*; all other graces we partake of in time; pardon of sin is a time-blessing; sanctification of the Spirit is a time-blessing; glory in heaven is a time-blessing; that is, there was a time when it began, though there be no time when it shall end. It is called *Eternal life*, Matt. 25:46; it is eternal life in the duration of it, but it is not eternal life in the rise of it: for we are but of yesterday, and had our natural lives but a little while since; and eternal life, in the strictest sense, we do not possess till our natural life in this world is at an end. Saith the apostle, *Blessed be the God and Father of our Lord Jesus Christ, who hath blessed us with all spiritual blessings, in heavenly places, in Christ, according as he hath chosen us in him before the foundation of the world, that we should be holy and without blame before him in love*, Eph. 1:3, 4. Electing grace is eternal, it had no beginning; and therefore it must have the precedency, and must have its influence upon all time-grace.

2dly, Election-grace is the *purest* grace, the most pure unmixed grace; there is no pretence of mixture here. A believer in Christ Jesus doth receive grace and peace multiplied to him, and I know that this grace is all free; but, if I may so say, it is not so purely free as electing grace is. That grace which was shown to a number of Adam's offspring in the purpose of God from eternity, if I may so express it, eternally, long before they began to be; certainly that must be pure grace. If we receive mercy from the Lord on our praying, or on our performances, though they deserve nothing at all, yet we are apt to put a bad sense on it, and are apt to think, 'This blessing I had because I sought it earnestly;' but in election-grace there can be no pretence for this: for that was long before we were; long before the foundation of the world, as the apostle expresses it, Eph. 1:4.

3*dly*, The grace of election is most *God-like*; take heed to this, the grace of election is, I say, most *God-like*; it becomes him, and his glory shines most eminently in it. He acts like a God in electing, and so like a God, that there is no pretence of likeness to it amongst any of the actions of creatures; and therefore it is resolved finally into this by the apostle, when he speaks so much of it; *Nay but, O man, who art thou that repliest against God? Shall the thing formed say to him that formed it, Why hast thou made me thus? Hath not the potter power over the clay, of the same lump to make one vessel unto honour, and another unto dishonour?* Rom. 9:20, 21. God acted like himself, when from eternity he foresaw all the work of his hands, and set apart some to honour, and some to dishonour: there was sovereignty in it; and the more sovereignty in God's acts, the more he acts like himself.

4*thly*, Election grace is a *pregnant* one, a large grace, a big-bellied grace, if I may so express it; all things else flow from it, all the grace that we partake of in this world, and in the next, comes from the womb of election: our pardoned state, our renewed pardons day by day, they all flow from the grace of election; election begins, and all the rest follow.

But before I come to speak how they follow, I would take notice of two things that seem contrary to this election. Election is a decree and purpose of God in his own heart, about the eternal salvation of a company of Adam's offspring; this is revealed to us in the word, to be the thought and purpose of God before the world began, *According to the eternal purpose which he purposed in Christ Jesus our Lord—according to his own purpose and grace, which was given us in Christ Jesus before the world began*, Eph. 3:11. 2 Tim. 1:9. Therefore, before I come to speak of the streams flowing from election, I would speak a little to those two grand impediments that seemed to lie in its way.

1*st*, The first thing that God did, seems to be a grand impediment laid in the way of election. God's creating man, and making the first man and woman perfectly holy, and entering into a covenant with them, on these terms, that upon their own perfect obedience (for which they were well qualified), they and all their posterity should be perfectly happy. Now who would have thought here, but that all mankind should have been thus happy? there appears nothing like election here. God makes man perfectly holy, and perfectly happy, and enables him so to continue; and he makes a covenant with him securing that happy state, only upon the condition of his perfect obedience: Now, would any man imagine, that when God made these transactions at first with his creatures, that there was any thing like election here; that a company only of this man's posterity should be saved, and a great company of them lost? Election seemed to be clouded by the first creation; nothing like it appeared, and yet it remained firm in the purpose of God: for God never meant to save any one man by the first Adam's standing; no, nor to save the man himself that way. I say, God never meant to save any man in the world by his own perfect obedience. He demanded perfect obedience from the first Adam, and qualified and fitted him for it, and he was able to yield it; but God knew that no man would yield it. And this seems to be one grand objection to election, and obstruction of it,—God creating man in a happy state, with ability to continue in it.

2dly, Another thing, that looks as dark the other way upon election, is God's permitting all mankind to fall. Creating man was God's work, and permitting man to sin was God's act: for sin could no more have entered into the world but by God's permission, than a creature could have entered into the world but by God's creation. The entrance of sin into the world was permitted by God; Will any be so bold, and so daring as to say, God could not have hindered Adam's sinning if he would? he would be a bold person, indeed, that would say so. God permitted sin to enter into the world, and he permits it to continue in the world; the providence of God about sin is the greatest glory that he gets in the world, though there are but few who have eyes to perceive it. Now the creating all mankind at first, in their head and root, perfectly holy and happy, seemed to have put a stop to election one way: some would think, 'Surely all Adam's posterity shall be saved;' that all his offspring should have been a happy company of saved persons. But when sin came in, all things seemed quite lost; then the natural conclusion ran the other way, 'Surely all the world will now be damned: for they are all made sinners.' *By one man's disobedience sin entered into the world, and death by sin*, Rom. 5:12. Therefore the devil might think (as doubtless he did think) I have now undone all mankind (for I do not think the devil knew any thing of election at that time): but this was the time wherein electing grace began to appear. Election-grace lay in the heart of God; he never designed to save man by his own obedience, nor did he design that all mankind should be lost by their own disobedience. Now began election to appear.

1st, It appeared in the first promise, that great promise which hath a great deal of gospel in it, the first gospel that we have in the Bible, and therefore we should the more prize it. *I will put enmity between thee and the woman; between thy seed and her seed, it shall bruise thy head, and thou shall bruise his heel*, Gen. 3:15. Sirs, the first birth of a divine purpose is a promise. A purpose is a thought in God's heart, what he means to do; and a promise is a word from God's mouth, assuring what he will do; and his promises are all commensurate to his purposes. The first appearance of election-grace is a promise, a promise of distinction; a promise that pointed forth the provision grace made for fallen sinners, and the blessed issue that it should have.

2dly, Election-grace appeared in the dispensation of grace towards men; for not only doth election appear in what God promised; but in what God doth. We find he dispenseth grace to some, and withholds it from others; and always with distinction. It is but a small account we have in the book of Genesis, and that but of a few persons; but there is still a distinction according the election of grace. The first two men that were born into the world, and it is like enough they were born into the world both at a birth; Cain, the first-born, and Abel his brother; and there, if I may so say, we find the line of election running upon one hand, and passing by upon the other; the elder brother is passed by, and left to be a murderer, and the younger brother is taken, and honoured to be a martyr of God, he is accepted of God, honoured to be a witness for him, and persecuted to death. Election appeared most singularly in Noah; this man was chosen and set apart, though the whole world was drowned; one man and his family was set apart, electing grace passed upon him, and he found grace in the sight of the Lord, and that was grace indeed; the whole world was drowned, and one man and his house only found grace: and not all that house neither. When, after the flood, the world was drowned again in profaneness and idolatry, a little more than four hundred years after the flood, electing grace fell upon Abraham; God chose him and called him: he is called God's chosen in several places of the Old Testament. Abraham had two sons, and there we find the grace of election running one way, and passing by the other way. Isaac had two sons, and there we find the same distinction is made; *Jacob have I loved, and Esau have I hated; the children not being born, neither having done any good or evil, that the purpose of God according to election might stand*, Rom. 9:11-13. This seems a strange thing, Sirs; Rebecca was near twenty years, she and her husband, crying to God for the blessing of posterity; for the promise lay, as it were, in her loins, and that made her the more earnest; and when she had the blessing of conception, and the children struggled together within her, she said, *If it be so, why am I thus?* 'Whence comes this trouble?' *and she went to inquire of the Lord; and the Lord said unto her, two nations are in thy womb, and two manner of people shall be separated from thy bowels, and the one people shall be stronger than the other people, and the elder shall serve the younger*, Gen. 25:22, 23. This is expounded by the apostle, *Jacob have I loved, and Esau have I hated.* And indeed it was a very dark-like dispensation, when the good woman had been so long earnest for the blessing of the womb, and had conceived two children, the Lord tells her, one is an elect person, and the other is not; they lay in the same womb, they were begotten by the same father; they were conceived by the same mother, as the answer to the same supplication to God; yet 'One have I loved, and the other have I hated!' This was an awful hint of a dispensation according to the election of grace. It was, saith the apostle, *that the purpose of God according to election might stand*, Rom. 9:11. And thus it went through all the Old Testament, till it came to the people of Israel, the nation of the Jews; and they, as a nation and a church, were chosen of God, and the rest of the world passed by; and thus it goes on to this day.

3dly, Another great fruit of election was, the sending of our Lord Jesus Christ, in the fulness of time, into the world. Election-grace sent Christ: This our Lord himself tells us, concerning his own agony, *Father, save me from this hour; nevertheless, for this cause came I unto this hour,* John 12:27. 'I knew that the design of God, in order to the saving of the lost world, was, that I should engage in this hard and bitter work, and I came into the world for this cause;' *For this cause*, saith he, *came I unto this hour.*

4*thly*, From election-grace flows the sending forth of the gospel, after our Lord's ascension, through the whole world. The election of God of old for a long while, lay among the Jews, and a few proselytes that were brought into the church; but when our Lord was risen again, and ascended into heaven, the gospel was sent through the whole world, and election-grace takes place every where. None knew where election-grace lay; it is a vein known only to God; we do not know where it lies; but wherever it lies, God will send forth his labourers to dig for it. When our Lord went to heaven, there were many veins of election scattered through whole nations. If I may so say, the devil was never so busy in sinning, and God and Jesus Christ were never so busy by his grace as they were at that time. The nations had many of the elect among them: indeed, if there be but one penny lost, the candle shall be lighted to search for it; if there be but one sheep lost, the great shepherd will search for it from mountain to mountain, and will bring it home upon his shoulders. But at that time election-grace ran through many parts of the world, and a great many were gathered in. It was our Lord's own words: *Lift up your eyes, and look on the fields, for they are ripe already for the harvest,* John 4:35. That was a happy time indeed! It may be, though it is very hard to be sure of it, and none should pretend to be sure of it, but I am apt to think that within thirty years after our Lord ascended to heaven, there were more converted to the faith of Christ than there hath been for some hundreds of years after, at another time. Election-grace was working then, and the vein of it was known to God. It is hopeful, blessed work to preach the gospel where election grace is going forth; where the line of election is laid in the purpose of God, preaching the word will have great effect.

5*thly*, and *lastly*, As to the fruit of this electing grace, there is the giving of faith to believe the gospel; the working of faith to believe the gospel, to believe in Christ. The gospel is sent to the elect, in the love of God, and upon them whom he hath a mind to call, in his due time he pours out his Spirit, and works faith in them. *To you it is given*, saith the apostle, *on the behalf of Christ, not only to believe on him, but also to suffer for his sake*, Phil. 1:29. *They who had believed through grace*, saith the apostle, Acts 18:27. Grace works believing in the word; the grace of election wrought upon their hearts in working faith in them: *As many as were ordained to eternal life believed*, Acts 13:48. Now when this grace of election is come this length, revealed in his promise, and in his covenant, and in the singular dispensations of it, as he sees good; when he hath sent his Son to ripen it, and to purchase all the fruits of this electing grace; when he hath sent his gospel to reveal all this to us, and at last sent his Spirit to work faith in us; and when all this is done, then the poor creature comes under the sprinkling of the blood of Christ, and the sanctification of the Spirit; which are the words of my text. There are two or three things farther that I would add about this.

1st, This is one of the most awful, and the greatest depth of God towards man; and is not to be searched into too curiously, nor is it to be known particularly, but by its fruits. I say, this election-grace of God is one of the greatest depths of God towards man about his salvation, and is not knowable of itself immediately, but by its fruits. Can we know what is in the heart of God? can creatures of yesterday know the eternal counsels of God? Unless he declares them, who can know them? and therefore this of election is only to be known by the effects of it. The devil gets great advantage by this over many poor sinners; when they hear of election, as an eternal, immutable purpose in the heart of God, about the salvation of men, the devil tries them this way, Dost thou know that thou art elected? No, saith the man; Then, saith the devil, thou mayest be eternally lost. But the thing itself is utterly unknowable but by the fruits of it. And therefore try it this way, 'Election-grace appears in its fruits; am I then under the sprinkling of the blood of Jesus? have I the sanctification of the Spirit unto obedience? if I have, then election-grace hath passed on me from eternity:' and this is the only way to know it.

2dly, Election-grace passes over, and passes through a world of mighty impediments; and this is the glory of it, and should be regarded by us. Election-grace passes over, and passes through many great impediments; if I may so say, election never regards what state the elected are in, but will overcome all difficulties. Who would have thought that the once poor wretch Saul was an elect vessel? that mad persecutor of Jesus Christ, when he was keeping the clothes of them who stoned Stephen, as one that would make himself an officer, and encourage them in their wicked work of murdering a servant of Jesus Christ; when he was breathing forth slaughter against the disciples of Christ, and thought it not enough to persecute them in Judea, but would even have persecuted them through the whole world? *Being exceedingly mad against them*, saith he himself, *I persecuted them even unto strange cities*, Acts 26:11. He hated Jesus Christ so much, that he would have gone from one end of the world to another, to have persecuted him and his followers: but yet he was an elect man; the grace of election ran through all this, and over all this. *It pleased God, that separated me from my mother's womb, and called me by his grace, to reveal his Son in me*, Gal. 1:15. The power of election overcame all. There are many of the elect children of God, that have been left to fall far nearer into hell, than many thousands who have fallen eternally into it. Many of the elect of God have been oftentimes even on the brink of the pit, but the secret cords of electing grace have taken hold of them, that they have not fallen in. Saith our Lord, Matt. 24:24, *They shall deceive, if it were possible, the very elect.* The devil shall never have this to boast of, that he ever prevailed against any one of God's elect. He may prevail against many rotten professors, but for an elect person, a true believer on Jesus Christ, a member of Christ's body, the devil shall never be able to twit Christ with this, 'Here is one of thine, that I am now master of.' Electing grace goes through a world of impediments, and that is the glory of it. *Oh how great is the depth both of the knowledge and wisdom of God! how unsearchable are his judgments, and his ways past finding out!* Known unto God are all his works, even from the beginning; we are surprised, we are amazed, we are stumbled by a great many things that come to pass, but there is nothing new in the world to God; all things are as he hath appointed them, as he hath foreseen them, and as he hath determined them. He hath raised up the stage of this world, and hath suffered sin to enter, and to make such havoc thereon, that the glory of his grace, in saving the remnant according to the election of grace might stand, might shine out, and appear in its glory. The elect of God now lie hid, and, as it were, buried in a state of nature, till grace brings them out; and they are, as it were, buried in a state of grace too, through manifold infirmities, even till they are brought home to glory; and then they shall know what the election of grace is, when it hath ripened its whole work upon all the vessels of mercy that were foreordained to glory. We should admire, we should adore, and tremble before this awful sovereign Lord God, that doth with his own as seemeth good unto him. We should, as our Lord did, give thanks, and say, *We thank thee, O Father! Lord of heaven and earth, that thou hast hid these things from the wise and prudent, and hast revealed them to babes; even so, Father, for so it seemed good in thy sight*, Matt. 11:25, 26. We must refer all to this sovereign will and pleasure of God, and leave with him all our own concerns, and all the concerns of his church and people, and conclude that all shall be well ordered, because ordered according to the counsel of his will. I would further say, that this election-grace is knowable, and the knowledge of it is of wonderful advantage: it is of great use to know that we are elect; and it may be known by the fruits of it, and it is a great blessing to know it. We are commanded *to give diligence to make our calling and election sure*, 2 Pet. 1:10; and many of the saints have attained to this knowledge, both as to themselves and others of the people of God. A little Application let me make of this,—That the grace of election is the spring of all that grace which God shews to the children of men.

SERMON IX.

1 Pet. 1:2.

Elect according to the foreknowledge of God the Father, through sanctification of the Spirit, unto obedience, and sprinkling of the blood of Jesus Christ: Grace unto you, and peace be multiplied.

I WAS speaking of election as the leading fountain, as a pregnant grace, as the first grace of God, and all that comes after it flows from it. This I took notice of, both with some glances on the spring, and with some remarks upon the streams that flow from it. I had not time then to enter on any Application; but would now add a few words of Use to what I then said, and so proceed to the last clause of the verse, Grace unto you, and peace be multiplied; which is the third thing that I observed to you, in this preface of the apostle to this epistle. An apostolical benediction; *Grace unto you, and peace be multiplied.* The Doctrine I am now to apply is this, That the grace of election is the spring of all that grace which God shows to the children of men. The text fairly leads us to this, *Elect according to the foreknowledge*, etc. If you go to the first rise in resolving this question, you see a great many in the world who have no acquaintance with Jesus Christ; they have no experience of the virtue of his blood: it never came upon them, and they never cared for it. But there are others who are sprinkled thereby, and who prize it above all things: Whence comes this difference? The one are elected to it, and the other not. So it is also as to the sanctification of the Spirit, some are sanctified by it, and a great many are not. The first rise of this difference is, they who are sanctified are elected to it, the others are not.

Use 1. The first thing in the Application of it is this, Behold here the grace of God! behold it! look rightly upon it. If a man takes up the grace of God from the fountain, through the streams, unto the issue of it, what a marvellous thing is the grace of God! It had no beginning in the rise of it, but was from eternity, boiling up in the heart of God; and it runs from the heart of God through the heart-blood of Jesus Christ, and through that it streams and flows down to us in grace and glory. What a marvellous sight is this! Alas! people do not know what the grace of God is; some know nothing at all of it; a great many know but little of it, and they look but little to it; but when grace is taken in its full extent, from its rise, through its channel, to its issue, what a marvellous thing is the grace of God! the free grace of God towards condemned sinners, that it should run this way to their eternal salvation! There are three things concerning the grace of God, that no man who looks rightly upon it but must perceive them. 1*st*, The absolute freedom of it, that there was nothing to move God to show grace, but only the grace that was in his own heart. 2*dly*, The riches of it. When we look upon the grace that a poor sinner needs, how exceeding rich must it be? What is the reason why the faith of poor sinners is so hampered and chained, that they find it so hard to believe the grace of God, when they see a great deal of sin in themselves? It is because they do not know the riches of God's grace. Grace and sin are enemies one to another, but grace is always stronger than sin, wheresoever God applies it. *Where sin hath abounded, grace doth much more abound*, saith the apostle, Rom. 5:20.

That poor creature is in a fair way to heaven, nay, he is in a sure way to heaven, and will surely come thither, concerning whom God saith, 'This sinful creature is striving to shew what sin can do, and I will strive to shew what my grace can do; his sin can destroy him, but my grace can and shall save him: it shall much more abound.' 3*dly*, There is the wisdom of grace; not only is it rich and free in its communications, but it is very wise in its management. Wisdom in dispensing grace appears in this, that the wise dispenser designs both the ends and the means too. The election of grace is not barely the choosing of a man to eternal life, but it is the choosing him thereto in and by the proper appointed means to reach that end. So saith the apostle, *We are bound to give thanks always unto God*; and well might he say so, that could add, *who hath chosen us unto salvation through sanctification of the Spirit, and belief of the truth*, 2 Thess. 2:13. But there is something besides in this wisdom, that passeth our understanding, and which we are to believe, but shall never know it fully till the last day. The apostle had been speaking of the same deep theme that I am upon, about election; see what use he makes of it, Rom. 11:33, *O the depth of the riches both of the wisdom and the knowledge of God! How unsearchable are his judgments, and his ways* *past finding out!* There was no mortal man in this world ever could tell a reason why grace makes such a difference; here is a poor sinner, and he is passed by; he is under the means of grace, and nothing touches him, nothing fixes on him; he hears from day to day, and feels nothing; but here is another, upon whom the word has its effect; he feels it, and is changed thereby: no man can give a reason for this, no other reason but this; *Even so, Father, for so it seemed good in thy sight.* That is the reason which Christ gives. However, I make no doubt, but that all the purposes of God about choosing and passing by the children of men, that this world are now so unable to receive, and to believe, will appear, in the day of Christ's coming, and the manifestation of all things, to have proceeded from the riches of the wisdom and the knowledge of God; though the reason be utterly unsearchable to us, yet there is something still in the eye of God. That is the *first* Use—Behold the grace of God!

Use 2. From hence behold the happiness of the partakers of this grace! Whatsoever condition they are in, though they be strangers scattered through all the regions of the earth, yet are they elected according to the foreknowledge of God the Father, and sprinkled with the blood of Jesus, and sanctified by his Spirit. They are a happy people; for the description here given of them in the text is an honourable one: not barely distinguishing them, but highly commending them; they are happy on this account. The apostle James hath a word concerning this, not far from this purpose; James 2:5, *Hearken, my beloved brethren, hath not God chosen the poor in this world, rich in faith, and heirs of the kingdom, which he hath promised to them that love him?* The apostle is there speaking by way of reproof for that vain frame which was amongst Christians in their assemblies, that when a man with a gold ring, and goodly apparel, came in, they shewed him respect; but the poor they did not respect. 'Now,' would the apostle say, 'how came ye to be so mistaken? Do not you know God's usual way? that they who are poor in this world, are often rich in faith: and very frequently they who are rich in this world are poor in faith?' Whensoever a poor creature falls under this great blessing of the sanctification of the Spirit, and the sprinkling of the blood of Jesus, as a fruit of electing-grace, they are highly dignified and truly happy.

Use 3. They are doubly happy who know this as to themselves. A great many people will assent readily to this truth, That they who are chosen of God to eternal salvation, through sanctification of the Spirit, and the sprinkling of the blood of Jesus, that these are a happy people; but they are specially happy who do know this *as to themselves*. That this is their great blessing, that they are thus chosen, that they are thus sanctified, that they are thus sprinkled, is a deep dispensation of God! that he gives so much, and yet gives so little knowledge of it! What if I should say, it is not fit for us to know all that we receive? it may be it would do us hurt to know all the love and tenderness that is in the heart of God towards us; we know that discoveries thereof bring snares along with them; but this is our misery, that the sight of our mercy should be a snare to us: yet surely, where mercy is seen, where it is well known, and well guided, it is a double mercy.

Use 4. How much more yet are they blessed who possess all that electing grace designed for them! They are happy who fall under this love of election and the fruits of it; they are yet more happy who know it; but they are most of all happy who are possessed of all that election designed for them; and this is the state of glory above. And therefore our Lord gives the crown of glory, at last, upon these terms: *Come, ye blessed of my Father, inherit the kingdom prepared for you before the foundation of the world*, Matt. 25:34. The foundations of the world were laid long ere you came into it, and you were a long while in the world before ye knew any thing of Jesus Christ, and the grace of God; 'but now,' saith our Lord, 'ye are come to possess all that eternal love that I designed for you.' The two greatest grounds upon which we certainly conclude, that the glory to be revealed is exceeding great, are, the eternal purpose of love in the heart of God, and the infinite price of the blood of the Son of God. It must be a great glory that God had so many thoughts about, and it must be a great glory that the Son of God paid so great a price for. There is nothing proves so plainly the love that God had in his heart for his people, and the infinite value of the blood of Christ, as a perceiving of that glory that we partake of by this purpose, and by this purchase. A poor believer finds it a hard matter to venture on Jesus Christ for eternal salvation, for pardon of sin and peace with God, and for all the privileges that we possess in this life; but, if I may so say, if we could see pardon of sin, peace with God, and all the other privileges that we possess in this life; and if, at the same time, we could see the crown of glory, we should find it a far easier matter to believe for them, than to believe for that: for doubtless the last prize of our calling will be greatly beyond all other blessings we partake of by the way. And thus I have finished the second thing that I took up in the apostle's preface to this epistle; his description of the parties to whom he writes, both from their outward condition before the world, as strangers scattered through several kingdoms; and also as to their condition before God, as elect according to his foreknowledge, sanctified by the Spirit, and sprinkled by the blood of Jesus.

III. I would now, *thirdly*, briefly run through and speak to the third thing in these two verses, and that is the apostle's wish or prayer, *Grace unto you, and peace be multiplied.* A wish that is expressed very frequently in the word of God; you will find it in all Paul's epistles, only with this variation, that in his epistles to Timothy, and in that to Titus, he adds *mercy* to *grace and peace*. Peter wrote but two epistles, and he hath this salutation in both of them; *Grace be unto you, and peace from God the Father, and from our Lord Jesus Christ.*

1*st*, Let us consider this with respect to the persons it is wished to, and prayed for; and they are called in the preceding part of the verse, *Elect according to the foreknowledge of God the Father, through sanctification of the Spirit unto obedience, and the sprinkling of the blood of Jesus: grace be unto you*. 'You have grace already, and peace already; therefore grace and peace be multiplied unto you.' Sirs, there is no praying for the multiplying of grace and peace to them who never had any; but the apostle saith concerning them, that they were partakers of grace and peace; *and now*, saith he, *be they multiplied unto you*.

2*dly*, Let us consider these words with respect to the person wishing it to them, and who is the writer of this epistle; *Peter, an apostle of Jesus Christ*: and an apostle's saying, *Grace unto you, and peace be multiplied*, when writing by the influence of the Holy Ghost, is equal to a promise. This is what I would a little take notice of. Promises are of two sorts, formal ones, and virtual ones. Formal promises are those that are so in the form of them, as it is in the covenant, Jer. 31:33, *I will put my law in their inward parts, I will write it in their hearts, I will be to them a*

God, and they shall be to me a people. Ezek. 36:26, 27, *A new heart will I give you, and a new spirit will I put within you; I will take away the stony heart out of your flesh, and I will give you a heart of flesh; I will put my Spirit within you, and cause you to walk in my statutes.* These are formal promises; when God speaks thus expressly, he is the speaker, and he is the promiser, and the doer; of these the apostle speaks, 2 Cor. 7:1, *Having therefore these promises, dearly beloved, let us cleanse ourselves from all filthiness of the flesh and spirit, perfecting holiness in the fear of God.* And the same apostle Peter, speaks of these in his second epistle, chap. 1:4, *There are given unto us exceeding great and precious promises, that by them we might be partakers of the divine nature.* But there are another sort of promises, that we call virtual ones; that is, though they are not in the form of a promise, yet they are really and materially one, and may be used by the faith of a believer as such. I shall instance in some of these. 1*st*, All the blessings of saints, as saints, recorded in the word, are promises to following saints for the same blessings. Pray observe; I speak not of mercies suited to special or extraordinary occasions, but of the blessings of God to believers in their course of walking with God, which are recorded in the word: these are grounds for the faith of every believer to expect the like. Saith the Psalmist, Psa. 32:5, *I acknowledge my sin unto thee, and mine iniquity I have not hid: I said, I will confess my transgressions unto the Lord, and thou forgavest the iniquity of my sin.* Well, and is not there an end? here is a distressed man seeking pardon, praying for it, and blessed with it: see what he adds, in the very next words; *For this shall every one that is godly pray unto thee, in a time when thou mayest be found.* What! may every godly man venture to put in after David? may such as we are venture to put in for the same blessing that David got? Yes, we may, warrantably on the same grounds. David was distressed with sin, and relieved with pardon; and every poor sinner in the same case may plead and speed as he did. *They that fear the Lord,* saith he, *will be glad when they see me, because I have hoped in thy word,* Psa. 119:74. 2*dly*, All the prayers of the saints recorded in the word, as to their own present case, they are prayers that may feed our faith, and may be used again by us. Psa. 34:6, *This poor man cried, and the Lord heard him, and delivered him from all his troubles*: and therefore any poor man may cry unto the Lord. And this is one great good that we get by the Psalms of David; a great part of the Scripture, both in the Old and New Testament too, contains the prayers of the saints. I acknowledge, they make a very bad use of them who compose a common prayer out of them; but every believer may make a prayer from them: whatsoever any distressed believer hath asked of God, any child of God may ask the same even to this day. 3*dly*, All the prayers of Jesus Christ for his church and people, are something more than real promises. I do not say that they are formal promises, but they are something more than real promises. Christ's prayers I say are so: a great instance we have of them in the 17th chapter of John throughout. Whatsoever Christ begged of his Father, for the relief and blessing of his children, every believer may pray it over again confidently. We may pray over Christ's prayer a great deal more confidently than we can the prayers of the saints; we may put our Amen to Christ's prayers a great deal more confidently than we can to Paul's: for our Lord was always heard, and his praying for us was a part of his saving us; he was a praying Saviour as well as a dying Saviour. 4*thly*, To bring the matter to the text, All apostolical prayers, directed by the Holy Ghost in their writings, are equivalent to a promise. I do not deny but the apostles, extraordinary men as they were, might sometimes miscarry in their praying; we find they sometimes miscarried in their practice. We find that Peter was blamed, and that justly, by Paul, for his dissimulation, Gal. 2; but whatsoever weaknesses they might have as men, in some parts of their work, yet, when they were made use of by the Holy Ghost as his penmen, in writing the Scriptures, they were under his infallible conduct; and therefore the prayers of the apostles, in their epistles, were equal to a promise. What the apostles, by the direction of the Holy Ghost, did pray for and wish to Christians in their days, every Christian in our day may lay claim to.

3*dly*, I would now consider these words *in themselves, Grace unto you, and peace be multiplied*. There are three things that may be taken notice of in this blessing wished to them: —the blessing prayed for, *Grace and peace*;—the connection of them, they are joined together, grace and peace;—and the increase and multiplication of them; *let them be multiplied*: 'not only grace be unto you, and peace be unto you, but let them be multiplied unto you.' This is a wish of the Holy Ghost's, by the pen of the apostle, and is, as I told you, often in the word;

in all Paul's epistles, and in both of Peter's. This is what can only be perceived and experienced by a spiritual man; if the apostle's expression had been, 'gold and silver be multiplied unto you; riches and health be increased to you; prosperity in this world be multiplied to you;' every Atheist would have understood him: but when he speaks of grace and peace being multiplied, it is a speaking of things that no ungodly man understands what they mean: they are spiritual things themselves, and the increase of them is spiritual too.

I. I shall speak of the things wished, *Grace and peace*; a little to each of these separately. 1*st*, What grace is. *Grace unto you*, saith the apostle. Grace meets with two acceptations; as it is in the heart of God, and as it is from the hand of God in the heart of a believer. Grace, as it is in the heart of God, is called the grace of God, and is frequently spoken of in the word; but this cannot be increased nor multiplied, because it is infinite. There is no elect child of God that may lawfully desire God to love him better than he doth, or Christ to love him better than he doth; no, none of these things is lawful; the measure of his love passes bounds, and therefore there can be no addition thereto. But take grace as it is the gift of God to a creature, and then it is capable of multiplication in the fruits, and in the manifestation of it; for that is what the apostle here means. *Grace unto you be multiplied*; not the love of God to you, but the fruit and manifestation of that love, be multiplied unto you. The other word here is *peace*, and peace is far more counterfeit than grace, and hath different acceptations. 1*st*, There is the world's peace; that all natural men are under. The world is never angry with an unrenewed man for his unrenewedness. *If ye were of the world*, saith our Lord, John 15:19, *the world would love his own*; 'the world and you would never quarrel, if you were not distinguished from it by grace.' 2*dly*, There is the devil's peace; and every natural man hath that too. The devil and such are at peace, there is no quarrel, no odds between them. *When the strong man armed keeps his palace, his goods are at peace*, saith our Lord, Luke 11:21. And all sinners are the devil's goods till Christ rescues them. Oh what a great house hath the devil! a great house and plentifully furnished! All sinners are the devil's goods; he possesses them, he rules them, he guides them as people do their own goods in their own houses, and use them to one end or another, even as they please. 3*dly*,

There is the sinner's peace in himself, and that is the worst of all; people are quiet within. How many poor sinners are there who never knew what it was to be in trouble for any thing within! Crosses without, and disappointments in worldly things, they understand what it is to be in trouble about these; but what it is to have inward trouble they never felt. This is a sad and an amazing thing; a great many poor sinners are perpetually quiet within: there is no reason for it, but there are causes of it. There is no reason for it at all; Is there any reason for a man to be at peace with himself that is at war with God? Is there any reason for a man's being at peace with himself, when God proclaims war in his law against him? The causes of this indeed are, many people are blind, and they see nothing; they are stupid, and they feel nothing; and they are dead, and can do nothing: all these three names are given to a man in his natural state, How then can it be expected that he should feel trouble? They are blind, hardened, stupid, and seared, so that they feel nothing. *They are dead in trespasses and sins*, Eph. 2:1; and therefore it is that they have peace and quietness within; but this is none of God's peace: the apostle does not pray that any of these may be multiplied: no; it is a great blessing to have all these false peaces broken. The apostle here means Christ's peace: and it stands principally in two things; peace with God, as to safety from all hurt from him; and peace of conscience, as to quiet within. 1st, There is peace with God; and this every elect child of God, that is a believer, hath; I do not say, that he always feels it, but he hath it. *Being justified by faith, we have peace with God, through our Lord Jesus Christ*, Rom. 5:1. Whosoever they be, man or woman, young or old, though they are cursed and condemned by the law of God, as much as ever it can, how great soever their transgressions are, how great soever the threatenings of God against them are, yet from the day that they lay their hands on this altar of God, Christ Jesus, everlasting peace between God and them is proclaimed. It may be they do not presently hear it; but whosoever have laid their hand upon this altar of God, they shall never perish by the weapons of his indignation. Poor Joab laid his hands on the typical altar of God, and see how it fared with him; when he was found to be one in the conspiracy of Adonijah, he fled unto the tabernacle of the Lord, and caught hold of the horns of the altar; and when it was told king Solomon, he sent

Benaiah unto him, and commanded him to come forth; *Nay, but*, saith the man, *I will die here*. 'Well,' saith Solomon, '*do as he hath said*; he is a traitor and a wicked man, and if he will not come out, slay him there:' *and Benaiah went up, and fell upon him, and slew him*, 1 Kings 2:28-35. Blessed be God, his justice will never say so concerning a poor sinner, that saith, 'I will die cleaving to the horns of God's altar; if that cannot shelter me, and be my sanctuary, here I will die.' No man shall be slain that makes this adventure; peace is proclaimed, and the weapons of indignation are put up immediately. *2dly*, There is peace of conscience, and that is peace within; peace with God is peace above; and these two are sometimes separated: however, peace of conscience is every believer's just right, and if he hath not the sense of it, it is his own fault. And this peace of conscience respects two things, a man's state, and his way. The peace which respects a man's state, is that peace which the reflecting on his believing gives him, called by the apostle, *The answer of a good conscience towards God*, 1 Pet. 3:21. What can a man's conscience speak for him before God? Nothing at all of good can it speak, from any thing it can *do*, from any thing it can *feel*, or from any thing it can *act*; only here is good news, it hath heard of *the resurrection of Christ from the dead, who died for our sins, and rose again for our justification*; and this is all that a believer's conscience hath to answer before God. Again, peace of conscience respects a man's way, the way wherein he walks. A man that is at peace with God, may yet walk in a crooked way, but God will find him out; and though it does not make a breach in a man's state of peace with God, yet it may bring on a testimony of God's fatherly anger. Peace of conscience not only respects a man's state, but also his walk; the apostle seems to have a respect to this, 2 Cor. 1:12, *Our rejoicing is this, the testimony of our conscience, that in simplicity and godly sincerity, not with fleshly wisdom, but by the grace of God, we have had our conversation in the world*. As if the apostle would have said, 'Every time that I think of the way wherein I walk, I find a testimony in my conscience that I desire to please God.' So much for this *first*, grace and peace *in themselves*.

II. The *second* thing to be spoken to is, their *connection, Grace and peace*; this is greatly to be noted, this phrase being used above twenty times in the New Testament. Grace and peace. Grace is the foundation, and peace is the building upon this foundation. There are two great faults about this matter; bad people's fault and good people's fault. 1*st*, There is the sinner's fault; they would fain have peace without grace; they have no concern about the special love and favour of God, yet they would fain be saved from hurt by him. 2*dly*, There is the believer's fault; they have grace, and do not build peace upon it. Every one that is a partaker of the grace of God, hath a solid foundation for peace laid in him, and he should build upon it. Grace is misimproved, or peace is mistaken, which is the cause why so many partake of grace, that do so little possess peace; either people do not improve the grace of God for all those ends for which it is given, or they mistake the peace that God gives. People generally think, that the peace here wished for to them is inconsistent with tribulation and affliction in this world; but the matter is quite otherwise.

Lastly, We are here to consider the *multiplying* of it. *Grace and peace be multiplied.* 1. Grace and peace is multiplied when the soul is filled with it. I will read one scripture to you concerning it, and there is not its fellow in all the Bible with respect to this point; and it is an apostolic prayer also, Eph. 3:16-19, *For this cause I bow my knees unto the Father of our Lord Jesus Christ, that he would grant you, according to the riches of his glory, to be strengthened with might, by his Spirit in the inner man; that Christ may dwell in your hearts by faith; that ye being rooted and grounded in love, may be able to comprehend with all saints, what is the breadth, and length, and depth, and height, and to know the love of Christ, which passeth knowledge, that ye might be filled with all the fulness of God.* Will you not think him to be a happy person indeed who hath this prayer fulfilled on him? He who hath Christ dwelling in his heart by faith, and his heart rooted in love, and the love of Christ shed abroad in his heart in all the dimensions of it, wondered at and felt by the soul; and at last to be filled with all the fulness of God. Then is grace multiplied indeed; then is a soul filled with grace, especially when these two things concur; when every power of the soul is filled with its suitable grace, and every grace in the soul filled with its suitable object. 1*st*, When every power of the soul is filled with its suitable grace: spiritual knowledge and understanding is the suitable grace for our minds; the grace of divine love is a suitable grace for the affection of love in our souls; Oh! what a blessed thing is it to have every power of the soul filled with its suitable grace! and then also, 2*dly*, To have every grace filled with its proper object. The object of all grace is our Lord Jesus Christ, but there are various representations of Jesus Christ, by which grace acts distinctly on him. Faith acts on Jesus Christ as an all-sufficient, able, trusty Saviour; love acts on him as altogether lovely; repentance acts upon him as one smitten for our sins, and as bearing the burden of our iniquities. Grace is multiplied when Christians have it suited to all their occasions; when the grace that is called for is in exercise, and they have it not to seek, but it is ready, lying by them, as it were. The apostle calls us *to come boldly to the throne of grace, that we may obtain mercy, and find grace to help us in the time of need*, Heb. 4:16. It is a great word the apostle uses concerning this; 2 Cor. 9:8, *God is able to make all grace to abound towards you, that ye always having all sufficiency in all things, may abound to every good work*. But I shall insist on these things no longer; only a word or two of Application.

1*st*, You may perceive that this is a prayer which you stand in great need of. Do not you need to have grace and peace multiplied to you? They never knew what the grace and peace of God was, who do not desire the multiplication of them. They are strangers to grace, who do not desire the increase of it; and they do not know the peace of God, who do not desire more of it. Grace and peace are never perfect in this life; and the greatest desires after them are raised by the greatest tastes of them. Have you not then need of this prayer?

2*dly*, You have good ground to pray over this prayer in the text: 'So say thy servants in thy word, Lord, *Grace and peace be multiplied*; Lord, fulfil this word!' The Lord help you to cry, and answer you when you cry! for these blessings you extremely need. Notwithstanding all the pains that we should take with ourselves about salvation, all is nothing to the pains which God takes with those whom he hath a mind to save. Where sovereign grace hath engaged itself, what mighty things are performed for the saving of the sinner! How many strong bolts and bars doth electing grace break through, that it may save the elected? Many are suffered to run on in their own ways to the pit, and have none to stop them; but when any of Christ's sheep are running on to ruin, the great Shepherd will stop and catch them, and bring them home upon his own shoulders: Oh what a blessed way is that we come to heaven in! upon the shoulders of our great Shepherd! We had been lost long ere now had it not been for his care. We have nothing in us which can further our salvation, and nothing in us that can hinder it, blessed be God! if Christ hath a mind to save us: for grace will always have the mastery of sin, and the dominion over it, wherever it is applied. As sin hath reigned unto death, so grace reigns through righteousness unto eternal life by Jesus Christ our Lord; and if that begins, it will carry on the work, and perfect what concerns us; and in a little time more, our way and our work will be done, and grace and peace shall be multiplied to us, till we come to that good land where grace and peace grow. They are indeed planted here, but they belong not to this world, this world is not the soil for them; they are plants of heaven, and they grow best there. O how will all the possessors of it bless that grace, when they come there, which they never knew before but by report! and that peace which cannot be fully known till we get thither! And there our grace will be without any mixture, and our peace without a mixture of any thing contrary to it; and then indeed grace and peace shall be multiplied to us. Lord, hasten that time!

SERMON X.

1 PET. 1:3, 4.

Blessed be the God and Father of our Lord Jesus Christ, who according to his abundant mercy hath begotten us again to a lively hope, by the resurrection of Jesus Christ from the dead: to an inheritance incorruptible, undefiled, and that fadeth not away, reserved in heaven for you.

YOU already know what is contained in the first and second verses of this epistle, directed by the apostle to the believing strangers scattered through several countries, who were elected by God the Father, sanctified by the Spirit, and sprinkled by the blood of Christ.

It now follows to speak of the apostle's entrance on this epistle; it begins with praise: and here the apostle Peter is like the apostle Paul, who generally begins his epistles this way; with praise unto God for his grace and mercy to them to whom he writes. In the beginning of the epistle there are three things to be remarked, which I would speak to in their order. 1*st*, The person his praise is directed to, *The God and Father of our Lord Jesus Christ.* A singular name of God, a name fitted to the faith of a believer; a name whereby God is known, and which we must learn to know him by, The God and Father of our Lord Jesus Christ.

2*dly*, The next thing in the words is the form and way of the apostle's praising; *Blessed be he*, saith he; *Blessed be the God and Father of our Lord Jesus Christ.*

3*dly*, The third and last thing in these words is, the matter of his praise; which branches forth itself into four things.

1*st*, There is the blessing itself, *begetting us again to a lively hope*: this is a strange kind of begetting, the raising a poor dead sinner to a lively hope, who, if I may so say, had nothing before but deadly fear; here is a lively hope brought in. 2*dly*, We have in these words the spring and rise of this gracious work; it is *according to his abundant mercy*; so we read it: but if the English would bear it, it is according to his much mercy, according to his great mercy; so the Greek runs. All the saving operations of God for, and upon the heirs of glory, they all arise from great mercy; mercy is the great high spring of all. 3*dly*, Here is the grand means of this great work of God in begetting us again to a lively hope; What way is this brought about? By the resurrection of Christ from the dead. All the hopes of believers rise from something done by Christ, and done upon him; our hope does not rise so much from any thing done by us, or done upon us; it is by the resurrection of Christ from the dead. *Lastly*, We have the great end of this work of God in begetting us again to a lively hope, the great end that it is directed to, and will issue in, and this we have in the 4th verse: it is to *an inheritance incorruptible, undefiled, and that fadeth not away, reserved in heaven for them.* It is little known now what the work of grace on a believer drives at, and what it will issue in. A poor dead sinner is wrought upon by the Spirit of God in the gospel, and nobody can imagine what this will turn to; saith the apostle, it is *to an inheritance incorruptible, undefiled, and that fadeth not away.* Before God hath done with him, it will be known it is for the possession of a vast boundless glory; a blessed estate is provided for them above.

I. It is the *first* of these that I would now enter upon; the name of the party the apostle gives thanks to, *The God and Father of our Lord Jesus Christ.* The apostle Paul, in his epistle to the Ephesians, calls God, *the God of our Lord Jesus Christ, and the Father of glory,* chap. 1:17. A little farther, in the same epistle, he saith, chap. 3:14, *For this cause I bow my knees unto the Father of our Lord Jesus Christ.* In these two places, the apostle speaks distinctly: in one of them, he calls God, *the God of our Lord Jesus Christ*; in the other place he calls him, *the Father of our Lord Jesus Christ*: but, in the text, they are both joined together; *the God and Father of our Lord Jesus Christ.* So doth the apostle Paul also, in his epistle to the Corinthians, 1 Cor. 1:9, *Blessed be the God and Father of our Lord Jesus Christ*; and again, in his epistle to the Colossians, *We give thanks to God, and to the Father of our Lord Jesus Christ,* Col. 1:3. It is plain by this description, that the apostle means the first person in the Godhead, God the Father; and he describes him by this, that he is the God and Father of our Lord Jesus Christ.

There are two things necessary in the opening up this to you, and laying it before you for your edification; 1*st*, I would shew you how this is to be understood; 2*dly*, How it is to be used.

1*st*, How this is to be understood, that God the Father is the God and Father of our Lord Jesus Christ. There are two names here, and I would speak to each distinctly: 1*st*, How is God the Father, the God of our Lord Jesus Christ? The meaning of it centres all in this, that God the Father is the God and Father of our Lord Jesus Christ upon this account, that our Lord Jesus Christ is the first in the covenant with God. Sirs, no creature can have a relation to God, as his God, but by covenant. The relation of God as a Creator relates to his framing all things. God is the creator of the sun, moon, and stars, and of all the works of his hands; but he is not the God thereof. The relation of a God always springs from covenant, and therefore the word doth not speak of it; and blessed be the Author of the word, that it is never spoken of! God is never said to be Adam's God; he was certainly so, for all that. The grace of God, in being a God to a creature, is owing only to the second Adam. It is only said, that Adam heard the voice of the Lord God in the garden; in the second and third chapters of Genesis, that give an account of Adam before the fall; we do not find it said that ever

God was Adam's God: he was Adam's creator, and Adam was really in covenant with God, and really had God to be his God, till he sinned; yet he stood so little a while in his state of innocency, that the Spirit of God never thought it worth mentioning to call Adam by this, that God was his God. Now, the relation of God's being a God to a creature, resulting from covenant, our Lord Jesus Christ, as man, is the head of this covenant; and therefore it is that God the Father is called the God of our Lord Jesus Christ. There was never so near and close relation between God and a creature, as there was between him and the man Christ. Jesus Christ hath the first room in the covenant. Never had there been a poor sinner advanced to this privilege, to have God to be his God, unless there had first been a great man, Christ Jesus, who had God to be his God. Therefore thus our Lord directs his disciples, *I ascend unto my Father and your Father, to my God and your God*, John 20:17. And there is great need that Christians should have this well fixed and established on their hearts:—that relation which God had to Christ, is the foundation of all that relation we have to God.

2dly, How is God the Father, the Father of our Lord Jesus Christ? I answer, God's being the Father of our Lord Jesus Christ respects principally these three things: *1st*, The inconceivable communication of the divine nature to the person of the Son. This is the highest and the greatest that we can arrive at; and we cannot arrive at it but by faith. He is called, Heb. 1:3, *the brightness of his glory, and the express image of his person*. He is called frequently, *the only begotten of the Father*, John 1:14.; 3:16. That from eternity the divine person of the Son was begotten by the divine person of the Father. The Father of our Lord Jesus Christ is then an expression of his divine nature. *2dly*, The extraordinary way of the bestowing the human nature upon Christ, entitles him to this name, of being the Son of the Father, and the Father's being a Father to our Lord Jesus Christ. There are not a few amongst us, whom God hath left unto a reprobate mind, and forsaken to their utter destruction, who think that Jesus Christ is a mere man; I no more expect the salvation of such a man, than I do the salvation of the devils. A man who believeth that Jesus Christ is no more than a mere man, is as far from salvation as the very devils themselves are. But yet, notwithstanding, the way of the communication of the human nature to Christ entitles him to a sonship to God: *Therefore*, saith the angel to the virgin Mary, *the Holy*

Ghost shall come upon thee, and the power of the Highest shall overshadow thee: therefore also, that holy thing that shall be born of thee, shall be called the Son of God, Luke 1:35. There was never a holy thing born of a woman but only this child Jesus Christ. Indeed at first God made two holy things, the first Adam and his wife; but there was never a holy thing born of a woman but Jesus Christ; *that holy thing that is born of thee shall be called the Son of God. 3dly*, Jesus Christ comes under this name, that God the Father is his Father, because of the special engagements of love that the Father bears towards him, and proves towards him. Never was there such a love as that the Father bore to the Son. All the love that we partake of is but a bit, a short reflection from this love. *Therefore*, saith our Lord, *I have declared unto them thy name, and will declare it; that the love wherewith thou hast loved me, may be in them, and I in them*, John 17:26. So much for the explaining of these names of God—that he is the God and Father of our Lord Jesus. I am now to shew you how we are to use this name of God; what uses it serves for.

1st, It serves to direct us in right thoughts of God; pray take heed to this; it serves, I say, to direct us in the right thoughts of God. There is a thought and a sense of God engraven in every man by nature; for nature's light and reason points forth to us, that there is a God. How came all things to be? Because there is a God. Why is there a world? but because there is a God that made it. Whence comes there to be a beginning of the creation? but because there was a Creator without beginning. Now this name of God directs us to right thoughts of him. The Old Testament saints laboured under a great disadvantage; they did not know this name of God; they knew as much of God as God thought fit to reveal of himself, and they knew as much of God as might be food to their faith; that God was a gracious God, and a God in covenant with Abraham and Isaac and Jacob, and the patriarchs; but this great name of God, *the God and Father of our Lord Jesus Christ*, they did not know. We find Jacob, when he is pleading and wrestling with the angel, *What is thy name?* saith he; as if the good man should have said, 'I know thou art God, but what is thy name? how shall I know thee again? what light wilt thou send forth, by which I may know thee more clearly and better?' *Wherefore is it that thou dost ask after my name?* saith the Lord; 'it is secret; the time is not yet come for the revealing of it; and thou must believe in the dark.' The poor Jews, and the poor Gentiles and Heathens, they did not know God by this name, *the God and Father of our Lord Jesus Christ*, and such are in a miserable case. But to bring this matter a little nearer; there are a great many Christians (if you will call them so, and we must call them so, because they will call themselves so, and would take it ill to be called by another name) that yet do not know God by this name, *the God and Father of our Lord Jesus Christ*. All their thoughts, and all their exercises, are about God as in himself, about God as revealed in his word, about God as revealed in his works, and clothed with so many glorious attributes, that the word speaks of; a God of infinite power and infinite wisdom, and infinite justice and truth. But, sirs, we have not the right God for all this. It is true, these are some dark glances at the true God; for the true God is certainly infinite in power, wisdom, justice, and truth: Ay, but who is this God? It was well observed by a blessed servant of Jesus Christ now in heaven, that the greatest part of people take up their religion in the knowledge of what God is; but they do not mind who this God is; they are concerned about the nature of the true God, but they do not know the person of this true God, who this God is; it is only the God and Father of our Lord Jesus Christ. It was a great word of blessed Luther, though few have ears to hear it well, and to understand it well; 'an absolute God,' saith he, 'is the idol of this world.' The grand idol of this world is an absolute God: a God not clothed with his grace and glory, shining in the face of Jesus Christ, is but an idol; a God that is not the God and Father of our Lord Jesus Christ, is but a dream of pagans. Blessed be God for the discoveries, that the light of his word makes to us, that the name of the true God is, *the God and Father of our Lord Jesus Christ*.

2dly, This truth, this name of God, gives us great directions in our thoughts of Jesus Christ; all our thoughts of Jesus Christ must be determined and fixed by the Father's relation to him, and his relation to the Father. When the apostle John is writing his short letter to a godly lady, *the elder*, saith he, *to the elect lady*; our precise Quakers, who will not give names of civil honour to persons of quality, should be ashamed in the reading that epistle, *the elder to the elect lady*: such was her quality in the world, and the apostle acknowdedgeth it. *The elder to the elect lady: grace unto you from God the Father, and from Jesus Christ the Son of the Father*: 'the Son of the Father;' remember that in all your thoughts of Jesus Christ, this must be continually in your mind, his relation to his Father. As we must not conceive of an absolute God, without his relation to Jesus Christ—for otherwise we cannot know him savingly—so we must not conceive of Jesus Christ without his relation to the Father; God the Father is the God and Father of our Lord Jesus Christ.

3*dly*, This may direct us to the knowledge of the original spring of our salvation; this is the scope of the apostle in these words; *Whence comes our salvation first? From the God and Father of our Lord Jesus Christ.* We do owe Jesus Christ himself, and all his great undertakings, and the eternal life that he hath brought in by that undertaking, we owe it all to the grace and love of the God and Father of our Lord Jesus Christ.

4*thly*, This name of God may instruct us about believing on Jesus Christ; I say, this may instruct us about faith in Jesus Christ. It is a strange thing, Sirs, that this matter of faith in Jesus Christ, for all that is spoken of it in the Bible, and for all that is daily spoken of it in the preaching of the word, yet still it remains a riddle to all unbelievers, and it will do so to the end of the world; and there is no help for it. It is a vain thing for a minister to dream that he is able by words to make an unbeliever know what believing is; they may as well think, to make a blind man, born so, know what seeing is. However, to speak a little of it from this name of God, that he is the God and Father of our Lord Jesus Christ: What is believing? You have heard many times concerning faith; I will tell you one thing more concerning it, from my text: faith in Jesus Christ is a poor sinner's claiming kindred with God by Jesus Christ. The poor sinner hears in the gospel of one called Jesus Christ, who hath God for his God and Father; the poor sinner hath God neither for his God nor his Father; God is an enemy to him, a stranger to him, and against him; but he hears of this blessed one Jesus Christ, that hath God to be his God and Father, and he comes in and claims kindred with God by Jesus Christ; for all our kindred with God is by faith in Jesus Christ. The poor sinner saith in himself, 'I am a stranger to God, and God is an enemy to me: I cannot claim a relation to God by my first father Adam; his sin hath broken that relation, and he thereby fell under the wrath and rebuke of God; but there is a new man come into the world, Christ Jesus, who hath God for his God and Father, and all that are in him have God for their God and Father too.' Remember, Sirs, and know from this name of Jesus Christ, what the precise nature of faith is; faith in Jesus Christ, is a poor sinner's coming in for kindred with God, and kindness from him, by Jesus Christ. The great reason of all our confidence in resting upon Christ by faith, is, that this Lord Jesus, whom we believe in, is a mighty one with God; God is his God and Father: God was never a God and Father to any, but he becomes a God and Father to all that are in him. If we lay hold but on the skirts of this Jesus Christ, we are immediately thereby made partakers of an interest in God as our God and Father.

5thly, This truth directs you about the worship of God. Wheresoever there is any notion of the being of God, there is immediately a conviction following of a debt of duty and worship to him; and according to the light that men have in the knowledge of God, such is the nature of that worship which they pay to him. When we come to know the true name of the true God, we come to know what is the true worship that we should pay to him. His name is *the God and Father of our Lord Jesus Christ*, and all the worship that is paid unto him, not under this name, is mistaken and false Worship. *First*, They that do not worship God under this name, they do not worship the true God. What! do not they worship the God that made the heavens and the earth? But this is not the true God for all that. I know indeed there is no idol that can make heaven and earth, and I know that all the attributes of God are proper to him only, and can be given to no idols; but they do not worship the true God for all this. *This is life eternal*, saith our Lord, *to know thee the only true God, and Jesus Christ whom thou hast sent*, John 17:3. Unless men worship God as sending Christ, and worship him as in Christ Jesus, they do not worship the true God. 'We are in him that is true,' saith the apostle, 1 John 5:20: and *this is the true God, and eternal life: little children, keep yourselves from idols*, in the very next words: as if the apostle should have said, 'All those gods are but idols, that are not known and worshipped as God is revealed in the face of Christ.' *2dly*, It is false worship, that is not paid to God under this name: for they who worship God out of Christ, do not worship him in the right place. The worship of God under the Old Testament, when all things went by types and shadows, was only to be in one place, whither all their worship was directed; to the temple, and to the mercy-seat especially: for that was the holiest of all in that ministration. But there is no place now where God is to be worshipped but in Christ Jesus. My meaning is, that there is no place now, that will make our worship to be more acceptable in than another. We may now worship God every where, there is no difference in places; it is a piece of Popish superstition to dream that consecrated churches are better places for worship than others: halls, houses, fields, are all alike as to this. *I will therefore*, saith the apostle, *that men pray* EVERY WHERE, *lifting up holy hands, without wrath and doubting*. 'In every place, be where they will.' But, if I may so say, there is one place that consecrates the worship, and if so be the worship is not performed there, it is stark naught; and that is *the true tabernacle that God pitched, and not man*, as the apostle's phrase is, Heb. 8:2, namely, in the temple and tabernacle of our Lord Jesus Christ. Thither all our worshipping of God is to be directed; and therefore a great many people's prayers will be cast back into their faces with abhorrence by God, on this very account: 'You have prayed, and worshipped me, and sought me; but your prayers were not put up in the right place; you forgot the Lord Jesus Christ, who is the only place to which all our worship to God is to be directed.' *3dly*, All such worship is naught, because it is not put up by a Mediator. You see in the text here, that the name of the Mediator is contained in the name of God; *Blessed be the God and Father of our Lord Jesus Christ*; the name of the Mediator, by which only you can prevail, is contained in the name of the God that you can only worship: therefore, saith our Lord, to the poor woman of Samaria, *Ye worship ye know not what*; 'You do not know the Father, because you do not know the Son;' *but we know what we worship; for salvation is of the Jews*; 'the Mediator is to come of them; and therefore all your worshipping is but worshipping an unknown God.'

6thly, and lastly, This name, *the God and Father of our Lord Jesus Christ*, may be of great use to us in directing our walk and conversation, and behaviour towards God. Is God the God and Father of our Lord Jesus Christ? then this may tell us how to guide all the providences of God towards us; write but this name upon all providences, and how easy and sweet will they be? these are the doings of the God and Father of our Lord Jesus Christ: so are all your mercies; all your mercies come from the

God and Father of our Lord Jesus Christ. *Blessed be the God and Father of our Lord Jesus Christ,* saith the apostle, Eph. 1:3, *who hath blessed us with all spiritual blessings in heavenly places in Christ Jesus.* Mercies are never rightly known, when their author is not rightly known. They are but confused thoughts that the most part of people have concerning the providences they meet with, as concerning the God that they worship. They meet with merciful dispensations, and they are pleased with them, but they are not profited by them; the reason is, because they do not know who sent them. It is *the God and Father of our Lord Jesus Christ* that hath shewn me this mercy. Oh, what a great endearment of mercy, to know the name of the sender of it! So it is also with respect to afflictions and trials; what a great blessing is it to know this! see how our Lord useth it himself, *The cup that my Father hath given me, shall I not drink it?* John 18:11. If it was a cup that men only gave me to drink, I might quarrel with it, and I should have just cause for it; if it was a cup the devil gave me to drink, I would reject it; but it is a cup that my Father hath given me to drink, and therefore I must drink it; and I will drink it, and drink it cheerfully. *The cup that my Father hath given me, shall I not drink it?* As if our Lord should have said, 'Can you make any doubt of the reasonableness of my cheerful submission to what my Father doth?' And as our Lord practised this himself, so it is what we are directed to by the apostle at large, in the twelfth chapter of the Hebrews, from the 6th to the 11th verse, where the whole topic of the apostle runs this way. Patience under tribulation, of what sort soever it be, is argued from this consideration, that he is a Father who doth it. No great wonder if there is struggling and kicking against the yoke of the Lord, when people do not know the heart and mind and love of him that sent it. *What son is he that the Father chasteneth not? if ye endure chastening, God dealeth with you as sons,* Heb. 12:7; and you should deal with him as a Father, in bearing it patiently. So much for this first thing in the words—the person the apostle directs his praise to, *Blessed be the God and Father of our Lord Jesus Christ.* The next thing that follow to be spoken to, is the form and manner of the apostle's praising, *Blessed be he,* a word frequent in the New Testament. *Blessed be the God and Father of our Lord Jesus Christ.*

SERMON XI.

1 PET. 1:3, 4.

Blessed be the God and Father of our Lord Jesus Christ, who according to his abundant mercy hath begotten us again to a lively hope, by the resurrection of Jesus Christ from the dead: to an inheritance incorruptible, undefiled, and that fadeth not away, reserved in heaven for you.

THE apostle's entrance on this epistle is with thanksgiving, as is the usual manner of the holy men of God that write unto the churches. This I have taken up in three things. 1*st*, The party that is blessed, to whom thanks is given, *the God and Father of our Lord Jesus Christ*. 2*dly*, The form and way of the thanksgiving, *blessed be he*. 3*dly*, The matter and the ground of this praise, *he hath begotten us to a lively hope, by the resurrection of Christ from the dead, to an incorruptible inheritance*; and this I divided into four things. 1*st*, The matter of the blessing, simply in itself, *begetting us again to a lively hope*. 2*dly*, The spring of it, *according to his abundant mercy*. All dispensations of grace to the children of men spring from the abundant mercy of God. 3*dly*, There is the ground and means of conveying this blessing; it is by the resurrection of Jesus Christ from the dead. *Lastly*, The grand issue and design of this great work; it is to an incorruptible undefiled inheritance reserved in heaven.

I have already finished the first of these; the name of the person to whom the apostle's praise is directed, *the God and Father of our Lord Jesus Christ*: how God the father is the God, and how he is the Father of our Lord Jesus Christ, I have also spoken to: I have also shewn how this truth is to be guided and improved by us in six particulars, that I would but just name, and then proceed. 1*st*, This may direct us in the knowledge of God: none know the true God, but they who know him under this name, *the God and Father of our Lord Jesus Christ*. 2*dly*, This may direct and instruct us in the knowledge of Christ himself: for as we cannot know the Father but by the Son, so we are not to know the

Son, but as he is in the Father: as the uncreated, invisible, and incomprehensible glory of God shines in the face of Jesus Christ, so the glory of Jesus Christ is never seen but when the glory of God is seen shining in his face. *3dly*, This directs us about the original high spring of our salvation. Jesus Christ is every where called the Saviour: for nothing could be done about our salvation, till Christ undertook it; but it was the Father that appointed him to be the Saviour, and our salvation in the first rise of it arose from an act of grace in the Father's heart about us. *4thly*, This may direct us what faith in Jesus Christ is; what believing on Jesus Christ is, and what its nature: believing on Jesus Christ is, a poor sinner, a stranger, an enemy to God, pleading for peace, for kindred, for friendship and blessings from God, through Jesus Christ. If God was not the God and Father of our Lord Jesus Christ, no sinner could lay any claim to kindness from him. *5thly*, This may direct you in the worship of God. It is the God and Father of our Lord Jesus Christ, that you must serve and pray to every day; if you forget this, you forget the God you call upon; and they who forget the God they pray to, it is little matter whether they forget the prayers that they make or not: it is all to one purpose whether their prayers be forgotten or remembered. *For this cause I bow my knees*, saith the apostle: Who is this, if one should say, that thou art so much in praying to, and so often upon thy knees in speaking to? saith the apostle, *For this cause I bow my knees to the God and Father of our Lord Jesus Christ*; as if he had said, 'I should never have a heart to call upon God, but that I know him by this name—*the God and Father of our Lord Jesus Christ.*' *Lastly*, This name of God is of great use to direct us in improving all the providences of God, whether they be mercies or crosses. They who do not see God's name written upon his dealings, can never make a good use of them. *The Lord's voice crieth unto the city*, saith the prophet, *and the man of wisdom shall set thy name*, Mic. 6:9. Unless people see God's name in his dealings, they cannot possibly profit under them.

II. That which now follows in the *second* place to be spoken to, is the form and way of the apostle's blessing this God and Father of our Lord Jesus Christ. *Blessed be he.* It is not only 'blessed is he,' though that be true, but 'blessed *be* he.' Concerning this praising of the Lord, I would first speak more generally of the duty of praise and thanksgiving in itself, and then speak of it more particularly, as relating to the apostle's aim and scope in this text.

1*st*, Concerning this duty in itself; we find these things plainly about it: 1*st*, That praise and thanksgiving is well deserved by the Lord; his excellency in himself, and his bounty and mercy towards us, call for it. There is nothing more a debt, and more a duty, than praise and thanksgiving is;—God is deserving of our praises. 2*dly*, Blessing of the Lord is frequently called for in the word, very often in the book of Psalms. *Bless ye the Lord; bless him all ye kindreds of the earth; bless him all ye nations*, Psa. 66:8, 68:26.—This is often called for; probably if it were well examined, there are more charges in the word for praises than for prayer. 3*dly*, We find that the saints were much taken up in this duty of blessing and praising God; most part of the Psalms are taken up this way. We can hardly find any account of any dealings with God, but praise made up part thereof. Nay, not only the saints, but their Lord and Master, was greatly given to this work of praise; we find him frequently at it, *I thank thee, O Father, Lord of heaven and earth*, Luke 10:21. When he was giving the wine at his table, he gave thanks, Matt. 26:27.—This duty of praising was frequently practised by the saints. Nay farther, 4*thly*, we find the saints frequently exciting themselves to this duty of blessing the Lord: *Bless the Lord, O my soul, and all that is within me bless his holy name; bless the Lord, O my soul, and forget not all his benefits*, Psa. 103:1, 2. Pray now, what doth a man do when he blesses God? When God blesseth us he does somewhat, and a great somewhat too; but when we bless God, we do just nothing, or that which is next to nothing at all. When we bless God, we can give nothing, for nothing can be given to him. Rom. 11:34, *Who hath given to the Lord, and it shall be recompensed to him again?* But is our blessing of God then nothing? No, there is somewhat in it, for all that; though our blessing him is not like his blessing us: his blessing of us, is wishing well, and doing well to us, it is his mending our state by his blessing: our blessing him, is wishing well to him; it is not doing him any good by mending his state, for that is perfect.—We find the saints in scripture stirring up themselves to bless and praise the Lord, though they know they can do but little at it.

Lastly, We find, concerning this praising, that heaven is prepared for it. Heaven is not only a state of glory, that will lay the partakers thereof under an everlasting debt to give praise; but it is a place where praise is to be given. There are a great many things to be done by us whilst we are here upon earth; we must pray, and we must believe and we must suffer, and we must have patience in tribulation, and we must rejoice in hope, and we must serve the Lord in all humility, and fear, and watchfulness; but none of these things are in heaven; there is only one work that is appointed for heaven, and heaven is appointed for it, and that is praising. We are to be to the praise of the glory of his grace, wherein he hath made us accepted in the Beloved. The name of the Lord Jesus Christ is to be glorified in us, and we in him, 2 Thess. 1:12. Heaven itself, and all the blessing that lead to it, are all appointed, bestowed, and dispensed purposely for the end of praise in general. It is deserved by the Lord, required by him, paid to him by his people, who frequently stir up themselves to the work; and we find that heaven is appointed for it.

2dly, What then is this blessing and praising God, so much spoken of in the word, practiced by the saints, and commanded by God? It stands in these three things: *1st*, Owning his perfect blessedness in himself, in all the appearances of it to his creatures. When we bless him, we only own what is in him; but we do not add any thing to him. It is only the inconceivable blessedness and perfection of God, that shine to us in his word and works, which we see and own when we bless him. *If thou sinnest, what dost thou against him? or if thy transgressions be multiplied, what dost thou unto him? If thou be righteous, what givest thou him? or what receiveth he of thy hand? Thy wickedness may hurt a man as thou art, and thy righteousness may profit the son of man*, as Elihu speaks to Job, chap. 35:6-8. All the service and obedience that is paid by his creatures add nothing to him; and all the sins and provocations that are amongst men detract nothing from him. His infinite perfect blessedness is incapable either of addition or diminution.—Our blessing of him is only acknowledging his blessedness. *2dly*, It stands in wishing well to him; in wishing the exalting and glorifying that fulness that is in him. How excellently have we this expressed to us in Nehemiah! chap. 9:5: upon that solemn day of their fasting (and they spent the day very well) they read in the book of the law of the Lord their God one fourth part of the day; and another fourth part of the day they confessed their sins, and the iniquities of their fathers; another part of the day they spent in worshipping the Lord their God; and another part of the day in praising him: but that which I refer to is their praising; they that were appointed for the work were set in their places, and the call was given unto them, *Stand up, and bless the Lord your God for ever and ever: Blessed be thy glorious name, that is exalted above all blessing and praise.* As if these blessed men should have said, 'We know it to be our duty to bless the Lord; but all our blessings fall short of what he is worthy of: he is far above all our blessings and praises, and they can never reach to an equal retribution or acknowledgment of the greatness and goodness of God.' 3*dly*, Our blessing of God stands in our commending him with praise and with thanksgiving. This word in my text is a form of praise; and praise and thanksgiving are two sundry things. Praise relates to the person that engages us; thanksgiving relates to a person with respect to benefits that we receive from them. It is possible a man may praise God when he does not give thanks. We may praise God for what he is in himself; but thanksgiving is upon the account of his bounty extended to us. His people are appointed for this, *to shew forth his praises, who hath called them out of darkness into his marvellous light*, 1 Pet. 2:9.

3*dly*, I shall speak farther concerning this great duty of giving praise and of giving thanks unto the Lord, as including one and the same thing. There are a great many duties that people commonly know, and commonly try, and as commonly spoil in the trying; and one great cause of their marring these works is, because they do not well know what their work is. I would therefore plainly and briefly show what this duty of praising and thanksgiving is: for this implies strongly, that there is cause for it. Mercy shewn and put forth, and bounty received, is the ground of praise and thanksgiving. There are three things about this, that if you would mind the work aright, you must think of, 1*st*, A meditation of your mercies; 2*dly*, Impression on the heart by it; 3*dly*, An expression of this. I name these things distinctly, not that they are really separable in themselves, but only for the better directing you to order your thoughts aright in this matter.

1*st*, The first thing in praising is, that the mercy we would praise for must fill the mind; there must be a serious thoughtfulness about it. Forgetting God's benefits is the moth of thankfulness, and mars it.

Bless the Lord, O my soul, and forget not all his benefits, saith the Psalmist, 103:2. And he acknowledges the unthankfulness of his predecessors; *Our fathers remembered not the multitude of thy mercies*, Psa. 106:7. 'They understood them not, they remembered them not.' Sirs, memory is a natural power that some people have a greater excellency in than others; this is known in all sorts of people, from their childhood to their old age. You would think it strange now that there should be any great sin in forgetfulness; but this is charged upon Israel, Deut. 32:18, *Of the rock that begat thee thou art unmindful, and hast forgotten the God that formed thee*. Is it a sin to have a bad memory? No, no more a sin than to have bad eyes or bad ears; for they are all natural infirmities; but yet there is a kind of forgetfulness that is a great sin. God's mercies and his goodness to us should be laid up in our memories, and treasured therein. God's mercies should have a great room in our memories. People will never do any great matters in godliness, till they learn to meditate thereon. The Psalmist, speaking of his praising the Lord, saith, *My meditation of him shall be sweet*. It is impossible that we can remember all God's mercies; but it is a very sinful thing to forget his special mercies; they should be treasured up in our memories as the most precious jewels that we can lodge there. Our memory is a kind of room, in which we must lay up what we would keep safe; and a marvellous house our memory is. Now meditation is nothing else, if I may so say, but a man's going from one chamber to another in this house, and to compare together, and to examine all God's loving kindness towards us. When the Psalmist charges it on himself not to forget all his benefits, the man is far from meaning that he could remember them all; but he was desirous to charge himself with them as well as he could, and laboured to remember them as well as he could. This is the first thing that we should mind in praising the Lord; for unless the mind be well employed, fixedly and seriously employed, in thinking upon the Lord's mercies, we shall never pay the debt of thankfulness and praise honestly and heartily.

2dly, After this thinking and meditation follow impression. Meditation is the work of the understanding; impression is the feeling of the heart. As long as meditation only floats in the brain, it is no more but a notion; but when meditation hath its due effect, and reaches and stamps the heart, that is the impression of mercy: the want of this is that which people are quite spoiled for in the matter of praise. They know the cause of thankfulness to God, they remember the mercies that he hath shewn unto them; but they do not apply it by such a powerful meditation that may work their hearts to some sense of it. This impression of mercy is a most necessary thing in order to praise; and it is raised from some of these; 1*st*, By a serious viewing of the mercy all round, looking upon it every way, how great it is, how seasonable, how useful, how profitable to us. There was a good woman, and a happy woman, Elizabeth, see how she expresseth her thanksgiving, Luke 1:25. She hid herself five months after she had conceived, saying, *Thus hath the Lord dealt with me*. The case was this, she had been a long time without children, and the Lord by an angel intimated that she should conceive with child, and that this child should be the harbinger and the forerunner of our Lord Jesus Christ; and when this was accomplished, it is said by the Holy Ghost, that she hid herself five months, and said, 'Thus hath the Lord dealt with me;' as if the good woman should have said, 'What great kindness is here! I am with child, and this child is the forerunner of our Lord Jesus Christ:' and an extraordinary one he was. 2*dly*, Impression is raised by the greatness of the giver. The majesty of God, who bestows the mercy, makes the smallest of his mercies to be great. A man who hath a low esteem of mercy, hath always a low esteem of the God that shews it. 3*dly*, This impression is raised from a deep sense of our own unworthiness; and therefore David's praise rises this way, 2 Sam. 7:18, *Who am I, O Lord God? and what is my house, that thou hast brought me hitherto?* All proud folks think little of great mercies; but a humble man will think much of a small mercy. *I am less than the least of all thy mercies*, saith Jacob, Gen. 32:10. He had a great deal of mercy, but he counted that the smallest of his mercies were bigger than he. 4*thly*, This sense and impression of mercy is raised from the debt that is laid on the receiver; a great giver, and an unworthy receiver, and a great debt laid upon the receiver by the giver for his giving. *What shall I render unto the Lord*, saith the Psalmist, 116:12, *for all his benefits?* They can never have a right sense of mercy, who do not know what mercy calls for. If it stood only in this, *that it is the bounty of God that gives, and we are happy in receiving*, this would make our hearts light, vain, and frothy; but when this is added thereto, 'all these givings of God, and all these receivings from him, are but so many debts and burdens laid upon thee,' this will make a man lie low indeed. *What shall I render to the Lord for all his benefits towards me?* This is the second head—an impression raised upon the heart.

3dly and *lastly*, This impression will work in outward expressions. Meditation is the work of the mind; impression is the feeling of the heart; and expression lies in all the outworkings of praise that may be: where the former are not, this cannot be; but where the former are, this will be, whether men will or not. If the mercy be known, and be felt, the expression of praise for it will be unavoidable, one way or other. I shall name a few of these ways; *1st*, The first expression of praise for mercy is in admiring and adoring the grace of the giver. This is the native expression of mercy, and of thankfulness for it, to be filled with a holy adoring and admiring the grace of the giver: this lies so near to the nature of praise, that it is inseparable from it. Thanksgiving, in the very first working of it, lies in an admiring the giver of the mercy. Thanksgiving is only an hearty expression of the goodness of him who hath given the mercy. Thanksgiving and mercy giving relate one to another: thanks are given by us, because mercy is given by God. *2dly*, Beside this expression of praise by the adoration of the heart, praise will break forth in words and in deeds, according as a man is able to shew it. There will be a stirring up of himself, and all that is within him, to bless his holy name, Psa. 103:1, 2. There is a striving to praise, in which a great part of the nature of praise doth consist. There is a stirring up ourselves to praise the Lord; this is what is required by the Lord, and frequently practised by his people: they do what they can, and they would do more than they can. So David, in that place already named, 2 Sam. 7:20, he looks upon his mercy every way: *And this was yet a small thing in thy sight, O Lord God; but thou hast also spoken of thy servant's house for a great while to come: and is this the manner of man, O Lord God? and what can David say more unto thee? for thou, Lord God, knowest thy servant*. What can David say more! Strange words indeed! Will not any body, think you, wonder that the great Psalmist of Israel is so soon run a ground? but David could not have praised better, he could not have praised more, than in that way of praising. *What can David say more?* 'I have said what I thought, and I have said what I can, and God knows I cannot say what I would, and thou, Lord, knowest thy servant; for thy word's sake, and according to thine own heart, thou hast done all these great things.' As if he had said, 'I know that my praise can never measure thy heart; according to thine own heart thou hast done these great things.' I say, praise will not only express itself in inward admirations, but also in outward thanksgiving, all manner of ways, and that both in word and deeds. *Whoso offereth praise glorifieth me; and to him that ordereth his conversation aright will I shew the salvation of God*, Psa. 50:23. Sirs, if I may so say, if our praise falls low, let our conversation rise higher; if our tongue cannot speak much, let our life speak more to his praise. A well-ordered conversation is a well-tuned song to the praise of the God of our mercies. *3dly*, We find this expression of praising, that when the believer hath done all that he can do at it himself, he will call in every one to help him. *I will bless the Lord at all times, his praise shall be continually in my mouth. My soul shall make her boast in the Lord. The humble shall hear thereof, and be glad. O magnify the Lord with me, and let us exalt his name together*, Psa. 34:1-3. Pray observe, the man resolves to bless God at all times, and to have his praise continually in his lips; what help then needed he in this work? Saith he, in the next words, *O magnify the Lord with me, and let us exalt his name together.* I will tell you freely; a believer, that hath a right sense of mercy on his heart, is just like a man that is carrying a great treasure home with him, he is loth to lose a penny of it, loth to lose any of it; but it is a great deal too heavy for him; and therefore he says, 'Oh for help! will any one help me to carry it safe home, that I may not lose any of this great treasure of mercy, but send forth the due praises to the giver of it?' What means the Psalmist so poetically, if I may so say, to call upon the whole creation to praise God, as in Psalm 148. Praise him, sun, moon, and stars, fire, hail, wind, snow, mountains, hills, trees, cattle, fowls, etc. He names almost every thing in the world, and gives an exhortation to them to praise the Lord. Why is the man so taken up? Why, the blessed man saw God's excellency, and perceived his bounty towards him, and knew his debt to God, and strove what he could to praise him, and was convinced he could do but little towards it; and therefore calls in every thing to help him to praise the Lord. Sirs, this is pretty well known, that when a believer is greatly distressed, he is mightily concerned to have help in prayer. With what earnestness doth many a poor believer beg the help of other believers' prayers! It is a good work, and it is a duty for them to ask it, and it is a duty required of them who are asked to pay it. But if ever you had a right sense of the loving-kindness of God, you will find as great need, and as great inclination, to beg the help of other people's praises, as ever you were to beg the help of other people's prayers. Never was there an affliction, never was there a sin, so sensible to the heart and conscience of a distressed believer, as the great loving-kindness of the Lord sometimes is: it is a heavy burden, but a sweet one.

4thly, Another expression of praise is, our sealing to the praises that others give unto God; in setting our Amen to all the praises that are given him; so that the poor believer is in this happy state, that though he cannot praise as he would, yet he knows there are better praisers of than he is, and if he cannot sing with them, he can add his Amen to them: though he cannot write after their copy, yet he can, in a manner, take the pen in his hand and set down Amen: Amen to all the praises that have been given to God from the beginning of the world to the end of it; in time and to eternity. And in this a great part of our praising lies. Alas! what can we do with a few words of praise from such narrow, straitened hearts as ours are? how small is the return that we are able to make for all the loving-kindness of God to us? 'Well,' saith the believer, 'I know it is but little that I can do, but yet there are some who can praise better; the Lord hath been praised from the beginning of the world, and he will be praised to the end of it; he is and will be praised by the blessed assembly above of saints and angels; and though I am not in their company, yet I belong to them, and I will put my Amen to their praises every day.' Sirs, the life of prayer stands in Amen; I do not mean in the word only, words are but form; the life of prayer stands in Amen, in that assent of faith which seals the petitions which we put up; that is the life of prayer: even so the life of praise stands in our Amen, which is the assent of faith to the praises we put up.

5thly, Another expression of praise is resolving on perpetual praise. Sirs, I would not have you think that you pay for the mercy you receive by the praise that you give: mercy is never paid for by praise; for grace to praise is new mercy, and our debt grows bigger by praising. But the believer expresses his thankfulness by resolving to praise for ever; and therefore the Psalmist expresses himself thus; *I will sing unto the Lord as long as I live; I will sing praise unto my God while I have my being*, Psa. 104:33. Aye, but thy life will be quickly at an end, David: 'But I shall have a being for ever, and the work of praise is resolved upon for ever. *I will sing praises unto my God, while I have my being*.' Sirs, take heed to your spirits in this; whosoever they be, who think they quit scores with God for mercy, by an hour or two, or a day of thanksgiving, such persons neither know God, nor mercy, nor themselves. Our praising is but our duty, and when we have done all we can, there is a great deal more owing; and we must never expect to pay God for his mercy, even unto the utmost days of eternity. We must resolve to praise him for ever: for his mercy endureth for ever, and everlasting mercy should oblige to eternal praise.

Lastly, The last expression of praise which I shall name, is praying praise to God; not only resolving to praise him for ever, but to pray him to exalt himself; to pray him to take the work of thanksgiving into his own hand, and, if I may so say, to give himself thanks. So doth the Psalmist; *Be thou exalted, O Lord, in thine own strength, so will we sing and praise thy power*, Psa. 21:13. A strange prayer! *Be thou exalted, O Lord, in thine own strength, so will we sing and praise thy power*. 'Do thou put forth thy power, and advance thy glory, then shall we praise thee better than we do; so will we sing and praise thy power.'

4*thly*, I shall add a few things farther relating to this duty of praising the Lord for his mercy. 1*st*, The worst and the meanest of men have a great deal of God's goodness and mercy shewn to them. *The Lord is good to all, and his tender mercies are over all his works*, Psa. 145:9. There is a wonderful deal of patience, and goodness, and long-suffering, that is put forth and extended to the most wicked, ungodly sinners, Rom. 2:3, 4. 2*dly*, All the expressions of God's goodness, love, and mercy, to men, lay them under a debt of praise to God; this is plain and easy, and the very naming of it may suffice—that all the expressions of God's goodness to men lay them under a debt of praise to God. 3*dly*, Special mercies call for special praises: as there are great things in God's law, and lesser, so there are great things in God's bounty, and lesser; so there should be greater praising, and lesser. He is a happy man who can weigh mercies! though every one is bigger than we deserve, yet there are some which are bigger than others in themselves: and the more special the mercy is, the more praise is due to God. *Lastly*, Though every mercy requires praise, and special mercy requires special praise, yet none can praise God truly, but a partaker of saving mercy: it is for saving mercy that the apostle's praise in the text is directed. Where is that praise performed which God will take? Only by believers. I know this is a theme that will hardly go down: other persons beside believers receive mercy, other persons beside believers owe praise, and other persons beside believers pay praise in their way; but there is no praise accepted by the Lord but that which is paid by believers. I would prove this in a few things, and then come, in the *last* place, to make some application. 1*st*, None but believers have their persons accepted; and no man's service is accepted but his whose person is first accepted. Unless a man stands safe, and in peace with God through Jesus Christ, there is nothing which he can do that will be accepted with the Lord. Abel was first accepted by the Lord, the Lord had first respect to him, and then to his offering; Cain's offering was rejected, because the Lord had no respect to his person: and this is the constant way of God; every one is accepted of the Lord in his performances, as he is in his person, and the acceptance of our performances, is only through Jesus Christ; and the acceptance of our performances is only because our persons are accepted in the Beloved. 2*dly*, None but believers know either God or themselves; and you may well conceive how unacceptable their praise must be, who neither know who the giver of mercy is, nor who the receiver is: and this belongs to the natural condemned state of all unbelievers—they neither know God nor themselves. 3*dly*, It is the believer only who is framed for praise; and can you think that any person can be fit for this work unless God makes them so? *These people*, saith the Lord, *have I formed for myself that they should shew forth my praise*, Isa. 43:21. See what a great preamble the apostle makes to this matter of praise; 1 Pet. 2:9, *Ye are a chosen generation, a royal priesthood, a holy nation, a peculiar people, that ye should shew forth the praises of him that hath called you into his marvellous light*. What! cannot they shew forth the Lord's praise till all this be upon them? No; all these privileges of your state are in order to the enabling you to the work of praise. *Lastly*, None but a believer can give praise unto the Lord, because none but such can make use of the Psalmist's argument; *O give thanks unto the Lord, for he is good, and his mercy endureth for ever*, Psa. 107:1. No unbeliever can say, 'I praise the Lord, for he is good, and his mercy endureth for ever;' he may say, 'I praise the Lord, for he hath done good to me;' but can you say, that he is good to you? The Lord doth good to a great many whom he is not good to; God indeed is always good in himself; but how can a man call God good to him, who does not know whether he be reconciled to him or not? Common mercies are from the goodness of God; aye, but that goodness of God which sends common mercies, hath many times a great deal of wrath in it, and vengeance at the bottom. Common mercies are always given in love to believers; but they are rained as snares upon the ungodly. That ease and prosperity, and plenty of all things in this world, which a believer partakes of, he gives God hearty thanks for, and he has good reason so to do; but if an unbeliever partakes of these, and remains still an unbeliever, they are but aggravations of his guilt, and heightened of wrath against him. Neither can the unbeliever use that other argument; *For his mercy endureth for ever*. All the mercy of God towards an unbeliever, is mercy that endureth but for a time. It is only the believer who can say, *I give thanks unto the Lord: for his mercy endureth for ever*; 'he is good already to me, and he will continue that goodness to eternity.' So that from all these things it is plain, that none but a believer can give hearty praise: no unbeliever can use the believer's arguments; and whosoever cannot use the arguments, will never be found exercised about the duty.

Application. I shall, in the *5th* and *last* place, make some application from what hath been said concerning this duty of blessing and praising God in general; and then I shall come to speak of it as it relates to the scope of the apostle in the text. And all the application that I shall make, shall be respecting two directions about this in the word, Psa. 34:1. *I will bless the Lord at all times*: and the other is that word of the apostle's, *Give thanks in every thing*, 1 Thess. 5:18. Some of these things I would name, and proceed.

1st, Praise and bless the Lord for all the mercies you have partaken of, busy yourselves about their number: give thanks for all the mercies that you partake of. Can I tell, can you tell the number of them? No; I know neither of us can. None can number their sins, and none can number God's mercies. Give praise to the Lord for all his kindness to you; for all his kindness to your bodies, for all his kindness to your souls; for all his kindness to your families; and for all his kindness to your friends. Oh! what great work is here! How many, or rather how few of your mercies have you made conscience to bless God for? Unholy and unthankful are joined together by the Spirit of God (2 Tim. 3:2), and they are commonly joined together in the spirits of men. *Unthankful and unholy!* Why do not people mind this duty of praising and thanksgiving more? Sometimes people will boast of their mercies, and raise their plumes upon the account of the favourable providences of God towards them, and grow proud of their outward mercies; this is a great abuse of them: but pray give thanks to the Lord for all his goodness to you. Whatsoever you have is mercy, and whatsoever mercy you have it is of his giving; and whatsoever he gives lays a debt upon you, and praising is your debt as far as you are able.

2dly, Praise the Lord in all your crosses. That is hard to do, you will say: but it is your duty, be it ever so hard. *I will bless the Lord at all times*, saith David, *his praise shall be continually in my mouth*, Psa. 34:1. Why, David, dost thou know what times may come upon thee? Thou mayest be driven from thy crown and kingdom, and be banished thy country, and forced to flee into the wilderness; 'But,' saith he, '*I will bless the Lord at all times, his praise shall be continually in my mouth.*' If Paul and Silas be driven from preaching Christ to suffering for him; if they be whipt and bound, and put in the stocks, yet they would sing praises unto God there;—bless the Lord for all your crosses. I never expect to see much good of that cross which the believer cannot make a song of praise for. You will never thrive in your souls, till you can take a cross in your arms, and bless the sender of it, and say 'This is less than I deserve; it was sent in love, and it will issue in my profit and advantage.' We should learn in every thing to give thanks. Sirs, this duty of praising and blessing God, is a great and a hard duty; a duty very easily forgot; a duty very hard to perform aright. He was a mighty man at this work, Job I mean, who had learned to bless God in every thing. You are never right at this work of praise, unless you can praise in every condition. This was Job's practice, Job 1:21, *The Lord hath given, and the Lord hath taken away, blessed be the name of the Lord.* He could bless his name in giving, and bless his name in taking away; he had the same thoughts of the name of God, whatsoever changes there were in his dispensations towards him. We understand a little how to bless the name of God, when he gives; this is the common carnal frame of a great many Christians; if God gives, they know how to give thanks, though but poorly, God knows; but if God takes away, they know not how to thank him for taking, for smiting, for correcting, for afflicting. Oh! how few are there, if I may so say, such skilful musicians, as to make a song of praise on a sharp rod? how few are there who can sing in the stocks? who can praise God in the furnace? and bless his name whatever condition they are in? It hath been well said, and it holds true in several things, That those who cannot be contented in every condition, will never be able to bless God, as they should do, in any. If God comes down to our humours, we can bless him; but if he takes his own wise way of dealing with us, how backward are we in this work of praise! This is the second thing,—Learn to bless God for crosses.

3*dly*, Praise the Lord, and give thanks unto him, for all his appearances in the world; for his public appearances: God sometimes comes forth to public view; to the observation and sense of men: I do not say every one sees God, but every one should see him when he makes these appearances of his. The Psalmist hath an exhortation, Psa. 46:10. *Be still, and know that I am God; I will be exalted among the heathen, I will be exalted in the earth.*

4*thly*, Give praise to the Lord for the gospel you enjoy; salvation is in it; Christ is in this gospel; Christ is offered to you in it; salvation is brought near to you in it: and so it will go with you all to eternity according as this mercy is valued. People may have different sentiments about a great many of the dispensations of God; but there is no allowing of a difficulty, or a contrary sentiment, about the dispensation of the gospel. There are several appearances of God in his providence, that people may be divided and mistaken about, and there is no great matter in the one opinion or in the other. Providence is so dark a book, that it is not every one who hath an eye clear enough always to read it right, and to make sense of it; but the blessing of the gospel is of that nature, that a man's eternal state depends upon his sense of it. Is the enjoying of the gospel a small thing in your eyes? a thing you have never given hearty thanks to the Lord for? I can assure you, in the Lord's name, you have not gotten any good by it, if you never gave hearty thanks to the

Lord for it: for all who get good by it, are certainly thankful for it. The greatest good is in it, and the greatest praise is due for it.

5thly, and *lastly*, All who are partakers of the blessings of the gospel should in an especial manner praise and bless the Lord for it; therefore, when the Psalmist had said, *O give thanks unto the Lord, for he is good, and his mercy endureth for ever*, Psa. 107:2; in the very next words he adds, *Let the redeemed of the Lord say so*. 'Let others say what they will, let the redeemed of the Lord say he is good, and his mercy endureth for ever.' 'But,' you will say, 'the blessing of the gospel is so great, and of that nature, that they who are partakers of it need no exhortation to praise for it.' But this duty of praise is so great, and the sin of believers so great in neglecting it, that it is very excusable in me to stir them up to it. This blessing of the gospel is manifold; if there be any turning of the heart towards the Lord, any faith in Jesus Christ, any experience of the goodness of God in the gospel, we should praise him for this. I will give you a motive or two to stir you up to this: *1st*, The blessing of the gospel is the most free of all mercies: all the goodness of God is undeserved; but there is something that is more especially free in the dispensation of his grace; his granting you help in difficulties is an undeserved mercy, his giving you your daily bread is an undeserved mercy; we no more deserve a bit of bread than we do eternal life; but though both be free, yet we may be allowed to say, there is more of the freedom of grace in the one than in the other: for the greater the blessing is, the more freedom there is in bestowing it. Saving grace is most freely bestowed, and therefore should be most heartily acknowledged; for our praise to God should arise according to the freeness there is in the dispensation of it. *2dly*, The blessing of the gospel in saving grace, is a blessing that flows from God's heart; a blessing that he gives in love. Common mercies, if I may so distinguish, they are only given from the hand of God; by his bountiful hand in a way of common providence; but the special mercy of God is always given in love. The Lord may make a poor man rich, and love him never a whit better than he did before; the Lord may raise a sick man to health, and the poor creature may lie under the anger of God in his health as well as in his sickness: but if the blessing of the gospel comes on you, God hath done it in love and great mercy. *3dly*, This should be praised for, because it is the most profitable to us: it hath the greatest blessing in it to us. Our praise should arise according to our profit; the greater good we get by the Lord's bounty, the greater praise do we owe to him that shewed it. Now, the success of the gospel upon us, is that which does us most good; for it mends our hearts, and secures our eternal state. *Lastly*, The blessing of the gospel should be praised for, because it ushers us into the channel of eternal mercy. Then shall we be able to praise him indeed; *for he is good, and his mercy endureth for ever*. By the blessing of the gospel we arrive where God's mercy flows for ever. The main thing that people should be concerned about, is to be once brought into that road, into that channel in which God's everlasting mercy everlastingly flows. The stream of God's common mercy flows but for a little while; in a little time it will be cut off and dry up, and the poor creature left like a fish upon the dry ground; but when a person once gets the blessing of the gospel, he is then brought into the channel of the everlasting mercy of God. Such an one can say, not only *his mercy endureth for ever*, but, his mercy *towards me* endureth for ever. There lies the accent of all: for what matter is it if the mercy of God doth flow for ever, if I be not in the road wherein it will flow upon me. The mercy of God will flow for ever, but they in hell shall not taste one drop of it; because they are out of the road of it. But this is the happiness of them who are partakers of the blessing of the gospel, that they are hereby brought into that road in which the mercy of God will endure for ever towards them.

I would add two or three words of advice about this duty of blessing and praising the Lord.

Direction *first*. Mind this work of praising the Lord, as a work by itself: take heed to this. Thanksgiving and praise is an ordinance of the Lord by itself; it is a duty by itself, and you should mind it by itself. Praising the Lord should indeed season all we do. When we pray, the apostle tells us, Phil. 4:6, we should *in every thing, by prayer and supplication, with thanksgivings, let our requests be made known unto God*. There are three words which the apostle useth for prayer; *prayer, supplication,* and *making our requests known unto God*: and in all these three, saith the apostle, mix thanksgiving. Remember now, praise is a distinct ordinance, as well as prayer; hearing, reading, praying, meditating, singing, receiving the Lord's supper, church-fellowship, all these are distinct ordinances, though many of them are still to be mixed together; but mind this work of praise as a thing by itself. Is it any great wonder that people are so unskilful in the work of praise? it is because they do not mind it by itself. There are many who know what it is to retire by themselves to pray; I hope so of you all, if not, I do not know what you do here: for I desire to speak to none but them who retire alone to pray. But pray now answer me, as in God's sight, Did you ever know what it was to retire to praise? For a poor creature to shut his chamber-door, and to retire alone, and say, 'God knows that all my business with him at this time is to praise his name; his mercy presses me, and I would fain praise him.' I deny not but we should mix praising with prayer, but I would have Christians try praising by itself; it is an ordinance of God, a distinct appointment, a duty by itself laid upon us; why therefore may we not try it by itself? And I do assure you, if ever you try it, you will find it hard work: it is like a poor creature setting his shoulder under the great and weighty burden of the loving-kindness of God. What is praise? true praise is nothing else (you may think it a strange description) true praise is nothing but the believer's cheerfully groaning under a weighty, oppressing load of mercy. You will never praise rightly till mercy oppresses you, and you become like people sinking under the weight, and groaning under the burden of it. See how David praises, 2 Sam. 7:20, *Who am I, O Lord? And what can David say more? for thou, Lord, knowest thy servant.*

Direction 2*d*. Let all your praise ascend unto God by Jesus Christ. Take heed to this; let all your praise be sent up by Jesus Christ: this is the apostle's direction, Heb. 13:15, *By him let us offer the sacrifice of praise to God continually, that is the fruit of our lips, giving thanks unto his name.* When we pray, we know that the blessings we ask are so great, that we can expect them no otherwise than as they are the purchase of Christ. We know our performances are so small, that we cannot dream of their acceptance with God, unless our great High-priest present them: but take good heed to yourselves, lest you grow proud in praising; and remember that you have as great need of Christ's intercession, to render your praising acceptable, as to render your prayers acceptable. We are to *offer up spiritual sacrifices, acceptable to God by Jesus Christ*, 1 Pet. 2:5. When the apostle was in that great frame for praising, Eph. 3:20, 21,

Unto him that is able to do exceeding abundantly above all that we can ask or think, according the power that worketh in us, unto him be glory in the church, by Christ Jesus, throughout all ages, world without end, Amen. It is as if he had said, 'I do not forget that our great High-priest must present our praises as well as our prayers.'

Direction 3*d*. *Lastly*, Concerning this work of praise, I would give you one advice more, and that is, Learn to be well acquainted with the book of Psalms, and the praising part of the word of God. The book of Psalms is a book of songs; and in the Old and New Testament too, there are a great many songs uttered by the holy men of God, and written by them, and ordered by the Holy Ghost to be in our Bibles, as God's mind and will to us; and if ever you would mind the work of praise well, you must be acquainted with the praising part of the word. The apostle Paul hath an exhortation, commonly known, but not well understood, Col. 3:16, 17, *Let the word of Christ dwell richly in you in all wisdom, teaching and admonishing one another in psalms, and hymns, and spiritual songs, singing with grace in your hearts unto the Lord; and whatsoever ye do in word or deed, do all in the name of the Lord Jesus, giving thanks to God and the Father by him.* Pray observe these two verses; the apostle names no more of the word, but the singing part of it. There is a great deal in the word of God beside psalms, and hymns, and spiritual songs; and there is another use to be made of the word than singing; it is also to be read: but the apostle confines his exhortation to the duty of praise, directs us in it, and proposes this as one great mean, *Let the word of Christ dwell richly in you*; and what part of the word of Christ is it that he means? The praising part of it; *admonishing one another*, saith he, *in psalms, and hymns, and spiritual songs*. Sirs, it is a great help to the duty of prayer, that we have so many of the prayers of the saints recorded in the word; though it is a rotten use that is made of the praying part of the word, when here a scrap, and there a scrap, is gathered together to a book of common prayer; an abomination that God will visit for, though man forget; which hath sent thousands of souls to hell in this nation, rocking them asleep in security. This is a great abuse of that part of the word. There are many poor believers that, in reading David's Psalms, have been made to say, 'Surely this man speaks as if he was in my soul's stead.' The same spirit was in believing David, as is in the poorest believer this day in London; no great wonder then that they fully perceive and understand the words of one another. Thus, as we find a great help in praying, from the praying part of the word; so we find a great deal of help for praising, by being well acquainted with the praising part of the word. I must say, and I believe very few are able to contradict me in this, that the greatest part of believers in all ages, of all the books in the Old Testament, have been most edified by the book of Psalms. I do not speak this with any kind of reflection on any other part of the sacred writ; the prophets are excellent; the prophet Isaiah is a most evangelical prophet; but for the spiritual pulse of a Christian, the book of Psalms is the greatest index thereof of any book in all the word of God. All the saints have felt it, and I dare say you have felt it, if ever you have been exercised unto godliness to any purpose.

Thus we have heard of this great duty of praising the Lord; the Lord help us to act it! to give unto the Lord the glory due unto his name! Oh what a mighty command is that! *Give unto the Lord the glory due unto his name*, Psa. 29:2 and 96:8. Who can tell what is the Lord's due? and who can give him what is his due? No creature can do it; for he is exalted above all blessing and praise: but we should bless him as we can, and hope that in his due time we shall bless him better than ever we can do whilst we are here. He hath blessed us with all spiritual blessings in heavenly places in Christ Jesus; we have not as yet received them all; but we wait for them all in the Lord's good time. We have a good many of them already; and we should praise and bless the Lord for what we have got; and we should praise him for what we hope for: and we should praise the Lord for what he hath offered to us, though we have not been so wise as to accept of the offer. But yet the Lord's grace in offering deserves our praise, even when we are ashamed of the bad entertainment we have given to the offer. How happy might we have been! how blessed a life might we have led, if we had given way to all that goodness and mercy which has been flowing in upon us! But many a striving hath there been between God and us; gracious on his, and wicked on our part.

SIX

SERMONS

ON

IMPORTANT SUBJECTS

FROM

GALATIANS 2:21

SERMON I.

GAL. 2:21.

I do not frustrate the grace of God: for if righteousness come by the law, then Christ is dead in vain.

THE scope of the apostle Paul in this epistle, is to reprove the church that he writes to, for a great and sudden apostacy from that faith of the gospel that they were planted in: the apostle Paul himself was one of the main planters amongst them; and quickly after his removal from them false brethren crept in amongst them, and perverted them from the simplicity that was in Christ: their great error lay here, in mixing the works of the law with the righteousness of Christ, in the grand point of the justification of a sinner before God. Throughout this epistle the apostle argues strongly against this error: they had not renounced the doctrine of Christ; they did not deny justification by faith in him; but they thought that the works of the law were to be added to their faith in Christ, in order to their justification.

I shall only take notice briefly of a few of his arguments against this error, as they lie in the context, to lead you to the words that I have read, and mean to speak to.

The former part of the chapter is historical, telling them what he had done, and what had befallen him some years ago; how he was entertained and received by the great servants of Christ at Jerusalem, Peter, James, and John, that seemed to be pillars, and were indeed so: see the first ten verses. The next thing that he breaks forth into, in point of arguing with them, is upon the account of Peter's dissimulation, and Paul's reproof of him: the point seemed to be very small; Peter had made use of his Christian liberty in free converse with the believing Gentiles; but when some of the brethren of the Jews came from Jerusalem, he withdrew himself, and separated from them, fearing them of the circumcision; 'fearing that they would take it ill:' a weak kind of fear it was, and upon this small thing the apostle set himself against him with great zeal. *I withstood him*, saith he, *to the face, because he was to be blamed*, ver. 11. By this withdrawing the use of his Christian liberty, he hardened the Jews, and he weakened the hands of the weaker Jewish converts, that thought the wall of partition between the Jews and Gentiles was not yet taken away.

1st, His first argument against mingling the works of the law with faith in justification, is taken from the practice of the believing Jews. What way did they take to be justified? *We who are Jews by nature, and not sinners of the Gentiles, knowing that a man is not justified by the works of the law, but by the faith of Jesus Christ; even we have believed in Jesus Christ, that we might be justified by the faith of Christ, and not by the works of the law; for by the works of the law shall no flesh be justified*, ver. 15, 16.

2dly, His next argument is taken from the bad effect and sad consequence of seeking righteousness by the law, ver. 17, which, because it is something dark, I would explain it a little in a few words: *But if, while we seek to be justified by Christ, we ourselves are also found sinners, is therefore Christ the minister of sin? God forbid.* 'If so be we that have sought righteousness in Jesus Christ, if we have yet any dealings with the law in point of righteousness, we are found sinners still; and if a justified man be found a sinner, why then Jesus Christ, instead of delivering us from the bondage of the law, is found a minister of sin.'

3dly, His third argument is yet strongest of all, and some way the darkest, ver. 20, *For I through the law am dead unto the law, that I might live unto God.* As if he should have said, 'For my part, all the use that I got of the law, the more I was acquainted with it, it slew me the more, and I died the more to it, that I might live to God; all that the law can do to me in point of justification, is only to condemn me, and it can do no more;' and whensoever the law enters into a man's conscience it always doth this; *When the commandment came, sin revived, and I died: the commandment slew me*, Rom. 7:9, 11.

4thly, His next argument is taken from the nature of the new life that he led, ver. 20, *I am crucified with Christ, nevertheless I live; yet not I, but Christ liveth in me: and the life which I now live in the flesh, I live by the faith of the Son of God, who loved me, and gave himself for me.*

Words of extraordinary form, but of more extraordinary matter: words that one would think seem to be some way cross to one another: but yet they set forth gloriously that gracious life that through Christ Jesus is imparted to justified believers. 'Christ died for me, and I am crucified with Christ; and yet I live, but it is Christ that lives in me, and Christ lives in me only by faith.'

My text contains two arguments more, drawn from a common natural head of arguing against error, by the absurdities that necessarily flow from it; and they are two the greatest that can be, 'Frustrating the grace of God,'—and 'making the death of Christ to be in vain.' And greater sins are not to be committed by men: the greatest sin, the unpardonable sin, is expressed in words very like to this, Heb. 10:29. *Of how much sorer punishment, suppose ye, shall he be thought worthy, who hath trodden under foot the Son of God, and hath counted the blood of the covenant, wherewith he was sanctified, an unholy thing, and hath done despite to the Spirit of grace?* And how near to one another are frustrating the grace of God, and doing despite to the Spirit of grace, and making Christ's death to be in vain, and counting the blood of the covenant an unholy thing!

There are two words to be explained before we go any further: *1st*, What is the grace of God? *2dly*, What is it to frustrate the grace of God?

First, What is the grace of God? The grace of God hath two common noted acceptations in the scripture.

1st, It is taken and used in the scripture for the doctrine of the grace of God, and so it is frequently used; the gospel itself is called the grace of God, Titus 2:12, *The grace of God, that bringeth salvation, hath appeared unto all men*: that is, the gospel; for it is the teaching grace of God that is there spoken of, called by the apostle, *the gospel of his grace*. And this grace of God may be received in vain. Many may have this grace of God and go to hell. Pray that you receive not the grace of God in vain.

2dly, By the grace of God in the word is understood the blessing itself; and this is never frustrated; that grace that called Paul, that grace that wrought mightily with him, that was not given him in vain: *the grace that was bestowed was not in vain, for I laboured more abundantly than they all; yet not I, but the grace of God that was with me*. The gospel of the grace of God is frequently frustrated, but the grace itself is never so.

Secondly, What is it to frustrate this grace of God? The word that I remember in the original is used, Mark 7:9, *Ye make void* (or reject), *the commandments of God*. It is the same word with that in my text: to frustrate the grace of God, is to defeat it of its end, to miss the end of it. Luke 7:30, it is said the Pharisees and lawyers frustrated the grace of God against themselves; or, as we read it there, *they rejected the counsel of God against themselves*. The true grace of God itself can never be frustrated, it always reaches its end, for it is almighty: but the doctrine of the grace of God is many times rejected; and the apostle here in the text speaks of it as a sin that they are guilty of that speak of righteousness by the works of the law. There is one thing that I would observe in general from the scope of the apostle, *viz.* that in the great matter of justification the apostle argues from his own experience: the true way to get sound light in the main point of the justification of a sinner before God, is to study it in thy own personal concern; if it be bandied about by men as a notion only, as a point of truth, discoursing wantonly about it, it is all one in God's sight whether men be sound or unsound about it; they are unsound in heart how sound soever they are in head about it. The great way to know the right mind of God about the justification of a poor sinner, is for all to try it with respect to themselves. Would the apostle say, 'I know how I am justified, and all the world shall never persuade me to join the righteousness of the law with the righteousness of Christ.'

There are four points of doctrine that I would raise, and observe from the first part of these words:

1*st*, That the grace of God shines gloriously in the justifying of a sinner through the righteousness of Christ.

2*dly*, It is a horrible sin to frustrate the grace of God.

3*dly*, All that seek righteousness by the law do frustrate the grace of God in the gospel.

4*thly*, That no sound believer can be guilty of this sin.

I would speak to the first of these at this time: 'That the grace of God shines gloriously in the justifying of a sinner by the righteousness of Christ alone.' When the apostle speaks of it, how frequently is this term *grace* added? *Being justified freely by his grace, through the redemption that is in Christ Jesus*, Rom. 3:24. *That being justified by his grace, we might be made heirs according to the hope of eternal life*.

There are four things to be explained here, that will make our way plain to the proof of this point. What is justification? Who is it that doth justify? Who are justified? And upon what account?

1*st*, What is justification? We read much of it in our Bible, and the doctrine of it is reckoned one of the fundamental points of the true Christian religion, and so indeed it is. This grand doctrine, the fountain of our peace, and comfort, and salvation, was wonderfully darkened in the Popish kingdom; and the first light of the reformation, that God was pleased to break up in our forefathers' days, was mainly about this great doctrine. Justification is not barely the pardon of sin; it is indeed always inseparable from it, the pardon of sin is a fruit of it, or a part of it. Justification is God's acquitting a man, and freeing him from all attainder; it is God's taking off the attainder that the broken law of God lays upon every sinner. *Who is he that shall condemn? It is God that justifies*, Rom. 8:35. Justification and condemnation are opposites; every one is under condemnation that is not justified; and every justified man is freed from condemnation. Justification is not sanctification; it is an old Popish error, sown in the heart of a great many Protestants, to think that justification and sanctification are the same: justification and sanctification are as far different as these two:—There is a man condemned for high treason against the king by the judge; and the same man is sick of a mortal disease, and if he dies not by the hands of the hangman today, he may die of his disease tomorrow: it is the work of the physician to cure the disease, but it is an act of mercy from the king that must save him from the attainder. Justification is the acquitting and repealing the law-sentence of condemnation; sanctification is the healing of the disease of sin, that will be our bane except Christ be our physician.

Justification and sanctification are always inseparable, but they are wonderfully distinct. Justification is an act of God's free grace; sanctification is a work of God's Spirit: sanctification is a work wrought within us, justification is something done about us, and therefore justification is every where spoken of in the word in the terms of a court act.

2*dly*, Who is he that justifies? I answer God only: *Who shall lay any thing to the charge of God's elect? It is God that justifies, who shall condemn?* Rom. 8:33. He only can justify that gives the law: he only can justify that condemns for sin: he only can justify that is wronged by sin, Mark 2:7. The Pharisees blasphemed, it was in their darkness; but yet the truth that they spake was good, though the application of it was quite naught: *Why doth this man speak blasphemies? who can forgive sin, but God only?* In the case of the man sick of the palsy, whose sins Christ first forgave before he healed him of the palsy—so that the forgiveness of his sins was his justification, and the healing of his disease was as if it were the type of his sanctification—their application was wrong, in that they did not know that Christ was God, and that he had power on earth to forgive sins: but the truth itself was sound—'none can forgive sins but God only.'

Justification is an act of the judge; it is only the judge and law-giver that can pronounce it: and *there is but one lawgiver*, saith James, *that can both save and destroy*, James 4:12. 'None properly offended by sin but God, and nothing violated by sin so immediately as the law of God.'

3*dly*, Who is justified? Every one is not justified. What sort of a man is he that is justified? Justification is the acquitting of a man from all attainder, and it is God's doing alone; but what sort of a man is it that is justified? Is it a holy man? a man newly come from heaven? Is it a new sort of a creature, rarely made and framed? No: it is a sinner: it is an ungodly man: 'God justifies the ungodly.'

The man is not made godly before he is justified, nor is he left ungodly after he is justified; he is not made godly a moment before he is justified, but he is justified from his ungodliness by the sentence of justification: when he is dead in sins and trespasses, quickening comes, and life comes, Eph. 2:1.

4*thly*, Upon what account is all this done? And this is the hardest of all. You have heard that justification is the freeing of a man from all charge, and that it is done by God alone, and given to a man before he can do any thing of good—for no man can do anything that is good till he be sanctified, and no man is sanctified till he is justified—but the grand question is, *How can God justly do this?* saith the apostle, Rom. 3:26, *That he might be just, and the justifier of him that believeth in Jesus.* How can God be just, and yet justify an ungodly man? 'To justify the wicked, and to condemn the righteous, are both an abomination in the sight of God,' when practised by man, Prov. 17:15. How then can God justify the ungodly? The grand account of this is, God justifies the ungodly for the sake of nothing in himself, but solely upon the account of this righteousness of Christ, that the apostle is here arguing upon: *Being justified freely by his grace through the redemption that is in Jesus Christ, whom God hath set forth to be a propitiation through faith in his blood*, Rom. 3:24, 25. When God justifies a man, the righteousness of Christ is reckoned to him, and God deals with him as a man in Christ; and therefore his transgressions are covered, and the man is made the righteousness of God in Christ, because Christ is made of God unto him righteousness, *Of him are ye in Christ Jesus, who of God is made unto us righteousness*, 1 Cor. 1:30. Where is the poor man's righteousness that is justified? It is in Christ Jesus. For, *He hath made him to be sin for us who knew no sin, that we might be made the righteousness of God in him*, 2 Cor. 5:21. And to be made the righteousness of God, is nothing else but to be made righteous before God in and through Jesus Christ.

These things considered, the proof of this point is very easy—That the grace of God shines gloriously in the way of justifying a sinner by the righteousness of Jesus Christ: I shall therefore add but a few things more in the proof of it.

First, In this way all is of God, and nothing of the creature's procuring, and therefore it is of grace. Grace always shines most brightly where man appears least; every thing that tends to advance the power and efficacy of man's working, always hinders the shining forth of the glory of the grace of God; but in this way of justifying us through the righteousness of Christ, grace shines forth most gloriously, because it is all of God: we do nothing in it. To instance in a few things here,

1*st*, The finding out of this righteousness by which we are justified is of God alone. If the question had been put to all the angels in heaven, and to many worlds of men, if this one question had been put, How can a just and holy God justify a sinner? no created understanding could ever have been able to find out how it could be done; it was the infinite wisdom of God alone that found out this way. He will send his own Son to be a sinless man, that shall sustain the persons, and bear the sins, and take away the sins of all that shall be justified. The native sense of all mankind is this: when we know any thing of God, we know that it stands with his nature to condemn sin, and hate the sinner; but how it can stand with his justice to acquit a sinner; it is God only that could find out that.

2dly, As the finding out of the way of our justification is of God alone, so the working out of it is Christ's alone. There was no creature of God's counsel in finding out the way, so there was no creature Christ's helper in making the way. All the great work of fulfilling the righteousness of the law was done by Christ alone; none could offer to help in the great work of bearing the weight of his Father's wrath, and bearing the burden of the justice of God, for the sins of his church. Our Lord was the alone bearer of this, he alone brought in everlasting righteousness, and *put away sin by the sacrifice of himself*, Heb. 9:26.

3dly, The applying of this righteousness is only of God also. It is the work of the Holy Spirit to bring it close unto the sinner by faith: and here we have as little to do as in the former. There was none of God's everlasting council in the finding out this way, nor had Christ any helper in the work of redemption; and we help the Spirit of God as little in his work of applying this: for till the grace of God prevails upon the heart, there is a constant struggling against it. There are many poor sinners that have struggled with the Spirit of God, seeking to save them, more than many believers have ever strove with Satan, seeking to destroy them. All unbelievers are led more tamely to hell by the devil, than believers are led quietly to heaven by the Spirit of God.

4thly, The securing all this by the everlasting covenant is of God only. We seal God's covenant by our faith for the benefit of it; but it is Christ's great seal that is its security, even the seal of his own blood. *This is my blood of the New Testament, which is shed for many, for the remission of sins*, Matt. 26:28. And so much for this first thing: The grace of God shines gloriously in the way of justifying a sinner by the righteousness of Christ; because it is altogether of God, the sinner hath no hand in it.

Secondly, This will further appear, if we consider what vile creatures the receivers of it are; they have nothing to procure it, nothing to deserve it, but a great deal to deserve the contrary. In Romans 5 they have three names; ver. 6, we are called *ungodly; In due time Christ died for the ungodly*. Ver. 8, we are called *sinners; Whilst we were yet sinners, Christ died for us*. Ver. 10, we are called *enemies*; *When we were enemies, were reconciled to God by the death of his Son*. Here are three names:

Ungodly! Sinners! Enemies! the highest words whereby ill-deserving can be well expressed; and it is the usual way of the Spirit of God, to lay open the worst in a poor sinner, when God is about to give the best; and all they that receive it, receive this grace under these names. *God be merciful to me a sinner*, saith the poor publican; and *this man*, saith our Lord, *went down to his house justified*, Luke 18:13, 14. *Jesus Christ came into the world to save sinners, of whom I am chief*, saith Paul, 1 Tim. 1:15.

And not only is it so that they are undeserving and unworthy, but they are also very proud and vain, and have a great opinion of themselves; and must it not be great grace then to justify such men? *Thou sayest I am rich, and increased with goods, and have need of nothing*, saith our Lord to the church of Laodicea, *and knowest not that thou art wretched, and miserable, and poor, and blind, and naked*; even when Christ is courting them to buy of him his gold and white raiment, Rev. 3:17, 18.

Thirdly, The grace of God in justifying a sinner through the righteousness of Christ appears to be very glorious, even in the very naming of it: it is the grace of God: it must be great grace, for it is the grace of God: it is the grace of a holy God: it is the grace of a just God: it is the grace of a powerful God: it is the grace of that God that can do every thing; every name that exalts the glory of God, doth also raise the value of this grace: it is the grace of God towards vile sinners, and that makes it great indeed. Let us consider this grace of God a little.

This grace of God is dear to God; and therefore it is the more grace. The grace of God in justifying us is dear to God; it cost the Father dear to part with his own Son; it cost the Son dear to part with his own life to bring in this righteousness; and, if I may so say, it cost the Holy Ghost dear to work the faith of this righteousness in the heart of a poor sinner. When we consider how all things else that God did were easily done but this: when the world was to be made no more is to be done, but 'Let it be;' but when the world was to be redeemed, 'Let it be' will not do; a body must be prepared for the Son, and that body must be sacrificed for sin, and be slain, and sustain the wrath of God, and the curse of the law; and all this to bring in an everlasting righteousness.

Again: This grace that was so dear to God comes to us good cheap, we give nothing for it: the Lord will take nothing for it, we have nothing to give: the apostle doth not think it enough to say *being justified by his grace*; but he adds, *being justified* FREELY *by his grace*, Rom. 3:24. *Whosoever will, let him take of the water of life freely*, Rev. 22:17. Taking implies some freedom in it, but taking freely is a redoubling of the expression. This grace of God, that is so dear to God, comes good cheap to us, it cost us nothing.

Again, This grace of God is everlasting; it is the eternal raiment of all believers, even of them that are in heaven. Saith the apostle, Rom. 5:21, *Grace reigns through righteousness unto eternal life, through Jesus Christ our Lord.* Observe, neither grace, nor righteousness, nor eternal life, nor Jesus our Lord, cease in heaven; they are all there together; Christ as the author of eternal life, and worker of righteousness; and the believer as the possessor of eternal life, and the enjoyer of this life; and grace as the high spring of all; grace is in heaven; the reign of grace is only in heaven. That of Rev. 19:8 is by most understood to relate to the other world; and it is said there, that 'unto the Lamb's wife it was granted to be arrayed in fine linen, clean and white;' and that fine linen is the righteousness of Christ, in which the saints stand everlastingly accepted before God. *Behold I and the children that thou hast given me!* saith our Lord, Heb. 2:13, and their glory in heaven is to behold the glory that he had with the Father, as their head, before the world began, John 17:24.

Again, It is grace, because it is very abundant: it is an usual thing in the Old Testament to call great things by the name of God, as the trees of God, the city of God, the river of God; now this grace of God is so called because it is great, exceedingly abundant: saith the apostle Paul concerning it, *The grace of our Lord Jesus was exceeding abundant towards me*, 1 Tim. 1:14. Did ever any of you know how many sins you had? Yet you must have a great deal more grace, or you can never be saved; there must be more grace than sin, or you cannot be saved, Rom. 5:20, *The law entered that sin might abound: but where sin abounded grace did much more abound.* I do not say, no man can be saved unless he hath more inherent grace than he hath inherent corruption in him; but, unless there be a greater abundance of the grace of God for covering of sin, than there is of sin to be covered, no man can be saved: the apostle adds a much more abundance to it. One would think there was enough of sin and guilt in the disobedience of the first Adam; and so there was:

but, saith the apostle, the matter is far greater here: *And not as it was by one that sinned, so is the gift; for the judgment was by one to condemnation; but the free gift is of many offences unto justification: for if by one man's offence death reigned by one, much more they that receive abundance of grace, and of the gift of righteousness, shall reign in life, by one, Christ Jesus*, ver. 16, 17 of that 5th chapter of Romans. There is abundance of grace, and of the gift of righteousness through Jesus Christ, needful to save any sinner. When the Lord makes this matter to balance in the eyes of his people, and there are great discoveries made to them of the aggravations and of the multitude of their sins; this is a common wicked thought arising in their awakened consciences: Can God forgive? Can God pass by so many and so great transgressions? It is a sinful thought, the plain meaning of it is, 'Is there more grace in God than there is sin and guilt with me?' We were all undone if it was not so; if Christ's righteousness was not more able to justify than the first Adam's sin was to condemn, no man could be saved.—The grace of God shines in this way of the justification of a sinner by the righteousness of Christ, in that there is an abundance of it imparted to all them that partake of it.

Application. You have heard that the grace of God shines gloriously in the justification of a sinner by the righteousness of Christ: in all your dealings, then, with God, mind grace mainly: they that never had an errand to God for the blessing of justification, they may possibly be saved; but they are not yet in the way to salvation that were never yet concerned about this question, How shall a man be acquitted before God? or that never treated with God about justification? In all your dealings with God still remember grace: when you come for justification, plead for it as grace: when you receive it, receive it as grace: and when you praise for it, praise for it as grace; and thus will you behave as the people of God have done. When you plead for it, plead for it as grace; bring nothing with you in your hand, offer nothing to God for your justification; it is a free gift: if God be pleased to give it, in his great bounty, you shall be saved. You have no reason to quarrel if God doth not give it: you have no reason to fear but God will give it. Though you do not deserve it, yet he hath promised it. As there is a fulness of righteousness in Christ to procure grace, so there is a fulness of grace in the tender of the gospel; and you are to believe that Christ is willing to make all this over to sinners.

When you receive justification, receive it as grace; sometimes we beg it as an alms, and sometimes in the gospel the Lord offers it as a gift, and we are to receive it as such. If the Lord tenders you the gift of righteousness through Jesus Christ, do not say you cannot receive it; do not say you are not meet for it; the question is, Are you in need of it? Are you not guilty? and is not a pardon suitable for the guilty? Receive it as a grace. The true reason why so many neglect right dealing with God for justification, and slight God's dealing with them about receiving it, is because their hearts stand at a distance from, and they have a sort of a quarrel with mere grace. As it is certain that nothing but grace can save the sinner, so it is as certain there is nothing more unpleasing to the sinner than grace; than that good, which when received he must always own the bounty of the giver, and never to eternity be able to say, 'My own hand hath made me rich:' Christ will bring none to heaven that are in that mind. He that will not be rich in Christ, must be poor and condemned still in the first Adam. *Know ye not*, saith the apostle, *the grace of our Lord Jesus Christ, who though he was rich, yet he became poor, that we through his poverty might be made rich*, 2 Cor. 8:9. The riches of a believer stands in the poverty of Christ; and every true believer counts Christ's poverty his riches.

SERMON II.

GAL. 2:21.

I do not frustrate the grace of God: for if righteousness come by the law, then is Christ dead in vain.

I TOLD you the last day (what you may learn by your own reading), that the scope of the apostle in this epistle is, to teach and defend the doctrine of the justification of a sinner by the righteousness of Christ, apprehended by faith alone. In the text the apostle hath two arguments for this truth, against the contrary error, with which the Galatians were plagued; and both arguments are taken from the absurdities that follow upon the contrary doctrine.

1st, That seeking righteousness by the works of the law, doth frustrate, and make void the grace of God.

2dly, That it makes Christ's death to be in vain: and there is nothing revealed by the Lord, in his word, more sacred, and more awful than these two—the grace of God, and the death of Christ; and therefore it must needs be a great wickedness to enervate, and overthrow both these. From the first part of these words I observed four things, and have already spoken to the first of them, and would speak to the next at this time.

1st, The grace of God shines gloriously in the justifying of a sinner through Christ's righteousness alone. All the revelations that are made of this great way of God's justifying a sinner, are all made with a high deference to the grace of God, as the original thereof.

2dly, I am now to speak to this point—That frustrating the grace of God is a great and horrible sin: the apostle here brings it in as such, and denies his concern in it; *I do not frustrate the grace of God.* The scope of his discourse leads me to this head: 'If I seek righteousness by the works of the law, I should frustrate the grace of God; but I do not seek righteousness that way, therefore I do not frustrate the grace of God.' Frustrating the grace of God is a great and horrible sin: there are two things I would speak to upon this head—To shew you how this sin is committed—and then, wherein its greatness doth appear; for there are many that commit this sin, and when they have done, think nothing of it.

1st, How is this sin committed that the apostle here vindicates himself from? *I do not frustrate the grace of God.* This sin is committed two ways: *1st*, By not receiving the grace of God when it is tendered. *2dly*, By seeking other ways and shifts for righteousness than the grace of God.

First, Frustrating the grace of God is, not receiving it; the grace of God is frustrated when it is not received: the right entertaining of it is by receiving it. The apostle exhorts the Corinthians, *We then, as workers together with him, beseech you also, that you receive not the grace of God in vain*, 2 Cor. 6:1. I have told you in what sense the grace of God might be received in vain, and in what sense it could not. The doctrine of the grace of God, the offer of the grace of God, may be received in vain, and rejected, as many times it is; but the grace of God itself cannot be received in vain, for it always worketh its effect wheresoever it lights. The grace of God is an irresistible principle of salvation: never man had one mite of the grace of God, but he was saved by it: Christ Jesus hath two quivers, if I may so say; there is a common quiver, out of which he draws some arrows, and shoots them at sinners, and they can fence against these well enough, and, never be hurt by them; but then he hath other arrows, that are marked with his love, and sent by his power, and there is no guarding against them. As there are arrows of destruction, so there are arrows of salvation, *Let thine arrows be sharp in the heart of the king's enemies*, is the prayer, Psa. 45. My work then is to shew how it is that the grace of God is not received.

1*st*, The grace of God tendered in the gospel, and the way of salvation by Jesus Christ, is not received when it is not minded. There is little hopes of that man's salvation that doth not think of salvation, or when the matter is neglected. *How shall we escape*, saith the apostle, *if we neglect so great salvation*, Heb. 2:3. The true sense of the original word lies mainly in this, not so much in a stated formal enmity to it, but only in a careless indifferency about it: the grace of God is not received when it is not minded. Therefore, would you know when you profit by the gospel, know it this way: if what you hear from the word doth not occasion many thoughts in your hearts, you get no good at all. If the matter of salvation do not become the matter of your serious meditation, you receive the grace of God in vain. God may say concerning such men, 'They will not so much as think of my proposals to them.'

2*dly*, People do not receive the grace of God when they do not see their need of it, when they do not see their absolute need of it. As long as a man hath this dream—and every natural man falls into such a dream—as long as a man thinks in his vain mind, that any thing else but the sovereign grace of God can save him; this man will never receive the grace of God. It is impossible that a man can receive it, till he see that nothing else will do his business.—Wo be to them that think any thing but grace can save them: they are in a forlorn state indeed!

3*dly*, They that do not believe that the grace of God alone can save them, they do not receive it neither; for as the grace of God is sent to men as that which they do simply stand in need of, and as that which nothing can supply the want of; so it is sent as a sovereign remedy, that whatsoever ails the poor creature it will do it for them.—So much for this first thing: They that do not receive the grace of God, are guilty of this great sin of frustrating the grace of God.

Secondly, This sin is also committed by men's taking other methods and shifts to obtain the favour of God than this grace alone; they frustrate the grace of God. I would speak a little to this under two heads: *1st*, I would shew you the cause of it. *2dly*, I would shew the effects that proceed from those causes.

(1.) Of the cause of it. The world is full of it; this heresy, if I may so say, runs through the whole earth; no man is quite free from it but only the sound believer; a man may be orthodox in his judgment, and subscribe to the orthodox doctrine, and Protestant truth; but every natural man is a heretic in this matter; he hath secretly something else in his eye to recommend him to God, and to make his state safe before God, besides the righteousness of Christ. Now the cause of this universal hankering after ways of people's own devising to do their business with God, without this grace of God through Christ, is what I would speak a little to.

It flows from nature: now nature is so strong a spring, that nothing but the mighty grace of God can turn it; it is so strong a principle. I would shew this in a little.

1st, The grace of God in saving sinners by Christ Jesus is above nature in its best state; it is above sinless nature. If you could suppose such a thing as this, that there was a man as holy as the first Adam was; if God should create another man as holy as the first Adam was, and bring to this man the doctrine of the righteousness of Christ, and of the grace of God in him, it would be above his nature. It is above sinless nature; it is that which Adam did not know, neither was he bound to know it, for it was not revealed to him; nor did he need to know it, for there was another way provided for his standing, that he might have kept.

2dly, This way is not only above sinless nature, but it is quite contrary to corrupt nature. If it be above sinless nature, it must needs be far above corrupt nature; but not only is it so, but it is also cross and contrary to it. There is in this corrupt nature four things that are its strength, and from that strength comes this enmity to this way of salvation.

[1.] There is in this corrupt nature dismal darkness and ignorance, expressed by the apostle in the abstract, Eph. 5:8, *For ye were sometimes darkness, but now are ye light in the Lord.* Not only are they dark and blind, but they are darkness and blindness. Now in this darkness, as to this matter, I will name two or three things: 1*st*, There is ignorance of the righteousness and holiness of God, Rom. 10:3. 2*dly*, There is ignorance of the holy law of God, Rom. 7:10. 3*dly*, There is utter ignorance of God's righteousness in Christ Jesus. A little to each of these:

1*st*, In every natural man there is an ignorance of the righteousness and holiness of God. I know that in man's nature there is a knowledge that there is a God, and that this God is a righteous, and a just God: the greatest heathens, by the mere light of nature, have arrived at some competent knowledge of this; but the exactness of this righteousness of God never did any natural men know; they do not know the unspottedness of his righteousness, nor how unsufferable to him the least impurity is. Would any bold sinners venture to present to God their rottenness and vileness, if they knew God's righteousness? The righteousness of God is such an awful thing, that no natural man can understand it, but he must be presently confounded!

2*dly*, Every natural man is ignorant of the strictness of the law of God: the severity of God's law in forbidding every sin, and in condemning every sinner, without any respect to any sin, or to any man that commits it. The law of God is an impartial rule of righteousness, that condemns every transgression; and it cannot do otherwise: it is the glory of the law so to do; its strictness makes it judge all sin; and its righteousness makes it condemn all sinners; and therefore, when this righteousness of God's law is once discovered, it presently breaks all the confidence of a natural man: *I was alive without the law once*, saith the apostle Paul, Rom. 7:9, *but when the commandment came, sin revived, and I died.* How could the apostle Paul be said to be without the law? I believe, that the apostle Paul, even in his natural state, was better acquainted with the law, and the Old Testament, than any man in London now is; for the Jews, even to this day, teach their children with great carefulness: now the apostle Paul was one of the best Jews in all that country. How then could this man be said to be without the law? He had the law in his mind, and in his memory, and in his hands, and was exceeding zealous for it—*I was*, saith he, *touching the righteousness which is in the law, blameless*, Phil. 3:6.—Aye, but the man only thought so, when he did not know the law of God; but when the commandment came, it made another manner of discovery. It condemned those things in him that he never thought to be sin before, and it made other things in him to be exceeding sinful. All natural men are under utter darkness about this; and therefore it is no wonder that they betake themselves to other ways than the grace of God in Christ.

3dly, All natural men are ignorant of the righteousness of God in Christ.

[2.] In every natural man there is pride. Every natural man is a proud man: proud towards God. That which goes under the name of pride amongst men is greatly mistaken. Pride towards man is a base thing; but it is pride towards God that I am speaking of. The poor sinner thinks that he is not quite so bare and empty, but that he hath something of his own wherein he may stand accepted before God—every natural man doth think so—it fares with a natural man as it doth with some poor men that are born of great families, whose fathers left them, as we use to say, a high birth, but a poor purse. Now this proud gentleman chooses a great deal rather to wear his own thread-bare coat, than another man's livery. Just so it is with sinners; their father Adam was a great lord: lord of this world, heir of righteousness, rich in stock—enough to have made all his posterity rich before God: but he broke and failed, and turned us all beggars into the world. But there comes another person, God's own Son, and he offers to clothe the poor beggar; but the poor proud man had rather go to hell in the rags that his father Adam left him, than go to heaven in the robe that Christ offers him, dyed in his own blood.

[3.] In every natural man there is awful trifling about the great concerns of salvation. The truth is, people are not thoroughly awakened, nor in good earnest about the matters of salvation. It lies not near their heart as a weighty question, *What shall I do to be saved?* These thoughts do not press them, 'I am a poor man that must shortly die, and this crazy carcase of mine will shortly moulder into the dust of the grave; but my soul must live for ever in, and enter upon an eternal state, as soon as the last breath of my body expires, and what shall become of me then?' The greatest part of the world trifle about this great question, 'What shall I do to be saved, to be secure to eternity?' What a shameful thing is it to think of this! I have often told them, that I have spoken to, and it is to be told, till it be mended, that it were a happy thing if people would but spend half that time, nay a quarter of that time, in secret thoughts about salvation, that they spend in hearing the word of salvation; and it is a hard matter if people cannot be prevailed with about this.—I can well assure you, that all the solid soul-thriving of the hearers of the gospel, is not so much in what they hear, in the preaching of the word, as in what they digest in their secret thoughts and meditations about it. Now is it any wonder that people take to any courses about their salvation, when they thus trifle about it? For if the end be not precious in a man's eyes, you can never expect to have him thoughtful about the means.

[4.] In all natural men there is unbelief of God's word. It is a hard question to resolve, What was the first sin? Any child can tell you, that the first sin of mankind was eating the forbidden fruit: it is true, the first sin was ripe in that action: but what was the first wandering thought from God? Whether it was the man's discontent with the state that he was made in; or aspiring after a higher state than that in which he was made; or a jealousy of God; or unbelief of the word of God; that unbelief was in it is most certain. The serpent began his temptation this way, *Yea, hath God said ye shall not eat of every tree in the garden? Hath God said you shall surely die? Ye shall not surely die*, Gen. 3:1, 4. The scope of his temptation was this, to bring in sin and ruin upon the world, by making sinless Adam to doubt of the truth of God's threatening; and he well knew that if once the awful faith of the truth of God's threatening was weakened in their minds, that they would soon make bold on the sin. God's threatening was as a kind of fence against the sin: *In the day that thou eatest, thou shalt surely die*. 'Assure thyself of death if ever you meddle with the forbidden fruit.' Satan knew that death was terrible to man, and that he would not easily rush upon it; aye, but, saith he, *God hath not said ye shall surely die, but you shall live, and be as gods*, if you transgress. Sirs, the Devil brought in the first sin and ruin upon mankind, by the unbelief of God's word of threatening. And he brings in the eternal ruin of men under the gospel by unbelief of God's word of promise: every natural man hath an evil heart of unbelief in him, as the apostle warns all to take heed of: Heb. 3:12, *Take heed, brethren, lest there be in any of you an evil heart of unbelief, in departing from the living God.* This matter of unbelief is many ways spoken of in the word: the way of salvation by Jesus Christ, and his righteousness, stands all in the word of God. If you ask the last question concerning a man's faith, you must resolve it into the word of God: there are, indeed, many questions that go before it, but this must be the last. If you ask, How may a sinner be saved? The answer is, By the righteousness of Christ. If you ask again, Who is this Jesus Christ, whose righteousness will be the salvation of all them that have it? He is the great Son of God, that took our sins on him. Well, but how shall this righteousness be mine? By faith alone: if I lay hold of it, and venture my soul on it, it is mine? Aye, but the last question is, How do you know that it shall be so? God hath said it in his word, *To him give all the prophets witness, that through his name whosoever believeth on him shall receive remission of sins*, Acts 10:43. Now every natural man having unbelief in him, God's word hath no weight on him. We find they proclaim their unbelief in every thing. When God commands, they proclaim their unbelief in disobeying; when God corrects them, they proclaim their unbelief in rushing again upon the same courses that God punishes them for; when God threatens and warns the sinner of his danger in such a sin, the man proclaims his unbelief by staying still in it: and what are all these but acts of gross unbelief? When God commands, the man thinks, that God means not as he speaks; when God threatens, the unbeliever thinks God will not do as he threatens—When God promises, saith the same unbelief, 'Though God speaks fair, he will not be as good as his word.'

Now, is it any wonder that every natural man takes another way of salvation besides the righteousness of Christ, when every natural man hath these four woful things in him? And, indeed, none can do otherwise till these four things are overthrown in him—till the darkness is removed by the illumination of the Spirit of God—and the pride be brought down by humbling grace—and the security of the conscience be brought down by awakening grace—and till the power of unbelief be broke by the Spirit's working faith. So much for the causes of this.

(2.) I am now to shew what the effects are that flow from these causes; or, what flows from this woful natural aversion in all men from the grace of God, and from their inclinations to frustrate it.

1st, Hence it comes to pass that the world is filled with fancies, and devices of men to please God.

This runs through the whole earth: the religion (if I may call it by that name) of the Pagans; the religion of the Turks, and the Mahometans, and of the Papists, however they may differ in a great many points of doctrine, and particular circumstances of worship, yet they all agree in this; all these religions, and all religions in the world, except the true, are filled with many devices of men to render themselves acceptable to God. The Lord brings them in, Micah 6:6, making this enquiry, *Wherewith shall I come before the Lord, and bow myself before the high God? Shall I come before him with burnt-offerings, with calves of a year old? Will the Lord be pleased with thousands of rams, or with ten thousand rivers of oil? Shall I give my first-born for my transgression, the fruit of my body for the sin of my soul?* Pray take notice here; one of the grossest idolatries that ever was in the world, and the most abominable act of it, is this, when parents, to pacify God for their sins, have offered their children in sacrifice to their idols; this hath been frequently practised in the world, and, it may be, is at this day in some parts of the world. Whence can this be! that there should be so strange a violation of one of the strongest bonds of nature? It is not to be supposed that these people did so because they did not love their children; no doubt but they loved them as well as you do yours: but only here lay the matter; they were under a strong conviction of sin, and under strong desires to please God: and they were ignorant of the true sacrifice, and, therefore, they offer to God what they think best, and what they love best; and that they hope God will accept most kindly from them. Sirs, you think there are many fopperies in Popery, fit only to be laughed at; and so indeed there are: their whipping themselves about that time of the year they call Lent: and great persons do this, kings, and queens, and lords, and great men; one would think it strange that so many great people should play the fool so; the true reason of it lies here, they have a conscience of sin, and they know they are sinners, and they do not know the true way of peace with God through the righteousness of Christ, and they are taught these foolish ways, and, therefore, they pursue them. And truly, if the light of the gospel should be darkened yet much more in England, I cannot tell how many silly professors amongst us might be drawn, even into this foppery. It is natural for all men, ignorant of the righteousness of God in Christ, to devise ways of their own to render themselves acceptable in the sight of God.

2dly, The next effect of this woful aversion from the grace of God, in justifying us by the righteousness of Christ, is in men's going to the law and the works of it. I do but name this, because I shall speak more largely to it by itself, under the third and next doctrine.

3dly, I would speak something to the sad effects of this, that are found even in them whom God saves. This aversion from the grace of God is so natural, that it puts forth itself strongly in them that the Lord is at work savingly upon; and I will name a few things about this, that some here can witness to; and I am sure that many more can witness to them than are here.

(1.) Hence it comes to pass that, in many who are saved in the issue, there is a long sorrowful trouble of mind that they live under; and all the world shall not persuade them what the true cause of it is. They are full of sorrow and complainings; no other language to be heard to God or man, but many sorrowful complaints; their corruptions are strong, their souls dead and dark, their consciences disquieted. And what is the true reason of all this? They are yet averse from giving glory to the sovereign grace of God in saving them by Christ. Many sorrowful hours, many of the elect of God have gone through in the strength of this corruption; and they have never seen it till a long while after. It is a shame and reproach to professors, and a dishonour to our Lord Jesus Christ, that so many, in whom the root of the matter is, have their hearts sinking within them when relief is so plainly provided for them. The true reason is, because they are averse, and not willing, nor inclined to be indebted solely to grace, and to have all their supplies singly from it.

(2.) From hence it also comes to pass, that there are so many out-breakings of sin, or at least the working of it in the hearts of many that the Lord hath a mind to save; and doth work savingly upon. How many poor creatures are there that know this? That from the time that the Lord first began to deal with them, and made them serious about salvation, their corruptions have grown more strong, and Satan more formidable and vexing; and, it may be, they are left of God to commit some gross sin, that they were never guilty of before. Whence comes this?

It is not only from the strength of temptation, nor is corruption grown stronger; but here lies the reason: Now God hath begun to awaken them, and they are not yet disposed kindly to yield themselves up unto the entire conduct of grace; not willing to give the grace of God its proper employment: but this is the way people generally take whensoever they are awakened, and made serious about salvation; then they fall to work, and set about duty—they pray, and bear, and read, and repent, and labour to reform their conversation, and in the mean time they are utterly unacquainted with employing Christ; and, therefore, the Lord in his righteous judgment leaves them to themselves, and lets them see that they must stand upon another bottom, or they will surely totter and fall; that they must be quite weaned from themselves, and all things made new in Christ, or nothing will be done rightly.

(3.) And thus some, as they live sorrowfully all their days, so they also die sadly; they have been leaning on their own righteousness as far as they could all their life long; sometimes hanging upon one twig, and sometimes upon another; and one breaks, and the other breaks, and here they get a fall, and there they get a fall; but at last, if the Lord hath mercy upon them, they are made to see the vanity of all these shifts; and then they betake themselves in earnest to that which is without them, to a righteousness that they have no hand in, that is wrought out by Christ alone, and given by pure grace.—So much for this first head, How this sin of frustrating the grace of God is committed.

2*dly*, I am now to shew the sinfulness, and the greatness, of this sin of frustrating the grace of God. The apostle is here vindicating himself from it: *I do not*, saith he, *frustrate the grace of God*. Now there are two things especially that aggravate all sins, and the more of them there be in any sin, the more sinfulness is there in that sin. 1*st*, The direct tendency of any sin to damnation. 2*dly*, The direct enmity that there is in any sin to the grace of God; and wheresoever there is a sin that is especially framed both these ways, that sin must needs be a great one.

(1.) This sin of frustrating the grace of God is directly against man's salvation, and tends directly to damnation. All sin against the law tends to damnation by its desert; every sin deserves hell. Every sin against the law of God works out wrath by deserving; but sin against the gospel works out wrath by special activity, by its apt acting; and there is a great difference between these two: a man that commits a sin against the law, he commits a sin that deserves death; but he that sins against the grace of the gospel, in that very sin he works out his own death. Other sins expose a man to the wrath of God as a judge, but this sin is like self-murder, the man executes the law upon himself. Every man by nature is under a sentence of condemnation, but rejecting the grace of God, leaves and binds a man under that condemnation: there is no other remedy for it, but only the grace of God through Christ; therefore rejecting that, is rejecting the only remedy.

(2.) This sin is directly against the glory of God. There is a great deal of the glory of God concerned in his grace. This grace of God tendered to us, through Jesus Christ, is God's great plot and contrivance for his own glory: and frustrating of it, is all that man can do to frustrate God, and to disappoint him in his main design. Blessed be God, no creature can do this; but, wo be to them that do all they can against it. The Pharisees *rejected the counsel of God against themselves*, Luke 7:30. Sirs, God would never have suffered the first Adam to have fallen, unless he had had a greater contrivance for his own glory in raising him up again. God would never have suffered the dishonour that sin's entrance brought upon him in the world, unless he had designed the bringing about of greater glory to himself by the manifestation of his grace. Therefore, *where sin hath abounded, grace hath much more abounded*; and that brings a great deal more honour to God than sin brings dishonour. The grace of God is the very bowels and the heart of God; and to frustrate this, is to kick against the very bowels of God. The grace of God is all through Jesus Christ, it flows through him; and therefore all reflections upon the grace of God reflect upon him. The grace of God is tendered to men by the Holy Ghost; and, therefore, refusing and frustrating the grace of God, is rejecting of the Holy Ghost. In a word, this grace of God is the great scope of the whole Bible; and to frustrate the grace of God, is to make the whole Bible in vain, both Old and New Testament too. The Holy Scriptures are able to make us wise unto salvation, but it is through faith that it is in Christ Jesus, 2 Tim. 3:15.

Application. There are only two words that I would speak to for the improving of this doctrine. Is frustrating the grace of God such a horrible sin? Then, *1st*, Do you all beware of it. *2dly*, Receive this grace of God; for there is no other way to avoid the frustrating of the grace of God, but only by receiving it.

1st, I would have you all beware of this sin of frustrating the grace of God; but, more especially, I would direct a warning of fear against this sin unto several sorts of persons.

(1.) Unto moral, civil, well-natured people, good livers, as we use to call them. Through the mercy of God, some are born of a better nature, as we call it, than others; of a sweet easy temper; and it is a great mercy to have a well-tempered mind, by a natural constitution, as well as it is to have a well-framed body. Now, when this virtuous natural temper hath the advantage of a godly education, these sort of people come quickly to look very well; and, therefore, they ought to take great heed. You civil, well-natured people, do you have a great care of frustrating the grace of God; for it is a sin that you are especially tempted to. There are some people so ill-natured, and of so bad a temper, that they need, as we use to say, a great deal of the grace of God to save them. And are there any that do not need the grace of God? The Lord save any of you from thinking so! He is in a woful case indeed, that thinks he doth not need the grace of God. Moral, civil people are in great danger of this sin: they think they have a good stock of their own to set up with, and therefore, they do not borrow of Christ.

(2.) People that have taken upon them the profession of religion, had need to take heed of this sin of frustrating the grace of God. They have taken upon them a profession, it may be they know not how, nor wherefore; but it is come upon them. If you be clothed with the garment of profession, have great care of this sin. There are many that profess the grace of God, that yet are strangers to the thing itself; and they are in a very dangerous case.

(3.) They that boast of outward privileges, should have a care of this sin of frustrating the grace of God: they were baptized when they were children, and have heard the word, and attended upon ordinances, and they begin to think themselves fair before God for the hope of eternal life. They are blameless in their walk, and conversation. Let such people, in an especial manner, take heed of this sin. I can assure you, that a blameless conversation hath been a great temptation to a great many to undervalue the grace of God, and the righteousness of Jesus Christ. These sort of people were never sick at heart, etc.

(4.) Awakened souls; they whose consciences are awakened, have great need to take heed of this sin of frustrating the grace of God. The Lord, sometimes, makes both light and fire too, to dart in upon the consciences of poor sinners, and they begin to see and feel what they never saw nor felt before; and when it is thus with them, sometimes, they think things are a great deal better with them than they were before; and, sometimes, they think it is a great deal worse with them; and they that in their awakening think it to be a great deal worse with them than it was before, are in a more hopeful state than they that think it is better with them: for it is not a thorough awakening, if the person thinks that awakening to be enough. Such people should take heed of this sin, lest they frustrate the grace of God: for there are two things that they are especially endangered by.

[1.] By the force of this conviction they set about duty, and that pretty warmly; and these are lovely things in the eyes of poor creatures that never knew before what praying and reading the word of God were; but when once their consciences come to be awakened, they begin to get alone, and cry to the Lord. Now, when the soul is in this case, it had need take great heed of this sin of frustrating the grace of God. How many poor awakened sinners are there that have made a pillow to sleep to hell upon with their own duties and performances, as if it were by the righteousness of the law! And thus they do not submit to the righteousness of God in Christ, nor do they attain to the rest that remains for the people of God. Rom. 10:3, Heb. 4:9.

[2.] If they do not sit down upon their duties, then, on the other hand, they are apt to be quite discouraged, and to give up all for lost. An awakened conscience, if it be thoroughly awakened, is upon the point of despair; and the point of despair is the point of ruin, or the point of salvation, as God pleases to issue it. It is the turning point.—When the poor sinner's conscience is awakened to see its lost and undone condition, in that case he is just on the point of winning or losing for evermore. If the man hearkens to God, and gives glory to his grace, by trusting in Jesus Christ alone for salvation, the bargain is made for evermore: but if the poor sinner turns aside, and stops in any thing short of this, then either the disease grows greater, or else a hardness comes in the room of it, that is worse than the disease itself. That is the first exhortation:—Have a great care of this sin of frustrating the grace of God.—And, to that end,

2*dly*, Give the grace of God a hearty welcome. There is no other way to prevent the sin of frustrating the grace of God, but by receiving and welcoming it. Welcome the grace of God for your work: but not for the devil's work. All God's work, that which God craves of you; all that you may give to the grace of God to do for you; all the work that you have to do with God, that you may give to the grace of God to do for you; only do not set the grace of God to do the devil's work, that is sinning; turning the grace of God into wantonness. The grace of God will do every thing for us, but the devil's work. And, if I may so say, he hath a great deal of the spirit of the devil in him, that will give so precious a thing as the grace of God to do the devil's work. Aye, but how shall we receive the grace of God? I answer, three ways. 1*st*, Doubt not your need of it. 2*dly*, Do not delay your accepting it. 3*dly*, Do not question your title to it.

(1.) Doubt not your need of it. If the Lord hath a mind to save you, I know very well there will be no great need of this caution. Every sinner that God saves effectually, is a person that not only thinks he is needy of the grace of God, but he thinks he is more needy of it than any body else in the world; that if there was any such man in the world, that could be saved without grace, he was the farthest from such a one: that if there was any man in the world that needed more grace than ordinary, he was the man.

(2.) Do not delay your accepting of grace whensoever it is revealed to you. Whensoever you have the offer of the grace of God, whensoever you are about the means of grace, labour to get this grace itself, Heb. 3:7, *Therefore the Holy Ghost saith, Today if you will hear his voice, harden not your hearts*. You may not hear his voice tomorrow; hardness of heart grows mightily by delays.

(3.) Do not question your title to it. I mean this, make no doubt but that it is as lawful and as allowable in God's sight for you to lay hold on the saving grace of God, as ever it was for any sinner in the world. I do not mean that graceless people should presently think that they have a title to the grace of God; for no man hath a title to it till he receives it. But this I say, the offer of the grace of God, in the gospel, gives fair warning and liberty for every one to embrace it. *He that will, let him come, and take of the water of life freely*, Rev. 22:17. And that which is thus freely offered, and freely given, should be thankfully welcomed, and thankfully received, when it is enjoyed.

SERMON III.

GAL. 2:21.

I do not frustrate the grace of God: for if righteousness come by the law, then Christ is dead in vain.

WHEN I first entered on these words, I told you what the scope of the apostle was in this epistle: he is here bringing forth arguments against that error that the Galatian churches were plagued with; and arguments for that truth of the gospel that he had planted amongst them, and taught them: the truth was this, That the righteousness of a sinner for justification was only in Christ. The error of the Galatians lay in this, That something of the righteousness of the law was to be mixed therewith. My text contains two arguments against this error, drawn from a common natural head of arguing against error, by the absurdities that necessarily flow from it. Now there are two grand absurdities that flow from this doctrine of the law in point of justification.—1*st*, That it frustrates the grace of God.—2*dly*, That it makes Christ's death to be in vain: and two more abominable things cannot be well thought of; and people have great need to fear, and to take heed of any doctrine that hath any tendency to either of them. The first of these the apostle expresses in his own person; *I do not frustrate the grace of God*. And here he speaks like a believer, and not like a minister nor an apostle; so he discourses from ver. 16 speaking of himself and the rest of the godly, like ordinary believers, that betook themselves to this way of relief by Christ's righteousness alone. I proposed four observations to speak to.

1st, That the grace of God shines gloriously in the justifying of a sinner through the righteousness of Christ: and this I have spoke to.

2dly, That frustrating the grace of God is a great and horrible sin; for so it is expressed by the apostle, *I do not frustrate the grace of God.* As if he should have said, 'Blessed be God, I am not in that road; I am not one that frustrates the grace of God; I am saved by it.' How the grace of God is frustrated, and how great the sin is, I spoke to the last day. The revelation of the grace of God, and the tender of it, and the urging of it, may be frustrated, and is by many: but the grace itself, in its powerful conveyance by the Holy Ghost on the hearts of men, always reaches its end. The grace of God is irresistible in its closest powerful application: this I also spoke to; and would only add a word or two further about the greatness of this sin of seeking righteousness by the law, and thereby frustrating the grace of God.

(1.) This is a sin that but few in the world can commit. The greatest part of them that go to hell cannot commit this sin; they never frustrated the grace of God. Indeed all that are finally guilty of it go to hell; but all that go to hell are not guilty of this sin. The greatest part of the world never frustrated the grace of God, for they never heard of it; and, therefore, our Lord pronounces a wo against Capernaum, against Chorazin and Bethsaida, and tells them that they were in a worse case than Sodom and Gomorrah, than Tyre and Sidon, Matt. 11:21. etc. because the grace of God was never offered them as it was to the others.—Sirs, let me tell you, the worst quarters in hell are for those persons that are nearest to Christ, and yet not in him by faith; of all sinners such drop deepest into the pit.

(2.) The devils are not guilty of this sin. There is not a devil in hell, nor out of it, that is so guilty of this sin of frustrating the grace of God, as thousands of professors in London are. The devils are haters of the grace of God; but the grace of God was never tendered to them: they only hate the grace of God as it is tendered to men, and envy it; but the grace of God was never offered to the devils. The way of preserving the holy angels, and the way of justice to the damned spirits, proclaim greatly the wonderful privilege that we have in the gospel. The holy angels are kept, and they received grace, for the election of grace fell on them: they are called the elect angels. When that great apostasy was in the upper house, all the reprobate angels fell of their own accord, and all the elect angels stood: and that election of grace towards angels ran through Jesus Christ, who was to be their preserving head. There is something that looks like this in the word of God.

But recovering grace to angels was never given; the angels that stood had preserving grace given them, to keep them in their first station; but the angels that fell had no recovering grace given them. *Christ took not on him*, saith the apostle, *the nature of angels, but was born of the seed of Abraham*. And thence it came to pass, that the devils themselves are not guilty of this sin of frustrating the grace of God. Surely then people had need to take great heed that they be not guilty of a worse sin than that which the devils can commit. There is no creature that hath frustrated the grace of God, but that creature that hath the offer of the grace of God.

(3.) Frustrating the grace of God is a sin that none that are in hell are guilty of. All that are finally guilty of it on earth are sent to hell, but none that are in hell are guilty of it; for when once that last sentence is executed upon them, the door of grace and mercy is for ever shut upon them. So that it is the gospel-sinner only who can frustrate the grace of God, who is guilty of that sin; and that but a small part of the world are guilty of it; that the devils in hell are not guilty of it, that all the damned in hell are not guilty of it, though they rage and roar, and blaspheme; and all sorts of wickedness we may well conclude to be in their miserable state; but frustrating the grace of God is a sin not to be found in hell, because grace enters not there.—So much shall serve for this second point of doctrine, That it is a horrible sin to frustrate the grace of God. I come now to speak to the next doctrine.

3*dly*, To seek righteousness by the works of the law, is to frustrate the grace of God: for this is the scope of the apostle's argument. It is to shew that there is no righteousness to be had by the law; and this is one argument that he proves it by, *I do not*, saith he, *frustrate the grace of God*. It is, as if he should have said, 'If I sought righteousness by the works of the law, I should frustrate the grace of God; but I do not seek righteousness by the law, for I am dead to the law, and therefore I do not frustrate the grace of God.' There are two things under this doctrine that I would speak to—1*st*, What is it to seek righteousness by the law?—2*dly*, How doth it appear that seeking righteousness by the works of the law is frustrating the grace of God? For they that are guilty of this sin of seeking righteousness by the works of the law, they are very loth to take in this, that they frustrate the grace of God: they will say, that they give all respect to the grace of God; even the self-righteous Pharisee could own the grace of God, Luke 18:11, *God, I thank thee that I am not as other men*. 'I thank God, that I am so good as I am;' when he was a poor, vain, self-conceited man all the while.

[1.] What is it to seek righteousness by the works of the law?—By law here I mean the holy spotless law of God. The law of man hath nothing to do in the point of righteousness before God. This seeking of righteousness by the law is righteousness in God's sight; the apostle states the matter so. No man is justified by the law in the sight of God. That a man is justified by the law in the sight of men, nobody can deny.—We should be very careful to justify ourselves in the sight of men by the law, and our conformity to it; but this righteousness here spoken of is righteousness in the sight of God, and righteousness by the law of God; and it stands in three things.

1st, Righteousness by the law is that which obtains a man's acceptance with God. That is righteousness by the law that procures a man's acceptance with God; upon the account of which he stands before God as a righteous man, and is dealt with accordingly. Now, he that seeks righteousness by the law in this sense, is one who dreams, that by doing, and obeying what the law requires, he may work out that for which he may stand righteous, and accepted in God's sight. And that is one way this sin is committed.

2dly, In this righteousness before God by the works of the law, there is an expectation of impunity for all that is past in transgressing the law. And we find that this must necessarily be the righteousness of a holy man, who stands in a state of acceptance with God; but the righteousness of a man who hath been once a sinner must be by having that which may bring him into a state of impunity and safety, or all the transgressions that he hath been guilty of before. Now, men are guilty of seeking righteousness by the works of the law this second way, when they do, or think to do, that for which God will forgive all their transgressions, and forget all that they have done; and of this the Pharisee made no question: though he was a sinner, yet he comes and prays, and expects acceptation in God's sight, and the forgiveness of his sins, upon the account of the good that he had done.

3dly, In this righteousness by the works of the law there is a title to eternal life.—He that, by what he doth, expects to have a right conferred upon him to eternal life, is a man that seeks righteousness by the law; *Good Master, what good thing shall I do that I may have eternal life?* said the poor young legalist, Matt. 19:16. 'I would fain have eternal life, and would fain have a right to it: Master, tell me what good thing shall I do to get it.' These are the three ways by which men seek righteousness by the law:—To do that whereby a man may obtain acceptance before God.—To do that for which he may obtain pardon and impunity from God.—To do that for which, he may have a right conferred on him to eternal life.—But, you will say, this is so gross Popery that there is no Protestant guilty of it. Alas! alas! every natural man is guilty of it—and it is only the almighty power of the Spirit of God that can erase it out of their hearts. I will offer you some plain proofs of this.

(1.) How many are there, when their hearts are examined, must own that their eyes are altogether on the precepts of the law, and not a thought on the promises of the gospel?— How many poor creatures are there that begin to be thoughtful about their salvation, insomuch that they make people that are about them, who are ignorant and charitable, think that they are hopeful Christians; but try these people this way, and you will find that all the exercise of their religion is about the precepts of the law, and they have no exercise at all about the promises of the gospel. He that minds only the precept, is only a doer; and he that minds not the promise, he is no believer: for the precept is the rule of practice; but it is the promise that is the foundation of faith.—Now, how can that man be reckoned a believer, that hath no heart-exercise about the promises?

(2.) A great many people are mightily taken up about their own works, and but very little about Christ's. Our righteousness doth not stand in our own works; but stands in Christ's works, what Christ did, and suffered for us in his life, and death, and resurrection; therein stands our righteousness.—Now, how many poor creatures are there that reckon it a great matter, and glory mightily in their own doings: if they pray, and hear, and read, and can but make any sort of reformation in their conversation, how big do these things appear in their eyes? But

Christ's life and death, and all his great performances for our salvation, are mean and low, and of small esteem with them. And do not these sort of people seek righteousness by the law? Aye surely.

(3.) They look for eternal life, but they look for it as a reward of works, and not as an inheritance given by gift and grace; and all servants and slaves must do so; and all natural men are slaves, they are children of the bond-woman, Gal. 4:31.: they work for fear of punishment, and in hopes of the crown: they work for wages; the wages they love, and would have; but the work they hate. Whereas the believer acts just the contrary; he loves the work, and he expects the wages as the gift of grace from the blessed Father he serves. The apostle makes a great distinction between these two, *Wherefore thou art no more a servant, but a son, and if a son, then an heir of God through Christ*, Gal. 4:7. Every man that is for righteousness by the works of the law is a servant; he looks upon God as his master, and the law as his master's will, and he sets about obeying with all his might. Now, is not this a good servant? Yes.—But all such servants go to hell: you must be children; for none but children are saved. And, indeed, there are none true servants to him, but they that are children; they are but slaves, and are cast out, that do not serve with their love, and expect the inheritance only as a gift of grace.—So much for that first thing, What it is to seek righteousness by the works of the law.

[2.] I am now to shew you, that seeking righteousness by the works of the law, is to frustrate the grace of God: and I would shew it—first in point of doctrine—and then in point of practice.

1*st*, As to point of doctrine.—In the matter of righteousness before God, the law and the gospel are perfectly opposite, and they are only so in this point. The law and the gospel agree sweetly together in all things else; but in this point of the righteousness of a man before God, the law and the gospel are quite opposite one to another. The gospel comes to bring in another salvation than the law thought of; and the law destroys the salvation of the gospel. The law and gospel, in point of righteousness before God, are exactly opposite: *And if by grace, then it is no more by works, otherwise grace is no more grace; but if it be of works, then it is no more of grace, for otherwise works were no more works*, Rom. 11:6. Grace and works, in the point of righteousness before God, are perfectly opposite: *You are saved by grace*, saith the apostle, *not of works, lest any man should boast*, Eph. 2:8, 9.

2dly, Let us bring this matter into practice, and you will find that all men express this in their frame; both the self-righteous man, and he that is not so—not only is it asserted in point of doctrine, that works and grace are thus inconsistent, but we always find it, even in the spirit and temper both of the one and of the other.

(1.) He that seeks righteousness by the law, is a man that never saw his need of grace: and you may be well assured that that man will frustrate the grace of God, who never saw his utter need of it. He was never so far emptied, but he expects and imagines that he shall be able to work out a righteousness for himself, and so is not brought under any conviction of his utter need of the grace of God—whereas he that is for the grace of God in Christ alone, is a man that hath a great need of the grace of God, and sees himself undone without it.

(2.) This self-righteous man sees no glory in the grace of God shining through the righteousness of Christ, there is no excellency in it to him. Every natural man is in this mind; he sees a great deal of glory in his own doings: in a beautiful conversation, in brave gifts, and in a shining walk before men; he sees a great deal of beauty and glory here. Every natural man thinks there is a great deal of glory in his own performances. The self-righteous Pharisee came boasting in his own performances: *God, I thank thee that I am not as other men are, extortioners, unjust, adulterers, or even as this publican: I fast twice a week, and I give tithes of all that I possess*, Luke 18:11, 12. These were great things in the man's esteem, and so they are in the eyes of every natural man. But for that righteousness that is lodged in Christ, that is wrought out by a man without him, by one that came down from heaven, and is gone up thither again; that hath all this righteousness seated in him, and gives it forth to us by mere grace; no natural man thinks any thing of this. But the believer is a man that hath an high esteem of the righteousness of Christ. How doth the apostle Paul speak of this? *I count all things but dung, that I may win Christ; and be found in him, not having mine own righteousness*, Phil. 3:8, 9.

(3.) Every natural man is averse from the grace of God, and therefore he must needs frustrate the grace of God. He is averse from it: but every believer is just of another mind.— Sirs, if all men's hearts were known to us, as they are to God, here is one thing that would determine every man's state. What way do you best like to go to heaven in? 'I would fain be very holy,' saith the poor man, 'that I may be very happy when I die.'—Saith the believer, 'I would fain be clothed with Christ's righteousness, and get eternal life as the gift of his grace; and I know that by being in Christ I shall be sanctified.' But no believer seeks sanctification as his righteousness, and title to glory: it is a preparation for glory, and the way that leads to glory, to all them that are saved according to that blessed method, Rom. 8:30, *Whom he justified, them he also glorified*; and by glorification there, both sanctification and eternal life are well understood by most.—So much for the third doctrine, That seeking righteousness by the works of the law frustrates the grace of God.

I would now speak a few words to the fourth doctrine, and then make some application of both together.

Doctrine 4*th*. No true believer in Jesus Christ can frustrate the grace of God. The apostle is here speaking of it in the account that he is giving of the grace of God working in him; *I through the law*, saith he, *am dead to the law, that I might live to God*; and 'I live by Christ, and by faith in him, and, therefore, I do not frustrate the grace of God.' He is not speaking of the great attainment, that some few Christians arrive at; but he is speaking of that which is common to the state of all Christians: *I do not frustrate the grace of God*.—Before I come to the proof of this, I would lay down a few cautions, to prevent mistakes.

1*st*, It must be allowed that a great many who have been made Christians have been long enemies to the grace of God; and there is not a greater instance of this than the good man that speaks in my text, the apostle Paul. He was a great heart-enemy to Jesus Christ: and he was an enemy to Christ, if I may so say, with a good conscience, according to the real light that the poor man's blinded conscience had: *I verily thought with myself that I ought to do many things contrary to the name of Jesus of Nazareth*, Acts 26:9.—'I never heard a name that I hated so much as the name of this Jesus of Nazareth; and I hated it from the heart, and my conscience prompted me to it.' When our Lord met him by the way, *Saul, Saul, why persecutest thou me?* little did the poor man think Christ died for him, and should be a blessed fountain of life to him.—A believer may be a great enemy to the grace of God, before the grace of God makes him a believer.

2dly, It may not be denied but that a true believer may take in doctrines contrary to the grace of Christ in their tendency, though he perceive it not. I should be lothe to think that all these Galatians, that are here so sharply reproved by the apostle Paul, were rotten-hearted people; there might be many sincere people amongst them, imposed upon by the cunning of them that lay in wait to deceive. There may be, through darkness, perplexed heads in many honest hearts, about several points concerning the grace of God. It is not for us to measure any body's state according to the principles that they profess, unless they be very bad.

3dly, It is not to be denied but that in a fit of temptation, even a true believer may abuse the grace of God; he may turn it into wantonness, and may grow light and vain, because of his mistaking the nature of the grace of God. Several have done so, and God knows how to tame them that do so; and the severest fatherly rebukes of the law are upon them that wax wanton because of his kindness.—These things being premised, I would briefly shew how it is that a good man cannot frustrate the grace of God.

(1.) Because good men are all grace's captives. Every believer, as a believer, and when he is made a believer, is made a captive of the grace of God. How are men saved, think you? We cannot see which way they are saved; the word goeth forth, and people hear it; but we do not know who gets good, and when they get good by it. I will tell you when men are saved; when the grace of God comes and lays hold of them, and claps hold of a poor sinner—'This man shall be my captive, and I will save him.'—All believers are captives to the grace of God, and, therefore, they cannot frustrate the grace of God; they are all subdued by this grace, and made *willing in the day of his power*, Psa. 110:3.

(2.) No believer can frustrate the grace of God, because he is dead to the law, as the apostle's word is in the context, Gal. 2:19. And there are two things needful to make a man dead to the law;—to know the law, and to know himself: and whosoever knows both these, is a man dead to the law. He that knows the purity, and the spotlessness of the law of God, and he that knows his own heart, and its vileness, this man will natively draw this conclusion. 'Surely this law can never do me any good—I can never fulfil it, and it can never save me: if there be not another way of salvation than by the law, I am gone for evermore.' *I through the law am dead to the law*, saith the apostle; 'I need no more, to make me despair of life by the law, than to see the law: it commands what I cannot do, it threatens what I cannot avoid nor bear;' and therefore, *I am dead to the law, that I might live to God*;—'my life must come in another way than by the law.'

So much shall serve for the opening of these truths. It would now follow to make some Application; which I shall do in two things, respecting all the doctrines that I have raised from this former part of the verse.—By these doctrines here delivered by the apostle, you are called to try the spirits, to try the doctrines you hear—and you are called to try your own state; for every doctrine that is contrary to the grace of God is a doctrine that Christians should hate. And your eternal state is to be determined by these things—What are your heart-thoughts of the law of God?—What are your heart-thoughts of the righteousness of Christ?—And what are your heart-thoughts of the grace of God?—And every one that knows truly what his inward sense of these things is, may soon come to some conclusion concerning his spiritual state: but I shall speak more fully to these things the next opportunity.

SERMON IV.

GAL. 2:21.

I do not frustrate the grace of God: for if righteousness come by the law, then is Christ dead in vain.

FROM this first argument of the apostle for the justifying of a sinner through the righteousness of Christ, and not by the righteousness of the law, I have raised, and opened, and spoke something to four doctrines:—

1*st*, That the grace of God shines gloriously in the justifying of a sinner through the righteousness of Christ.

2*dly*, That it is a dreadful sin to frustrate the grace of God.

3*dly*, That all who seek righteousness by the law, they do frustrate the grace of God.

4*thly*, That no true sound believer can be guilty of this sin:—Frustrating the grace of God is a sin that no believer can commit.

I would now come to make some application of these, which I mean to prosecute from these two heads:—

I. To warn you to take heed and to try the spirits, as the apostle exhorts, 1 John 4:1, according to this doctrine.

II. Try your own state according to your heart-thoughts of this matter.

I. You are to try the spirits—you are to try the doctrines that you hear.—When the greatest measure of the Holy Ghost was poured out upon the churches, and when extraordinary officers were raised up amongst them, and in a time when some of the apostles were living, by one of them was this exhortation given, 1 John 4:1, *Beloved, believe not every spirit, but try the spirits whether they are of God.*—And it is very observable, that the scope of that text, that the apostle there lays down, leads us plainly to the doctrine that I am upon, *Believe not every spirit, for there are many false spirits, and antichrists, that are gone out into the world.*—But you will say, How shall we know them? Saith the apostle, ver. 3, *Every spirit that confesseth not that Jesus Christ is come in the flesh, is not of God: every spirit that confesseth that Jesus Christ is come in the flesh is of God.*—Now, by a very usual phrase, that was well understood then, and is not hard to be known now, by *spirit*, doctrine is meant—every doctrine that tends not this way is not of God. Aye, but you will say, Where are there any that say Christ is not come in the flesh, save the Jews? The apostle seems to make this a grand mark of antichrist. Now in antichrist's kingdom (and that is a fitter name for them than that of the church, for with the church they have nothing to do) it is every where asserted, that Christ is come in the flesh; for they have made a great part of their religion to consist in carnal, wicked representations of Jesus Christ; they have made a goddess of his mother, and they have made a puppet-show of his life and death, by their ridiculous representations: aye, but the main thing that Christ came into the flesh for, that is forgotten by them:—and of this the apostle speaks, ver. 10, *He hath sent his Son to be the propitiation for our sins.* Christ's business in this world was to be made a sacrifice for sin: and they that do not hold him forth as a sacrifice for sin, do, in effect, say he is not come in the flesh. Now, concerning these doctrines that I would warn you against, I would branch them forth into a few heads.

(1.) There are doctrines darkening the grace of God, and the righteousness of Christ, that you should beware of. The gospel is called by the apostle, 'the gospel of the grace of God,' twice in one discourse to the church at Ephesus, 3:2, 7; and 'the word of his grace,' Acts 20:32. What judgment then should Christians make of such men's spirits, that are called ministers, and will be called so, and yet you may hear them preach from one end of the year to another, and never hear a word of the grace of God, or the righteousness of Christ?—if they be sound in the faith, it is well; but the very concealing of these things is a great sin, and a great snare to people; the very name of the gospel is 'the gospel of the grace of God:' it is miscalled by the name of 'the gospel,' if the grace of God runs not through every vein of it.

(2.) There are doctrines perplexing the grace of God; they make it dark, and they make it intricate: they perplex the doctrine with methods, and they perplex people's consciences with their doctrine. There is no church canon in all the world that is much worth regarding, but that which we have in Acts 15; for those that were called by the name of

General Councils, for the first three hundred years after Christ, have many weaknesses and follies in them; and they began to savour of a begun degeneracy, though in the main points of the truths of the gospel they remained sound. In Acts 15:1 certain men that came down from Judea had taken up this conceit, and *taught the brethren, that except they were circumcised after the law of Moses, they could not be saved.* Observe where they laid the stress of this thing, 'except ye be circumcised after the law of Moses, *ye cannot be saved.*' You know very well, that the apostle Paul looked upon circumcision as a very indifferent thing: sometimes, in his travels, he ordered some to be circumcised, but at other times he would not; he looked upon it as a matter of indifference, for the avoiding of scandals, and so the apostle reckoned it no great matter: *Circumcision is nothing, and uncircumcision is nothing.* Aye, but when once it came to be broached into a doctrine, and a necessity laid upon it.—*Except ye be circumcised after the law of Moses, ye cannot be saved*—let us see what this awful reverend assembly at Jerusalem say to it; the apostles, and elders, and brethren, a blessed company they were, a blessed church, worth all the churches in England, without any reflection. Ver. 24, *Forasmuch as we have heard that certain which went out from us have troubled you with words, subverting your souls, saying you must be circumcised, and keep the law; to whom we gave no such commandment*: they trouble you, and they pervert your souls.—Sirs, There are four questions, that must always be preserved plain; plainly delivered, and plainly known by all good men: 1*st*, What is that righteousness in which a sinner can stand safe before God? The plain answer to it is, That it is the righteousness of Christ only. 2*dly*, How come we by this righteousness? The gospel answer is, By grace alone; it is given us as a free gift, we do not buy it. 3*dly*, How are we possessed of this righteousness? By faith alone; there is no putting on this raiment but by faith alone. 4*thly*, What warrant hath a man to believe on Jesus Christ? The plain gospel answer is, Only the promise of the gospel. And here are two things I would caution you about; and the most part of people's mistakes lie about them. 1*st*, The law is no gospel but as it leads to Christ; the law not leading to Christ is against the gospel, and the gospel against the law; but the law leading to Christ serves the gospel, and the gospel serves the law by fulfilling it. 2*dly*, The doctrine of holiness, as it flows from Christ, is gospel; but the doctrine of holiness, without Christ, is no gospel. To make this plain: Whosoever they be that teach people to be holy, and tell them how they may be holy, and urge them very hard that they must be very holy, for this end, that when they are holy they may believe on Jesus Christ; these people pervert and perplex the gospel: but if people be persuaded of the necessity of holiness for salvation, and that they must believe on Jesus Christ that they may be holy, this is gospel.—That is the second thing, Have a care of those doctrines that perplex and confound the truths of the gospel.

(3.) There are mixing doctrines: they that would mix something with the grace of God: the grace of God they will not disown; the righteousness of Christ they will not deny, but they will put something in with them in the matter of justification. Take heed of this matter; it is a shame that this should be talked on as a matter of controversy; it is a point that every one's conscience should be fully satisfied in, as they expect salvation from the hand of God. Indeed good men may jar and jangle about terms that neither of them well understand; but when the matter comes to a particular person's own case, there should be a full satisfaction in this point—that the righteousness of Christ for our justification must stand pure and unmixed. It is a corrupt thing to mix any of the works of the law with the grace of God: and herein lay the error of the Galatians; the grace of God, and the righteousness of Christ, they liked very well; but they would join the law of Moses therewith. Let the law of Moses keep its own place, and be the rule of our sanctification; but in our justification, it hath no room at all: God never gave it any room there, and all they are fools that do: it never served any man that way.

(4.) There are blaspheming doctrines, opposing and blaspheming the grace of God; and the land is full of them. You may have heard of a sort of people, the Socinians, and they are gross enemies to the grace of God. These strike at the very root of the grace of God, and the righteousness of Christ. If Christ be not the true God, how can he save a sinner? It is impossible that the righteousness of a creature can atone for the unrighteousness of a creature. It is the Godhead of Christ, that adds that infinite virtue to his sacrifice, that we are saved by.—So much for this first exhortation 'Try the spirits.'

2dly, I would exhort you to try your own state by this doctrine: *I do not frustrate the grace of God*: and as this hath been handled, it calls you to try yourselves about three things:—1*st*, What are your real thoughts of God's law? 2*dly*, What are your real thoughts of Christ's righteousness? 3*dly*, What are your real thoughts of the grace of God? A little to each of these.

(1.) What are your real thoughts of God's law?—And although you may think this a remote-like mark, yet it is not so remote, but it comes near to the point: judgment will be made of a man's state before God, according to his real thoughts of the law of God. Good men have always great and high thoughts of God's law, and they have low thoughts of themselves. Psa. 119:128, *I esteem all thy precepts concerning every thing to be right, and I hate every false way. The law is holy, the commandment is holy, just, and good: the law is spiritual; but I am carnal, sold under sin*, Rom. 7:12, 14. But you will say, 'Do not every body think so of the law of God?' I answer, No. No natural man hath a good thought of the law of God. Every corrupt, unrenewed man hath one of these three thoughts concerning the law of God;—

[1.] The natural man thinks the law of God easy to be kept. It is a graceless proverb that some people have in their mouths sometimes, and it flows from the corruption of their hearts, 'That it is an easier thing to please God than it is to please man.' Indeed, if they would take God's way, it is an easy thing to get his favour; but according to the sense that it is commonly spoken in, it is a wicked saying, and flows from this wicked meaning—that the natural man thinks the law of God easy to be kept; and thereupon the Scribes and Pharisees (and so do all that seek righteousness by the law), they expound the law of God so largely that one would think any body might keep it. Therefore, when our Lord hath a mind to break down this fortress of self-righteousness, he explains the law of God in its true strictness. The Pharisees' doctrine was, that nobody broke the sixth commandment, but he that murdered a man—that no man broke the seventh commandment, but he that committed adultery with his neighbour's wife—that nobody broke the ninth, but he that foreswore himself: and, indeed, if this had been all the interpretation of the law of God, that part of it that concerns our duty towards man had been no hard thing. Blessed be God, a great many good people, and bad people too, have not been guilty of these gross transgressions:—but when the spiritual meaning of the law comes to be considered, who is innocent? *I had not known lust*, saith the apostle, *unless the law had said, Thou shalt not covet*, Rom. 7:7. 'The commandment came to me in another sense, with that brightness that soon convinced me of sin.' This is the first thought that people have of the law of God—that it is easy to be kept.

[2.] When they are beat from this, and they find the law of God to be so strict a rule that it reaches to the word, and thoughts, and heart, to the least motion either from within or without—then they begin to hope that the threatening will not be fulfilled: if God gives so severe a law, that reaches to all, even to the least sins, then they hope God will not punish every sin with the curse of the law. The Lord, by Moses, warns the people of this, Deut. 29:19, *And it come to pass, when he hears the words of this curse, that he shall bless himself in his heart, saying, I shall have peace, though I walk in the imagination of my own heart, to add drunkenness to thirst.* The secure man is very unwilling to take up the holiness and the strictness of the law of God as forbidding every sin; but he is far more unwilling to believe that God means to execute the threatened vengeance for these sins. And what sorry pleas have they? *God is merciful.* Aye, so he is, but not to them that despise his law. God is not merciful to any law-breaker; but God is merciful in providing a law-keeper to save us; but he hath no mercy for the law-breaker. If a man expects life by the law, he must die by it.—'Aye, but Christ hath died for sinners;' and so he hath; but Christ was sent to fulfil the law, and not to take it away. Christ came not to make the law of God less strict in commanding than it was, nor less severe in threatening; but Christ came to take both upon his own back: and all that believe in him shall be saved from both. Christ took not away the law, but fulfilled it; and it is the reckoning of that fulfilling of the law by Christ to us, that is our salvation; and thus *the righteousness of the law is fulfilled in us*. The righteousness of the law was fulfilled by Christ, and this is reckoned to a believer; and so the righteousness of the law of God is fulfilled in him; fulfilled by Christ, and so fulfilled in the believer in him.

But now suppose the light of the word drives a man from both these vain imaginations, and he sees the law to be so holy that no man can escape its threatenings; when the natural man is thus beat from these two, then,

[3.] He rises up in rebellion against the law, and blasphemes the law of God. Sirs, there are a great many poor creatures that complain grievously that many blasphemous thoughts follow them: I do believe that next unto the advantage that Satan may have over some bad-tempered minds, and ill-disposed bodies, I am apt to believe that the main root of all these blasphemies, is this point of doctrine that I am upon. When the poor creature was secure, he thought he could easily fulfil the law of God, or avoid the curse of it; but when he comes to see both these to be in vain, then, unless grace subdues the man's heart, it naturally rises in rebellion against the law of God. 'Why did God give such a strict law, that nobody can keep, but every one must be destroyed by it?' These very thoughts arose in Paul's mind, Rom. 7:13, *Was then that which was good made death to me? God forbid.* The apostle Paul never knew himself to be a sinner till the law came; and the more close the law came it slew him the more, and quickened sin in him more. Now, how can any one think well of that law that slays the sinner, and enlivens the sin? 'God forbid, saith the apostle, that I should say this was the end for which the law was made; but this was a blessed end in Christ's hand:' *By the commandment, sin appeared to be exceeding sinful,* that Paul might see his exceeding need of a Saviour. And there are two things that raise these rebellious thoughts against the law of God.

(1.) When clear light about the law shines upon the man's conscience, then all the Babel-building of their own works are thrown unto the ground: their praying, reading, hearing, holiness, it is all thrown, to the ground by the law of God;—the law condemns them utterly in point of righteousness. The law indeed commands them in point of practice, and it commends them as things pleasing to God; but in point of righteousness before God, the law condemns them utterly, the only language of the law is this, 'Do all, and live; fail in the least, and die:'—and thus the man sees all his own righteousness is gone. And how unwilling are people to yield to this? What a great matter is it for a man to be able to do so? When a poor awakened sinner, that never knew the grace of God, or the righteousness of Christ, when he hath by the force of good education, or the power of the word, been brought under some conviction of sin and duty, he then sets about praying, and reading, and hearing, and reforming, and, it may be, hath been doing something at this for several years; but in the mean time was an utter stranger to Jesus Christ. Now what a great matter is it for a man to forego all this, as if it had no worth in it? But why should not a man be willing to part with it? *I count it all but dross and dung*, saith the apostle, that I may win Christ, Phil. 3:8. This blasphemous frame is expressed in Ezek. 33:10, and it hath reference to the point that I am upon: *Therefore, O thou Son of man, speak unto the house of Israel, Thus ye speak, saying, If our transgressions and our sins be upon us, and we pine away in them, how should we live?* The meaning is this, 'The Lord is here, by his severe prophet, plaguing us with reproofs from the word of God for our sins, and the execution of God's threatenings are upon us in his judgments; now if we be sinners, and God deals thus severely with us, what shall come on us?' Saith the Lord, ver. 11, 'There is a way of escape, *Turn and live*; but have a care you do not trust to your own righteousness: for if you do, you are gone for good and all.' Ver. 13. *When I say to the righteous, he shall surely live, if he trust to his own righteousness, and commit iniquity, all his righteousness shall not be remembered; but for his iniquity that he hath committed he shall die for it.*

(2.) When the sinner once finds that he is forced to forego all that he hath got already, he then also sees that there is no hopes for the time to come; that he hath no hopes at all of a righteousness by the law; and this the poor sinner reckons like the putting him into hell: he is as sorry to part with the rotten props of his own righteousness, as if the taking it away was the casting him into hell; when it is the only way to save him from it. No man can be a believer on Jesus Christ, but he that despairs of righteousness by his own doings. This is the first thing I would have you examine yourselves about, What are your secret thoughts of the law of God? There is no righteousness can come by it; and that is the excellency of the law; it is none of the law's fault, but its glory, that no righteousness can come by it: it is a rule of righteousness, but it is no means to confer righteousness upon a sinner. The law can give eternal life to a sinless man; but it can give no life to a sinner: *If there had been a law that could have given life, verily,* saith the apostle, *righteousness should have been by the law*, Gal. 3:21. 'Righteousness should certainly have come that way.'

2*dly*, Try what your thoughts are of the righteousness of Christ. By the righteousness of Christ, I do not mean his divine excellency, as he is the Son of God, equal with the Father; nor the excellency of the man Christ Jesus, on whom the Spirit was poured forth without measure: but, I mean, that righteousness that this God-man wrought out for us, as our Redeemer, for our justification, by his life and death; this is called the righteousness of God, Rom. 10:3. And every one may know his state towards God by his thoughts of this:—every despiser of it is a stranger to God, and every spiritual admirer of it is a man acquainted with God.

[1.] The believer hath high and esteeming thoughts of it, as an only righteousness, and as a very glorious one. Let us compare a little what righteousnesses there are, have been, or can be. The first righteousness lasted but a little while; that of the first Adam and Eve; it may be, it was not a day old; however, it was a very short one. Now, there is no comparison between Christ's righteousness and this: it is true that this comes the nearest to it: and the apostle Paul takes notice of this parallel, Rom. 5. The first Adam stood in the room of all his posterity, and they all stood in him, and with him as long as he stood; and this was a pretty glorious obedience that the first man performed, and if he had continued in it, the time of his trial, it was to have been reckoned for the benefit of all his posterity; but it was but the righteousness of a man; it was but the righteousness of a creature; it was a righteousness that would have *continued* happiness, but it could bring no happiness to them that had once lost it. If such a thing could have been imaginable, that the first Adam had stood, and one of his posterity had fallen, the first original righteousness would never have been able to have obtained pardon for that sinning offspring of Adam. But the righteousness of our Lord Jesus Christ is that which brings in a pardon, and a title to eternal life, to them that had forfeited all. There is another righteousness, a little one, hardly worth that name, that is performed by believers, in obedience to the holy law of God; but this comes no way near to it. If we may speak of the righteousness of the law, that is in hell: There are some poor creatures that do not imagine what hell is; they think it is the place that in all God's creation may be best spared: but let me tell you, hell is as useful a place as any;—it is there where the righteousness of the law is proclaimed: every lash that is there given by the justice of God to the damned, proclaims aloud the righteousness and the holiness of the law.

But I hope none will make any comparison between that righteousness that the law squeezes from the damned by their punishment, and that righteousness that the law found in Christ when it bruised him for our iniquities.—Every believer hath high thoughts of this righteousness of Christ.

[2.] And not only so, but every believer hath venturing thoughts on this righteousness of Christ: The man not only thinks highly of it, but he builds upon it, and betakes himself to it. The righteousness of Christ is like a curious ark or ship, whereby all that are embarked in it, shall be safely landed in heaven. Now it signifies nothing for a poor man to stand upon the shore, and to commend the ship, and say it is a brave vessel; he must get into it: if ever he hath a mind to escape the destruction of the world, he must get into the ark, Christ.—The apostle hath an elegant similitude, *By faith Noah, being warned of God of things not seen as yet, moved with fear, prepared an ark, to the saving of his house; by which he condemned the world, and became heir of the righteousness which is by faith*, Heb. 11:7. Pray observe; The state of Noah, and every man's state by nature are alike. God tells Noah, 120 years hence I will drown this whole world; and not a man, nor beast, nor fowl of heaven, shall escape. Sirs, it is not so long, by one half almost, to that time when we shall be all in eternity! 120 years was but a small time to them, who lived 700 or 800 years. We are just in the same case: warning is given us by the course of nature, and by the word, that in a few years more we may be all turned out of this world: and our dying is of equal importance, as to our eternal state, with Christ's coming; what difference is there if thou shouldest die this week, or if Christ should come to judge the world this week? Thy eternal state is equally concerned in both. Now, God tells Noah, 'I have provided an ark for thee; I will drown the whole world; but I will provide an ark for thee.' But after the man had builded it, he must get into it, or he could not be saved by it. Now, here comes in the tidings of the gospel; we are not bid to prepare an ark, but we are told that God hath already prepared an ark, his own Son, who was hewed and framed by the justice of God, that he might be made a fit lodging for poor sinners. Now, the work of all them that would be saved, is to get into Jesus Christ, and to betake themselves to this righteousness, and when they have done so, to rest quietly there. But yet this righteousness of Christ, as much as it is, and should be, spoken of in the preaching of the word, yet multitudes of professors never once thought of it; they often think we must be holy, and that Turks understand as well as you: But pray how do you think to come by your holiness? Without righteousness? Never man shall be holy without the reckoning of Christ's righteousness to him; without which you can never partake of Christ's spirit to sanctify you. This seeking, and studying, and framing a holiness, without employing Christ, doth these two things:—it dishonours Christ utterly:—and it renders holiness altogether impossible. It is utterly impossible there should be a spark of true holiness in that heart that is a stranger to faith in Christ Jesus. Morality, and Pagan civility, there may be; but true gospel holiness is a blessed consequence of faith in Jesus Christ.

3dly, Try your state by your thoughts of the grace of God:—what your thoughts of God's holy law are; and what your thoughts of your own righteousness are:—and then what your thoughts of the grace of God are. And wheresoever the grace of God is, there will be right thoughts of it framed in the heart; and they will be many, and serious, and very deep, and reverent; for the matter is very great. What greater thing can a man be exercised about than the grace of God towards great sinners? Oh, what a weighty subject is this for meditation! and this I dare say, that he that hath but few and mean thoughts about the grace of God, never had one dram of the grace of God in himself: for all the grace that is in believers is but as a little drop from this great fountain; and wherever it is really communicated, the fountain from which it flows will be greatly admired.—There are a few things concerning these thoughts that I would speak a little to.

(1.) See that your thoughts of the law, and of the grace of God, and of the righteousness of Christ, be such as are squared with the word of God:—we must think of these things as God hath spoken of them in his word; and not frame thoughts to ourselves, from our own imagination.—What saith the word of God concerning the law, and the righteousness of Christ, and the grace of God appearing therein?

(2.) Let your thoughts of these things be such as you have when you are nearest to God.—Pray take heed to this: all that are Christians, understand a little of this, what it is to be nearer to God one time than another. If you are true Christians, you will know what this means; if you are not, this direction belongs not to you. There are sometimes when believers are nearer to God than at other times; and always, when a man is nearest to God, his thoughts of the things of God are best:—he would be a happy Christian that could always retain the same sentiments and sense of the things of God that he sometimes hath. When a person is near to God, and he hath lifted up upon him the light of his countenance; when the glory of God appears before the eyes of a man, what doth the man then think of the holy law of God, of the righteousness of Christ, and of the grace of God? Oh, there is nothing else that makes any considerable appearance in the eyes of a man at that time. I am very well persuaded that the most confident pleaders of the cause of self-righteousness, the men that plead most for being justified by the righteousness of the law, if God would but speak to them, and bring them near to himself, they would lay their hands upon their mouths and speak no more. *Behold I am vile*, saith Job, *what shall I answer thee? I will lay my hand upon my mouth. Once have I spoken, but I will not answer; yea, twice, but I will proceed no further. I have heard of thee by the hearing of the ear, but now mine eye seeth thee, therefore I abhor myself, and repent in dust and ashes*, Job 40:4, 5 and 42:5, 6.—Labour, I say, to retain the same impressions of these great things of God, that you had when you were nearest to God.

(3.) Labour to have such thoughts of the law of God, and the righteousness of Christ, and the grace of God, as you find exercised souls have. Labour to entertain the same thoughts of these things, as you find the generality of exercised souls have. What a learned scholar saith of these things, is not so much to the purpose; for they may mistake in many things; but what is the current, general sense of all them on whose consciences God ever wrought; in whose consciences there is any light? What is the general sense that they all have of these things? Labour for that. Was there ever any Christian under the hand of the Spirit of God, that had any difference in this point? Never one in this world: they all forsake the law, and despair of life by it; they all commend the righteousness of Christ, and betake themselves to it: they all admire the grace of God, and venture their all upon it. Whatsoever difference there may be about this or the other ordinance, or in other lesser things, yet as to those things, in which the very nature and heart of the new creature lies, there is no scruple at all about them.

(4.) Labour for such thoughts of these things as you know you must have, and will have when you come to die. Labour for such thoughts of the law of God, and of the righteousness of Christ, and of the grace of God, as you will have when you come to die. Dying thoughts are commonly the truest. When a man is launching into eternity, when the man hath, as it were, put one foot off from the shore of time, and is leaving this world—what a poor mean thing is this little cottage of self-righteousness? It is as nothing in the man's eyes; but that great palace of the righteousness of Christ, and the great tenor of free grace, in bestowing it on the unworthy—what a glorious thing doth it appear to be? Dying people do not use to brag of their lives, and their great attainments: *Lord Jesus, receive my spirit*, saith dying Stephen, Acts 7:59. 'I am waiting for one good turn more from Christ. Now, I am dying, Lord, take my soul.' *Although my house be not so with God*, saith dying David, *yet he hath made with me an everlasting covenant, ordered in all things, and sure: this is all my salvation, and all my desire*, 2 Sam. 23:5.

(5.) Labour to have such thoughts of these things as all men will have, both good and bad, both on the right hand and on the left hand of the Judge, at that great day. The world will once be all of a mind, that is questionless; in the main things all believers are of one mind now: and in the main things all unbelievers are in one mind; and unbelievers reckon Christ crucified weakness and foolishness: and all believers reckon him the wisdom and the power of God; but when the last day comes, they will be all of one mind exactly, both good and bad; they on the right hand, and they on the left hand too. If this question were to go round to all the miserable assembly at the Judge's left hand, What think you of the law of God?—'Oh! it is a holy, powerful, dreadful law,' would they say. 'We lie under it for evermore, and feel the lashes of it.' What think you of the righteousness of Christ? 'It is a safe garment, happy they that are clothed with it; we have refused it, and therefore we are destroyed.' The despised grace of God is there precious to them: we use to say, 'Truth is the daughter of time:' if I may reflect upon the words. 'Truth is the daughter of eternity:' and this day of eternity will bring forth truth to all men, as to these three points:—The holiness of the law of God—The virtue of the righteousness of Christ—and, The dominion of the grace of God. These are points that all the damned in hell, and all the glorified in heaven, will eternally have the same sentiments of; but with wonderful difference as to their share therein. The damned hear nothing but the curse of the law: but it is the happiness of the glorified in being delivered from it. Rom. 5:21, *That as sin hath reigned unto death, so grace reigns through righteousness unto eternal life by Jesus Christ our Lord.* The words just going before are, ver. 20, *Where sin abounded, grace did much more abound.* There are two great things that have filled this world:—there were but two men in it that are worth talking of—the first Adam and the second; and if you know these well, it is no great matter what you are ignorant of. The first Adam is the law; the second Adam is the gospel: to the former belongs hell; and to the latter heaven. Now, these two great men brought in two great things:—the first man brought in that woful thing we call sin; and the second man brought in that brave thing we call grace; and both these are great principles: sin reigns, and all that it reigns over it destroys; it reigns unto death: and grace reigns, and all it reigns over it saves; *Grace reigns unto eternal life, through righteousness, by Jesus Christ our Lord.*

SERMON V.

GAL. 2:21

[Latter Clause.]

If righteousness come by the law, then Christ is dead in vain.

I DO not frustrate the grace of God; for if righteousness come by the law, then is Christ dead in vain. You have heard of the connection of this verse with the preceding part of the chapter: and of its relation to the scope of the apostle, and to that point of gospel doctrine that he is there proving; and that is, That a man is not justified by the law, but by Christ, or by faith in him. And this verse contains two arguments, the first of which I have already spoken to, and finished. In the former part of the words, *I do not frustrate the grace of God*, would the apostle say, 'If I seek righteousness by the works of the law, I should frustrate the grace of God;' and from this I have spoken at some length to four points of doctrine.

1st, The grace of God shines gloriously in justifying a sinner by faith in Jesus Christ.

2dly, That it is a horrible sin to frustrate the grace of God.

3dly, That all who seek to be justified by the law, do frustrate the grace of God.

4thly, This is a sin that no godly man, no sound believer, can be guilty of;—and this I observed from the apostle's saying, *I do not frustrate the grace of God*. And this was spoken by him as he was a believer, and not as an extraordinary officer of the church.

I am now to enter upon the apostle's second argument, in the latter part of the words, *For if righteousness come by the law, then Christ is dead in vain*. You may see, by the different character, that the word come, is there added by our translators, to make the sense more smooth: according to the running of the word in the original, it is, *If righteousness by the law, the Christ is dead in vain*.—'If it be by the law, if it come by the law, then Christ is dead in vain.' There are implied, and contained in these words two negatives, and two positives; and I would speak a little to each. The two negatives are these:—

I. That the righteousness that justifies a sinner comes not by the law.

II. That Christ died not in vain.

The two positives that are contained in the words are these:—

I. That if righteousness came by the law, then Christ died in vain.

II. That it is a horrible sin to make Christ's death to be in vain. And how a sinner can be guilty of it, you shall hear.

I. The first negative in the text is, That righteousness comes not by the law; and this is implied, when the apostle speaks of it, as a principle from whence so absurd a conclusion would follow: it is plainly intimated that righteousness comes not by the law, because the apostle saith, if it did do so, *Christ was dead in vain*.

I would speak a little to this—that the righteousness of a sinner for justification before God, comes not by the law. There is nothing that a man doth according to the law, there is nothing that a man suffers according to the law, that can be his righteousness before God; and there is something of both these attempted by men, but both in vain. This I would prove, that no sinner can have righteousness by the law.

(1.) The law discovers sin, and that is the apostle's argument, Rom. 3:21, *Therefore by the deeds of the law shall no flesh be justified in his sight; for by the law is the knowledge of sin.* There is no sin in the law; but the knowledge of sin by the law, is the knowledge of a contrary by its contrary. The law is perfectly holy; but this strict rule discovers the crookedness that is in man's heart. *By the law is the knowledge of sin,* Rom. 3:20. *But that no man is justified by the law in the sight of God, it is evident, for the just shall live by faith.* Gal. 3:11. It was evident to Paul, and it is evident to believers, but it can never be evident to an unbeliever, that no man is justified by the law, or by the works of it.

(2.) No man can be justified by the law, because the law condemns every sin, and every sinner for every sin. The law of God is so strict, that it condemns every sin. Now, that which condemns, cannot justify; for these two are contrary, Gal. 3:10, *As many as are of the works of the law, are under the curse.* The apostle Paul was a bold divine, he spoke the truth of God boldly, and cared not what men thought of it. Had the apostle said, 'As many as break the law, are under the curse,' we would have thought that pretty tolerable; but saith he, *As many as are of the works of the law, are under the curse.* Why so? Because their works are not perfect: for it is written, saith the apostle, *Cursed is every one that continueth not in all things which are written in the book of the law to do them.* The law curseth every one that cannot fulfil it: if a man could fulfil the whole law of God, and transgress but in one point, yet that one sin would be condemned by the law, and the sinner for it.

(3.) No man can be justified by the works of the law, because every man is a sinner. Rom. 3:19, 20, *What things soever the law saith, it saith to them that are under the law, that every mouth may be stopped, and that all the world may become guilty before God: therefore by the deeds of the law shall no flesh be justified in the sight of God; for by the law is the knowledge of sin.* The question that the apostle is there upon, is on this point, that is so great a point in the Christian religion: How shall a sinner be justified before God? It is not how a holy man may be justified;—it is not how a man that never sinned may be justified: but it is, How shall a *sinner* be justified? A man that is flesh be justified? Now, saith the apostle, there no *flesh* justified in the sight of God.

(4.) The law knows no mercy. Mercy and grace belong to another court than the law: *The law came by Moses; but grace and truth came by Jesus Christ,* John 1:17. Condemnation for sin belongs to the law, but justification from sin belongs to the gospel. The law hath nothing to do with the one, and the gospel hath nothing to do with the other. The law hath nothing to do to condemn them that the gospel absolves. But you will say, 'Is not this a great fault in the law, that it cannot justify a man?' The apostle speaks some way like this in Heb. 7:18, 19. Though I do believe that the apostle there rather means the Old Testament dispensation, than this law, in its more general comprehensive sense, that I am now speaking of; *For there is verily a disannulling of the commandment going before, for the weakness and unprofitableness thereof; for the law made nothing perfect, but the bringing in of a better hope did; by the which we draw nigh to God.* This is a common thought arising in the hearts of men, 'Is it not a fault in the law, that it cannot justify a man? Is it not a fault that the law can send men to hell; but not bring them to heaven?' I answer, No: It is the excellency of the law; not its fault, but its glory; for let us consider a little what the law doth about righteousness.

[1.] The law discovers and reveals a perfect righteousness; there is no surer, no better rule of righteousness in this world, than the holy law of God: therefore, when our Lord is dealing with a poor carnal legalist, a puffed-up young man, that came to him in great haste; with great zeal, running to him, like a man that would be in heaven before any body else, *Good master, what good thing shall I do to inherit eternal life?* saith our Lord, 'You know, no man can come to heaven, but he that is perfectly righteous; now the only rule of perfect righteousness is the law of God: and, seeing thou art in the vein for doing, *keep the commandments.*' The poor man, not knowing his own heart, nor the breadth of God's law, replies, *All these things have I kept from my youth up.* Saith our Lord, 'I will prove thee a breaker of the law, and a gross one too; *Go and sell all that thou hast, and give to the poor; and follow me, and thou shalt have treasures in heaven.*' Not that a title to eternal life comes to any man by giving his estate to the poor; but our Lord hereby discovers the rottenness of the poor self-justiciary's heart, that the man quickly, before all the company, discovered that his estate was more valuable to him than eternal life. Our Lord would have him give an evident proof, that his heart was disengaged from the world, and then follow him, and he should be saved; but he went away sorrowful, for he had great possessions, Matt. 19:16, etc. There is a perfect rule of righteousness in the law of God, for the most perfect creature that ever was; for sinless Adam in his state of innocency. *The law of God is perfect*: so it is often called in the word of God.

[2.] This righteousness that the law of God discovers, it also commands by its authority: all manner of righteousness is commanded by the law of God.

[3.] All sin is threatened by the law of God; yea, the want of this righteousness which it commands, is threatened by the law.

[4.] By the law the promise of eternal life is made to the righteous; for the law of God, completely considered, hath the promise of eternal life to all the obeyers of it: but never man shall reach it, because the righteousness of the law is impracticable: it requires that righteousness that no man can perform; and, therefore, what it promises no man can attain to. This the apostle calls the impossibility of the law: so it is in the original; we read it, *What the law could not do, in that it was weak through the flesh*, Rom. 8:3. The true reason why the law cannot give life, is because of the *flesh* of them that are under it: no man can fulfil the righteousness of the law, and, therefore, no man can attain to life by the law.—So much for the *first* negative implied here, That no righteousness can come by the works of the law.

II. The other negative is this, That Christ died not in vain. Now, this word, in vain, respects two things:—1*st*, That is said to be done in vain, which is needless. 2*dly*, That is said to be in vain, that is unprofitably done. Now, neither of these can be said of the death of Christ: there was great *need* of his dying, and great *good* came by his dying, and, therefore, he died not in vain.

(1.) There was great need of Christ's dying, and that upon manifold respects; I will name a few.

[1.] In regard of the decree of God, there was a necessity of his dying; and this our Lord had in his eye, when he was come just upon the borders of dying, John 12:27, *Now is my soul troubled, What shall I say? Father, save me from this hour; but for this cause came I unto this hour*; where our Lord hath respect to the necessity of his dying, upon the account of the divine appointment.

[2.] It was necessary upon the account of the covenant between the Father and the Son: Christ promised to die, and, therefore, he must be as good as his word:—*A body thou hast prepared me; then said I, Lo, I come (in the volume of the book it is written of me), to do thy will, O God.* And what was that will of God? Dying was his will, and the blessed consequences of it. Heb. 10:5, 7.

[3.] It was needful upon the account of the scriptures: and this our Lord insists on frequently. The scriptures of the Old Testament foretold Christ's death: there were many predictions and prophecies of it; many types and shadows of it; therefore our Lord tells his disciples, Luke 24:44, *These are the words that I spake unto you, whilst I was yet with you, that all things must be fulfilled, which are written in the law of Moses, and in the prophets, and in the Psalms, concerning me.* And again, *Thus is it written, and thus it behoved Christ to suffer, and to rise from the dead the third day*, Luke 24:46. There was a necessity of it for the fulfilling of the scriptures, and, therefore, our Lord rebuked Peter, when he offered to make a defence for his master: *How then shall the scriptures be fulfilled, that thus it must be?* Matt. 26:54. 'Put up thy sword, man, this is no place for that work: the scriptures are fulfilling.'

[4.] There was a necessity of Christ's death for the salvation of his people. Their justification, and their salvation, were only brought about by the death of Jesus Christ.

II. And that leads me to the *second* head—Christ's death was not in vain: for there was great fruit and profit by it.

[1.] It brought in an everlasting righteousness, which should stand accepted before God: this is what our Lord wrought out by his death, foretold by the prophet Daniel, chap. 9:24, *To bring in everlasting righteousness.*

[2.] There was not only a righteousness brought in, but by Christ's death there was a purchase made; a purchase of grace and glory for his people. The death of our Lord Jesus Christ purchased great things for us, even all things that we enjoy. It did not indeed purchase the covenant of grace; for the covenant of grace sent Christ; but yet it purchased all the blessings of the covenant; for the grand condition of that covenant was, that Christ must buy all the good things contained in it by the price of his own blood.

[3.] Christ died not in vain, for his blood confirmed and sealed the charter: *This is my blood of the New Testament, which is shed for many, for the remission of sins, drink ye all of it*, Matt. 26:27, 28. Christ's death confirmed the covenant, and made it a Testament, Heb. 9:15, 20.

[4.] Christ's death was not in vain, but for great profit: for thereby a way to heaven was made plain to believers, a patent way to heaven. How blessedly doth the apostle speak of this, Heb. 10:19, 20, *Having therefore, brethren, boldness to enter into the holiest by the blood of Jesus: by a new and living way which he hath consecrated for us, through the vail, that is to say, his flesh.*—The meaning is, his flesh rent; the consecrating of the way, was by rending the flesh of Jesus Christ.—The righteousness that justifies us—the blessings that make us happy—the covenant that secures them—and the way to heaven, are all by the death of Jesus Christ:—and they are strangers to all these things, who do not know that their way to them, lies through this vail of the slain Son of God.—So much for the two negatives.

2*dly*, I am now to speak to the two positives in the words.

(1.) That if righteousness comes by the law, then is Christ dead in vain. I have told you that righteousness comes not by the law, and that Christ did not die in vain. Now, the apostle joins them together, and shews what a strange aspect they have one upon another. *If righteousness come by the law, then Christ is dead in vain.* This is an inference that will necessarily follow, If righteousness comes by the law, then Christ died in vain, to work out righteousness:—if righteousness comes by the law, Christ's death was in vain in the main end of it, *viz.* to work out righteousness.—My friends, I would have you consider this with yourselves, and this one thought may serve to rectify many mistakes:—Our Lord Jesus Christ did not die to make hard things easy, to make a hard way to heaven easy; but Christ died to make impossible things *certain*. He did not die to make it more easy to get to heaven than it was before; but he died to make *certain* a way to heaven, that was *impossible* before. Rom. 8:3, *What the law could not do, in that it was weak through the flesh, God, sending his own Son in the likeness of sinful flesh, and for sin condemned sin in the flesh*:—and again, Gal. 3:21, *If there had been a law that could have given righteousness, verily righteousness had been by the law*. But because there was no law that could give righteousness to man, therefore Christ came to bring about that which was altogether impossible. How unworthily do they think of Jesus Christ, and the grand concern of his death, that look upon it only as purchasing a new law, whereby men might come to heaven on easier terms than they could by the old! Christ came to purchase a new way to heaven: a way that none could make but he: a way without which none could ever have come to heaven:—and really (though I acknowledge that about things unrevealed, and about the secret things of God, men should be sober) that notion of the possibility of the salvation of the Heathen, that never heard of Jesus Christ, is condemned in this text. If a Pagan, that never heard of Christ, may be saved, then is Christ dead in vain. If the end that Christ died for, can be reached any other way, then certainly Christ died in vain. If the righteousness that Christ died for, could have been attained any other way; if the fulfilling of the law, that Christ underwent, in order to this righteousness; if these could have been done any other way, Christ died in vain. But these things are not so.

(2.) The second positive is, That making Christ's death to be in vain, is a horrible sin.—The apostle is here arguing from absurdities; and he argues from two of the greatest that can enter into the minds of men.—'If you seek righteousness by the law, you frustrate the grace of God, and what a wretched creature is that!—If you seek righteousness by the law, you make Christ's death in vain; and can you do any thing worse, than to kick against the grace of God, and to make the death of Christ in vain?' These sins are very great. But you will say, Can any man make Christ's death in vain? No. No man, nor any devil neither, nor all the devils together, can frustrate the virtue of Christ's death; it is above the reach of hell and earth. The devil, and the wicked world, thought to make Christ's life in vain, by putting him to death; to put an end to his doctrine, and life, and disciples, by killing him; and to put an end to all, by keeping him in the grave: but to make Christ's death in vain, is utterly impossible: it is so certain, so reverend a transaction of Divine Providence, contrived in so much wisdom, that its end must necessarily be reached. But, though no man can make Christ's death to be in vain really—yet,

[1.] A man may make it in vain to *himself*; he may reduce himself into the same case as if Christ had never died. *Behold, I Paul, say unto you, that if you be circumcised, Christ shall profit you nothing*, Gal. 5:2. A strange word! *Christ shall profit you nothing!*—Was the apostle Paul a man that preached an unprofitable Christ? No: but *You* render him *vain*, if you seek righteousness by the law. Ver. 4, *Christ is become of no effect to you; whosoever is justified by the law, is fallen from grace*. A justified man by the law, there never was in this world: but the apostle speaks of it here as supposing the best; supposing they had got all that they could have devised, for their justification by the law; supposing that they had obeyed the law more perfectly than any sinner ever had done, saith the apostle, 'This is all the benefit you would reap by it, Christ's righteousness would be of no effect to you.'—A man makes Christ's death to be in vain to *himself*, when he doth not lay hold of its power, and virtue by faith.

[2.] A man makes Christ's death to be in vain, by doing all that *he* can to make it so; though he doth not do so in fact. And you will find this the rule of God's dealing; he measures men's wickedness, and judges of their actions, by the native design of them; though they never reach it. In all acts of dishonouring God, and rebellion against him, God deals with men according to their sinful *intentions*, in these sins, though they fall far short of taking effect. A sinner, by his self-righteousness, cannot make Christ's death to be in vain; but he doth all that he can to make it so: and this is what the apostle means here when he saith, *If righteousness come by the law, then Christ is dead in vain.* 'You do all that you can to make Christ's death in vain.'

I should now come to speak something of the greatness of this sin, of making Christ's death in vain; of entertaining any principles or practices, that have a tendency that way. But I cannot enter upon this now.

SERMON VI.

Gal. 2:21.

[Latter Clause.]

If righteousness come by the law, then Christ is dead in vain.

I *DO not frustrate the grace of God, for if righteousness come by the law, then Christ is dead in vain.* The most sacred things revealed to us in the word of God, are these two—the grace of God—and the death of Christ; and they are joined close together; they are two things that all who have a mind to be saved must constantly have in their eye;—the grace of God—and the death of Christ: and yet there are not a few that despise both; that frustrate the one, and make the other in vain: and this charge the apostle lays upon an error, that he is reproving the Galatian churches for, and that was their seeking righteousness by the law, and the works of it. I have spoken unto these words, as containing two strong arguments against seeking of righteousness by the works of the law.

1*st*, That thereby the grace of God is frustrated.

2*dly*, That thereby Christ's death is made to be in vain;—as far as the wickedness of man can do the one or the other.

Upon this second argument I was the last time, and spoke something to four notes that I drew from it; two of them negatives, and two of them positives.

1*st*, That there is no righteousness, for the justifying a sinner, that can come by the law. Never man got to heaven by the law: never a man got to heaven by his own good doings. All go to hell for their own evil doings; but no man, since sin came into the world, ever went to heaven by his own good doings. That I proved.

2*dly*, The other negative contained here is, That Christ hath not died in vain:—for the apostle doth certainly imply that he did not die in vain, when he aggravates the sin of seeking righteousness by the law, as inferring so horrible an absurdity; for he is pointing forth the heinousness of this sin in very dreadful colours, on purpose to make it hated.

The two positive truths contained here are these:—

(1.) If there was any righteousness could come by the law, Christ's death would be in vain. Christ had died in vain, if any man could have stood accepted before God, without the virtue of his death. The virtue of Christ's death, was of efficacy for the rendering men accepted before God, even before he came into the world. The fathers, that died before Christ came, were saved by the same faith, that believers on Christ were saved by, after he came. So saith the apostle, Acts 15:11, *But we believe, that through the grace of our Lord Jesus Christ, we shall be saved, even as they*; comparing the Old Testament and the New Testament dispensation together.

(2.) The second positive was this, That making Christ's death to be in vain, was a great and horrible sin. I told you, it was impossible to make it vain really, or to hinder any of its excellent fruits. As no man could hinder the solid causes of it, so no man can hinder the strong fruit of it:—the fruit of the death of Christ is quite out of the reach of men or devils. When our Lord was in his humbled state, the devil could, upon permission, carry his body up to the pinnacle of the temple: but he had no power to hurt him. When he was in this world, one wicked disciple betrayed him, and the rest cowardly forsook him; his enemies prevailed against him in the hour and power of darkness, and took away his life; but for the fruit and virtue of his death, that is lodged higher than man can reach: yet men may make Christ's death to be in vain.

1*st*, To *themselves*.—A poor creature, that hath not faith in Christ, gets no more good of him, than if Christ had never died, or if Christ's death had been in vain; than if he had never died, or had died to no purpose.

2*dly*, God will always reckon with men according to their design in sinning. All sin is a breaking of God's law; but yet God's law will not be broken, but will break all the breakers of it:—sin is counted, and charged as a dishonouring of God; and yet the Lord's honour is advanced in the ruin of the sinner.

I proceed now to shew you the dreadfulness of this sin, of doing any thing that hath a tendency to the making Christ's death to be in vain. I would, 1*st*, aggravate this sin in its just measures; and, 2*dly*, come to the Application, and shew how common a sin this is.—It is a great sin to make Christ's death in vain, in the way wherein it is practicable; and in that sense that the apostle here means.

1*st*, Let us consider God; whensoever we are to take the just measure of any sin, we are to take it with respect to God. This is the grand aggravation of all sin, that it is against God. When David is confessing, with deep remorse, his vile sins of adultery and murder, which were sins against his neighbour; *Against thee, thee only, have I sinned,* saith he, *and done this evil in thy sight*, Psa. 51:4. Now let us consider what this sin doth with respect to God;—and here we must take up some account of God, according to the gospel revelation of him: for as Jesus Christ is not revealed by the law, so neither is the sin of rendering his death to be in vain, aggravated by the law, as it is by the discoveries made of God in the gospel. It is a sin against God the Father, and against God the Son, and against God the Holy Ghost.

(1.) To make this sin appear in its greatness, first, it is against God the Father wofully. The greatest contrivance that ever the infinitely wise God had, for the glory of his name, was the working out of eternal redemption, by the death of his own Son, for a company of lost sinners. This is the chief of the ways of God: all things revealed of him, and of his counsel, and of his purpose, and of his actions, are all but low, in regard of this; all others are subservient to this act of Divine Providence: this is the chief of the ways of God. Let us see what treasures of his glory are concerned therein.

[1.] There is infinite wisdom in contriving a way, that the understanding of angels and men could not find out, and when it is revealed, it cannot be fully known. It is said concerning the angels, that they *desire to pry into those things*; into those things that the Spirit reveals, *concerning the sufferings of Christ, and the glory that should follow*, 1 Pet. 1:11, 12. Now, if the glorified angels in heaven be students of Jesus Christ, and of the glory of his sufferings, and of the glory that was the fruit thereof, how much more should men do so! There is a *manifold wisdom of God* that shines therein, and is perceived by, and made known to them. Eph. 3:10, *To the intent that now unto the principalities and powers in heavenly places, might be made known, by the church, the manifold wisdom of God, according to his eternal purpose, which he purposed in Christ Jesus our Lord.* Now, where the wisdom of God is so much concerned, judge you what a provocation it must needs be, when foolish man does all that may be to defeat this wisdom. *Christ as crucified*, is called *the wisdom of God, and power of God*: but unto poor ignorant man he is foolishness and weakness, 1 Cor. 1:23, 24.

[2.] In this way of saving us by the death of Christ, there is the great grace, and mercy of God, that he would magnify. Now, what a great sin must it be to count all this in vain? *God so loved the world, that he gave his only begotten Son, that whosoever believeth on him, should not perish, but should have everlasting life*, John 3:16. *God commendeth his love to us, in that whilst we were yet sinners, Christ died for us*, Rom. 5:8. And shall this love be so far despised, as that a man shall endeavour to make it be in vain?

[3.] This is a contrivance, also, for the magnifying the holy law of God. The Lord is so zealous for his law, that he will part with it for no man's sake. He will not abate an ace of the rigour of his law, for the saving of the world: but he hath found out a way to give the law all its due, and yet to give the poor sinner all that he needs. This is marvellous the law gets all the righteousness it demands, and the sinner gets all the justification he needs: the law shall be honoured, and justice shall be satisfied, and the sinner shall be saved, and not destroyed: *God is just, and the justifier of him that believes in Jesus Christ*, Rom. 3:26.

(2.) This sin is also aggravated, as it is against God the Son. Let us consider what Christ's death was; it was the greatest concernment of a divine person. It was a great deal better to say, all the martyrs died in vain: it were a far less sin to say, as the ungodly world doth, 'That they threw away their lives, with their folly and preciseness, when they might have saved them with a word, or a bow, or a cringe, to the idols of the nations.' It were a great sin to say so you know how the apostle aggravates this as a great absurdity, as to the doctrine of the resurrection: *Then they also that are fallen asleep in Christ are perished*, 1 Cor. 15:18. But that was a small matter, in regard of making Christ's death to be in vain, which was a special concern of a divine person. The blood shed, was the *blood of God*, Acts 20:28. And can God's blood be shed in vain? It was the lowest step, and the crowning act of Christ's sufferings: all that went before would not serve; the low estate he was born in, and the manifold afflictions he lived in; his being seized on in the night with soldiers, and lanterns, as a thief; his being bound, his being scourged, his being nailed to the cross in torment—this will not do neither. The crowning, and saving act of our Lord Jesus Christ was his dying. It was also the grand pledge of our Lord's love, the great discovery, the great proof of his love to his people. *He loved his church, and gave himself for it*, Eph. 5:25. *He loved us, and washed us from our sins in his own blood*, Rev. 1:5. *Greater love hath no man than this, that a man lay down his life for his friend*, i.e., 'A greater testimony of love than this can no man give, than to part with his life for them that he loves,' John 15:13. Now, judge you, what a great sin it must needs be for a man to lay an imputation of vanity, and unprofitableness, on this great pledge of the love of our Lord Jesus Christ, to say he died in vain?

(3.) This sin of charging Christ's death to be in vain, is a sin against the Holy Ghost; it is sinning against the Holy Ghost. We find concerning the Holy Ghost, that he framed that body that our Lord lived in, and died in; he was conceived of the Holy Ghost, Matt. 1:20. Next, Christ was anointed by the Spirit without measure:—which was our Lord's text at Nazareth. *The Spirit of the Lord is upon me, because he hath anointed me to preach the gospel to the poor*, Luke 4:18.—*The Spirit of the Lord is upon me*. The Holy Ghost did assist him, and witness to him, in his death and at his resurrection. And therefore, when Stephen was preaching Christ, to Christ's murderers, he aggravates their sin by this, *Ye stiff-necked, and uncircumcised in heart and ears, ye do always resist the Holy Ghost; as your fathers did, so do ye*. Especially, this sin is greatest when the Holy Ghost is convicting men, by the law, of their vileness; and convincing men, by the gospel, of the relief that is offered by Christ Jesus:—and a great many struggle against the Spirit of God in both these cases. It is a long while before the sinner yields to the conviction of the Spirit, that all things are naught within, and that there is nothing right in them; and it is as long, many times, before they yield to the Holy Ghost, in venturing their souls on Christ as a sufficient Saviour.—And thus you see how this sin is aggravated, as being against God the Father, God the Son, and God the Holy Ghost. But to come a little lower.

(4.) This sin of making Christ's death to be in vain, is a dreadful sin against *others* also. It is a sin against sinners—and against believers also. It is so far a sin against others, that every unbeliever, every stubborn refuser of life and salvation by Christ's death, doth, in a manner, teach all others to run on in the same way of destruction that he takes:—He that saith Christ died in vain, doth in a manner cut the throats of the whole world; for all that are saved, must be saved by the virtue of his death. It is also a great sin against believers. The apostle aggravates this in the case of scandal; and the scandal that the apostle there speaks of, was in the untender use of Christian liberty. You sin against Christ, and then you, also, *cause your weak brother to perish, for whom Christ died*, 1 Cor. 8:11, 12. The word [*perish*] there, might well have been rendered in another English word that is less offensive: '*Through thy knowledge shall the weak brother perish*, or rather, *stumble and fall*, for whom Christ died for when you sin so against the brethren, and wound their weak conscience, you sin against Christ.'—Now, the thing that I drive at is this; If the apostle thus aggravates the untender use of Christian liberty, without a due regard to the weakness of other Christians, that may be overthrown and hurt thereby, how much more must this sin be aggravated, of endeavouring to make Christ's death to be in vain? For,

[1.] This strikes at the foundation of the Christian's faith: for if a man hath any faith at all, it must be built on Christ's death; that you will make no question of: that faith which is not built on a dying Christ, is but a perilous dream, God awaken all from it that are in it! When the apostle is placing the foundation of his confidence, in that song of triumph, Rom. 8:33, 34, the very first word of it is, *Who shall lay any thing to the charge of God's elect? it is Christ that died.*

[2.] This sin strikes against the foundation of all the Christian's peace and comfort. Not only is the believer's state secured by his faith in Jesus Christ; but his quiet, and the calm of his conscience, are maintained also the same way. If the virtue of the death of Christ be taken away, all the joy of believers goes with it: for it stands only in this. The death of Christ is of eternal virtue and value, and, therefore, the believer's joy springs up perpetually.

[3.] This sin strikes against all the praises of the saints on earth, and of the glorified in heaven. To make Christ's death in vain, would drown all the music both of heaven and earth. No believer here could give any praise; and there would be no praises there. The song of Moses and the Lamb rises from this—the Lamb was slain; *Worthy is the Lamb, that was slain, to receive power, and riches, and wisdom, and strength, and honour, and glory, and blessing*, Rev. 5:12. They sing that praise eternally, because they eternally feel the virtue of his blood.

Application. I come now to make some improvement of this point.—If it be so dreadful a sin to make the death of Christ to be in vain, How fearful a thing is it, that yet this sin is so common? I know multitudes think themselves as free from it, as the Galatians, to whom Paul wrote, thought themselves free from the error he charges them with: but men's imaginations are no proof of their innocency. It is here charged upon them that they *were* guilty of it; otherwise they would not thus have been charged, by the Holy Ghost, with the sin of making Christ's death to be in vain, as much as man can do, and as to *themselves*. I will instance in a few things, as proofs of this.

1st, To begin with that instance in the text, of *seeking righteousness* by the law:—Whosoever they be that seek righteousness by the law, these men make Christ's death to be in vain. If they do so, *Christ is become of no effect to them; Christ profits them nothing*, Gal. 5:2, 4. 'But who are these,' say you, 'that seek righteousness by the law?' I might answer this question with another, Who doth not? Every body doth, in one measure or another. Seeking righteousness by the law, is when a poor sinner thinks he can be able, some time or another, to do that which God will be gracious to him for: whether it be a work of the law, or a work of the gospel, it is all one for that: when a man thinks to do that for which God will accept him as a righteous man, and account him no more a sinner—this is one that makes Christ's death to be in vain: for if it were possible that any man could be righteous before God, by any thing that he could do, saith the apostle, *Christ is dead in vain*.

2dly, All apostates from the Christian profession are chargeable with this sin of making Christ's death to be in vain; and there are not a few of them in the age we live in. They are so dreadfully painted forth in the word of God, that, if I may so say, their very picture hath scared many an honest heart; many honest-hearted believers have been scared dreadfully with seeing the picture of these apostates. It is said, *They crucify to themselves the Son of God afresh, and put him to open shame*, Heb. 6:6. *Of how much sorer punishment, suppose ye, shall he be thought worthy, who hath trodden under foot the Son of God, and hath counted the blood of the covenant, wherewith he was sanctified, an unholy thing, and hath done despite to the Spirit of grace?* Heb. 10:29. These persons once made a profession that there was virtue in the blood of Christ; but now they are come to renounce it.—I am truly afraid of this thing; it hath often come in my mind: we have a generation amongst us, that are plagues come from hell; men called Deists, which is nothing else but a new court word for an Atheist: and they that are called Socinians, which is only a more civil word for a Turk; people who do not believe that Jesus Christ is the Son of God, but only a good man that died at Jerusalem. They believe not that Christ died for any other ends than to testify the truth of his doctrine, and to set us an example to suffer patiently for the truth. My thoughts are not only about the horror of this heresy, that all should tremble at; but my real jealousy is, that there are amongst them not a few that have sinned the sin against the Holy Ghost; that have come up to blaspheming the Spirit of God, and the blood of the Everlasting Covenant, shed by the Son of God. The Spirit of God hath written their doom, and let the saints wait in fear and patience, till God execute it: for execute it he will, were their quality ever so high, their number ever so great, their wisdom and power ever so strong. They are combined against the Son of God, and he will be avenged upon them; and let the faith and prayer of the saints hasten it.

3dly, All that *seek not* righteousness, and eternal life, through Jesus Christ, and his death, they are guilty of this sin, of thinking, and counting that Christ died in vain. All that do not seek eternal life by Christ, are guilty of this sin. And how many such poor creatures are there, that for as often as they have read the Bible, and for as often as they have heard the gospel preached, yet to this day they never saw any need of the death of Christ for themselves? They run away with a notion, that it was needful the Son of God should come into the world, and die for men: but they were never convinced of this, that it was simply needful for *thee*, and for *thy* salvation; that unless the Son of God had come, and laid down his life for *thee*, thou couldst not be saved.—Every man must be convinced of his *personal* need of Christ's death, that ever expects to get any good thereby.

4thly, A great many poor creatures never saw any glory in the death of Christ. I do acknowledge that the cross of Christ was the greatest and thickest vail upon his glory; when he was forsaken by his followers; when he was insulted over by his enemies: when heaven and earth forsook him: and hell was enlarged against him. What was more low than the man Christ, when he died? Yet, notwithstanding, to a believer, the great beaming forth of the glory of God shined in the face of Christ crucified. Herein shined the manifold wisdom and grace of God. Every lash, in a manner, that the Father laid upon the Son, proclaimed aloud the love of the Father, that put him to that suffering, and the love of the Son that underwent it. The poor Jews were but sorry believers, John 11:36; when they saw Christ weeping at Lazarus's grave (although I believe Christ wept not so much for Lazarus, as in contemplation of the common calamity of mankind; and it may be, this was the first grave that ever Christ was so near to in his life), *Behold*, say they, *how he loved him!* Surely, then, Christ's cross should far more teach us to cry out, 'Behold, how he loved his people!' than Lazarus's grave, and Christ's weeping over it, did the Jews, to say, *Behold, how he loved him!* Christ's dying for his people, proclaimed his love to them indeed; but yet a great many see no glory in all this.

5thly, Many poor people have no business with Christ, about the virtue of his death; they have no employment for him about that thing, to have the virtue of the death of Christ applied to them for their salvation. This is that the apostle was so mighty earnest for, but they have no thought, no understanding of it: *That I may know him, and the power of his resurrection, and the fellowship of his sufferings, being made conformable to his death*. What was this conformity to the death of Christ, that Paul was here labouring for? Was it only wishing that he was a dead man? No, no; he would have and find the virtue of Christ's death quickening him: raising him up, and saving him more and more.

I will tell you, there are some things about the grave of Christ, that should make every believer's heart to be much about it, and to make us visit it daily by faith.

(1.) There the law is buried, there the old husband is laid, that we can never be well till we are divorced from. The apostle tells us several things concerning this, Col. 2:14, 15, *Blotting out the hand-writing of ordinances, that was against us, which was contrary to us, and took it out of the way, nailing it to his cross.* There were few eyes so good, as to be able to see the condemnation of the law, nailed to the cross of Jesus Christ; to see sin condemned by him, as the word is, Rom. 8:3, *He condemned sin in his flesh,* being made a sacrifice for it. Therefore, when the apostle is, in the 7th chapter of the Romans, speaking of the difference between the law and the gospel—between a natural state and a believer's—he resembles it plainly to this, to the state of a woman that hath two husbands. The first husband was the law, and a dreadful one it was; no fruit was brought forth by that marriage, but that which was unto death.—Now, she must be sure that this husband be dead, before she can be lawfully married to Jesus Christ. Ver. 3, *If whilst her husband liveth, she be married to another man, she shall be called an adulteress: but if her husband be dead, she is free from the law; and so she is no adulteress, although she be married to another man.*

(2.) In the grave of Christ, by faith, believers are to see that their sin is buried.—Saith the apostle, Heb. 9:26, *He hath put away sin by the sacrifice of himself.* 'He put away sin:' he hath so far put it away, that it shall never rise up in judgment against any that the virtue of Christ's death is applied to: thereupon the apostle grounds his triumph on this, *It is Christ that died,* therefore the believer cannot be condemned (Rom. 8:34).

(3.) In Christ's death there is a charter sealed by his blood. And how should believers be exercised in looking to Christ's death on this account? There are many seals to God's covenant: seals on God's part, and seals on our part: God puts to the seal of his word, and of his oath, and of the sacraments, and of manifold repeated promises: and believers they put to their seal of faith. John 3:33, *He that hath received his testimony, hath set to his seal that God is true.* But the best and greatest seal is Christ's death, confirming the covenant. *The covenant was confirmed before of God in Christ,* saith the apostle, Gal. 3:17.

Lastly, To bring the charge of this sin yet more close; even believers themselves are not innocent of it:—not only all that seek righteousness by the law:—not only all apostates from the faith of the gospel:—not only they that seek not righteousness and life by the virtue of Christ's death;—but even believers themselves, are guilty of this sin—there is something in *their* frame that saith, 'Christ hath died in vain.'

[1.] There is conscience of sin arises many times in believers. The apostle, speaking of the Old Testament administration, finds fault with it as defective upon this account, That it did not make him that did the service perfect, as pertaining to the conscience. Heb. 9:9 and 10:1, 2, *They could not make the comers thereunto perfect, for then would not they have ceased to be offered? because that the worshippers, once purged, should have had no more conscience of sins.* Pray observe the scope of the apostle in both these chapters: he is there telling us what shadows the Jews had of that grand sacrifice, that was to be offered by the true High priest, Jesus Christ, in their daily, and weekly, and monthly sacrifices; but the greatest of all was in that grand sacrifice of atonement, that was offered up once a-year. 'Now,' saith the apostle, 'all these sacrifices do not make the comer thereunto perfect as to his conscience:' that is, 'they did not deface all conscience of sin in the Israelite: but there was a secret fear still that their sin was yet in remembrance before God.' And what is the argument with which the apostle proves that these sacrifices did not make the comers thereunto perfect? Saith the apostle, 'It is proved by this, *Because they were so often repeated.*'—The daily sacrifice was repeated every day, and the weekly sacrifice, every Sabbath-day; and the monthly sacrifice every new moon; and the yearly sacrifice, once a-year, upon the seventh month. 'Now,' saith the apostle, 'If these things could have made the comers thereunto perfect, they would not thus have needed to have been repeated.' And from this argument, he concludes the insufficiency of the legal sacrifices to quiet the conscience, and he also proves the sufficiency of Christ's sacrifice to quiet the conscience by its oneness. *But this man*, saith he, ver. 12, *after he had offered one sacrifice for sin, for ever sat down on the right hand of God*: and again, ver. 14, *By one offering, he hath for ever perfected them that are sanctified.* The case lies plainly here—every true believer, that hath acted faith on Jesus Christ distinctly, and hath lodged his eternal salvation, and his everlasting acceptance with God, on the virtue of Christ's sacrifice, this man chargeth Christ's death with being in vain, if conscience rise again, and he hearken to it. I know, sin *will be*, and conscience *will* check for sin; but remember this, Christ died not in vain; the virtue of Christ's death remains still: it made that peace that no future transgressions shall be able to weaken or impair.

[2]. In the case of sanctification. Saith the poor believer, 'The work of holiness, and sanctification, goes on slowly:' and truly so it doth; and we should see it, and bewail it greatly: Well, what then? Hath Christ died in vain? Christ's dying is sanctification: *For their sakes I sanctify myself,* saith our Lord, *that they also might be sanctified through the truth,* John 17:19. *He gave himself for us, that he might redeem us from all iniquity, and purify unto himself a peculiar people, zealous of good works,* Titus 2:14. It were a great blessing, if believers had but skill to draw, by faith, sanctifying virtue from the death of Jesus Christ. This is what the apostle is upon, Romans 6 throughout. *How shall we that are dead to sin, live any longer therein?* But how are believers dead to sin? Have they not sin living in them? *We are dead to sin in Christ,* saith the apostle; 'he died for sin, and he hath dominion over sin, and we reckon ourselves dead to sin, but alive to God, through Jesus Christ,' ver. 11.

[3.] There is weakness of faith in believers, as to the glory to come. Not only are there many qualms of conscience, and many defects in their holiness: but when believers think of the glory to come, and the great prize of their high calling, and see it great, and high, and far above them, the more they see of the glory of it, the more they see they are unworthy of it. 'May such a vile wretch as I expect this great reward of eternal life?' Yes: for Christ bought it; he hath not died in vain.—It will be best known at that day, what Christ died for, and for whom; when all the kings that he hath bought, and all the crowns that he hath purchased for them, and all the kingdoms shall be seen, it will then be known Christ died not in vain.—Every shaking of faith, as to any blessing that Christ's death purchased for his people, every shaking of that faith, hath this woful charge to be given in against it, that Christ then hath died in vain. Indeed, if the crown of life was to be enjoyed as a reward of thy works, it were a vain thing to expect it: if it were to come in as a reward for our performances, it were a dream to expect it: but, since it is the gift of God, through Jesus Christ our Lord—since Christ hath bought it—every believer should expect it: 'As great as it is, as unworthy as I am; yet, notwithstanding, the confidence of faith should be maintained.' Therefore, now, for the consolation of believers, labour by faith to drink in these two things:—That righteousness comes not by the law—and, That Christ hath not died in vain:—and what strong consolation will they yield!

(1.) Righteousness comes not by the law; and there is great comfort in this. Righteousness comes not by the law, to any man out of Christ: and there is no condemnation comes by the law, to any man *in Christ*.—If so be that men will give glory to God, and renounce their own righteousness, and all their expectations of relief that way, and betake themselves to God's device of salvation by Jesus Christ, and believe on him, as they can expect no good by the law, so they should fear no hurt by it; for, as sin hath made it impossible that the law of God should justify us, so the grace of God in Christ, hath made it impossible that the law should condemn a believer in him.—Therefore, saith the apostle, *There is now no condemnation to them that are in Christ Jesus*. Why so? *The law of the Spirit of life, in Christ Jesus, hath made me free from the law of sin and death: for what the law could not do, in that it was weak through the flesh, that God hath done by Jesus Christ, that so the righteousness of the law might be fulfilled in us*, Rom. 8:1-4.

(2.) Feed also upon this by faith, That Christ died not in vain. There is nothing you can want, nothing that you can pray for, nothing that you can ask for in time, nor enjoy to eternity, but it is contained in this, *Christ died not in vain*:—For Christ died to all those blessed purposes that are needful to make them happy for ever, that are sharers therein. Whensoever you come to have any dealings in earnest with God about salvation, and your justification, and eternal life, always remember these two things: The grace of God—and Christ's death. The law hath nothing to do in this case; it cannot *help* you whilst you are under it, but condemn you: and if you be believers, the law cannot hurt you, for you shall be absolved: for this is a righteousness without the law, *But witnessed to by the law and the prophets*, Acts 10:43.

LETTERS

A LETTER FROM THE LATE REVEREND MR ROBERT TRAILL TO HIS WIFE.

My dear and beloved Wife,

THE storm has scattered our poor family, and has driven me here to this strange land; and new storms arising do keep you, that you cannot come to me here, and you know what hinders me from coming to you: but blessed be our Lord and our God, that we know that we may meet often before the throne in prayer and supplications one for another; and it is a mercy that we have yet leave to commune one with another in letters. I do often remember you, neither do I eat my solitary morsels without minding you, and thinking on the days when you and the children were about our table: but alas! the days of our liberty and peace were not improven by me as they ought, and should have been; and now all that I can do in that land of my exile, next unto prayer for you, is to write to you at this distance. The Lord, whose gift a good wife is, did choose you for me, and has made you a mother of six children unto me, and has preserved you to me a help and yoke-fellow unto this my old age, yea, has made you comfortable to me in my sufferings to which he has called me. It has been no small refreshing to my spirit to think that you do cheerfully, and I hope comfortably, bear the part of these crosses which the Lord hath put upon me. I am fully persuaded, that if we can take any loss that we have met with in the Lord's way, and for his honourable cause, joyfully and without murmuring, it shall turn to our good, and it shall well and abundantly be repaid by him, who gives the hundred fold even in this life, though with persecution. Fret not against unjust men, who have driven me so far away from you; but pray for them, that the Lord may give them repentance to the acknowledging of his truth and of their own backslidings from it. Ye know that they have done worse to others than to me; princes have been hanged by their hands, and they have shed the precious blood of faithful witnesses: and I am sure you would rather have me in the banishment far from you, than to have had me at home with you as a Bishop, or a Dean, or time-serving Minister. The longer you live, you shall the more clearly see the Lord's hand to be wise and good in all that has befallen us: I hope his thoughts towards us are peace, and not evil, to give us an expected end. O pray for yourself and for me, that he who has given us, upon the behalf of Christ, not only to believe in him, but also to suffer for his name, would also give us grace that we may suffer cheerfully, and would also carry us through cleanly and faithfully: he who hath called, yes, he who hath called us, also will do it. He sends no man a warfare upon his own charges, and he fits and furnishes for suffering work, and bids us commit all the steps of our way unto the Captain of our salvation, even to Jesus, who is the author and finisher of our faith, *who for the joy that was set before him, endured the cross, despising the shame, and is set down on the right hand of the throne of God*, Heb. 12:2.

But not wishing to trouble you with a long letter, I shall have done by recommending to you a few things:

1. I recommend to you to make yourself acquaint with the Lord, as he hath revealed himself to you in his word, Job 22:21, 22, and seek his face in earnest and fervent prayer; for a right seeking, and patient waiting will do you much good, Luke 18:1-9. Let the word of God dwell richly in you, and often look into that glass which will both give you a sight of your own heart and ways, that you may loathe yourself: in them you see a sweet sight of Christ's kind heart towards humbled and mournful sinners, that you may love him, and seek to taste and see that he is good: and blessed are they that trust in him.

2. When now you are deprived of that large allowance of public ordinances which formerly you enjoyed, be much in secret duties; he can make this morsel eaten in secret both sweet and strengthening unto you: next unto your Bible, some good godly books, as worthy Mr Rutherford's Letters, a book which has done much good to some souls, and will do good to more! and that good little book of Mr William Guthrie's.

3. Have a care of the children, now especially, as I am so far removed from you and them: see what good you can do for their souls, in often

praying for them, and admonishing them in the Lord, as you see their case doth require. You have some of them more ordinarily with you than the rest: let their time together be well improven. Have a care of Margaret, your youngest daughter, whom the Lord keep with you now in your old age: warn her to seek the Lord early in the morning of her age; for those who seek him early shall find him: charge her to eschew the vanities and follies of a present evil world, and to walk and carry herself as becomes the daughter of a poor banished minister. I have some good hopes that the Lord who saved her from death here in Holland, and brought her safe home with you to the land where she was born, will glorify himself in his mercy and free grace toward her; the Lord grant that it may be so: I hope you and she both will join your amen to this. You have your second son with you: he may be helpful to you and to the small remnant of that scattered family, that you have with you; and when his eldest brother shall return, he likewise will be helpful to you in family duties. I bless the Lord for them both, that he has begun to make himself known to their souls, and to incline their hearts to seek him, and to cleave unto him in this backsliding time: the Lord increase his grace in them, and keep them stedfast in nearer communion with himself.

4. Be not troubled with perplexing thoughts about the world: the meek in the earth are waxing nearer to an end; and you see no way, in human appearance, how their place shall be filled up again. Believe, that he that provides well for his own that trust and wait on him, will make, that the barrel of meal shall not waste, nor the oil in the cruse fail, until the day that the Lord send the rain upon that poor land, 1 Kings 7:14. Has he not promised that those who walk uprightly before him, and whose confidence is in him, shall *dwell on high: the places of defence shall be the munition of rocks, their bread shall be given them, their water shall be sure?* yea, your eyes shall yet see the King in his beauty, and ye shall yet again behold the land that for the present seems to be very far off. That scripture, Philippians 4:6-7, ought to be often and seriously meditated upon.

Lastly, I would entreat you, dear wife, to be much in chalking out, and trying your evidences for heaven, and often praying, that the Lord would write them clearly and distinctly on your heart, and would help you to read them, and to rejoice in them, or rather in him who has made the purchase for you, and freely given you the evidence of it: he knows that it would be no small comfort in this my old age; and I am persuaded yet to hope to see you and the Lord's Jerusalem in that land in peace, before I see death. But this would much sweeten the delay, and this though it were till death, to have the lively hope that ye and I shall enjoy the Jerusalem that is above, where righteousness and peace dwell, and where no storm can come to scatter us again. Pray, pray for this to you and me, yea, and for all the children the Lord has given us. Sure am I there is room enough for us all there. O let us run to him who has gone thither to prepare mansions for all whom the Father has given to him in the eternal decree of election, and for whom he has laid down his life as a price for our redemption! And we cannot better know that (even we, poor sinful wretched,) we are of the blessed number, than by our coming to him, to seek and find salvation in him, who has passed his word, yea, his oath on it, that he will cast none out that come to him; and he is a king of his word, and will not fail to perform what he has promised. Let us grip to these immutable things, his word and his oath, in which it is impossible for him to lie, that we may have strong consolation, when we flee for refuge to the hope set before us. Now, I leave this on you; lay hold upon him who has tenderly cared for me all my lifetime, and has been in a special manner kind to me in this place of my exile, giving me now and then sweet feasts in this wilderness, for which I desire you may bless him: and cast all your cares upon him, for he will care for you: he is my God, and will be the God of my relations after me; and when I come to fall asleep, and to be taken off the stage, I hope there shall be a family serving the Lord in their generation better than ever I did in mine; himself grant that it may be so! The abundant grace of our Lord, and the sweet consolation of his blessed Spirit, be with you, my dear heart, and with the six children, and with the eldest daughter's children and husband. This is the frequent and fervent prayer of your loving husband,

Robert Traill.

A LETTER
FROM THE LATE REV. MR ROBERT TRAILL
TO HIS CHILDREN.

[Rotterdam, March 1665.]

Dear Children,

Grace, mercy, and peace be to you, from God our Father, and from the Lord Jesus Christ.

I HAVE often, in this time of my exile, had many earnest wishes for your eternal salvation, and some weak prayers to the hearer of prayer, for all of you, that ye may be saved from the wrath to come, and may, in the day of the Lord Jesus Christ, be owned of him, set on his right hand, and taken in to dwell with him forever; that ye be of the blessed number of these of whom he will be admired, and in whom he shall be glorified, *in that day, when he shall come in flaming fire, to take vengeance on all them that know not God, and obey not the gospel of our Lord Jesus Christ,* 2 Thess. 1:7-10; and that poor, wretched, unprofitable I may have to say in that day, *Behold me, and the children thou hast given me*, which were for a while for signs and wonders in the world, and now are for signs and wonders of thy rich mercy, and free undeserved grace. The Lord hath often put it into my heart, to write unto you all in one letter, that I may stir you up to the serious and frequent thoughts of that which is your greatest concernment, even your eternal salvation; that ye may make that your main task, *to work out your salvation in fear and trembling*; and, for that end, *to give all diligence to make your calling and election sure: for if ye do these things, ye shall never fail: but an entrance shall be administered unto you abundantly, into the everlasting kingdom of our Lord and Saviour Jesus Christ,* 2 Pet. 1:10, 11. There are three things mainly that have made me thus to write unto you. *1st,* Because this is a duty lies upon Christian parents. The Lord did shew unto Abraham, the father of the faithful, that he expected this at his hand, in reference to his relations, Gen. 17:19, *For I know that he will command his children and his household after him, and they shall keep the way of the Lord.* And the Spirit of God, in the New Testament, does much press this duty. 2*dly*, Because my obligations to Christ, and to his free grace, are so many, and so great, that, had I never so many children, I would think myself bound, to the utmost of my power, to consecrate them all to him: and to press upon them, by all that love could suggest unto me, that they would serve the Lord God of their Father. 3*dly*, Because among the many other challenges I have now in my solitary hours, in this house of my pilgrimage, for neglect of duties in my days of peace, this is one, that I did not improve my time aright, *when the candle of the Lord did shine upon my tabernacle*, and ye were as olive plants about my table. Alas! I did not press upon you, as I ought and might, the serious thoughts of eternity, and of your soul's salvation; and therefore I am the more obliged now to do it, at this distance; and who knows but it may sink deeper into your hearts, that it comes thus by a letter from an aged, banished father? I remember that I was often moved, in prayer with that family over which the Lord had set me, to pray for preparation against a time of scattering, though I did not then think that it should have been such, and so far off, before death; but now it is come, and that which death will make is following: the Lord give us the sanctified use of the one, and serious preparation for the other. 4*thly*, Because I am under the bond of a promise and vow to the Most High God, taken on, before him, and unto him, at your baptism, that I should endeavour to train you up for himself, that ye might learn to know, fear, and serve him. I remember, I presented every one of you to that sacrament, except one who was presented, in my absence, by a faithful and worthy minister, who is now at his rest, and who doubtless did pray for the blessing and fruit of that ordinance unto the child he did present; and, I hope, his prayer was heard; and that the Lord, who has chosen for her a good husband, and made her the mother of children, shall own her as one of the daughters of Zion, who shall be found in the register of these of whom it is written. They were born there, by the new and better birth. Yea, the Lord has been graciously pleased to let me live so long with you, till I have entered all of you (except the youngest, who, I hope, shall not want his part of the covenant blessing), unto that other sacrament of the Lord's supper, that so you might therein, by your own proper act and deed, make an open and avowed resignation of yourselves to the Lord, *as your God, and your father's God*, and declare before the world, that in him alone ye have salvation, and that ye will live and die to him; and so might perform what was promised for you by your parents in that first sacrament, when you could not restipulate by yourselves, but behoved to do it by another, till ye should come to years of knowledge, that ye might then give your own actual and formal consent; which, I hope, ye have done, as often as ye have been partakers of that other sacrament. *5thly*, Because the Lord has made me, again and again, in this my Patmos, to cry unto him, more than ever before, for grace and glory to myself, and to my seed; and to lay out before him that sweet and large promise, Deut. 30:6, *And the Lord thy God will circumcise thine heart, and the heart of thy seed, to love the Lord thy God with all thine heart, and with all thy soul, that thou mayest live*; yea, now and then to act faith, and to pray upon it, and to win unto some hopes that it shall be made good for all of you. Sure I am, there is room enough for all of you in heaven, were ye more than ye are: there is mercy and grace enough in Jesus Christ, to bring you thither; and nothing can keep you out, but unwillingness to enter in by him, who is *the way, the truth, and the life*, and who makes it one of his greatest complaints against perishing sinners, that they *will not come unto him, that they may have life*. And the *6th* and *last* thing, that hath moved me to scribble these lines, is, That the few and evil days of my pilgrimage are fast wearing to an end, the shadows of the evening are stretched out, and my sun is near the setting, neither know I, if I shall see you any more in a present world: and therefore, while the Lord lets me yet dwell in this frail tabernacle, I would desire to mind you of these things which concern your eternal peace; and that ye may remember these things, when I shall be no more within time, either to speak or write to you.

I would recommend to all of you, both sons and daughters, and that, in this backsliding time, *when so many are turning back from Christ, and walking no more with him*, ye would strengthen your resolution not to leave him; for to whom should ye go, in turning away from him, seeing he only has the words of eternal life? John 6:66-68, *From that time many of his disciples went back and walked no more with him. Then said Jesus unto the twelve, Will ye also go away? Then said Simon Peter unto him, Lord, to whom shall we go? for thou hast the words of eternal life. Say ye not, A confederacy to all those to whom this apostate generation say, A confederacy; neither fear ye their fear, nor be afraid: but sanctify the Lord God of hosts in your hearts, and let him be your fear and your dread,* Isa. 8:12, 13. The Lord himself speaks in this to your hearts and mine, with a strong hand instructing us. Now, I conceive, that this would much conduce to help you to stedfastness in a backsliding time, often to make actual resignation of yourselves to the Lord, I mean, on your knees in prayer, humble and hearty prayer; to give up yourselves, souls and bodies, to him, who is your Lord, Creator and Redeemer, who has bought you by a dear price, that ye should be his, *and that ye should live to him, and not to yourselves.* This actual resigning yourselves to him, and explicit and formal covenanting with him, would please him well, would give the devil and your own corruptions a great dash, and would make you understand some scriptures more clearly and more comfortably; as Psa. 16:2, *O my soul, thou hast said unto the Lord, Thou art my Lord: my goodness extendeth not to thee.* Psa. 27:8, *When thou saidst, Seek ye my face; my heart said unto thee, Thy face, Lord, will I seek.* Jer. 30:21, 22, *And their nobles shall be of themselves, and their governor shall proceed from the midst of them, and I will cause him to draw near, and he shall approach unto me: For who is this that engageth his heart to approach unto me, saith the Lord? and ye shall be my people, and I will be your God.* Zech. 13:9, *They shall call on my name, and I will hear them: I will say, It is my people; and they shall say, The Lord is my God.* But of this worthy and stedfast Mr William Guthrie has written well; which little great book I recommend to all of you. And now, my dear children, whose everlasting salvation my soul prays for, and desires to believe, and whose holy and Christian conversation in the way thither, I earnestly beg, meditate often on that scripture, Titus 2:11-14, *For the grace of God, that bringeth salvation, hath appeared to all men: teaching us, that, denying ungodliness and worldly lusts, we should live soberly, righteously, and godly in this present world; looking for that blessed hope, and glorious appearing of the great God, and our Saviour, Jesus Christ: who gave himself for us, that he might redeem us from all iniquity, and purify unto himself a peculiar people, zealous of good works.* And pray for grace to obey that great and excellent gospel lesson, *that ye may assure your hearts before him, and that it may be well with you in the great day of the Lord.* And shall I mention to you what worthy Mr Bolton said on his death bed to his children? (I hope the mentioning of it shall do you no harm, but good). 'I charge you,' said he, 'O my children, not to meet me in the great day, in a Christless graceless condition!' I hope, every one of you will endeavour, and make it your main study and care, to be found in Christ in that day, 'not having your own righteousness, but that which is through faith in him.' The Lord himself grant that it may be so; *and the Lord God, my God, and my father's God, who has fed me, and provided for me all my life long until this day, and the great angel of the covenant, which redeemed me from all evil, bless the lads*, and lasses also. And so I recommend you to him, as your God all-sufficient, *and to the word of his grace, which is able to build you up, and to give you an inheritance among all them that are sanctified through faith that is in him. And now the very God of peace sanctify you wholly*: and I pray God, *that your whole spirit, soul and body, be preserved blameless unto the coming of the Lord Jesus Christ. Faithful is he who calleth you, who also will do it.* Children, pray for me your aged father, who desires to live and die in the hope, that we shall, with joy, meet before the throne; and that ye take these lines, as some weak help to carry you thither. They are from

Your loving and affectionate father,

ROBERT TRAILL.

ADDITIONAL SERMONS

The following sermons, which did not appear in the 1810 edition of Traill's works, are taken from *Select Practical Writings of Robert Traill* (Edinburgh: Free Church of Scotland, 1845).

SERMON ON HEBREWS 12:29

For our God is a consuming fire.

THE transgression of the wicked saith, within the heart of every man to whom God hath given spiritual understanding, that there is no fear of God before their eyes. The formal and fearless approaches unto the Lord in all his ordinances, which have now become so common among professors, ought to say to us, that they have but little of this fear. The beginning, yea, the whole of religion, consisting in a great measure in this holy fear, and being denominated from it frequently in scripture, it cannot but be a sad evidence of the decay of religion, when this fear is so evidently wanting or weak: and therefore, to be exercised a little (if we would in the right manner) in the consideration of this matter, as it is at all times suitable to them to whom the vitals of religion are savoury, so, in a special manner it is pertinent for those, who have the solemn ordinance ensuing[1] in their eye and aim.

There are three false grounds upon which Satan and our own corrupt hearts are ready to plead against this so precious and necessary a grace, and the exercise of it. The *first* is more gross, yet such as carries away thousands to destruction; that is—an apprehension that God is all mercy and goodness. It is true his mercy and goodness are infinite; and yet, so is his justice. We shall not stand to shew either the grounds and reasons of this woful mistake, or to discover it largely; it is enough that it is here removed, by the Holy Ghost declaring somewhat of the terrible majesty of God, in a figurative expression. The *second* is—some think that the New Testament dispensation doth not so require the fear and dread of God, as the Old Testament did, as it did also then

[1] We find in the margin of the original MS., that this sermon was preached April 22, 1669, on the Thursday before the administration of the Sacrament. We learn also in the same note, that this was the first discourse which the author preached in London.

more manifest his dreadfulness, both at the giving of the law, and in his punishments, sometimes extraordinary, for the breaches of it; but under the New Testament, he manifesteth his mercy, and calleth for love. The scope of the apostle in bringing in this word, doth evidently obviate the mistake of this: for from the 18th verse to the end, he instituteth a comparison, and stateth the differences between the two dispensations; and in the preceding verse, doth draw a conclusion, from all the love and mercy revealed in the gospel, which is the worship with fear; and backs it with the argument in this our text. The *third* ground of mistake may be—granting the dreadfulness of God in himself, and in the New Testament dispensation also; yet, that a saving interest in this God, as ours in Christ, doth remove all this dreadfulness, and calls for nothing but love, and delight, and familiarity. This ground of mistake the Holy Ghost obviates, by declaring, that even *our God*, our covenanted God, is a *consuming fire*.

This word then containeth a very weighty declaration of the dreadfulness of God, under the borrowed term of *a consuming fire*. It is the gracious condescending way of the Holy Ghost, in scripture, to speak of God according to our capacities, and to manifest him by such names and descriptions as may convey to our understandings some sense and knowledge of him. By this word, then, we are to understand, that as fire, and a consuming fire, is a dreadful creature, so when the name of it is ascribed unto God, we are to take notice of his dreadful and terrible nature and majesty.

The words then being plain, we shall not stand to start and raise questions and difficulties from them. We have then these instructions from them:

Obser. 1. The Lord Jehovah is a most dreadful and terrible God. Obs. 2. And that as he is so in himself, so this attribute of his doth still continue, notwithstanding of a saving and covenant relation unto him. Both these are in the words themselves. Obs. 3. This truth hath a great influence, as a motive and argument, upon our serving of him with reverence and godly fear. The connecting word *for* beareth this.

As to the first,—The dreadfulness of God in himself—we may well say of this subject, as Jacob of that place, *How dreadful is it!* Much of the dread of it upon the heart, would enable us to speak and hear of it to better purpose than otherwise we do. We shall not prosecute it as a common-place, or multiply notions concerning it; but would plainly and briefly make it clear from the word. And as the metaphor here doth evidently point out a relation to some object which, as fuel, is in hazard of being devoured by this consuming fire, so, in speaking of this terribleness of God, we shall prosecute it as relating to us. Consider him then, *1st*, As in himself; *2d*, In his works; *3d*, In his ordinances.

First, Although every thing in God (if we may use the phrase, nothing being in him which is not himself:) every attribute of God doth demonstrate this, we shall name but a few:

1. Consider his incommunicable attributes, which paint forth somewhat of his nature and being—his infiniteness, absolute sovereignty, eternity, independency, and inexpressible glory—and we, poor, finite, dependent beings, at the next door to nothing, lately brought out of nothing by his infinite power, and by the same every moment preserved from returning into it. This infinite distance betwixt him and us, will work dread in every considerate soul. It is a great wonder, that the whole frame of nature is not swallowed up by the glory of his majesty. Upon account of this, Abraham dreads to speak unto him: upon this account, the angels in a holy dread cover their faces; and Job, upon a discovery of this, abhors himself in dust and ashes: from this it is, that no man can see God and live; that is to say, a discovery of God in his majesty, is enough to confound a creature into nothing. *No man hath seen him at any time*, saith he who is God—the Holy Ghost. This his glory is light inaccessible. *Whom no man hath seen, nor can see*—a strange word! Light is that which manifesteth every thing, and yet, it is a cover unto God from the eyes of all creatures.

2. Consider the holiness of his nature. *Holy, holy, holy!* (Isa. 6; Rev. 4): *Thou only art holy* (Rev. 15:4). And therefore we, by the unholiness and vileness of our nature, our hearts, and lives, are upon this account as stubble fully dry before him. Is it not a wonder then that he, who is of purer eyes than that he can behold iniquity, doth not every moment consume us who drink up iniquity as water? How can a sinner, then, not fear?

3. Consider this dreadful and holy One as sitting in judgment, and exercising his justice in making laws, and giving sentence against the

breakers thereof. *His eyes behold the things that are equal; he sitteth in the throne, judging right.* And here we are to be considered as breakers of his laws from the womb to the grave. Oh! how dreadful is this attribute of God! and how stupid must senseless hearts be!

4. And as this holy just One pronounceth righteous sentences, so there cometh next to be considered his infinite truth in accomplishing, and his irresistible power in executing them. No creature can, either by subtlety or strength, escape his hand.

Secondly, Consider the dreadfulness of this God in his works. The very sight of the glory of the heavens and earth—of the frame of nature, every way admirable—of his ordinary and extraordinary works—ought to stir in us a dread of this God: his ordering of all creatures, his accomplishing of all his purposes, his maintaining of this All—his sovereign distributing of blessedness and misery to men and angels, according to his wise decrees. Heaven and hell are dreadful things, and should awaken our hearts to greater fear.

Thirdly, But to come nearer to our present work. How much of his dreadful glory is to be seen in his church, and ordinances in dispensing of them, and the blessing or curse of them. He is terrible out of his holy places (Psa. 68:35; Gen. 28:17).

In his ordinances this consuming fire draws near to us, and we to him, though with offers of mercy and salvation; yet to abusers there is a certain fearful looking-for of judgment and fiery indignation, which shall devour the adversaries. In prayer, we speak to him. Abraham, and Moses, and Jacob,—with what fear are they in this duty! The prophets begin with this, *Thus saith the Lord*, to strike secure hearts with some awe of their Master. Here we hear him speaking to us. Do we communicate?—Damnation, judgment, and wrath are then to stir us up to a careful, heedful way of performing that duty.

But it may be said that all this is true; but we, who have a saving interest in this God, need not entertain such impressions. I answer, Happy indeed are they who upon good grounds can say so! Such, indeed, ought not to fear to be ever actually destroyed by this consuming fire. But yet there is a fear called for from such, and this leads us to the second note.

Obser. 2. Even God in covenant with his own is a dreadful God

(Deut. 28:58). We find such in scripture entertain the most deep impressions of his terribleness; and that is, *1st*, Because only such do know him, and none can know him but they must fear him. It is a most native effect of a discovery of God, to have a holy dread and fear of him. *Men do therefore fear him* (Job 37:24). Surely the want of fear floweth from ignorance. *2d*, The Lord, though in covenant with his people, is still the same God, and in him are all those things which move holy fear. It is true that his justice having received satisfaction from their Surety, shall never break out against them to destroy them; and that, upon the account of their covenant-relation unto him, they may with comfort and delight travel through all the attributes of God, even such as are most terrifying. Yet, notwithstanding of all this, all those things are still in our covenanted God, which are the grounds of fear and reverence. *3d*. And as he is still the same, so we are but very little changed, and there is but a little of that removed that lays us open to destruction from this consuming fire. It is true that there is a change in the state of believers in their justification and adoption, which is a begun change in their natures in sanctification: yet still they are creatures—still there is much unholiness in their hearts and lives, and all sin in itself is equally hateful to God, and contrary to his holy nature; still they are under his holy law, and bound to obedience, though not as a covenant of life, yet as the rule of their life; still they are in hazard of his anger (though not as an unappeased enemy, yet as an offended father), and of the fruits of it, upon their breaking of his laws. *4th*, The experience of the Lord's people who have felt somewhat of the wrath of God upon their own hearts for sin doth prove this, and calleth for fear. Not only at first conversion, when by a mighty hand he makes a conquest of them, the design whereof, though it be great mercy and salvation in his heart, yet his way of managing it towards many proclaimeth that anger in his face, and strokes in his hand; but after conversion, many experiences have the saints of the dreadfulness of God. It was so eminently with David (Psa. 102 and 51:5). The saints have some attributes of God to move fear and dread, which others have not: his goodness, love, pardoning and healing mercy, the manifestations of that love and mercy (Hos. 3:5; Psa. 130:4),—unto a considerate soul, how ready are these to stir up holy fear and dread!

The application and use of this doctrine the Holy Ghost here maketh, which is our third note.

Obser. 3. The dreadfulness of God ought to enforce a reverent and holy fearful way of serving him. This is evidently the scope of the Holy Ghost, in bringing in this reason to back the former exhortation. So Psalm 2:11, *Serve the Lord with fear, and rejoice with trembling* and, in the next verse, it is backed with the same argument; because there is burning wrath in him, gross sinners are in hazard of being destroyed; and this is said to be in the Son, the Mediator.

And in general, this sense of the dreadfulness of God, calleth for these three things in our way of serving him.

1. In all our approaches to him, and in all his approaches to us in his word or works, to have, and keep up upon the heart, a due deep sense of the infinite distance that there is betwixt him and us; and of his glory and majesty, and our vileness and nothingness. We find frequently in Scripture, that the more near the Lord did draw to his people, even in gracious communications of himself, the more of this was upon their hearts. How did the Lord's condescension to Abraham humble him? How did his merciful proclaiming of his name to Moses humble him? So was it with David (2 Sam. 7:18). Have a care that you forget not yourself, when he admitteth you to nearness to himself.

2. A second general observation in our way of serving of him, which this dread should stir us up unto, is, always to approach unto him, and converse with him, in the Mediator. Without this, there is no possible escaping of being consumed in our approaches unto him. This is a blessed act of holy fear, and is of great concernment unto our safety. Not only in our first reconciliation with God we must have Christ with us, but we are to abide in him; to put him on as our apparel, as our armour to defend from wrath; and always to dwell in him, and to have him dwelling in us.

3. In all your worship and walk, beware especially of sin. This is the very throwing of ourselves into this fire. It is sin which mainly makes us as fuel before this fire: it is upon the account of sin that ever the Lord did break out, to destroy and consume any.

But before we come to the more particular application of those truths, we would obviate some objections that may arise in the heart against them, the clearing whereof may give some light and understanding in the matter in hand.

First, It may be said, that this is legal doctrine, and inconsistent with that boldness in approaching unto God, which is allowed unto his own. To this I answer,

1. It cannot be denied but that such is the weakness and infirmity of the Lord's people, that it is hard for them to distinguish the boundaries betwixt some graces in their actings; so that when the love and favour of God are borne in with power upon their hearts, to the filling of them with joy, it is no easy matter to keep up holy fear in exercise; and when his holiness and majesty are manifested, it is hard not to find some abating of love and delight. But this floweth from our own infirmity and weakness, and not from any opposition betwixt these two graces. And the infirmity which is the cause of this, is twofold: *First*, The infirmity of grace, and the weakness of the new man even in the best; and their having the old man in some vigour and power yet remaining. This, as it keepeth the best from such an intense and vigorous acting of any grace as is called for, so it disposeth them, to make different graces to clash one against the other. To instance it in the particular in hand—when the Lord by the breathing of his Spirit, and the manifestation of himself, doth draw out the soul to act the grace of holy fear and dread of God, unbelief, which in some measure remaineth with the best, is very ready to render that prejudicial to the acting of faith and love, by misapplying of the discovery of his dreadfulness, unto the stirring up of a doubt of his love and favour unto such vile ones as we are. And on the other hand, when he draweth near to fence the soul with consolations, and the sense of his favour, it is ready to forget itself, and the sense of his greatness—which greatness and majesty of his, though they be nothing abated by his gracious condescension to the soul, yet is the soul ready to esteem it so, because in a great measure even the best are ignorant of God. And therefore it is no wonder, since the best find such a difficulty in reconciling in their thoughts these attributes of God, which to our shallow understanding seem different—as his justice and mercy, majesty and love—that it should also be very hard not to make these graces clash together which act upon these different objects—the attributes of God. But, *secondly*, The infirmity and weakness of our very

constitutions have some influence upon this; for the graces of the Spirit being seated in our souls, and in the actings of them the powers and affections of the soul being increased, it is no wonder, since our souls are not capable of acting strongly with different affections, nor able to entertain an impression of fear and dread in an intense degree, which is not prejudicial unto that of love and joy,—that even upon this account, we are in hazard of making the actings of different graces prejudicial, and in a manner opposite unto one another. But we shall not stand on this.

I answer, 2. That there is no such fear of God called for from the doctrine of his majesty rightly understood, as is any way legal, or opposite unto faith and love: for it is deep heart-reverence and holy awe that are called for, which, as we find in some measure in the kindly affections of children to their parents, is very well consistent with love, and trusting them with the care of all their movements. So also is it very well consistent in the Lord's people with faith in, and love unto him. And therefore, when we read of the fear and fearers of God in scripture, we are not to take it, as holding forth that passion of fear which is an apprehension of some ill coming; but rather, this reverence and holy awe, which may be, where there is no fear of wrath as coming. And so, here, the serving of him acceptably, with reverence and godly fear, upon the account of his being a consuming fire, though the exhortation, as it concerns the visible church, ought not to be taken as exclusive of the fear of consuming by him; (since many in the church are enemies to God, and so, are commanded to fear that, as a mean to make them submit unto him:) yet, as it is an argument pressing the regenerate to reverent service of God (which is the scope of the Holy Ghost here,) it imports no ground of such an unbelieving fear, in them who have fled for refuge, to lay hold upon the hope set before them.

3. I answer—That though these things, reverence and love, be not inconsistent, yet are we at some times, and in some cases, called more to the exercise of the one than of the other: so that as a disconsolate soul is warranted to be more in the meditation of the mercy, and love, and condescension of God, that thereby the heart may be stirred up to act faith and love, for the removing of that distemper; so, a secure and backslidden saint, is called in such a condition, to the meditation

of God's holiness, majesty, and hatred of sin, that thereby he may be stirred up unto repentance, and returning to God. Not but that there is much need of the anointing which washeth all things, to instruct us in the way of duty here; nor that the Lord doth not sometimes recover backslidden souls (as at first he occasionally converts some,) by a sovereign merciful leading by the bands of love. But we find this the Lord's ordinary way in scripture of dealing with his people, of mixing threatenings with promises, and manifestations of his holiness and justice with those of his mercy; and thus, to distribute to every one their portion. And according to this is his ordinary method with his own, as their experience can testify.

But that we may also answer an objection which may be in the heart, though not avowed—it may be said, That there are not now such proofs of the dreadfulness of God in his dispensations, as were formerly in the Old Testament, when many immediate judgments were poured out upon sinners.

I answer. 1. Look by faith down to hell, and all such objections would for ever vanish. 2. The Old Testament dispensation of the gospel was administered more in external encouragements and punishments, and the New Testament in spiritual ones; and as the one are more choice and merciful, so the other are more terrible. And if we shall compare the one with the other, we shall find, that it is no less dreadful to approach unto God in the New Testament ordinances, than it was in those of the Old Testament. Look to the Popish church accursed, or the dreadful spiritual plagues that fall on thousands within the Reformed churches, and we shall be forced to say, with the Bethshemites, *Who is able to stand before this holy Lord God?*

But now, to draw some practical conclusions, for a more particular application of all this:

1. We see what a doleful condition those are in, who are not in Christ, and have no saving interest in this dreadful God. His holy nature makes him hate them; his justice pronounceth sentence against them; his truth and power execute it. Every moment's breath they draw is from his patience. They are as dry stubble before this consuming fire. Oh, if it were but believed, what work upon hearts would it raise!

2. And as it is thus with them, so we should learn to lament over the sins of the church of God in these days; and over our own hearts, wherein are such evident tokens of the want of, or at best of the weakness, of this holy dread. I shall name only some plain proofs of it, which as they flow from the want of the due impression of his dreadfulness, so, where it is, they are in a great measure removed—which may both make this grace of fear more desirable, and the want of it more hateful.

1. From this floweth, as a sad proof, the disorderly loose walk of the greatest number of professors. How many fools are there now who make a sport of sin? And what is this, but to sport with a consuming fire? Strict walking with God, keeping up a watch over the heart, ordering the tongue in savoury and edifying discourse, accurate, exact, and circumspect walking, are reduced into notions by the far greater part. And whence floweth all this, but from ignorance of him with whom we have to do? How rare is the power of religion, and the shining of it, in the conversations of Christians!

2. Consider the manner of worship of many, and examine your own. When many come to pray, they rush irreverently unto the work, and carry themselves so in it as if they were coming to present a compliment, or, at best, to discourse with a man like themselves. How rare is it to feel the heart deeply pressed with the sense of that dreadful majesty to whom they make the address! Come they to hear the word? Many carry themselves as if their only errand were to get a proof of the parts and gifts of the speaker, or to get more brain-knowledge, that they may be more qualified to talk of the matters of God. And oh! how few who take heed how they hear,—who come to get a message delivered to them from the living God, and who tremble at the word! And all this cometh from the want of the due fear of God, who in that ordinance speaks to them. How do many approach unto God in the sealing ordinance? Holy fear of receiving unworthily, and the dreadful plagues that follow upon it; preparation made conscience of, is not every one's exercise that sitteth down at that holy table. And this floweth from the want of the due impression of this, that it is one of the most solemn approaches that the Lord maketh to us, and that we make unto him. If the fear of taking his name in vain in that ordinance were upon the heart, there would be seen another sort of work in preparing for it than is commonly to be seen.

3. And in as far as heart-exercise may be guessed at, by the manner of walking and of worshipping God, we may lament that in all appearance this is in a great measure gone, and all because of the want of the due fear of God. And in reference to this, I would only pose you with these questions, and let the conscience of every one answer them to the Lord, who speaketh to them from heaven. 1. What find you of a constant care of keeping up constant communion with God, walking as in his sight, taking his law for your rule in all your ways? If this be gone, you are at a great loss: Herein lies a great part of the lively exercise of religion. Take you godliness to be no more than an outwardly blameless conversation and frequenting of the ordinances? This is a gross mistake. 2. If you have convictions of your shortcoming, what do you with them? Do you quench or entertain them? Surely the security and sleeping of many, even within the reach of this consuming fire, doth proclaim that there is little fear of him: fear would set us to our feet, and make us haste to escape. 3. Wherewith do you entertain your affections throughout the day? What is it that hath the flower of your thoughts in the morning, and the last at night? Is it God? or somewhat which you would be ashamed to name to a man like yourself? How can the fear of God be in that man, we may say, as John of the love of God in another place.

Use.—Since, then, it is so that the want of this due impression of the majesty of God is so evident, and bringeth forth such sad fruits, it is exceedingly of your concernment to endeavour to have this, as you tender the welfare of your souls,—as you would grow up in his way, and bring forth fruit to his praise. They must be at a sad pass who desire not this. And as you would have these deep impressions of the majesty of God,

1. Strive for the knowledge of him. It is the ignorance of God that is the most universal cause of all the sin and misery in the world, and in the church. It is a hard matter to convince many of their ignorance of God; and why? Because they can answer some questions anent his nature, and the persons, and anent his attributes. And yet they demonstrate their ignorance by their want of fear in their walk and worship, for it is impossible to separate the knowledge and fear of God.

2. Remember that both are promised in the well-ordered covenant, and therefore it is your part to plead those gracious promises (Jer. 31

and 32; Ezek. 36), and patiently and believingly wait for the accomplishment of them.

3. Converse much in the serious meditation of him,—a duty which of all is the most clear token of a lively serious Christian. What wonder is it to see one fearless of God, who doth rush on in his course, as the horse doth into the battle? But let a man set aside some time every day, or in the silent watches of the night, to muse and think again and again of God, and of what is revealed of him in his word and works, and let the heart be exercised therein, and you will find light and life flowing in upon your soul; you will find the holy fear of that glorious One quickening your soul.

4. Beware of every thing which hardeneth your heart against his fear; not only all sin in the general, but those things in particular which you find in experience most to influence your hearts to stupidity. Every soul exercised in searching himself will know what is his own iniquity.

And in all, and with all, be sensible of the work being above your own strength; and that, though you be called to some views of duty, in reference to the obtaining of this fear of God, yet this is only to put you in God's way wherein he ordinarily meeteth his own. But you must be endued with power from on high: there must be an impress of his own hand upon your heart, to bring out this grace to exercise. Pant, therefore, for it, and wait on him, and he will manifest his glory unto you, and stir up this holy fear in you.

SERMON ON ISAIAH 63:16

Doubtless thou art our Father, though Abraham be ignorant of us, and Israel acknowledge us not: thou, O Lord, art our Father, our Redeemer; thy name is from everlasting.

ISAIAH, by the spirit of prophecy, foreseeing the woful captivity that was to come not many years after his death, is here anticipating the due exercise of the godly under it, and wrestling with God for the removal of his wrath, and returning of his merciful favour towards them. His prayer is most fervent (ver. 15), and in this is an argument made use of for pressing the same. The verse contains a confident asserting of God's special interest in that people, even in the view of a formidable-like objection; for understanding whereof, we are to canvass two senses put upon the words. One is, that this hints at the saints in heaven,—their ignorance of what is done below, and how it fareth with God's church. This is ordinarily in this sense used for refuting the fond foundation of prayer to saints in heaven, from their alleged particular knowledge of the state of those on earth; the falsehood of which doctrine, with that of its sandy foundation, may otherwise be solidly concluded, without the drawing of this scripture to a sense that doth not very natively agree with its scope and drift. The other sense, which we shall confirm, is this,—that the prophet here, in the name of the church, asserteth by faith a gracious interest in God, even when conscience convicteth of a sad unlikeness to their forefathers, to whom this relationship was first graciously granted, and in them to their seed. And that this, and not the other, is consonant to the place is evident, from the pertinency of this sense unto the scope, and the necessity of drawing the other to any convenient sense by some force; for what sense can the latter part have commodiously as an objection against their faith, that they are not acknowledged by Israel? But the conviction of unlikeness to their predecessors in their grace and actings for God, is a strong and forcible objection, which nothing but a strong faith well managed can overcome. This sense agreeth with the acknowledgments of guilt made before and immediately after (ver. 17).

Or we may take both as hinted, and containing this sense: 1. 'Thou art our Father; though the worthies with whom thou enteredst first into covenant, and who were faithful therein, are now ignorant and unmindful of us, yet the relation between thee and us stands;' 2. 'And though they, if they were alive and saw us, would disown us as their children, because of our great unlikeness to them.' (See John 8:39, 40.) And since the two words of 'ignorance' and 'not acknowledging of them' give some ground for this larger sense, we shall take it.

In the verse there is, 1. A confident assertion of an interest in God as our Father, made by the prophet in his own name and in that of the people of God. 2. The objections in the said passage, whereof this assertion is owned, 'Though our worthy forefathers be both ignorant of us, and if they knew us would disown us, for our unlikeness to them.' 3. A returning to the former assertion of faith, with further enlargement and confirmation from this,—'Our Redeemer,' and his 'everlasting name.'

We shall briefly touch at something, from the general scope and connection of the words with the preceding and following.

Observ. A special interest in God is a sufficient warrant for asking of him any suitable and needful blessing. If you ask the prophet's reason for his bold-like expostulation and prayers (ver. 15), his answer is here: 'What wonder that children expect the sounding of their father's bowels toward them in distress?' (See Psa. 18:1, 2, 3, 6.) Christ's preface to the pattern of prayer hints this.

We need not stand to shew what is a special interest in God, especially, being to speak of the nature of that particular expression of it which is here used. It is a covenant relation. But to prove and confirm you in the faith of this, is our first work.

1. This special interest in God secures by promise and right all that is needful for his people; nay, I may say, by begun possession; for, 1*st*, He that hath an interest in God hath an interest in all blessings, for all are in him as the fountain, and all stream natively from him. He is all in all; he alone makes up all wants (Psa. 73:26). 2*d*, This interest is yet further secured in all blessings, by the large promises of that covenant whereof this interest in God is the main and fundamental article. 3*d*, And this is yet further secured by the infinite faithfulness and power of the Promiser.

2. The Lord commands and allows this improvement of an interest in him, and commends it when done. He reveals himself in all his excellencies, that his people may live upon him, and giveth the pledge of his promises that they may live by them, and gain by trading on them. (See Jer. 3:19.)

USE.—1. Then this interest is of exceeding value, since it is a relevant warrant for such pleadings. How would men value such an interest in a king as might warrant them to ask any thing within the compass of his limited power? If they that want it knew its value, they would not live without it; and if they that have it knew it better, they would lead a better life, and a more comfortable.

2. Labour to keep the faith of this clear, if you would be in a good case for prayer, and prevailing with God therein. I shall name now only this good help to keep the faith of an interest clear, and it is, a constant diligence in the study of walking suitably to an interest in him. Nay, suppose there were unbelieving doubtings about our interest in him, yet this care of performing the duties lying on one who hath an interest, will be found a safe, ready, and speedy way for putting an end to such unbelieving debates. As, for instance, suppose thou question thy interest in God as thy Father, yet study to render him that love, reverence, and obedience that a child oweth, and it will not be long a dispute with thee.

Two things may be objected against this practice: one, against its lawfulness; another, against the hopefulness of its succeeding. And though it may anticipate what is to be spoken on this purpose, yet it is not impertinent to the clearing up of this offered help, especially since we cannot reach the subject at this time.

First, For its lawfulness. 1. Commands of God clear it up. Love, and fear, and all due obedience, are exacted lawfully and by divine authority of them that are not in a gracious relation to him. All that the godly ought to do by virtue of their gracious relation to God, the ungodly are under commands to do them also, though in the due order and method of divine prescription; otherwise, want of an interest in God should be an excuse for the greatest part of the bold rebellions of sinners against God.

2. Common relations to God exact, as due from men, the same dutiful behaviour towards God, which a more special interest hath a

more effectual way of obliging the godly unto. And, therefore, we find the Lord pressing men to their duty from such common relations, and the godly making special use of such sometimes, when a more special interest hath been darkened (Job 10:8, 9; Psa. 119:93): sometimes in a holy delightful reckoning of all their relations to God; for a wise believer looks on none of them as contemptible (Psa. 139:14).

Secondly, For its hopefulness of succeeding to the clearing up of a gracious interest in God, these things make somewhat:

1. That walking answerably unto a common relation or an honest study thereof, can hardly be found in any who hath not a special interest in God. The Lord will have a fair quarrel even with them that have no other relation to him, but as he is their maker and maintainer, that they have not duly obeyed him (Rom. 1:20, 21).

2. Commonly the darkness of our knowledge of our special interest in God proceeds from the feebleness of our endeavours to answer the duties of such a relation, as the sad experience of many on the one hand doth confirm it; and, on the other, the experiences of the diligent hand testify, that it was the way to enrich them with assurance of their interest, as well as with the possession of other special blessings. In handling of the words, we shall first handle the objection that the prophet's faith triumphs over, in itself: and so, the order of our discourse shall be on these heads—1. The deceased godly are unacquainted with the state of the survivors. 2. The posterity of them whose privileges they enjoy, may be very unlike their predecessors. 3. Convictions of both may stand with a strong faith. 4. Assurance of a special interest in God may be attained by the people of God.

Observ. 1. The godly deceased are ignorant of the state of the survivors. It is said of the wicked, that they know not the lot of their posterity (Job 14:21). Concerning the godly, the scripture speaks not expressly. But the truth of this may be confirmed,

1. From the silence of scripture about their knowledge of affairs done below, which at least should limit the vanity of men in asserting the contrary as an article of faith, especially, on so fond a foundation as that 'glass of the Trinity' that the Papists talk of, wherein they behold such things, and for so idolatrous an end, as the giving them the worship due to God and Jesus Christ.

2. It may be hinted and guessed at by their happy state, wherein they are settled. If the knowledge of the sins of others, especially of their relations and posterity, was so grievous to them when on earth, and encompassed with sin, how probable is it that this knowledge would be far more grievous to them, when perfectly sanctified? But if it be said, that sanctified and pure affection would allay this grief, as it will in the day of judgment, when they see vengeance executed on them; the answer is, that the cases are not alike, since there is a difference between sin, and acts of justice for it; God's glory is in the one, and his dishonour in the other.

3. This their ignorance may be concluded, from the probable incapacity they are at for knowing it. Their distance from, and want of converse with the inhabitants of the world, and the inability of the soul for attaining such knowledge without nearness and converse, may say more against it, than can be said for it; for the alleging of any extraordinary mean of knowing, ought not to be produced without warrant from the word, or sound reason deduced from thence. Hence it cannot be so denied of angels, who are often about their Master's work on earth.

4. This their ignorance of the state of survivors may be guessed at, by the impertinency and uselessness of such a sort of knowledge. If it can be proved that such a knowledge is useless, there is good reason to deny it. How, it cannot be useful to them, for their work and labour ceaseth (Rev. 14:13); and so, interceding with God for the survivors, since it is evidently a labour, is not probably their exercise; and unprofitable knowledge is not suited to their state. Yet to speak on such a dark subject with sobriety and moderation, without any peremptory determination, since the scripture's voice is not peremptory therein, these things we offer to your thoughts:

1. It is probable that what the saints knew when in life, of the state of the church and people of God, they remember in heaven, since it is unreasonable to think, that by the glorified state of the godly there is any impairment in their natural faculties, but rather an increase.

2. They know certainly, that they, and the rest of the people of God with them in heaven and on earth, are not yet full partakers of all the blessings that their Lord purchased for them; and it is likely that they

want not holy and happy desires of full faith, for the perfection thereof, both in themselves and others, and in vengeance on their enemies (see Rev. 6:9, 10); though it be not safe to build doctrines peremptorily on such dark prophetic places (see Rom. 8:19, 22); albeit that also is a dark place.

3. It is not improbable that the bright displaying of the glory of Christ's kingdom, in some eminent acts of mercy to his church, and judgment on his enemies, may be manifest to them (see Rev. 18:20, and 19:1, 6, 8), and the way that this hastens the wished-for day of the Lord. But these are but conjectures, and as such I deliver them, leaving to every one a liberty to dissent according as they apprehend the foundation to be weak on which they are built. But the former grounds against any particular knowledge of particular persons and states, have more solidity.

Use.—1. You that have relations whose special welfare you desire, labour *now* to know their state, and to be helpful to them: for death will put you out of the reach of knowing how it is with them, or of helping them if you knew it.

2. Then look upon your godly friends deceased as lost to you, as to any immediate usefulness; their example, and their precepts, and warnings, may still have force; but as to them, you now stand on your own legs, and want the props of the help and comforts of their sympathy.

3. Then learn to lament the more the loss of godly men. It is a gain to themselves, for they exchange earth for heaven; a sort of gain to Jesus Christ (if we may so speak of him), who is our only gain in life and death (Phil. 1:21), who gains a glorified holy member, for a sinful defiled one; a gain to the church invisible, in that its number is the nearer being filled up. But to the church militant, it is a loss, and a considerable one; which should stir us up to turn our complaints into prayers, that God would fill up the want, by the converting of others, and increasing his grace on the survivors.

Observ. 2. The posterity of them whose privileges they enjoy, may be so unlike their predecessors, as that they may deserve to be disowned by them: though Israel be the *prince with God*, he might disown us, as being not Israel, though of Israel. (See Rom. 9:6, 32, 33.)

In handling of this sad truth, the multitudes of instances of unlikeness will go far to prove it. And this we shall confirm, not so much from the unlikeness of Israel or Judah at this time that the prophet speaks of, but of our unlikeness to our predecessors whose privileges we enjoy. Amongst these predecessors of ours, we shall—1. Name the worthies in the text and the Old Testament saints; for we Gentiles are their posterity, not by natural generation (and if so, it were a very small matter, if it go alone,) but by a gracious implantation. (See Rom. 11:17, 22, 24, and Rom. 4:11.) Abraham is called the Father of all believers, by the eminent room he had in the church, as a pattern of faith.

2. The primitive Christians are our predecessors, whose privileges we enjoy, and the same administration of the gospel that was first delivered unto them.

3. Our predecessors are the generation of Christians in these lands, the fruits of whose blood, and sufferings, and venturous actings for the gospel, we now enjoy in some measure.

And we shall compare ourselves with them for these ends:

1. That there may be some mention unto the Lord's praise of his mighty acts, and effects of his grace on the generation foregoing. And it is a great part of our work to shew forth his praise this way. (See Psa. 145:4, 6, 7, 10, 11, 12.)

2. To preserve and send forth the savour of the name of the righteous, that it may be had in everlasting remembrance (Heb. 11:4).

3. Because such comparisons are very humbling, as well as chastening and convincing.

4. To stir up and encourage from this conviction unto more faithful and painful walking with God, since attainments of saints do hold forth what is attainable.

To begin then with the first sort—the Old Testament saints—and to clear up how justly we may be disowned by them as their successors; before we speak of our unlikeness to them as to duty, we must shew their unlikeness to us as to privileges—and this will aggravate the case to our disadvantage sadly.

1. The revelation of the mind of God was far more sparing and dark to them, than to us (Heb. 1:1, 2). Here a little, and there a little, did they receive thereof: but the water of the sanctuary, which to them was by showers, or a little river, is to us a sea of knowledge of God's will.

2. Their ordinances were far more dark and carnal than ours, so that it is called *the letter* (2 Cor. 3), and ours that *of the Spirit.*

3. The church made up of them, was a little inclosure of a few Jewish families at first—at best and greatest, but of one nation, and a few proselytes out of the heathen—whereas the church is now diffused through many nations, and many benefits flow from its multitude. For all these their disadvantages in point of privilege, we are at more disadvantages in point of duty and attainments, and sadly unlike to them in these particulars.

4. The scope of the historical part of the Bible, is not to give us any full account of the graces and excellencies of the Old Testament saints, but only in occasional hints now and then (except in the book of Psalms); whereby we may charitably conclude, that there were many more excellent things found with them, than are recorded. But for ourselves, we may know all.

5. In the deep providence of God, they were winked at in many things, which now, the express revelation of God's will makes intolerable. This I name, for the obviating of the prejudice that is usually entertained, by reading of their failings, especially in polygamy, and in marrying of near relations. It may be almost said, that uncharitable undervaluing of them on the account of such weaknesses, proceeding mainly from the ignorance of God's mind in them, is a greater guilt in us, than their falling was to them.

6. In general, the church was then a minor, and in bondage (Gal. 4:1, 2, 3).

Our sad unlikeness to them, I shall branch it forth, first from the two in the text; and then, from some others elsewhere famous in the word.

Abraham. This is the father of the faithful, honoured with the name of *the friend of God* whose children we may be ashamed to reckon ourselves, for our unlikeness to him,

1. In his faith and confidence in God's promise (Rom. 4:19, 20). His faith was seen in his obedience in going out of his own land, to a strange country; in expecting posterity, when, by the course of nature, it was impossible; in his universal obedience unto divine commands that crossed the promise. But for us, we are commonly in this case; 1. A promise, with a great prop from sense, is some stay to the soul,

but none without it. 2. Hence is our obedience as narrow, as our faith is feeble. Let it not be said that he was sure the promise was made to him, whereas our doubting proceeds from our questioning our right to the promise; for this is but a delusion of Satan and of our own hearts, as is proved, *first*, In that general and unlimited promises in the word, are as good as the most particular that can be desired; and, *secondly*, The trial, when seriously managed, will produce a discovery, that it is the truth of the promise that is the real question in the heart, whatever else for the fashion be pretended. And though serious searching may discover this to any, yet I add these confirmations of it; 1. Probabilities of accomplishment satisfy the soul in its alleged faith, more than discoveries of our right to the promise, or of the faithfulness of the promise; and when these are wanting, ofttimes nothing can stay the heart. 2. There is ofttimes gross unbelief felt in resting on promises of outward provision, when the right to them is not so much in question. What the causes of this treachery are, deserveth a more exact inquisition: but we shall not insist further on it at this time, than this—that the grounds of unbelief are here most visible, and the desires of the heart most fervent; and therefore, it is the harder to be stayed. 3. That promises which have a general reference to the church, and Christ its head, and exaltation of his kingdom, are hardly satisfying to many, though they be most clear (Psa. 110), when outward appearances are wanting. Yea, in this, eminent saints have failed, as Baruch and Elijah (Jer. 45; 1 Kings 19).

2. We are unlike to Abraham our father, in his bold and reverent familiarity with God. He walked with him, and dealt with him, with a most sweet mixture of these true qualities: witness that brave pleading for Sodom (Gen. 18). But we are commonly on the one or other extreme, of presumption or discouraging diffidence, and are commonly tossed from the one to the other in our exercises, and rarely preserve both in an equal mixture. Witness, 1. Our common strange way of approaching to him, either as a terrible adversary, or one so high above us, that there is no sort of familiarity allowable. Men oftentimes in the beginning of their prayers, use such prefaces, as if their acquaintance with God were just then a making. 2. The predominion of fear, of unbelieving fear, when the heart is in any serious temper; as of vanity and lightness at other times.

Object. 1. But the Lord conversed with Abraham ofttimes in a visible shape (as Gen. 18), and therefore his boldness was better founded. Ans. 1. Do you think that that shape, and manner of appearance, did abate aught in that holy man of the reverent awe of God which was on his heart, in more special approaches to him? 2. We have God dwelling in our nature in Jesus Christ, whereof that was but a prelude—which warrants this familiarity in a high measure of faith. (See Gal. 4:1-6.) This makes a great change to our advantage, and gives great ground for familiarity.

Object. 2. But is it not evident that God calls for fear and awe; and his excellency and his holiness are enough to make us keep at a great distance? Ans. Since it is so, he is so great and glorious, that unless he had prepared a way for coming to him, and obliged us by his command to take and use it, it had been presumption to have approached with this familiarity. But there is little true reverence in making respect a plea for disobedience. Think you that God's dwelling in our nature in Christ—that the privilege of adoption to which we are brought by him—that the free spirit of children in our hearts, and the Lord's express commands to boldness and freedom, in improving of his usefulness for us engaged by promises—that these are not warrants sufficient to embolden us?

Object. 3. But how shall we mix them? 1. Mix them often in your meditations and thoughts of God, and you will find such a mixed frame. 2. Give the predominant care to keep from that extreme to which, by nature, or temptation, or special weakness, you are most inclined. 3. Do what you can to maintain such thoughts of God which you are helped unto, when admitted most into his fellowship—such thoughts as influence grace most, and render your pleadings most savoury to yourself, when in a specially reflecting frame, and most acceptable to him. 4. Study faith and tender walking. It is an evil conscience that makes men entertain strange thoughts of God oftentimes.

The second instance is Israel: Jacob, that man of manifold afflictions and trials, forced to flee from his father's house, afflicted by his father-in-law, pursued by his brother, grieved about his children, and at length driven to Egypt with his family, and there dieth. The Lord's people from him are commonly called Israel. This holy man is eminent for his wrestling with God. Gen. 32:26; Hos. 12:3, 4, where it seems he was so mighty in bodily and spiritual exercise combined. He hath his refuge unto God in a great strait; and when opportunity is offered, he behaveth princely (as the word is) in it—not like unto our faint, cold, languid desires, scarcely worth the name of prayers, let alone of wrestlings. 1. We, if there be difficulty in the work, are ready to give over, and to wait for a better time. It is special valour to wrestle, which implies opposition. 2. A few cold wishes will serve the turn with us, but he could spend a night in wrestling. 3. Opposition from our own unbelieving hearts will discourage us; but such, from God himself, doth not put him off his duty. 4. If we perform the duty in any tolerable manner, we are satisfied; but nothing but a blessing will satisfy him. Oh! who is it that wrestles long, and gives not over, if it were a whole night, till he get the blessing?

I shall now add unto these two famous instances, some few things, wherein we are far inferior to the saints of old.

1. In living as strangers and pilgrims, albeit the promises of the future life after death were more shadowy than they are unto us. (See Heb. 11:9, 10, 13.) This continued in Jacob (Gen. 47:9), and even in David's time, when God's people were settled in Canaan (Psa. 39:13, and 119:19; 1 Chron. 29:15). But we are as settled inhabitants, with fond hearts, purposes, hopes, and endeavours, laid out on worldly things.

2. We are unlike them in zeal for God, and his glory, word, ordinances, sabbath, and worship. How bitter were their lamentations for the Lord's withdrawing; how bold their testifyings against all courses of defection from God, often with great danger to themselves! As for us, we are well satisfied with dishonour done to God, if there be no real immediate hurt to ourselves: yea, if our own petty enjoyments be secured, there is little moan made for the calamity of others, and the uncertainty of the case of posterity.

3. We are unlike to them in longing for the Messiah's coming. They longed, watched, and prayed for his first coming; but we, little, for his second coming. Though that degenerate generation amongst whom he came did not know him, and handled him as a deceiver, yet many and fervent were the longings of their fathers for him.

Our next predecessors are the primitive Christians, whose posterity we are yet unworthy to be reckoned, though we enjoy their privileges; yea, in that point, have advantages above them.

1. In the first age, immediately after Christ's ascension, there was the great affliction of Christ's removal from them, the greatest trial that ever a poor company of believers were tried with, as may be guessed at, by Christ's using so many words of comfort against it. Whereas it is long since he went away, and it is the nearer by so much to his second coming.

2. They had the Jewish temple and ceremonies yet standing, though dead, yet not decently buried; which bred them no small temptations and trials amongst themselves and from enemies. (See Rom. 14.)

3. The New Testament dispensation of the gospel and the doctrines thereof, delivered to them by word of mouth from the apostles and evangelists, and all the proofs thereof drawn from the Old Testament, which needed a great portion of the Spirit in the dispensers, as it was afforded to them. Whereas we have their doctrine consigned to writing by themselves, and that through the Spirit's direction.

4. And then, and immediately after, there was the great scandal of the cross of Christ—a man lately put to death as a malefactor! Whereas we have this confirmed to us by all the wonderful effects that, by the power of the Holy Ghost, this doctrine hath since had in the world.

5. A most stubborn hatred against the very name of Christianity, rooted by the devilish idolatry of the world and the power of the Roman monarchy arrayed against them. Whereas now it is not so in any place, though the purity and reality of profession be yet persecuted, and it is likely will ever be in some measure.

It is true they had advantages above us in other respects, which did help sufficiently to balance these disadvantages. But we are sadly unlike them,

1. In their wonderful charitableness to their poor brethren (Acts 2:44, 45). Great were their expenses in supplying the apostles and others, in their great travels in advancing the gospel; many strong proofs did they give that their hearts were detached from this world, and bound in love to the brethren. But for our charity, it is evident, that, take away the laws of a well-governed land for the provision of the poor, and the reputation of the profession which stands in giving somewhat on charitable occasions, if all were left to free-will offerings, charity would amount to a small sum.

2. Their mutual love, and harmony, and union, which, considering all things, was a wonderful grace; to-wit, the great extent the church was speedily enlarged into, the diversity and multitudes of nations and languages of professors, and the great line of separation which God himself had made, and for many ages continued between Jew and Gentile. But now, not only Christians of one nation, but of one congregation, do rarely live in love and peace.

3. Their great, and cheerful, and patient sufferings, and their forgiving spirit. Persecutors themselves were sometimes wearied with them for the cheerfulness of their sufferings: they were often in an excess about it, and rushed upon death through the faith of the glory and reward of sufferings. But for us, a little fining is more heavily taken than death was by them; and suffering even for a good cause, is commonly reckoned no small calamity.

4. Their great and constant pains in promoting the gospel, and spreading the name of Jesus through the world, which the Lord blessed with a wonderful success. But these advents are gone. Nations professing Christianity even in some purity, manage trade with the heathen and infidels, for advancing the interest of riches; but how little that of religion is minded, no man can be so blind as not to see it, and every tender heart ought to regret it as a sad degeneracy.

Not to bring in the instances of the apostles, in one of whom—Paul—we may find enough to put us all to the blush; whose pains, and prayers, and tears, and travels, and work, and sufferings, in advancing the gospel as a minister, and honouring it as a Christian, are so high, that many may think them rather matter of admiration than of imitation, though he expressly, by the Holy Ghost, enjoins this last, (1 Cor. 11:1)—predecessors are nearer to us—the worthies that lived before us in this land, about the time of the Reformation from Popery, who were also under great disadvantages in respect of us, though they also have gone far beyond us. As, 1. The darkness they were in as to many points of doctrine, and especially about the worship and government of God's house, which the Lord hath since clearly revealed from the word. 2. The smaller measure of the gifts of praying and preaching which were then dispensed, as it may be evident, in comparing what is on record of their labours, with what is common now. 3. The great and universal opposition of the church in those days, unto the truths they professed, and to themselves, as preachers and professors thereof. The Popish doctrines then were but a coming to the light, and the light but a growing for the discovery thereof. 4. The rareness of the scriptures themselves, which were kept from the people by unworthy bishops, and bloody laws. Yet under all these disadvantages, we are far outstripped by them,

1. In their stedfast suffering for such truths as were neither so much cleared up as either they are now, or as such are which have been the trial of this generation, neither were always fundamental; yet they did adhere to them at all hazards, and many, to the loss of their lives in a cruel manner.

2. In their great valuing of the smallest means of grace, even the bare reading of the word. Oh! if there were such an edge on professors as was then, ministers would have other sort of congregations to preach unto.

3. In their honest plainness and sincerity in walking up to their light. They were not detainers of the truth of God in unrighteousness, as so many are, who are owners of knowing heads, and unholy hearts; heads full of light, but hearts void of true spiritual life, and sense, and tenderness. Oh, how many apes are there, and imitators of these worthies in the land! How many counterfeiting their outward carriage, while crossing their doctrine; and most professing their doctrine, while hating their practice.

One great objection I must remove for the rendering this sad comparison the more humbling and convincing, and for preparing our way for application; and it is this, That all these predecessors of ours had singular helps and advantages above us, which make the case very different: As, 1. The Old Testament saints had extraordinary means of converse with God, whereof we are now deprived. 2. The New Testament saints had an extraordinary measure of the Spirit. 3. Our immediate predecessors had also a great measure of this, suited to their emergencies and work. I answer, as to the first, Extraordinary manifestations of God by visions, dreams, and oracles, are no such great advantages as we commonly think, who are deprived of them. 1. Ungodly men had them, so that they are not in themselves sanctifying things: Cain, Balaam, Saul, a number of the most ungodly had them.

2. They were not constant, but now and then. 3. Oftentimes they were attended with great terrors on the godly that met with them, and terrible fears of death; and therefore, were nothing comparable to that soft and calm voice of the Spirit speaking clearly in the word.

2. As to that extraordinary measure of the Spirit that the New Testament saints had, a great part of it was for the increase of gifts, and giving other gifts of tongues and miracles useful in that age. But true holiness was still conveyed in the same way, and increased by the same means that now it is. And thereof further we find, that there were no small numbers of hypocrites and apostates found amongst them, even in the best of those days which the church ever beheld.

So that take all things together, and we shall find, 1. That the advantages that Christians had of old, are balanced by others which we possess. 2. That the main grounds on which they walked, and by which they attained to such eminency, are the same that we have: God himself to study, and know, and converse with—the covenant of peace between him and them that emboldened them in all their addresses to him—means especially of prayer, whereby to obtain all blessings from him, according to his promises—a rule of his will for a rule of their walk, wherein we may say, by reason of the great light we enjoy, that we are not inferior unto any of the generations of the saints—the same grace to animate and strengthen—and the same recompense of reward.

THREE SERMONS ON MATTHEW 7:13, 14

SERMON I.

Enter ye in at the strait gate: for wide is the gate, and broad is the way, that leadeth to destruction, and many there be which go in thereat: because strait is the gate, and narrow is the way, which leadeth unto life, and few there be that find it.

THE exhortation of Christianity and religion is to make sure of salvation; wherein heaven and salvation are represented to us as the end of a journey, and a palace to be entered into by a particular gate. The motives are enwrapped together, *first*, from the multitude that take the more easy way unto destruction; *secondly*, from the great difficulty there is in taking, finding, and keeping the way that leads to life; which is a cause, that both few seek it, and many take up with what is more easy.

We need not to stand to speak of Christ's wisdom, in speaking of the mysteries of the kingdom of heaven in parables. It was his constant custom, and a blessed pattern it is; and happy are they that have, by his Spirit, a gift of making the things of God plain, by such similitudes. It is a way that hath these advantages: 1. It makes things plain, when the similitudes are apt and pertinent, for it brings them down to people's senses by sensible and obvious things. 2. It hath a very native influence of taking with the fancy and affections, as hath been successfully practised by all the great orators and masters of persuasion. 3. It sticks in the memory, even as the sight of a man's picture makes one remember him better than the description of his person, or an account of his name. 4. It promotes heavenly-mindedness. The many parables in scripture from sowing, and fishing, and planting, and building, and walking, and running, and fighting, may, and ought to bring spiritual subjects to our thoughts, when we see or hear of such things. Two faults in this matter are carefully to be avoided. 1. Light and trifling similitudes or resemblances, that may reflect on the gravity of divine matters. 2. Too hard and strait pressing of them. They serve only for illustrating, and not for proving, and are not to be pressed beyond their scope and drift.

The other thing we shall speak of in general is this, that even Christ himself is much and often speaking in his ministry, of the rousing and awakening subjects in religion; as the fewness of the saved, the difficulty of salvation, and the hardness of the labour required about our soul's eternal welfare. And if Christ be much on this subject, then, his servants should take laws of him, and imitate his practice, and hear such doctrine gladly, especially since, 1. Nothing is more profitable, than to prevent a cheat in your eternal state; and this is its design; and this cheat is usually carried on by such a principle as this, that salvation is common and easy. 2. Nothing is more suitable, since these heart-plagues and accursed principles are sown in the heart of every man by natural corruption, and watered by the devil's temptations. And, 3. It is specially useful and seasonable in such a time of trying and stumbling, when we may see the shells of many a wrecked professor.

And to enforce this subject on your thoughts, as a preparative to the hearing of it, consider some things in Christ's pressing it, which make it far more weighty.

1. He came down from heaven, in the purest and strongest love to fallen sinners, and gave unquestionable proofs of it. Surely, then, he would not lay unnecessary burdens on them. Many a burden that we could not bear, he bore on himself, and leaves none in the room thereof but what is simply needful (Matt. 11:28, 29, 30).

2. He knew better than any, both the number of the saved, and the difficulty of salvation: he knew his own little flock, and all the hardships they were to endure, so that his testimony is yet more to be weighed.

3. Never was any in his name more full and large in offers general and unlimited of a right to him, and in promises of salvation by him (Matt. 11:28, 29; John 7:37, and 5:40).

4. In his own ministry, he was generally sweet and alluring, according as is hinted in Matt. 11:10, 20. He was not a severe John Baptist, but was a kind tender-hearted pastor.

5. He knew men's hearts best. Ministers guess by their own experience and the word; but he hath an immediate view of men's hearts, and

therefore, his testimony, both concerning their duty, difficulty, and danger, is far more weighty.

6. He was the clear discoverer, and mainly the author of the way to heaven. He had infinite mercy in preparing it, suitable wisdom to know it, and all authority to determine it, as the only way that all must take and follow.

7. We may speak also of his own experience in this matter; that though his case was singular, both as to his difficulties and assistance, yet even this is proposed to us, as a moving pattern for our imitation (Heb. 5:7, and 12:2, 3). If the heir of heaven, by birthright, did enter therein through much hardship, much more are we to lay our account with the like.

Let us therefore, from these things, be stirred up to hear what our Lord teacheth us in this plain exhortation; which for the more orderly handling of the matter, passing the order of the words, we shall reduce to these heads: 1. There are two different states that all mankind enter into after this life; the one is called life, the other destruction. 2. There are two different ways that lead thither. 3. It fares with men as to their eternal state, according to the way in which they walk in this life. 4. The difference of the ways is the cause of the difference of the numbers that walk in them. And then, after the handling of these, we shall come closer unto the exhortation given by our Lord, with its grounds.

Observ. 1. There are two different states of all mankind after this life, and no more. Many different states are there in this life as to our outward concernments of body, mind, or other interests; but the greatest of all is that which is the true emblem of this—even the state of men's souls, in peace or enmity with God. This is commonly acknowledged, and the inference is plain in it, both in its predictions (Rom. 2:5, 6, 7; 2 Thess. 1:8, 9), and in the account of the form of the judgment to come (Matt. 24:34, 41, 46). That there are but two is also evident, both from the scripture's silence of any others, and the peremptoriness of the grounds of men's being determined and sent to these, even as they are found in the first or second Adam. That they are different states, is commonly acknowledged, yea, the difference is vast, and greater than being and not being.

Use.—This plain truth calls more for application unto consciences, than any great pains in informing the mind about it. This calls for,

1. Frequent and serious meditation of it. Men think often too much on any change in their condition, if it be but probable, whether sad or joyful; but this certain and great change hath little room in your thoughts. You sometimes want matter of meditation: here is that which may still be fresh—a great, certain, speedy, eternally-lasting change that is to pass upon you. Suppose a great prince is sending for you all, to carry you into a strange land, where some of you shall be miserable slaves, and others advanced to great state and dignity,—if I may thus allude to the proud king's commission. (See Isa. 36:16, 17.)

2. Undervaluing, and thinking little of your other present states. They are all but trifles in comparison of this. Present states are but small, future are uncertain. It is sadly strange, though very common, to see people living in this world as they were never to leave it, and minding a future state as if they will never be in it—so common is it to see gross unbelief veiled with fair and full professions of belief.

3. In thinking which of the two shall be yours. If there were many, or if the difference between the two were small, this meditation were the less needful: but now it is so necessary, that, indeed, it is inseparable from the real and serious belief of the truth. To help you in this,

Observ. 2. There are two different ways wherein all men walk toward this different state. We shall not urge any difference between the way and the gate, since the words are parabolical, and the inquiry seems neither sober nor profitable. One way leads not unto both, or either. The ways are as far different in their kinds as the states are in theirs; yea, the difference is that of contrariety and opposition. Not to speak of the difference named in the text, reserving it unto the particular notes, but of that which is proper and elsewhere in the word—ways are distinguished mainly thus, 1. From that which the walker leaves; 2. That which he aims at and approaches to—as is known in familiar talking of such things. Now, these ways differ in both exceedingly. He that walks in the way to life, leaves sin, the world, and its vanities, and draws near unto God, pursues after holiness and communion with God; the other walks, by a leaving of God more and more, for, being born with his back towards God, though he be often called on, he returns not, but goes on in pursuing after vanity and a happiness in somewhat besides God. (See Heb. 10:38, 30.) So that the ways differ exceedingly, not to speak of the different rule by which they walk, and other differences handled from Romans 8:1, 4.

Only take it in a few plain words—1. The godly man's way is in a course of communion with God in Jesus Christ; the wicked's way is in estrangement from him: this they love and pursue (1 John 1:3; Psa. 73:25, and 16:7, 8). 2. The one, in a study of conformity to him in holiness; the other, to a conformity unto the world in vanity (Rom. 12:2). 3. The one, in a way of faith and trusting God; the other, in unbelief, and resting all upon the force of sense and reason. Now, that these differ, is no question, and that there are no other ways wherein men walk, but in one of these, is evident. What may be said of infants, and such as are without the church, is another question, which belongs not to our purpose.

Use.—But here comes the most needful question, Which of these ways do we walk in? We cannot walk in both, no more than be in both states hereafter. To enforce this,

Observ. 3. It fares with men as to their endless state, according to the way they take and walk in now. This is already cleared in its grounds and proofs. (See Rom. 2:5, 6, 7.) It is not more unsuitable unto God's goodness and faithfulness to send a holy believing soul into hell, than it is to his holiness, justice, and truth, to bring an unholy unbeliever to heaven. So that here, the gate is shut by dreadful bars against the presumption of the unholy man, and is shut in mercy against the fears of a holy tender believer. You may then hence know what shall be your future state, if you can find out your present way.

Observ. 4. There is a great difference betwixt the numbers of the walkers in these different ways. There is a great train in the one, and but a few in the other, as is commonly testified in the word; yet is this to be understood only comparatively, for even the godly, considered by themselves, make up a vast multitude. (See Rev. 7:9.) And, that we may consider this first as a caution of the other, these things shew that they are a great number who enter into life:

1. The price that was laid down was surely for some considerable purchase—that though there be still an infinite disproportion between

the infinite price and the purchase, yet, surely, it was laid down for the remission of the sins of many.

2. Of this sort have some been in all ages since righteous Abel; since men began to *call upon the name of the Lord* (Gen. 4:26), wherein Adam himself hath been priest and prophet, to this day have there been always some walking in the way to life.

3. Consider what a great harvest was gathered in after that blessed heat and rain of the Holy Ghost on the apostles, so that even of the Jews (Acts 21:20) there are many thousands, and many more of the Gentiles.

4. Consider what a great cloud of witnesses for the truth, by sufferings, there has been in many ages and countries, even of sufferers unto death, of whom all charity commands to believe, that they entered into life, according to Christ's promise made to sufferers for his name's sake.

5. Consider how largely the gospel hath been spread by the mercy of the Lord's blessing on his servants. See but of one man (Rom. 15:19). Even in the apostles' days, the church was greatly spread; and more, thereafter, throughout all the Roman empire, a great part of Asia and Africa. And this sheweth there were great numbers, in that days of the spreading of the light of the gospel, use to be times of its power; and that the Lord still hath some to gather in, or ripen, where it is continued.

And particularly as to the place of the world we live in, if we consider, 1. The long time the gospel hath been amongst us; 2. The many rich gifts he hath bestowed on his servants; 3. The rare acts of providence in preserving, as well as in bringing in the gospel amongst us; 4. The multitude of professors tolerably blameless; 5. The many godly parents that have a godly posterity, as a witness from heaven against the men who say that children are out of God's covenant, and deny the duty of instructing them; we may safely conclude, that there is a considerable number in the land that shall enter into life, as there are many already entered therein.

Having thus cautioned this truth, we shall now confirm it in that only sense wherein it is true, and wherein here it is asserted: and it is observable, that it is commonly spoken by way of comparison, as here, either with them that perish, or of the sincere with hypocritical professors (Matt. 22:14 and 20:16). And though it be commonly acknowledged, yet because it is not duly pondered, we shall lay forth the truth of it before you from these considerations.

1. Consider what a vast multitude is deprived of the very means of the knowledge of the way to heaven. Alas! the Bible is in but a few languages. Many millions of sinners have never heard Christ's name, and never had the messengers of peace proclaiming salvation to them in his name. A subject of very sad meditation is this. Many worshipping sun, moon, and stars, and the devil himself in a visible and deformed shape—their case is hopeless, and so hath it been for many generations, and likely so to be, till the Lord wonderfully appear for their delivery from the snare of the devil.

2. Consider what a great number of those that have any thing of the means of salvation, have them so mixed and corrupted, that there is little success, and little hope thereof. These corruptions are, 1. In doctrine; where, as Paul speaks, they corrupt the simplicity of Christ's gospel by their human inventions; as the Popish church, which has the Bible, but bound up from the people; Christ as Mediator preached, but saints joined therein with him; justification by faith, but by conjoined works; hell and heaven taught, but purgatory added thereunto. Now, where such doctrines are taught, there is little hope of any sound conversion to be wrought thereby. 2. Corruptions in worship, which when great, render it altogether unacceptable. Prayer is offered unto God, but through idols; sacraments are lamentably corrupted, and mutilated, and clouted with men's foolish inventions; and that of the Lord's Supper turned into the most abominable and ridiculous idolatry in the world—to worship a bit of bread, and immediately to eat it, and yet, that, as the real substantial body of Jesus Christ. Now, what hope is there of any communion with God, or communication of grace from Christ, in such ways of worship? Besides, their public prayers and service in an unknown tongue, and thus, the common people are deprived of the hearing of the word read, which in such a case, is more valuable than all their preaching. 3. Corruptions in government and discipline, which in this case of the Papists are so great, that they render their salvation yet more hopeless: As, 1. The whole frame of that Babel stands upon the pretended infallibility of their church, which is

the very root of that wicked kingdom. And this being more carefully taught than any of the fundamentals of religion, and easily believed by a people nursed up in profaneness and ignorance, and in natural carelessness about their salvation, makes their case very dangerous. 2. Their wicked Hierarchy, or Satanarchy rather, is very dangerous to souls. By this, the priests rule over the consciences of the people, and bishops over the priests, and the Pope over the bishops—and thus he becomes indeed the son of perdition, yea the cause and father of the loss of many souls. 3. Their damnable devices of satisfaction for sins, and indulgences for sins to come, and thus they make merchandise of souls, in a more gross manner than is to be found in any religion in the world. This hath these pernicious consequences: 1. It looseth the reins unto profaneness; 2. And leads men into the natural sin of hypocrisy and feigned shows, of devised and imposed duty, instead of true and real holiness; 3. And leads away from Jesus Christ, and brings them to depend on self-justification. In a word, it is a religion framed by Satan and wicked men, to answer a carnal heart's desires to the full, and is indeed a sorcery, and a most prevailing one (Rev. 18:23). And the judgment is: *If any man worship the beast and his image, and receive his mark in his forehead, or in his hand, the same shall drink of the wine of the wrath of God which is poured out without mixture into the cup of his indignation; and he shall be tormented with fire and brimstone, in the presence of the holy angels, and in the presence of the Lamb* (Rev. 14:9, 10).

3. Consider that where the truth is in some good measure purely delivered as to the matter, there are but a few that are ministers of the New Testament indeed, full of the Holy Ghost, and bearing their Master's image, and going at his call, and feeding in his name. And though conversion doth not necessarily follow on a minister's godliness, and his lawful call, yet commonly there is little success where there is such a carnal ministry, as that place (Jer. 23:32) holds forth in some degree: *Behold, I am against them that prophesy false dreams, saith the Lord, and do tell them, and cause my people to err by their lies, and by their lightness; yet I sent them not, nor commanded them: therefore they shall not profit this people at all, saith the Lord.* This is a blessed appointment of Jesus Christ, and of absolute necessity to the well-being of the church, and of constant continuance therein (Eph. 4:12, 13, 14), and it is highly

to be esteemed. But there is no reason that the honour of the office should cover the faults of them that are clothed with it. Faults that cannot be hid, that are plagues in many ministers throughout the churches, are, 1. Undertaking the work, and setting themselves in the way of preparation unto it, without any call from God, or spiritual sanctifying impression which might conclude a call. 2. Studying of human learning for the increase of gifts, rather than studying true conformity to God in holiness, which is a great qualification. Hence is it seen, that the most learned, and men of greatest gifts, have least or no grace; though sometimes it be otherwise, to testify, that learning and grace are not inconsistent. 3. The much mixture of man in the dispensing of the gospel (1 Cor. 1:17, and 2:4), so that preaching by many is done as a proof of their parts and learning, rather than the pure and lowly mean whereby Christ hath resolved to save believers. 4. The little standing in God's counsel, and acting with a dependence on him, and the influences of the Holy Ghost, which is a cause of much sad work (Jer. 23:22).

Now, all these faults in ministers have these prejudices attending them as to the people: 1. Some from the evidence of these things have rejected the ministry, and spoken evil of it,—a great sin, though it is sad that they should have such a temptation; and which is more pernicious to them, do join themselves to such in whom greater faults are to be found. 2. The Holy Ghost works not, or rarely, with their ministry, but in justice withdraws, when he is not employed nor depended on more than he may and ought to be by any godly man in any employment of the mind. 3. And even these workings are not missed by people; but as such ministers come in their own name, so the people hear them as such, and never inquire after more than what is man's therein; and instead thereof, have their heads stuffed with notions, and knowledge sometimes increased, and affections tickled by some human devices and flashes of wit,—which things are mighty pleasing to a carnal heart, both to give and take, both by precept and example. 4. And such carnal ministers usually lead the people, both by precept and example, into such a sort of practice of godliness as is found with themselves; for ordinarily, except where the fear of God overawes, or where a man is gross in his walking, no man will deliver such a frame of practical godliness to others which is cross to his present attainments or resolutions at least. But of this more fully, when we speak of ourselves and our own case.

4. Consider, besides all these things, and though all these were removed, how small a number of them that have the gospel purely preached, and by faithful ministers, do profess any thing; I mean, do not so much as take on an honest-like name of Christians. Few will be found, if you search them out wisely; and that will be by searching after their professed obedience to law and gospel. 1. By the consideration of the law, many sorts of hearers are visibly cast out. To begin with the third commandment, all swearers and forswearers, that commonly and fearlessly take his dreadful name in vain, are out of the way of professors: all sabbath-breakers: all eminently unfaithful in their relationship, and in the duties thereof: bad husbands, wives, parents, children, masters, servants: all hearts misordered, and persons under the prevalent power of passion, malice, and envy: brawlers, chiders: all unclean beasts, that burn in their filthy lusts, though in the heart only: all thieves, extortioners, and such as get unjust gain: all noted liars, that make no conscience of their words, especially in backbiting and speaking evil of others: all covetous persons. 2. As to the gospel, they are not to be reckoned professors who give any visible token of contempt and despising of its ministry, and turn away their ear from hearing the word: who are openly negligent in performing the duties which are required of them, as family and secret worship in prayer, and reading God's word: whose conversation is nowise influenced thereby as to any change, but who live just as if they were under heathenism.

5. Consider how many professors who are not guilty of any of these gross evils, yet have a tainted profession. I mean, in such spots as observers may perceive as evidences of their unsoundness. Many such things there are. A temptation suitable to their corruptedness coming, is welcomed by many, as the thirty pieces by Judas: a trying time, when suffering for the profession cometh, and then are they burnt up by this sun.

6. Consider how many untainted professions are unsound before God. When trials are not great, unsound professors may rub them out: when temptations are not strong, common restraining grace may

prevent their being carried away who yet may be heart-workers of iniquity, and may be dust in God's balance, though all the world besides cannot see their lightness. This sad truth should not be improved into an uncharitable censoriousness of others, but to a jealousy over ourselves, and a belief of this grave truth, that few enter into life.

And as I brought the caution of the truth home unto ourselves, so shall I also in this, and shew you on what considerations it is evident that there are few comparatively that shall be saved in this land, and who walk in the way to life. And in this I shall use such freedom as, I judge, becomes an ambassador of Jesus Christ.

Consider, 1. How evidently the multitude walk in the way of profaneness, which leads to hell. He is a stranger to England that is ignorant of it. Now, how many thousands of such there are, would be found no easy work to reckon. Such all carry the brand-mark of the devil. This profaneness prevails generally in some places, and too much every where. London may be a scantling of this.

2. Consider how many souls are poisoned and murdered by their teachers. Not to speak of the Papists, who in England are in a far more hopeless case as to salvation than if they were shut up in cloisters in Spain or Italy; neither need I speak of the gross errors and damnable heresies that many are fed with unto destruction; neither shall I name any party. But in general, whoever are fed with doctrines contrary to those foundations, and drink them in, must certainly perish:—1. To the doctrine of the Trinity of persons in the unity of the Godhead. 2. To the incarnation of the Son of God. 3. To the satisfaction paid to justice for sin. 4. To the justification of a sinner by a believing laying hold of this satisfaction. 5. To the authority of the written word, both in revealing truth to be believed, and prescribing duty for practice. But I would speak rather of such teachers as have the greatest multitude committed to their charge, and the main allowance in the time for the discharge of their calling; and I do it not out of reflection on them, nor out of partiality, but from a real compassion on the perishing multitude of this nation, and to stir you up unto the like sense, and to pray for the Lord's pitying them.

And of them, without any breach of charity it may be said, 1. As to their persons; 2. And then, their way of ministry.

1. As to their persons, which is very considerable for misleading the hearers. 1. The generality of them know not God, nor his Son Jesus Christ, in any saving experimental way: they walk not with him, nor have his image on them. It is a greater matter to know God savingly, and to have real acquaintance with him, than is commonly thought. Their common, carnal, and earthly-mindedness, and walking after the flesh, doth sadly prove it.

2*d*, They run unsent. How few have a real call from Jesus Christ, to dispense his word and gospel. Their way of entering by simony and unlawful means, and into the rooms of faithful believers; their evident caring for the fleece rather than the flock, doth sadly shew it.

3*d*, They are generally insufficient and unable for the work they pretend to be about. The sufficiency of several is no cover for the lamentable insufficiency of the generality.

4*th*, They are generally negligent in their calling. Though in these parts, on obvious accounts, there is some more diligence in preaching, yet there is little of this through the land. And as for the Nonconformists their neglect of this, their case varieth, for the generality of their hearers are an uncertain company, that scarcely look on those they hear as their pastors. 2. As to their ministry, we may find, besides what is hinted, these things, which are very dangerous to souls. There are those errors commonly taught,—1. That people are regenerated in baptism. 2. That such as are obedient unto the church are all good Christians, and accordingly are spoken of, in life and after death; which is a marvellous hardening of the wicked. 3. Speaking evil of strictness, and preciseness, and spirituality, when they do so of them that study the same, who are generally neither lovers of them nor beloved by them. Now, who can tell the pernicious consequences of such doctrines, which, alas! are to be read off the conversation of the generality of their hearers? 4. For worship, fopperies, and mocking of religious worship; and mingling many human devices, and symbols, and badges of conformity with, or inclination to, the Mother of Harlots, especially in their prayers and sacraments. All which shew that it is no wonder that we conclude the generality of England's inhabitants to be in the broad way to hell.

Consider, 3. How many that have escaped these evils, and are some way clothed with a profession of the faith of purer doctrine and practice, of purer worship, are yet sadly unsound at heart. The evidences given in the general may be here particularly applied for confirmation of this truth as applied unto us. I shall add a few more.

1. How many ignorant ones crowd in amongst professors, that are ever learning, and never come unto the knowledge of the truth. 2. How many perishing under secret lusts, as secret leaks in a fair-like vessel, which appear most in a storm. 3. How many carnal compilers with every wind of temptation, with every turn and change—men that count gain godliness, and hardly can be persuaded of the lawfulness of any course that may expose them unto suffering; and resolve still to save their stake, be the game played as it will.

In short, the characters of godliness in the word, agree unto a very small number; so that select and sum up from all, and you may see that the saved, in comparison of them that perish, are very few.

Use.—Lay aside any deceitful principle about the multitude of the saved, and be no more confident upon the same; but exercise jealousy the more, and search more.

Observ. 5. The difference of the numbers of them that obtain these two states, is because of the difference of the ways that lead thither. All that know of life and destruction, desire the better, and to escape the worse. But their hindrance is, the difference of the ways. The way to destruction is open, broad, and easy; the other way to life is strait, difficult, and narrow. Of the particular properties of the two ways, we shall speak afterward, if the Lord will. Now only of this general: If the way to life were as sweet, and safe, and taking with flesh and blood, it would be filled with travellers: but it is not so, and as we shall hear, cannot be so. Let us then lay this to heart, that it is men's unwillingness to meet with labour and difficulties, that discourages many—it is their being bewitched with the present ease of a sinful path. Admire, then, the folly of mankind who are thus taken with the circumstances of the way when the issue and lodging-place are so far different.

SERMON II.

MATT. 7:13, 14.

Enter ye in at the strait gate: for wide is the gate, and broad is the way, that leadeth to destruction, and many there be which go in thereat: Because strait is the gate, and narrow is the way, which leadeth unto life, and few there be that find it.

ETERNAL concernments are so weighty in themselves and of so near importance to every man, that nothing can be a greater kindness, than to give real help and warning hereabouts. But through men's unbelief, it is commonly little valued, and little improved.

Having already given you the general truths hinted in the words of my text, we shall now enter upon the particular handling of these words. And they afford to us these things, as the subject of our exercise:

1. That the way to heaven is narrow and strait, and to hell broad.

2. It is the Lord's will, that men should walk in the narrow way.

Of the first of these—that the ways to heaven and hell are greatly different, not only in their issues, but in the paths themselves—in handling of this, we shall shew, 1. Why the one is called Life, the other Destruction: 2. Why the course that leads thither, is called a Way: 3. Shew the different properties of these two ways.

First, Of the different ends:—Heaven is called life, not only from the common signifying of all happiness by the term Life, but because it is the thing promised in the first covenant (Gal. 3:12), albeit now attainable only by the second and better covenant; and because it is truly life, in comparing it with the present life of nature.

1. Compare it with the life of nature; this union of soul and body in a tolerable harmony. 1. This life, at best, is a moving towards death. Man is on a journey from one grave to another, from one womb to another, in our common mother the earth. Life now is but as a candle: while it is burning, it is wasting. There is no such thing in heaven. There, time is concluded; eternity is the only period (and this concludes all periods) of its duration. 2. This life, even though it wanted this period, hath

many miseries in it, that take away its deserving such a name; such as, its sorrows, crosses (Rev. 21:4, 5). 3. One generation thrusts another away. Life is now a flitting moveable: the fathers must give place to their children, and they to theirs. In heaven there is no such thing.

2. Compare it with the life of grace, or that new life that the Lord by regeneration begets in his children. That life is but a life of preparation unto this in heaven, as the child in the womb is to his coming into the world. Its best is but an earnest of what is possessed fully afterwards.

3. It wants not its own twinges, and faintings, and swooning fits; many spiritual diseases there are in the regenerate, besides all their hard work. Yet it is more deservedly called life, if compared with the other.

The state of men in hell is called Destruction, the most terrible name of any evil:—not a destruction of their being, nor of their sense of a miserable being; these are preserved: nor of any evil thing in them; all of this sort remains. But it is called thus, 1. Because there is a perfect and full removing of every thing that is really comfortable unto them; it reaches both soul and body. 2. Every evil thing is present—evil company, an evil place, an evil and miserable condition; universal torments in soul and body of an eternal endurance, without ease.

Ere we proceed, we shall apply this into your consciences.

Believe both firmly. Do you believe the sad state, as well as the joyful one? It is men's self-love that makes them more ready to believe the great things of good than evil, as deserved in spiritual matters; when yet, in other things, it is more ordinary to do the contrary. This great truth of the greatness of heaven's happiness is best believed, when these things have their due weight with the soul: 1. The faithfulness of the promises. 2. The spring and end of it—that free grace may be glorified. 3. The worth of Christ's purchase, and the price paid for it. 4. The aspiring nature of the new life, like an infant framed to live in a more open place. 5. The greatness of the tastes and earnests of it got in this life.

As to hell in its greatness of misery—when, 1. The faithfulness of the threatening and threatener; 2. The design of the threatener—the glory of his justice; 3. The deserving of sin, which the knowledge of the greatness of the party offended, and holiness of his law broken, do mightily shew; 4. The first fruits of this, in horror of confusion, and rage against God, and his law, and holiness, in some of the wicked—when these things are duly pondered, then may men attain the faith of this. Believe them—for as they are the main principles of your religion, so are they of most effectual influence upon men's hearts and lives, when the faith of them is once well digested. The true belief of these plain propositions commonly professed will produce a deep impression, a high esteem, and due exercise about those things; which may serve as marks of your faith.

1. Time, precious time, and especially, time under the gospel:—that is the only thing between us and our eternal lot; precious for its use of preparation for it, and for divine long-suffering acted on, and in time. It should be redeemed by many, well improved by others; and it may be holily wearied of by others, whose hope is lively.

2. God's favour in Christ:—how should this be esteemed, prayed for, and praised for, and thankfully kept: this is our right to happiness.

3. Holiness and sin:—how should men's affections change in reference to these, which are the ways to those great and different states.

4. This life and all its concernments:—this faith would make us go up and down, as unconcerned how this world goeth; like a man carried in a vessel over the seas, travelling to take up an abode for all his days, is not concerned in learning the art of sailing, which others that intend to live on and by it will do.

I leave it with these few notes: 1. It is the greatest difficulty in religion, to believe firmly these things. 2. The greatest advantage to a believer in his walk and exercise, is from the belief of them. 3. The greatest and most common cheat in religion, is about the pretended and alleged faith of them.

The *second* thing to be handled is, the term of *the way*, and *the gate*, applied unto that course and exercise which the Lord hath appointed for going to heaven, and for those which men walk in to hell.

This way of expressing, not to urge it too strictly, holds out to us, 1. That these different practices of godliness or ungodliness (for so shall we call them, until we determine them more particularly), have these different states as their end: they lead to them, as a way doth unto some place, from which it gets its name of such a way. So, ungodliness is the way to destruction, 1. By threatening from God. 2. Desert in itself. 3. And it is a sort of earnest of it: There are begun degrees of destruction in the ungodly. Godliness is the way to life, 1. By promise; 2. Fitness and meetness for it (Col. 1:12). 3. It is also an earnest of glory.

2. That there is labour and travel requisite in walking in them. Whenever you hear of a way, you hear of what implies travel. It is true, there is great difference in ways, and in the manner of travelling, as it is here; but even the wicked want not their pains in the way.

3. Travel in it must be progressive. He that walks in a way, and goes not forward, doth nothing. In the way to heaven, some are farther advanced than others, and at some times more than others. And so it is with them that walk in the broad way: sometimes they may be not far from the kingdom of God, and sometimes at hell's mouth.

4. From the term *gate*, we learn that there is an orderly and methodical entering on, or finishing of that way: but because we would not press parabolic phrases too strictly, we pass it. And having formerly spoken of this also, we forbear the application of it.

The *third* thing to be handled is, the properties of these two ways; the one called strait, and the gate narrow; and the other the reverse. I shall handle these things distinctly, ere I add any application.

I. That the gate to life, and the way to it, is strait and narrow. In handling of this, I would, first, Give you some things that confirm that so it is; secondly, Shew wherein the straitness of it lieth.

First, That the way to life is hard and strait, 1. It is seen in the confessions and practices of multitudes that walk in the broad way: some never think on it; some are affrighted from it, when thinking thereupon. Upon this same account it is seen, that the way to life is narrow, 2. In that the truly godly find it very hard, and the longer, both the sweeter and the harder. They at first seem to attain something of sweetness in religion; but afterwards, the work and the trials are better seen. 3. In the hypocrite's pain, which he finds in the external show of this strait way (Mal. 3:14), though it be certain, that the hypocrite is not acquainted either with the sweetest, or hardest part of religion. But besides the testimony of the word, the surest confirmation of this, and the clearest, will be by giving a particular account of the straitness of this gate, and narrowness of this way to life.

As the second thing wherein this stands, I shall give you a brief account of the way to life, and of the difficulty in each of them. And they all are but so many stages in this way, and passages that a believer must go through.

1. The new birth (John 3:3, 6). A man is never in the way to heaven till this change pass over him. This is a change, 1. Of nature. Oh! how hard is it for folks to put off their nature! They think they make excuse for any fault, when it is said to flow from their nature. This is a creation (2 Cor. 5:17). 2. It is a most perfect change of inclination and affections, that what was loved is hated now, and what hated is loved now: and people know what a pain there is in turning the inclination. 3. It is a change wrought by another power than theirs, which renders it some way the harder, though the more sure and possible. Now, compare this new birth with the natural birth, or with death, which is as the soul's birth into glory; and the differences are very evident. Alas! how many are there that stand at this gate, and by no means will pass it. What!—change their natures and cast off all their beloveds?—they cannot hear of it.

2. The strait gate of the covenant. Shall I call it strait, that is cast up so wide with a universal invitation? Yet I may venture to call it so. It is so strait, that no man with any of such baggage can enter it, or will be willing. 1. The proud unhumbled sinner cannot enter in here. He that comes not empty and lost in his own sight, cannot be admitted to make such a bargain with God for salvation. 2. The resolved idolater that will not sell all for Christ in this bargain, and will not give up with all other lovers, to make a new covenant with Christ, cannot enter. (Matt. 13:44.)

3. There is the new life, which is a part of this narrow way. This follows on the new birth, and is the soul's promise in the covenant, that he will lead a new life (Rom. 6:4). This new life is a great and rare thing. We shall not insist at large on it, but on a few properties of it.

1. It is a life of faith (Gal. 2:20; Heb. 10:38). Formerly, the man lived by sense and reason: now, he doth by faith, looking on a promise as a good security; and employing God, and acting faith on it, whenever he is in any strait.

2. It is a life of sincerity and uprightness, or a sincere life. Hypocrisy and deceitful shows he striveth against, and in a great measure overcometh; for there is now uprightness in the inward parts, and no corner of the heart that is reserved for any evil to lodge in, though it may be found there in too great abundance (2 Cor. 2:17).

3. It is a life of holiness. The Holy Ghost is its author, the holy law of God the rule, and the holy Jesus the man's pattern and example.

4. A growing life, and that all a man's days. This new life being duly cared for, attains growth as long as a man lives.

This life is called *new*, because the man lived not this way before: and the rest of the world do not so, nor ever did, nor will do. It is different from the life of the world, in that it hath another food for its strengthening, and air for its breathing; another father, or another and more special way of begetting, another end it lives for and aims at, with other vital actings.

The third thing that shews the narrowness of the way to heaven, is the cross. This is laid in the way, and every man must resolve to take it up when he wins to it, and follow Christ. *Whosoever will come after me, let him deny himself, and take up his cross, and follow me* (Mark 8:34). It is true, that every man meets with his crosses less or more; but Christ deals very plainly with his people, in telling them, 1. That their happiness is not to be expected in this life, but in the seed and seal of it: he draws them to heaven by faith, to know what his love hath prepared for them (1 Cor. 15:19; Matt. 19:28, 29). That they must lay their account in resolution with the greatest suffering, even of the loss of life, rather than to deny the least of his truth and words (Matt. 10:38; Mark 8:38). 3. And that all their life long, and every day, they may meet with such things. The fourth thing that shews the narrowness of the way to heaven, is the work that is to be done by them that walk therein. As,

1. The work of mortification (Mark 9:43, 45; Col. 3:5,) and that especially to be extended unto the most beloved lust. How painful this is, many may know; nay, many venture on hell, rather than thus to part with them. It stands also in some acts of faith, as, 1. That such a lust is forbidden of God, under pain of his displeasure. 2. In a striving resolution to gratify it in nothing. 3. In calling for help, both to mind and practice this resolution in our walk. 2. The work of self-denial. Whatever the lust be, as self-interest is very large, it must be denied, and the interest of God's glory and service must sway the soul in all things (Mark 8:34).

3. Tender and considerate watching.

4. The work of running on in this way, and making daily progress (1 Cor. 9:24; Phil. 3:10, 11).

5. The work of fighting and wrestling with spiritual enemies (Eph. 6:10, 11); to watch, and learn skill to put on, and handle wisely our spiritual armour with which the Lord has furnished us.

The fifth and last thing which shews the straitness of the way to heaven, is the new trials that a Christian meets with, and none but he, and these from the Lord himself, for wise ends; of which hereafter,—as, 1. The swoonings and faintings of the soul through the Lord's withdrawing. (See Psa. 23:3.) 2. The labour of wrestling with him, when his face is hid—a hard but ordinary trial.

I may yet add further, the gate of death is a strait and narrow gate, by which believers enter into life:—that after the trial of all these last, this remains, as the greatest difficulty; not to speak of it in a natural sense, but only as it is a trial, wherein a miscarrying is irretrievable: die amiss, and all is gone:—and also, as the soul is often in the least fitness for any work then. But the encouragements of faith in this are great and strong: Christ the conqueror is with his own in these trials.

II. That the way to destruction is broad and easy, is seen,

1. In that men are born with their faces and hearts towards this way; their inclinations lead them strongly to it:—there is no need of any change on them to fit them for it.

2. They have multitudes of temptations suited to their sinful inclinations that, as a wind, drive them on in it. Many lusts are gratified by walking in this path, and many wise and noble after the flesh are treading in it.

3. The Lord is often provoked, and may soon be, to take off any restraints that stand in their way (Psa. 5:10, 11).

4. They ordinarily shift off easily all crosses for Christ's sake, by complying with their carnal inclinations.

5. They walk at liberty from any inward spiritual bonds on their hearts and way. So it is called *a walking after the imagination of their own hearts* (Deut. 29:19); opposed expressly to a walking after the rule of the word.

Caution.—Notwithstanding of all these things, yet there are circumstances of another nature, that shew their ways to be yet contrary to those: As,

1. The way to life, on all these accounts, is easy, 1. Because of the

kindly delight that the new nature hath in all its difficulties and labour. 2. The lively hope of the glorious end of the way (2 Cor. 4:16, 17, 18). 3. The gracious support and help of infinite strength. 4. The communications of joy and delight they feel in their works;—a part of the encouragements allowed them in this life.

As also, the way to destruction is strait, 1. In that all the walkers therein are in bonds and fetters to Satan, and their own lusts (John 8:34). 2. In that God often meets them with his warnings, and makes conscience fly in their faces, as the angel in Balaam's. 3. They want not their own graceless cursed crosses, and ofttimes in as great a measure, as the truly godly do. 4. The fear of the issue is enough to embitter all for the present.

Use.—Is the way to heaven narrow and strait?—Then, how shameless is the graceless world, to reproach the way of the godly as strict! It is the most shameless slander that ever the world made. To call the godly ungodly is but a lie against them; to reproach the sincere as hypocrites, or the peaceable as seditious,—this is all little in regard of this,—to reproach them for that which is their glory, and that even in scripture words; to reproach them as puritans and precisians. Of the same nature is their commendation of men, as being men of latitude, and of a large walk in the matters of God. That we may insist a little more on this inference that is so clear and pertinent, let us sift out the causes of this reproach.

1. Carnal men naturally think all too little for this world, and any thing almost too much for the world to come.

2. They generally conceive good hopes of themselves, when walking according to this graceless principle.

3. As they like not doctrines that cross these precepts and practices of theirs, so, far worse, practices different from, and contrary to theirs; for practice is a more living and abiding testimony than doctrine. Hence we see, that let professors profess what they will, if they agree in practice with the world, they are liked by it well enough. For instance—in a place given to scandalous misspending of time in tippling, if a professor invited to share with them, should simply say, he cannot in conscience come so near an appearance of evil; this would vex the graceless company more, than if another should join with them, and even in their company speak of the strictness of the way to heaven.

4. False doctrine, or false application of true doctrine by ministers, hardens sinners mightily in their prejudice against strictness in God's ways: as also, the godly their placing too much of religion in little and small things, especially if of an indifferent nature in themselves.

2. Then it is a good token of a right way, that it is narrow and strait; and a shrewd suspicion of a false one, that it is broad—I mean, if it be represented as a way that leads to heaven: for the way of gathering churches of professors is quite different from this, and it is a woful mistake in people to confound them. There are three false ways that are broad: 1. The way of intellect and morality—the Pharisee's way. (See Matt. 6:19, 20.) 2. The way of external conformity to the letter of the law—an outward service. 3. The way of any church order under heaven, is but a broad way to heaven, let men make it never so strait; for as long as men only are judges of our way, there is a great latitude for hypocrisy, and much double dealing with God, if men's hearts be not sound.

Use 3.—Then, make a wise choice;—it is laid before you, as even life and death, and their several ways. It is sad, that men should be at a stand what to choose; but much more, that they should make a bad choice, even to choose death.

I conclude with these few remarks: 1. The way and the end are inseparable; therefore take both, or leave both. If you would have life, walk in the narrow way to it: if you will walk in the broad way, resolve to meet with destruction.

2. The narrow way grows the longer the broader and easier, and the broad way the longer the narrower, till a man be in hell. It is joy to a godly man, that so much of his way is past: it is sore to the other, that it is so with him, and that there is so little remaining.

3. Unless time be preferred to eternity, there is no comparison between the two. A time of trouble at worst—an eternity of ease, and joy, and life: a time of delight at best, and an eternity of destruction thereafter;—is there any choice here with a reasonable man?

SERMON III.

MATT. 7:13, 14.

Enter ye in at the strait gate: for wide is the gate, and broad is the way, that leadeth to destruction, and many there be which go in thereat: Because strait is the gate, and narrow is the way that leadeth unto life, and few there be that find it.

WE shall yet again enter on a further account of the hardness of the way to heaven, and of the broadness of the way to hell, both by further enlarging on what was glanced at, and from new particulars: but the latter we shall bring in in the application. Besides what is said we shall now,

1. Speak somewhat by way of caution, to prevent mistakes.

2. Some native doctrinal inferences from the whole purpose.

3. Some lamentation and exhortation. I. For caution, take these things,—

I. For all these things that shew the way to life to be narrow, yet unto the godly man it is a most pleasant way. Oh! with what delight doth he walk therein, with the heart lifted up in the ways of the Lord, as Jehoshaphat (2 Chron. 17:6, Psa. 1:2, and 119:32, 59). It is a way of great breadth, though not for sin, yet for duty and delight (Psa. 119:96). He makes haste and progress in it (Psa. 119:60, Phil. 3:13, 14). And on the contrary, the way of sin, and unto death, is dark and strait, and that because of the nature of the new exertion in the soul (Rom. 7:21, 22, 23). This makes many things sweet and easy that otherwise are hard. How much toil will a mother undergo about her own child? Why, all is natural to her. The strivings, and wrestlings, and fightings, are hard indeed unto the flesh; but the new man likes them the better. See if it be not so with you in your toil in religion. Though there be something within that tires somewhat of work, there is somewhat within also that makes tiresome work sweet. The way of life is a pleasant way, because of the lively faith and hope of the prize (Rom. 8:18, 24, 25; 2 Cor. 4:16,

17, 18; Heb. 10:34). It is pleasant from the support and help of infinite strength (2 Cor. 12:8, 9, 10; Isa. 40:31). It is pleasant from the sweet enjoyments of fellowship with God they feel in the mean time. The simple and plain meaning of this truth is then in these: 1. That the way to heaven is full of great difficulties. 2. They are such as an unregenerate man cannot away with. 3. And such as a godly man, without courage and strength from heaven, would never wrestle through; but with that strength, sometimes finds them easy:—and again, it is for his advantage to find them hard and strait.

Second caution—Whatever breadth and wideness there is in the way to destruction, it is ofttimes on other accounts found strait. They find it bitter, and tire of it (Hab. 2:13). All the walkers therein, are bondslaves to sin and Satan (John 8:34, 44). God often meets them with warnings by his word and rod, as the angel did Balaam, and thereby conscience straitens them. Ahab, in the way to hell, met Elijah as an enemy (1 Kings 21:20). Their fear of the issue embitters all for the present; and the vanity and emptiness of all their idols to stay their hearts with solid satisfaction. The meaning of this then is—to corrupt nature the way to hell is easy, and that it is commonly felt so by the wicked.

II. Draw some doctrinal inferences from the whole purpose.

1. We see, then, that the Lord hath constituted a great difference betwixt the ways that lead men to their estates in another world, as to the gratifying of the flesh: the one strait to it, the other easy. We have said enough to confirm this; the words are also clear for it. The reasons of this are, 1. Conformity to Christ the head, in the godly, who entered into glory by a strait way, as has been said. 2. It cannot otherwise be, supposing the Lord's design on his people to glorify himself, in the bearing them up, and in the exercise of grace. 3. Corruption being left in both—in the one wholly, in the other in part—makes it to be so as it is. 4. That the Lord may leave it to men's choice though he graciously determine his own, by his hand, to choose life, whatever hardness be in the way.

2. No man's testimony concerning the two ways can be of such service as a godly man's who hath walked in both—as none know so well without experience what hell and heaven are, as the devils that have tasted of both; and we see their malice bewrayeth it:—unless we

except our Lord Jesus, who had a sort of experimental knowledge of both, as his readiness to save sheweth. And the witness of the godly is seen, 1. In that they all have turned out of that way, and never turn in again. 2. And they testify a vast difference between them, not only as to the issue, but the way itself. And what means all their shame, and sorrow, and mourning for their walking in the broad way, but a testimony against the one, and for the other?

3. We see the true reason of the difference in the number of the saved and damned, is from the interest of the flesh, denied by a few, and indulged by the greater part: and we may wonder at the folly of men making so bad a choice of their way to eternity, as commonly they do.

III. Lamentation and reproof.

1. Over the godly who are questioning their way, because of the difficulty they find therein, whereas it ought rather to confirm them that they are in the right; or who at any time look with envy on the ease of the foolish (Psa. 73).

2. Over the ungodly, who bless themselves that they never found any such hardship and straitening in godliness. It is strange but true, that the ungodly find these the most easy, that the godly find most hard; as faith not only of divine truth, but of their interest in Christ—or that repentance is an easy thing with them—or the sincerity of their hearts: they think their hearts were always right:—or about prayer, and all religious duties. And this is because they know not the true nature of all these great things.

3. Over those who frame to themselves a religion free of all its difficulties. Men in professing to take the rule of the word for the rule of their religion, do often wrench and cut away all things that are hard therein in applying it.

Lay aside that foolish and common opinion, that the way to heaven is easy. Oh, by all means beat it out of your minds! I shall in pressing this exhortation shew, 1. The commonness of the mistake. 2. What are the causes of it. 3. What is its danger. 4. How it may be removed.

1. To shew the commonness of this opinion about the easiness of the way to heaven, it may serve to see men's confident hopes of getting safe thither, with their laziness in striving, or taking pains. This is unquestionable, that many of the most confident are most lazy. It is a common

thing to see men of these sorts to be confident of heaven, 1. That never mortified one corruption, especially their darling one, nor ever endeavoured it. 2. Nor ever wrestled with God in prayer, as a hard work. 3. Nor ever watched over their hearts. 4. Nor ever deny themselves. 5. Nor ever sanctify a day to the Lord in a spiritual manner. 6. Nor ever submit to a cross, that a little warping can prevent or shift.

2. What are the causes of it. 1st, Men's own hearts are inclined to such a way, and so are easily prevailed with to think it is so. This inclination is strengthened by these: 1. A rooted ignorance of God in his greatness, holiness, and truth,—the root of all wickedness. 2. Ignorance of the nature of heaven and eternal life: he that knows the end and prize lost, is likeliest to know what running and fighting are called for. 3. Ignorance of their enemies, their own hearts, and others: he that knows not his heart's corruption is not likely to take much pains to have it made better. 4. Undervaluing of eternal things, especially when compared with temporal.

2*d*, Satan is busy in persuading to this, being cunning enough and well acquainted with his own interests. If he could, he would keep all ignorant; and if that cannot be, he strives to make them lazy, and lose their crown.

3*d*, Mistakes of the practice of the godly. The ungodly see not the secret duties of the godly, nor their inward work in public duties, and therefore think them like themselves.

4*th*, The ensnaring practice and principles of a careless world about them. If they be like their neighbours and others, they think well of themselves.

3. What is its danger. Its danger is great. This keeps them in the broad way, and great with peace of mind, and against all warnings and convictions. Hence is it sadly seen in experience that multitudes of professors keep it, and are most rarely awakened of any body else.

4. How it is to be removed. 1. By the rule of the word. 2. The practice of the saints, as David and Paul (1 Cor. 9:26, 27). 3. By an honest experiment. The last consideration is that of the text, which we shall now enter on.

It is Christ's special will, and our special duty, to enter in, and keep on in the strait way that leads unto life. This is the scope of the words.

If any scruple or doubt should remain about this, these things clear it: 1. It was Christ's special errand as a priest, to remove the otherwise immovable impediments lying in this way. 2. As a prophet, to teach the church the way. 3. As a king, to lead them in it, and help them on against all impediments that remain. 4. In his state of humiliation, he went before us in this way as a pattern. 5. In that of exaltation, he assureth us of the happy issue of striving; and in the room of his people, and as their head, hath taken possession of the kingdom. 6. The great principle that moved him, and the end he aimed at, was to have his Father's love, and wisdom, and grace, and his own, glorified in bringing sinners to heaven. As God, he accomplished the work by merit and strength; as man, by suffering and example. So that it is abundantly clear that Christ envies not your walking in the way to life, but rather invites, commands, encourages, threatens, to stir you up to walk therein. That it is our special and main duty is also clear, not only on the former grounds, but, 1. Because this alone tends to the saving of the soul. 2. No duty whereby God can be actively glorified by us can be performed save in this way. But there is no difficulty in this point, or necessity of clearing it. If it be the way, and the only way to heaven, then every one will judge it necessary to walk in it. Our work, then, mainly in opening up this exhortation, and preparing for its practice, stands, 1. In clearing what it is to enter in at the strait gate. 2. In clearing the motives and arguments whereby Christ presseth it; and then we shall also press it.

1. What is it to enter in at the strait gate? It is,

1*st*, To begin, and set forth well and rightly, in the practice of godliness. A good beginning is the one-half of the work.

2*d*, It is to hold on and continue therein. Though the word *enter*, at the first view, and in the parabolic phrase, seems not to imply this, yet necessarily it is implied, in that heaven itself is the end; and all the course that leads thither is spoken of as a gate and a way. Though our Lord's way of speaking may shew that the main difficulty is in right beginning, and that they that begin, and enter in, never go out of it again.

2. What are his arguments to press it? They are, the wideness of the way to destruction, and the multitude of walkers therein,—which say to us these things:

1. That the greatness and commonness of danger should be a sharp spur to duty. The Lord allows a lawful exercise of self-love; and oh that it were more in exercise amongst you! The report of destruction should make salvation more lovely, and all the means that lead unto it, even those that are hardest.

2. The multitude of walkers in a way, of itself is no sound argument for its goodness, nor that it shall have a good end. Christ would not have his people to follow the multitude: they are to be a singular people as to their way of walking.

The second argument is from the nature of the way that leads unto life, which saith,—

1. Our Lord is very free and faithful in warning his people of all inconveniences they may meet with in the way; which being duly pondered, may prevent many stumblings.

2. The difficulty of the way to heaven makes many hold on in the way to hell. The wicked know the straitness of the way to heaven. I named this amongst the general truths. But now, how come they to know the way to be strait, since they never walked in it? They know it by what they hear in the word; by what they see in the saints; by what they feel in the form of religion; by what their lusts teach them to fear there is in godliness;—and this, compared with what they feel in the broad way, varies the case from what hath been already spoken of them.

Now, to press this exhortation on you in the close of all this purpose, I would desire you to gather and compose your spirits, and reflect on what hath been said, and proved, and cleared, 1. That there are two different states after this life abiding all men: there must you shortly be. 2. There are two different ways that lead thither. 3. It fares with men according to the way they take. 4. There is a wide difference between the numbers of the walkers in the two ways. 5. And that, from the great difference in the ways. We have also taken a closer view of the words, and shewn you, and proved, that the way to heaven is narrow, and to hell broad, by several illustrations, though many more might be adduced, and they that are named never insisted on. And lastly, that our Lord is willing you should walk in the way to life, and escape destruction; and hath bound it on you by his command, as your duty; and hath sent me to proclaim this his will, and to declare to you your duty.

My question then is, Do you believe these things or not? If you do not, propose your scruples: how easy a work it is to clear them! And what use do you intend to make of them! Say not, you expect to hear that of me, for if you believed these divine truths, you would use them quickly. But I will tell you what use you *do* make of them, ere I tell you what you *ought* to make. 'I make use of all,' may one say, 'for further informing of my understanding about these things and thus people learn still to know more and more, and mind to practise nothing. Some will make use of these things for rendering them more censorious and suspicious of others. It is far easier to instruct one how to see a mote in another's eye, than a beam in his own; and he is far more inclined to the one than the other.

The use you *should* make of all this, is to look upon your own way, and see wherein you find it strait and narrow. Oh, for the Lord's sake, try yourselves in this! It is not past hope, even though all be amiss. Do you walk in a way so broad as to give room to any allowed sin, or willingly neglected duty? Then you are not in Christ's strait way. Or is it so strait that you perceive you can make no progress therein with such a load? Then is it good. How came you into that way? Was it by Jesus Christ? And is it in him that you yet walk? Or are you dreaming that there is no farther use of Christ in helping you to heaven, but in dying for you? Oh, sad mistake! Must he not dwell in you by his Spirit,—lead, and guide, and protect you? Is your way so broad, that you can escape your enemies? Or so narrow, that you must go *through* them? Have you the multitude walking with you, or are you much alone? The way of whole parishes travelling to heaven is not the king's highway. A believer, though he have company, yet in a manner he is alone: he hath as much work as if there were none but himself.

After reflecting on and examining of your way, if you find you are in the strait way that leads to life, then, I exhort you, be cheerful: go on in the strength of the Lord. Your way hath a good end, and you shall shortly feel it: your helper is strong. Be painful and diligent; strive on, wrestle, press through all! Weary not of well-doing; mind your work heartily; your reward is sure. Bring forth your faith and patience, and use them nobly, for great shall be your victory in the latter end of the day.

As for you whose consciences may convince you that as yet you have not walked in this way, and know within yourselves that you have a pretty easy work in godliness, know of a truth and certainty that this way will bring you to destruction, for God threatens it! How terrible is it, for God inflicts it and lays it on! Meditate awhile on this. Will the Most High alter his word that hath gone out of his mouth in righteousness, for ease to your sinful flesh? Where hath he said that the lazy shall be crowned, or that a fighter against God, and a friend of sin and Satan, shall be rewarded with eternal life? Then, leave it betimes—even now: make a good choice. The ways and the ends are set before you. Consider how frail and uncertain your life is; how uncertain the gospel's continuance with you is, and any power attending it; how the way will be to you the straiter, the longer that you delay entering in thereat. And if you have a mind to be saved, hearken to these admonitions. Put away your foolish opinions about those ways, and fill your understanding with the certain truth of God in this matter. Lay aside your lazy practices, and take pains about your souls. Enter in at the strait gate, and walk on in the narrow way that leads unto life. And let these be your practices: Enter in Jesus Christ, and have him dwelling in your hearts by faith, and abide in him, and walk in him. Lay aside every sin, especially your besetting sin. Take up every duty, and every thing that is in duty,—the inward spiritual part thereof. And thus you will find the way sweeter than you think for, and an abundant entrance shall be ministered unto you into the kingdom of God.

SERMON ON EPHESIANS 3:8

Unto me, who am less than the least of all saints, is this grace given, that I should preach among the Gentiles the unsearchable riches of Christ.

IN these words, the blessed apostle repeateth the same thing he spoke in the preceding verse, of his call, and being constituted a minister of the mysteries of the gospel, and that of free grace; with the addition of a very humble designation he giveth to himself,—*less than the least of all saints* and a very high and deep expression of the great subject of his preaching,—the unsearchable riches of Christ. This last word of the text only we intend to insist on, as being most pertinent for us. And before we come to observe any thing, we would first a little clear the words. And,

1. By *riches of Christ*, ye are not to understand that riches which consists in outward and worldly valuable things, though indeed Christ be the most sovereign owner of all the gold of the earth; but we are mainly to understand that treasure and storehouse which is in him, of all divine perfections of grace and glory, of which more another time. It is a phrase that denotes the plenty of the riches, their excellency, and their suitableness to answer all necessities.

2. They are said to be *unsearchable*,—not that it is unlawful to search into them, in as far as they are revealed; or that by such searching, by the Lord's grace and Spirit, a man may not attain unto some sight and knowledge of them. Nay, this apostle doth in this chapter, verse 4, and in 2 Corinthians 11:6, avow his knowledge in the mystery of Christ; but only, that they are so many and great that no finite understanding can search them out unto perfection; as it is said of God (Job 11:7, 8). And here, by the way, we have an argument for the divinity of Jesus Christ. If there be *unsearchable* riches of Christ, he must be something more than a creature.

The riches of Christ are unsearchable; or his excellency, and the treasures of it in Jesus Christ, are unsearchable. For the opening and clearing of this precious truth, and making way for the manifold usefulness of it, we would take notice of these two things: 1. What the riches and excellencies of Christ are. 2. How they are unsearchable: what sort of searching into them is commanded, and what forbidden.

As to the first,—the riches and excellencies of Christ. This is one of the vastest subjects of all the truths of God, or rather, it containeth the whole truths of the gospel; yea, all that is revealed in the word, of God and man, may be reduced to this. It is the main subject of the gospel; the main of preaching is here; the main of a Christian's meditation in this life is here. Yea, it is very likely that the main exercise of the glorified above is about this. It is, then, doubtless, an excellent theme to discourse upon, and there is much need of holy hearts and affections in speaking and hearing of it.

We are, then, no further to speak or think of it than is revealed; and indeed there is more revealed than saint or angel can duly speak or think of. And yet all that is revealed, is far from declaring plentifully the matter as it is. Consider, then, in the first place, the excellency and riches of his person. God the Son, equal in all divine perfections with the Father (Heb. 1:3); the brightness of his glory, and the express character or image of his person. To discourse upon his excellency on this account, were to undertake to speak of all the glorious perfections and attributes of God which are revealed in the word, which is a vast subject and dreadful. But because he is man also, we are to consider that nature in him. That holy sinless flesh which he took upon him wants not its own excellencies. But especially the *soul* of Jesus Christ, that singular and rare creature (for it was made, and doubtless with as transcendent excellencies as a creature was capable of). Oh, what treasures of holiness and purity, of grace and glory, were there, and are there in it! And his riches on this account is evidently useful, since it was requisite that the Mediator should be God-man.

But to come a little lower, in the second place consider, that from this personal union of his human nature with his divine person, and his undertaking of the work of redemption in that manner, there was a pouring out of the Spirit without measure upon him, so that he became the fountain of all fullness of grace and glory. The fullness of the Godhead dwelt in him from all eternity, personally, in some sense, and that is in his person; but now, upon this undertaking, it dwelt in him bodily (Col. 2:11, and 1:19). This pleased the Father, that in him shall all fullness dwell. A Mediator so qualified we stood in need of, as will be seen in the particulars of the management of this text.

Thirdly, Consider his riches and excellency in the discharge of the office of Mediator, being thus so sufficiently qualified for it. And this taketh in all that he did and suffered; all he did before he came in the fullness of time, and all that he now doth, and shall do to the last day. But only to touch a few particulars, consider,

1. The freedom of his mercy in taking upon him this office of Mediator. Nothing constrained him: he was absolutely free. If his own love in a manner constrained him, the more lovely and excellent is he. What happiness wanted he? What can be added to him? If all men had perished, he had lost nothing. But indeed, when he hath taken on him the work of saving his own, none of them can perish. Had he such a desire to have a company of sinful men and women to be with him for ever? Who can sufficiently admire it? Our misery calls for this riches of grace and mercy.

2. Consider his excellency of love, not only in taking it on, but when such and such things were called for by the justice of God, from the Surety. This is more wonderful. If the redemption of all the elect had cost him but one petition or word to justice, it had been matchless love to have bestowed it. But when it was required that he should be a man, and such a man,—and lead such a life, and die such a death,—to be accused by the law, deserted of his Father and of all creatures, and to have Satan and the world let loose upon him,—oh, what love is here, and how great riches and excellency!

3. And as he refused not to undertake the employment, because of foreseen dangers and difficulties, so when he undertook it he did not faint nor was discouraged because of them. He was born of a mean woman; he was persecuted from his cradle to his grave. All temptations, all trials from God, and men, and devils, were in his cup. And after several years' living thus a man of sorrows (it was his name, sorrowful), and acquainted with the saddest griefs (these were his most constant companions), near his death, the entire cup of wrath, and the dregs of it, for the numberless sins of all the elect, was presented unto him; and after some holy submissive smugglings of sinless human nature at the receiving of such a deluge of wrath, it was drunk up, and the full price

paid upon the cross for these souls for whom from all eternity he had bargained with the Father. What riches and excellency of love are there in this! (Rev. 1:5, 6.) He not only drank up the wrath which our sins deserved (which was indeed the cause of his death), but because there was a remaining spottedness in our souls, he took his own blood, and washed us in it. He not only drank that which was as poison to kill him, even the wrath due to our sins, but he took his heart's blood to wash away the stains that those sins had made in our souls. Our sinfulness and pollution call for his richness of mercy.

4. As his love and courage were admirable in going through these things, so his humility, meekness, and compassion come next to be considered. He was not only by line of the blood-royal, as the son of David according to the flesh, but especially, as God-man, he was the heir of all things. Yet his first cradle is a manger, and his entertainment in the world very coarse. When he came out to his public ministry, how poor and contemptible was his outward appearance to the world! He declares himself that he was below the very foxes and birds, as to the constancy and settledness of his shelter. He came to save the world, and yet every man almost was against him, except a few despised ones. But he was not discouraged, though grieved with their ingratitude. He ate with sinners, and he laid his holy hand upon the leper's skin. He did not cry, nor lift up nor cause his voice to be heard in the street. Our stubbornness and rebellious carriage called forth this condescension.

5. His riches of wisdom do eminently appear in the matter of redemption. The manifold wisdom of God doth appear here. It is one of the most glorious and deep contrivances; it is the chief of the ways of God we may well say. Justice is fully satisfied, mercy notwithstanding eminently shines. Sinners are saved, and pardoned freely. The wisdom of it stands in his choosing so fit means for attaining the end; the only fit ones; and in ordering these means wisely, for reaching that end. His end is to reconcile God and man, and to bring man into the favour and friendship of God. God's justice stands in the way of bestowing favour upon man; man's sinfulness separates betwixt God and him. Justice must be satisfied; and both man's guilt and debt, and the power of sin must be removed, ere the Lord accept of him. Blessed Jesus hath

first justice to satisfy, which he doth, by laying down his own blood; a most sufficient price. This, as a price, reconciles God to us, and in its efficacy washes the souls of his people; and when applied by faith, renews them, and works in them love to God. And more particularly his wisdom appears, in applying himself unto us, and taking on him these offices and employments, in the discharge whereof, he fully maketh up all we stand in need of. Because we are enemies to God in our hearts, he subdues us as a king, and bringeth us into subjection, and removeth our natural rebellion. Because we are guilty of sin, he maketh atonement for us to justice, by the sacrifice of himself; and that this sacrifice may have still its efficacy in our renewed transgressions, he still maketh intercession for us. Because we are ignorant of God and his will, he revealeth these things unto us by his word and Spirit, that we may savingly know these things which belong to our peace and salvation. We have many enemies in our way to heaven: he subdueth these, taketh away their deadly sting, and defendeth from any mortal harm from their assaults. He giveth laws unto us as a king, how to carry ourselves in our duty; he giveth as a prophet, discerning, to know and understand them; enableth us to give obedience; and when that fails, he obtaineth pardon for failings. What a manifold wisdom doth appear in all this, and what riches of wisdom!

6. The riches of his righteousness do appear in the matter of redemption. *I counsel thee*, he says, *to buy of me gold tried in the fire, that thou mayest be rich; and white raiment, that thou mayest be clothed, and that the shame of thy nakedness do not appear; and anoint thine eyes with eye-salve, that thou mayest see* (Rev. 3:18). This righteousness is what Christ hath not only as a holy man or God, but that which he attained in our name by his perfect obedience and satisfaction, which is imputed unto us.

7. Consider the riches of his power and might. He is the arm of the Lord,—he on whom our help and strength are laid. 1. His overcoming and removing, as it were, justice out of the way of his people's happiness, proves this. 2. His subduing all of them, for all were once rebels and enemies to himself. 3. In preserving his own interest in the hearts of his people, and in his church, against so much opposition from so many enemies; which speaketh much riches of strength and

power. 4. In making his enemies tremble before him, by his presence in his church and ordinances; making them to fear, as before an army with banners.

8. Consider the riches of his glory and majesty shining in all this great work. Not only as God, equal with the Father, is his glory infinite; but even in the discharge of his mediatory work, his glory was and is conspicuous. *We beheld his glory, the glory as of the only begotten of the Father, full of grace and truth* (John 1:14), and *He manifested forth his glory* (John 2:11). All his miracles were glorious things, though blinded sinners could not behold him. His suffering was a most glorious business as ever was accomplished, albeit the outside of it, and what was discernible by carnal eyes, seemed to be quite contrary. So also there is great glory in the sufferings of his people ever since; and all the glory is his, for it is for his cause and by the assistance of his Spirit they suffer. 1. It is for the glory of his person. 2. Of his works of preaching and miracles. 3. Of his sufferings and death. 4. Of his resurrection. 5. Of his ascension. 6. Of his guiding his church till the end. 7. Of his last coming to judgment.

Now, a word, how it is they are unsearchable, and how far lawfully we may and ought to search. They are unsearchable, because infinite and incomprehensible by our shallow understandings. Angels do pry into them, and with a holy kind of curiosity desire to know more and more of the mysteries of the gospel; but even their understanding, though far above ours, cannot comprehend them fully. We may search into them upon these conditions: 1. That we go not beyond what is revealed in the word. Our natural curiosity is here carefully to be bounded and limited *to the law and to the testimony: if they speak not according to this word, it is because there is no light in them* (Isa. 8:20). 2. That we in searching from the word, labour to have the Spirit to open these things unto us, and to sanctify our hearts to receive them suitably. An irreverent fearless searching into these things even from the word, may ruin us as much as going beyond the word: for as we cannot be preserved from error in judgment, if we be not guided by the light of the word; so, there are heart-errors we cannot escape, if we have not the Spirit with the word. 3. Our end in searching must be sincere; not to satisfy our understandings, by attaining to some apprehensions of these noble things, but to have the graces of the Spirit in our souls revived, and in life, love, reverence.

For the uses of these truths, they are more than can be numbered easily.

Use 1. I would recommend this duty to you, to be much in the meditation of the riches and excellency of Jesus Christ. It may be, some may think the time better spent in studying to know some profound notions and truths concerning other points of religion. This I am sure of, that the solid life of religion, and power of godliness, consist in these points that many giddy people may think common and easily known; and that it is a sad token of a decayed backslidden soul, when such things are become unsavoury, and when they itch after other things more remote from heart-exercise in godliness. But to those who savour the things of God, I would recommend this study unto them, and that from these advantages:

1. By this mean you shall attain unto more conformity unto Jesus Christ in his glorious holiness. And is not this very desirable? Conversing with him by faith and love would make it remarkable to enemies that you have been with Jesus (Acts 4:13). Beholding his glory worketh a glorious change into the same image in the beholder: *We all with open face beholding as in a glass the glory of the Lord, are changed into the same image from glory to glory, even as by the Spirit of the Lord* (2 Cor. 3:18).

2. By this you shall attain unto fellowship with him (1 John 1:1, 2, 3). And this is the very life of a believer, the health of his countenance.

3. You shall hereby attain unto a quickening and reviving of all the graces of his Spirit in you. All graces act in him and his fullness, and there is not a more native way of getting these brought out into actings, than by serious meditation on this blessed object.

4. And lastly, and consequentially from the former, you shall attain unto such sweet manifestations of these riches in him which no tongue can express,—which are best known by feeling. You will see his loveliness, and find manifestations of his love to you in particular. You shall know what that joy unspeakable and glorious (1 Pet. 1:8), that fullness of joy is (1 John 1:4); yea, to be filled with all the fullness of God (Eph. 3:19).

Use 2. It is this blessed One, and his riches and excellency, which we would recommend unto all that are yet strangers unto him. Riches are a great attractive: where are there any comparable to those in him? If your hearts be capable of affection to a lovely object, here is the fairest of the sons of men. If you desire happiness, come here and get it. Are you afraid of wrath and hell?—come here to the shelter and high tower.

Use 3. We would recommend them unto the Lord's own. Here is strong consolation, and good hope through grace. In these cases, doth the sense of sin in its guilt exercise you?—see here riches of merit in him to satisfy justice on your account: act faith on him, and you are secure from all hazard. Is the strength of temptations your exercise, and the power of a body of death?—here are riches of healing and sanctifying grace. Do you doubt of your interest in God, and of your title to heaven? I answer from this, 'Have you an interest in these riches or not?' If you think you have not, then labour to have an interest in them, and you have it, if you ask it seriously. If you dare not deny a claim to Christ, and yet doubt of your salvation, you sin greatly; for he will lose none of his own, and hath confirmed it by his word and oath. Are you exercised with the case of the Lord's public work, and of the interests of his glory and kingdom in the world? It is a noble exercise; oh, if it were more common and ordinary! Yet, fear not; he will deal prudently; he shall be exalted and entitled, and made very high. He cannot faint nor be discouraged: he will accomplish his purposes, gather in his elect, and perform all his promises to his people, and his threatenings against all his enemies. The greatest part of his work is already done: justice is satisfied, the price is paid and accepted, and the captives shall go free. It is long since he said, *He comes quickly*, and he will perform it in due time; and then shall we see more of the excellency and riches of Christ than we either could believe, or hear, or think of; the wicked to their eternal sorrow, and the godly to their everlasting joy.

Use 4. What a sad matter is it that such an excellent one hath so little of our love and affection! All loveliness is in him, and all our love is called for; and where it is elsewhere bestowed, it is but sinfully wasted upon vanity. As in all things he hath the pre-eminence in point of perfection in himself, so ought he above all things to have the pre-eminence in the affections of our souls. There are three attractives of love among men—excellency and worth, near relationship, and obligations and favours; all of which are eminently in him.

USE 5. Of instruction. Are there unsearchable riches in him, and in some sort unsearchable emptiness and poverty in us?—here is a blessed match and meeting. Think not to live upon your own store and stock, but upon his. When you want any thing, come hither for supply, for here only it is to be had. Fear not that this treasure can be exhausted. It is a great sin to desire to live upon our own sufficiency. The poor in spirit are pronounced blessed, but only such as seek the unsearchable riches of Christ.

SERMON ON PHILIPPIANS 2:12, 13

Wherefore, my beloved, as ye have always obeyed, not as in my presence only, but now much more in my absence, work out your own salvation with fear and trembling; for it is God which worketh in you both to will and to do of his good pleasure.

THERE be two great evils in judgment and practice, which in all ages of the church have, upon the right and left hand, made many to pervert the straight ways of the Lord. One is, a pleading for and practising of a carnal liberty from gospel duties and commands, upon a woful mistake of the nature of gospel privileges, and of the dispensation of the grace of God therein. This is a turning of the grace of God into wantonness. Another extreme is, a turning of gospel commands into legal, and a pleading so for obedience thereunto; self-ability (abstract from the influences of grace) to perform that obedience, and a proper merit resulting from that performance, that confidence in the flesh is proclaimed, and the grace of God made a cypher. What influence the former hath had in the raising and maintaining of the heresies of the Antinomians, Familists, Quakers, etc., none but strangers in our Israel can be ignorant. And what influence the other extreme hath had in raising the Arminian, Popish, and Socinian heresies, all that are acquainted with the case of the church of God, both abroad and at home, do know but too sadly. Yea, how great an influence the darkness and confusion in the minds of many of the Lord's people concerning the due harmony of the sovereign influence of the grace of God, with the natural liberty of the will concurring; the due acknowledgment of the necessity of that influence, and the obligation to the practice of duties, notwithstanding of the want of it, hath upon their spiritual condition, every one who hath an ear to hear, and a heart to understand, and grace to search his own heart, doth in some measure know.

Therefore, though it be not so wholly suitable to the nature of this exercise, to prosecute debates with the adversaries of truth; yet because of the advantage that those on either extreme do pretend to have hence for their error, and the real advantage which this place doth give to refute the one and the other, I shall therefore, ere I come to the practical improvement of them, glance a little at both. In which handling, I shall divide the text, give the literal meaning, clear it from their objections, point out the things here held out, with their influence on our practice in religion.

These words come in among the gracious exhortations which the Holy Ghost giveth by Paul's pen unto these believing Philippians. In the beginning of the twelfth verse, the apostle, having praised their former obedience, whereof he was a witness whilst among them, and expressed his charitable confidence of their continuance and increase in that obedience, even in his absence, as an insinuatory preface unto what he was to say; he then setteth down a most weighty exhortation, and backeth it with an encouraging argument, in verse 13th. In the exhortation are three things: 1. The act itself in the duty enjoined, *work out*. 2. The subject-matter whereabout this act is to be exercised, *your own salvation*. 3. The qualification of this act about this subject, *with fear and trembling*.

As to the first, there needs little to be said of it, it being so very clear. It is not simple working, but a *diligence* in working called for, and continuance in that diligence, until the perfect end of the work be attained. This is the force of the original word.

The second—the subject-matter wherabout this act is to be exercised—*your own salvation*. We shall not stand upon the various acceptations of this word in scripture, as sometimes signifying the means of salvation (Heb. 2:3; 1 Pet. 1:9); sometimes the saving effect of those means upon the called (2 Tim. 1:9); sometimes the accomplishment of this begun salvation in heaven. We take it not here as importing both beginning, progress, and perfection of salvation; for he is speaking to those in whom the work was already begun, as in chap. 1 verse 6. But the evidence of the scope bindeth us to aver, that here the apostle presseth them to a diligent advancing, and a constant progress in the work and course of their salvation, the way of truth and holiness, wherein already they were engaged. This salvation is called *their own*, not that the doctrine of it was of their own devising and framing; or that their walking up unto that doctrine by faith and obedience, was of their own strength (in that sense, salvation is only of the Lord, and Christ is the inventor of the doctrine, and the author and finisher of the work of salvation); but that it was theirs by a gifted right and possession. They were the parties to whom the doctrine of salvation was imparted, in whom it was begun, and on whom it was to be accomplished.

The third thing is, the qualification of this commanded exercise, *with fear and trembling*. This, enemies to the certainty and assurance of faith, and to the perseverance of the faithful, draw to their advantage. In opposition to which mistake, I shall only give the meaning of this word, and confirm it from the analogy of faith, and the context, omitting what the deluded Quakers may allege hence for their energumenical shakings, as unworthy of any regard. All agree, that by *fear* and *trembling* one and the same thing is signified. This qualification of duty is several times used, sometimes in cases different from this, as in 1 Corinthians 2:3; Ephesians 6:5; sometimes in cases that are as it were parallel with this, as Psalm 2:11; Romans 11:20. All which do clear us in this, that it is only humility, sense of our own weakness and infirmity, which is here called for; and if you will, include in it the filial fear of God; which do no way plead for doubting and diffidence as to the issue, which is the thing their adversaries plead for. For the security of saints, and the certainty of their perseverance, is not founded upon any thing in themselves, but upon the veracity of the promiser, the always effectual intercession of Christ, and the indwelling of the Spirit. So that a holy fear of falling because of sinful weakness, can no ways shake these foundations.

But that we may further clear the nature of the fear called for, omitting many distinctions used by divines in this case, we shall only name this: Fear is either of the issue—hell; or of the means leading to it—sin; both either absolute or conditional. Absolute fear of hell is despair; diametrically opposite to faith, and forbidden by all these commands in scripture, requiring faith and trusting in the Lord, as a part of our worship. Conditional fear of hell; that is, 'I fear hell, if I walk in the ways leading unto it,' is a sanctified mean of God's appointment for escaping it, by eschewing of those ways that lead unto it. Absolute fear about the means; that is, that I be given up wholly to a final neglect of the means of grace, and to a total revolting from God, in the practice of sin without repentance, is all one with despair; and is forbidden by the whole tenor of the covenant of grace. Conditional fear about the means, that is, 'I fear, if I watch not, and do not lean unto Christ's strength, I may fall into sin,' is also a sanctified mean for escaping of sin, and so of the fear of hell. And this is all one with Calvin's distinction upon this place. 'There is a fear,' saith he, 'which begets carefulness in duty with humility (which is here required); and a fear which begets anxious doubting in whatever required.' Hence it is observable in experience, and evident in spiritual reason, that the more there be in any, of this holy conditional fear, and the more fruitful it be in its native effects of humility, diligence, self-denial, and trusting in their Lord's strength, the more clear is the man's assurance of salvation. And this sense of the words, is much confirmed by the subsequent words. For what an absurd consequence would the adversaries make of it! 'God works both to will and to do: therefore, do you your duty *doubtingly*, without any assurance of the end.'

This leads us to the second, wherein we have, 1. The causal particle *for* knitting these words, as an encouraging argument with the former. 2. Who it is that is the author of this encouragement;—God. 3. Wherein his help consisteth; efficaciously working both to will and to do: *efficaciously* as the original imports. 4. The fountain from whence this help flows—his free will, *good pleasure*. Not that which simply denotes his sovereignty in doing or not doing as he pleaseth (which would not so agree with the scope); but that kindly favour which he bears to his own in Jesus Christ, which though he manifest it sovereignly in some sort, yet is it always with a respect to their good.

Concerning almost all of these, the enemies of truth do move debates. But not to be tedious in these matters, especially in an exercise of this nature, I shall only hint at some few things, which may clear the truth, and remove any objection the adversaries do propound against them. As, 1. That such commands as are here do not infer any thing but obligation to duty; and no ways any ability to perform them, or any merit in performance. 2. That the determining influence of the grace of God upon the will is consistent with its natural liberty. 3. How that the acknowledging of this influence doth take away any ground of being called co-workers with God in the business of our salvation, in the Popish and Arminian sense, and yet giveth no ground to the libertine extreme. 4. How that this assorting of the whole into grace is an argument to diligence.

I. First, That this command to *work out* doth not import self-ability to obey, nor any merit to result from obedience, is so clear from the connection of the argument with the command, that I would not so much as have started it, if the natural corruption of men's hearts were not so extravagant as it is, and that adversaries do make use of it, and the learned, in commenting upon the place, do remove it.

1. The prime import of all commands to duty, is a revelation of God's will of obedience; and as they hold forth what his will is about duty, so they infer an obligation to performance.

2. That the Lord being holy and just, requireth nothing but what is or was in the power of the person commanded to obey, either in his own person or in his representative.

3. That gospel commands, in their prime import, are of the same nature with legal; and consequently, men are punished for disobedience of the one as well as of the other, because, legally considered, they were in their representatives endued with power to obey.

4. Yet gospel commands, as given by the Lord to his own covenanted people, are sanctified means for working and procuring of obedience. Not that they are a moral mean, to stir up the godly to exert any strength in themselves in performing acts of obedience; but, 1. Because they discover the Lord's will, and their obligation to obedience thereto: 2*d*, Because from this accidentally is discovered their inability to yield obedience as in themselves, which produces self-denial. 3*d*, From this floweth, by the Lord's blessing, acts of faith upon the fullness and sufficiency of their Surety, wherein stands their stability and strength for all things (Phil. 4:13). Yea, we may say, that in all gospel commands, as tendered to those in Christ, there is included a promise of grace to obey; and in this they are distinguished from legal commands. But the simple reading of these words, and the considering of the connection of the argument with the command, is enough to silence such cavillers, if the verdict of the Holy Ghost pronounced against their error were enough to silence them: the words that follow, containing the fullest expressions of the entire help of God's grace, which a godly man stands in need of, both for willing and doing; and consequently, of the weakness of a regenerate man, as in himself considered.

II. The second thing to be cleared is, How the determining influence of the grace of God upon the will (here asserted) consisteth with its natural liberty. This is a depth wherein many learned heads and unholy hearts have drowned; and, indeed, it is a very great one. It shall suffice us to lay down the positive truth, that there is no inconsistency betwixt the two; which may thus be cleared:

1. All creatures being necessarily dependent, both in their being and operation, upon the First Cause, man's will being a creature, it cannot, either in sound reason or divinity, be asserted that it is independent from this general concourse or influence wherein stands the very being and working of every creature.

2. This holy Creator and Preserver of all things having necessarily before him, as his end in creation and providence, his own glory, hath by his wise decrees determined so the actings of all his creatures, as may best subserve his infinitely wise designs. So that man's will must again fall under a determination because of such decrees.

3. And as the will of man is thus necessarily liable to a double determination, as it is a creature, so in its being made such a creature, a subordinated faculty, to be led and determined by the understanding, it again falleth under a restriction of that unlimited liberty pleaded for; for being in itself a blind faculty (or a rational appetite, as some define it), it cannot move towards any thing but what the understanding holdeth out as good, either true or apparent. Hence may be seen somewhat of the manner of the Lord's influence upon the will of man; for it is evident that the illuminating influence of grace upon the understanding is perfective of its natural capacity of discerning, both *in via contemplanda*, which is the theoretical judgment, and *in via agenda hic et nunc*, which is the practical, both in its first and absolute judgment concerning things good or bad, and in its comparative judgment concerning things better or worse;—from which determinations of the understanding, follows such a commanding of the will to choose or refuse, that it cannot but elicit the one of these acts, and that most freely.

4. Hence it follows that the natural liberty of the will doth not consist in an absolute indifferency to act thus or otherwise, good or bad, but in the special towardness, cheerfulness, and liberty of its acting; for the only necessity inconsistent with this, is that of force and

coaction. And indeed, the asserting of the will's liberty, as adversaries do, doth not only loose this proud faculty from its due dependence on the concurrence and decrees of its Maker, but lifteth it up unto a higher pitch of liberty than can lawfully be ascribed to God himself, who cannot will what is ill; and to angels and glorified saints, who are graciously determined to will only what is good.

III. How that the ascribing of this unto God doth deny our being workers together with God, in the Popish sense, and yet is opposite unto the Libertine extreme.

The Papists would so divide the work, that they may share the glory between God and man,—the Libertines would make a man a brute or a stone. Against the first, we say, that either it must be at the first of conversion, or in the progress of sanctification. At the first of conversion, the Lord's work is entirely enlivening; and man's influence on the effect is such as a dead man can have upon his own quickening, which in nature is evident can be none at all (Eph. 2:1, 2). And though, in the infusion of the new life, there be indeed gracious habits infused, qualifying the man for gracious actings, yet these habits are not sufficient either to preserve themselves from total decay, or to determine their possessor unto the least gracious operation, without a present actuating influence from the fountain whence they first ran. For we do not maintain the activity, yea, nor immortality of grace, as flowing from its own positive nature, but rather its relative (so to speak); that is, it is no self-sufficient habit, but the continuance of its sufficiency, that flows from the continuance of its dependence on the first fountain; which dependence the Lord, by the well-ordered covenant, hath determined to be incorruptible,—a grace, therefore, immortal. Therefore, in the bringing out of these gracious habits into gracious actings, the actual influence of actuating grace is absolutely needful: *Abide in me, and I in you. As the branch cannot bear fruit of itself, except it abide in the vine, no more can ye, except ye abide in me* (John 15:4). *Without me* (χωρις εμου), or separate from me, and my influence, as the root, *ye can do nothing*—which was spoken to branches already in the vine. Here the believer (as Calvin expresseth it in his *Institutes*), '*passivé agit*,' or, as others, '*actus agit*,'—being acted upon graciously, he acts graciously. How evidently these clear principles exclude all boasting, is evident; but we will not stand on this.

But to guard against the other extreme: We do not say that a godly man is wholly passive in gracious actings; for, 1. He acts with these same natural faculties in all gracious operations, wherein the gracious habits are seated—as judgment and affections. 2. Neither are we wholly to deny, yet very warily to understand and admit it, that as other moral habits are strengthened by repeated acts, so, in the growth of sanctification, the habits of grace do acquire a greater positive strength than at first infusion; and consequently, a man far advanced in holiness hath a greater disposition, easiness, and facility (simply considered) in exerting gracious operations, than another in whom the habits are not so much corroborate by exercise in the Lord's ways. Hence the scripture distinction of Christians into fathers, young men, and children. But though we are to keep at a distance from any thought of the best their being able to do any thing that is good, without actual influence of grace, yet is it consonant to spiritual reason and experience to say, that the influences needful for actuating strong gracious habits unto gracious actions, are simply not so powerful and mighty (sufficient they must always be) as necessarily are in bringing forth decayed languid habits into act (Psa. 51:10).

The last thing is, How that this argument can have influence upon diligence in obedience. Carnal reason and its carnal patrons do plead, that this is the highway to render men secure and careless in duty. And it cannot indeed be denied, that it may have such an effect, and often hath, on sensual men not having the Spirit. Not to stay upon a debate which, as to its practical use, may afterward be spoken to, we would only say, 1. That the apostle in our text is speaking to godly persons who were already diligent in their work—who, being partakers of the divine nature, were capable of being moved with gracious principles. 2. Evangelical arguments are all encouragements and promises, which as they are only the portion of the godly, so, such do find strong influence accompanying such arguments, for the inspiring unto diligence. The adversaries plead only for legal arguments, and such as natural reason teacheth. Yea, what stronger argument can be used to a poor soul ready to faint because of the greatness of its work, than this, 'Arise, and be doing; for the Lord will work in you both to will and to do?'

But now, it is high time to come to the observations contained in these words, omitting what may be observed from the connection, since there is such plenty of excellent matter in the words themselves.

OBSERV. 1. The great improvement which the Holy Ghost calleth the saints to lay to heart, and the great duty which a faithful minister layeth upon his flock, is that of their own salvation. This design of the apostle in writing to his flock (such the Philippians were, see chapter 4 verse 1), and the scope of the Holy Ghost in recording it for the church in all ages, doth make out the truth of this—a truth shining so in its own evidence, and confirmed by the scope of the whole book of God, that it were superfluous to prove it.

USE. Let it then be the subject of your most serious thoughts; and these two considerations in particular, 1. That it is *salvation*, a matter of highest concernment. 2. It is your *own*—a matter of your nearest concernment. The former claimeth evidently a superiority above worldly interests. Oh! how low are they in respect of salvation. It supposeth danger, and the greatest danger: none need salvation, but such as are lost. None can lay it to heart aright, but those who lay to heart their lost condition. *What shall I do to be saved?* the question of every serious soul, importeth both. The latter—your interest in it—calls for a superiority in concernment beyond that of others simply considered. Every one should be careful of another's soul, but more of his own soul's salvation—such suitable concernment therein, as nature's light draweth a man to what most nearly relates to himself. And that is very great, and *the* greatest.

OBSERV. 2. To be rightly exercised about this matter, much labour and pains is called; this is the *strait* gate; and that even from such as have been exercised therein diligently, as the Philippians were. This is confirmed, 1. From its importance. It is the one thing needful, and therefore our singular endeavours are called for in pursuing it. 2. From the great and mighty opposition that is made unto a man in this work, from many and strong enemies. Strong impediments in the way of an important design call for much diligence. Force is against us, and subtlety, and continuance in both by our enemies. 3. From the commonness of a mistake in this matter, that it is easy; and from want of diligence therein. STRIVE *to enter in at the strait gate: for many, I say unto you, will seek to enter in, and shall not be able* (Luke 13:24).

USE. What shall be said of those who have not yet begun to be exercised in this great matter? Is salvation an indifferent thing? Is it attainable without pains? Whatever diligence hath been used by any in it, continuance and increase therein are called for. Trifling endeavours are reprovable here, as unsuitable to so great and important a business.

OBSERV. 3. In diligence with this great work, much humility and sense of our own infirmity are called for, with fear and trembling. And the grounds of this are evident, if we consider ourselves, and compare ourselves with our enemies—our weakness, with the greatness of the work; or if we reflect on our former experience in verification of this. And they are evident, if comparing both, we look wisely to what is to come. Opposition of enemies constantly increaseth, and the violence of their assaults.

USE. How unreasonable is confidence in ourselves in this great work! How reprovable are proud undertakers in their own strength! This calleth for a constant remembrance of all those humbling considerations, and self-denial in that remembrance. But lest it should degenerate,

OBSERV. 4. Whatever ground of fear there be as from self, yet it is the great encouragement of the saints that the Lord is the helper in this work. The absolute sufficiency of this helper in this work, is evident, from his infinite fullness and sufficiency in himself, which is a great depth. But it may be more evident, by taking some parts of this sufficiency, and comparing it with the wants of the saints, and its perfect suitableness will appear. Infinite power is for the supply of great weakness against strong enemies; infinite wisdom, for the cure of folly in dealing with politic enemies; infinite love, for putting forth such wisdom and power for their good. And unchangeable truth is engaged by promises and oaths, that such power, wisdom, and love, shall never leave them.

USE. How reprovable are they who do not set about this work because of discouragements; and such as carry it on discouragedly!

OBSERV. 5. Entire help is given by this sufficient helper. It is not an empty title. *To will and to do*—this is actual help, and that, entirely suited to our necessity: for there are but two things necessary unto all actions,—will, and power of performance; and both are here.

Use. Learn to acknowledge him, and wait for his help entirely. Both in willing and doing, set about nothing in this work in your own strength, and doubt not of his.

Observ. 6. The fountain whence all this floweth is his free will and good pleasure. Of his will he begat us freely (James 1:18); and freely he doth all.

Use. Look not to any thing of desert in yourself. Bless him for his help vouchsafed. Be not peremptory, but wait patiently, when help seemeth to be delayed. His sovereignty is to be acknowledged.

Observ. 7. The consideration of this entire help is a great argument to diligence.

Use. Try what ye find of the force of this, and try yourselves by it.

SERMON ON 1 CORINTHIANS 2:10

But God hath revealed them unto us by his Spirit, for the Spirit searcheth all things, yea, the deep things of God.

NEITHER do the faithful preachers of the gospel, nor its conscientious hearers, make any doubt of this matter of mourning,—that the frame of men's minds who are exercised about these things, is sadly unsuitable unto their greatness and importance. For convincing you of this, if not the curing of this distemper, we have made choice of this scripture.

Two things are main causes of this distemper; and the due faith of them would be the cure. 1. Men's not pondering with whom they have to do in the preaching of the word. Little do the careless hearers of the gospel dream that it is God the Holy Ghost that is dealing with them in the preached word. 2. Ignorance of, or not adverting unto the greatness and importance of the truths delivered unto them. Few think that they are the depths of God.

We shall take a view of the preceding part of the chapter which is needful for understanding the apostle's scope, and so for getting and reaching his mind. We have an account of his way of behaving in his ministry amongst them; and that, we may branch out into these heads:

1. That he came not with a vain flourish of worldly rhetoric and carnal wisdom (verse 1), because this, he hints, had been unsuitable unto the grave work he had to do amongst them—even the testimony of God: a testimony that had abundance of majesty and truth for its convoy, and had been but disparaged with carnal paintings of words.

2. That his behaving thus was according to his settled resolution (verse 2). He had laid down this brave resolution to preach Christ and him crucified amongst them, though there was no want of worldly wisdom amongst that people; which even many of them, after conversion, and who were ministers, did too much follow; whom also he is probably reflecting on, as afterwards in chapter 4 verse 18, he doth it more expressly.

3. We have a positive account of his humble behaviour (verse 3), in words that may astonish us, that even a holy fear of miscarrying in so great a work, and a deep sense of his weakness, as of himself for this great work, was deeply lodged in the spirit of this eminent apostle; so that if we compare this with the wonderful assistance that he had, and large measure of all gifts given him, it is a rare proof of grace and humility in him.

4. We have a further account of his way of preaching, both in enlarging on the former negative, and in asserting the positive, wherein he states an opposition between the two; teaching, in the first place, that a faithful minister should hide man and human parts, and wisdom, as much as may be, in dispensing the gospel; and in the second, that ordinarily there is most of the power and demonstration of the Spirit attending such ways of dispensing the gospel, wherein all carnal wisdom is most denied. That you may not mistake this, I shall clear up what is this evidence of the Spirit that attends preaching, and what there is of man contrary to it.

The evidence and demonstration of the Spirit and of power, is the efficacy of the word on consciences, produced by the influences of the Holy Ghost: this efficacy is, by a displaying of the authority of God, and a forcible bearing in of the light of truth on the mind, and its power on the heart and conscience. *We have renounced the hidden things of dishonesty, not walking in craftiness, nor handling the word of God deceitfully; but by manifestation of the truth, commending ourselves to every man's conscience in the sight of God* (2 Cor. 4:2). In these times, we confess, that this evidence of the Spirit was sometimes conveyed by the means of miracles: but these did only confirm the truth as God's, while the making it effectual on the heart, was by another and nearer operation of the Spirit on men's hearts. And what is that which is opposite unto it? In general, it is when men think to do this, and work such an effect on people's hearts, without the Spirit's help. As, *first*, When they propose with such clearness of forcible reason what they think is enough to persuade any rational man to yield his assent unto it, that they think no man can shut out the light. *Secondly*, When they use such forcible motives to persuade, that they think no man can resist them. Now, though this way be in itself very lawful, if scripture light and arguments be made use of, yet its fault is, when the Holy Ghost is not duly depended on, as the only bearer in of light and life upon the soul, and men give too much to the means in themselves.

5. We have the end he aimed at in this way,—that their faith might not be seen to be wrought by, and to stand upon man's wisdom, but God's power (verse 5), intimating clearly, that the faith of the hearers is much according to the way of the preachers. A false unsound profession may be begotten by a carnally-wise way of handling the things of God, and so, they may be said rather to gain disciples, than the Lord's true believers, by such ministrations.

And this leadeth us to the words which are brought in as an answer to another objection,—How came you then to know such a mystery? He answers, by revelation of the Spirit. In the words we have, 1. The way whereby the apostle and the godly come to the knowledge of the mystery hid from the world—God's revealing them by his Spirit. 2. The sufficiency of this way and mean proved—*for the Spirit searcheth all things, even the deep things of God.*

For the explaining of these things, there is great heed to be taken of the words. We must know what is meant by 'God.' It is specially here meant of the Father, who, as he is the *father of lights*, so also in a special manner, of all the knowledge of himself and his will that is to be found amongst men. *Revealed*, that is, hath taken off the hiding veil that was on them. *Unto us*, to me, Paul, and Sosthenes, and other faithful servants of Jesus Christ. *By his Spirit*, by the special efficacy of the Holy Ghost, whereby what we of ourselves could never come unto the knowledge of, by his working are clearly discerned. Next, as to the sufficiency of this mean—this revealer is the great searcher of all things; that is, he is well acquainted with all, even the depths of God, as a man is, with such things as he hath searched out unto the bottom, and unto perfection: which, by the way, is a solid proof that the Holy Ghost is God.

Our main design in pitching upon this verse, was for the last words of it; yet we shall speak somewhat also unto the other things in it, but more briefly, and for preparing our way unto the other principal thing.

Observ. 1. All discovery of the saving truths of God flows from his gracious revelation thereof by his Spirit. In handling of this we shall, first, Show what this revelation is; secondly, Prove it by the insufficiency of any other mean to attain such a discovery.

1. What is this revealing of divine truth by the Spirit? We are, for understanding of this aright, to distinguish the several revelations that the Lord hath given to his church. And these are, 1. The revelation made unto the fathers and prophets of old, varied in circumstances, until Moses' time, by visions, and oracles, and tradition from father to son; thereafter, by the lawgiver Moses; and thereafter unto the prophets—all which were but more clear breakings forth of the same divine truth, consonant to itself, and harmonious as to the matter, though with different circumstances; and this by the Spirit of Christ (1 Pet. 1:11). 2. That rare and matchless revelation by the Lord himself, who had the Spirit without measure (Heb. 1:1). Which albeit for the authority of the Messenger it was matchless (so is he called in Mal. 3:1), yet in that dispensation, there were for wise reasons many truths then kept back. 3. The revelation unto the apostles, and by them to the church; who had the greatest measure of the Spirit of God attending them, that ever mere men had—according to the promise in John 14 and 15, and its fulfilment in Acts 2:4. The revelation that is made unto the church by the sealed and complete canon of the Holy Scriptures, the native product of the Holy Ghost (2 Pet. 1:21; 2 Tim. 3:16). This is the great revelation; and by this, the Spirit revealeth now unto the church the deep things of God. And there needs no more but what the godly obtain—the same Spirit that did indite them by his penmen,—to make them plain and powerful on our hearts. In the second place, we shall prove the insufficiency of any other means to attain the knowledge of these things. And this is evident from, 1. The gross ignorance of them that have had nature's light most refined; the Greeks and Romans before Christ's time. Not only supernatural truth was not reached by them, but any ordinary Christian may now discover how lame they were, even in pursuing after and attaining the knowledge of truths accessible by nature's light—as in their multitude of gods, and gross sins in practice. 2. The lamentable blindness of the world, and all nations everywhere that want this revelation altogether, or have it let out unto them by little, and unfaithfully, as in the Popish church. 3. The sad ignorance of them that have this revelation read by and to them, and

explained and expounded daily unto them. Surely it saith, that men, by themselves, can never attain the knowledge of these things. 4. The main truths are evidently out of the reach of nature's light. There are many that nature's light revealeth, such as the being of God, the unity of the Godhead; his power, wisdom, and spiritual nature (Rom. 1:20; Acts 17) the immortality of the soul, a life of retribution and rewards—and that there is another world of spiritual inhabitants, as many apparitions have proved even to the heathen. But the Trinity of persons, the union of two natures in the Son of God, and the whole continuance of salvation, and several other things about the two covenants, are undiscoverable by nature's light.

USE 1.—Be deeply thankful for this revelation. Alas for the sin of ingratitude and unthankfulness, and that, for this greatest mercy! To move you to a deep thankfulness, consider, that this is the most gracious revelation that God ever gave to mankind. It is of the greatest things in themselves, and of things of the greatest usefulness even for eternal salvation. And consider, that it is a most full and clear revelation. Even they that had extraordinary ways of revelation, had but a little of that revealed, that is plentifully now revealed unto us all in the word. It is a most sure way of revelation, not exposed unto those doubts and mistakes in which even extraordinary ways did leave men. *We have also a more sure word of prophecy; whereunto ye do well that ye take heed, as unto a light that shineth in a dark place, until the day dawn, and the day-star arise in your hearts* (2 Pet. 1:19). It is every way sufficient for the end designed (2 Tim. 3:15): the Spirit's going along with it, makes it sufficient for saving knowledge. It is a revelation given unto a small part of the world—and what are you better than the Indians that dwell in the shadow of death?

USE 2.—Oh! labour to make a good use of it. Improvement is all and the main thing this matter calls for. It stands, 1. In opening your eyes, and lending your ears to what is revealed, and in studying it. The study of the word, as the great revelation of the Holy Ghost, is rarely practised. Shall the Holy Ghost reveal, and men not open their eyes, and lend their ears? 2. In studying and taking heed thereunto, as his revelation. Many study and read the word, without this sanctifying qualification of all such endeavours. It is just with the Lord, that when men in a careless and profane contempt slight this aid, he should give them up unto blindness and erring mistakes. 3. In seeking humbly and fervently the help of the Holy Ghost in this search. Little profiting by it is to be hoped for without this. 4. And in all, driving at that end that the revelation is made for, to make you wise unto salvation; and unto all the means that lead unto it, and fit and prepare you for it. Unsanctified aims in studying divine truth, have led many into woful error.

The next thing is, concerning the omniscience, and perfect knowledge of God the Holy Ghost; of which we shall not speak, save for clearing of the matter, *for the Spirit*. And that you may know, saith the apostle, how sufficient this is, it is a revelation from him who is all-knowing; who *searcheth all things*, not for increase of knowledge, as a man searcheth out unknown things, but to shew the perfection of his knowledge of them; even as a man doth, of what hath cost him a most narrow and exact search. The Holy Ghost is fully and perfectly acquainted with all the great and deep things of God. Being one in essence, and all essential perfection, with the other two blessed persons, it cannot be otherwise. This serves to prove, that the Holy Ghost is God, and that the scriptures are a true, safe, and wise revelation of God's will unto men, since they come from one so well acquainted with all. But that which we intend mainly to insist on is the last.

The mysteries of the Christian religion are *the deep things of God*. And that this is the meaning of the expression *deep things of God*, is clear from the following words, *For what man knoweth the things of a man, save the spirit of man which is in him? even so, the things of God knoweth no man, but the Spirit of God. Now we have received, not the spirit of the world, but the spirit which is of God; that we might know the things that are freely given to us of God. Which things also we speak, not in the words which man's wisdom teacheth, but which the Holy Ghost teacheth; comparing spiritual things with spiritual* (verses 11, 12, 13). Here he proves by a clear similitude, that the Holy Ghost only is fully acquainted with these; that all the godly have this spirit revealing those things to them; and that those things thus revealed, were the subject of his preaching. And the following words, *But the natural man receiveth not the things of the Spirit of God: for they are foolishness unto him: neither can he know them, because they are spiritually discerned* (verse 14) prove, why they are called *deep things*—even because they are not obvious to a *natural man*.

In handling of this great and grave truth, we shall show, 1. What are these deep things of God. 2. Why they are thus called; and, 3. Prove it in some particular truths.

1. What they are. Not to speak of any depths not revealed, for this were to darken counsel by words without knowledge, they are—scripture truths, such as we owe the knowledge of only to revelation, and which are no other ways attainable—gospel truths, or such as broke up mostly with the manifestation of Jesus Christ in the gospel—and such as have the closest reference unto God's glory and the salvation of man. This is from their end, the great end of God's manifestation of himself unto the world.

2. Why are they called the deep things of God? Because of their own great depth: they are profound deep things, because of their relation unto God, and that, as being the author of the revelation of such truths, and the author and framer of the truths in themselves, and their relation to him, as the main matter and subject of them. They are the deep things that God hath made and revealed, and mainly, are depths about God, and to him, as the great end, even his glory and praise.

3. We shall prove it in particulars; and this is a most large subject, yet, because of its great usefulness, both for informing the ignorant in the sum of Christian doctrine, and convincing the careless of their depth, we shall enlarge on it, only premising, that we have deep attention, deep humility, and deep reverence in hearing these things. We cannot speak of them all without an extraordinary length, and therefore we shall pitch only on the chief of the deep things of God, under these heads, 1. Such depths as are revealed about God himself. 2. Such as have an immediate relation unto man: for saving knowledge may be comprised under these two heads, the knowledge of God, and of ourselves.

I. These depths that are about, and concerning God himself, are, 1. His nature and being. The light of nature can discover a little of the being of God, and of his nature; but that full and deep account thereof that the scriptures give, it by no means can reach. 2. His infinite incomprehensibleness. A created understanding can no more contain and comprehend his being, than a child's hand can span the heavens and earth (Job 11:7, 8, 9). How great a length do men's understandings go in search of the creatures! 3. His great and deep justice and judgments (Psa. 36:6; Rom. 11:33), especially manifested in punishing sin with eternal vengeance. 4. His all-seeing eye; his perfect knowledge and omnipresence. It is a sad thing, that our thoughts of God are so far from what they ought to be. 5. The depth of divine patience in delaying threatened and deserved judgments.

2. The mystery of the Trinity is a great depth that many have drowned in, while they have not been humbly satisfied with the revelation of this in the word, but have offered to wade and fathom it by the force of their shallow understanding. One God in three persons is the greatest of all the depths of God; concerning which I have only to say, the light of nature could never discover it—and now that it is discovered, it is the main doctrine of all foundations of our religion, so that a denier of it, is by no means to be reckoned a Christian. And such monstrous apostates there are in the land, which should make us mourn and fear. And consider the dreadful consequents of denying this great truth. He that denieth the Son to be God, necessarily must deny his satisfaction to justice for sin, and the justification of a sinner, by a believing laying hold on this satisfaction; and accordingly he denies it. He that denieth the Holy Ghost to be God, must deny, and always doth, the omnipotency and sovereignty of his grace in converting a sinner, and in perfecting of him. And these things are so close unto one another, that the deniers of the power of grace, are ofttimes left to the denying of the divinity of the Holy Ghost, the worker thereof. Consider concerning this depth, that there is none that calls for more deep reverence and fear in thinking thereof: and you ought also to have a more exact fear of any blasphemies that are vented directly or indirectly against the same. Come not near the tabernacles of those wicked men that blaspheme the God of heaven. It is astonishing to think what sort of professors they are that fear not at the sight and report of such blasphemies; I mean mainly the Quakers, the chief leaders of whom do expressly, and in print, blaspheme these doctrines, and therefore the which society is to be abhorred, unless they disown such blasphemies.

3. The third depth, is that of the incarnation of the Son of God. *The Word was made flesh, and dwelt among us (and we beheld his glory, the*

glory as of the only begotten of the Father,) full of grace and truth (John 1:14). Here are two natures in one person. *Without controversy great is the mystery of godliness; God was manifest in the flesh, justified in the Spirit, seen of angels, preached unto the Gentiles, believed on in the world, received up into glory* (1 Tim. 3:16). This is the sum of the gospel. *What the law could not do, in that it was weak through the flesh, God sending his own Son in the likeness of sinful flesh, and for sin, condemned sin in the flesh: that the righteousness of the law might be fulfilled in us, who walk not after the flesh, but after the Spirit* (Rom. 8:3, 4). That this is a great depth, and that no natural man can reach it by nature's light, is evident. But to take a careful view of it, consider, 1. The inequality of the natures united, and the strictness of the union—God and man in one person. Oh, wonderful! the man's blood is called God's (Acts 20:28). The person God-man receiveth divine worship even when born. *And again, when he bringeth in the first-begotten into the world, he saith, And let all the angels of God worship him* (Heb. 1:6). 2. The low depth of humiliation that God in this nature underwent, without any real abasement (Phil. 2:6, 7). All the creation is astonished at his sufferings. 3. The design of all this—the glory of grace in saving sinners, by striking up a new and brave way to heaven, so that that song only may for eternity be sung by its inhabitants, *Unto him that loved us, and washed us from our sins in his own blood, and hath made us kings and priests unto God and his Father; to him be glory and dominion for ever and ever. Amen. Thou art worthy to take the book, and to open the seals thereof: for thou wast slain, and hast redeemed us to God by thy blood out of every kindred, and tongue, and people, and nation; and hast made us unto our God kings and priests: and we shall reign on the earth. Worthy is the Lamb that was slain to receive power, and riches, and wisdom, and strength, and honour, and glory, and blessing* (Rev. 1:5, 6, and 5:9, 10, 12). The praises of such sinners, and their souls were so dear to him, that he underwent so much to purchase them.

4. The fourth deep is Predestination—that out of the same mass of fallen mankind, the Lord's sovereignty pitched on some to be the objects of his mercy, and left the rest to perish for their sins. *For he saith to Moses, I will have mercy on whom I will have mercy, and I will have compassion on whom I will have compassion. So then, it is not of him that willeth, nor of him that runneth, but of God that sheweth mercy*

(Rom. 9:15, 16). And this is a great depth (Rom. 11:33). Here also many stumble, by the pride of their hearts, and treacherous winning of Satan. That this is a great depth, none can question; and all that search into it, find it so to be. For the understanding whereof, these things may help: 1. This is an act of God, as a sovereign Lord, and not as a judge. 2. He oweth nothing to any of his creatures, as they are his creatures, until he engage himself graciously by promise. 3. He oweth nothing to his sinful creatures, as sinful, but vengeance, the desert of their sin. If then, in the sovereignty of his love, he pitch on some, and leave others to their desert, who can quarrel? The *excellency* of this depth is seen, in that he hath wisely contrived a way for executing this decree by his son Jesus Christ, and reaps glory both to his mercy and justice eternally.

5. The fifth depth of God is, his creating and making all things of nothing. Oh, what a stately frame hath he made! That it is so, every one seeth; that God made it, any man may by reason know. Stones and earth are not likely things to make themselves (Psa. 104:24). How marvellous are they all! (Psa. 111:2, 3). The saints are frequently travelling in this deep, with wonder and adoration. This depth is the more seen, if we consider,

1*st*, The freedom of this great work. He might have suffered all things to have lain eternally in the womb of their mother nothing; he needed not any creation yet gave he a being to such a huge number of creatures in the air, earth, and water, besides the celestial bodies and their inhabitants.

2*d*, The wonderful wisdom that is therein in compacting the creation so wonderfully and orderly, in hanging the earth in the midst of the air, and the heavens round about and above it everywhere; in the orderly motion of the heavens; in bounding the sea, and making it so useful unto man by fishes and trading—his breaking up so many veins of fountains and rivers for the inhabitants of the earth:—in the winds that purge the air, and help unto sailing; in the course and motion of the sun for distinguishing the seasons of summer, winter, spring-time, and harvest; in broaching the clouds, that their waters may refresh the earth, and in such a manner to distil, as may benefit and not hurt.

3*d*, The power that is seen therein. Oh, what a strong arm must it be, that settled the foundation of the earth, and gave the heavens such a whirling motion at their first creation, that they never stand still,—in making so glorious a light as the sun, and so beautifully spangled a firmament—in making so great a sea, and limiting it so, that it overflows not the earth!

6. The sixth depth, is divine providence. This is, God's sustaining and governing the world that he hath so wisely made. Oh! what a depth is here of wisdom and power. Who could guide this world, but the same arm that made it? Let us launch out a little into this depth. There is the Lord's supporting of all things that he hath made: this is like a continued creation, a keeping them out of nothing, which were lately brought forth thence (Acts 17), and his wise providing of food for every thing living. *These wait all upon thee, that thou mayest give them their meat in due season. The eyes of all wait upon thee; and thou givest them their meat in due season* (Psa. 104:27 and 145:15). What a great house doth he keep! But especially his deep acts of government are to be considered: he is the governor in the midst of the nations. Let us take notice of his providence toward the world,—1. Sovereignly: he sheweth himself in shaking and changing nations as he pleases, and kings and kingdoms. *And all the inhabitants of the earth are reputed as nothing: and he doeth according to his will in the army of heaven, and among the inhabitants of the earth: and none can stay his hand, or say unto him, What doest thou?* (Dan. 4:35). He sits upon the floods; they have their shaking fits, even as human bodies. 2. In that he is still accomplishing his pleasure, and carrying on his wise, just, and holy designs, whatever men intend; yea, makes use of them that know him not, to accomplish his pleasure. But mainly do his depths of providence reach his church and people, 1. In making their enemies bring about their mercy. The murderers of Christ little knew what a blessing his church was to get by his death: Cyrus executes God's will, and fulfils prophecies that he little knoweth of (Isa. 44:28, and 45:1-8). 2. In ripening them for mercy by strokes. They are humbled thereby, and fitted for receiving his deliverance. But because this leads us unto the other head of the depths of God, we shall therefore conclude with a word of application upon this branch of the subject.

Are the truths concerning God such depths? Then away with pride, and any opinion of understanding, as of ourselves to reach them, and find them out. Much humility is called for in searching into them, and much reverence, and sense of the greatness of the matter. They are the depths of God, and this should make us fear. Then, labour to know God better; there are many depths of God that yet ye little know. Only take along with you still the lamp of the word—there must be no searching without this. And study God for the increase of grace, rather than of brain-knowledge. Search till you be brought to wonder and adore. Adore him, and invoke him in holy fear, in fervent love, with high praises, and with great trust and confidence.

II. As for those depths of God which concern man, I shall first speak unto that which is already past—the covenant of works made with our first parents (Gen. 2), and the breach thereof (Gen. 3), and the punishment following on it. Which depth contains these things: 1. The Lord's creating our first parents out of the earth indeed, as to their bodies, but their souls of a higher original, and placing them in a most happy condition; and as to his friendship and favour, giving them dominion over the lower creation, and endowing them with great excellencies of body and mind. 2. His free engaging with them in a covenant, by fulfilling the condition whereof, their happiness might have been perpetuated to them, and their posterity. 3. His leaving them to the freedom of their own will, and not freeing them of temptations, though furnishing them with strength sufficient for standing out against them. 4. His speedy executing of the threatened punishment upon their disobedience: wherein we see his curse upon them, his extruding them from paradise; and that all their posterity are born rebels to God, by guilt, and their own natural inclinations to ratify it.

That this is a great depth, is evident from these sad things that have followed on it: 1. That all are by nature enemies to God, and hateful to him. 2. That all the actual transgression that defiles the world, came in at this gap. 3. And all mankind that are in hell, came in hazard of it at first by this. 4. And that the Lord, though he hath provided a remedy, yet in the depth of his judgment he keeps up the knowledge of it from the greater part of mankind. 5. From men's corruption of nature, the greater part of them that hear of the remedy, receive it not.

2. The second depth concerning man, is the new covenant of grace by and in Jesus Christ,—a blessed depth!—a blessed plank for

shipwrecked mankind to escape death by. This depth the angels desire to dive into (1 Pet. 1:12, Eph. 3:10). This depth hath in it all the other deep things of God, to wit, the nature and attributes of God which shine here wonderfully; his wisdom, grace, justice, and mercy:—the mystery of the Trinity,—of the incarnation of the Son of God,—of predestination;—of a new creation, the greatest depth of divine providence. This is the great master axiom of divine wisdom, the brightest glass of his glory, casting the most glorious reflexions.

In this, consider 1. The parties covenanting, God the Father, and Son. It must be a stately bargain that they two make, full of majesty, wisdom, and truth. 2. The condition of this covenant—that the Son shall take on him our nature, and satisfy justice, and so save his people. 3. The fulfilling of these conditions in the Son's faithfulness to his Father, and the Father's faithfulness to the Son: the one discovers the depth of Christ's sufferings; the other, of his purchase. Here is Christ's hell and our heaven. 4. For whom all this is done, and all this contrivance made—for sinners—unworthy, vile creatures. 5. What is made the condition on their part for obtaining a right to all this—receiving Christ's offer of himself as a competent Saviour by faith—an easy way for making so great a purchase, or rather, for the appropriation of his purchase unto ourselves!

Thus have we given you a hint of the depths of God; and for these ends—that you may know and lay to heart how nearly God is concerned in gospel truth: that you may see how unfit you are for searching them unto perfection: that you may study them more and more, since they have such a relation to him: that in the search, you may employ the Spirit of God to enlighten and guide you. Proud and careless searchers into the things of God, must necessarily stumble foully. Oh that people were wise and humble in these matters, and had the fear of God in their hearts!

TWO SERMONS ON HEBREWS 6:4-6.

For it is impossible that those who were once enlightened, and have tasted of the heavenly gift, and were made partakers of the Holy Ghost, and have tasted the good word of God, and the powers of the world to come, if they shall fall away, to renew them again unto repentance; seeing they crucify to themselves the Son of God afresh, and put him to an open shame.

BECAUSE the depth of the purposes in these words requires somewhat more than ordinary explication, and application also, I thought it fit to insist on them in this exercise also,[1] and not to satisfy myself with our brief exposition. Many truths may be deduced from them, as we hinted in expounding; but it is the scope we shall attend unto mainly, and that, as it is relating to us, rather than to such a kind of apostacy of which none of us can possibly be guilty.

On all hands it is granted, that an account of the sin against the Holy Ghost, and its punishment, is here held forth unto us, as is most plain; and that there is such a sin, which man through his corruptions and Satan's temptations may arrive unto, as shall render his salvation desperate. It is called from Matthew 12:31, 32, a *sin unto death* (1 John 5:16), for the pardon whereof in another, we are not to pray. And here, and in Hebrews 10:29, it is spoken of as certainly damnable. All sin indeed is damnable in its nature; all sins may be damning in effect, without repentance and pardon; but this is always certainly damning. The handling of the purpose here to your edification, labours under singular disadvantages, as—the difficulty that there is in finding out the nature of this great sin. The Lord hath left it so dark in the word, that many of his servants have had their different apprehensions about it, whereof I might give you a large list, though in these times, wherein light shineth more clearly about many other gospel truths, there is a greater agreement about it. It is—the deepest apostacy after the highest

[1] This and the following Sermon form the first part of a series in the original MS. consisting of four discourses, of which the last two are merely notes, and therefore unfit for publication.

common operations of the Spirit. It is some disadvantage also, that Satan is so ready to assault many of the godly, with temptations about this; and where they prevail, they are the worst of all his darts. Yet have I adventured to handle this subject on these accounts, 1. To use it as a reason against security and arrogancy in godliness, and as a preventive of the same deadly evil. 2. To encourage the truly godly, and arm them against Satan's temptations to this evil, or persuading them that they are guilty of it. 3. Because it comes in very seasonably upon the preceding purpose of men's standing out against Christ; which is so deep a subject, that it requires a strict and exact handling. And, 4. To prevent or remove the scandal to the gospel by men's apostacy.

Our method in our discourse is this—1. To remove any mistakes that this portion of the word not rightly understood may occasion. And the main end is this—that they that have saving and true grace, may fall away:—and therefore, we shall prove, how it is not of such, but merely of *professors* that the apostle speaks. And for clearing our path in this, we must compare these verses with verses 7 and 8, and especially 9, 10, 11, and 12, where he is speaking certainly to the truly godly amongst them. And so we have these comparisons, 1. Here are *gifts* and *tastings*, that is, faith working by love. 2. How few are the men called and counted amongst Christians, that are sensible souls fleeing for refuge to Christ. 3. Here are things glorious indeed, but not accompanying salvation; but in some, going before it, in others, without it. 4. Here the apostle supposeth a possibility of falling away, of those who are persuaded to the contrary. So that it is evident, that the danger hinted in these words concerns bare professors only, and not them that are true converts; yea, it is remarkable, that in this same chapter, the apostle saith as much for the certainty of the faith and perseverance, and salvation of true believers, as any where in the word. *God, willing more abundantly to shew unto the heirs of promise the immutability of his counsel, confirmed it by an oath: that by two immutable things, in which it was impossible for God to lie, we might have a strong consolation, who have fled for refuge to lay hold upon the hope set before us: which hope we have, as an anchor of the soul, both sure and stedfast, and which entereth into that within the veil* (verses 17, 18, 19).

Our next work shall be, to premise some truth from the words themselves, that may clear our way: 1. That these attainments the apostle speaks of, are in themselves excellent things, and greatly to be valued; being great tokens of a more special favour of God to them to whom they are given, than to them from whom they are withheld. 2. The having of them, as it is a mercy, so the truly godly have them all, and more. 3. The apostle doth not threaten any that have these things, save such as do not duly use them to an increase and obtaining of what is better still.

Our discourse now shall be on these heads, 1. What great attainments a mere professor may have. 2. How deeply he may fall from them, and notwithstanding of them. 3. What is the danger of such an apostacy.

I. Such as shall be damned eternally may attain unto great things in religion. The truth of this is so plain, and so well known in the word (see Matthew 7:21, and 13:20, 21), that we need not stand to prove it farther, than by confirming the particulars; and we shall content ourselves with what is here. In handling this truth, we shall, 1. Show what these attainments are. 2. Why the Lord gives them to such characters. 3. What is wanting of that which would preserve them from apostacy.

First, What these attainments are. We shall insist on the five steps which the apostle names here:

1. He may be *enlightened*—natural darkness and blindness in the things of God are removed. This saith, that he may have the means—and the worst of men have had the best of these, as the Jews, who had Christ's ministry, and that of his apostles—and these means may have a good effect on him, in enlightening his mind in the knowledge of truth. And this effect that is here named, may extend so far, that he may have a literal knowledge of the word, and the truth thereof: of this there is no question. He may have a supernatural knowledge of many profound things in the word, by a special gift of knowledge or illumination, so that he may in this be above many of the truly godly, as to that sort of knowledge. It is likely that Judas knew more than the thief when he became penitent. And, indeed, there is nothing that a believer knoweth, but this apostate may know, though not in the same manner; and thus, the righteous who are ignorant, may be far inferior to those who come short of heaven. The measure of his knowledge may be great; even that of all things concerning God, his own heart,

and the doctrines that are contained in the word. And the fruits of that illumination may be great. He may see such an excellency in Christ's church, as to join with it; and such danger in gross sin, that he may leave it; and attach such blamelessness to his walk, that no man can discern his rottenness.

2. He may *taste of the heavenly gift*—he may have a sort of faith, whereby Christ, and his grace and mercy may be tasted by him. This is a mighty attainment, whereof we spoke in the explication: but that we may draw the line the more accurately, we must now further handle the nature of this faith whereby he tastes. We say, then, that he hath an historical faith believing the truth of gospel tidings: this is a little tasting of justifying faith, for it is like it. He may meditate and contemplate on this truth; and this cannot be, without some savour of it and its goodness. And he may apply these things to himself, as his portion, and far more must this be savoury to him. *He heareth the word, and anon with joy receiveth it; yet hath he not root in himself, but dureth for a while*: for *a while* only he believeth.

3. Such believers are *partakers* of the more special (not *most* special) workings *of the Holy Ghost*. There may be alarming convictions; but Felix, Herod, and Judas, wanted not these: to be awakened with a fright of hell, is no token of a godly man. Or there may be debasing discoveries of self, so that they have not been ashamed to confess their sin, to God's glory and their own shame: even Judas had this. Or external reformation flowing from fear of wrath, and that sensibly working on the heart, as in the case of Ahab. There may be within them a secret restraint on corruption, by the hand of God, not only by his providence (Gen. 20), but by motions on the heart. There may be a spirit of zeal for a good cause when it is afoot in a particular season, as that of the Jewish multitudes, when they cried *Hosannah!* They may have great gifts, such as that of prayer, whereby they are able to speak to God in pertinent petitions as to words, with good appearance of tender affections, and great fervency; and also as of understanding the things of God, so of expressing them to the edification of others, in preaching and in conference. And they have some exercise of conscience in the discharge of these, not only as reflecting on the right season of doing, and of influence stirring them up to do them, but in looking on them

when done; yea, and in finding difference as to assistance therein at one time and another: even Saul knew and lamented when God had departed from him.

4. And *taste the good word of God*—that is, they find its relish and sweetness. When they find it touching their condition, yea, when some of its discoveries of duty are made, they may relish them, as Herod, who heard John gladly, and did many things. Also, not only its suitableness, but its power may be felt, to the stirring up of delight and wonder, as in the case of many of Christ's hearers; and turning them to good resolutions and purposes. Its mysteries may delight them (and what wonder?) so that the feet of its ministers maybe *beautiful upon the mountains*; and its promises of pardon, and peace, and acceptance being thought to be theirs, may by them also be tasted and relished.

5. They may taste of the *powers of the world to come*. Besides what is said of this in the explication, these may be added: he may fancy heaven and that blessedness to be his, and venture and lose much for them—he may in some good measure undervalue the earth in comparison of them. By the *powers of the world to come*, we may understand its virtues and properties, both of which this man may taste. And of its virtues and effects—such as the making a man solicitous and careful about knowing how to get it (Luke 18:18), and painfulness in the means of obtaining it. This is one of its powers also. There is also joy in the thought of its being his, and the endurance of suffering, rather than forfeit this right, though not much nor long; and he may have a lower esteem of this world than he formerly had, and like Balaam, think little and joyfully of death, as a passage to heaven. And he may taste of its properties: its vast greatness may puzzle his understanding, and make him cry out, with David, *Oh, how great is thy goodness, which thou hast laid up for them that fear thee; which thou hast wrought for them that trust in thee before the sons of men!* (Psa. 31:19). Its goodness and excellency may draw forth his affection of love and delight, and its being to come, his expectation and looking for it.—So much of the first thing, as to what great attainments a hypocrite may win to in godliness; not that every one attains so much, but the Lord gives them to some.

Second. Why doth the Lord grant so great things unto them that get no more?—a deep question! that might safely enough be answered with silence, or with the words of the householder, *May not I do what I will with mine own?* Yet may we offer at some wise reasons of this depth of Providence.

1. It is to declare his willingness to save, and to make it the more evident, that men's ruin is of themselves: for in this case is all done, that can be done, in the way of means; and more than is done to many, and more than he is bound to do for any. He brings them on a great way, to leave this on their consciences, and on the consciences of others, that he delights not in the death of sinners.

2. The Lord doth this to make his grace the more conspicuous—his special saving grace; conspicuous in its freedom, and in its power also. When two are carried an equal length in the preparation to a saving interest in God, the one is taken, and the other left.

3. That his own people may not stay, and sit down on any measure of attainments, but still may press on; so is he pleased, for this end, to communicate so much of his common grace to them that may backslide, that all may press forward for more.

Third. But you may say, 'What is wanting to saving grace in all these things?—they seem to be greater attainments than many of the people of God win to.' This leads to the question, 'What is wanting of that which would preserve from apostacy?' I answer, Every thing here in the text hath somewhat wanting: As,

1. Their illumination: it wants still these: they never see themselves quite undone, and empty of all good, so as to loathe themselves, and be quite diffident of themselves, and to go out of themselves. Always there is somewhat that the unsound sinks into, and hath a good opinion of. And they never saw Christ, as the only enriching treasure for the man himself. Fine notions of Christ's accomplishments they may have in the general; but of his being all in all, and that he is suited fully to them, this they see not.

2. As to their faith, it is called temporary, because it lasts not; but this is not visible until defection; therefore we must search it farther out. Whatever faith a man may have of divine truth, and whatever application may be made of Christ to himself, he wants these things of a sound faith: 1. He wants the bottom and ground-work of saving faith, and that is, denial of self and all self-sufficiency. The guilt of sin

on his conscience may stir him up to employ Christ in some way; but utter emptiness of all good in himself, as well as of safety from himself, never can, nor doth move him. 2. And therefore he fails in the very act of faith, which is, a receiving of Christ wholly, and resting in him, as he is made of God to us wisdom, and righteousness, and sanctification and redemption, and offered to us (1 Cor. 1:30). God hath exalted him to be a Prince and Saviour (Acts 5:31), and as such he is to be received. 3. And lastly, he is a stranger unto the life of faith, or abiding in Christ, and drawing virtue from him (John 15; Gal. 2:20). These are mysteries impracticable unto the man of highest common attainments. Now, all these three are knit together, and follow one on another. As to this, their shortcoming flows from this mistake;—they imagine they need Christ as a Saviour, and a giver of grace, and then, when they have got that which they think to be grace, they look on it as somewhat sufficient of itself, with their careful improvement of it, to advance the work of their salvation. Whereas the true believer seeth as much necessity of taking up his abode in the city of refuge, as of fleeing to it; and knows, that as his first new life flowed from his engrafting into Christ, the true stock, so his fruitfulness depends on the daily communication of his virtue.

3. As to their partaking of the Holy Ghost, here is a vast difference;—they know nothing of the regenerating sanctifying virtue of the Holy Ghost, which is the main benefit sinners receive by him. They want still the change of the heart and nature; they are still bad ground (verse 8), still *dogs* (2 Pet. 2:22).

Object. But how shall I know, that there is such a change by the Holy Ghost on me, but by such things as you have ascribed to the common operations? I answer, Better marks than any of these may every godly man find out of himself; As, 1. A single regard unto God's glory, which can never affect an unsanctified soul. To make it the man's chief aim, the attaining of it his chief joy; his dishonour his chief sorrow, are no where to be found but in a sanctified soul. 2. And as to external reformation, those indications that are in the sound man, are in the heart, and from thence in the life, while the other man is still in an evil condition; and therefore, that reformation of the former, is more sound, and even, and universal. And it hath an aim also towards perfection; perfect holiness is lovely, to a holy sincere man. 3. As to gifts, the godly man, whatever share he hath or wants of these, hath what is far better than they are, and never wants such a measure of them as is simply needful. In prayer, for instance, though it may be he talks not so much nor so well as to words, as one of greater gifts, yet he still talks better—for his heart is more at the work, his aim is more honest, his reflections more spiritual, and his attainments more gracious and sanctifying.

4. Their tasting of the good word of God, whatever it hath in it, it wants much that the sound man hath. They taste not all in the word of God, for some things in it they are strangers unto; as, its enlivening power quickening them by it, and according to it, which David (Psa. 119) so often prays for. See also 1 Peter 1:23, where it is described as a living seed cast into their heart, raising them up unto a new life: this they know not. Its promises may quicken them to joy, but it never removes their natural death. Its feeding fructifying power also they know not of. They taste it only for trial, but do not feed on it. But a godly man finds this his bread, whereby his soul lives, and grows, and brings forth fruit unto God. It is the children's bread that children's nature only hath an appetite after. Some things of the word also they taste, that they do not relish and savour, as – its convincing power: when it comes close to them, and that daily, to make new discoveries of their distemper, this they have no relish of. David takes it as a commendation of the word, that it warns him (Psa. 19:11, 12). The unsound man can take its conviction now and then in good part; but when it is full at the work of discovering sin, and comes close upon his practices, he cannot endure it. And the unspotted holiness and strictness of God's word, is no relishing thing to him, but he is ready inwardly to blame it, as being too strict; whereas the godly man will, like Paul (Rom. 7:12), call the law good, even when he cannot fulfil it.

5. Though he may taste of the powers of the world to come, he wants what a godly man may have. For he wants the experience of the due meetness for it that every godly man in some measure possesses. He is ready, that is, willing, but not meet and prepared to receive it; and therefore you will find, that he may pray for it, and not make ready for it. It hath no such power on him, as to induce him to prefer it, as a spiritual happiness, above all things in the world; but still, there are some things he loves better—somewhat which he is more afraid of

losing, than of this blessedness, as trials do discover: the cares of the world, or the persecution of it, draws him away. And the spiritual and true earnest of it is still unknown to him; and though it may, in some measure, be also unknown to a godly man, yet seeing the apostle speaks of such an attainment of the hypocrite, that the sincere themselves do not always obtain, we may well lay this against that, as a proof of its wanting that which it seems to have. The earnest of glory is all one with that of the Spirit. *In whom* (Christ) *also, after that ye believed, ye were sealed with that holy Spirit of promise, which is the earnest of our inheritance, until the redemption of the purchased possession, unto the praise of his glory.—Who hath also sealed us, and given the earnest of the Spirit in our hearts.—Now he that hath wrought us for the self same thing is God, who also hath given unto us the earnest of the Spirit* (Eph. 1:13, 14; 2 Cor. 1:22, and 5:5). These expressions may help us to guess at the thing. The earnest being of the nature with the principal sum, as well as a securing of it, and the Holy Ghost being its author, we may know that it must have these things to make it up,—some near degree of fellowship with God; some sensible advance in conformity to him; and a holy delight and satisfaction resulting therefrom. Something like this, but a counterfeit, may the ungodly hypocrite have; but it is attained this way,—he looks on heaven as a state of excellent happiness, by his historical faith; his false spirit tells him it is his; and his heart rejoices in the hopes of it, though he still remain a stranger unto holy, sanctifying fellowship with God. The unsound man, for all his tasting of its powers, is yet unacquainted with these virtues that the meanest of the godly partake of; its main powers are not yet tasted. It takes not off his eye from sensible things, unto invisibles (2 Cor. 4:18). It puts not a bitterness into all his contentments, in comparison of it. A godly man is a stranger, and all his desirable mercies are but pilgrim's fare to him, that is often seasoned, and hath the bitter sauce of the remembrance where he is, and how far from home. It makes not all sufferings light, and tolerable, and small, in regard of it (see Rom. 8:18; 2 Cor. 4:17); then joyful (Matt. 5:12; Heb. 10:34). An unsound man may suffer for heaven, but he looks on this suffering as a great disadvantage, and is sorry that the way is not more easy; and therefore, when sufferings come to a height, he falls off. It makes the godly man count all the pains in labouring for it to be but small, and unworthy of it; but the unsound man thinks he may take pains enough, and possibly too much; and therefore he becomes a censurer of them that go beyond him in diligence, that they may make more ado than there is need.

Use 1.—Since it is thus that bare professors, in whom the root of the matter is not found, may go so far, then this speaks terror unto those that are short of them; and they are many: it says, 'If you come short of them that have not true grace, you must be far more behind than they.' For the enforcing and clearing of this subject, know, that many of those who go to hell, are not by much so near heaven, as others who yet shall be there also:—many sail to hell by the coast of heaven, still expecting to land safely, till the storm come, and drown them in perdition;—and that all these things in some measure all the godly have had, and many remarkably, ere the gracious change was felt or came on them. And therefore, though the having them will not prove you godly, yet the want of them will prove you to be ungodly.

Now, a slender reflection might suffice for conviction, that many want what is here. As for illumination—are there not many grossly ignorant, and who know not the letter of divine truth; and many who have that, have no more? A hypocrite may have great discoveries of the things of God, as we have already said. For faith—there are many that give an ignorant implicit assent unto divine truth and the gospel, that never came unto a tasting of the sweetness of the gospel; they have never felt any relish of a Saviour. For the partaking of the Holy Ghost many have no knowledge that there is a Holy Ghost, by any experience of his workings in awakening and convincing them. As for the taste of the word—many feel nothing in it of goodness and savour, nor of its pertinency to them, nor of its bitterness in reproving them. And as little power hath the world to come on them. If they can get thither when they die, they care not for any of its virtues. How terrible should this be to you, who are short of the attainments of those that yet may be in the gall of bitterness! The security of the age we live in, and the arrogancy of professors, call aloud to ministers to proclaim to them their hazard.

Use 2.—Be exhorted to take the warning in the scope of the apostle: go still forward in godliness, until you come the length that no hypocrite can attain; and this will be a work for you all your life long. For though the sincere though weak believer be quite above the reach of a bare profession, yet every sincere man hath these things, that will make his endeavours in advancing constant:—He is humble, and thinks little of his attainments, though never so great:—he is illuminated, and seeth both how small his attainments are, and how much is yet before him: hence, holy fear, and jealousy of himself and his treacherous heart, and so is he the more diligent—and he hath a love to progress, both from his single regard to God's commandment, and the love which the new creature within him hath toward further holiness.

If this fruit be reached in you, it is the design of the Holy Ghost in writing this, and mine in handling it: if not, I shall witness for God, that you were warned of the greatest danger that can befall you, and that you slighted it; so that when it overtakes you, you may justify God, and condemn yourselves. Oh! consider what a dreadful thought it will be in hell, to think, 'A little more advancing would have removed me out of the way of this danger.' Certainly none fall deeper into hell, than they that fall from the top of heaven's walls. He that hath given you what you have, is as ready to give you what you want, and more. A misery wilfully contracted must yours then be.

SERMON II

HEB. 6:4, 5, 6.

For it is impossible for those who were once enlightened, and have tasted of the heavenly gift, and were made partakers of the Holy Ghost, and have tasted the good word of God, and the powers of the world to come, if they shall fall away, to renew them again unto repentance; seeing they crucify to themselves the Son of God afresh, and put him to an open shame.

WE have been speaking unto this truth, that mere professors may have great attainments. We shall now handle these—that professors of high attainments may fall away most sadly; and that there is a fall that is irretrievable; and what that is, shall be described further from the word.

Professors of the highest attainments in common grace, may fall away dreadfully: the apostle's supposition proves its possibility. The scripture gives us some instances. In the case of Saul, we find him, according to the times, gifted with a spirit for government, walking for a while in God's way, and then he suddenly falls. Judas, an apostle, Christ's hearer and domestic servant, of whom, though we read nothing particularly to his advantage, yet, doubtless, many good things were with him, and his fellow-disciples never suspect him; and yet, at length he falls away. Herod may be reckoned amongst them, and Demas, and several apostates named in the word. Our own experience testifieth this, in that we have seen many, who when religion was in fashion and favour, did profess highly, pray often, reform many things, and walk blamelessly; who could talk of convictions, and awakenings, and joys, on some experience; and of the force of the word, and benefit of ordinances; yet many have turned profane, many corrupted in their principles—of whom, though it is like, the Lord hath his own whom he may still reclaim, yet, doubtless, many have justified this truth from their experience. For further confirmation of this, take and use in a good sense the world's wicked observation, 'A young saint an old devil.' Though it is likely the devil did teach men this, to frighten them from religion in their young days, which are the fittest season of setting about it, yet experience shows, that none are more wicked when of age, than such as have been under convictions unprofitable when young. The world's censure of professors, that they are worse in many things to deal with than other folks, though there be much of prejudice and partiality in it, yet some truth it has as to many. Observe also, that men when awakened by sickness or danger, and who sleep again, go on more seriously and boldly in sin, than ever they did; and are farther out of the reach of a conviction, than any, or than themselves formerly were.

We shall adduce further evidence from scripture to confirm this truth.

1. The truly godly themselves who have saving grace, may fall back in a great measure—and much more they. The instances of such are various; some by a sudden fit of temptation being drawn on unto great

sin, and quickly recovering, as Peter; some lying longer under its power, as David, whose decay seems to have been very great, and for many days. And the force of the reason is strong; for common operations are nowise so powerful to restrain corruption and prevent apostacy, as the truth of God's grace in the heart.

2. Men under the highest of common operations may fall utterly away, because what they have, are not sufficient preservatives and antidotes against defection. Thus, mere illumination cannot preserve; because a man, as long as he is unrenewed, may walk contrary to his light, and even then too much. His tasting of faith cannot preserve; because though somewhat of Christ's sweetness be tasted by him, yet there is in Christ what he distastes, and thus he prepares his way to apostacy. His partaking of the Holy Ghost, ordinary or extraordinary, is no bar to hold out defection; for it is no sanctifying participation, and so, is no more than a certain qualification for some works naturally good. His tasting of the good word of God and the powers of the world to come are not sufficient neither; for they are but *tastings*, and not a feeding thereupon, which alone yields strength unto a man to keep him from falling.

In general, all these are such things as he hath, or such things as he tastes. Two things he hath,—illumination, and gifts of the Holy Ghost; such may be taken from him; and even when they are present with him, they cannot preserve him from apostacy. The things that he hath a taste of are excellent—faith, the word, and works:—but this is the want—that he hath a taste, and no more. And so this bewrayeth either the unsoundness of his aim and intention, that he meddles only with Christ, and the word, and heaven, to get a taste and trial of them, and no more; or the unsoundness of his temper, that he can endure no more but a taste of these things: and certainly it tells their unprofitableness to him. Christ is ordained to be lived on, and by faith (Gal. 2:20), and only so far *tasted* in the beginning, as to encourage to follow on to know him, and to be built up on him (1 Pet. 2:3, 4), to be dwelt in (John 15), to have him dwelling in the heart (Eph. 3:17). The word is to be fed upon by beginners as milk (Heb. 5:12, 13; 1 Pet. 2:1, 2). Children must live by tasting of the milk, as grown men on it as food proper for them. Man liveth not by bread, but by the word; heaven is not to be tasted, but dwelt in (Phil. 3:20). It is to be the mark a Christian shoots at. And therefore as to all these things that he tastes of, he wants the due virtue, and influence, and power. Yea, there is also the inconstancy of these things: he may lose the relish of them; yea, the very tastings may be taken away, and so, any little effect that tasting might have, is also removed. And this may come to pass, partly by the corrupt temper of his heart; partly, by the Lord's judgment taking away the opportunities of tasting from him, that hath no mind to feed on this fare. Again, this may betray his weakness, that it prevails not against the sinful savour of other things. This tasting then bewraying, as is said, the unsoundness of the heart; and the short-livedness of these things, saith, that the benefit of them cannot be reaped by him, while he is such; and what benefit is reaped, is not enough to preserve him from decaying.

The third reason of this truth is, that such want the necessary and only sufficient preservatives against defection. As, 1. He wants the new nature: all he has amounts not to innovation and a new creature; and it is evident at the very reading of these words, unto any acquainted with the style and phrase of the Holy Ghost, that it is his design here to speak only of common attainments. Now, that the new nature is an excellent preservative against defection, is evident. This new nature, in a native way and principle which is the strongest and most lasting, produceth love to God from whom it had its being; to his truth and word, the instrument of its being, and means of its nourishment and growth; and also, it hath as native, a loathing of any departure from God and his way, though darkness and delusion in a particular may prevail.

2. They want true faith, a special mean of preventing apostacy (see Heb. 3:12; and 10:38, 39), and that it is not with them, we showed already. That it is useful to prevent apostacy, is many ways demonstrable: 1. Because it is the mean on our part of our union with Jesus Christ, the fountain of our strength; and so, the way to get communications of grace needful from him, is to exercise this grace on him. 2. It is the main shield we have to oppose to the temptations of Satan (Eph. 6:16), and of the world (1 John 5:4). So Moses found it (Heb. 11:26-29).

3. They want an interest in God's favour and friendship, and so, want that care, and kindness, and watching over them for good, that his

people meet with. The waterings and refreshings, preventing mercies, surprisals of mercy, and wise turning-about of begun falling, to the advancing of future stedfastness, which the Lord gives to his people, and whereby he prevents utter apostacy, they are strangers to.

4. The Holy Ghost's sanctifying abode in their hearts they want, which is the great preservative of the people of God. (See 1 John 2:27). They have a sort of qualifying abode for the material part of duty, but no more. These may serve for the clearing and confirming of the truth of this, that common grace is no preservative against defection. In farther prosecution of this purpose concerning the possibility of the fall of men of highest attainments in common things, I shall, 1. Distinguish the sorts of falling away and apostacy; 2. Show how they are carried on and advanced; 3. Show what is their danger.

1. What sorts of falling away professors are in danger of. The general distinction is—an apostacy may either be in principles or profession, or else in practice; and that both of them may be damnable, we shall hear anon. An apostacy from the profession of Christian religion is threefold—through ignorance, when many that have not come to any sound understanding of their profession, forsake it; such were the carnal Jews (John 6:66)—an apostacy from the profession through infirmity and carnal fear, as Peter's was; although it is dreadful, when their profession is cloaked and covered for a while for some base ends—and an apostacy from the profession through resolute wickedness; and this may be sometimes with a check, and sometimes without it. The first of these belongs not to us. An apostacy in practice, is that decay and falling from the practice of those duties, that the profession retained obligeth unto; and this is total or partial: partial, as in the case of the godly, who often fall into it; total, as in that of hypocrites only, who may return just to the same state from which their common workings brought them, (2 Pet. 2:19, 20). Only, I would have you to regard these things about this distinction of apostacies; to wit, that where there is a great measure of any one, there is no want of a measure of the other—that if they were separable, apostacy from the profession is the worst, because most to God's dishonour, though the other also be dishonourable and destructive—that a great degree of either is damning—and they are so linked together, that in the full handling of one, we must speak of the

other, for principles of profession have an influence on practice, and bad practice has an influence to darken the judgment.

2. The next thing promised to be handled is, How such apostacies are carried on. And this question is useful for convicting those who are under them; for preparing us all against them, and Satan's devices and our own heart's treachery in the matter—and for instructing us both in repentance and reformation—for the method of sin's advancing, instructs in the method of reformation and repentance.

As to the apostacy of ignorance it concerns not us, for we speak of that of illuminated professors. As to the other, though we have distinguished them, yet now, shall we offer to give a thread of the scope downward again, premising only these things, 1. That the depth of the sovereignty of Satan's cunning and the heart's treachery, renders it impossible to search out this mystery of iniquity unto the bottom. 2. As it is the design of the Spirit of God in his common operations, to draw men unto that pitch of attainment and happiness from which there is no falling, so is it Satan's, in tempting, to pull men into irrecoverable misery. 3. As men's wickedness often mars the success attainable by the improvement of the Holy Ghost's workings, so the Lord's goodness, sometimes special, sometimes common, stops the career into inevitable apostacies; and therefore, often where saving grace is not, yet the depth of apostacy is prevented, sometimes by restraint on temptations, and sometimes by a restraint on the corruptions in men.

Now, to offer some light upon these black stairs to the pit, we are to remember how far the man is gone upward as is said. 1. His first preparative to backsliding is standing still. He thinks he is so well advanced, that he is now shot-free: now he hath got what will save him; and he looks down upon those below him, with a sort of loftiness and disdain. 2. Then come heart-quarrels against further advancement. As the pride of his heart appears in the former case, so does its unrenewedness and want of sanctification in this. Wanting the new nature that kindly inclines unto progress, he thinks that further progress is needless, or may be troublesome and prejudicial unto his carnal interests, the love whereof is not rooted out. 3. Satan and his heart do now propose unto him his idol, some one corruption or other, that in the former advancing was, it may be, for a while put to the door: now is it presented, and entertained, it is likely, more secretly, but as warmly as ever. It hath the throne, although it gives not forth such open laws as formerly. 4. Then may his light and this reinstatement struggle awhile together, and with an issue of this sort—that either his light is displeasing, for its crossing him in his enjoyment, or that idol may now and then be a little discountenanced, though never hated, according to the clearness of his light and convictions, as they ebb or flow. 5. While it is thus with him in this carnal warfare, possibly a trial may come, wherein resolvedly he must take part with his light or his sin; for the former may be in his ordinary practice, the latter in his way wherein he must walk, and that with choice and deliberation. And here a hotter and sorer combat must be, and we suppose, without a powerful restraint, he now makes a bad choice, and resolvedly crosseth his light, for satisfying of his carnal aim and scope. 6. When he is arrived at this, that he walks in a way that is not good, with a deliberate purpose, and hath left the way of God in profession or practice, then is it possible that he may arrive at a positive and avowed resolute dislike of that way and truth that formerly he walked in, and which was so prejudicial to his lusts. And the more there remains in him of the light of that truth, then more hotly doth the fire of enmity in his heart break forth. This is a considerable step, and far downward, and near the pit. But this is not all. 7. He comes now to a hatred and dislike of Jesus Christ himself, whose truth he once knew and professed. He thinks him a hard master, now when he hath left him; that his laws are more intolerable and grievous, and his promises unworthy, and insufficient to balance his designs of seeking happiness. 8. And then he comes to hate those pains and workings on his heart, whereby any savour on his heart at any time was wrought of this way, and his offered and once pretended guide. 9. And lastly, his enmity against the worker, the Holy Ghost, may break out, and that the more, that in all this backsliding of his, he hath met with the more warnings, stops, and terrors, in his course.

Another way to guess at the method of such apostacies, shall be from the words themselves, wherein we have five steps of advancement, and so the apostacy must be from all; and we must begin at the top of this ladder. 1. His tasting the powers of the world to come is fallen from, it may be from carelessness, and the bewitching relish of other things (see Matt. 13:22); and this chokes his further growth. Heaven, the end and scope of all godliness, grows an unsavoury thing with him, for he never had a spiritual savour of it; and this little taste may be put away by his savouring the things of the earth. 2. His savouring of God's word decays also naturally, because of the former. He that hath lost his relish of heaven, what taste can God's good word have unto him? 3. He then comes to lose his partakings of the Holy Ghost: gifts decay either through his carelessness, or justly are taken away. 4. His sort of faith decays with it: Christ becomes unsavoury also. He hath now no relish of a Saviour; the tidings of him are tasteless and disgusting. 5. And lastly, he falls from his light and knowledge also, either by struggling with it, and the Lord's withdrawing thereof, or by his wilfully putting it out—which is a sin possible for a man left of God, and given up to Satan to do. 3. What is the danger of apostacy? 1. This is one of its great dangers, that every declining is restless, and tends unto a growth. No man can stand still in this course, unless he is kept by restraining, or brought back by saving grace. 2. Because recoveries are very rare, even from apostacies that are not simply incurable. There is so much provocation in them, that the Lord ordinarily recovers not so many plagues of heart; and these so strongly are contracted, that rarely they are recovered from. 3. And because there is a step in apostacy that is incurable, that is the danger which the Spirit of God here propoundeth. And therefore here we shall both show its nature and its irrecoverableness, and how it is reasonable that it should be so.

For its nature—there is considerable difficulty here; yet shall we endeavour to walk as warily as we can, to shun inconveniences on both hands. The word gives us no definition; but it gives us the names of this sin. It is a *sin against the Holy Ghost*, that is, against him in his workings, and as working is the object of this, if we may so speak (Matt. 12:31). He that speaks a word against the Son of Man, having no conviction of his godhead and office, it shall upon repentance be forgiven; but not so this sin, which is against the Holy Ghost's workings: he hath *done despite unto the Spirit of grace* (Heb. 10:29). It is also a blasphemy against the Holy Ghost, and relates to the case where the Pharisees, convinced in their consciences by the Holy Ghost of the appearance of God in Christ's mighty works, did yet call him a devil; not that it stands simply in words, but only as the blaspheming words proceed from the heart, as in that instance they did. And it is an apostacy that is utter and total: *For if we sin wilfully after that we have received the knowledge of the truth, there remaineth no more sacrifice for sins, but a certain fearful looking for of judgment and fiery indignation, which shall devour the adversaries* (Heb. 10:26, 27). And it is a *sin unto death* (1 John 5:16), and unpardonable; that is, such as never shall be forgiven. *All manner of sin and blasphemy shall be forgiven unto men: but the blasphemy against the Holy Ghost shall not be forgiven unto men* (Matt. 12:31). There is no repentance for such as commit it (Heb. 6:6); nothing is left to them, but an expectation of vengeance.

The scriptures as they name the sin, so they specify the persons that commit it. They are professors; it is not the sin of heathens: they have *trodden under foot the Son of God, and counted the blood of the covenant wherewith* THEY WERE SANCTIFIED, *an unholy thing, and have done despite unto the Spirit of grace* (Heb. 10:29). And they have knowledge, illumination, and other gifts, as this, and the other places we have cited do all prove. It is then a sin to be found in professors of the highest stamp.

The scriptures tell us what the committers of this sin do. They blaspheme against their conscience and knowledge (Matt. 12:31); they crucify Christ afresh, call him a deceiver, and approve of the Jews crucifying him. On that account they *put him to open shame*; they openly renounce his name, and give the world to know that they have tried him, and find nothing in him worthy to be adhered unto. But Hebrews 10:29, is a further and clearer explication of this. They *tread under foot the Son of God*, that is, openly and basely despise him—*count the blood of the covenant wherewith they were sanctified an unholy*, common *thing*; that is, reckon Christ's blood sealing the covenant wherein once they were externally, and so, federally holy, no more than common blood, nay, not so much—and *do despite unto the Spirit of grace*; despitefully reject the Holy Ghost, who was at labour formerly with their hearts, to convert and sanctify them, and work grace in them.

This much might satisfy, but we shall now briefly deduce some conclusions from the foregoing, without offering any peremptory definition from them.

1. This sin, then, is against Christ as a Saviour, and in his office of Redeemer, and that, witnessed unto by the Holy Ghost in the sinner's conscience; and so, it is called both a sin against Christ and the Holy Ghost in different respects, but the latter more properly; or both thus conjunctly—it is against Christ evidenced to the conscience by the Holy Ghost to be the Redeemer of the world; or against the Holy Ghost witnessing this to the conscience. 2. This sin is an act of the highest contempt, and despite, and wilful rejecting; and such it must be where the evidence is so pressing.

How can this sin be committed? As it is thus defined, many question its possibility, and that, because of these circumstances: It is a sin above that of the devils, who are greater and older sinners than men: it is such an avowed rushing on eternal misery, when man's reason and self-love should struggle against it;—and there is no temptation to it. In answer to these objections, we shall give some general reasons to obviate them, and prove the possibility of committing it; explain scripture instances; and give a more particular reply. In general, we give for answer, that the heart's wickedness is an unsearchable depth, and our reason will soon be aground in searching it; nor can it well be told what may be produced of such a creature as man is, when these things concur—total desertion on the part of God; the being utterly left unto Satan's temptations; and the irritating power of spiritual challenges and convictions. As for the scripture instances, we need only allude here to that of the Pharisees, who knew that Christ was led by the Spirit of God, and yet they fell into this blasphemy. But to answer particularly, it is no absurdity to say that there are some aggravations in the sin of men, which are not in that of devils; as all gospel sins, which flow not so much entirely from sinful nature in itself considered, as from it when suitable circumstances draw it out. As for the rushing on eternal misery which it implies, it is a question, if they always know this, when they commit it: belike the Pharisees themselves knew not all their danger. In ordinary sins against knowledge, somewhat of this madness is found, and there is no wonder if it should be found in this. Their stupidity of conscience is come to that height, that it is no wonder they run on. As for the want of temptations to commit this crime; if by a temptation you mean an offer of advantage, that should take with a reasonable man, it is true, there is none here as in other cases. But if we take temptation so largely, as to comprehend Satan's diligence in stirring up, the heart's inclination to yield, some fancied satisfaction to move, then, the sinner against the Holy Ghost sins not without a temptation. His fancied advantages may be many, as was the case with the Pharisees, and as it is with the worst of apostates at all times; yet in such high acts of raging madness against God, man acts rather like a devil, than a reasonable creature.

We are now to show the unpardonableness of this sin, and the reasonableness that it should be so. And though it might be enough to satisfy us that God saith it, yet we may consider its reasonableness, which will appear from a consideration of these points; 1. This is the highest affront unto the Son of God who hath undertaken our redemption. To neglect his salvation through carelessness, is damning (Heb. 2:3); to contend with him and his offers in pursuit of our lusts, is yet worse; to stand out against him to the last breath in the madness of rebellion, is terrible. But after some acquaintance and professed subjection, deliberately to pour out contempt on his sacrifice of atonement, and thus give the defiance to God, is intolerable. 2. This is the highest and utmost opposition unto such operations of the Holy Ghost, as may be saving, and that, after the clearest and most convincing evidences that can be given. 3. This is the highest ripeness of sin; this is sin in its own proper colours; thus the man who commits it, is like the devil, or like one in hell. 4. It is the full ripeness of spiritual plagues that do highly indispose unto all returning. Hardness of heart is great and ripe, like the devil's; conscience is stupid, or filled with hopeless fear, and that indeed no pleasure to the man, and yet not heavily his burden.

Because we cannot now enter on the further handling and applying of this terrible purpose, I shall now only draw these inferences from what is said.

1. Then there is no ground for Satan's disquieting of any with their having committed this sin, who are displeased with any thing they have done in opposition to Christ and his Spirit; who have any honest longings to be at peace with God in him; who find any longings of love and liking towards him; and who can entreat the Holy Ghost to work yet more within their hearts.

2. We see then that there is great reason to beware of any thing that leads towards this dreadful sin, that it may be escaped; such as long continuance under the offers of the gospel, without making up a hearty peace, and closing with Christ, which is our security against this sin; and sins against knowledge and conscience, even against the law. These are sad preparatives, and lead on to this sin against the Holy Ghost.

3. Walking in the way and course that is not good. This is more than the former, for this is deliberate and resolved; whereas the violence of a temptation by a surprise may draw Peter and David into the other.

4. Beware of the pardonable sins against the Holy Ghost, if you would escape that which is unpardonable. These are four in scripture terms, which I shall only apply unto our present purpose:

1*st*, Desisting the saving assaults of the Holy Ghost (Acts 7:51), a dreadful sin! which yet all in some measure are guilty of, who yield not their hearts at the first calls of the gospel; and indeed, the unpardonable sin itself, is a high degree of this.

2*d*, Quenching of the Spirit (1 Thess. 5:19), which whatever be in it as it stands in that chapter, this is in it as to our purposes—when awakening, heart-warning, sin-consuming operations are quenched; when men cast water thereupon, as if they were in hazard of being burnt up thereby.

3. Grieving of the Holy Ghost (Eph. 4:30), which though it be a sin, as the former, that the godly may and often do fall into, yet we rather apply it in this sense to the ungodly; and thus it is, when the Spirit of God is at work, and is in some joyful hopeful temper of having gained somewhat on the heart, the man immediately provokes and proves all to be lost labour.

4. Vexing of the Spirit of God (Isa. 63:10). That is the sin of rebellion, and it hints, as it were, the Spirit of the Lord being put to irresolution and vexation how to guide and gain them, when one mean after another is used, and all in vain: *O Ephraim, what shall I do unto thee? O Judah, what shall I do unto thee? for your goodness is as a morning cloud, and as the early dew it goeth away* (Hos. 6:4). Love is tried, and that prevails not; terror, and that works not (See Matt. 11:16). None of his dealings please them; but as it was with Israel, they find fault with every thing. We have thus been handling as dreadful truths as are to be found in

the word—that men of unsound hearts may attain to great things in godliness, or in the appearances of it; and that hypocrites of the highest attainments may fearfully fall. But it may be said, 'This is the way to dishearten us in religion to tell us such things.' I answer, If God do not tell you them, do not believe us. Besides, there is not the least discouragement in all this, but rather matter of humility, and searching, and awakening, and therefore do we use it. Its design is not to discourage, and it is abused if this be felt. And what hazard, say you, are you in of apostacy like this in the text? You are in hazard of heart-declinings, which may be damning. You know not what temptations you may be exposed unto, of renouncing the truth of the gospel; and the prevailing of such temptations may accomplish all the misery spoken of here. May apostates go far forward to heaven? Then search yourselves, and see how far you go beyond them.

FINIS.